ANCIENT ISRAELITE RELIGION

ANCIENT ISRAELITE RELIGION

Essays in Honor of
FRANK MOORE CROSS

Edited by
PATRICK D. MILLER, JR.,
PAUL D. HANSON,
S. DEAN McBRIDE

FORTRESS PRESS   PHILADELPHIA

Library of Congress Cataloging-in-Publication Data

Ancient Israelite religion.

"Bibliography of the works of Frank Moore Cross": p.
Includes index.
1. Bible. O.T.—Criticism, interpretation, etc.
2. Bible. O.T.—Theology. 3. Middle East—Religion.
4. Bible. O.T.—Comparative studies. 5. Cross,
Frank Moore. I. Cross, Frank Moore. II. Miller,
Patrick D. III. Hanson, Paul D. IV. McBride,
S. Dean (Samuel Dean), 1937–   .
BS1171.2.A53   1987   296'.0933   86–45919
ISBN 0–8006–0831–3

1452A87   Printed in the United States of America   1–831

CONTENTS

CONTENTS

CONTRIBUTORS

N. Avigad, The Hebrew University of Jerusalem
Klaus Baltzer, University of Munich
Phyllis Bird, Garrett-Evangelical Theological Seminary
John J. Collins, University of Notre Dame
Michael David Coogan, Stonehill College
William G. Dever, University of Arizona
David Noel Freedman, University of Michigan
Jonas C. Greenfield, The Hebrew University of Jerusalem
M. H. Goshen-Gottstein, The Hebrew University of Jerusalem
Jo Ann Hackett, Indiana University
William W. Hallo, Yale University
Paul D. Hanson, Harvard Divinity School
John S. Holladay, Jr., University of Toronto
Thorkild Jacobsen, Harvard University (Emeritus)
J. Gerald Janzen, Christian Theological Seminary
Jon D. Levenson, University of Chicago
Norbert Lohfink, Philosophisch Theologische Hochschule Sankt Georgen
P. Kyle McCarter, Jr., Johns Hopkins University
Abraham Malamat, The Hebrew University of Jerusalem
George E. Mendenhall, University of Michigan
Carol Meyers, Duke University
Eric M. Meyers, Duke University
Patrick D. Miller, Jr., Princeton Theological Seminary
Roland E. Murphy, The Divinity School, Duke University
Joseph Naveh, The Hebrew University of Jerusalem
Robert A. Oden, Jr., Dartmouth College

Brian Peckham, Regis College, Toronto
Helmer Ringgren, University of Uppsala
J. J. M. Roberts, Princeton Theological Seminary
Michael E. Stone, The Hebrew University of Jerusalem
Shemaryahu Talmon, The Hebrew University of Jerusalem
Jeffrey H. Tigay, University of Pennsylvania
Moshe Weinfeld, The Hebrew University of Jerusalem

PREFACE

Frank Moore Cross, Jr., was born on July 13, 1921. He attended Mary-ville College (A.B., 1942) and McCormick Theological Seminary (B.D., 1946). While still in seminary, he wrote an award-winning essay which subsequently was published under the title "The Tabernacle: A Study from an Archaeological and Historical Approach," *The Biblical Archae-ologist* 10 (1947) 45–68. It was the firstfruits of a veritable stream of significant scholarly publications to flow from his pen. From McCormick he went on to the Johns Hopkins University, where he studied under William Foxwell Albright, one of the foremost Semiticists of our century. He received his Ph.D. degree in Semitic languages in 1950. It was at Johns Hopkins that the broad directions of his scholarly interests were set. After returning to teach for a time at his alma mater, McCormick Theological Seminary, Frank Cross, at the relatively young age of thirty-six, was appointed in 1957 to one of the oldest and most prestigious posts in his field: the Hancock Professorship of Hebrew and Other Oriental Languages at Harvard University. For nearly thirty years, he has occupied this chair with brilliance and distinction. From 1958 to 1961 he also served as curator of the Harvard Semitic Museum, and since 1974 he has served as its director. His interest in archaeology has been longstanding. In 1955 he was codirector of an expedition to the Judean Buqe'ah; in 1963–64 he served as Archaeological Director of Hebrew Union College in Jerusalem; and from 1975 to 1979 he was Principal Investigator, Punic Excavation of the American Schools of Oriental Research—Harvard—Michigan Expedition to Carthage. More recently he has participated in underwater excavations off the coast of Sardinia.

One measure of a scholar's contribution to his profession are the offices and honorary appointments that he holds. Frank Cross has had many of these. Among them, he has been a Fellow of the American Council of Learned Societies, the American Academy of Arts and Sciences, and the Institute for Advanced Study at the Hebrew University in Jerusalem. He is a member of the American Philosophical Society and of Phi Beta Kappa. Last but not least, he has served as president of two major learned societies, The American Schools of Oriental Research and the Society of Biblical Literature.

Cross has also been a productive scholar literarily, his bibliography numbering two hundred items. Even more significant than the quantity, however, is the quality and substance of his writing. His articles and books are never tedious or dull. Always lucid and thought-provoking, they frequently break fresh ground, setting new directions for research and delineating parameters for further exploration.

He has concentrated his research and writing in three major areas. The first is the area of Hebrew and Northwest Semitic epigraphy and paleography. The groundwork for this was already laid in the two doctoral dissertations, *Early Hebrew Orthography: A Study of the Epigraphic Evidence* and *Studies in Ancient Yahwistic Poetry*, which he wrote in collaboration with David Noel Freedman. Since then many articles on various epigraphic finds, Hebrew scripts, and the evolution of the alphabet have established his reputation today as one of the foremost Semitic epigraphers.

A second area of research and writing in which Professor Cross quickly established himself as one of the knowledgeable authorities is the area of the Dead Sea Scrolls, and especially the impetus they provided for the textual criticism of the Hebrew Bible. His volume, *The Ancient Library of Qumran and Modern Biblical Studies* (1st ed., 1958; rev. ed., 1961 and 1980), is a classic in the field and one of the most informative and readable introductions to the Scrolls. Cross's theory regarding the evolution of local texts is one of the more provocative and potentially most fruitful developments in the textual criticism of the Hebrew Bible.

A third major area of Cross's scholarly contribution is the religion of Israel, to which this volume is devoted. This interest was already foreshadowed in his very first publication, the essay on the Priestly Tabernacle mentioned above, and it has manifested itself from time to time in a series of important essays. Outstanding among these are his article "Yahweh and the God of the Patriarchs," *Harvard Theological Review* 55 (1962) 225–59, and his article "'ēl" in the *Theologisches Wörterbuch zum Alten Testament.* Several of these essays were gathered in revised and expanded form in a volume published by the Harvard University Press in 1973 under the title *Canaanite Myth and Hebrew Epic: Essays in the History of the Religion of Israel.* This volume is easily one of the most interesting and thought-provoking works on the subject to appear in this century. It is a model of scholarly writing, exemplifying masterly control of data, creative synthesis, careful reasoning, and lucid writing.

In addition to being a prolific author himself, Cross has also served as a distinguished editor. He is editor of Harvard Semitic Monographs, associate editor of the *Bulletin of the American Schools of Oriental Research*, and chairman of the editorial boards of Hermeneia and Harvard Semitic Studies. He also serves as a member of the editorial boards of *The Biblical Archaeologist, The Harvard Theological Review, Zeitschrift für die alttestamentliche Wissenschaft,* and Catholic Biblical Quarterly Monograph Series.

No review of Cross's many accomplishments would be complete without at least alluding briefly to his gifts as a teacher and the lasting impact he has had on his students. Through them his influence extends throughout many of the leading universities and seminaries in North America and other parts of the world. It was also in part his stimulus as a teacher and scholar that led to the formation of the Colloquium for Biblical Research, under whose auspices this volume was initially planned and subsequently executed and from whose membership the editors of this volume were selected. Several of its members are also contributors of chapters in this volume and one of them, Werner E. Lemke, prepared this biographical sketch. The Colloquium for Biblical Research was founded in 1963 by seven of Cross's students, then all doctoral candidates at Harvard Unversity. Since then, the Colloquium has expanded to include distinguished graduates from other institutions. Its members meet annually in extended sessions for the purpose of sharing research in fields of ancient Near Eastern studies focusing on the Bible. It is only proper and fitting that this organization has assumed sponsorship of a volume honoring one who has contributed so much to this field. It is with profound gratitude and deep affection that we join others in paying tribute to a master scholar and teacher of us all.

INTRODUCTION

Ancient Israelite religion is a subject much studied but far from fully understood. The primary base of data for reconstructing or describing that religion—the Hebrew Bible—has been known and examined minutely for two millennia. Yet new evidence of direct bearing on the history of the religion of Israel continues to appear as a result of the archaeological investigations being carried on—in extensive fashion—in this century. The literature of the Bible, the revelatory scriptures of two of the great religions of the world, Judaism and Christianity, is an outgrowth of that religious history though not precisely coincident with it in all its parts and development. Here of course is sufficient reason for major attention to the subject. Further, the effort to understand with greater clarity the history and culture of the ancient Near East, one of the seedbeds of civilization, requires considerable attention to the religion and culture of Israel, a part of that world which had an impact on the ensuing religious history of the world far beyond what one would expect from a nation of such modest size and power.

In the midst of many other inquiries into the Bible over the past three quarters of a century, the religion of Israel has persisted as a subject of interest. During that time the strong focus on the Bible as a theological source has sometimes eclipsed its role as a source for Israel's religious practices and beliefs, but efforts to deal with particular problems as well as survey the whole have not been lacking (see Bibliography at end of Introduction). Most of the major treatments of ancient Israelite religion have been the work of a single scholar and essentially based upon the biblical literature. While all of these are useful and valuable contributions to the field, there is need now for a work of more comprehensive scope with regard to both the material covered and the scholarly resources employed. This work, dedicated to Frank Moore Cross, one of the historians of Israel's religion who has clearly recognized the need for a more comprehensive approach and demonstrated its value in his own work, has been planned to fill that need. It is no small indication of Cross's standing in the field and the esteem in which he is held by friends and colleagues throughout the world that it has been possible to produce such a work as this. The continuity between his own work on the religion of Israel and this volume does not reside in any particular reconstruction of that religion but in the desire to address the subject with a broad range of data, models, and expertise.

The types of data that must be drawn upon in analyzing and reconstructing Israel's religion are four: (1) biblical texts, which cover the broad range of that religion's history and are composed and refracted in a complex process of tradition and literary history; (2) extrabiblical primary sources, that is, those written remains which come from the time and space that ancient Israel occupied, specifically the corpus of epigraphic material uncovered in excavations of (presumably) Israelite sites and those closely related to Israel or in direct contact with Israel, for example, the Mesha stele and some Ammonite texts; (3) extrabiblical secondary sources, that is, the larger body of written remains from the ancient Near East surrounding Israel during the last two millennia B.C.E. (the relevance of the much earlier Eblaite material for Israel's religious history is so uncertain and controverted that it has not been included in this volume); and (4) archaeological data, that is, the nonepigraphic, building and artefactual remains, especially from Palestine proper but also including similar relevant data from the wider environment. All of these kinds of material evidence are brought to bear on ancient Israel's religion in this volume. Particular attention is given to the last three because they have generally not played as significant a role as they deserve in large-scale studies of that religion and they inevitably require a range of expertise and knowledge that few individuals can bring by themselves to such an enterprise.

The biblical literature is the primary focus in Part Two of this volume; the extrabiblical and archaeological material is the primary focus in Part One. It is obvious, however, that these types of data should not and can not be looked at separately without relating them to one another. The division of the book into two parts, therefore, is only partially legitimate but does represent a focusing of the chapters. Those in Part One give primary attention to *comparative Near Eastern, epigraphic,* and *archaeological* data; those in Part Two give primary attention to *biblical* data. In many, if not most, cases the chapters relate to both biblical and nonbiblical materials. For example, M. Weinfeld's treatment of the tribal league at Sinai draws upon Egyptian as well as biblical data, although the latter are primarily in view. P. K. McCarter's chapter, however, in dealing with two important aspects of the religion of Israel under the monarchy, specifically the question of the existence of local cults of Israel's god, Yahweh, and the relationship of (the) asherah to that deity, focuses primarily on the important epigraphic material from Kuntillet ʿAjrud but also ranges broadly across Ugaritic, Akkadian, and biblical texts to deal with the issues at hand, as indeed do other chapters whose primary focus is epigraphic, for example, those of J. A. Hackett and J. H. Tigay. In a quite opposite fashion—and intentionally so—some chapters focus solely upon a single corpus of texts without reference to other kinds of data precisely in order to elucidate the contribution of that particular corpus to our understanding of Israel's cultural and religious history. Examples of such an approach are D. N. Freedman's delineation of the earliest understanding of Yahweh in Israel's religion as discerned from a study of the corpus of early poetry and N. Avigad's examination of the socioreligious information derived from a study of the corpus of Israelite seals. Even in these cases, however, it is instructive that Freedman finds the biblical literature illumined by reference to Canaanite religious developments and the texts from Kuntillet ʿAjrud and that Avigad quite naturally places the glyptic evidence in conversation with information drawn from the Bible.

The study of an ancient religion involves several perspectives and questions, all of which are reflected in the chapters published here. The issues of *origins* and *historical development* are taken up in a number of ways. To get at beginning stages one must identify the earliest evidence and from that seek to reconstruct the earliest features (e.g., Weinfeld and Freedman). Later stages, however, are equally important, if not more so. Certainly that is true for the rise of kingship and the formation of a national state, the subject of chapters by G. E. Mendenhall, C. Meyers, and J. J. M. Roberts. It is worth noting that these chapters deal with the ideology of kingship, but not in the now familiar terms of sacral or divine kingship. The issues raised here have to do with the relationship of kingship and the state to legitimating traditions, to temple-building as a historical, social, symbolic, and religious activity, and to presumed pagan influences.

Contemporary study of Israel's religion has given much attention to the Josianic reform in the late seventh century B.C.E. and the Deuteronomistic movement(s) associated with it as well as to the exilic and early postexilic period. There, it has been suggested, is where one may find the religious roots of much of the biblical literature. In other words, the latest periods may be in some sense as formative as the earlier ones. For this reason a number of chapters are devoted to these later stages and the religious movements and crises reflected therein and their outcomes (N. Lohfink, K. Baltzer, P. D. Hanson, E. M. Meyers, J. G. Janzen, and S. Talmon).

The examination of the origins and historical development of an ancient Near Eastern religion in its whole or in its parts inevitably raises *comparative* questions, that is, issues arising out of the relation of Israelite religion to its religious environment. Several chapters in this volume focus in whole or in part on the context or world out of which Israelite religion developed and in which it flourished (e.g., W. W. Hallo, T. Jacobsen, A. Malamat, P. D. Miller, J. C. Greenfield, B. Peckham, and other articles dealing with primary epigraphic remains). In some cases, major features of Israelite religion, such as sacrifice, the aniconic tradition, and prophecy are examined in the light of new data from the ancient Near East (Hallo, Jacobsen, and Malamat). In other cases, essays focus more broadly on features of various religions or the literary remains testifying to religious developments among neighboring peoples, cities, or states, identifying aspects of significance for understanding Israelite religion (e.g., Miller, Greenfield, Peckham, and Hackett).

One of the issues that increasingly occupies the attention of students of Israel's religion is the question of the relation between *public* and *popular* expressions of that religion, between *official* and *unofficial, normative* and *aberrant*. These distinctions are not all the same. There are manifestations of popular religion fully in accord with normative and public expressions. There are public and national facets of the religion that at certain periods may be quite out of accord with normative understandings. The very extent to which the biblical literature itself represents a majority or a minority understanding of Israel's religion is by no means a clearly decided issue. This means that the biblical literature needs to be carefully examined for signs of a greater religious complexity than previously recognized (e.g., P. Bird on women in the Israelite cultus) but also that one must investigate other sources to identify religious elements that are not as transparent in the primary reports and documents, that is, the biblical literature. Here is one of the reasons for devoting a number of chapters to the archaeological remains from Palestine and its environs, both epigraphic (e.g., Greenfield, Peckham, J. Naveh, M. D. Coogan, Hackett, McCarter, Tigay, and Avigad) and artefactual (W. G. Dever and J. S. Holladay). These chapters are not necessarily designed explicitly to explore the relationships or distinctions referred to at the beginning of this paragraph, but they illumine them in many respects and in some cases (e.g., McCarter and Tigay) offer major proposals for integrating biblical and epigraphic evidence in reconstructing aspects of Israel's religion. A notable example of the potential impact of inscriptional data on our understanding of the complex components of Israel's religion is the considerable reference in these pages to the finds from Kuntillet ʿAjrud (e.g., Miller, Coogan, McCarter, Tigay, Holladay, Weinfeld, and Freedman) and Deir ʿAllā (Malamat, Greenfield, Coogan, Hackett, and Mendenhall).

In terms of method and approach, it is increasingly clear that reconstructing ancient Israelite religion cannot be done in satisfactory fashion without drawing upon *sociological* and *anthropological* data and models to illumine features otherwise unclear and in some cases to help fill the gaps in our knowledge with imaginative hypotheses that grow out of a broad base of data and analogies from comparable social and cultural systems. Important examples of such an approach are given here in greater and lesser degrees in the chapters of Dever, Holladay, C. Meyers, Bird, and Hanson.

Finally, the core of any presentation of Israel's religion involves the articulation and interpretation of *primary features* of that religion as it is known from official and nonofficial sources. Most of this volume does that in fairly direct fashion, but certain topics deemed by the editors to be of particular importance have been selected for special concentration— for example, monarchy (Mendenhall, C. Meyers, and Roberts), covenant (Oden), women (Bird), love and marriage as a religious motif (H. Ringgren), wisdom and piety (R. E. Murphy, M. E. Stone), reform (Lohfink), apocalypticism (J. J. Collins), torah (J. D. Levenson), and the relationship between Israel's religion and biblical theology—both Christian and Jewish (M. H. Goshen-Gottstein). Such a list indicates something of the scope of this book even as it reminds one of the many other features that might have been included had one but "world enough and time" (and space, etc.). It is hoped that the volume as a whole, while by no means exhaustive, will be sufficiently comprehensive, illustrative, and judicious to be of lasting value to the student of Israel's religion.

BIBLIOGRAPHY

For brief overviews of the contemporary investigation of particular problems and issues, see P. D. Miller, Jr., "Israelite Religion," *The Hebrew Bible and Its Modern Interpreters* (ed. D. A. Knight and G. M. Tucker; Philadelphia: Fortress Press, 1985) 201–7, and W. Zimmerli, "The History of Israelite Religion," *Tradition and Interpretation* (ed. G. W. Anderson (London: Oxford University Press, 1979) 351–84. Relatively recent comprehensive surveys may be found in H. Ringgren, *Israelite Religion* (Philadelphia, Fortress Press, 1966), Th. C. Vriezen, *The Religion of Ancient Israel* (Philadelphia: Westminster Press, 1967), G. Fohrer, *History of Israelite Religion* (Nashville: Abingdon Press, 1972), and W. H. Schmidt, *The Faith of Israel* (Philadelphia: Westminster Press, 1984).

ABBREVIATIONS

AAR	American Academy of Religion
AASOR	Annual of the American Schools of Oriental Research
AB	Anchor Bible
Abot R. Nat.	*Abot de Rabbi Nathan*
AcOr	*Acta orientalia*
ADAJ	Annual of the Department of Antiquities of Jordan
AES	*Archives européenes de sociologie*
AfO	*Archiv für Orientforschung*
AION	*Annali dell'istituto orientali di Napoli*
AIPHOS	*Annuaire de l'institut de philologie et d'histoire orientales et slaves*
AJA	*American Journal of Archaeology*
AJBA	*Australian Journal of Biblical Archaeology*
AJSL	*American Journal of Semitic Languages and Literatures*
AnBib	Analecta biblica
ANEP	*Ancient Near East in Pictures,* J. B. Pritchard, ed.
ANET	*Ancient Near Eastern Texts,* J. B. Pritchard, ed.
AOAT	Alter Orient und Altes Testament
ARM	Archives royales de Mari
ARW	*Archiv für Religionswissenschaft*
AS	*Anatolian Studies*
ASOR	American Schools of Oriental Research
b.	*Babli, The Babylonian Talmud*
BA	*The Biblical Archaeologist*
BAR	*Biblical Archaeologist Reader*
BARev	*Biblical Archaeology Review*
BASOR	*Bulletin of the American Schools of Oriental Research*
BETL	Bibliotheca ephemeridum theologicarum lovaniensium
Bib	*Biblica*

BibOr	Biblica et orientalia
BIES	*Bulletin of the Israel Exploration Society*
BJRL	*Bulletin of the John Rylands University Library of Manchester*
BKAT	Biblischer Kommentar: Altes Testament
BMB	*Bulletin du musée de Beyrouth*
BTB	*Biblical Theology Bulletin*
BWANT	Beiträge zur Wissenschaft vom Alten und Neuen Testament
BZ	*Biblische Zeitschrift*
BZAW	Beihefte zur Z*AW*
CAD	*The Assyrian Dictionary of the Oriental Institute of the University of Chicago*
CAH	*Cambridge Ancient History*
CBQ	*Catholic Biblical Quarterly*
CBQMS	Catholic Biblical Quarterly—Monograph Series
CIS	*Corpus inscriptionum semiticarum*
CMHE	*Canaanite Myth and Hebrew Epic*, F. M. Cross (Cambridge: Harvard University Press, 1973)
CRAIBL	*Comptes rendus de l'Académie des inscriptions et belles-lettres*
CRINT	Compendia rerum iudaicarum ad novum testamentum
CSSH	*Comparative Studies in Society and History*
CTA	*Corpus des tablettes en cunéiformes alphabétiques*, A. Herdner (Paris: Paul Geuthner, 1963)
EAEHL	*Encyclopedia of Archaeological Excavations in the Holy Land*, ed. B. Mazar and E. Stern (Jerusalem: Massada)
EI	*Eretz-Israel*
EM	*Ensîqlôpediâ Miqra'it*
EncJud	*Encyclopaedia Judaica*
EvTh	*Evangelische Theologie*
ExTim	*Expository Times*
FOTL	Forms of Old Testament Literature
FRLANT	Forschungen zur Religion und Literatur des Alten und Neuen Testaments
GARS	*Gesammelte Aufsätze zur Religionssoziologie*, Max Weber (Tübingen: J. C. B. Mohr [Paul Siebeck], 1921)
GAW	*Gesammelte Aufsätze zur Wissenschaftslehre*, Max Weber (Tübingen: J. C. B. Mohr [Paul Siebeck], 1933)
GKC	*Gesenius' Hebrew Grammar*, ed. E. Kautzsch, trans. A. E. Cowley

HALAT	*Hebräisches und aramäisches Lexikon zum Alten Testament*, W. Baumgartner et al.
HAT	Handbuch zum Alten Testament
HES	*Harvard Excavations at Samaria* (1908–1910)
HKAT	Handkommentar zum Alten Testament
HR	*History of Religions*
HSM	Harvard Semitic Monographs
HTR	*Harvard Theological Review*
HUCA	*Hebrew Union College Annual*
ICC	International Critical Commentary
IDB	*The Interpreter's Dictionary of the Bible*, ed. G. A. Buttrick, et al. (Nashville: Abingdon Press, 1962)
IDBSup	Supplementary volume to *IDB*
IEJ	*Israel Exploration Journal*
JANESCU	*Journal of the Ancient Near Eastern Society of Columbia University*
JAOS	*Journal of the American Oriental Society*
JBL	*Journal of Biblical Literature*
JCS	*Journal of Cuneiform Studies*
JEA	*Journal of Egyptian Archaeology*
JES	*Journal of Ecumenical Studies*
JJS	*Journal of Jewish Studies*
JJSoc	*Jewish Journal of Sociology*
JNES	*Journal of Near Eastern Studies*
JQR	*Jewish Quarterly Review*
JR	*Journal of Religion*
JSJ	*Journal for the Study of Judaism in the Persian, Hellenistic and Roman Period*
JSOT	*Journal for the Study of the Old Testament*
JTC	*Journal for Theology and the Church*
KAI	*Kanaanäische und aramäische Inschriften*, H. Donner and W. Röllig (Wiesbaden: Otto Harrassowitz)
KD	*Kerygma und Dogma*
MAOG	*Mitteilungen der altorientalischen Gesellschaft*
MDOG	*Mitteilungen der deutschen Orient-Gesellschaft*
MT	Masoretic Text
MUSJ	*Mélanges de l'université Saint-Joseph*
MVAG	*Mitteilungen der vorderasiatisch-ägyptischen Gesellschaft*
MWSJ	*Max Weber's Studie über das antike Judentum: Interpretation und Kritik*, ed. W. Schluchter (Frankfurt: Suhrkamp, 1978)

NCB	New Clarendon Bible
OBO	Orbis biblicus et orientalis
Or	*Orientalia*
OrAnt	*Oriens antiquus*
OTL	Old Testament Library
OTS	*Oudtestamentische Studiën*
PAAJR	*Proceedings of the American Academy of Jewish Research*
PEQ	*Palestine Exploration Quarterly*
PRU	*Le palais royal d'Ugarit*
PVTG	Pseudepigrapha Veteris Testamenti graece
QDAP	*Quarterly of the Department of Antiquities in Palestine*
RA	*Revue d'assyriologie et d'archéologie orientale*
RB	*Revue biblique*
RelRev	*Religious Studies Review*
RIDA	*Revue internationale des droits de l'antiquité*
RQ	*Römische Quartalschrift für christliche Altertumskunde und Kirchengeschichte*
Sanh.	*Sanhedrin*
SBL	Society of Biblical Literature
SBLASP	SBL Abstracts and Seminar Papers
SBLDS	SBL Dissertation Series
SBLMS	SBL Monograph Series
SBLSCS	SBL Septuagint and Cognate Studies
SBT	Studies in Biblical Theology
Šeb.	*Šebiʿit*
SHR	Studies in the History of Religions
SJLA	Studies in Judaism in Late Antiquity
SJT	*Scottish Journal of Theology*
ST	*Studia theologica*
StudOr	*Studia orientalia*
TDOT	*Theological Dictionary of the Old Testament,* ed. G. J. Botterweck and H. Ringgren
THAT	*Theologisches Handwörterbuch zum Alten Testament,* ed. E. Jenni and C. Westermann
TLZ	*Theologische Literaturzeitung*
TWAT	*Theologisches Wörterbuch zum Alten Testament,* ed. G. J. Botterweck and H. Ringgren
UF	*Ugarit-Forschungen*
UT	*Ugaritic Textbook,* C. H. Gordon
VT	*Vetus Testamentum*
VTSup	Vetus Testamentum, Supplements
WHJP	*World History of the Jewish People*

WMANT	Wissenschaftliche Monographien zum Alten und Neuen Testament
WO	*Die Welt des Orients*
WZKM	*Wiener Zeitschrift für die Kunde des Morgenlandes*
ZA	*Zeitschrift für Assyriologie*
ZAW	*Zeitschrift für die alttestamentliche Wissenschaft*
ZDPV	*Zeitschrift des deutschen Palästina-Vereins*
ZTK	*Zeitschrift für Theologie und Kirche*

ANCIENT ISRAELITE RELIGION

PART ONE

SOURCES AND CONTEXTS

1

The Origins of the Sacrificial Cult: New Evidence from Mesopotamia and Israel[1]

WILLIAM W. HALLO

In 1975, I. J. Gelb discussed the role of singers, musicians, snake charmers, and bear wards in ancient Sumer in an article which, no doubt with a nod to J. Huizinga,[2] he entitled "Homo Ludens in Early Mesopotamia."[3] If I turn in this chapter from this "playful" side of the Sumerians to their more "murderous" aspect, it is with an eye not only to Gelb's study but also to a monograph published just three years earlier by the Swiss classicist W. Burkert under the title "Homo Necans: Interpretations of Ancient Greek Sacrificial Rites and Myths."[4]

In his important study, Burkert surveyed the anthropological and more particularly the Greek literary evidence for the origins and motivations of animal sacrifice. His conclusion, to which this summary cannot begin to do justice, is that the sacrificial rites as described in Greek literature or observed to this day in "primitive" cultures reflect a prehistoric origin which can be reconstructed approximately as follows. Prior to the domestication of plants and animals, hunting and gathering groups divided between the sexes the essential functions of victualing themselves, with men assigned to the hunt and women to the gathering of edible plants. But the hunt required collective action and the aid of traps and weapons, and these mechanics held a potential threat in that they could conceivably be turned inward against members of the group. Hence the catching and dispatching of the animal prey were gradually hedged about with "ritualistic" restrictions designed to reduce the likelihood of internecine conflict among the hunters.

With the domestication of plants and animals, the earlier sexual specialization tended to disappear, but the replacement of wild prey with domesticated victims created new problems. Now the bull, cow, goat, or lamb led to the slaughter was not only defenseless but familiar and more or less humanlike in appearance and disposition. Thus, dispatching it could not be justified in terms of self-defense or as an act of manly valor

What Josiah in effect instituted reconciled the older prohibition against "profane slaughter" with the newer centralization of the cult: If the only authorized altar was to be in Jerusalem, then slaughter without benefit of altar had to be permitted outside Jerusalem as a matter of practical necessity.[14]

This theory of the evolution of the Israelite sacrifice, essentially based on Milgrom, differs significantly from earlier theories. The classical Wellhausenist position, for example, which still finds adherents today, insists on the chronological priority of Deuteronomy over the Priestly Code and thus regards the provisions of Leviticus as intended to abrogate those of Deuteronomy, rather than vice versa. A novel modification of this view would make the abrogation temporary: An early postexilic reform was intended by those who returned from Babylonian exile to discourage pagan practices among the peasants they had left behind and "perhaps also to increase the prestige and income of . . . the small shrine which had replaced the grand Temple of Solomon," but the new law became impracticable and soon enough a dead letter.[15]

R. de Vaux, in his authoritative treatment of the subject, reconstructs a dual origin for Israelite sacrifice. The importance of blood and the consumption of meat by the faithful, already illustrated by the paschal sacrifice, represents the earliest stage, associated with the desert wanderings and derived from, or at least similar to, pre-Islamic Arab practices. In Canaan and Greece, on the other hand, indigenous usage tended to favor the burning on the altar of the entire sacrificial animal (holocaust) or at least a significant part of it (thysía), and this usage gave rise to the Israelite concept of whole burnt offering ('ōlâ) or partial burnt offering (zebaḥ) respectively. The latter, the commoner of the two (at least at first), left part of the victim to be consumed by the priests and part to be eaten by the worshipers in a sacral meal. But whatever the historical analogues to nomadic or autochthonous precedent, Israelite sacrifice was transformed and sublimated. It did not serve to appease, to feed, or to achieve union with the deity. Rather, it came to constitute, in varying proportions, an act of donation to, communion with, or exculpation by the deity.[16]

Let us then turn to the Mesopotamian evidence, by far the most richly documented of all in the preclassical world. For here we have not only, as in Israel and elsewhere, the canonical (literary) formulations of how sacrificial rites are to be performed, or what can be designated "prescriptive rituals," but also the archival (economic) texts, the after-the-fact accounts of the actual course of events taken by the ritual and duly recorded from the objective point of view of those charged with detailing the expenses incurred for each step of the ritual against the possibility of a future audit by a higher authority. These are the so-called "descriptive rituals" and they survive in far greater numbers than the "prescriptive rituals" and from many successive periods.[17] The "economy of the cult"[18] that can be reconstructed with their help leaves no doubt that, in Mesopotamia, animal sacrifice, though ostensibly a mechanism for feeding the deity, was at best a thinly disguised method for sanctifying and justifying meat consumption by human beings—a privilege routinely accorded to priesthood, aristocracy, and royalty and sporadically, notably on holidays and holy days, to the masses of the population.[19] As noted by de Vaux,[20] the late Jewish author of "Daniel, Bel and the Dragon" saw through the Mesopotamian pretense involved in the "care and feeding of the gods"[21] and took a dim view of it.[22]

But the ritual texts, whether prescriptive or descriptive, tell us little about the true motivation for the sacrificial cult or the related question of its origins in the native conception. For this we must turn to the higher forms of literature, notably the mythology. Until now, this has served to underline the "official" interpretation which stressed the divine need for sustenance. Indeed, if there is one common thread running through both Sumerian and Akkadian myths about the relationship between gods and men, it is that men were created to relieve the gods of the need to provide for their own food. Thus, for example, in the Sumerian myth known as "Cattle and Grain" or "Lahar and Ashnan"[23] man was created (lit. "given breath") "for the sake of the sheepfolds and good things of the gods."[24] To quote W. G. Lambert, "The idea that man was created to relieve the gods of hard labor by supplying them with food and drink was standard among both Sumerians and Babylonians."[25]

This conception is even thought to find a faint echo in the primeval history of Genesis. For the epic (J) version of the creation begins: "When the Lord God made earth and heaven—when no shrub of the field was yet on earth and no grasses of the field had yet sprouted, because the Lord God had not sent rain upon the earth and there was no man to till the soil" (Gen 2:4b–5). And it continues, after the creation of man (Gen 2:15): "The Lord God took the man and placed him in the garden of Eden, to till it and tend it."

But a newly recovered Sumerian myth puts matters into a rather different light and permits considerably more precise analogies to be drawn with biblical conceptions. The myth, or mythologem, is embedded in an ostensibly epic tale dealing, as do all other Sumerian epics, with the exploits of the earliest rulers of Uruk, that well-nigh eternal city where writing first emerged in full form late in the fourth millennium and where cuneiform continued in use almost to the Christian era, the city whose name is preserved in the table of nations as Erech (Gen 10:10). The earliest rulers of Uruk were preoccupied with heroic campaigns against distant Aratta, the source of lapis lazuli and other precious imports from across the Iranian highlands to the east, perhaps as far away as Afghanistan. On one of these campaigns the crown prince Lugalbanda fell ill and had to be left behind in a cave of the mountains by his comrades, with only enough food and fire to ease his dying days. Left for dead, he prayed to the sun at dusk, followed by the evening star, then the moon, and finally the sun again at dawn—and there the text effectively broke off in the first systematic presentation of the plot by C. Wilcke in 1969.[26]

The thread of the epic is taken up at this point by a large tablet from the Yale Babylonian Collection first identified by S. N. Kramer, copied by me in 1965, incorporated into a preliminary but unpublished edition by S. Cohen some years later,[27] and finally edited by me in full and with the help of numerous fragmentary duplicate texts from other collections for a volume in honor of Professor Kramer.[28] From all of this, the following sequel can be reconstructed.

The prayers of Lugalbanda were answered: He arose from his sickbed and left the cave. He refreshed himself from revivifying "grass" and the invigorating waters of the nearest stream, but then he faced a problem: The food left for him by his comrades-in-arms had given out; the fire they had left had died out. How was he to nourish himself henceforth? He was still in the mountains, or at least the foothills of the Zagros, surrounded by wild plants and wild animals. The plants are pointedly contrasted with the domesticated varieties familiar to him from the cultivated plains of Uruk, and the animals consume them with relish. It is implied, however, that they are not fit for human consumption. In this extremity, Lugalbanda decides to make a virtue of necessity and turn carnivorous. But this is easier said than done when a solitary man confronts a thundering herd of aurochsen. He must select one that is weak and languid from overeating[29] and try to trap it as it mills about the meadow. To do this, he must bait the one trap he has presumably constructed. As I translate the relevant passage, he does so by baking some delectable cakes—admittedly a questionable procedure in these circumstances but one that would justify a subsidiary aetiology inserted in the text at this point, namely, the invention of fire, or at least of fire-making! The embers of the last campfire left by his companions having died out, Lugalbanda must start a new fire by striking flintstones (?) together until they generate a spark. And even then, "not knowing how to bake a cake, not knowing an oven" (11. 284, 289) he has to improvise. But one way or another, the aurochs is caught and then tethered by means of a rope made on the spot from the roots and tops of the wild juniper tree uprooted and cut with a knife. The process is then repeated with two goats, taking care to select healthy ones from those in sight.

But with the practical problems disposed of, Lugalbanda's real problems are just beginning. His companions have left him supplied with an ax of meteoric iron and a hip dagger of terrestrial iron (the latter presumably used already to cut the juniper trees), but how can he presume to wield them against his quarry? Only the appropriate ritual can solve this problem. Providentially, the answer is vouchsafed in a dream, by none other than Za(n)qara, the god of dreams himself. He must slaughter the animals, presumably at night and in front of a pit, so that the blood drains into the pit while the fat runs out over the plain where the snakes of the mountain can sniff it, and so that the animals expire at daybreak.

Upon wakening, Lugalbanda follows these prescriptions to the letter, needless to say. But he goes them one better—significantly better. At dawn he summons the four greatest deities of the Sumerian pantheon—An, Enlil, Enki, and Ninhursag—to a banquet at the pit. This banquet is called in the text *gizbun* (written logographically as *ki-kaš-gar* [lit. "place where beer is placed"]), a Sumerian word later equated with Akkadian *tākultu,* the technical term for a cultic meal or divine repast.[30] Lugalbanda pours libations of beer and wine, carves the meat of the goats, roasts it together with the bread, and lets the sweet savor rise to the gods like incense. The intelligible portion of the text ends with these two lines (ll. 375–76): "So of the food prepared by Lugalbanda / An, Enlil, Enki, and Ninhursag consumed the best part."

What is offered here is a first glimpse at a tantalizing new bit of evidence regarding early Sumerian religious sensibilities. Admittedly, the text can be translated differently here and there by other interpreters or, upon maturer reflection, by myself. But some salient points are already more or less beyond dispute. They are enumerated here, together with the conclusions that I propose to draw from them.

1. The highest deities of the Sumerian pantheon—three gods and one goddess who traditionally represent and govern the four cosmic realms—physically partake of the best of the meat at a sacred meal convoked in their honor. Presumably, then, they sanction the slaughter of the animals that has made this consumption of their meat possible.

2. The slaughter itself is carried out according to divinely inspired prescriptions, by a divinely chosen individual, with weapons made of rare metals. Presumably, then, we are to understand it as sacred, not profane, slaughter, indeed as the aetiology of the sacrificial cult.

3. The capture of the animals is related in the context of an elaborate narrative that is ostensibly of epic character but presumably has the typical mythic function of explaining a continuing phenomenon observed

9

in the present by appeal to a real or, more often, imaginary one-time event in the past.[31] In this case, then, we are led to conclude that we are presented with an aetiology of meat-eating that explains its origins as derived from the straits in which Lugalbanda found himself, thus replacing a prior, vegetarian order of things.

4. Other and perhaps lesser aetiologies are found in the epic cycle of Uruk. Our own text thus seems to include the invention of fire; another, the Epic of Enmerkar and the Lord of Aratta, includes the invention of writing.[32] That neither invention is placed chronologically quite where modern research would date it does not detract from the deduction that Sumerian epic was a conscious vehicle for mythologems in general and for aetiologies in particular.

5. Finally, the new text offers a fresh perspective on the comparable biblical conceptions as current scholarship sees their evolution. In both cases, an original dispensation provides for vegetarianism in the divine as well as the human (and perhaps even animal) realm, with mankind assigned the task of domesticating and cultivating the vegetation. Although in the biblical case the domestication of animals followed as early as the second human generation (Abel), its purpose may be construed as limited, in the time-honored Near Eastern manner, to the exploitation of their renewable resources, such as wool, milk, dung, and draft power.[33] Although Abel sacrifices "the choicest of the firstlings of his flock,"[34] and his sacrifice is accepted, it is not until Noah's sacrifice of the animals that he had brought safely through the flood that humanity is specifically given dominion over the animals and allowed to consume them.

In the Sumerian flood story, the flood hero (Ziusudra), celebrating his emergence from the ark, "slaughtered a large number of bulls and sheep" in "a stock phrase often found in Sumerian literature"[35]—but the text breaks off at this point before we learn whether human beings shared in the feast. In the Old Babylonian Epic of Atra-hasis, the passage about the end of the flood is fragmentary, but the sacrifice is described simply as an "offering" *(nīqu)* of which the gods sniff the smell as they gather around like flies and which they then eat.[36] Finally, in the Neo-Assyrian version of the flood as incorporated in the Gilgamesh Epic, the sacrifice is specified as burned over cane, cedarwood, and myrtle *(qanû erûnu u asu),*[37] thus attracting the gods, again like flies, to the sweet savor. Thus the cuneiform tradition may not have linked the inauguration of meat-eating with the immediate aftermath of the flood as did the Bible. But Lugalbanda, as the third member or generation of the postdiluvian dynasty at Uruk,[38] could represent the corresponding Sumerian conception of this innovation.

With relatively minor differences, then, Babylonian and biblical myths reflect remarkably similar conceptions of the origins of the sacrificial cult. Where the two cultures diverged widely was in its subsequent evolution. In Mesopotamia, the sacrificial cult was literally taken as a means of feeding the gods and specifically, beginning with the end of the third millennium, their cult statues.[39] In Israel, where anthropomorphic conceptions and representations of the deity were proscribed, and where the worshiper already participated in the consumption of the earliest (paschal) sacrifice, the later cultic legislation explicitly provided priesthood and laity with a share of the sacrificial offerings. Thus Israelite sacrifice, though in origin designed, as in Mesopotamia, to sanctify the very act of consumption, "ultimately served as well to sanctify other human activities and to atone for other human transgressions."[40]

NOTES

1. In its original form, this material was first given at the University of Puget Sound, Tacoma, Wash., on 13 March, 1983, R. G. Albertson presiding. In slightly different form, and under the title of "Homo Necans in Early Mesopotamia," it was read to the 193d meeting of the American Oriental Society, Baltimore, 22 March, 1983.

2. J. Huizinga, *Homo Ludens: A Study of the Play-Element in Culture* (Boston: Beacon Press, 1955).

3. I. J. Gelb, "Homo Ludens in Early Mesopotamia," *StudOr* 46 (= Armas I. Salonen Anniversary Volume, 1975) 43–76.

4. W. Burkert, *Homo Necans. Interpretationen altgriechischer Opferriten und Mythen* (= Religionsgeschichtliche Versuche und Vorarbeiten 32, 1972). This has meantime been translated by P. Bing under the title *Homo Necans: The Anthropology of Ancient Greek Sacrificial Ritual and Myth* (Berkeley and Los Angeles: University of California Press, 1983).

5. The word "sacrifice," which means "to make a thing sacred" or "to do a sacred act" *(sacrum facere),* was used in Latin to describe "various rites which arose from the common meal when that meal was held . . . for the purpose of entering into union with [the divine]" (R. K. Yerkes, *Sacrifice in Greek and Roman Religions and Early Judaism* [London: Adam & Charles Black, 1953]) 25–26.

6. "What we call by the Latin word 'sacrifice' is nothing else than a sacred meal" (L. Bouyer, *Rite and Man* [Notre Dame, Ind.: University of Notre Dame Press, 1962] 82). Note that the Greek terms for "offering" *(thýos, thysía)* acquired the sense of incense, presumably because for the celestials the smoke of the burning offering was adequate, according to L. L. Mitchell, *The Meaning of Ritual* (New York: Paulist Press, 1977) 17–21.

7. R. Girard, *La violence et le sacré* (Paris: Bernard Grasset, 1972); trans. by P. Gregory as *Violence and the Sacred* (Baltimore: Johns Hopkins University Press, 1977).

8. W. W. Hallo apud W. G. Plaut, B. J. Bamberger, and W. W. Hallo, *The Torah:*

A Modern Commentary (New York: Union of American Hebrew Congregations, 1981) 743; previously apud Plaut, *Numbers* (1979) xxvi.

9. Translations are according to the New Jewish Version (NJV) unless otherwise indicated.

10. See *EncJud* s.v.

11. J. Milgrom, "A Prolegomenon to Leviticus 17:11," *JBL* 90 (1971) 149–56.

12. J. Milgrom, "Profane Slaughter and the Composition of Deuteronomy," *HUCA* 47 (1976) 1–17; idem, "A Formulaic Key to the Sources of Deuteronomy," *EI* 14 (1978) 42–47 (English summary, pp. 123*f.).

13. A. R. Hulst, "Opmerkingen over de Ka'ašer-Zinnen in Deuteronomium," *Nederlands Theologisch Tijdschrift* 18 (1963) 337–61.

14. Cf. already J. Milgrom, *IEJ* 23 (1973) 160.

15. Bamberger apud Plaut, *The Torah*, 874; previously idem, *Leviticus* (1979) 179. Cf. also B. A. Levine, *In the Presence of the Lord* (Leiden: E. J. Brill, 1974) 47–52.

16. R. de Vaux, *Ancient Israel: Its Life and Institutions* (trans. J. McHugh; New York: McGraw-Hill Book Co., 1961) 440–41.

17. B. A. Levine, "Ugaritic Descriptive Rituals," *JCS* 17 (1963) 105–11; idem, "The Descriptive Ritual Texts of the Pentateuch," *JAOS* 85 (1965) 307–18; idem, "Offerings to the Temple Gates at Ur" (with W. W. Hallo), *HUCA* 38 (1967) 17–58; A. F. Rainey, "The Order of Sacrifices in Old Testament Ritual Texts," *Bib* 51 (1970) 485–98.

18. For this concept of R. M. Sigrist, see W. W. Hallo, *State and Temple Economy in the Ancient Near East* (ed. E. Lipiński; Orientalia Lovaniensia Analecta 5, 1979) 1. 104–5. See now R. M. Sigrist, *Les s a t t u k k u dans l'Ešumeša durant la période d'isin et Larsa* (= Bibliotheca Mesopotamica 11, 1984).

19. See now the dramatic proof of this proposition for ninth-century Babylonia by Gilbert J. P. McEwan, "Distribution of Meat in Eanna," *Iraq* 45 (1983) 187–98.

20. De Vaux, *Ancient Israel*, 434. Cf. also Jer 7:21.

21. A. L. Oppenheim, *Ancient Mesopotamia: Portrait of a Dead Civilization* (Chicago: University of Chicago Press, 1964) 183–98.

22. Cf. now also R. C. Steiner and C. F. Nims, "You Can't Offer Your Sacrifice and Eat It Too: A Polemical Poem from the Aramaic Text in Demotic Script," *JNES* 43 (1984) 89–114.

23. Unedited; see the texts listed by R. Borger, *Handbuch der Keilschriftliteratur* (Berlin: Walter de Gruyter) 1 (1967) and 2 (1975), under G. A. Barton, *Miscellaneous Babylonian Inscriptions* (New Haven: 1918), no. 8, and the discussion by G. Pettinato, *Das altorientalische Menschenbild und die sumerischen und akkadischen Schöpfungsmythen* (AHAW 1971/I) 86–90.

24. Translated thus or similarly by S. N. Kramer, *Sumerian Mythology* (Memoirs of the American Philosophical Society 21, 1944; 2d ed.; New York: Harper & Row, 1961) 73; idem, *From the Tablets of Sumer* (Indian Hills, Colo.: Falcon's Wing Press, 1963) 221; idem, *History Begins at Sumer* (Philadelphia: University of Pennsylvania Press, 1981) 109.

25. W. G. Lambert and A. R. Millard, *Atra-ḫasīs: The Babylonian Story of the*

Flood (Oxford: Clarendon Press, 1969) 15. Cf. in detail G. Komoróczy, "Work and Strike of the Gods: New Light on the Divine Society in the Sumero-Akkadian Mythology," *Oikumene* 1 (1976) 9–37.

26. C. Wilcke, *Das Lugalbandaepos* (Wiesbaden: Otto Harrassowitz, 1969).

27. Cf. also S. Cohen, "Studies in Sumerian Lexicography, I," in *Kramer Anniversary Volume*, ed. B. L. Eichler et al., AOAT 25 (Neukirchen-Vluyn: Neukirchener Verlag, 1976) 99–101.

28. W. W. Hallo, "Lugalbanda Excavated," *JAOS* 103 (1983) 165–80. See there for a detailed exposition of the text.

29. See Hallo, "Lugalbanda Excavated," 175 line 293. T. Jacobsen proposes an alternative translation: "the curly (haired) aurochs, fatherly, protective" (private communication).

30. Cf. R. Frankena, *Takultu: de sacrale maaltijd in het assyrische ritueel* (diss., Leiden, 1953).

31. Hallo, "Lugalbanda Excavated," 170.

32. G. Komoróczy, "Zur Ätiologie der Schrifterfindung im *Enmerkar-Epos*," *Altorientalische Forschungen* 3 (1975) 19–24.

33. Cf. K. Butz apud Lipiński, *State and Temple Economy*, 305–39 on dung *(putru)* in the Old Babylonian economy; G. Maxwell, *A Reed Shaken by the Wind* (London: Longmans, Green & Co., 1957) on its role among the Marsh Arabs of contemporary Iraq; A. Sherratt, "Plough and Pastoralism: Aspects of the Secondary Products Revolution," *Patterns of the Past: Studies in Honor of David Clarke* (ed. I. Hodder et al.; Cambridge: Cambridge University Press, 1981) 261–305.

34. See NJV. Lit.: "from the firstlings of his flock and [specifically] from their fat [parts or pieces]," i.e., the parts later—in Levitical legislation—especially reserved for the deity or, in the Blessing of Moses, for strange gods (Deut 32:38); cf. Lugalbanda I 350 and 360.

35. M. Civil apud Lambert and Millard, *Atra-ḫasīs*, 145 line 211 and 172 ad loc. Additional references: Pickaxe and Plow (uned.), 25–29; Uruk Lament (MS M. W. Green), 129–15; UD.GAL.NUN hymns (W. G. Lambert, *OrAnt* 20 [1981] 85–86).

36. Lambert and Millard, *Atra-ḫasīs*, 99.

37. *ANET*, 95 line 158.

38. Cf. W. W. Hallo and W. K. Simpson, *The Ancient Near East: A History* (New York: Harcourt Brace Jovanovich, 1971) 47.

39. W. W. Hallo, "Cult Statue and Divine Image: A Preliminary Study," *Scripture in Context II* (ed. W. W. Hallo, J. C. Moyer, and L. G. Perdue; Winona Lake, Ind.: Eisenbrauns, 1983) 1–17.

40. Hallo apud Plaut, *The Torah*, 743; previously apud Bamberger, *Leviticus* (1979) xxvi.

2

The Graven Image

THORKILD JACOBSEN

TO THE PROPHETS: VANITY

The ancient Mesopotamian cult statues, graven images, which form our subject here, were not, admittedly, highly thought of by the prophets and the psalmists of the Bible.[1] Isaiah, the most scathing of them, says of the maker of idols and the wood he carves:

> Half of it he burns in the fire; over the half he eats flesh, he roasts meat and is satisfied; also he warms himself and says, "Aha, I am warm, I have seen the fire!" And the rest of it he makes into a god, his idol; and falls down to it and worships it; he prays to it and says, "Deliver me, for thou art my god!" They know not, nor do they discern; for he has shut their eyes, so that they cannot see, and their minds, so that they cannot understand. No one considers, nor is there knowledge or discernment to say, "Half of it I burned in the fire, I also baked bread on its coals, I roasted flesh and have eaten; and shall I make the residue of it an abomination? Shall I fall down before a block of wood?"
>
> (Isa 44:16–19)

A scathingly sarcastic indictment indeed, but keenly observed and, as far as one can check it, literally true. The Mesopotamian cult statues were indeed normally made of wood and overlaid, "decked," with thin sheets of gold and silver on which details of dress and so forth were engraved. Nor is there any reason to doubt that the carpenters who made the wooden cores would normally and as a matter of course have disposed of cuttings and leftover bits of wood for their work by using them as firewood for domestic purposes.

Must we, then, accept the prophets' verdict as it stands and conclude that the ancient Mesopotamians, a highly intelligent and civilized people, failed so utterly to consider in their heart that they would fall down to a block of wood? It seems almost inconceivable, a challenge, rather, to further investigation to see whether perhaps there was more to it than is immediately evident from the prophets' accounts, some aspect that might make the apparent incongruity less glaring.

15

IDOL OR RELIGIOUS ART?

One's first question will, of course, be whether the prophets in their religious zeal may have misunderstood, as outsiders, what they saw? Western tradition is not averse to images, even to religious images, but no one could rightly think that even as deeply felt and deeply moving a work as Michelangelo's *Pietà* is an idol or that his magnificent paintings in the Sistine Chapel are. At the high altar in the Cathedral of Copenhagen stands a more than life-sized, very beautiful marble statue of Christ by Thorvaldsen. No one has ever seen in that more than its beauty and the occasion it gives for pious thought. Could it not be that the ancient Mesopotamians looked at their cult statues somewhat in the same manner, for their beauty and as encouragement to pious thought only?

The answer must, I think, be a clear "No!" The entire character of Mesopotamian worship, the service to the statue as to a god with offerings and prayers, constant references to it as "the god," or by the name of the god it represents as Marduk, Shamash, and so forth, show clearly that no such explanation will do. There was identity—whatever that may have meant—of god and statue. A few examples may serve to illustrate.

THE CULT STATUE WAS THE GOD

King Agum kakrime of Babylon (1602–1585 B.C.E.) tells in his inscription that:

> When in Babylon the great gods by their holy pronouncement had decreed the return to Babylon of Marduk, Lord of Esagila and Babylon, I, in order that Marduk would turn for me his face toward going to Babylon, prayed to Marduk with (cries of) woe and wails, made plans, paid heed, and so I turned Marduk's face toward the taking of him to Babylon and thus came to the aid of Marduk who loves my reign. By means of the (sacrificial) lamb of the diviner I made enquiry of Shamash (the sungod) the king, and so sent to a faraway land, the land of the Haneans and so they (i.e. the Haneans) verily led hither by the hand Marduk and Sarpanitum, who loves my reign, To Esagila and Babylon I verily returned them. To a house which Shamash had confirmed for me (as suitable) in the enquiry (by divination) I verily took them back.[2]

What is here described as the return of Marduk and his divine consort Sarpanitum was the return of their statues which had been taken to the land of the Haneans as spoil sometime in the past, and the fact that it *was* a matter of statues is abundantly clear from the fact that Agum kakrime goes on immediately to tell how he assembled craftsmen and provided lavishly gold and precious stones for them to decorate the statues in proper style. Presumably they had been stripped of their overlays of precious metals and the like when they were taken as spoils.

A very similar case is the return of the statue of Marduk that had been taken as booty by Elam and was recovered by Nebuchadnezzar I of Babylon (1124–1103 B.C.E.) in a successful campaign against that country. He tells how he prayed with great fervor to Marduk after the victory and how Marduk's

> broad heart had compassion so that he turned his head (lit. "neck") toward the center of Urukug ("The holy city" i.e. Babylon) and . . . hied hither from evil Elam, took the road of jubilation, the path of rejoicing, the trail of pleasure into the midst of Shuanna (i.e. Babylon). The people of the country, all of them, took note of him, the tall stature, perfect, noble, resplendent, and the lord entered to take his seat in his restful abode.[3]

Very clearly "Marduk" is here the statue returning from Elam.

Lastly, a passage from an inscription of Nabonidus (556–539 B.C.E.) dealing with Sennacherib (705–681 B.C.E.) may be quoted:

> He (Sennacherib) took Marduk by the hand and led him to Assur. He dealt with the country (i.e. Babylonia) consonantly with the divine anger, and the prince Marduk did not cease from his anger. For twenty-one years he made his residence in Assur.[4]

Again, "Marduk" stands for the statue of Marduk that Sennacherib carried off to Assyria.

The evidence for identity of god and cult statue in the minds of the ancient Mesopotamians seems clear and consistent.

THE CULT STATUE WAS NOT THE GOD

Unfortunately, however, equally clear and consistent evidence can be quoted to show that to the ancients god and cult statue were two different and quite separate things.

Each of the major deities—for example, Marduk, Shamash, and Ishtar—had temples in several Mesopotamian cities, each with a cult statue of the deity. So while the deity was one, his or her statues were many. Moreover, deities such as the sun-god Shamash and Ishtar the goddess of the morning and evening star were also seen as present in their respective heavenly bodies.

In rituals in which Shamash served as judge in cases brought by human beings against demons and ghosts besetting them, he was hailed in the morning as he rose in the east over the mountains to take his stand as judge on high, and he was sped on his way at evening at sunset as, after the day's work, he passed into the inner heaven in the west.[5]

Quite similarly Ishtar—or with her Sumerian name Inanna—is hailed as the evening star, for instance, in a hymn that begins:

The great queen of heaven, Inanna, I will hail!
The only one, come forth on high I will hail!
The great queen of heaven I will hail!

The pure torch that flares in the sky,
the heavenly light shining bright as the day,
the great queen of heaven, Inanna, I will hail!

The holy one, the awesome queen of the Anunnaki,
the one revered in heaven and earth,
    crowned with great horns,
the oldest child of Suen, Inanna, I will hail!

Of her majesty, of her greatness, of her exceeding dignity,
of her brilliant coming forth in the evening sky,
of her flaring in the sky—a pure torch,
of her standing in the sky like the sun and the moon,
known by all lands from south to north,
of the greatness of the holy one of heaven
to the lady, I will sing![6]

Thus one and the same deity could have many cult statues, could in addition be hailed in a heavenly body of which it was the deity, and—to complete the confusion—could be seen as distinct and separate from it as when the Old Babylonian Gilgamesh Epic distinguishes carefully between Shamash, the god, who is written *Šamšu* and is given the determinative for deity, and the sun, the word for which is written *šamšum* with final *m* of mimation and is not given the divine determinative.[7] The evidence is thus clearly contradictory: the god *is* and at the same time *is not* the cult statue.

"TO BE" AND "NOT TO BE"

The contradiction of *is* and *is not* in the matter of the cult statue is so flagrant and cuts so deep that there must seem to be little hope of resolving it unless one goes to the most basic levels of understanding and attempts to gain clarity about the very fundamentals of ancient thought, about what exactly "being" and "nonbeing" meant to the ancients. We must consider, if only briefly, the ontology of the ancients, their ideas of what constituted "being" and "reality," their criteria for judgment of true and false.

We moderns—most of us at least—live in two intersecting worlds, the world of tangible things and the world of intangibles; we are *dualists*, of mind and of matter, of material and of spiritual.

As to what is real, our main criterion is that of coherence. A dream may be extremely vivid and the dream experience may seem very real; yet, if on awakening we find that it stands in no causal connection with the

18

We shd be careful before adopting ideas like this.

stream of experience before we went to sleep, we dismiss it as unreal, it was a dream merely. For the ancients there was no such dismissal. Their world was one, they were *monists*. They too distinguished between experience when awake and dreams, but to them the difference was not, as for us, one of kind, that is, real or unreal, but one of degree. Both kinds *This does not sound good enough as a distinction.* of experience were real, but not in the same degree, not of the same staying power. Anything established its existence by coming to one's awareness, but some things were fleeting only and did not stand up under closer examination. They were *sarr* ("fleeting," "momentary," "insubstantial," "false", "lies"). Others held up, were durable, *kênu* ("firm," "lasting", "true"), so that—to make up an example—if one thought a guest had arrived, that guest thereby existed, but if on opening the door, one found that no one was there, that guest had proved *sarr* ("fleeting"), had not stayed, was not *kênu* ("true"). The world, all that existed, therefore, was a matter, in our terms, of the mind. It was what had come, and would come, to awareness in the observer. This way of thought gave to concepts and words a reality value that we would not allow them. For instance, when a man had built himself a new house he went through an elaborate ritual to expel "the brick-god" from it. An image was made of the god, it was placed in a little boat with provisions, and the boat was set adrift on the river with farewell wishes to speed the god along.[8] The concept of "brick" for which the brick-god stood was that of the separate, loose brick, and that separateness had to be removed from the house, in which the bricks were to shed their separate identity and become part of a solid wall. Kipling has a short story built on much the same way of thinking. It concerns a steamer on its maiden voyage, and to begin with we hear the chorus of separate voices of engine and steel plates and other parts of the ship, until at the end they all fall silent and only one voice, the deep basso of the ship as a whole, subsuming its parts, is heard— accordingly, the word, or rather what it calls to mind, has reality as soon as it has come to awareness. When Shamash, the sun-god, ordered Samsuiluna of Babylon (ca. 1749–1712 B.C.E.) to build his temple, that temple thereby existed—but in an indefinite "somewhere," not where it should be, and it remained in limbo because a serious rebellion kept Samsuiluna and his troops that should do the building busy fighting. Only after his victory could he, as he says, "put Shamash's word in its place," that is to say, "realize it," build the temple it has brought into his awareness.[9] *Enûma elish*, the Babylonian epic of creation, offers a particularly striking example. There the gods give Marduk the powers of the great gods, which causes their words to realize themselves, to come true *(kênu)*. They test this by asking him to say that a constellation be annihilated, and then again that it be reconstituted. He says so, and the

19

constellation ceases to exist; then he orders it to exist again, and it reappears.[10] On the human plane, one may take a look at the terms for accusation and proof as they are used, for example, in the famous Code of Hammurabi. Here the term *ubburu* creates a form of being for the accused, an identity in which he is wrapt, "invested." *Ubburu* means "encircle," "twine or wrap around," and the proving of the accusation as "true" is expressed by a phrase that means "fixing him" in that identity, "causing him to endure in it," *kunnu* ("to make enduring"), construed with the accused as direct object and the preposition *ina* ("in") for what he is accused of, his alleged identity as criminal.[11]

As ideas may come slowly to mind and then be realized in action, we distinguish between the idea and its realization sharply. Not so the ancients. For them it was a single process of an existent gradually becoming more and more substantive, enduring, and lasting. Since things and events thus exist before they become in our terms "real," they can be sensed, much as a doctor can tell the existence of a disease from its symptoms before its actual outbreak. If desert plants appear in a city, for instance, the desert identity is already infecting that city, is in it as latent and will realize itself; the city will be deserted and become wilderness.[12] If a child is born with the head of a serpent, the form of the god in serpent shape, Ningishzida, is present and will fill with its being: Ningishzida will ravage the country.[13] The form is a symptom of latent existence, a promise, or a threat of filling with its content.

THE SIPPAR CULT RELIEF

The relevance of all of this to the understanding of the cult image will be seen if we consider a representation of the cult image of the god Shamash in Sippar, fashioned in the reign of the Babylonian king Nabu-apal-iddina (885–852 B.C.E.).[14] The inscription tells us that

> Shamash, the great lord residing in the Ebabbara that is in Sippar,[15] whom in the turmoils and troubles of Akkad (i.e. Babylonia) the Sutean, the evil enemy, had effaced, destroying[16] the lineaments, whose cult had been forgotten so that his appearance and attributes had vanished beyond grasp in that nobody had seen them[17]—his appearance did Simmashshihu, King of Babylon, make inquiries about, but he smiled not on him[18] and he did not lay eye on his image and attributes; so he had the sundisc[19] (that is) in front of Shamash roofed over and instituted regular offerings for it.

This state of affairs lasted[20] until the reign of the pious King Nabu-apal-iddina. Then, we are told (iii.11–25),

> the great lord Shamash, who for a long time had been wroth with Akkad (i.e. Babylonia) and angrily averted his neck, became appeased in the reign of

Nabû-apal-iddina, King of Babylon, and turned his face hither. A picture of his statue, a plaque of baked clay, of it and its attributes, was discovered on the other side of the Euphrates river, on the west side.

This plaque was then shown to the king by the high priest of Sippar, and the king, who had been told—presumably by signs or omens—to do so, happily ordered the fashioning of the cult statue according to the model furnished by the plaque (iv.14–28):

> By means of the expertise of Ea, and the workmanship of the carpenter, goldsmith, sculptor, and gem-cutter gods he truly and with care fashioned the statue of the great lord Shamash with ruddy gold and clear lapis-lazuli and by the purification rite of Ea and Asalluhe, before Shamash he "washed its mouth" in É-kar-zagina(k) (i.e. "The house of the pure quay"), which is on the bank of the Euphrates, and it took its seat in its abode.

The relief that accompanies this inscription shows a giant seated figure. It is bearded and wears the horned tiara of a god. Above it is a canopy with a decoration of circular disks shown below the edge. The front of the canopy merges into the body of a two-headed serpent-man who holds in his hands reins with which he guides a huge sun disk on a stand on the floor before the figure. Below the scene as a whole are wavy lines. Fortunately for us these various things are explained in epigraphs placed next to them.[21]

The main such epigraph reads

Image (or "Statue") of the great lord Shamash
who dwells in the Ebabbara in Sippar[22]

and obviously refers to the seated figure, the cult image, which in the inscription is designated as "his statue" and "it," as opposed to "his attributes." The attributes must then be the huge sun disk on the stand in front of the seated figure, its throne, its horned crown, and the two-headed serpent-man, whom an epigraph identifies as the sun-god's chief constable.[23] To the attributes belong also the canopy and its circular ornaments. They are identified in the accompanying epigraph as the deities Sin (the moon-god), Shamash, and Ishtar (goddess of the morning and evening star).[24]

It is thus clear that neither the huge sun disk on the stand nor the small one shown under the canopy is the god—even though the latter is called Shamash in the epigraph. They are merely the god's attributes.[25]

Nor is the actual sun in the heavens, which they portray, even the god, for, as we saw, it is carefully distinguished from him in the Old Babylonian Gilgamesh Epic, where it is written *šamšum* as a mere thing, without divine determinative.

Lastly then, there is the seated figure, the cult image itself. Is that finally the god, as so many texts suggested? No, it cannot possibly be, for we are told in col. iv. 24 that "its mouth was washed before Shamash" (*ma-har* ᵈ*Šamaš*), which clearly distinguishes it from the god himself. Similarly with the former cult image that was destroyed by evil enemies. Although the text speaks of it as if it were the god and says, "the great lord Shamash ... whom ... the evil enemy, the Suteans, had effaced, destroying the lineaments" (i.6–8), it is abundantly clear that the god himself was in no way annihilated. He was angry—that was probably why he let the image be destroyed—and did not allow a new cult statue to be made until long afterward when he relented in the reign of a pious king and had the plaque showing how it should look found across the Euphrates on the west side.

There is thus no alternative to the conclusion that the god was thought of as in some manner transcendent, not to be equated—as we use the word—with any of the cult furnishings, the sun disk, or the cult statue, nor with the visible sun itself. He was a power above them and beyond them.

What, then, was the cult image? This text and many that speak in similar terms make it quite clear that the image represented a favor granted by the god, that it was a sign of a benign and friendly attitude on his part toward the community in which it stood.

How was it a favor? What did it do? Here what we have seen about things and events coming gradually into existence helps toward understanding: They are there as latent before becoming fully manifest, foreshadowed by the occurrence of their forms, which impose themselves on things as early symptoms. The desert plants in the city and the serpent's head on the newborn child show the form on its way to realizing itself fully. In that way, when the god relented, his or her form in the cult image showed itself in Sippar in the finding of the plaque, to become manifest in the refashioned cult statue. And the cult statue itself, as the form of the god, would foreshadow the presence of the god, filled with its specific content.

Seen in this light, then, a cult statue is a foreshadowing of and a stage in a divine presence, a theophany. Here the god can be found, can be approached. If he becomes angry and denies his presence to a community, he lets the cult statue of him be lost or transferred elsewhere.

In saying that the cult statue is the form of the god filling with its specific divine content we do not wish to suggest the image of a vessel filled with a different content, or even of a body with a god incarnate in it. We must think, rather, in terms of a purely mystic unity, the statue mystically becoming what it represents, the god, without, however, in any way limiting the god, who remains transcendent. In so "becoming," the statue ceases to be mere earthly wood, precious metals and stones, ceases to be the work of human hands. It becomes transubstantiated, a divine being, the god it represents.

This incredible ability to become transformed was achieved through special ritual acts and through the power of the word to create and change reality, as when Marduk's word in *Enûma elish* had power to destroy, and then reconstitute, a constellation. That same awesome power informed sacred formulas and incantations available for, and accompanying, the ritual. In the text on the Shamash tablet from Sippar this last decisive phase of the fashioning of the image is concisely stated. The finished statue underwent a purification rite of "mouth-washing" at "the house of the pure quay" on the bank of the Euphrates.

THE "MOUTH-WASHING" RITUAL

Fortunately the ritual thus referred to is known to us in rather full form from elsewhere, fragments of ritual instructions from the library of Ashurbanipal and a Neo-Babylonian complete set of instructions that differs from the older versions mainly in that it preserves the remarkably archaic core of the ritual that they omit. Perhaps that core had come to be felt as no longer acceptable.[26] Except for the section dealing with the workshop, we shall therefore use it as basis, supplementing it, or pointing to differences, whenever indicated.

The ritual begins in the workshop when the statue is ready from the hands of the craftsmen and waiting only for a propitious day. The house is cleaned and swept, unclean persons leave, and the statue is placed in a room set apart. Various materials to be used in the rite are made ready and hallowed by means of blessings. The incense to be used is addressed as originating in "the cedar-scented forest," and the holy-water basin and its deities are likewise blessed. So is the flour to be strewn on it and the water it contains. There follow the sacrifice of a ram and a libation of beer. The workmen who worked on the statue—which is referred to merely as a piece of wood, "the plank" *(gištuppu)*—are present, and the goldsmith, apparently as the last to work on the statue, is called upon first, has red wool and two other kinds bound around his right hand, a scarf for a turban around his left. The officiating priest then pretends to cut off the goldsmith's hand with a knife of tamarisk wood (the red wool symbolizes the blood), and the goldsmith swears an oath, saying: "The god Gushkinbanda, Ea of the goldsmiths, verily made it. I did not make it!" Then the carpenter who fashioned the wooden core of the statue has the same done to him and swears that Nin-ildu, Ea of the carpenters, made it, not he. The meaning of what is here done is of course clear: The fact that the statue is the work of human hands is ritually denied and thus magically made non-existent, nullified.

The statue is then addressed thrice with the words: "From this day you go to Ea your father, may your heart be content, your liver rejoice, may Ea your father become full of joy at seeing you!" It is then taken to the riverbank preceded by a torchbearer. A new incantation is intoned and kept up all the way to the river. It begins: "Grown big as you sprouted, as you sprouted, O tree standing in the forest." The sense of this part of the ritual is also readily understood once one realizes that the magic process that began with making null and void, as never existing, the work of the craftsmen now continues by magically setting the clock back. "From this day you go to Ea your father" means that from this moment you move backward in time toward your origin, the irrigation waters of the river, Ea, who fertilized the earth and made the tree grow. The statue, which in the workshop was already back to its unworked form, the gištuppu,[27] the plank from which the carpenter fashioned it, is now moved one step farther toward its beginnings, to the standing tree in the forest from which the plank was cut, and it is now on its way still farther back, from the forest to the waters that first gave it life, its father, the river-god Ea.

At the riverbank, where offering tables have been set up, the statue is placed on a reed mat facing toward the setting sun, that is, toward night and the dark of nonexistence. Offerings are made to Ea and his son Asalluhe, and emblems of Ea, a turtle of silver and a tortoise of gold, are thrown into the river together with a saw and a chisel of copper. That is, the tools with which the statue was fashioned go back to where they came from, to Ea, who in various forms is also the various craftsmen-gods, in order to make all as it was before the tools were used for making the statue. Two further incantations praising Ea are chanted, beginning, "King, lord of the deep" and "Enki, king of the waters below." Enki is Ea's Sumerian name. The invigorating ceremony called "mouth-washing" is then performed, as it is subsequently repeated at various points of the ritual. It is a generally strengthening and invigorating rite which is not specific to this ritual for a statue but is used very generally as a restorative. As its background I should like to see the sense of well-being and refreshing that this physical act conveys. I remember a summer day in Iraq after being out in the desert surveying ancient mounds all day with high winds and dust in our clothes, mouths, noses, and everywhere, reaching a small town and being given soap and water to wash not only our faces and hands but also the inside of our mouths. It woke one to new life. In the rite of mouth-washing, of course, that power in it is magically enhanced by incantations and blessing of the water.

To come back to the main line of the ritual, after the mouth-washing the offering tables are cleared away and the statue taken to an adjoining orchard while the priest intones an incantation beginning, "The mouth of him who comes is washed," and repeats itself three times. In the orchard the statue is placed in a reed shelter on a mat covered with linen. Its face is now toward sunrise, toward the coming day and its own coming to life and being born. It is in its birthplace among the trees of the forest. At this point one of the other versions places the doing away with the craftsmen's tools. They are put on the mat beside the statue and then removed.

Leaving the statue in the orchard, the priest then goes down to the river, where he offers up flour, which he throws into it, and also makes a libation. He then addresses the river in its capacity of "father," saying: "Father 'Waters below'! To determine destinies . . ." —the rest is unfortunately not given—and a following incantation: "Quay of the waters below, quay of the waters below." This latter incantation we have elsewhere in a very brief early version which runs: "It is the quay that makes things come out right, the quay of the waters below, the quay of the sacred waters, the quay of Enki. From out of their midst I scoop water, I cleanse the tamarisk! In its being the quay that makes things come out right . . ." and so forth.[28] It should be noted here that the waters are destined for the tamarisk, the preferred wood for making divine images and known therefore as the muscle and bone of gods. It is to play a decisive role in what follows. The priest then scoops up water and fills the holy-water basin which he takes to the chapel of the goddess Kugsud.[29] There he sets it up and places it in various plants, herbs, and precious stones together with oil, cedar perfume, honey, and butter. Next he fills a wooden trough of tamarisk wood with water from the holy-water basin and transfers to it the precious stones, herbs, and oils. This trough, filled with holy water, he places on the sun-dried brick of the birth-goddess Dingirmah. That done, he prepares offerings for the birth-goddess, the deities of the holy-water basin, and the various craftsmen-gods, as well as for the statue. He does the same for all the great gods in their astral forms as stars of the night, and each time he intones an incantation beginning, "O tamarisk, sacred wood!" which praises the tamarisk as the wood from which gods are made and gods are purified. This clearly has reference to the trough of tamarisk on the brick of the birth-goddess.

Here again, fortunately, the implications of the succession of ritual acts is clear. The waters from the river are the life-giving waters of the "father," the river-god Ea, and represent his fructifying semen. The trough of tamarisk into which they are poured represents the womb of the "mother," the wood, which is to conceive and to give birth to the cult statue. It is furnished, in addition to its own substance, wood, with other ingredients for a statue, precious stones, among them gold and silver ore, and it is placed on the "brick of the birth-goddess," that is, on the primitive birth stool and block for cutting the umbilical cord that was her implement and emblem.[30] Around it, as birth helpers, stand the other deities that are powers to form and shape the embryo, namely, the craftsmen-gods—she herself has as one of her names that of "The Carpenter in the Womb"—and all the gods are called in to help and to witness the birth. Each is reminded in the repeated incantation of the sacred nature of the mother-to-be, the tamarisk, which, as mentioned, was *the* wood for divine images. The night is to see the birth of the deity whose statue has been made not on earth but in heaven among the assembled gods; it is to appear the next morning.

In the morning the ritual action begins on the riverbank at sunrise with offering tables set out for Ea, the sun-god, and Asalluhe. Chairs are placed for them on a layer of reed cuttings, an awning of red cloth is stretched out over them, and linen drapes are drawn before them. Holy-water basins and offerings are made ready. The officiating priest then thrice intones an incantation beginning, "(O you) who were born by himself in heaven," probably addressed to the statue, and another which may be restored as, "(O) Shamash, great lord of both heaven and earth" addressed to the sun-god. Next Ea and the engendering powers of his waters are celebrated in two hymns, one beginning, "You are the life-giving waters, the river rising (in flood)," and—perhaps after one more lost here—the other, "The divine task of the flood is unique, is holy." These are to be seen in the context of the standard ancient Mesopotamian metaphor for the male sexual climax and ejection of semen (*šà-zi-ga*, "the river in flood"). It is Ea as engendering father—the father, the waters below—who is here being celebrated on the occasion of the birth of a son. Offerings are then presented, libations libated, and two further incantations to Ea, Shamash, and Asalluhe intoned, the incantation priest standing at the left side of the statue in the orchard on the riverbank and turned toward the seats of the three gods. Then the coming day is hymned in a chant, which is fortunately preserved in its major parts. In the Ashurbanipal version, where it is styled for a statue of the moon-god, it reads:

You day on which a god was formed, a pure image perfected,
You, on which a god was made manifest unto all countries,
one endued with awesome splendour, consummate in nobility, an imperious
    noble one,
surrounded by halo, the features decked in awe-ful dread,
peerlessly sparkling, a new moon come into view pure!
O you (day) on which this new moon was formed on (the horizon) the rim of
    heaven and of earth:

26

This new moon has come forth out of the forest of Hashur-cedars
a heavenly creation, fashioned by man,
a perfect new moon done truly with care
of (the goldsmith-god) Gushkinbanda's workmanship.
(Yet), this new moon cannot—not having undergone the rite of mouth-
    washing—
smell incense, eat food, drink water![31]

At this point the text of the Ashurbanipal version is broken, but we can see from the parallel versions that mouth-washing was performed and that afterward an incantation beginning, "Sacred image, fit for great offices" was intoned. There is a gap after this line, but the end of the incantation is preserved:

(the goddess Ningirim took a holy-water basin)
brought in it holy water.
The god Ninzadim, the chief jeweller of Anu,
worked on you with his holy hands.
Enki, who brought you in his sparkling clean hands,
brought you in honey and butter,[32]
has thrown blest water at your mouth,
has opened by lustration-craft your mouth,
You are verily holy like Heaven, holy like Earth.
May any lapse of the tongue be absent.

The incantation priest then goes up to the statue and whispers in its right ear: "Ea has determined as your lot divinity and rule, walk around: You can move about, bless a blessing, make the gesture of blessing with your right hand! You are free! You are released!" The Neo-Babylonian ritual has here the denials of their work by the craftsmen which, following the older versions, we have dealt with as part of the ritual on leaving the workshop. After that, according to the Neo-Babylonian version, the priest performs the symbolic action of "opening the eyes" of the statue, the precise nature of which is not stated but which is obviously done in preparation for the walk by the statue to its temple. The incantation priest intones an incantation beginning, "As you leave, as you leave" and then one beginning, "Image born in heaven." The waxed surface of the statue is polished with hot water, and incantations celebrating the robe, the crown, and the throne of the seated statue are recited. Lastly the incantation "Tarry not in heaven" is recited, clearly an appeal to the god to descend from heaven where he was born and "participate" in the image. Two incantations speed the statue on its way, one beginning, "May the foot at the ground traversed . . ." and the other, "After he has walked through the streets." They are kept up until the statue arrives at the gate of its temple, where it receives greeting gifts. Then it is led in, and an incantation, "My master, for your heart to be content . . ." is sung until it reaches the door of the cella. As it is enthroned in the cella, an incantation, "The celestial evening meal," is sung and a following one, "Fit for the august throne-dais." The priest then prepares offerings and performs a final mouth-washing of the statue. An offering table for the god is prepared, he is laved with water from the wooden trough prepared for his birth the night before, and an incantation, "Asalluhe son of Eridu" is seven times recited. "Food of godhead" is then presented to the statue, and that night the priest goes to the river for a concluding rite. The new cult statue has been installed in its temple ready for its divine duties and offices.

CONCLUSIONS

In sum, then, the ritual has turned the clock back, thus nullifying all human work, and has prepared for a birth in heaven of the god in question by sympathetic magic on earth. It greets the newborn god the next morning, entreats him to come down from heaven, and escorts him to his temple, where he is enthroned. Truly, a weird and extraordinary performance! The central rite in which the image is engendered and born of water and wood is as primitive and crude as one could find anywhere—almost fetishistic—and it is not difficult to focus on that and dismiss, as just a lot of hocus-pocus, the various incantations with which this primitive rite is hedged around and explained as being other than what it patently is.

That, apparently, is more or less what the prophets did. To them, the image was exactly what it was in the primitive rite, "a block of wood," and it remained that—and only that.

To the prophets, the Mesopotamian idols constituted a potential religious threat. And so they spoke as they had to speak—out of polemical zeal for the truth. But for us today, Bel Merodakh and the other idols have ceased to be any religious threat whatever, so we can perhaps afford to look at them with a little more forbearance and try to understand a little more of what they were actually thought to stand for.

Here we may suitably begin with the axiom so well stated by Humpty-Dumpty when Alice questioned whether a word he used could mean what he said it meant: "The question is who is to be master, the word or I?" Because of this, because the meaning of a symbol is determined from without it, so to speak, the question, when one has to do with symbols, is always first and foremost about how the symbol is, or was, interpreted by the people who use it, what *they* think it stands for.

It would be easy to connect the star on top of the Christmas tree and on countless Christmas decorations with star worship. But in actual fact it must be understood in the light of the Star of Bethlehem, as a sign leading to Christ—in no sense itself divine. For that is what the users of the symbol see in it. Or, take a less happy symbol, the swastika. Here it is quite irrelevant that the swastika represents the sun, the flaming wheel rolling across the heavens. After Hitler it became a symbol of Nazism and of acceptance of those unattractive tenets, and as such its present-day usage must be understood.

This means, then, that we really must take the various incantations and what they say seriously if we want to understand what the image stood for at the time of the ritual as we have it, that is, 600–500 B.C.E. and later.

The god—or rather the specific form of him that was represented in this particular image—was born in heaven, not on earth. In the birth the craftsmen-gods that form an embryo in the womb gave it form. When born in heaven it consented to descend and to "participate" (in L. Lévy-Bruhl's sense) in the image, thus transubstantiating it. The image as such remains a promise, a potential, and an incentive to a theophany, to a divine presence, no more.

So in conclusion, as a plea that I have not here grossly overspiritualized ancient Mesopotamian religiosity, let me quote a prayer to Marduk by Nebuchadnezzar from the early sixth century.

Without Thee, Lord, what has existence?
For the king Thou lovest, whose name Thou didst call
who pleaseth Thee, Thou advancest his fame,
Thou assignest him a straightforward path.

I am a prince Thou favorest, a creature of Thine hands.
Thou madest me, entrusted to me the kingship over all people.
Of Thy grace, O Lord, who providest for all of them,
cause me to love Thy exalted rule.
Let fear of Thy godhead be in my heart,
grant me what seemeth good to Thee.
Thou wilt do, verily, what profiteth me.[33]

NOTES

1. Cf. Jer 10:13–15; Isa 44:9–20; and Ps 135:15.

2. V.R. pl. 33 cols. i.44—ii.17. Cf. Jensen apud Schrader, *Keilschriftliche Bibliothek* 3/1, 134–52 with literature. Delitzsch's reading ù at the beginning of i.46 was kindly confirmed by Geller and Finkel. The reading sila₄ in ii.8 is likewise due to Delitzsch. See his *Die Sprache der Kossäer,* 56 n. 2.

3. IV R. pl. 20 no. 1.9–18. The text reads (9) . . . šà-bi daǧal-la arhuš tuk-a gú-bi niǧin šà-bi-ta Uru-kù-ga (10) .... (11) *[libba-šu rap-šu rêma] er-ši-ma ki-šad-su u-sah-hi-ra ana qé-reb Uru-kù-ga* (12) [x x x(x)] ǧen-a-ni šà-bi-ta níǧ-hul Elam-maᵏⁱ-ke₄ kaskal a-li-ri har-ra-an asilal hé-en-da-

še-še-ga šà Šu-an-na-ta mu-un-dib (13) [*xxx(x)*]-*ku i-ku-šam-ma iš-tu qé-reb lim-ni-ti E-lam-ti har-ra-an šu-lu-lu*(!?) *ú-ru-uh ri-ša-a-ti* (14) [*ṭu-du ma*]-*ga-ri iṣ-ba-ta ana qé-reb Šu-an-na*^ki (15) ukù ma-d [a(?)a l a m] s u k u d-da hé-du₇ še-er-ma-al ⟨zalag⟩ šu-li-li-eš maš dağal-le-da i-bi har-ra ak-a-e-dè (16)*ib-tar-ra-a ni-ši ma-a-ti la-an-šú e-la-a šu-su-mu e-tel-la na-par-da-a šu-lu-la kul-lat-si-na pu-tuq-qa-šu* (17) n a m-b a-n i-í b-d u₉-n a ù-m u-u n b a-n i-i n-r i d u₆-m a r-r a-b i n í-d ú b-d ú b-b u (18) *i-ru-um-ma ir-ta-me šu-bat-su né-eh-ta.*

4. ¹⁴*qá-ti rūbi* ᵈ*Marduk* ¹⁵*iṣ-ba-at-ma* ¹⁶*ú-še-ri-ib* ¹⁷*qé-reb Aššur*ki ¹⁸*ki-ma uz-zi ili-ma* ¹⁹*i-te-pu-uš māti* ²⁰*ul ip-šu-ur* ²¹[*ki*]-*mil-ta-šú* ²²*rūbu* ᵈ*Marduk* ²³*21 šanāti* ²⁴*qé-reb Aššur*ki ²⁵*ir-ta-me šú-bat-su.* S. Langdon, *Die neubabylonische Königsinschriften* (Leipzig, 1912) 271 Nabonid Nr. 8 i.14–25.

5. For greeting hymn, see V.R. 50–51 from the 3d house of the series *bît rimki.* For literature, see R. Borger, *Handbuch der Keilschriftliteratur* 1 (Berlin: Walter de Gruyter, 1967) 407 Pinches V R.t.50–51. For farewell hymn, see Bertin, *Révue d'assyriologie* 1 (1886) 157ff., and Abel and Winckler, *Keilschrifttexte zum Gebrauch bei Vorlesungen.* For literature, see Borger, *629,* and Winckler.

6. E. Chiera, *Sumerian Religious Texts* no. 1 and duplicates. See the edition by D. Reisman, *Two Neo-Sumerian Hymns* (Ph.D. diss., University of Pennsylvania, 1969;) 147–211. For literature, see R. Borger, *Handbuch der Keilschriftliteratur* 2 (Berlin: de Gruyter, 1975) 31, Chiera, *Sumerian Religious Texts* no. 1.

7. B. Meissner, "Ein altbabylonisches Fragment des Gilgamos Epos," *Mitteilungen der Vorderasiatische Gesellschaft* 7/1 (Berlin, 1902) 1–16 col. i.5 ᵈ*Šamšu*su nominative; i.10, 11 ᵈ*Šamši*si (genitive denoting the sun-god); but *ša-am-ša-am* (accusative) in col. i.13 denoting the sun. Mimation individualizes and so corresponds to "the" or "a" in English. Case ending without mimation is used when the word denotes a unicum within the universe of reference of speaker and hearer; thus it is frequent with proper names. See W. von Soden, *Grundriss der akkadischen Grammatik* (Rome: Pontifical Biblical Institute, 1952) 63d. Forms without case ending and mimation merely assign to a class; in the case of a proper name such as Shamash, to a class with one member only. Note that beside the notion of a single sun-god there was also a notion that there were many different suns, one for each day. See W. von Soden, *Akkadisches Handwörterbuch,* p. 1158 *šamšu(m),* and different sun-gods, see S. Langdon, *Sumerian Epic of Paradise and the Fall of Man* (PBS X/1, University Museum, University of Pennsylvania, Philadelphia, 1915) pl. 1 col. ii.19: i-n e-šè ᵈU t u-u d-n e-a u r₅ h é-n a-n a m-m a, "Now, on that day and sun-god it verily became thus."

8. See the Series ᵈKulla (H. Zimmern, "Ein babylonisches Ritual für eine Hausweihe," *ZA* 23, 369ff., and 25, 195f.).

9. F. Thureau-Dangin, "L'inscription bilingue B de Samsu-iluna," *RA* 39 (1942–44) 5–17, esp. lines 95–97 (Sumerian version) and 97–99 (Akkadian version) on p. 10. For literature, see Borger, *Handbuch der Keilschriftliteratur* 3.

10. Tablet IV.19–28. For text, see W. G. Lambert, *Enûma eliš: Babylonian Epic of Creation* (London: Oxford University Press, 1967). For translation, e.g., A. Heidel, *The Babylonian Genesis: The Story of the Creation* (2d ed.; Chicago: University of Chicago Press, 1951).

11. Cf., e.g., Codex Hammurabi 1 *šum-ma a-wi-lum a-wi-lam ú-ub-bi-ir-ma ne-er-tam e-li-šu id-di-ma la uk-ti-in-šu mu-ub-bi-ir-šu id-da-ak.* Literally trans-

lated: Suppose a man wrapped (i.e., accused) a(nother) man in that he cast murder over him (the image is that of a fowler casting a net) but has not held him firm (i.e., has not proved it upon him), the "wrapper" (i.e., the accuser) is to be killed. See also 106 where an agent has denied taking money from the merchant: *tamkārum šu-ú i-na ma-har i-lim ù ši-bi i-na kaspam le-qé-em šamallam ú-ka-an-ma* ("that merchant will before a god and witnesses convict the agent of taking the money [lit.: will make firm the agent in the taking of the money]").

12. *Šumma âlu* Tablet I.139. C.T. 38.1.1. Cf. Nötcher, *Or* 31, p. 52: *šumma šam ki-di ina âli innamir alu šuātu i-har-ru-ub* ("if a desert plant is seen in the city, that city will become wilderness"). Cf. the following line: "If a mountain plant *(Ú-KUR-RA)* is seen in a city, that city will become wilderness."

13. E. Lichte, *The Omen Series šumma izbu* (New York, 1970) 46.6. Cf. 36.50, in which a woman gives birth to wind, i.e., labors in vain. It presages famine, loss of produce.

14. L. W. King, *Babylonian Boundary Stones and Memorial Tablets in the British Museum* (London, 1912) no. XXXVI, with literature.

15. Conceivably to distinguish it from the temple of Shamash of the same name in Larsa.

16. We assume *uhalliqu* to be in hendiadys with the preceding *usahhû*.

17. We understand *na-țil* as a Permansive 3 per. sg. G with conditioning force, that is, indicating that the action of the verb persists in, and lastingly conditions, the subject, as, e.g., in *alik harrana* in the Yale Gilgamesh fragment vi.24, which means that Enkidu has traveled the road and so knows it. Here *națil* means that nobody survived who had seen the image and so would know how it looked. Cf. T. Jacobsen, *Toward the Image of Tammuz* (Cambridge: Harvard University Press, 1970) 433 at end of page.

18. Lit.: "He gave him not his face," *pa-ni-šu la id-din-šu*, which means "he paid no attention to him." For this meaning, see von Soden, *Akkadisches Handwörterbuch*, 702, *nadānu(m)* II.3.cα. We see no reason to assume a separate meaning "to reveal oneself" for the occurrence here involved (thus King's translation followed by von Soden), much as it fits the context.

19. The term used is *niphu* ("flare," "effulgence"). It must refer here to a concrete cult object since it is "roofed over." Apparently it is the large sun disk shown on a stand in front of the seated statue of Shamash in the relief which is carved with symbols of rays of flashing light.

20. There were even periods when the offerings to the sun disk temporarily were discontinued.

21. The correct interpretation of these epigraphs was given by A. Poebel in *AJSL* (1936) 52, 111–12.

22. (1) *ṣa-lam ᵈŠamaš bêlu rabû* (2) *a-šib É-babbar-ra* (3) *šá qé-reb Sippar*ki.

23. (1) *nāgir ᵈŠamaš* (2) Muš-igi-min ("the chief constable of Shamash, Mush-igimin"). The name is Sumerian and means "two-faced serpent." See Poebel (work cited in n. 21).

24. (1) *ᵈSîn (EŠ) ᵈŠamaš u ᵈIštar (XV) ina pu-ut apsî (ZU + AB)* (2) *ina bi-rit ᵈMuš ti-mi nadû (ŠUB*rⁿeš*)-ú*, "Sin, Shamash, and Ishtar. They lie between the divine Muŝ (i.e., Muŝ-igi-min) of the posts (i.e., of the canopy) opposite the Apsû." Apparently these divine emblems are shown not in their actual place. They

belong on the front edge of the canopy, which the sculptor could not show in his side view of the statue; they must, however, have been too important to leave out and so he rendered them in frontal view where he had room, behind their actual place. The canopy with its representation of the three major heavenly bodies may be taken to symbolize heaven, the floor line on which the dais under the throne rests, the earth, and the wavy lines below it the subterraneous fresh waters, the Apsû. The setting of the image thus symbolizes the cosmos. It may be added that the canopy may well have had side curtains not shown, curtains that could be let down or drawn to form a tent or aedicula such as are often shown in clay models of cult statues in their cellas. They would serve to shield the image from profane looks.

25. With this fits that "the sundisc (that is) before Shamash" which Sim-mashshihu roofed over and for which he instituted offerings (i.18–20) quite clearly was not satisfactory, no valid substitute for the god's statue *(ṣa-lam-šú)*. Equally clear is the fact that it is treated as a thing only and distinct from the god.

26. The ritual is part of the *mīs pî* series to be edited by Dr. C. B. F. Walker of the British Museum. Dr. Walker has generously allowed us to see his unpublished MS edition, for which we are most grateful. For the section here treated, see the publication of the Babylonian version (BM 45749) by Sidney Smith in *Journal of the Royal Asiatic Society* (1925) 37ff. and the treatment of it by E. Ebeling in his *Tod und Leben nach den Vorstellungen der Babylonier* (Berlin, 1931) no. 26 on pp. 100–108. Cf. the related text published as no. 27 on pp. 108–14. Ebeling, on p. 100, also lists the relevant literature and on pp. 100–102 interprets the text correctly in every essential. For the Ashurbanipal version, see H. Zimmern, *Beiträge zur Kenntniss der babylonischen Religion* (Leipzig, 1901) nos. 31–38 and IV R. pl. 25.

27. The full term is g̃ i š-d u b-n u n-n a ("the plank of the prince," i.e., of Ea). It is used in I R. p. 25, 19′ and 24′. The text occasionally forgets that the statue is not yet a god and refers to it as "that god," e.g. in line 9′.

28. H. Zimmern, *Sumerische Kultlieder aus altbabylonischer Zeit,* 2d series (Leipzig, 1913) no. 187 col. ii. 11′–19′. It reads: én-é-nu-ru (11′) kar-si-sá kar-Ab.zu (12′) kar-kù kar-^{d}En-ki-ga (13′) šà-bi-ta a im-ma-ra-e$_{11}$ (14′) šinig im-ma-ra-[si]kil (15′) kar-si-sá kar-Ab.zu[ì] me-a-ba (16′) kar-kù kar-^{d}En-ki-ga ì-me-a-b[a] (17′) šà-bi-ta a im-ma-ra-[e$_{11}$-a-ba] (18′) la-cuna. The last lines, 15′–17′, may be rendered: "in its being the quay that makes things come out right, the quay of the waters below, in its being the sacred quay, the quay of Enki, in that I scoop up water from it . . ."

29. The name means "holy sprinkler." She is apparently a personification of the branch used to sprinkle holy water from the holy-water basin.

30. On this brick, see M. Stol, *Zwangerschap en Geboorte bii de Babyloniërs en in de Bijbel* (Leiden, 1983) 57f.

31. IV R. pl. 25 col. iii lines 42–66.

32. A reference to the honey and butter in the holy-water basin.

33. S. Langdon, *Die neubabylonische Königsinschriften,* 122f. lines 55–72. It must be admitted, though, that the piety of this prayer may have its roots in Aramaic rather than native Babylonian religiosity.

3

A Forerunner of Biblical Prophecy: The Mari Documents

ABRAHAM MALAMAT

For the previous studies that we have devoted to prophecy at Mari and in the Bible we had at our disposal only ten out of the presently known twenty-eight "prophetic" documents from Mari.[1] In the meantime eighteen documents have been added to the "prophetic" corpus from Mari and several works have appeared that discuss the entire material (save one new document published in 1975; see below).[2] The full body of data now available enables us to advance our understanding of the topic at hand, inviting at the same time certain revisions.

TWO PATTERNS OF PROPHESYING AT MARI

Let us commence our discussion in an unconventional manner. We cite a Mari letter that is not really related to our subject but that may possibly serve as a key for understanding the reality behind the practices of prophesying at Mari. Bahdilim, the palace prefect of Mari under its last king, Zimrilim, advises his lord: "[Verily] you are the king of the Haneans, [but] secondly you are the king of the Akkadians! [My lord] should not ride a horse. Let my [lord] ride in a chariot or on a mule and he will thereby honor his royal head!" (ARM VI 76:20–25). According to this statement, the two strata making up the population were, on the one hand, the West Semitic (Haneans, the dominant tribal federation of the kingdom) and, on the other hand, the old-time Akkadian component. The symbiosis between these two elements usually left its imprint on every walk of life, including religion and cult. We therefore witness at Mari, and for the present practically at Mari alone, the coexistence of two patterns of predicting the future and revealing the word of the gods.

On the one hand we find at Mari, as at every Mesopotamian center, the practice typical of Akkadian civilizations, namely, divination and specifically the art of extispicy. This field was served by specially trained experts and above all by the *bārû*, the haruspex. At Mari, we are familiar with a number of such experts, the best known of whom was Asqudum, whose spacious mansion was recently uncovered east of the Mari palace.[3] These professionals usually dealt with the crucial matters of the Mari kingdom, such as seeking omens for the security of the city, the conduct of war, and military enterprises.[4]

Alongside the academic and supposedly "rational" system of predicting the future, we are confronted at Mari, and chronologically for the first time ever, with an atypical phenomenon for Mesopotamia: the remarkable manifestation of intuitive divination or, rather, prophecy, acquiring the word of the god through informal channels. This type of prophesying should properly be seen as a link in a chain of social and religious practices exclusive to Mari and in part similar to what is found in the Bible. These include the covenant-making ceremony, the ban as penalty for transgression, and the more controversial procedure of census-taking accompanied with ritual expiation.[5] This assemblage of procedures, which could be described as a system of interrelationships, is undoubtedly an expression of the other component of the Mari experience—the West Semitic tribal heritage.

Does the above warrant the conclusion, not usually considered,[6] that the message of the diviner-prophets was pronounced originally in West Semitic dialects, conventionally designated as "Amorite"? Should this be the case, then, in the documents before us the words of prophecy have already undergone translation into the chancery language, Akkadian, either by the officials writing to the king or by scribes who are not mentioned at all. Such an assumption may also explain the fact that the "prophetic" texts display a relatively greater number of West Semitic idioms and linguistic forms than the rest of the Mari documents. There is, however, still no basic study of this matter. If these assumptions are in fact correct, they point to a considerably complex process of transmission of the prophetic word—*ipsissima verba*—until it reaches the king's ear.

INTUITIVE PROPHECY

Whatever the case, informal prophesying at Mari places biblical prophecy in a new perspective, for inherent to both is the intuitive element. In neither of them is the prophecy the direct result of a mantic or magic mechanism that requires professional expertise but is the product of the experience of divine revelation, namely, a psychic, nonrational phenomenon. The essential nature of prophecy of this type entails certain dominant characteristics, three of which are most significant:[7]

1. The prophetic manifestations are spontaneous and result from inspiration or divine initiative in contrast to the mechanical, inductive divination that is usually initiated by the king's request to acquire signs from the deity. Compare in this connection the utterance of the Israelite

prophet: "I was ready to be sought by those who didn't ask for me; I was ready to be found by those who didn't seek me. I said, 'Here am I, here am I'" (Isa 65:1).

2. The prophets are imbued with a consciousness of mission and take their stand before the authorities to present their divinely inspired message.

3. A more problematic characteristic is the ecstatic element in prophecy, for the definition of ecstasy is not unambiguous. We would do well to lend this concept a broad and liberal definition, letting it apply to anything from autosuggestion to the divinely infused dream. Only in rare instances does this quality appear in the extreme embodiment of frenzy, and even then it is not clear whether it is accompanied with loss of senses, for the utterances of the prophets are always sober and purposeful and are far from being mere gibberish.

These particular characteristics, which are not necessarily found in conjunction, link the diviner-prophet at Mari to the Israelite prophet more than any other divinatory type known to us from the ancient Near East (except for the *rāgimu* [fem. *rāgintu*], "the pronouncer," "speaker" of the Neo-Assyrian period, addressing Esarhaddon and Ashurbanipal). Nevertheless, in a comparative study of Mari and the Bible we must direct our attention to the great difference in the source material: firsthand documents versus compositions that underwent a lengthy, complex literary process. Furthermore, the documentation concerning prophecy at Mari is restricted to a very short span of time, perhaps the last five to ten years of Zimrilim's reign. In comparison, the activity of the Israelite prophets extended over an expanse of centuries, especially if we include for our present purposes both the early, "primitive," as well as the late, "classical," prophets, which were not so decidedly distinct from each other, as many scholars would have us think.[8] In other words, Mari presents a synchronic picture, from one particular point in time, while the Bible permits a diachronic view that enables us to follow the development of the prophetic phenomenon.

SIMILARITY AND DIFFERENCES IN PROPHECY AT MARI AND IN THE BIBLE

Despite the external, formal similarity between the diviner-prophets at Mari and the Israelite prophets, there is an obvious gap in the content of the divine message and in the function it assumes and apparently also in the position occupied by the prophet within the society and the kingdom. In Israelite society it seems that the prophet usually enjoyed a more or less central position, even though there are kinds of prophets that are peripheral. At Mari, however, the prophets apparently played only a marginal role.[9] Admittedly, this distinction may be merely an illusion deriving from the nature of the sources at our disposal. Judging according to place of origin and activity, in both corpora many prophets are from rural localities—in Mari from the provincial towns of Terqa, Tuttul, and others, and in the Bible Amos from Tekoa, Micah from Moresheth, Jeremiah from Anathoth, and his rival Hananiah from Gibeon—while others reside in the respective capital cities.

As for contents, the prophecies at Mari are limited to material demands on the king, such as constructing a building or a city gate in a provincial town (ARM III 78; XIII 112), urging the offering of funerary sacrifices (ARM II 90; III 40), demanding the dispatch of valuable objects to various temples (A 4260), or requesting property for the god (A 1121; the reference is certainly to a landed estate granted to a sanctuary and its priestly staff). Furthermore, many of the more recently published prophecies refer to military affairs and, above all, the concern for the welfare of the king and his personal safety. He is warned against conspirators at home and enemies abroad (ARM X 7; 8; 50; 80), especially Hammurabi, king of Babylon (see below), who was actually about to conquer Mari in a short time. This sort of message is significantly distinct from biblical prophecy, which presents a full-fledged religious ideology, a socioethical manifest, and a national purpose alongside the universal vision. This picture of a glaring contrast may well be considerably distorted. At Mari, nearly all the "prophetic" documents were discovered in the royal-diplomatic archive of the palace (room 115), and this would explain their tendency to concentrate on the king. Prophecies directed toward other people presumably existed, but on account of their nature they were not preserved. In comparison, had only the historiographic books of the Bible—Samuel, Kings, and Chronicles—survived, we would be faced with a picture resembling that at Mari, in which Israelite prophecy as well was oriented primarily toward the king and his political and military enterprises.

On the other hand, a recently published prophetic message from Mari (A 2731) contains a first glimmer of social and moral concern.[10] A diviner-prophet in the name of the god Adad from Aleppo urges Zimrilim: "When a wronged man or woman cries out to you, stand and let his/her case be judged." This command has an exact parallel in Jeremiah's prophecy concerning the kings: "Execute justice in the morning, and deliver from the hand of the oppressor him who has been robbed" (Jer 27:12; cf. Jer 22:3).

A tangible example of imposing obligations on the king of Mari may be found in one letter (ARM X 100) in which a divinely imbued woman writes to the king directly, with no intervention of a third party (although apparently a scribe was employed). The woman (whose name should be read Yanana) addresses Zimrilim in the name of Dagan concerning a young woman—perhaps her own daughter or perhaps a companion—who was abducted when the two women were on a journey. Dagan appears in the woman's dream and decrees that only Zimrilim is capable of saving and returning the lass to the writer. The gist of the matter is that a woman who was wronged turns to the king seeking justice in the spirit of the prophetic commands adduced above.

All told, it is, for the present, difficult to determine the nature of the analogy between the prophecy at Mari and that in Israel, the two being set apart by a gap of more than six centuries. Furthermore, there are no intermediary links whatsoever. It would be therefore premature to adopt the view that Mari presents the prototype of prophecy in Israel.[11] But one cannot belittle this earliest manifestation of intuitive prophecy among West Semitic tribes at Mari, which is still an enigma. Nonetheless, we can put forward in this regard two reasonable assumptions that are not mutually exclusive:

1. Intuitive prophesying was basically the outcome of a specific social situation—an originally nonurban, seminomadic, tribal society. Urban sophistication, no matter how primitive, naturally engenders institutionalized cultic specialists, such as the *bārû* (haruspex), the foremost of the diviner types in Mesopotamia and part and parcel of the cult personnel of any self-respecting town or ruler.

2. The phenomenon of intuitive prophecy was a characteristic of a particular cultural sphere, which extended across the west, from Palestine and Syria to Anatolia in the northwest and to the east as far as Mari. This assumption is based mainly on the ecstatic element in prophecy, attested throughout this region, albeit rather sporadically. It is found outside the Bible, in such cases as the prophets in Hittite sources, at Byblos mentioned in the Egyptian Tale of Wen-Amon, and in Syria in the Aramaic inscription of Zakkur, king of Hamath, and according to references in classical literature.[12]

After these general observations, let us now present the data at hand concerning prophecy at Mari. Since 1948, twenty-eight letters have been published, all addressed to the king and containing reports on prophecies and divine revelations. The senders of the letters are high-ranking officials and bureaucrats from all over the kingdom. About half are women, mostly ladies of the palace headed by Shibtu, Zimrilim's major queen. Several of the letters contain two separate visions, and thus the total number of prophecies reaches as many as thirty-five—a very respectable quantity. In a few cases the correspondent is the prophet himself (even though we deem the letters to have been written down by a scribe;

compare Baruch son of Neriah, Jeremiah's amanuensis). Thus we find correspondents prophesying in the name of Shamash of Sippar (A 4260), the court lady Addu-Duri (ARM X 50), and a woman named Yanana (mentioned above; ARM X 100). As we already noted at the outset, the words of the diviner-prophets, whether transmitted through intermediaries or even if dispatched directly to the king, were generally formulated with utmost lucidity, a fact perhaps due to the time elapsed between the actual prophetic experience and committing the vision to writing. How much more so is this the case in connection with biblical prophecy, which underwent continuous editing, even though certain prophecies may have been preserved in their original form.

PROFESSIONAL PROPHETS AT MARI AND THEIR RESEMBLANCE TO ISRAELITE PROPHETS

The diviner-prophets at Mari were of two types: professionals, recognizable by their distinctive titles (as were the biblical *rō'eh, ḥōzeh, nābî',* and *'îš 'ĕlōhîm*), and lay people, with no title whatsoever (see below). We know thus far five different titles at Mari, which may be seen as designating "cultic" prophets, if we may use a term accepted in biblical studies.

1. A priest *(šangûm)* is mentioned once as a prophesier (ARM X 51). He was imbued with a prophetic dream containing a warning for Zimrilim; in the Bible too the prophet Ezekiel was originally a priest, and so too the priest Pashhur son of Immer prophesied (Jer 20:1–6).

2. There are three references to prophesying *assinnu*s (ARM X 6; 7; 80),[13] a term not yet completely elucidated. On the basis of later sources, he had been considered a eunuch, a male prostitute, or a cultic musician. This functionary served in a temple in Mari and prophesied in the name of the goddess Annunītum, apparently while disguised and acting like a woman, perhaps like a present-day transvestite or coccinell. Therefore, he prophesies in the name of a female deity, who would normally be associated with women rather than men.

3. In one solitary case a prophetess is mentioned bearing the title *qabbatum* (not to be read *qamatu!*) (ARM X 8), derived undoubtedly from the Akkadian verb *qabû* ("to speak," "to proclaim").[14] It is tempting to link this term to the Hebrew root *qbb*, mentioned frequently in connection with the prophecy of Balaam, who announces *māh' eqqōb lō' qabbōh 'ēl*... (Num 23:8; the form *qabbōh* is irregular and possibly it is to be derived from a root *qbh*).

But the best known of the professional prophets at Mari are the *muḫḫûm* and the *āpilum,* whom we have already discussed in the past. Suffice it here to add certain new details and examine problems that have arisen in the meantime.

4. The *muḫḫûm* (fem. *muḫḫūtum*), as the etymology indicates, was some sort of ecstatic or frenetic. The *purrusum* form of the noun is peculiar to Mari (in other Akkadian sources we find the form *maḫḫûm*). This nominal form designates bodily defects and is functionally like the Hebrew *qittēl* form used in such words as *'iwwēr* ("blind"), *pissēaḥ* ("lame"), and *gibbēn* ("hunchback"). Thus this type of prophet, because of his peculiar behavior, was perceived of as a madman, similar to the biblical *mĕšuggā'*, a term used occasionally as a synonym of *nābî'* (2 Kgs 9:11; Jer 29:26; Hos 9:7). To these conclusions, which we have already reached in our previous studies,[15] we should now add the instances of the verb *immaḫu* (third person preterite) derived from the same root as *muḫḫûm*. The verb is used in the N stem resembling *nibbā'* (see also *hitnabbē'*) in the Bible and has the ingressive meaning "became insane," "went into a trance" (ARM X 7:5–7; 8:5–8).

In addition to the five nameless *muḫḫûs* mentioned in the "prophetic" documents, there is now new administrative material available in three recent volumes of the Mari documents.[16] They do not contain the prophetic messages as such but list four *muḫḫûs* by name along with the deities they serve. These prophets figure in lists of personnel who received clothes from the palace, just as in previous lists there was already one reference to an *āpilum* (ARM IX 22:14 and see below). These data certainly imply that these two prophetic types derived material support from the royal court. But it is surprising that all four *muḫḫûs* have strictly Akkadian and not West Semitic names: Irra-gamil, *muḫḫûm* of Nergal; Ea-maṣi, *muḫḫûm* of Iturmer (ARM XXI 333:33'/4'; XXIII 446:9', 19'); Ea-mudammiq, *muḫḫûm* of Ninhursag; and lastly a prophetess named Anu-tabni, *muḫḫūtum* of the goddess Annunītum (ARM XXII 168:8' and 326:8–10), as befitting women who appear in the service of female deities. I have no satisfactory explanation for the nature of the names of the newly attested prophets, for we would generally expect West Semitic names. It is, however, possible that those prophets who were dependent on the court of Mari had already assimilated into Akkadian culture. In any case, the direct contact with the royal court calls to mind the court prophets in Israel, the likes of Nathan, the *nābî'*, and Gad, the *ḥōzeh,* who served David and Solomon, or the Baal and Asherah prophets, who functioned in the court of Ahab and Jezebel.

5. Finally, we turn to the *āpilum* (fem. *āpiltum*), a prophetic title exclusive to Mari, meaning "answerer," "respondent" (derived from the verb *apālum,* "to answer").[17] In contrast to the noun, the verb is frequently associated with mantic techniques. Unlike the rest of the prophets, the *āpilum* acts on occasion in concert, in groups similar to the bands of prophets in the Bible *ḥebel/laḥᵃqat nĕbî'îm).* He is attested over a

wider expanse than any of the other prophets, from Aleppo in northern Syria to Sippar near Babylon in the south.

The *āpilum* of Shamash of Sippar addresses the king of Mari directly without any intermediary, demanding a throne for Shamash and one of the king's daughters for service in his temple.[18] He also requests objects for other deities, among them an *assaku* (a consecrated object) for Adad of Aleppo (A 4260). Within these geographical extremities we find an *āpilum* of the Dagan temple in Tuttul (near the confluence of the Balih with the Euphrates) and an *āpiltum* in the Annunītum temple in the city of Mari itself. It is noteworthy that in these very same sanctuaries both the *muḫḫûm* and the *muḫḫūtum* functioned as well, indicating that two essentially different types of diviner-prophets could be found side by side. Furthermore, in the Dagan temple of Terqa even three types of prophets were at work simultaneously: a *muḫḫûm*, a *qabbatum,* and a dreamer of divine dreams.

AFFINITY TO HEBREW TERMINOLOGY AND CONTENT OF BIBLICAL PROPHECY

It seems that the very terms *āpilum* and *muḫḫûm* have counterparts in biblical terminology concerning divine revelations. To the biblical terms *ʿānāh, ʿōneh* ("answer," "answerer"), as indications of divine revelation, discussed by us elsewhere,[19] we may now add several pertinent passages.

Most significantly, the verb *ʿānāh* is at times used to describe the prophet's acting as God's mouthpiece, whether actually responding to a query put to the deity or not. This is clearly seen, for instance, in 1 Sam 9:17: "When Samuel saw Saul, the Lord *answered him*, 'Here is the man of whom I spoke to you! He it is who shall rule over my people.' " This is also the case of Jeremiah's words that invalidate the use of the expression *maśśāʾ YHWH* as a legitimate designation for a divine revelation, requiring in its stead the figure of speech: "What has the Lord *answered* and what has the Lord said?" (Jer 23:37). The term *maʿăneh ʾĕlōhîm* (lit. "God's answer") denoting the word of the Lord occurs once in the Bible, in Micah's prophecy (Mic 3:7), which also makes the illuminating use of *ʿnh* in connection with the oracles of Balaam: "Remember now, O my people, remember what Balak king of Moab devised and what Balaam the son of Beor *answered* him" (Mic 6:5). The verb *ʿānāh* does not indicate here any response to a specific question that Balak put forward to Balaam but rather the prophetic oracle Balaam was compelled to deliver on behalf of Israel. It is not impossible that this foreign diviner, who is never called *nābîʾ*, was a prophet of the *āpilum* ("answerer") type. That is hinted at also by the cultic performances resorted to by Balaam, on the one hand (Num 23:3, 14–15, 29), and by the band of the *āpilu*, on the other (A 1121, esp. lines 24–25), both aimed at acquiring the divine word.[20]

It is of interest that the recently discovered Balaam inscription from Deir ʿAllā, dating to the end of the eighth or early seventh century B.C.E., and apparently composed in either an Ammonite or an Israelite-Gileadite dialect, enumerates various types of sorcerers, including a woman designated ʿnyh. The term most likely means "female respondent," that is, a semantic equivalent of the Mari term āpiltum.[21] This interpretation gains cogency by the following words referring to the woman: rqḥt mr wkhnh ("a compounderess of myrrh and a priestess"). Even more significant is the Aramaic inscription of Zakkur, king of Hamath, from about 800 B.C.E. In his hour of peril, the king turns to his gods "and Baalshamayn responded to me (wyʿnny) and Baalshamayn [spoke to me] through seers and diviners (ʿddn)" (lines 11–12).[22]

The possible intersection between the prophetic activity of the āpilum and the muḫḫûm is probably indicated in a letter containing the message of a muḫḫûtum—a prophetess. She implores the king of Mari not to leave the capital to wage war and declares: "I will answer you constantly" (attanapal; ARM X 50:22–26). In other words, there are cases where a muḫḫûm would be involved in the act of "answering" (apālum).

Before turning to the lay prophets, let us examine two prophecies of similar content and reminiscent of the biblical "oracles against the nations," one of an āpilum (spelled here peculiarly aplûm) and the other of "the wife of a man," that is, a lay person. Both reports were transmitted to Kibri-Dagan, Zimrilim's governor of Terqa. The āpilum/aplûm "arose" in the name of Dagan of Tuttul "and so he said as follows: 'O Babylon! Why doest thou ever (evil)? I will gather thee into a net! . . . The house of the seven confederates and all their possessions I shall deliver into Zimrilim's hand!' " (ARM XIII 23:6–15). The prophecy, which contains several motifs well known from biblical prophecies of doom,[23] reflects the deteriorating relations between Mari and Babylon on account of Hammurabi's expansionist aspirations. The other prophecy explicitly mentions the name of Babylon's king, Hammurabi, as an enemy of Mari (ARM XIII 114). A divinely inspired woman approaches Kibri-Dagan late one afternoon with the following words of consolation: "The god Dagan sent me. Send to your lord; he shall not worry [. . .], he shall not worry. Hammurabi [king] of Babylon . . ." (continuation broken). The urgency of the matter is indicated by the fact that the letter bearing this encouraging message was dispatched the very day after the utterance.

From these two prophecies, and possibly from most of the visions concerned with the king's safety, it is apparent that they were recorded at a time of political and military distress afflicting Mari. This too would be

This is the sort of thing we cannot know for certain. (arg. ex sil.)

analogous to Israelite prophecy, which particularly thrived in times of national emergency, such as during the Philistine threat in the days of Samuel and Saul, Sennacherib's campaign to Jerusalem, and especially Nebuchadnezzar's invasion of Judah. The crisis factor was certainly one of the principal forces engendering prophetic manifestations both in Mari and in Israel.[24] However, in contrast to the Bible with its prophecies of doom and words of admonition against the king and the people, the messages at Mari were usually optimistic and sought to please the king rather than rebuke and alert him. Such prophecies of peace and salvation (see ARM X 4; 9; 10; 51; 80), colored by a touch of nationalism, liken the Mari prophets to the biblical prophets of peace or "false prophets," and surely the corresponding prophecies are greatly similar. Indeed, one of the prominent "false" prophets in the Bible, Hananiah of Gibeon, Jeremiah's rival, rashly proclaims in the name of the Lord (and not in the name of a foreign god) the impending return of the Judean exiles from Babylonia, "for I will break the yoke of the king of Babylon" (Jer 28:4). How reminiscent this is of the *āpilum*'s prediction against Babylon (see above, ARM XIII 23). In both instances the message is pleasant to the ear and whitewashes the crisis situation, for the prophets of peace serve the establishment and express its interest (compare the four hundred prophets at Ahab's court who prophesy "with one accord"; 1 Kgs 22:13).[25]

In contrast to Mari, the Bible is replete with prophecies unfavorable to the king and to the people. Their heralds, the so-called prophets of doom or "true" prophets, are constantly harassed by the authorities. One well-known case is Amos, who in the royal sanctuary at Bethel foretells King Jeroboam's death and the exile of the people (Amos 7:10–13). In reaction the priest Amaziah, by order of the king, expels the prophet disgracefully to Judah. Jeremiah provokes an even more violent response, in the days of both Jehoiakim and Zedekiah. Pashhur, the priest in charge of the Temple in Jerusalem, when confronted with the prophet's words of wrath, "beat Jeremiah the prophet, and put him in the stocks that were . . . in the house of the Lord" (Jer 20:2).

On the other hand, at certain times we find close cooperation between the king, the priest, and the prophet. A priest occasionally officiated as an intermediary between king and prophet, as when King Hezekiah sent emissaries to Isaiah (2 Kgs 19:20 = Isa 37:2–4) and Zedekiah to Jeremiah (Jer 21:1–2; 37:3). Similarly, Hilkiah, the high priest, headed the royal delegation that Josiah sent to the prophetess Hulda (2 Kgs 22:12–20). The roles are inverted at Mari, where a prophet's report could be conveyed to the king via a priest. According to two documents (ARM VI 45; X 8), prophetesses appear before the priest Ahum, who served in the temple of Annunītum located in Mari proper. Once Ahum reports the message to Bahdilim, the palace prefect, to be relayed to the king, and at another time he transmits the prophetic words to Queen Shibtu.[26] In this latter case, a new element appears to which we have only briefly alluded previously—the frenetic here was a mere maidservant, called Ahatu, who had no prophetic title, being simply a lay person. This brings us to the lay prophets.

LAY PROPHETS

More than half of the "prophetic" documents from Mari deal with lay persons not functioning as professionals attached to a sanctuary. Among these so-called lay prophets we find such designations as a "man," a "woman," a "man's wife," a "youth," a "young woman" (or "maidservant"), and certain persons who are mentioned merely by their personal names. In one case, we encounter a prophetic message elicited from a "man and a woman" (lit. "male and female"), who prophesy jointly (ARM X 4). Because this latter manner of prophecy is uncommon and astounding in Mari, it should be examined briefly.

Queen Shibtu writes to her husband that she has asked a man and a woman to foretell the fortunes of Zimrilim's forthcoming military expedition against Ishme-Dagan, king of Ashur. The mode of predicting the future here is exceptional and has led to different interpretations among scholars.[27] We present here the key sentence at the opening of Shibtu's letter in accordance with a recent collation: "Concerning the report on the military campaign which my lord undertakes, I have asked a man and a woman about the signs *(ittātim)* when I plied (them with drink), and the oracle *(egerrûm)* for my lord is very favorable" (ARM X 4:3–37). Shibtu immediately inquires about the fate of the enemy Ishme-Dagan and the oracle "was unfavorable." Further on, Shibtu cites in full the prophecy proclaimed by the two persons, which contains several motifs found in biblical prophecies.[28] How are we to perceive this kind of divination? It has been suggested that the man and the woman themselves served as a sign and portent, partly on the basis of the words of Isaiah (Isa 8:18): "Behold, I and the children the Lord has given me are signs and portents in Israel," but this interpretation seems forced. It seems, rather, that the queen turned randomly to select a man and a woman and offered them a drink, perhaps wine, so as to loosen their tongues and acquire an *egerrûm* oracle, which is based on "chance" utterances. It has already been suggested that this type of oracle is reminiscent of the divinatory method referred to as a *bat qôl* (lit. "a trace of a voice," usually translated "echo") in Talmudic sources, where it serves as a substitute for authentic prophecy.[29]

Among the lay prophets, as well as among the transmitters of prophetic reports, there is an unusually large proportion of women, mostly from Zimrilim's entourage. One of the king's daughters turns to her father, stating explicitly: "Now—even though I am (only) a woman—may my father and lord harken unto my words. I will constantly send the word of the gods to my father" (ARM X 31:7'–10'). Some women, including female dreamers, send their prophecies directly to the king without mediation (ARM X 50; 100). More than anyone else, Queen Shibtu serves as an intermediary for conveying prophetic messages to her husband, the king. Also among the professional prophets, as we have seen, there are a considerable number of women. This brings to mind the prophetesses in the Bible, the outstanding ones being Deborah wife of Lappidoth (Judg 4:4) and Huldah wife of Shallum (2 Kgs 22:14). In both instances, the Bible specifies in particular that they were married, probably to stress their stable position and reliability; this is the case of the "wife of a man," one of the Mari prophetesses (ARM XIII 114:8).

Are there any characteristics that separate the professional prophets from the lay? Two prominent distinguishing features have been noticed by scholars: (1) In the case of the professional, and only the professional, the actual message is preceded by the verb "to arise" *(tebû)*—"he/she arose"—which alludes to the stimulation of the prophets in the temple (perhaps getting up from a sitting or crouching position).[30] Synonymous expressions are used as well in connection with the prophets of the Bible (Deut 13:2; 18:15, 18: 34:10; Jer 1:17; etc.), and note in particular Ezekiel: "And set me upon my feet: (Ezek 2:2; cf. 3:22–24; Dan 8:17–18; 10:10–11). (2) Among the lay prophets the dream is prevalent as a prophetic means, while this medium is totally absent among the professionals.

PROPHETIC MESSAGE DREAMS

From a third to a half of all the published prophecies from Mari originated in dreams. Thus, phenomenologically speaking, there are two distinct categories of acquiring the divine word. The professional prophets enjoyed direct revelations while awake; the lay persons, on the other hand, were usually dreamers of dreams. Divine revelations through dreams were a widespread phenomenon throughout the ancient Near East, including Israel.[31] But at Mari, as well as in the Bible, alongside regular revelatory dreams we find a specific subcategory of "message dream," namely, a dream in which the message was not intended for the dreamer himself but rather for a third party (as for the Bible, see Num 12:6; Jer 23:25–32; 29:8; Zech 10:2).

The above two categories of prophesying now illuminate with greater clarity the parallel distinction made in the Bible, especially in the legal corpora: "If a prophet arises among you, or a dreamer of a dream, and gives you a sign or a wonder . . ." (Deut 13:1–5). In an incident involving Saul, the Bible explicitly differentiates between as many as three distinct divinatory methods: "The Lord did not answer him, either by dreams or by Urim or by prophets" (1 Sam 28:6; and see v 15).[32] Jeremiah still regarded the dreamer as a distinct type of prophet (Jer 27:9). But he already belittles the dream, contrasting it with "the word of God" and associating it with the false prophets: "Let the prophet who has a dream tell the dream, but let him who has my word speak my word faithfully. What has the straw common with wheat?" (Jer 23:28). This deflated status of the dream as a source of prophetic inspiration finds clear expression in the rabbinic dictum comparing sleep to death just as "a dream is withered prophecy" (Gen. Rab. 44:17).

The letters that report dream revelations are usually structured according to a regular scheme: the writer's presentation of the male or female dreamer; the opening formula of the dreamer: "(I saw) in my dream"— *(ina šuttīja)*, which is an obviously West Semitic form identical with biblical Hebrew *bahălômî* (Gen 40:9, 16; 41:17);[33] the content of the dream which is based on a visual or, more often, on an auditory experience (hearing the voice of the god); finally, comments of the writer of the letter. In many cases these include a statement that, along with the report of the prophet, a lock of his or her hair and the hem of his or her garment are dispatched to the king.

Let us dwell here upon one illuminating incident at Mari where the same dream recurred twice, night after night. The dreamer was a mere youth *(ṣuḫārum)* to whom a god appeared in a nocturnal vision. The dream was eventually reported to the king by Kibri-Dagan: "Thus he saw (a vision) as follows: 'Build not this house . . .; if that house will be built I will make it collapse into the river!' On the day he saw that dream he did not tell (it) to anyone. On the second day he saw again the dream as follows: 'It was a god (saying): "Build not this house; if you will build it, I will make it collapse into the river!" ' Now, herewith the hem of his garment and a lock of hair of his head I have sent to my lord . . ." (ARM XIII 112:1'–15'). The boy, who apparently had no previous prophetic experience, did not at first realize the source of his dream; only when it recurred the next night did he become aware of its divine origin and of the mission imposed upon him. This immediately calls to mind young Samuel's initial experience while reposing in the temple at Shiloh (1 Samuel 3). The Lord informs him in a nocturnal vision of the impending demise of the Elide clan, but in this case it was only after the fourth beckoning (on the very same night) that Samuel became convinced of the divine nature of the vision.[34]

In general, novice and inexperienced prophets were unable to identify revelations when they first encountered them (in the case of Samuel
see 1 Sam 3:7); hence the repetition of the manifestation, whether at
Mari or in the Bible. As for the latter, most illuminating is the initial call
vision of Jeremiah, who is reluctant to accept his prophetic mission,
pleading his youthfulness before God (Jer 1:6–7). After having had his
confidence bolstered, God tests him by a vision: "And the word of the
Lord came to me saying: 'Jeremiah, what do you see?' and I said: 'I see a
rod of almond *(šāqēd).*' Then the Lord said to me, 'You have seen well for
I am watching *(šōqēd)* over my word to perform it" (Jer 1:11–12). God
in his response confirms the reliability of the prophet's perception, a
totally unique event in the realm of prophetic visions in the Bible. It
proves that Jeremiah passed the test and is fit to undertake the prophetic
mission.[35]

A NEW PROPHECY FROM MARI AND THE QUESTION
OF PROPHETIC RELIABILITY

We shall conclude our discussion of prophetic dreams with the last one to
be published—one that has not yet been brought to bear upon the issue
of prophecy at Mari.[36] In this fragmentary document (A 222) the name of
the male or female writer has been lost as has been the name of the
recipient, most likely King Zimrilim, as in the rest of the letters. We read:

> (The writer): The woman Ayala saw *(iṭṭul)* in her dream as follows:
> (The dreamer): "A woman from the place Shehrum (5) (and) a woman from
> Mari in the gate of (the temple of) Annunītum [line missing] which is at
> the edge of the city—quarreled among themselves. Thus (said) the woman
> from Shehrum (10) to the woman from Mari: 'Return to me my position
> as high priestess *(enūtum)*; either you sit or I myself shall sit.' "
> (The writer): By the *Hurru*-bird I have examined this matter and (15) she
> saw (the dream well—*naṭlat*). Now her hair and the hem of the garment I
> am sending along (20). May my lord investigate the matter!

The nature of the dispute between these two women is not entirely
clear, although it may involve rivalry between two localities and their
representatives over the seat of the high priestesshood. But highly illuminating is the concluding passage where the writer reports that he
confirmed the validity of the vision by means of augury, referring probably to examination of the behavior and flight patterns of the birds. This
divinatory device, well known in the classical world, was performed at a
very early period in West Asia.[37] The examination proved that the woman
actually did see *(naṭlat)*. On the basis of the synonymous and inter-
changeable verb for "to see (a dream)" *(amāru)*, the intention could be
that the woman was indeed competent and experienced in the art of

46

dream oracles.[38] Thus the meaning is, as the editor of the text translated: "Elle a bien en ce songe!" just like the words of God to Jeremiah, "You have seen well" *(hēṭabtā lir'ôt)*! The writer does not stop with his own examination of the dream but sends the woman's personal items—her hair and the hem of her garment—to the king for his own examination. This unique practice, attested in connection with the Mari prophets, is mentioned on nine different occasions, that is, in a third of all the "prophetic" letters. This peculiar procedure has led to several scholarly interpretations, all of which remain in the realm of speculation. Since a lock of hair and a piece of garment were very personal objects—objects that could have served as some sort of ID card, we may assume that this procedure was assigned to determine the identity and even the very existence of the prophet and to confirm the authenticity of his or her message, as we have tried to demonstrate elsewhere.[39]

The credibility of prophetic revelation was obviously a sensitive matter, not to be taken for granted. Thus it was often verified by means of accepted mantic devices, which were considered more reliable and preferable to intuitive prophesying.[40] If we ignore the still obscure practices of sending the hem of the garment and the lock of hair of the prophesier, we encounter the following examples: Queen Shibtu writes to Zimrilim that she personally examined a prophet's message prior to sending it to the king and found the report to be trustworthy (ARM X 6); in another letter, a lady of the royal household reported a vision and then advised the king: "Let my lord have the haruspex look into the matter . . ." (ARM X 94); in a third letter, another woman implores the king to verify the vision of an *āpiltum* by divinatory means (ARM X 81); the same woman advises the king following the prophecy of a *qabbatum* (see above) to be alert and not to enter the city without inquiring of omens (ARM X 80).

In contrast, in Israel the prophetic word, whether accepted or rejected by the king or the people, is never subjected to corroboration by cultic means; it is simply vindicated by the test of fulfillment (cf. Deut 18:22; Jer 28:9; Ezek 33:33).

NOTES

1. A. Malamat, "Prophecy in the Mari Documents," *EI* 4 (1956) 74–84 (Hebrew; English summary, pp. vif.); idem, "History and Prophetic Vision in a Mari Letter," *EI* 5 (1958) 67–73 (Hebrew; English summary, pp. 86*f.); idem, "Prophetic Revelations in New Documents from Mari and the Bible," VTSup 15 (1966) 207–27; idem, "A Mari Prophecy and Nathan's Dynastic Oracle," *Prophecy: Essays Presented to G. Fohrer* (ed. J. A. Emerton; BZAW 150; Berlin: Walter de Gruyter, 1980) 68–82.

2. We list here only general works on the entire corpus of "prophetic" materials and not studies of individual Mari documents: F. Ellermeier, *Prophetie in Mari und Israel* (Herzberg: Verlag Erwin Jungler, 1968); W. L. Moran, "New Evidence from Mari on the History of Prophecy," *Bib* 50 (1969) 15–56; idem, *ANET³*, 623-25, 629–32; H. B. Huffmon, "Prophecy in the Mari Letters," *BAR*, 3 199–224; J. F. Craghan, "The ARM X 'Prophetic' Texts: Their Media, Style and Structure," *JANESCU* 6 (1974) 39–57; E. Noort, *Untersuchungen zum Gottesbescheid in Mari* (AOAT 202; Neukirchen-Vluyn: Neukirchener Verlag, 1977); R. R. Wilson, *Prophecy and Society in Ancient Israel* (Philadelphia: Fortress Press, 1980) 98–115; A. Schmitt, *Prophetischer Gottesbescheid in Mari und Israel* (BWANT 6/14; Stuttgart: Kohlhammer Verlag, 1982); I. Nakata, *Acta Sumerologica* 4 (1982) 143–48.

3. See J. Margueron, "Rapport préliminaire sur la campagne de 1979," M.A.R.I. 1 (1982) 9–30; ". . . de 1980," ibid., 2 (1983) 9–35; ". . . de 1982," ibid., 3 (1984) 8–14, 197–206. On the archive of Asqudum discovered on the site, see now D. Charpin, "Les archives du devin Asqudum dans la résidence du 'chantier A' " M.A.R.I. 4 (1985) 453–62.

4. The texts have recently been collected by S. Parpola, *Letters from Assyrian Scholars to the Kings Esarhaddon and Assurbanipal* (AOAT 5/2; Neukirchen-Vluyn: Neukirchener Verlag, 1983) 2. 486–91. For extispicy in Mesopotamia in general and at Mari in particular, see now I. Starr, *The Ritual of the Diviner* (Bibliotheca Mesopotamica 12; Malibu, Calif.: Undena Publications, 1983), and index s.v. "Mari" (p. 141); and cf. J. Bottéro in *Divination et rationalité* (Paris, 1974) 7–197.

5. See A. Malamat, "The Ban in Mari and the Bible," *Biblical Essays— Proceedings of the 9th Meeting of Die Ou-Testamentliche Werkgemeenskap in Suid Africa* (1966) 40–49; idem, "Mari," *BA* 34 (1971) 18–21; E. A. Speiser, "Census and Ritual Expiation in Mari and Israel," *JBL* 79 (1960) 157–63; M. Held, "Philological Notes on the Covenant Rituals," *BASOR* 200 (1970) 32–37; and see now H. Tadmor, "Treaty and Oath in the Ancient Near East: A Historian's Approach," *Humanizing America's Iconic Book: SBL Centennial Addresses 1980* (ed. G. M. Tucker and D. A. Knight; SBL Centennial Publications; Chico, Calif.: Scholars Press, 1982) 127–35.

6. An exception is J. M. Sasson's remark in his review of Noort's book (above, n. 2) in *AfO* 27 (1980) 130a.

7. Noort (*Untersuchungen zum Gottesbescheid*, 24ff.) rejects the characteristics mentioned below as typical of prophesying at Mari and accordingly denies any relationship to biblical prophecy. But his approach is too extreme in requiring every single characteristic to appear in each and every "prophetic" text. He has been justifiably criticized by, e.g., I. Nakata, *JAOS* 102 (1982) 166–68.

8. This identification has gained currency ever since the overemphasis on the Canaanite origin of early Israelite prophecy by G. Hölscher, *Die Profeten* (Leipzig, 1914), and cf. J. Lindblom, *Prophecy in Ancient Israel* (Oxford: Basil Blackwell, 1962) 47, 105ff. In contrast, subsequent scholars occasionally pointed out the continuity of certain early elements through the period of classical prophecy; see, e.g., M. Haran, "From Early to Classical Prophecy: Continuity and Change," *VT* 27 (1977) 385–97 (with previous literature).

9. The question of center and periphery in the status of the prophets has been raised only in recent years under the influence of sociology. See Wilson, *Prophecy and Society*, which emphasizes the peripheral role of all Mari prophets when compared with the central role of the *bārû*; and see most recently D. L. Petersen, *The Roles of Israel's Prophets* (Sheffield: JSOT Press, 1981). The author considers the *nābî'* and the *hōzeh* to be "central" in both Israel and Judah, while the *rō'eh* and the *'îš hā'ělōhîm*, as well as the *běnê něbî'îm* ("sons" of the prophets), are regarded as peripheral.

10. This document has recently been joined to the text A 1121, published long ago; see B. Lafont, *RA* 78 (1984) 7–17. For earlier treatments, see M. Anbar, *UF* 7 (1975) 517ff. and Malamat, "A Mari Prophecy," 73 and n. 6.

11. Here I fully agree with Noort, *Untersuchungen*; see his summary on p. 109; I do reject, however, the remarks such as those of Schmitt, *Prophetischer Gottesbescheid*, 13.

12. The West as a separate sphere of culture from the East (Southern Mesopotamia) with regard to certain basic religious elements has been appreciated by A. L. Oppenheim, *Ancient Mesopotamia: Portrait of a Dead Civilization* (Chicago: University of Chicago Press, 1964) 221ff. For the ecstatic prophesier in Hittite sources, see *ANET*[3], 395a; for the prophet from Byblos, see most recently A. Cody, "The Phoenician Ecstatic in Wenamun," *JEA* 65 (1979) 99–106. The author derives the Egyptian word *'dd* from the West Semitic *'dd*, which in the Aramaic inscription of Zakkur (see below) designates a type of diviner-prophet, and see Malamat "Prophetic Revelations," 209 and n. 2.

13. For this prophesier, see most recently Wilson, *Prophecy and Society*, 106–7 with bibliography.

14. For this term and additional bibliographical references, see now *CAD* Q, 2b.

15. Malamat, "Prophetic Revelations," 210–11 and n. 4, for additional references and earlier literature. Cf. now J. Renger, *ZA* NF, 25 (1969) 219ff.; *CAD* M/I 90 including Old Babylonian references outside Mari.

16. J. M. Durand, *Textes administratifs des salles 134 et 160 . . .*, ARM(T) 21 (1983); J. R. Kupper, *Documents administratifs de la salle 135 . . .*, ARM(T) 22 (1983); G. Bardet et al., *Archives administratives de Mari* 1, ARM 23 (1984).

17. Malamat, "History and Prophetic Vision," 71ff.; idem, "Prophetic Revelations," 212f. and n. 2, for the various spellings *apillû, aplû, āpilum*; see now *CAD* A/II, 170a; idem, "A Mari Prophecy," 68ff.; M. Anbar, *RA* 75 (1981) 91.

18. Interestingly, compliance with this prophetic demand seems to be alluded to in the female correspondence. Further on in our document the name of Zimri-Lim's "daughter" is given as Erishtī-Aya. Indeed, a woman by this name sends several doleful letters to her royal parents from the temple at Sippar; see ARM X 37:15; 43:16; etc. Cf. F. R. Kraus, *Königliche Verfügungen in altbabylonischer Zeit* (Leiden: E. J. Brill, 1984) 98 and n. 224.

19. Malamat, "History and Prophetic Vision," 72–73.

20. Balaam was certainly not a prophesier of the *bārû* type, as was long ago suggested by S. Daiches, "Balaam—a Babylonian bārū," *H. V. Hilprecht Anniversary Volume* (Leipzig, 1909) 60–70. This claim has often been correctly refuted; see recently A. Rofé, *The Book of Balaam (Numbers 22:2—24:25)* (Jerusalem:

Sinor, 1979; Hebrew) 32 n. 53. Offering sacrifices in preparation for deriving the word of the deity as is found in the Balaam pericope is similarly alluded to in the beginning of the Mari texts ARM XIII 23 and A 1221 (cf. Malamat, "A Mari Prophecy," 69–70); it is explicitly mentioned in a "prophetic" document that has so far been published only in French translation, A 455: ". . . One head of cattle and six sheep I will sacrifice . . . ", i.e., seven sacrificial animals. In what follows, a *muhhûm* "arises" and prophesies in the name of Dagan. Compare the seven altars, seven bulls, and seven rams that Balaam had Balak prepare before delivering his oracle (Num 23:29–30).

21. See the Deir ʿAllā inscription, first combination, line 11; J. Hoftijzer and G. van der Kooij, *Aramaic Texts from Deir ʿAllā* (Leiden: E. J. Brill, 1976) 180, 212. The editors interpreted ʿnyh as female answerer indicating a prophetess, following our conclusion about the title *āpilum* at Mari and its relationship to biblical terminology. This opinion has been accepted by Rofé, *The Book of Balaam,* 67 and n. 33, among others. Indeed, in the dialect of this inscription, verbs with a third weak radical are spelled preserving the *yod* before the final *he,* like Hebrew *bōkiyāh* (courtesy B. A. Levine). This term has nothing to do with "poor woman," despite the Hebrew homograph ʿnyh, as various scholars contend; see, e.g., A. Caquot and A. Lemaire, *Syria* 54 (1977) 200; P. K. McCarter, *BASOR* 234 (1980) 58; H. and M. Weippert, *ZDPV* 98 (1982) 98; J. A. Hackett, *The Balaam Text from Deir ʿAllā* (HSM 31; Chico, Calif.: Scholars Press, 1984) 133 s.v. "ʿnyh."

22. See J. C. L. Gibson, *Textbook of Syrian Semitic Inscriptions* (Oxford, Clarendon Press, 1975) 2.8ff. The author translates the word ʿddn as (prophetic?) "messengers" on the basis of ʿdd in Ugaritic (p. 15), and cf. above n. 12. For a possible connection between prophecy at Mari and at Hamath, see J. F. Ross, "Prophecy in Hamath, Israel and Mari," *HTR* 63 (1970) 1–28.

23. Especially the motifs of gathering into a net and delivering into the hand, which are found frequently in both ancient Near Eastern and biblical literature in connection with vanquishing the enemy; see Malamat, "Prophecy in the Mari Documents," 82, and "Prophetic Revelations," 217f.; cf. J. G. Heintz, VTSup 17 (1969) 112–38, who relates these motifs to the "Holy War" in the ancient Near East and the Bible.

24. This has been indicated by, among others, B. Uffenheimer, *Early Israelite Prophecy* (Jerusalem, 1973; Hebrew) 27, 37; Noort, *Untersuchungen* 93, 109; and recently J. Blenkinsopp, *A History of Prophecy in Israel* (Philadelphia: Westminster Press, 1983) 45. Remarkably, just before the conquest of Mari by Hammurabi there is a noticeable rise in future-telling activities of the *bārû;* see Starr, *Ritual of the Diviner,* 107.

25. For the "false" prophets and their dependence on the Israelite establishment, see among others M. Buber, *Der Glaube der Propheten* (Zurich, 1950) 253ff., F. L. Hossfeld and I. Meyer, *Prophet gegen Prophet* (Fribourg: Universitätsverlag, 1973); S. de Vries, *Prophet Against Prophet* (Grand Rapids: Wm. B. Eerdmans Publishing Co., 1978).

26. Moran ("New Evidence from Mari," 20) holds that ARM VI 45 deals with the same event as ARM X 50, while Sasson (*AfO* 27 [1980] 131b) associates it with ARM X 8. Neither suggestion is compelling. ARM X 50 does not mention a

priest by the name of Ahum, while ARM X 8 mentions a prophetess by name but without title, and ARM VI 45 speaks of an anonymous *muḫḫūtum*. It may be assumed, therefore, that before Ahum, a priest in Mari, both professional and lay prophesiers would occasionally appear.

27. On ARM X 4, and the mode of prophesying, see the recent studies: A. Finet, "Un cas de clédonomancie à Mari," *Zikir Šumim* (F. R. Kraus Festschrift; ed. G. van Driel et al.; Leiden: E. J. Brill, 1982) 48–55; J. M. Durand, "In vino veritas," *RA* 76 (1982) 43–50; M.A.R.I. 3 (1984) 150ff. C. Wilcke, *RA* 77 (1983) 93.

28. Note, above all, the motif of the gods marching alongside the king in time of war and saving him from his enemies, a motif resembling the intervention of the Lord in the wars of Israel. This involves as well driving the enemy into flight (cf. "Arise, O Lord, and let thy enemies be scattered," Num 10:35; see also Ps 68:2) and eventually decapitating the foe who will be trampled under the foot of the king of Mari. Cf. M. Weinfeld, "Ancient Near Eastern Patterns in Prophetic Literature," *VT* 27 (1977) 183ff.

29. For this type of oracle, see *CAD* E, *egirrû*, 45: ". . . oracular utterances . . . which are either accidental in origin (comp. with Greek *kledon*) or hallucinatory in nature." For the parallel with Hebrew *bat qôl*, see D. Sperling, "Akkadian *egirrû* and Hebrew *bt qwl*," *Journal of the Ancient Near Eastern Society of Columbia University* 4 (1972) 63–74.

30. See in particular Moran, "New Evidence from Mari," 25–26; Weinfeld, "Ancient Near Eastern Patterns," 181–82.

31. Malamat, "Prophecy in the Mari Documents," 83; "Prophetic Revelations," 221–22 and n. 1 on p. 222, for literature on the dream in the Bible. For the ancient Near East, see the basic study of A. L. Oppenheim, *The Interpretation of Dreams in the Ancient Near East* (Philadelphia: American Philosophical Society, 1956).

32. An exact parallel to these three alternative means of inquiring of the deity may be found in the Plague Prayers of the Hittite King Murshili II; see *ANET*[3], 394b–95a, and S. Herrmann, *Die prophetischen Heilserwartungen im Alten Testament* (Stuttgart: W. Kohlhammer, 1965) 54f.

33. The West Semitic form was pointed out by Held; see apud Craghan, "The ARM X 'Prophetic' Texts," 43 n. 32. The standard Akkadian form would be *ina šuttim ša āmuru/attulu;* compare a similar West Semitic usage in one of the first prophecies published: *ina panīya* (lit. "in front of me," meaning "on my way"); Malamat, "Prophecy in the Mari Documents," 81.

34. See Malamat, "Prophetic Revelations," 223ff. The phenomenon of an identical dream recurring several times is known especially from the classical world; see J. S. Hanson, "Dreams and Visions in the Graeco-Roman World and Early Christianity," *Aufstieg und Niedergang der Römischen Welt*, II, 23/2 (Berlin: Walter de Gruyter, 1978) 1411, and the passages from Cicero, *De divinatione,* cited there.

35. See A. Malamat, *Jeremiah Chapter One—The Call and the Visions, Iyyunim* 21 (Jerusalem, 1954; Hebrew) esp. 39–40.

36. The document was published by G. Dossin, "Le songe d'Ayala," *RA* 69 (1975) 28–30 (attributed by him to King Yahdunlim!); and see the comments of

J. M. Sasson, *JAOS* 103 (1983) 291. His interpretation of *enūtum* (see below) as "utensils" rather than "priesthood" is unsatisfactory.

37. Divination by bird behavior is a typically Western practice; cf. Oppenheim, *Ancient Mesopotamia,* 209–10. This practice was especially widespread among the Hittites; see A. Kammenhuber, *Orakelpraxis, Träume und Vorzeichenschau bei den Hethitern* (Heidelberg: C. Winter, 1976). The book deals only briefly (p. 11) with the kind of bird mentioned in our document: *MUŠEN ḪURRI;* see for this bird A. Salonen, *Vögel und Vogelfang im Alten Mesopotamien* (Helsinki, 1973) 143–46; and cf. J. P. McEwan, *ZA* 70 (1980) 38, 58ff.

38. See *CAD* A/II, *amāru* A 2, p. 13: to learn by experience (especially stative . . .). The stative form with the meaning "experienced" or "trained" is especially prevalent in the Mari idiom, and we may therefore assume the same nuance for the stative of *naṭālu: naṭlat* in our document.

39. Malamat, "Prophecy in the Mari Documents," 81, 84; "Prophetic Revelations," 225ff. and notes. For other explanations, see now Uffenheimer, *Early Israelite Prophecy,* 29–33; Ellermeier, *Prophetie,* 97–110; Moran, "New Evidence from Mari," 19–22; Noort, *Untersuchungen;* and Craghan, "The ARM X 'Prophetic' Texts," 53ff. Note in two documents (A 455:25; ARM X 81:18) the illuminating but problematic addition appearing after the dispatch of the hair and hem; in the latter: "let them declare (me) clean" *(lizakkû);* according to Moran, "New Evidence from Mari," 22–23: ". . . it is the haruspex who 'tries the case' and it is his response that will in effect declare the prophetesses clean." Cf. now ARM X, 267, ad loc.; Noort, *Untersuchungen,* 85–86; and S. Dalley et al., *The Old Babylonian Tablets from Tell al Rimah* (London: British School of Iraq, 1976) 64 f., no. 65.

40. See Moran, "New Evidence from Mari," 22–23; Craghan, 41–42; and H. W. F. Saggs, *The Encounter with the Divine in Mesopotamia and Israel* (London: Athlone Press, 1978) 141.

41. This study was prepared by a grant from the Fund for Basic Research, administered by the Israel Academy of Sciences and Humanities, and during my term as Fellow of the Institute for Advanced Studies of the Hebrew University.

4

Aspects of the Religion
of Ugarit

PATRICK D. MILLER, JR.

The discovery some fifty years ago of the ancient city of Ugarit and its extensive literary remains at Ras Shamra on the coast of Syria was an epochal event, first of all for our understanding of the social, political, economic, and religious history of the ancient Near East in the second millennium and, secondly, for the background of the language, literature, and culture of the Bible. Certainly the Ugaritic discoveries are of signal importance for the history of religion in the ancient Near East. They provide us with detailed, extensive—and also elusive—information on religious practices in second-millennium Syria-Palestine at a major city, a crossroads and a center that manifests continuities with practices and conceptions before and after in the broader sphere of Syria-Palestine. One needs to look at that center and its religious history in its own right as well as for its significance for the larger religious environment of which it was a part. The pages that follow do not attempt a full survey of that religious history but focus on three major aspects of it: the pantheon at Ugarit, the general character of the religion and religious ideas evidenced there, and the cultus, with particular attention to sacrifice.[1]

THE REALM OF THE GODS

The world of the gods as reflected in the texts from Ugarit was well populated and complex. Ugaritic religion, like the religions of neighboring cultures, saw the gods as forming an assembly and a pantheon that reflected the following characteristics: complexity, systematization including order or rank, and development or change. These characteristics are what I wish to explore in the following pages.

The pantheon of Ugarit is unique. It is not duplicated elsewhere and clearly belongs to its locale, reflecting the Syrian or Northwest Semitic context out of which it comes. But the setting of Ugarit at a major geographical and political center also means that the impact or influence from other countries or peoples on the conception of the divine world is extensive. Deities of West Semitic, Hurrian, and Mesopotamian origin are all present. Very few deities of any significance cannot be recognized from our previous knowledge of Canaanite-Phoenician, Hurrian, Meso-potamian, and other sources. This is no accident, however, and of no little importance. There is a self-conscious concern for the interrelationships of these various pantheons, reflected not only in the presence of documents in Akkadian, Hurrian, and Ugaritic all at the same place but even more in the fact that there is an extensive intermingling of the deities. A liturgical or sacrifice text can begin in Ugaritic and be addressed to 'ttrt and then immediately shift to Hurrian and deal with the goddess in her Hurrian form of Šauška. There are god lists of Babylonian character, of Hurrian character, and Ugaritic. But even more important is the clear effort to relate these, as, for example, in the Ugaritic pantheon texts (RS 20.24 and 26.142) and the polyglot AN or god list where the deities of the Ugaritic pantheon are listed frequently in terms of their Akkadian or Hurrian equivalencies. Here is reflected not only the complexity of the world of the gods but the clear concern to systematize that world and uncover its external as well as internal relationships. Probably as well as anywhere in the ancient world one can see here the interrelationships of the various views of the divine realm while perceiving also that the desire to order and understand those relationships is a self-conscious need and activity of the culture itself and not merely a device and fetish of modern scholarship. The significance of Ugarit for the history of religion rests to no little degree on the way in which its strategic location led to the interaction of religious elements from varying cultures, thus providing us with a partial prism for perceiving the spectrum of the religious world of the Middle and Late Bronze Ages.

At the center of that religious world as it is reflected at Ugarit were the deities El and Baal, the former the patriarchal head of the pantheon, the latter the rising young storm-god and cosmogonic warrior (see below). One of the pieces of data, however, pointing to the complexity of the pantheon at Ugarit is the fact that on the god lists there are various *ilu*s and *baʿlu*s mentioned whose relationship to the high gods El and Baal is not entirely clear. Further, while the pantheon, or elements of the pantheon, constituted an assembly, there were also subgroups of divine beings allied with El and Baal as well as other gods and goddesses, often functioning as coterie to the deity, for example, *dr il* ("the circle of El"), *dr il wpḫr bʿl* ("the circle of El and the assembly of Baal"), *il tʿdr bʿl* ("the helper gods of Baal"), *bn aṯrt* ("the children of *Aṯirat*"), and the like. The functions and roles of such groups of deities are what one would expect from comparative data—allies of the deity in battle, a deliberative planning body where gods take counsel together, a festive assembly or gathering for banquets and feasts. Similar roles were played by the divine council or heavenly assembly surrounding Yahweh in Israelite religion.[2] Indeed the council of Yahweh has its closest analogies in the council of the gods as it is depicted in the texts from Ugarit, not only in its functions but in the character of the assembly as a nondemocratic, anonymous group of divine or semidivine beings who receive and carry out the decree of the ruling deity.[3]

The character and roles of the individual deities also manifest both complexity and fluidity as well as anticipate in various ways what we know of later Canaanite and Syrian religion from biblical, Phoenician, and classical sources. The classic case of this is the "complex pattern of relations"[4] among the three goddesses Atirat (later Asherah), Attart (later Ashtart), and Anat. Their functions and roles clearly overlap, and they exist in changing and sometimes ambiguous relationships to the gods with whom they are associated. The mythological and epic texts from Ugarit, and to some extent other kinds of texts, provide us now with the history and story of these goddesses, so that one can discern more clearly their various roles and relationships than was the case when our knowledge of them was more fragmentary and confined to the later sources.

The Ugaritic texts have contributed significantly to our understanding of the background of emergent Yahwism in early Israel as they have uncovered the nature, complexity, and mythology of the head of the Canaanite pantheon, El, a god who was known from East Semitic, Northwest Semitic, and South Semitic sources but whose mythology was largely unknown to us except in the late work of Philo Byblius. Now we are able to see his profile sharply etched as a patriarchal figure, father of gods and human beings, chief of the pantheon, creator, bestower of blessing, and one who guides human destinies, stern, compassionate, wise, fearful at times, drunken carouser, highly virile or sadly impotent (depending upon how one reads the Shahar and Shalim text [*CTA* 23 = *UT* 52]).[5] El rules the divine world in the mythological texts, guides and blesses the kings in the epic texts, and receives sacrifices and offerings in the cult of Ugarit. With regard to El's place in the Canaanite or Syrian theogony, previously known from Philo Byblius, the Ugaritic texts have demonstrated the relationship with the Sumero-Akkadian and Hurro-Hittite tradition. They have also revealed the complexity of that tradition, showing, for example, that Kumarbi, the Hurrian god par excellence but lacking roots in Syrian religion, was identified not only with El, as one might expect, but also apparently with Dagan, a deity who did not play a role in Hurrian mythology and religion. Here, as in other regards, Ugaritic religion became the meeting place for Syrian and Hurrian religion, creating a dynamic syncretism that allowed for variation depending on the particular theological or cultic emphasis, which may in one instance be an agricultural concern, thus Kumarbi = Dagan, while in another case it may be the question of divine rule, and thus Kumarbi—El beset by Baal = Tešub.[6]

The presence of El names—for example, El Olam, "the Everlasting God" (Gen 21:33); El Elyon, "God Most High" (Gen 14:18–24); and El Shaddai (Gen 17:1; 28:3; etc.)—in the patriarchal narratives of Genesis as epithets or names of Yahweh suggests an early or close identification with Yahweh. Furthermore, El epithets continue to be associated with Yahweh in Israelite religion, the divine name El hardly ever appears in the Bible as the name of a non-Israelite deity, and El names were frequent in the Israelite onomasticon, particularly in the early period and in the postexilic era. This evidence seems most plausibly explained if Yahweh is considered as originally an El figure who developed a separate identity and cultus "as the cult of Israel separated and diverged from its poly-theistic context,"[7] a thesis put forth most strongly by F. M. Cross, who sees even the name Yahweh as originally a hypocoristicon of a liturgical title of El.[8] The shared imagery or role of patriarchal father and judge who rules over the council of the gods and manifests himself to human beings in dreams or auditions tends to confirm the early and close identification of Canaanite El and Israelite Yahweh.

Looking beyond the particular figure of El, one sees the complexity of the divine world of Ugaritic religion also in the way in which deities play different roles in different types of material, a phenomenon familiar from Sumero-Akkadian religion as well as other cultures. We do not have different pantheons at Ugarit, and the differences among the gods of the myths, those of the cult, and those of popular religion (as revealed in the proper names)[9] are not extensive. In *CTA* 29, what J. C. de Moor has characterized as the canonical god list,[10] most of the principal deities of the mythological texts are there: El, Baal, Anat, Atirat, Yamm, Kotar, Pidray, Attar, Šapš, and others. But several things are clear also:

1. A sense of order and rank is indicated.
2. There are other lists with significant variations.
3. While the deities at the top of the rank are not surprising, one notes that some deities, such as Atirat, Anat, Attart, Šapš, and Yamm, have lower and more subordinate places here and in sacrificial lists than their roles in the mythological texts might lead one to expect.

If, however, J. Nougayrol is correct in perceiving in the list two ranks, one being lines 1–18 headed by three major gods and then lesser deities and the other being lines 19ff. headed by the six goddesses who are spouses to the major gods and followed by lesser deities, then the order and ranking of the list as a whole would correspond more to what one would expect from the mythological and epic texts.

4. Some foreign deities such as Išhara and Dadmiš appear regularly in the god lists and offering texts but not at all in the mythological texts.

The deity Šapš is an informative example of the complexity of the divine world as perceived at Ugarit. It is not uncommon to find in the handbooks the judgment that the sun deity has a minor role or lacks prominence at Ugarit. It is true that Šapš plays a relatively minor role in the mythological texts, though even there one finds clues to a more prominent place, as in the references to Šapš' rule of the Rephaim. But from other contexts it is clear that Šapš plays a quite significant role in the religion of Ugarit and one not dissimilar from the role of Šamaš in Mesopotamian religion. In some manner Šapš is referred to in as many genres of literature as any other deity except Baal and Attart.[11] Her popularity is evident in the cult and in popular religion, the latter evidenced by the frequency of *šapš* as a component in proper names.[12] She is the recipient of offerings and sacrifices[13] and plays a major role in the serpent charms.[14] That, together with her association with the Rephaim evidenced in earlier and more recently published texts, points to an association with healing activities. In a letter to the king of Ugarit "the eternal sun" *(šapšu ʿalami)* is invoked in the sequence *bʿl, špšʿlm, ʿttrt, ʿnt,* and all the gods of Ališiya, that is, in second position behind Baal and before Attart and Anat.

The history of religion at Ugarit also reveals a *history in the divine world.* Our data are fragmentary but show some change and development in the realm of the gods. The case of Dagan is a clear example. He plays no part in the mythological and epic texts and thus remains at Ugarit a shadowy figure whose character as a grain-god may be clear but whose mythology and history are hidden in darkness. We do, however, find indicators that Dagan played a major role somewhere along the line and continued to exercise some influence in popular religions as well as the cult of Ugarit. Personal names with a *dagan* component are present, although not numerous.[15]

The deity appears prominently on sacrificial lists. If one of the two temples at Ugarit belonged to the cult of Dagan, as would appear to be the case from the steles dedicated to him there, then his significance for the religion of Ugarit, while puzzling in its character, is unquestionable. The fact that Baal is called *banu Dagan* ("son of Dagan") in the mythological texts where Dagan is absent suggests the possibility that Baal has taken over the function and place of Dagan. This is further implied by the fact that Dagan occupies a high place in the god lists but often had to yield his place in rank to Baal (who is always present) and sometimes was omitted altogether from the lists. We have, therefore, the complex situation where Dagan seems to belong to earlier stages in the history of Ugaritic religion in the light of his absence from the mythological and epic texts, his gradual displacement from the god lists, and the infrequency of Dagan personal names. At the same time, the presence of Dagan on sacrificial lists, occasionally in names, and as god of one of the two temples at Ugarit suggests a very active cult at later times. In the light of the reference to Dagan at Tuttul in one of the incantation texts,[16] one suspects again that we have evidence for Ugarit as a crossroads in the history of ancient Near Eastern religions. The presence of a major temple to Dagan in Ashdod, one of the major Philistine cities (1 Samuel 5) attests to the continuing role of this deity among the religions of Syria-Palestine.

A final example of the history of the gods at Ugarit is what happens when deities are combined in the form "X and Y" (X w Y). De Moor lists thirty-three of these combinations, some capable of being reversed (Y and X) and some deities appearing in more than one combination.[17] Some of the combinations involve deities having obvious relationships (*b'l wdgn; špš wyrḫ; 'nt w'ttrt*), and it is likely that originally the combination was simply a matter of associating two deities while they maintained their individuality. Gradually, however, certain combinations came to be more closely bound together, so that they came to be perceived as a single deity, and one could use the singular in referring to them (e.g., *ktr wḫss, mt wšr, nkl wib, qdš wamrr*). Some of the pairs could be broken up and used as parallel elements in parallel cola. The w (= "and") could be dropped, apparently because it had lost its meaning. The result is a single name made up of what were originally two names (X Y).[18] Here, of course, is where and how the Ugaritic texts provide us something of the early history of the Syrian goddess Atargatis. Not only do Attart and Anat both have association with Baal[19] but they are quite explicitly paired together or in parallel cola in several texts.[20] This encouraged tendencies toward identification. In later Syro-Phoenician religion, the connecting w (= "and") was lost altogether in the complete identification of the goddesses in the goddess Atargatis.

The three major goddesses of Ugarit, therefore, continue to play a role in religious developments of the first-millennium Mediterranean world.[21] In relation to Israelite religion there is no clear evidence of any knowledge of worship of Anat, Baal's sister and consort at Ugarit. Both Attart (= Ashtoret, or in the plural Ashtarot) and Atirat (= Asherah), however, are identified as Canaanite goddesses whom the Israelite people and kings on occasion worshiped, a practice condemned by the Deuteronomists. Con-

58

sistent with extrabiblical Phoenician evidence, the cult of Ashtoret is identified specifically with Sidon in Phoenicia and as a foreign religious element brought into Israel by Solomon and later eliminated by Josiah (1 Kgs 11:5, 33; 2 Kgs 23:13). In plural form, Ashtarot, this goddess is also generally associated with Baal in Deuteronomistic descriptions of Israelite apostasy (Judg 10:6; 1 Sam 7:3–4; 12:10). The goddess Aṭirat, consort of El, appears frequently in the Hebrew Bible both as the name of a Canaanite goddess, Asherah (e.g., 1 Kgs 15:13; 2 Kgs 21:7; 23:4), and as her cult symbol or idol (e.g., 1 Kgs 14:15; 2 Kgs 21:3; 23:6, 15).[22] In all such cases there is implicit or explicit condemnation of the worship of the goddess or use or worship of the cult object.[23] Recently discovered extrabiblical evidence from Kuntillet 'Ajrud and Khirbet el-Qom referring to "Yahweh and his *asherah*" has raised the question of whether this term could identify also either a cult object of Yahweh (cf. Deut 16:21) or his consort.[24]

THE GENERAL CHARACTER OF THE RELIGION OF UGARIT

Canaanite religion is regularly characterized in summary references or studies as a fertility religion. How does that apply to or hold true of Ugarit as a representative example? There are indeed major dimensions of the Baal-Anat mythology that seem to reflect a concern for fertility in the natural order: the death of Baal after or as he comes into the realm of Mot; Anat's winnowing and sowing of Mot; the vision by El of Baal alive accompanied by the words:

> The heavens rain fat;
> The wadis flow with honey.

All of this reflects in the mythology an attempt or desire to explain and deal with the problem of drought. Annual or sabbatical cycles may or may not have been involved. Drought was a devastating problem, and there may have been regular rites to try to deal with that whether or not Baal died every year. Procreation and cultic rites associated with that were also concerns of Ugaritic mythology (e.g., *CTA* 23 = *UT* 52).[25] But to seek to interpret the Baal cycle is to become aware that the mythology is much more complex than this and cannot be reduced to a description of it as reflection of a basically fertility religion any more than one can do that with Israelite religion (where drought was of equal concern and the deity viewed as dispenser of fertility, rain, and the like).

Equally significant in the mythology of Ugarit is the concern for cosmogony, the establishment of order and rule in the universe, and here again Ugarit reflects common concerns of Near Eastern mythology generally. At the heart of the Baal myth is the conflict with Yamm, representing the chaotic powers of the universe. The victory of Aliyan Baal over Yamm leads to the establishment of his kingship and the building of a magnificent house for Baal, a palace or temple. The associations with *Enûma elish*, as indeed with conceptions of the God of Israel, are apparent immediately, although they are by no means simply identical. In Israel the primal events of Yahweh's rule over that people and his claim to supremacy in the divine realm centered in the exodus and Yahweh's victory over the divine king of Egypt.[26] The earliest preserved account of that conflict, the hymn of praise in Exod 15:1–18, recounts the battle between Yahweh and Pharaoh's army, the destruction of the enemy forces in the sea by the incomparable divine warrior, and the leading of the people of Yahweh into his sanctuary. The song ends with a declaration in exaltation of Yahweh's kingship. The same mythic pattern is echoed in other poems such as Deut 33:2–5 and 26–29; Psalm 24; and Psalm 68[27] as well as in the prophetic and apocalyptic materials of such later works as Isaiah 40—66 and Zechariah 9—14.[28] Ugaritic, Mesopotamian, and Israelite religion shared a common theology to the extent that kingship over the cosmos was demonstrated in battle with the unruly forces, and the throne and abode of the king of the gods is established forever. There were political implications of this in Mesopotamia and Israel, and one may assume that the same was true at Ugarit inasmuch as the temple to Baal excavated there reveals his dominance—along with Dagan—of the religious establishment of that city.[29]

The complexity of the religious understanding implied in the mythology of Ugarit is further sensed when one realizes that kingship in the divine world belongs to El as well as to Baal. This is explained in various ways; for example, kingship is passing over from the otiose El to the vigorous young Baal,[30] or one is static and one is dynamic.[31] Whether or not the notions of static or dynamic are proper ones, I am inclined to see this complexity as not simply due to a transition stage in the generations of divine power but reflective of the broad scope of the divine rule that manifests itself in conflict with powers of disorder, in creative and procreative activity, and in protecting and directing the community and its rulers. All these manifestations become centralized in Yahweh in Israel, but they are present and anticipated in the functions and responsibilities of the gods of Ugarit as described in the mythological texts.

THE CULTUS—SACRIFICE AND THE KING

A number of texts deal quite directly with cultic matters.[32] One text (*CTA* 23 = *UT* 52) is apparently a ritual drama having to do with procreation and acknowledging the presence of the king and queen at the affair. But there is no proof of an actual *hieros gamos,* and what actually went on in the ritual is quite unclear. Other texts give us some impression of the religious personnel at Ugarit, and the archaeological work has revealed much of the typical paraphernalia of the cult and especially the great temples of Baal and Dagan.

In the case of the Baal temple, we have an example of the interaction of the cosmic and the earthly, the mythological and the cultic; for the building of a house for Baal is a significant part of the Baal-Anat cycle and is reflected in the building of a house for Baal at Ugarit.

The largest number of religious texts outside the mythological texts have to do with sacrifice and accompanying rituals. There is a fairly large variety of kinds of sacrifices as well as materials or animals for sacrifice. A number but not all of these terms are familiar from Israelite sacrifices. B. Levine has observed that the presence of *šalamīm* in conjunction with "burnt offerings" places Ugaritic practice clearly in the sphere of Northwest Semitic ritual and close to Israelite practices rather than in association with the practices of other parts of the Near East where generally sacrifices were placed before the deity for viewing but taken away for human consumption rather than burning. Levine even suggests that Ugaritic sacrificial practice at this point may be closer to Israelite than pre-Israelite Canaanite practices.[33]

The ritual texts when compared with the mythological texts reveal an important aspect of the conceptuality involved in the ritual of sacrifice: The rituals of sacrifice carried out in the human realm are reflected in or reflections of similar activities in the divine realm, and thus the sacrifice to the gods and the banquet of the gods overlap at least with regard to terminology. The Keret texts are instructive in this regard. El begins his instructions for Keret's wife-seeking expedition by giving detailed directions for the king's ritual preparations, including ablutions, prayer, and sacrifice. Keret is told first to wash his hands and arms, an action to be connected with the several occasions in ritual texts where the king is said to wash himself and is called "purifier" *(brr)*. The goddess ῾Anat also washes herself in connection with sacrificial rite. Ritual purification, therefore, as a part of sacrificial rites is reflected in narrative epic texts, mythological texts, and descriptive rituals and is an act performed by gods and kings. El then tells Keret to prepare various sacrifices, the materials of which are reflected in the ritual texts. These sacrifices Keret takes to the top of the wall, an action that may be related to the descriptive ritual text *CTA* 35 = *UT* 3 where the king apparently sacrifices on a roof (*gg*—cf Zeph 1:5a). Keret then lifts his hands heavenward in prayer and sacrifices to El and Baal. The parallel terms for these sacrifices (*dbḥ* and *mṣd*) are the same terms that El uses to describe the

61

feast he prepares for the gods in *Ugaritica* VI, one of the clear signs that the human sacrifice to the gods can reflect or be projected as the divine banquet of the gods.

The association of sacrifice with prayer to Baal not only is attested in the epic texts but also is found in an important ritual text (RS 24.266 = KTU 1.119) published in *Ugaritica* VII. The text includes the instructions for purifying the king discussed above as well as various kinds of sacrifices of animals (e.g., throat, liver) as well as libations (*šmn šlm*, "oil of peace"?). The king not only washes himself as does Keret but, also like the legendary king, makes sacrifices. Within this context, ritual instructions are given for praying to Baal when the city of Ugarit is under attack by an enemy. The prayer is formally a vow, not unlike what one finds in Num 21:1–4 and Judg 11:30–32, where vows are uttered in situations of military conflict seeking divine help against the enemy. The deity is promised sacrifices if the enemy is repulsed. There is a priestly bracket around the prayer to Baal describing first the situation of crisis that would elicit such a prayer/vow and at the end the positive response and deliverance of the deity. Not only does this correspond to the narrative contexts of the biblical texts cited above but it is analogous to the biblical laments or complaints where the divine response is expected and indicated in various ways. Indeed many of the complaint psalms may reflect the involvement of the king in sacrifice and other ritual activity to secure the help of the deity.[34]

Elsewhere in the Keret texts the king prepares sacrifices or feasts using terminology found in the mythological texts and the ritual texts. For example, Lady Hurriya summons Keret and his guests to eat and drink Keret's *dabḥu* even as El issues a similar summons to the gods to come eat and drink in his house. In these cases, the divine and human *dabḥu* is more a feast than a sacrifice. Keret later is reported to be preparing a sacrifice—*dbḥ* and *'šrt*. The latter term is somewhat uncertain and may refer to libations, but we find it also in the list of dedications offered in the prayer to Baal as well as in the Baal-Anat cycle and the Aqhat epic where Baal both gives and receives such a sacrifice or feast. Here, therefore, we have a sacrificial or festive act that takes place among the gods (*CTA* 3.1.19), among human beings (*CTA* 16 = Krt C.I.40–41), and as a human act for human beings (*CTA* 17 = *UT* 2 Aq. VI.30–31).

While other texts could be cited, these are sufficient examples to bear witness to the role of the king in sacrificial activity (see further, *Ugaritica* V.11, which also gives instruction to the king and queen about offering and eating sacrifices), the close correspondences between mythological texts, epic texts, and ritual texts, and the way that divine and human realms pattern each other in the important sphere of sacrifice.

The activities of the Ugaritic kings in the epic and ritual texts as well as some of their epithets—Keret is called "son of El"—have raised the question of their possible characterization as divine in the royal ideology of Ugarit. Suffice it to say, there is insufficient evidence to substantiate such a claim, although one may in some sense speak of a sacral character to kingship in Ugarit in the light of the ritual texts where the king is the principal figure on a number of occasions, although what he does is limited, that is, he goes through purification by lustration, participates in sacrifice, and is involved in the ritual of carrying statues of certain deities into "the house of the king."[35]

The point at which one may speak in some sense of "divine" kingship is in the growing evidence for a cult of the dead at Ugarit. The key text is RS 34.126, which appears to be a funeral liturgy for a recently deceased king. The ritual serves to provide the dead king with essential services and secure the blessings for his successor. In this context the *rpum*, apparently the long-dead ancestors, and the *mlkm*, the recently dead rulers, are invoked to take part in the ritual. In the Ugaritic king list (KTU 1.113) a deceased ancestor is referred to as an *ilu* = "god." This does not necessarily mean a high god of the pantheon, but rather a divinized ancestor who has become a part of the *rpum* and through the funerary cult has some relation to those living.[36] It is not clear what is the relationship of the cult of the dead to the *marzihu/marzeah*, a social and religious association of persons who engaged in apparently regular festive celebration and banqueting that was sometimes associated with funerals and, at Ugarit, seems to have involved the *rpum*, the departed ancestors.[37] In part, at least, the association seems to have engaged in mourning rites and memorials for the dead through their activities of eating and drinking. In any event, the *marzeah* is a further example of religious or cultic continuity between second-millennium religious practices in Syria and the practices of Arameans, Phoenicans, and Israelites (see Jer 16:5) in the first millennium.

NOTES

This chapter is a revision of an article that appeared first in the *Journal of Northwest Semitic Languages* 9 (1981) 119–28.

1. Several general or broad-ranging studies of the religion of Ugarit have appeared through the years. Among the more valuable and useful ones are the following: R. de Langhe, *Les textes de Ras Shamra Ugarit et leurs rapports avec le milieu biblique de l'Ancien Testament* (Paris, 1945); O. Eissfeldt, "Kanaanäisch-ugaritische Religion," *Handbuch der Orientalistik* 8/1 (Leiden: E. J. Brill, 1984) 76–91; H. Gese, "Kult und allgemeine Kennzeichen der syrischen

Religionen im 2. Jahrtausend," *Die Religionen Altsyriens, Altarabiens und der Mandäer* (Stuttgart: W. Kohlhammer, 1970) 173–81; J. Gray, *The Legacy of Canaan:The Ras Shamra Texts and Their Relevance to the Old Testament* (VTSup 5; Leiden: E. J. Brill, 1965); A. F. Rainey, "The Kingdom of Ugarit," *BA* 28 (1965) 102–25; W. F. Albright, *Yahweh and the Gods of Canaan* (London: Athlone Press, 1968), chap. 3; J. M. de Tarragon, *Le culte à Ugarit* (Paris: J. Gabalda, 1980); P. Xella, *I testi rituali di Ugarit,* I (Rome: Consiglio Nazionale della Ricerche, 1981).

2. P. D. Miller, "The Divine Council and the Prophetic Call to War," *VT* 18 (1968) 100–107; idem, *The Divine Warrior in Early Israel* (HSM 5; Cambridge: Harvard University Press, 1973); E. T. Mullen, Jr., *The Assembly of the Gods: The Divine Council in Canaanite and Early Hebrew Literature* (HSM 24; Chico, Calif.: Scholars Press, 1980).

3. Note the following concluding comment of Mullen, *The Assembly of the Gods,* 283–84: "With the exception of the phenomenon of the prophet as herald/ courier of the council, the Israelite view of the assembly agrees in every detail with that of the council of the gods seen in the Ras Shamra texts. We must conclude that the major source of influence upon the council motif in early Hebrew literature comes from Canaan and not from Mesopotamia. Yet the parallels among the councils in all three cultures strongly suggest that the concept of the council of the gods was a common motif in the ancient Near East."

4. W. F. Albright, *Archaeology and the Religion of Israel* (Baltimore: Johns Hopkins University Press, 1956) 74.

5. Contrast, e.g., the interpretations of M. H. Pope, *El in the Ugaritic Texts* (Leiden: E. J. Brill, 1955) 37–41, and Cross, *CMHE,* 22–24. Both of these works are fundamental in a broader sense for understanding the nature and role of El.

6. E. Laroche, *Ugaritica* V 524ff.

7. F. M. Cross, "'ēl," *TDOT* 1. 260. This article (pp. 242–61) is one of the most valuable and comprehensive treatments of the character of El at Ugarit and the relation of El to Yahweh of Israel.

8. Cf. Cross, "'ēl," and idem, *CMHE,* 44–75.

9. Cf. in this regard the important study of Israel's religion by R. Albertz, *Persönliche Frömmigkeit und offiziele Religion* (Stuttgart: Calwer Verlag, 1978), together with the literature cited there.

10. J. C. de Moor, "The Semitic Pantheon of Ugarit," *UF* 2 (1970) 187–228.

11. Ibid., 217.

12. See F. Gröndahl, *Die Personennamen der Texte aus Ugarit* (Rome: Pontifical Biblical Institute, 1967) 195, 354, and 414.

13. In addition to the offering lists, note *CTA* 23 = *UT* 52.54.

14. See *Ugaritica* V, Text 7 (RS 24.244) 564ff.

15. Grondahl, *Die Personnennamen,* 122–23, 381.

16. *Ugaritica* V, Text 7 (RS 24.244) 1.15.

17. De Moor, "The Semitic Pantheon of Ugarit."

18. Ibid.

19. See in the Baal and Anat cycle and Aṭtart's role in *CTA* 2 = *UT* 137 and 68.

20. E.g., in *Ugaritica* V, Text 1 at El's drunken feast in his palace and in Keret

(*CTA* 14 = *UT* Krt 145–46), as well as *PRU* V 158. 1. 1.6, and *Ugaritica* V, Text 8 (RS 24.251) 1.14.

21. See the discussion in R. A. Oden, *Studies in Lucian's "De Syria Dea"* (HSM 15; Missoula, Mont.: Scholars Press, 1977) 73–98; and Albright, *Yahweh and the Gods of Canaan,* 105–18.

22. The most extensive treatment of Asherah in the Hebrew Bible remains that of W. F. Reed, *The Asherah in the Old Testament* (Fort Worth: Texas Christian University Press, 1949). Cf. Oden, *Studies,* 88–94, 149–55, and references there.

23. The carryover into biblical times of the fluidity of these goddesses as they were represented at Ugarit is well indicated in the following quote from Oden, *Studies,* 97–98:
"The Old Testament, both in Hebrew and in Greek dress, exhibits a confusion between the names and roles of 'Ašerah and 'Aštart; and this confusion when combined with the conflate forms '*ntw'ṭtrt* (Ras Shamra) and '*ntrt (Egypt)* suggests the early mingling of all three major goddesses. I Kings 11:5, 11:33, and 2 Kings 23:13 concur with late Phoenician evidence in associating 'Aštart with Sidon, a city which is, in the Keret epic, associated with 'Ēlat/'Ašerah. A reference to 'Ašerah *(la'ăšērâ)* in the Hebrew text of 2 Chronicles 15:16 is a reference to 'Aštart *(τῇ 'Ασταρτῃ)* in the Greek text, while Aserah's cultic symbols are *hā'ăšērîm* in Hebrew but in Greek in 2 Chronicles 24:18. Demonstrating that the confusion worked in both directions, 'Aštart is *hā'aštārôt* in the Hebrew text of 1 Samuel 7:3 and 12:10, but τά 'άλση (7:3) or τοῖς 'άλσεσιν (12:10) in the Greek text, phrases usually reserved for 'Ašerah's cultic symbols. Both 'Aštart and 'Ašerah are mentioned in the same breath with Ba'l; yet assuming the Ba'l of the Old Testament is Ba'l Haddu neither 'Aštart nor 'Ašerah is primarily the consort in the Ugaritic myths of Ba'l whose mate is regularly 'Anat. Indeed the variable pairings of the Canaanite deities is itself impetus for the fusing of the three great goddesses into a single figure. And this variety obtains not only in the Old Testament, but also, and already, in the texts from Ras Shamra."

24. See the discussion of these finds in the following chapters in this volume: chap. 8 (Coogan), chap. 10 (McCarter), and chap. 11 (Tigay).

25. See in this regard now the comprehensive study of *CTA* 4–6 by B. Margalit, *"A Matter of Life and Death"* (AOAT; Neukirchen-Vluyn: Neukirchener Verlag, 1980).

26. Cross, *CMHE,* chap. 6.

27. Cf. Miller, *The Divine Warrior,* 74–128.

28. Cf. P. D. Hanson, *The Dawn of Apocalyptic* (Philadelphia: Fortress Press, 1975), chaps. 2 and 4; idem, "Zechariah 9 and the Recapitulation of an Ancient Pattern," *JBL* 92 (1973) 37–59.

29. For further discussion of the continuities and discontinuities between Baal as he is represented at Ugarit and Yahweh, see such works as Cross, *CMHE,* chap. 7; N. Habel, *Yahweh Versus Baal* (New York: Bookman Associates, 1964); and P. D. Miller, "God and the Gods," *Affirmation* 1/5 (1973) 37–62.

30. E.g., A. Kapelrud, *Baal in the Ras Shamra Texts* (Copenhagen: G. E. C. Gad, 1952), 133.

31. E.g., W. Schmidt, *Königtum Gottes in Ugarit und in Israel* (2d ed.; BZAW 80; Berlin: Alfred Töpelmann, 1966).

32. The most comprehensive presentation and discussion of textual data is found in the works by Tarragon and Xella cited in n. 1, above.

33. B. Levine, "Prolegomena," in G. B. Gray, *Sacrifice in the Old Testament* (reprint; New York: KTAV, 1971), xxxiv–xxv.

34. For a translation of the prayer to Baal text (KTU 1.119), philological commentary, and discussion of biblical analogues, see P. D. Miller, "Prayer and Sacrifice in Ugarit and Israel," *Text and Context* (ed. W. Classen; JSOT Supplement Series 48; Sheffield: JSOT Press, 1987).

35. See the discussion of the ritual involvement of the king in Tarragon, *Le culte à Ugarit,* chap. 4.

36. I am indebted to the careful analyses of these texts by Ted Lewis in his Harvard dissertation, "Cults of the Dead in Ancient Israel and Ugarit." On the subject generally, see M. H. Pope, "The Cult of the Dead at Ugarit," *Ugarit in Retrospect: Fifty Years of Ugarit and Ugaritic* (ed. G. D. Young; Winona Lake, Ind.: Eisenbrauns, 1981) 159–79.

37. For a summary presentation and discussion of the *marzeah* evidence, see P. D. Miller, "The MRZḤ Text," *The Claremont Ras Shamra Tablets* (ed. L. R. Fisher; Rome: Pontifical Biblical Institute, 1971) 37–49.

5

Aspects of Aramean Religion

JONAS C. GREENFIELD

The main source for the religion of the Aramaic-speaking peoples during the biblical period is epigraphic. This material has been drawn on by scholars since the end of the last century but remains sparse. With the recovery of the Sfire inscriptions (*KAI*, 222–24) an important source of useful information in the fields of language, literary style, treaty requirements, and curses became available, but there is little that is of direct use to the student of Aramean religion. The use of gods as witnesses to treaties is a well-known phenomenon of ancient Near Eastern treaties; the very god list was not "Aramean" and cannot be used for the discussion of the Aramean pantheon. The recently published bilingual from Tell Fakhariyah also adds philological and cultural information but is, at least in its first part, based on an Akkadian model and must be used with care. In this study we have attempted to use both the older and the newer material in conjunction with information concerning Aramean religion to be derived from the biblical text.

Aramaic texts from Anatolia or North Arabia of the Persian period have not been used, since these represent on the whole the autochthonous religions albeit in Aramaic dress. This present study is entitled "Aspects of Aramean Religion," since a choice had to be made among various possible items, and those which impinged on the biblical texts were given priority. Therefore, only the god Hadad, from the whole of the Aramean pantheon, is discussed, since he is the only Aramean god mentioned in the Hebrew Bible. A full-scale discussion dealing with later periods awaits the future when possible representational material from reliefs, coins, and seals will have been studied.

HADAD

The head of the Aramaic pantheon was the god Hadad whose cognomen was Rammān "the thunderer," the Rimmon of the biblical text.[1] The god Rammān is directly referred to twice in the Hebrew Bible: (1) the temple of Rimmon *(bêt Rimmôn)* in 2 Kgs 5:18 and (2) the mourning of Hadad-Rimmon referred to in Zech 12:11. There is, however, no reference to Hadad in the guise of Rammān in any of the Aramaic inscriptions that have reached us, although there are some personal names in cuneiform sources and on seal impressions in which the name Rammān is the theophoric element. It is Hadad (or in the form Hadda in some personal names) that is dominant in our sources as the leading god of Arameans. The kings of Damascus bear the throne name Bar Hadad, and the Bible speaks of Hadadezer, the Adad-idri of the Annals of Shalmaneser III, the king of Aram. The god Hadad appeared as a member of the West Semitic pantheon in the Old Babylonian period and is found in many West Semitic (= "Amorite") personal names.[2] In the territory of Yamhad, Hadad of Aleppo was the dominant deity and is known to us from a variety of texts from that period and later. Hadad of Aleppo was at a later date absorbed into the Assyrian pantheon and appears with the Sibitti as a final element in the lists of Mesopotamian divine witnesses in treaties.[3]

Hadad is the equivalent of the Akkadian storm-god Adad.[4] There is, however, no developed mythology of Adad in Akkadian literary material,[5] and the iconography of Adad has only recently been sketched.[6] The same is true of the Aramaic material, which mentions the god but gives very little information. We must turn to the Ugaritic texts, both mythological and epic, and to some references with literary overtones in the Amarna letters to learn about Ba ʻlu-Haddu, who plays a prime role in the Canaanite pantheon.[7]

It is in the ninth century, when the Arameans are settled in the western marches of the Assyrian empire, in Syria and in parts of Anatolia, that we can document Hadad's dominant role. In the first millennium a functional bifurcation had taken place—Baal became a Canaanite god and Hadad an Aramaic one. In the Tell Fakhariyah inscription the god Hadad of Sikanu, the sanctuary city of Guzanu, is celebrated.[8] King Hadda-yišʻi (written *hdysʻy* in that inscription) set up an image of himself in the temple of Hadad of Sikanu and extolled Hadad as his lord *(mrʼh)* and as the lord of the Habur river *(mrʼ hbwr)*, a unique epithet. Hadad's role as grantor of fertility is hailed, with the standard epithets of both Marduk and Adad applied to him. Thus Hadad distributes sustenance to his "brother" gods, a role fitting for the head of the pantheon. There is also reference to Hadad's role as recipient of offerings in funerary rites (see below). There can be no doubt that this sanctuary of Hadad, so close to the sources of the Habur, was a continuation of an earlier one dedicated to Adad or a similar deity and it continued to function as such also in the later Neo-Assyrian period.[9]

It is in the inscriptions from Zincirli (Samaʼl, Yʼdy) that Hadad is listed at the head of the pantheon. In the Hadad (*KAI*, 214) and Panamuwa (*KAI*, 215) inscriptions we find the following list with some internal variations: *hdd, 'l, rkb'l, šmš, ršp*. Hadad was clearly the head of the pantheon, taking precedence over El, but the dynastic god was Rakib-el, who is hailed as such in the Kilamuwa inscription (*KAI*, 24, l.16). Rakib-el is thanked together with Tiglath-pileser III by Bar-Rakib (*KAI*, 216; 217) for his good fortune.[10] Hadad, along with the other gods, is credited by Panamuwa I (*KAI*, 214) for standing by him since his youth and for giving him rule over Y'dy. But Hadad is singled out (1.8) for giving Panamuwa the "scepter of succession" *(ḥtr ḥlbbh)*,[11] and in gratitude the statue of Hadad was set up. The inscription refers in detail to a memorial rite, to be discussed below. As in the Tell Fakhariyah inscription (11.16–22), it is the wrath of Hadad that is to be feared (11.22–24). The god lists at the beginning of Sfire IA (*KAI*, 222) are of a general nature. The first half is "Mesopotamian," while the second half is West Semitic.[12] Hadad's importance emerges from the fact that he is called upon to execute the curses in this inscription (11. 25–26, 36, 38–39).

In the Zakkur inscription (*KAI*, 213) it is Elwer before whom a statue (of the god or of the king?) is erected.[13] Elwer has been equated in the Assyrian lexical lists with Hadad.[14] Elwer may indeed be a form of Hadad, or we may have at play here the tendency, typical of the later periods, to make equations of this sort. On the other hand, the god thanked by Zakkur for saving him from his enemies is Ba'lshamayn. Are Elwer and Ba'lshamayn also equivalent?[15] And what is the relationship of Ba'lshamayn with Hadad?

The Aramaic inscriptional material is indeed sparse and references to Hadad virtually cease, yet one should note that at Hierapolis *(mnbg)* Hadad was the leading god into the fourth century B.C.E., and probably later.[16] Hadad occurs on coins from Hierapolis as *hdd mnbg* together with the goddess *'th* (= Ateh).[17] A leading priest of Hierapolis of this period, Abdhadad, is found on a unique coin as *'bdhdd kmr mnbg*, "Abdhadad priest of Manbug," and his devotion to the god Hadad is recorded on the reverse of this coin.[18] It is on coins from Hierapolis that we first meet the goddess Atargatis *('tr'th)*, usually interpreted as a composite name *'tr< 'ttr* and *'th*, an Aramaic form of *'nt*. In later periods, when Atargatis is the dominant figure, Hadad is often her consort.[19]

A temple to the god (Haddad-) Rammān is mentioned in 2 Kings. No inscription relating to this temple has been found, but there can be little doubt that it was on the site of the latter-day temple to Zeus in the Hellenistic period and was known in the Roman period as the site of the temple of Jupiter Damascinus. On this site was built the Byzantine cathedral of St. John, which served after the Arab conquest as the foundation for the great Umayyad mosque. A fragment of an orthostat from the Aramean period was found there during repairs.[20] From the Tell Fakhariyah and Zakkur inscriptions we learn that it was in the temple that the inscribed statues were set up, while the Sfire inscriptions relate that the steles on which the inscriptions were written were set up in the temples.[21] In various biblical passages there are references to Aramaic religious practices in the temple in Damascus. In 2 Kgs 5:18 the Hebrew verb *hištaḥăwah* surely stands for Aramaic *sĕgad*. The *masgādā* is not referred to in any of the Aramaic inscriptions from Syria but is found in CAP 44, where an oath is taken by *Ḥ[rm]* by *msgd'* and *'ntbyt'l*. In this text the place of prostration is raised to divine status and an oath is taken by it.[22]

In the account of the practices introduced by Ahaz in line with what he saw in Damascus, the Bible refers to sacrifices, meal offerings, and libations (2 Kgs 16:10–15). The usefulness of these verses as a source for Aramean religious practices is limited, for the rites listed are typical of most sacrificial systems. There is also the possibility that what was seen was Assyrian modes of worship introduced to Damascus, and these, rather than indigenous Aramean practices, may have been copied by Ahaz.

MEMORIAL RITES

One ritual about which we do have some information is the memorial rite for departed ancestors.[23] This is mentioned in the Hadad inscription (*KAI*, 214.16–22): When the descendant of Panamuwa who will follow him on the throne will sacrifice to Hadad and invoke the name of Hadad, he should also invoke the soul/spirit of Panamuwa and say, "May the soul of Panamuwa eat with you and may the soul of Panamuwa drink with you; then it (the sacrifice) will be acceptable as a gift *(yrqy bh šy)* to Hadad, El, Rakib-el, and Shamash."[24] The need to appease the spirit of the dead was common to the peoples of the ancient Near East, and its traces may be found in unsuspected places. The *kispu* ceremony and related rites are well known at Mari and elsewhere during the Old Babylonian period and can be traced through the Neo-Babylonian period.[25] In my study of this rite in the Hadad inscription, I drew attention to the declaration made when giving the tithe to the Levite, "I have not given of it to the dead" (Deut 26:14). The donor testified that no part of the tithe was used in a memorial ceremony in which the *manes* of the dead was called upon to participate. It is also possible that the *zebaḥ mišpāḥâ* ("family feast"), (1 Sam 20:29) held on the New Moon (the day on which the *kispu* was normally held) was just such a memorial feast. In the light of the widespread occurrence of the *kispu* and its reflex in this passage, we have interpreted the phrase in the Tell Fakhariyah bilingual, "May Hadad, my lord, not accept his bread and water from him" (Aramaic 1.16) also to refer to a *kispu*-like offering.[26]

MOURNING

Mourning for a public figure is often recorded in the Hebrew bible. Thus for Samuel, we read, "Samuel died and all Israel lamented him" (1 Sam 28:3), while the threat of not being properly buried and bewailed was very serious as can be seen from Jer 22:18–19. Record of such mourning is found in the Panamuwa inscription (*KAI*, 215), "and my father Panamuwa died in the service of his lord Tiglath-Pileser king of Assyria while on campaign . . . and the kings, his brothers, mourned him and all those on the royal campaign also mourned him and he (the king) set up a memorial for him on the road." Two other inscriptions memorialize the dead: Sinzeribni (*KAI*, 225) and Si'gabbar (*KAI*, 226). Both were priests of the moon-god, called by his Aramaic name Sehr *(šhr)*, at Nerab. The first had an Akkadian name containing the name Sin, while the other had an Aramaic name containing the element *si'*, a West Semitic shortening of that name. These inscriptions are accompanied by "portraits" of the dead in relief.[27] They are both beardless, which in a contemporary Assyrian relief would indicate that they were eunuchs, but the Si'gabbar inscription indicated that he had children who mourned him. Si'gabbar declared that when he died, he saw his fourth generation mourning for him. The theme of the fourth generation is well known from biblical texts as in the tale of Joseph (Gen 50:24) and of Job (Job 42:16) and also from the memorial inscription that Nabonidus set up for his mother Adad-guppi.[28]

MARZEAḤ

Another institution that scholars have often connected with the cult of the dead is the *marzeah*.[29] This important institution is mentioned twice in the Hebrew Bible: Amos 6:4–7 and Jer 16:5. Chronologically the *marzeah* ranges from Ugarit in the late Bronze Age to Palmyra in the third century C.E. and geographically from North Africa to Syria. The connection with the cult of the dead depends on the interpretation given to the biblical passages. I have elsewhere proposed that the *marzeah* was also a social institution that brought together the wealthier members of the community.[30] There are no references to the *marzeah* in the Aramaic inscriptions of the biblical period from Syria and its environs, but it is mentioned in an ostracon from Elephantine and in Nabatean and Palmyrene inscriptions. It is safe to assume, on this basis, that it was also well known to the Arameans.

PROPHECY

The faith in prophecy on the part of the kings of Aram is exemplified in the Hebrew Bible in three tales. The first is found in 2 Kings 5. In this tale, the king of Aram dispatches his general Naaman, who is suffering from leprosy, to the king of Israel to be cured by the "prophet." Elisha saved the day for the bewildered king by undertaking to cure Naaman, who, when cured, recognized the greatness of the Lord. In the narrative there is an element that adds for the reader to the plausibility of this tale of miraculous healing being also acceptable in the court of an Aramean king. The element is that Naaman had expected Elisha to raise his hand or wave it over the afflicted part of the body and thus effect the cure. This was undoubtedly a magic act, perhaps an early form of "laying on of hands," but Elisha's suggested cure—dipping seven times in the Jordan (despite the magic heptad)—required an act of faith. It should be noted that in the course of time, the more physical act prevailed, for "laying on of hands" for curing, in conjunction with prayer, is known from the *Genesis Apocryphon* (col. 20, 11.28–29) and is prominent in the New Testament.[31]

The second tale is 2 Kgs 6:11–12, when the king of Aram seeks to find out who was the "mole" in Israel's service and is told that Elisha is gifted with a sort of extrasensory perception, knowing what the king of Aram speaks in his bedchamber. Finally, according to the biblical account, Elisha's prediction of Hazael's attaining the throne of Damascus (2 Kgs 8:13) served as motivation for Hazael's actions. These tales are part of the Elisha cycle and clearly have a dual purpose—the praise of Elisha and through his acts the glorification of Yahweh. Nevertheless, if belief on the part of pagans, in this case the Arameans, in the powers of the prophet and the efficacy of his oracles was not widespread, these tales could not have been propagated successfully.

As is well known, the institution of prophecy, if we use this term in a general manner to include visionaries, ecstatics, and receivers of oracles, was not an innovation of the first millennium. The subject of extrabiblical prophecy has received renewed attention in recent years. A great deal has been written about prophecy at Mari, and there can be no doubt that the Mari texts contain such pertinent material, although one must be careful not to force the Mari texts into the patterns of biblical prophecy.[32] There are also some Hittite oracular texts,[33] but of greater relevance is the dream recorded in Hattusilis' autobiography in which Shaushga appeared to Hattusilis, assuring him that she stood by him, holding his hand. Shaushga said, "Fear not," a phrase that occurs in oracular dreams (especially those of the patriarchs) and prophecies in the Bible.[34]

The mythological and epic texts from Ugarit provide some instances of oracular dreams. Thus Keret induced a dream by means of incubation (Keret 11.32–34) and is instructed in this dream to sacrifice to the gods, to muster his troops, and to go on a campaign to acquire a wife. The vision ends with the pertinent words, "and Keret awoke and (it was) a dream, the servant of El and (it was) a vision" (11.154–55). In the Baal cycle, after Ba'lu had been dead for some seven years, El saw in a dream/vision that the "heavens rain fat, the wadis flow with honey" (*CTA* 6 iii10–13) and declared that Ba'lu is alive. There may be other examples of oracular dreams in the Ugaritic texts. The vision recorded in the Wen Amun story remains enigmatic and the best that can be said for it is that it records the words of one possessed and it appears as an Egyptian phenomenon rather than a West Semitic one.

Before dealing with "prophecy" in an Aramaic inscription, two instances from Northwest Semitic inscriptions of the biblical period should be noted. The first is the Mesha inscription, in which Mesha recorded that Kemosh, the national god of the Moabites, had ordered him to attack Israel (1.14). We are not informed of the means by which the order was given to Mesha. Was it directly in a dream or a vision, or was it by means of a priestly oracle, or by some other means? The Deir 'Allā text in which we read that the gods appeared to Bal'am at night also contains a vision, but the text as a whole is fraught with difficulties and is not readily understandable.[35]

For a clear example of the prophecy we turn to the Zakkur inscription found at the beginning of the century at Afis, celebrating Zakkur's deliverance at the hands of Ba'lshamayn from a league of Aramean and Luwian states.[36] After praying to Ba'lshamayn he received an answer *(wy'nny/b'lšmyn)* via *hzyn* and *'ddn*. The first word is cognate to Hebrew *hōzeh* and means simply "seer"; but the second, *'ddn*, is without a cognate and has not to date been convincingly interpreted.[37] It was perhaps a sort of ecstatic or oracular prophet, or one like the *āpilū* known from Mari texts, who bring the divine answer. Since both words are in the plural, it is clear that Zakkur had a battery of prophets working for him. Ba'lshamayn's answer was *'l tzhl* ("fear not"), and the answer has the elements of the *Heilsorakel*.[38] Moreover, as I noted some years ago the answer given to Zakkur, *'nh hmlktk w'nh 'qm 'mk w'nh 'hslk . . .*, "I have made you king and I have stood by you and I will deliver you . . . ," contains elements of the *Danklied* known from several psalms.[39] This then is the clearest example of a form of prophecy in a Northwest Semitic text. Ba'lshamayn (aided perhaps by Adad-nirari III) kept his promise; the stele erected in the temple of Elwer commemorated that fact.

PRAYER

There are few references to prayer in the extant Aramaic inscriptions. The Tell Fakhariyah inscription is based on an Akkadian model, so that the reference to Hadad as '*lh rḥmn zy tṣlwth ṭbh*, "the merciful god to whom it is good to pray" (1.5), and the statement that Haddayišʿi set up the statue *lmšmʿ tṣlwth wlmlqḥ 'mrt pmh*, "that his prayer be heard, that his utterance be acceptable" (11.9–10), cannot be considered in its own right in a discussion of Aramean religion. Nevertheless, it is interesting to see the epithet *rḥmn*, the equivalent of Akkadian *remēnu*, an epithet of Adad, applied to Hadad, for this word will become widespread as a divine epithet in the Semitic world.[40] The Bar Hadad inscription (*KAI*, 201) found in northern Syria, that is, in Aramaic territory, and set up by an Aramean king, is dedicated to a Phoenician deity, Melqart of Tyre, rather than to an Aramean deity. Can it be used in this discussion? At the end of the inscription there is the phrase that indicates that the stele was set up, *zy nzr lh wšmʿ lqlh*, "for he vowed/prayed to him and he heard his voice." The formula is reminiscent of a widespread formula found on the many '*š ndr* inscriptions scattered throughout the Phoenician world, and it has many biblical parallels. But as H. L. Ginsberg, who treated this inscription in detail many years ago, showed, the later Palmyrene formula *dy qrlh wʿnyh* ("for he called him and he answered him") indicates that the formula used in the Bar Hadad inscription was in all likelihood also indigenous to the Arameans.[41] In the Zakkur inscription, discussed above for its prophetic portion, the phase used for prayer is graphic *w'śʾ ydy 'l b'lšmyn* ("I lifted my hands to Baʿlshamayn") (1.11). This gesture of prayer is known from pictorial representations from the ancient Near East, and the phrase itself has many literary parallels. On the coin from Hierapolis referred to above, the priest '*bdhdd* is shown with his hand raised in prayer.[42]

NOTES

1. For Rammān, see J. C. Greenfield, "The Aramean God Ramman-Rimmon," *IEJ* 26 (1976) 195–98.

2. It should be noted that in the personal names of the earlier periods the form Haddu/Hadda and its variants are found; cf. H. B. Huffmon, *Amorite Personal Names in the Mari Texts* (Baltimore: Johns Hopkins University Press, 1965) 156–58, s.v. "ʾDD."

3. H. Klengel, "Der Wettergott von Halab," *JCS* 19 (1965) 87–95; B. Lafont ("Le roi de Mari et les prophètes du dieu Adad," *RA* 78 [1984] 7–18) presents a full edition of an important text dealing with this deity. A Malamat ("A Mari Prophecy and Nathan's Dynastic Oracle," *Prophecy: Essays Presented to G.*

Fohrer [ed. J. A. Emerton; *BZAW* 150; Berlin: Walter de Gruyter, 1980] 68–82) has examined some of the comparative aspects of this text.

4. See D. O. Edzard, "Wettergott," *Götter und Mythen in vorderen Asien* (ed. H. W. Haussig; Stuttgart: W. Kohlhammer, 1965) 135–36.

5. H. Schlobies (*Der akkadische Wettergott* [*MAOG* 1/3, 1925] is long since out of date but remains the only comprehensive treatment.

6. A. Abou-Assaf, "Die Ikonographie des altbabylonischen Wettergottes," *Baghdader Mitteilungen* 14 (1983) 43–66; A. Vanel (*L'iconographie du Dieu de l'orage dans le proche-orient ancien jusqu'au VIIe siècle avant J.C.* [Paris, 1965]) deals indiscriminately with various "storm-gods." H. Genge (*Nordsyrisch-südanatolische Reliefs* [Copenhagen, 1979]) has assembled most of the reliefs of the storm-god, but the distinction between Aramaic Hadad and Luwian Tarhu is not always clear.

7. See M. H. Pope, *Götter und Mythen*, 253ff. Thus any interpretation that we might have for Zech 12:11 will be based on Ugaritic texts dealing with the death and return to life of Ba'lu. Since there is no Aramaic material parallel to this passage, it is not discussed here.

8. A. Abou-Assaf, P. Bordreuil, and A. R. Millard, *La statue de Tell Fekheryé et son inscription bilingue assyro-araméenne* (Etudes Assyriologiques 7; Paris: Editions Recherche sur les civilisations, 1982); J. C. Greenfield and A. Shaffer, "Notes on the Akkadian-Bilingual Statue from Tell Fekherye," *Iraq* 45 (1983) 109–16.

9. See E. Lipiński, "Aramaic-Akkadian Archives from the Gozan-Harran Area," *Biblical Archaeology Today* (ed. J. Amitai et al.; Leiden: E. J. Brill, and Jerusalem, 1985) 340–348, esp. 345). In a contract from the time of Kapara at Gozan we read of the "burning" of seven sons before Adad and of the dedication of seven daughters as sacred prostitutes as punishment for breaking the contract; see W. F. Albright, "The Date of the Kapara Period at Gozan (Tell Halaf)," *AS* 6 (1956) 82; K. Deller, *Or* N.S. 34 (1965) 384; M. Weinfeld, "The Worship of Molech and of the Queen of Heaven and Its Background," *UF* 4 (1972) 145.

10. It has become fashionable to write Bir-Hadad and Bir-Rakib. There is some justification for this, but I prefer the less modish form.

11. See F. M. Fales, "Note de semitico nordoccidentale," *Vicino Oriente* 5 (1982) 75–83, esp. 76–77.

12. The West Semitic list consists of a pair of otiose gods 'El and 'Elyān and fundamental natural phenomena: heaven and earth, depths and springs, day and night.

13. I have vocalized *'lwr* as Elwer rather than Iluwer, which is an Akkadian form.

14. See Schlobies, *Der akkadische Wettergott*, 8. In the God list AN:*anum*, Adad is glossed as Iluwer and Ilumer. Their relationship with Itur-Mer, known from Mari texts, and with Ber is yet to be established.

15. In reverse 1.23–24 I would read *b'lšmyn w'l/[qn'rq]*, the equivalent of *b'lšmm w'lqn'rṣ* of the Karatepe inscription rather than *b'lsmyn w'l/[wr] . . .* the usual restoration.

16. For Hierapolis, cf. G. Goossens, *Hierapolis de Syrie* (Louvain, 1943), for

Hadad pp. 116–17, 132–34; and R. A. Oden, *Studies in Lucian's "De Syria Dea"* (HSM 15; Missoula, Mont.: Scholars Press, 1977) 47–55.

17. See H. Seyrig, "Le monnayage de Hierapolis de Syrie à l'époque d'Alexandre," *Revue numismatique* VIe Série, vol. 13 (1971) 11–21 with a note on the inscriptions by A. Caquot (17–21).

18. This is coin no. 1 of this Hierapolis series. The priest has his hand raised in prayer. The inscription reads, according to the excellent photograph that Prof. A. Caquot and Mme H. Lozachmeur sent me: *zy ydmr lhdd* ("who adores Hadad"). Professor Caquot, who previously read *ydmh*, concurs with the reading *ydmr*. I have discussed this coin and its iconography in an article "To Praise the Might of Hadad" to appear in the forthcoming *Mélanges P. Grelot*.

19. Some important studies are quoted by Goossens and Oden. For Hadad and Atargatis at Acco, see M. Avi-Yonah, "Syrian Gods at Ptolemais-Accho," *IEJ* 9 (1959) 1–12. For Hadad at Palmyra and other late Syrian sites, see J. Teixidor, *The Pantheon of Palmyra* (Leiden: E. J. Brill, 1979) 73–74, 102–3, and H. J. W. Drijvers, *Cults and Beliefs at Edessa* (Leiden: E. J. Brill, 1980) 85–96, 111–12, etc. Note that alongside Hadad there developed during the Neo-Assyrian period two subsidiary Hadad deities. The first is (H)adad-milki, which occurs in names from this period as a theophoric element. This was noted by K. Deller, *Or* N.S. 34 (1965) 328–86. In the as yet enigmatic list of foreign gods in 2 Kgs 17:20–21, *'adarmelek* is surely a distortion of this name, as some scholars have seen. For the *'adarmelek* of 2 Kgs 19:37, see S. Parpola, "The Murderer of Sennacherib," in *Death in Mesopotamia* (ed. B. Alster; Copenhagen, 1980) 171–82. The second Hadad deity was Apladad, "heir of Adad," for whom cf. E. Lipiński, *Or* N.S. 45 (1976) 53–74. Professor K. Deller (letter of 8 January 1986) informs me that U.U, which he previously read as Adad-milki, should now be read simply Adad but that the spelling dIM-mil-ki still holds true. See now S. Parpola, *Orientalia Lovaniensia Periodica* 16 (1985) 274 n. 7, who states that U.U = *Dadda/i (Dāda/i)*. How is one to read the name dU.U.-DINGIR-*a*+*a* (K. Deller, *Baghdader Mitteilungen* 15 (1984) 227, 1.3)? Is it Adad-ilāhā or Dadda-ilāhā?

20. Cf. Greenfield, "The Aramean God Ramman-Rimmon," n. 23. For Jupiter of Damascus, see R. Fleischer, *Artemis von Ephesos und verwandte Kultstatuen* (Leiden: E. J. Brill, 1973) 378–79, pls. 167b–168a, b.

21. In Sfire IIc (*KAI*, 223) 11.2–3, 7, *bty 'lhy'* are not "sacred stones" as usually translated but simply "temples."

22. Cf. J. T. Milik, "Dieux Madbaḥ et Masgada," *Bib* 48 (1967) 577–80; E. Puech, "Note d'épigraphie latine palestinienne; le dieu Turmasgada à Césarée Maritime," *RB* 89 (1982) 210–21.

23. See J. C. Greenfield, "Un rite réligieux araméen et ses parallèles," *RB* 80 (1973) 46–52.

24. The root *rḍy* takes the form *rqy* in Early Aramaic and *r'y* in later Aramaic. The Aramaic form of the name vocalized as Reṣin in the MT (<*Raḍyan*, n.b. IQIsa *rṣy'n*) is found in the inscriptions of Tiglath-pileser III as both *Raqiānu* and *Raḥiānu*. The root is also found in the name *hdrqy* known from a seal reading *lhdrqy 'bd hdb'd*, for which see A. Lemaire, "Le sceau CIS II 74 et sa signification historique," *Semitica* (1978) 11–14.

25. See the literature quoted in my article referred to in n. 23 above, to which

add the following: M. Bayliss, "The Cult of Dead Kin in Assyria and Babylonia," *Iraq* 35 (1973) 115–25; Ph. Talon, "Les offrandes funeraires à Mari," *AIPHOS* 22 (1978) 53–55; J. Bottéro, "Les morts et l'au-delà dans les rituels en accadien contre l'action des revenants," *ZA* 73 (1983) 157–203 and some of the pertinent essays in *Death in Mesopotamia*. See now A. Tsukimoto, *Untersuchungen zur Totenpflege (kispum) im alten Mesopotamien* (Neukirchen-Vluyn: Neukirchener Verlag, 1985).

26. See J. C. Greenfield and A. Shaffer, "Notes on the Curse Formulae of the Tell Fekherye Inscription," *RB* 92 (1985) 47–59, esp. 52–53.

27. These funerary steles are reproduced in many recent books and catalogues; cf. Genge, *Nordsyrisch-südanatolische Reliefs*, II, Abb. 117, 118; see the discussion of this type of relief in J. D. Hawkins, "Late Funerary Monuments," in *Death in Mesopotamia*, 213–25.

28. See simply *ANET*[3], 561b. B. Landsberger had already related this theme in the Adad-guppi text to the Ši'-gabbar inscription.

29. For a survey of recent literature, see N. Avigad and J. C. Greenfield, "A Bronze *phialē* with a Phoenician Dedicatory Inscription," *IEJ* 32 (1982) 118–28.

30. J. C. Greenfield, "The *Marzeaḥ* as a Social Institution," *Acta Antiqua* (Budapest) XXII (1974) 451–55.

31. See D. Flusser, "Healing Through the Laying-On of Hands in a Dead Sea Scroll," *IEJ* 7 (1957) 107–8; J. A. Fitzmyer, *The Genesis Apocryphon of Qumran Cave I* (2d ed.; Rome: Pontifical Biblical Institute, 1971) 140.

32. The most recent comprehensive survey is that of E. Noort, *Untersuchungen zum Gottesbescheid in Mari* (AOAT 202; Neukirchen-Vluyn: Neukirchener Verlag, 1977). Cf. the essay by Malamat in this volume.

33. See A. Kammenhuber, *Orakelpraxis, Träume und Vorzeichenschau bei den Hethitern* (Heidelberg: C. Winter, 1976).

34. Cf. A. L. Oppenheim, *The Interpretation of Dreams in the Ancient Near East* (Philadelphia: American Philosophical Society, 1956) 197–206. The Hittite texts were translated by H. G. Güterbock,

35. The Deir 'Allā inscription, despite the exertions of some scholars, is not in Aramaic. In 11.1–2 of combination I, we read of Bal'am: 'š. ḥzh. 'lhn. h'. wy'tw. 'lwh. 'lhn. blylh. wyḥz. mḥzh. kmś'. 'l ("he is a seer of the gods and the gods come to him at night and he saw a vision like the oracle of El"), following J. A. Hackett, *The Balaam Text from Deir 'Allā* (HSM 31; Chico, Calif.: Scholars Press, 1984).

36. For various aspects of this inscription, see J. F. Ross, "Prophecy in Hamath, Israel and Mari," *HTR* 63 (1970) 1–28; J. C. Greenfield, "The Zakir Inscription and the Danklied," *Proceedings of the Fifth World Congress of Jewish Studies I* (Jerusalem, 1969) 174–91; cf. too H. J. Zobel, *VT* 21 (1971) 91–99. So too E. Puech in *Biblical Archaeology Today*, 356.

37. See Ross, "Prophecy in Hamath," 4–8; Greenfield, "The Zakir Inscription," 176.

38. See Greenfield, "The Zakir Inscription," 182–89.

39. Ibid., 179–80.

40. Applied to God in the Jewish tradition, to Ba'lshamen at Palmyra, and to Allah in the Islamic tradition.

41. H. L. Ginsberg, "Psalms and Inscriptions of Petition and Acknowledg-

ment," *Louis Ginzberg Jubilee Volume* (New York: American Academy for Jewish Research, 1945) English section, 159–71.

42. The recently published catalogue *Au pays de Baal et d'Astarté, 10,000 ans d'art en Syrie* (catalogue, Musée du Petit Palais, 26 October 1983—8 January 1984) contains, p. 219 (no. 250) a cylinder seal with an Aramaic inscription *ḥtm brq ʿbd ʿtršmyn,* "the seal of BRQ the servant of Attarshamayn." A worshiper (priest?) stands before a goddess, probably Attarshamayn, an offering table between them; the worshiper's hands are extended in an attitude of prayer. The author of this catalogue entry, P. Bordreuil, raises the possibility that the inscription that he describes as "araméen ancien" may have been added to an older seal.

6

Phoenicia and the Religion of Israel: The Epigraphic Evidence

BRIAN PECKHAM

The books of the Old Testament describe in cumulative detail the distinctive characteristics of Israel and the traditional quality of its relationship with Yahweh. They include oblique or incidental references to religious ideas, objects, and events that gradually became redundant or reprehensible in this process of discrimination. The late Phoenician and Punic inscriptions, conversely, record attitudes and practices that confirm the traditional structure of Israelite religion and illustrate both its persistent progress and its contemporary differentiation.

The Old Testament systematized the evidence in homogeneous literary and historical works. For instance, the transition from the conviction that Yahweh is God to the realization that Yahweh is unique made the gods of the nations redundant and allowed the appropriation of their cosmological epithets to describe Yahweh's transcendence.[1] Similarly, disdain for other religions made it possible to treat the eventual condemnation of primitive rites such as child sacrifice as a repudiation of the reprehensible practices of the nations.[2] Conversely, a tradition such as the venerable assembly of the gods that persisted in Phoenician practice and belief was also maintained in all phases of Israelite historiography, worship, and speculation.[3] Similarly, the superstition that sustained the magic of symbols such as the *mĕzûzâ* was replaced in the Old Testament, but without prejudice to the power of the symbol itself, by a more vivid reliance on tradition, instruction, and interpretation.[4]

The Phoenician inscriptions are also literary and historical works,[5] but they lack a comparable organizing context. The theory of a Phoenician empire based on the Levantine mainland and expanding inexorably westward is difficult to sustain.[6] Phoenicia was neither a nation nor a political entity but comprised a few principal cities and their dominions, which, through commercial interest, by historical necessity, and with the complicity of the Greeks, established separate and independent settlements in various parts of the Mediterranean world.[7] These apparently began in Cyprus, spread northward into Cilicia and Anatolia, and through the Aegean to the west.[8] They share a world but not a history, and their written records provide only random and fragmentary evidence for the reconstruction of a common literary tradition.[9]

The Tyrian inscriptions are not from the city itself but from its dependencies or environs. They include funerary monuments, dedications to different gods, building inscriptions, and votive texts. They can be used in conjunction with texts of the Bible to reconstruct some aspects and implications of late Phoenician religion.

The earliest is the dedication to Baʿal Lebanon by the governor of Carthage in Cyprus during the reign of Hiram II of Tyre.[10] This god was one of the four terrestrial Baʿals venerated by the people of Phoenicia,[11] and the cosmic significance of the mountain was recognized in contemporary and later songs of the Old Testament.[12] The cult of this Baʿal, derided in the story of Elijah on Mt. Carmel,[13] included acceptable practices such as prayer, sacrifice, and ritual awakening but was condemned by the Deuteronomistic historian for its intolerable rites of mourning.[14]

The other inscriptions from the region of Tyre are devoted to chthonic gods and analogous issues of life and death. An inscription from Sarepta about a century later commemorates a statue that was made for the goddess Tannit-Astarte *(ltnt ʿštrt)*.[15] A later inscription from Carthage mentions that Astarte and Tannit were worshiped in Lebanon,[16] and there is inscriptional evidence for the cult of Astarte at Tyre,[17] but this reference to Tannit is unusual and her collocation with Astarte is unique.[18] However, at ʾUmm el-ʿAmed south of Tyre, the principal god in the third and second centuries was an associate metamorphosis of Astarte, Mulkʿaštart, who, like Tannit, specialized in the ritual sacrifice *(mlk)* of children.[19] This practice was described by Hosea, condemned by Ezekiel, and repudiated as worship of an alien god *(mlk)* by the Deuteronomistic historian and other writers in the sixth century.[20] But it was usual in the region of Tyre, flourished in the western cult of Baʿal Ḥamōn, and was a natural expression of the contemporary belief that stability, world order, and salvation were derivatives of kingship.[21]

A similar reflex is exhibited in the funerary steles called *mṣbt*.[22] In Israel and Phoenicia they represented the expectation of enduring life in the sequence of generations and were erected by children for their parents, by husbands for their wives, or by individuals for themselves.[23] But they belonged to a complex of rites for the dead whose association with the cult of Astarte eventually made them unacceptable in Israel.[24]

The religion of Tyre was cosmopolitan and slightly effete,[25] but it sustained beliefs and practices that had an analogous importance in the contemporary Israelite religion. An early sixth-century inscription from Sarepta, for instance, is dedicated to Shadrapa (*šdrp'*), presumably the genius of healing.[26] But in the appproximately contemporary works of Jeremiah and the Deuteronomistic historian, and in the earlier writings of Hosea, healing is considered an attribute of Yahweh.[27] The conception is indigenous to neither religion, since Shadrapa is vague and peripheral in a region familiar with Eshmun and Aesculapius and healing is subordinate to larger issues in the Old Testament.[28] But the contemporaneity of a common aspiration emphasizes its distinctive interpretation in the Old Testament and its profound repercussion in the Mediterranean world.

The epigraphic materials from Sidon and its dominions include royal building inscriptions, dedications and funerary texts, votive inscriptions, temple records, and rituals. They are from Sidon, Cyprus, Cilicia, Anatolia, Greece, the Aegean, and the western Mediterranean, and range in date from the ninth to the third century B.C.E. They preserve items of traditional value, illustrate conventional attitudes, and obviously are related to texts and interpretations of the Old Testament.

The most important mainland inscriptions are the epitaphs of the kings of Sidon. They contain ideas, words, and idioms that demonstrate knowledge of Hebrew and suggest some acquaintance with its literary traditions.[29] They also contain information on practices and attitudes that becomes clearer in other inscriptions from the area and illuminates specific texts of the Old Testament.

They are concerned, for instance, with some aspects of kingship that occupied the Deuteronomistic historian. The Deuteronomistic formula of the kings usually ends (e.g., 2 Kgs 16:20) with the notation that the king slept with his fathers *(škb)*, was buried with his fathers *(qbr)*, and was succeeded by his son *(mlk thtyw)*. The Sidonian inscriptions also refer to the death of the king as sleep *(škb)*, mention his burial *(qbr)*, and are concerned with legitimate dynastic succession *(bn wzr' thtnm)*.[30] They share this historian's legal assumptions by alluding to the king's obligation to protect orphans and widows and by appealing to divine authority to justify and enforce ritual prohibitions.[31] They assume, with the Deuteronomistic writer, that the dynasty is under divine protection and that royal piety is manifest in the building and maintenance of temples.[32] But they have an exalted notion of the king that the Deuteronomistic historian found unacceptable: the contrast they assume between king and populace *(mmlkt/'dm)* is the contrast that the Deuteronomist assumes between God and human beings *('l/'dm)*;[33] the shrines they consider fitting for the king *(mqm)* are the shrines rejected by the Deuteronomistic historian as centers of false worship.[34]

81

Similar exalted notions of kingship are evident in the inscriptions of Kilamuwa of Zinjirli and Azitawadda of Adana.[35] The king is a father and a mother to his people as Yahweh is to Israel.[36] The king satisfies his people's need for food and clothing,[37] assures their boundaries and gives them peace,[38] and is the source of the benefits that the Old Testament ascribes to Yahweh.[39] The few prerogatives of kingship in these inscriptions that the Old Testament does not transfer to Yahweh can be predicated of Solomon but are applied systematically to the people.[40] Azitawadda, for instance, made peace with the other kings and through his justice and wisdom *(bṣdqy wbḥkmty)* became a father to them: Solomon ruled over all the kingdoms between Mesopotamia and Egypt and was famous for his wisdom, but wisdom and justice belong to the people who observe the law.[41] Similarly, the blessing of life and peace *(ḥym wšlm)* and length of days *('rk ymm)* that is given to Azitawadda is also given to Solomon and promised to the people.[42] Or, the annual and seasonal sacrifices that marked the culmination of Azitawadda's military and building operations were also celebrated by Solomon and mark Israel's tranquil possession of the land.[43]

The Sidonian royal inscriptions are concerned primarily with preserving the undisturbed tranquillity of the dead. Potential violators of the royal tombs are exhorted, cajoled, and finally threatened not to open their coffins or disturb their rest. There are simple prohibitions, pleas for special consideration, assurances that there is nothing of value in the tombs, appeals to divine sanctions, and curses against the perpetrators and their descendants.[44] Each of these elements is corroborated by particular texts of the Old Testament[45] and illuminated by their common perceptions of death. For a Sidonian king, the tranquillity of death is sleep with the Rephaim *(mškb 't rp'm)* that can be disturbed *(rqz)* either by opening the coffin *(ptḥ 'rn/ḥlt)* to search for treasure *(bqš)*, by taking it out of the tomb *('l yqbr bqbr)*, or by removing it from its resting place *(mqm)*. A contemporary dirge in Isaiah ridiculing the king of Babylon (Isa 14:3–23) portrays the same ideas about death and burial.[46] For the king, death is a sleep from which there is no return (v 8, *šākabtā lo' ya'āleh . . .*). When he dies, Sheol is disturbed (v 9, *rqz*), the Rephaim are roused to meet him (v 9, *rp'm*), and there is astonishment at his burial (v 10, *ḥullêtā*).[47] This fate is contrasted with the king's pretensions that he would rise (v 13— *'e'ĕleh*) and be enthroned with the gods above the stars of El (vv 12–14). Instead, as the Sidonian kings feared, he has been deprived of his resting place *(škb)* and cast out of his tomb *(qbr)*; neither he nor his descendants will ever be invoked (vv 18–23).[48]

Invocation of the dead was a specific feature of the symposia *(mrzḥ)* dedicated to the gods. An inscribed bronze cup, presumably from the region of Sidon and slightly later than the royal inscriptions, was dedicated *('rb)* at the symposium of the sun *(lmrzḥ šmš)*.[49] A contemporary inscription from Marseilles, in the official florid script of Carthage, summarizes its ritual prescriptions by exempting the poor *(dl)* but requiring donations for the priests from every clan *(mzrḥ)*, family *(špḥ)*, or symposium *(mrzḥ)*, and the individual *('dmm)* offering sacrifice.[50] A first-century inscription from Athens commemorates the dedication *('rb)* of an inscribed stele *(mṣbt)* in honor of a leader of the symposium and is dated on the fourth day of the festival *(mzrḥ)*.[51] These three texts attest that the symposia were held in honor of a particular god and were attached to a particular temple,[52] that they were marked by drinking, memorial offerings, sacrifice, and the appropriation of funds,[53] and that they were celebrated annually by local associations of merchants.[54] Their connection with ritual observances for the dead may be supposed and is clarified in texts of the Old Testament that describe symposia in Jerusalem and in Samaria.[55]

A symposium, according to Amos, was characterized by music, sacrifice, drinking, and mourning for the dead.[56] It was celebrated in honor of Yahweh at Bethel and Gilgal by the merchants of Samaria and their wives and was funded with the money they took from the poor *(dl)* by extortion and fraud.[57] It was a regular, perhaps annual, event that they awaited with great anticipation, and Amos used it as a paradigm for the day of Yahweh, a day of death and actual grief for the defeat and destruction of the nation.[58] The symposium illustrates the influence of the new merchant class on the development of Israelite religion, and its association with rites for the dead made its application by Amos to the fate of the people the standard of later biblical interpretation.[59]

Sidonian religion was conservative and uniform in all of its domains. The worship of the sun *(šmš)*, for instance, is attested in an eighth-century invocation from Karatepe and in a fourth-century dedication from the mainland.[60] The elaborate curses that protected the memory of the dead are found at Zinjirli in the ninth century, at Karatepe in the eighth, in Cyprus beginning in the ninth century, and at Sidon and Carthage in the fifth century.[61] The full panoply of gods that were worshiped at Sidon continued to be revered in Cyprus and throughout the western dependencies.[62]

The principal gods of Sidon were Astarte and Eshmun. The fifth-century royal inscriptions invoke all the gods *('lnm hqdšm)*, record the construction of a pantheon *(btm l'ln ṣdnm)*, and mention temples for the tutelary gods of the city *(bt lb'l ṣdn wbt l'štrt šm b'l)* but also give precedence to the worship of Astarte and Eshmun.[63] Astarte is called mistress and queen *(rbtn ḥmlkt)*, has a priesthood comprising the king

83

and the queen mother, has a temple overlooking the sea, and was enthroned in the temple of the highest heavens *(šmm 'drm)*. The temple of Eshmun was built at a spring in the mountains *('n ydll bhr)*, but he was also enthroned with Astarte in the temple of heaven on high *(šmm rmm)* and the temple of the land of the dead *('rṣ ršpm)*.[64] The rites of Astarte and Eshmun were observed throughout the Mediterranean world and are illustrated both in the Old Testament and in inscriptions from the Sidonian center at Kition in Cyprus.

Eshmun represented the cycle of life and death. He was Astarte's lover and the darling of women, and his rites included weeping and lamentation, planting gardens, eating pork, and processions through the city observed by his mistress.[65] They were familiar to the Deuteronomistic historian, who told the story of Jephthah's daughter wandering in the mountains bewailing her virginity, who described David's procession through the city observed by Michal from the window above, and Jehu's triumphal entry into Jezreel watched by Jezebel.[66] They were noted by Ezekiel, who was appalled to find women sitting at the entrance to the Temple weeping for Tammuz.[67] They are described in the Book of Isaiah in passages that announce the rebirth of the nation and condemn those who sacrifice in gardens, eat pork, and look for life among the dead.[68] The cult of Eshmun expressed a perennial hope that flourished in Judah during the exile. But the cycle of life and death soon lost its charm for the writers who had to explain how the nation had faced extinction and survived.

The cult of Astarte, queen of heaven, is known from the Book of Jeremiah and from a contemporary Cyprian inscription.[69] The inscription from Kition records payments made to participants in a festival meal for Astarte and Eshmun/Adonis[70] and obliquely describes some elements of the ritual. The festival took place at the new moon under the auspices of the god of the new moon.[71] It included the building of a temple for Astarte of Kition,[72] a procession through the streets of the city,[73] singing and lighting a fire for the queen of heaven,[74] sacrifice,[75] baking bread for Astarte and cakes for the participants in the festival,[76] shaving,[77] and the construction of pillars for Adonis.[78] It was familiar to the contemporary author of the Book of Jeremiah, who described a ritual that took place in the streets of Jerusalem (Jer 7:17—*běḥuṣôt yĕrûšalayim*) and that included some of the same elements: the children collected wood, presumably for the temple of Astarte but ostensibly for the fire, their fathers lit the fire for Astarte, the women made bread for the queen of heaven, they burned incense and offered libations, and they offered sacrifice and cut their hair in mourning.[79] The ritual coincided with the conjunction of astral and seasonal phenomena, and its purpose was to celebrate the simple satisfactions of life and to appease the power of evil and death.[80] It was ultimately unacceptable to the Old Testament tradition that rejected the dichotomy of good and evil and attributed both life and death to Yahweh (Jer 44:20–23, 26–28).

The alluring aspects of this cult of Astarte are evident in an earlier inscription from Cyprus.[81] It is written on the outside of a bowl from the temple of Astarte at Kition and contains an offering and a prayer:[82]

1]kr ml š'r z glb wypg ['l'š]trt w'[nty
2   −wytqr[b w]ytm lšw m[nḥty
3   − 'r z 'yt bkm lš' dd [
4 ml š'[r] = / / / ' ' ' ' ' ' ' ' ' ' bnd[r] tmš
5   ]mṣ' [   ]š' hd[
6 tmš

This means:

1 These strands of hair he trimmed and entreated Astarte and she [answered him].
2 He presented himself and made a complete offering [of his gifts,
3 "May this arouse the weepers to look for the beloved [. . . ."]
4 These strands of hair 139 by the vow of Tamassos
5 . . . .
6 . . . .

The prayer (lines 2–3) is enclosed in the dedication (lines 1, 4). It describes how Tamassos presented himself before Astarte and, when he had completed his offering, called on the mourners to look for their beloved. The language is liturgical, familiar in part from Old Testament prayers and ritual prescriptions,[83] in part reminiscent of the Song of Songs,[84] but associated in this text with weeping for Adonis. The dedication resembles the offering of hair prescribed in fulfillment of the nazirite vow,[85] but in its association with mourning for the dead was expressly forbidden by the Deuteronomistic historian.[86] The inscription illustrates how the worship of Astarte fulfilled the most common aspirations of men and women in the Mediterranean world but was bound with conceptions of unwitting recurrence that the Old Testament historical traditions were unable to sustain.

The inscriptions from Byblos and its domains all are dedicated to the same goddess, the mistress of the city *(b'lt gbl)*.[87] They depict the ideals of kingship familiar from the Sidonian series but in a manner peculiar to the city and its satellites. They portray the usual devoted service to the gods but also list the benefits that were expected to accrue to constant worship. They maintain the traditional theology of life and death implicit in the cult of Astarte but express it in a simple and straightforward liturgy.

The kings of Byblos subject themselves to the gods, make donations to their temples, and expect their protection.[88] They are equally convinced of the benefits of kingship and are concerned with the perpetuation of their name,[89] but they differ from the Sidonian monarchs in their clearer conception of the monarchic ideal of justice. In the mid-fifth century, Yeḥawmilk of Byblos based his expectation of a long reign *(t'rk ymw wšntw 'l gbl)* on the fact that he was a just king *(mlk ṣdq)*.[90] His predecessor and namesake Yeḥimilk expressed exactly the same hope in the mid-tenth century because he was just and upright in the sight of the gods *(kmlk ṣdq wmlk yšr lpn 'l gbl qdšm)*.[91] The earliest king of Byblos prays that whoever disturbs his grave will lose both his throne *(ks' mlkh)* and the legal authority *(ḥṭr mšpṭh)* that gave the city stability *(nḥt)*.[92] The same pious attitudes devolve on the populace in Israel where kings are the ultimate source of authority *(mšpṭ)* and are expected to be upright *(yšr)* but where long life is the reward for everyone who observes the law.[93]

Long life is the principal benefit expected by the worshipers of Astarte —her titles include "Mistress, Life, Goddess, Queen"—and life itself is one of her attributes.[94] From the mid-tenth century onward, the kings of Byblos pray that she will extend the days and years of their reign.[95] In the fifth century, Yeḥawmilk also prayed that she would reward his justice with blessing and life *(tbrk ... wtḥww)*.[96] In the Byblian colony at Lapethos in Cyprus, later inscriptions are dedicated to a variety of gods but attest the same conception of life: A fourth-century bilingual is dedicated to Athena and to "Anat, Strength, and Life" *(l'nt m'z ḥym)*;[97] a contemporary inscription records offerings to Astarte, Osiris, and Melqart and the dedication of a statue of the worshiper as his memorial among the living *(lskrn bḥym)*;[98] an early third-century inscription mentions the dedication of a statue of the suppliant during his lifetime *(sk[r bḥym])*, a commemorative bust of his father that was offered when he was alive *('bḥy 'by)*, and the provision for regular sacrifices to be offered for his own life and the life of his descendants *('l ḥyy w'l ḥy zr'y)*.[99] A fifth-century inscription from the Byblian settlement at Pyrgi ends with a prayer that contrasts the duration of a lifetime *(wšnt lm'š)* with the enduring years that accrue to the worship of Astarte *('lm bbty šnt km hkkbm 'l)*.[100]

This devotion to life is matched by a peculiar concern for the condition of the dead. The kings of Byblos follow the custom of inveighing against potential violators of their graves[101] but also describe their present aspect in the tomb. One king says that he lies in his coffin covered with myrrh and bdellium.[102] He and his son protest that their bones must not be disturbed.[103] The mother of a later king says that she is lying in her coffin, according to the custom of the royal house, wearing her robes and tiara and a gold mask.[104] A similar concern for the physical and representational attitude of the dead is manifested by the suppliants from Lapethos, who dedicated memorial images of themselves and their families in the temple while they were still alive.[105]

The theology of life and death that these memorials articulate is expressed more succinctly in the fifth-century dedication to Astarte from Pyrgi. This commemorates the dedication of a shrine to Astarte (lines 1– 5), recalls the circumstances that led to its construction (lines 5–9), and ends with a prayer (lines 9–11). The construction dates back to an earlier month in the year and to the request that Astarte made (line 6, *k˘štrt 'rš bdy*) on the day that the god was buried (lines 8–9, *bym qbr 'lm*). The dedication of the shrine to Astarte took place in the temple of the same god (lines 1, 2, 5—*'šr qdš 'z 'š p'l w'š ytn . . . bmtn 'bbt*). The king's concluding prayer is that, though years may come and go (line 9, *wšnt lm'š*), the god might continue in his temple as long as the stars are in the sky (lines 9–11, *'lm bbty šnt km hkkbm 'l*).[106] The entire text agrees with the other Byblian inscriptions in visualizing death as burial and life as an ephemeral imitation of the enduring celestial realm. It expresses the belief familiar from the Sidonian series that life and death compose an inevitable but manageable sequence that could be enacted annually and was manifested particularly in the successive years of a king's reign. But it was enacted differently and more dramatically in the Byblian colonies: at Pyrgi with the burial of the god, the intervention of Astarte, and a prayer for continued life; in Cyprus and Rhodes and Carthage in a representational liturgy celebrating the revival of the god and his reunion with Astarte *(mqm 'lm mtrḥ ʿštrny)*.[107]

The ritual and some elements of the liturgy were familiar to Hosea in his struggle to distinguish Yahweh from Baʿal and the recurrent pattern of the seasons.[108] The relationship between Yahweh and Israel is described as the marriage between Baʿal and Astarte but is distinguished from seasonal occurrence and redefined in the traditional language of covenant.[109] The sin of the people is described as a promiscuous relationship between the god and the goddess, and their contrition is compared to the ephemeral hope of resurrection on the third day.[110] Their reliance on a king of their own choosing and some commensurate gods is condemned as a rejection of Yahweh their king, who assures the succession of generations and the productivity of the seasons.[111] But in the end the analogy of the gods has its limitations, and Hosea concludes with the alternative of divine sonship and its illustration in the history of Jacob.[112]

The religious traditions incorporated in the inscriptions from the principal Phoenician cities and their dominions are analogous to those preserved in the Old Testament. They were familiar to the writers of the Old Testament, who shared many of the same ideas, ideals, and aspirations. They were diversified and consistent but never achieved the complexity and coherence that the Old Testament developed through centuries of reflection and interpretation. They were often repudiated and never left unchanged as Israel gradually distinguished itself and its God from the rest of the world. At their most mundane, evident in the tiresome and unimaginative steles from North Africa, they became redundant and died. At their best, they survived in the metamorphosis of the Mediterranean world.

NOTES

1. Cross, *CMHE*, 13–75. The J narrative uses the name Yahweh in telling the story of Israel but calls Yahweh *'ēl* or *'ĕlohîm* in describing Israel's relations with the rest of the world (Genesis 2—3; 6:1–2; Num 23:8, 19, 22–23; 24:8). The Deuteronomistic History supported the centralization of worship (Deut 12:13–14; 2 Kgs 18:22) with the conviction that Yahweh is unique (Deut 6:4, *yhwh 'ḥd*) and discouraged the association of Yahweh with any place except Jerusalem. The later Deuteronomistic historian argued that Yahweh is the only God (Deut 4:35, 39) and that the gods of the nations were sticks and stones (Deut 4:28), but applied to Yahweh the tokens of their cosmological preeminence such as *'ôlam,* the epithet of Šamaš (*KAI,* 26:A, III, 19), or *qōnēh šamayim wā'āres,* an elaborated epithet of El (*KAI,* 26:A, III, 18).

2. Ezek 20:25–26; Deut 12:29–31; 18:9–14; Num 3:11–13, 40–43. Cf. M. Weinfeld, "The Worship of Molech and of the Queen of Heaven and Its Background," *UF* 4 (1972) 133–54; O. Keel, "Kanaanäische Sühneriten auf Ägyptischen Tempelreliefs," *VT* 25 (1975) 413–69.

3. The assembly of the gods is invoked at Karatepe (*KAI,* 26:A, III, 19 *kl dr bn 'lm),* at Arslan Tash (*KAI,* 27:12 *rb dr kl qdšm),* at Byblos (*KAI,* 4:4–5 *mpḥrt 'l gbl qdšm; KAI,* 9:B, 5 *wkl 'ln gbl; KAI,* 10:10, 16 *l'n 'lnm, 't pn kl 'ln gbl),* at Daphne in Egypt (*KAI,* 50:3 *wkl 'l thpnḥs),* at Sidon (*KAI,* 14:9, 18, 22), and elsewhere. In the Old Testament the assembly has an explanatory function in the J narrative (Gen 3:22; 6:1–2; 11:7; Exod 34:10, 14) and in Job (Job 1—2), a structural function in hymns and prayers (e.g., Exod 15:11; Pss 29:1; 82:1; 89:7), and a theological function in the establishment of the prophetic tradition (e.g., 1 Kgs 22:19–23; Jer 23:18–22).

4. Deut 6:4–9; P. D. Miller, "Apotropaic Imagery in Proverbs 6:20–22," *JNES* 29 (1970) 129–30. There is contemporary evidence for the *mĕzûzâ* in the Phoenician incantations from Arslan Tash: F. M. Cross and R. J. Saley, "Phoenician Incantations on a Plaque of the Seventh Century B.C. from Arslan Tash in Upper Syria," *BASOR* 197 (1970) 42–49; F. M. Cross, "A Second Phoenician Incantation Text from Arslan Tash," *CBQ* 36 (1974) 486–90. The *mĕzûzâ* in

Deut 6:4–9 summarizes the covenant with Yahweh (*'lh,* Deut 29:11, 13) as the *mzzt* of Arslan Tash I refers to an everlasting agreement with the gods (*'lt,* lines 8–16). The force of the incantations is obvious in the story of the first Passover in Egypt (Exod 12:7, 22–23; Arslan Tash I:5–8), their language is used to describe Balaam as a diviner (Arslan Tash II:11 *t'n btm 'ny;* Num 24:3–4, 15–16 *š tm h'yn*), and their imagery of winged creatures, fire, roving eyes, and wheeled vehicles is found in the fantastic visions of Ezekiel 1 and 10.

5. J. C. Greenfield, "Scripture and Inscription: The Literary and Rhetorical Element in Some Early Phoenician Inscriptions," *Near Eastern Studies in Honor of W. F. Albright* (ed. H. Goedicke; Baltimore: Johns Hopkins University Press, 1971) 253–68; M. O'Connor, "The Rhetoric of the Kilamuwa Inscription," *BASOR* 226 (1977) 15–29; F. M. Fales, "Kilamuwa and the Foreign Kings: Propaganda vs. Power," *WO* 10 (1979) 6–22.

6. H. J. Katzenstein, *The History of Tyre* (Jerusalem: Schocken Books, 1973).

7. W. Röllig, "Die Phönizier des Mutterlandes zur Zeit der Kolonisierung," *Phönizier im Westen* (ed. H. G. Niemeyer; Madrider Beiträge 8; Mainz am Rhein: Verlag Philipp von Zabern, 1982) 15–30; B. B. Shefton, "Greeks and Greek Imports in the South of the Iberian Peninsula: The Archaeological Evidence," *Phönizier im Westen,* 337–70.

8. J. N. Coldstream, "Greeks and Phoenicians in the Aegean," *Phönizier im Westen,* 261–75; idem, "Some Cypriote Traits in Cretan Pottery, c. 950–700 B.C.," *Acts of the International Archaeological Symposium "The Relations Between Cyprus and Crete, ca. 2000–500 B.C."* (Nicosia, 1979) 257-63. Tyrians traveled to Sardinia from Tarshish by the end of the ninth century (F. M. Cross, "An Interpretation of the Nora Stone," *BASOR* 208 [1972] 13–19); Sidonians, as Greek tradition insists, were the first to arrive in Crete (F. M. Cross, "Newly Found Inscriptions in Old Canaanite and Early Phoenician Scripts," *BASOR* 238 [1980] 1–20) and most of the later Phoenician inscriptions from Greece and the islands were written by former residents of Sidon and its colonies in Cyprus (W. Röllig, "Alte und neue Inschriften aus dem ägäischen Raum," *Neue Ephemeris für semitische Epigraphik* (Wiesbaden: Otto Harrassowitz, 1972) 1. 1–8; P. M. Fraser, "Greek-Phoenician Bilingual Inscriptions from Rhodes," *Annual of the British School at Athens* 65 [1970] 31–36).

9. It is possible to distinguish, with varying degrees of precision, between the script types and traditions of the different Phoenician centers (B. Peckham, *The Development of the Late Phoenician Scripts* [Cambridge: Harvard University Press, 1968]).

10. *KAI,* 31 (ca. 750 B.C.E.); E. Lipiński, "La Carthage de Chypre," *Studia Phoenicia I–II* (ed. E. Gubel et al.; *Orientalia Lovaniensia Analecta* 15; Louvain, 1983) 209-34. Another fragmentary fifth-century inscription from Limassol mentions a local king and may be evidence that Carthage had become an independent state by that time (O. Masson and M. Sznycer, *Recherches sur les Phéniciens à Chypre* [Paris: Droz, 1972], 91–94).

11. Cross, *CMHE,* 28 n. 86. Ba'al Ḥamōn is known from numerous Punic inscriptions; Ba'al Ṣapōn was worshiped by Phoenicians in Egypt (*KAI,* 50) and at Carthage (*KAI,* 69); Ba'al Ḥermōn was a god of the Sidonians (Deut 3:9; Judg 3:3).

12. 2 Kgs 19:23; Ps 29:5–6; *CMHE,* 151–56.

13. 1 Kgs 18:17–28; R. de Vaux, "Les prophètes de Baal sur le Mont Carmel," *Bible et Orient* (Paris: Editions du Cerf, 1967) 485–97.

14. Rites of awakening (1 Kgs 18:27) are assumed in many Old Testament prayers (e.g., Pss 35:23; 44:24; 59:6; 78:65; Isa 51:9; Jer 31:26), and Phoenician and Punic votive inscriptions routinely commemorate sacrifice and the answer to prayer, but ritual phlebotomy (*gdd,* 1 Kgs 18:28) was condemned by the author of the Deuteronomistic History (Deut 14:1; cf. Jer 16:6; 41:5; 47:5).

15. J. B. Pritchard, "The Tanit Inscription from Sarepta," *Phönizier im Westen,* 83–92 (ca. 650–625 B.C.E.). On Sarepta as a dependency of Tyre, cf. J. Elayi, "Studies in Phoenician Geography During the Persian Period," *JNES* 41 (1982) 95.

16. *KAI,* 81:1 *lrbt l'štrt wltnt blbnn.*

17. An inscription from 'Umm el-'Amed records the construction of a niche for Astarte in the sanctuary of *mlk'štrt,* and another from eṭ-Ṭayibē dedicates a throne in her honor; cf. P. Magnanini, *Le iscrizione fenicie dell'Oriente* (Rome: University of Rome, 1973) 17, 26.

18. Cross, *CMHE,* 28–36. Tannit is also mentioned in an inscription from Wasṭa, just north of Tyre; cf. J. T. Milik, "Le graffito phénicien en caractères grecs de la grotte d'Astarte à Wasṭa," *MUSJ* 21 (1954) 5–12; cf. n. 62, below.

19. Magnanini, *Le iscrizione fenicie,* 16–23. The site is called *ḥmn* in the inscriptions, and *mlk'štrt* is its god (*'l ḥmn,* Magnanini, nos. 2, 3, 13–14). He has a priesthood (*khn mlk'štrt,* no. 5), worshipers (*'bdy,* no. 4) that are included in his veneration (*b'l ḥmn,* nos. 4, 13), and assistants who are called gods and angels (*'lm/'lnm, ml'k,* nos. 4, 13). A second-century inscription from Spain (Hispania 10, J. M. Solá-Solé, *Sefarad* 21 [1961] 251–56) also makes a point of including the worshipers in the dedication to the god (*l'dn l'zz mlk'štrt wl'bdm l'm 'gdr*).

20. Hos 9:11–14, 16; 2 Kgs 17:31; 23:10; Amos 5:26; Isa 57:5–10; Jer 32:35; Lev 18:21; 20:1–5. Child sacrifice is the explicit topic, and criticism of Jerusalem rituals is the implicit motivation of the E version of Genesis 22. Its earliest attestation in the Phoenician world is in contemporary seventh-century inscriptions from Malta (*KAI,* 61).

21. W. F. Albright, *Yahweh and the Gods of Canaan* (London: Athlone Press, 1968) 204–12; B. Delavault and A. Lemaire, "Une stèle 'molk' de Palestine dédiée à Eshmoun? RES 367 reconsidéré," *RB* 83 (1976) 569–83. This belief was articulated in Israel after the fall of both kingdoms in poetic compositions that described Yahweh as king and defined the benefits of divine rule (e.g., Psalms 24; 47; 93; 95–99).

22. There are four of these steles from 'Umm el-'Amed (Magnanini, nos. 6, 7, 10, 12), numerous examples from Kition in Cyprus (M. G. Guzzo Amadasi and V. Karageorghis, *Fouilles de Kition, III: Inscriptions phéniciennes* [Nicosia, 1977], nos. B, 1–6, 40, 45), and some from the western Mediterranean.

23. The Phoenician steles were erected by children for their parents (Magnanini, no. 6; Amadasi and Karageorghis, B, 2, 3, 5, 6), by a man for himself and his wife (Amadasi and Karageorghis, B, 1), or by individuals for themselves. The Deuteronomistic History, similarly, records that Absalom, during his own lifetime, erected a stele *(mṣbt)* for himself since he had no son to perpetuate his

name (2 Sam 18:18), that Jacob erected a pillar for Rachel (Gen 35:20), and that Moses set up pillars for the twelve tribes of Israel (Exod 24:4).

24. The ritual function of the steles is described in the E and Deuteronomistic stories of Jacob at Bethel (Gen 28:18–22; 31:13; 35:5–8, 14) where they are associated with vows and progeny and accompanied by libations. They are always connected with sacrifice, idols, and *'ăšērîm* (Exod 34:13; Deut 7:5; 12:3; 16:22; 1 Kgs 14:23; 2 Kgs 17:10; Isa 19:19; Hos 3:4; 10:1–2; Mic 5:12–13) and may have been a property of the cult of Astarte: at 'Umm el-'Amed (Magnanini, no. 4) and at Pyrgi (cf. n. 100, below) the *'šr* or *'šrt* is reserved for Astarte in the temple of another god, as in Jerusalem the *'ăšerâ* and its statue were placed in the temple of Yahweh (2 Kgs 21:3, 7; 23:4, 7).

25. Inscriptions from Tyre and vicinity mention the worship of El (Magnanini, no. 8) and of Ba'alšaměm (Magnanini, no. 1). Personal names have Egyptian *('sr, ḥr, 'bst)* and local *(b'l, 'šmn, 'lm)* theophoric elements. A second-century bilingual inscription from Malta (*KAI*, 47) is dedicated to Melqart (= Heracles), "Lord of Tyre" *(b'l ṣr)*, and Melqart is invoked in the treaty of Esarhaddon with the king of Tyre (R. Borger, *Die Inschriften Asarhaddons Königs von Assyrien* [Graz, 1956] 107–9), but no local inscriptions mention him. Attempts to make Melqart a national god or an emblem of Tyrian supremacy obscure the plurality of Phoenician religion and the particularity of Tyrian traditions; cf. C. Bonnet-Tzavellas, "Le dieu Melqart en Phénicie et dans le bassin méditerranéen: culte national et officiel," *Studia Phoenicia I–II*, 195–207.

26. J. B. Pritchard, *Recovering Sarepta, A Phoenician City* (Princeton: Princeton University Press, 1978) 100–102, fig. 98. An inscription of the same date (ca. 575 B.C.E.) from Amrit is also dedicated to Shadrapa; cf. M. Dunand, "Les sculptures de la favissa du temple d'Amrit," *BMB* 8 (1946–48) 96.

27. Gen 20:17; Exod 15:26; Isa 6:10; Jer 3:22; 8:22; Hos 5:13; 6:1; 7:1; 11:3; 2 Kgs 20:8.

28. G. Levi Della Vida, "The Phoenician God Satrapes," *BASOR* 87 (1942) 29–32; Comte du Mesnil du Buisson, "De Shadrafa, dieu de Palmyre, à Ba'al Shamīm, dieu de Hatra, aux IIᵉ et IIIᵉ siècles après J. C.," *MUSJ* 38 (1962) 143–60; A. di Vita, "Shadrapa e Milk'ashtart dèi patri de Leptis ed i templi del lato nord-ovest del Foro vecchio leptitano," *Or* 37 (1968) 201–11; N. Lohfink, "'Ich bin Jahwe, dein Arzt' (Ex 15, 26)," *"Ich will euer Gott werden." Beispiele biblischen Redens von Gott* (ed. H. Merklein and E. Zenger; Stuttgart: Verlag Katholisches Bibelwerk) 11–73.

29. *KAI*, 13–16. A detailed analysis of the relationships between the inscriptions of the Eshmunazor dynasty and the texts of the Old Testament was made by Greenfield, "Scripture and Inscription," 258–65. Almost every important word and expression in the inscriptions is more familiar from Hebrew than it is from Phoenician, and even the name of one of the kings *(tbnt)* seems to be derived from Judean traditions (e.g., 1 Chr 28:11–12, 18–19). Sidon acquired Judean territory in the Plain of Sharon in the mid-fifth century (*KAI*, 14:18–20).

30. *KAI*, 13:2, 5; 14:4–10. In the Deuteronomistic History the covenant with David concerns his offspring (*zr'*, 2 Sam 7:12; 2 Kgs 11:1). The importance of burial for a king is evident in the imprecation against potential violators of the royal tombs (*KAI*, 14:8) that they be deprived of rest *(mškb)* and burial *(w'l yqbr*

bqbr). In his inscriptions Bod'aštart stresses his legitimate succession by referring to himself as the heir of Yatonmilk *(wbn ṣdq ytnmlk)* and grandson of 'Ešmun'azor I *(KAI,* 16). The Book of Jeremiah used a similar expression *(ṣmḥ ṣdq,* Jer 23:5; cf. *KAI,* 43:11) to describe legitimate succession in a difficult and irregular situation.

31. 'Ešmun'azor bewails his fate as an orphan son of a widow *(KAI,* 14:3, 13 *ytm bn 'lmt)* as a plea for protection from those who might despoil his tomb, and the Deuteronomistic historian makes concern for these classes a criterion of justice and observance of the law (Deut 10:18; 14:29; 16:11; 24:17–21; 26:12–13; 27:19). Tabnit appealed to Astarte to enforce his prohibition against opening his tomb *(KAI,* 13:6 *k t'bt 'štrt hdbr h')* as the Deuteronomistic historian appealed to Yahweh to enforce ritual prohibitions *(kî tô'ăbat yhwh 'ĕlohêkā hû',* Deut 7:25; 12:31; 17:1; 18:12; 22:5; 23:19; 25:16; 27:15).

32. Against a king who might violate his tomb, 'Ešmun'azor invokes the gods to destroy his line forever *(KAI,* 14:8, 22 *'l ykn lm bn wzr'/l'lm)* and to subject him to a more powerful king who would cut him off *(KAI,* 14:8–10 *'š mšl bnm lqstnm)*. The Deuteronomistic historian declares that the promise was made to David and to his line forever (2 Sam 7:12, 16 *zr'/'d 'lm)* and repeats the assurance that the Davidic dynasty will never be cut off *(lo' yikkārēt lĕkā 'îš,* 1 Kgs 2:4; 8:25; 9:5). Similarly, 'Ešmun'azor *(KAI,* 14:13–18), Bod'aštart *(KAI,* 15–16), and Ba'alshallim (E. T. Mullen, Jr., "A New Royal Sidonian Inscription," *BASOR* 216 [1974] 25–30) all record construction and dedication in the temples of Sidon, and this is a principal theme of the Deuteronomistic historian, who commends kings for their interest in the temple (e.g., 2 Samuel 7; 1 Kings 8; 2 Kings 22—23) and condemns them for their dedications to other gods (e.g., 2 Kgs 16:10–16; 23:11–12).

33. *KAI,* 13:3 *('dm)*; 14:4, 6–7, 10–11, 20, 22 *(mmlkt/'dm)*. The contrast between God and humans *('l/'dm)* is explicit (e.g., Isa 31:3) and is expressed in Ezekiel's diatribe against the prince of Tyre (Ezek 28:2, 9). The Deuteronomistic historian, by contrast, insists that the Davidic king is just a man in the line of David: Yahweh is the king's father and he is Yahweh's son, but he will be disciplined as a man (2 Sam 7:14 *bĕšēbeṭ 'ănāšîm)* and the perpetuity of the dynasty does not exceed the norm of mankind (2 Sam 7:19 *wĕzō't tôrat hā'ādām)*.

34. 'Ešmun'azor's casket and tomb are in the shrine that he built *(KAI,* 14:4 *bmqm 'š bnt)*. It is distinguished from the temples of the gods *(bt, KAI,* 14:15–18) and resembles the shrines that the Deuteronomistic writer condemns for their association with altars, pillars, idols, and Asherim (e.g., Deut 12:2–3; 2 Kgs 23:14).

35. *KAI,* 24–26; Greenfield, "Scripture and Inscription," 265–68. Sidon's traditional relations with Cilicia and Anatolia are suggested by the alliance between Sidon and Sanduarri of Kundi and Sizu in the time of Esarhaddon (J. D. Hawkins, "Some Historical Problems of the Hieroglyphic Luwian Inscriptions," *AS* 29 [1979] 153–67) and by the evidence of language and ideology. Inscriptions from these areas share rhetorical flair, topics, themes, and lexical items (e.g., *'mr, 'dr, ytm, ksp/ḥrṣ, mlk/'dm)*.

36. *KAI,* 24:10–11 *(w'nk lmy kt 'b wlmy kt 'm wlmy kt 'ḥ)*; *KAI,* 24:13 *(km*

nbš ytm b'm); *KAI,* 26:A, I, 3 *(ldnnym l'b wl'm)*. Hosea describes the father-son relationship between Yahweh and Israel (Hos 1:2–9; 11:1–4; 13:13) and is followed by Jeremiah (Jer 3:4, 19; 31:20), the Deuteronomistic historian (Deut 8:5), and others (e.g., Ps 89:27). The conception is integral to the ideology of kingship and covenant (2 Kgs 16:7) and naturally supposes the kingship of Yahweh (Hos 10:3). The motherhood of Yahweh is transferred to the land (e.g., Hosea 2), or to Sion (e.g., Jer 31:15–22), or to a leader like Moses (Num 11:12–14).

37. *KAI,* 24:11–13; 26:A, I, 5–6; 26:A, III, 7–9. Yahweh, as king, supplies food and clothing (e.g., Deut 8:3–4; 10:18), and the Deuteronomistic historian describes Israel's propensity to forget Yahweh when it has eaten and is satisfied (Deut 8:11–20; 11:13–17).

38. *KAI* 24:6–8; 26:A, I, 4–5, 17–18; 26:A, II, 2–9. In the Old Testament the land is the gift of Yahweh, and the extension of boundaries is a specific benefit of the covenant (Exod 34:24; Deut 12:20). It is particularly the Deuteronomistic historian who considers that peace *(měnûḥâ)* is the effect of divine providence (Num 10:33; Deut 12:9; 1 Kgs 8:56).

39. Kilamuwa describes his effort to liberate the land from foreign domination by comparing himself to a devouring fire that consumes the hand and the beard of the oppressors (*KAI,* 24:6–7), and similar imagery is used to describe Yahweh's jealousy for his people (*'ēs 'okělâ,* Exod 24:17; Deut 4:24; 9:3; Isa 29:6; 30:30; 33:14).

40. M. Weinfeld, "The King as Servant of the People: The Origin of the Idea," *JJS* 33 (1982) 189–94.

41. *KAI,* 26:A, I, 12–13; 1 Kgs 3:3–14; 5:9–11; 11:41; Deut 4:6–8; 9:4–6. According to Ezekiel (Ezek 28:1–10), wisdom was the distinguishing divinizing quality of the prince of Tyre.

42. *KAI,* 26:A, III, 4–5; 1 Kgs 3:10–14; 5:4; Deut 6:2; 29:18; 30:15–20.

43. *KAI,* 26:A, III, 1–2; Exod 23:14–17; 34:19–24; 1 Sam 1:21; 1 Kgs 8:2, 62; 9:25. According to the Deuteronomistic historian, Josiah's successful campaigns ended with the restoration of Passover (2 Kgs 23:21–23) as Jeroboam's imperial design had culminated in the celebration of the same festival (2 Kgs 12:25–33).

44. Prohibitions are introduced by *'l* or by *'l 'l* (*KAI,* 13:3–5; 14:4–5, 21). 'Ešmun'azor supposes that his status as orphan and son of a widow entitles him to special consideration. Tabnit states that there is no silver or gold in his coffin, and 'Ešmun'azor says it is useless to look for anything in his coffin (*KAI,* 13:4–5; 14:5). Tabnit appeals to Astarte, and 'Ešmun'azor appeals to all the holy gods (*KAI,* 13:6; 14:9, 22). The curses are directed against the living and the dead.

45. Greenfield, "Scripture and Inscription," 258–65.

46. A similar conception of royal death and burial is found in Ezekiel's lament over the king of Egypt (Ezek. 32:17–32); it uses the epithets that Azitawadda applied to himself (*'dr, n'm,* Ezek 32:18–19; *KAI,* 26:A, I, 2, 13), is familiar with the contrast between death and the land of the living (*'rṣ ḥym*) that is found in the Sidonian inscriptions, refers to the resting places and tombs of the kings *(mškb, qbr),* and alludes to the divine aspirations of the royal dead (Ezek 32:21 *'ēlê gibbôrîm).*

47. The Rephaim are the dead leaders and kings of the world (Isa 14:9) to whom the Deuteronomistic historian assigns an ancestral realm (Gen 14:5; 15:20; Deut 2:11, 20; 3:11, 13; Josh 12:4; 13:12).

48. The dirge ridicules the king's vanity but not his idea of death. The story of Saul at En-dor (1 Sam 28:3–25) has the same suppositions: The dead are sought out (*bqš*, 1 Sam 28:7), are disturbed (*rgz*, 1 Sam 28:15), and ascend as gods (*'ĕlohîm . . . 'olîm*, 1 Sam 28:13); the curse falls on the violator of the tomb and on his descendants (1 Sam 28:16–19).

49. N. Avigad and J. C. Greenfield, "A Bronze *phialē* with a Phoenician Dedicatory Inscription," *IEJ* 32 (1982) 118–28. The goblet and its inscription (*qb'm//'nḥn 'rbt lmrzḥ šmš*) are from the early fourth century. The script is Sidonian, with expected similarities to the script of Kition in Cyprus.

50. *KAI*, 69:15–17 (ca. 325 B.C.E.).

51. *KAI*, 60. The inscription refers to the fifteenth year of the people of Sidon (*'m ṣdn*), distinguishes between citizens and members of the association (*hṣdnym/gw*), mentions a former head of the association (*nś'*) who had been its representative in the temple, records the decision to erect and inscribe a memorial stele at the entrance to the temple, and emphasizes the association's contribution to the temple for the cost of the stele.

52. The Marseilles tariff refers to the symposium of the god (*mrzḥ 'lm*), presumably Ba'al Ṣapōn, whose cult is regulated in the text (*KAI*, 69:1, 16). The Athenian decree refers to the temple of the god (*bt 'lm*) and more specifically to the Ba'al of Sidon (*'lm b'l ṣdn*, *KAI*, 60:6).

53. The importance of drinking is illustrated by the dedication of the bronze cup. Sacrifice is explicitly the topic of the Marseilles tariff. The Athenian decree mentions a memorial stele and illustrates the great importance that the *mrzḥ* attached to money. Money seems to have been a general fixation of symposia; cf. B. Porten, *Archives from Elephantine* (Berkeley and Los Angeles: University of California Press, 1986) 179–86; P. D. Miller, "The *mrzḥ* Text," *The Clarement Ras Shamra Tablets* (ed. L. R. Fisher; Rome: Biblical Institute Press, 1971) 37–49; J. C. Greenfield, "The *Marzeaḥ* as a Social Institution," *Acta Antiqua* 22 (1974) 451–55.

54. It is evident from the date formula of the Athenian decree (*KAI*, 60:1, "On the fourth day of the *mrzḥ*, in the fifteenth year . . .") that the symposium of the Ba'al of Sidon was celebrated once a year. The *mrzḥ* and its organization (*gw*) are distinguished from both natural (*mzrḥ*, *špḥ*) and civic (*'m*) institutions. Its preoccupation with money identifies it with commercial interests.

55. Amos 6:1–7; Hos 9:1–7; Jer 16:5–9.

56. The symposium is described in Amos 6:1–7, but its elements are emphasized in various parts of the book: music (Amos 5:23; 8:3, 10), sacrifice (Amos 2:8; 4:4–5; 5:21–24), drinking (Amos 2:8; 4:1–3; 5:11), and mourning (Amos 5:1–3; 8:3, 10). The same topics were used by the later revision of the book in its polemic against the sins of Jeroboam: music (Amos 6:5b), drinking (Amos 2:9–12; 9:14), sacrifice (Amos 3:13–15; 5:25–27; 7:7–17), lamentation (Amos 5:16–17; 6:9–10).

57. Amos specifically mentions Bethel and Gilgal (Amos 4:4–5; 5:4–6). The women are condemned for drinking with the men (Amos 4:1–3). The men are

involved, it seems, in international trade and the royal economy (Amos 6:1 *nĕqubê rēʾšît haggôyim ûbāʾû lāhem bêt yiśrāʾēl*). They are condemned for buying and selling the poor (Amos 2:6–8; 8:4, 6), for acquisitiveness and oppression (Amos 3:9–11), for getting rich at the expense of others (Amos 5:10–12), and for offering in sacrifice the product of their greed (Amos 5:22; 8:5).

58. The irony in Amos consists in restoring the lamentation for the dead (Amos 8:9–10) that the symposium inexcusably omitted (Amos 6:6). Anticipation is reflected in the style (Amos 1:1—2:16; 3:3–8) and is stated explicitly (Amos 5:11, 18–20). Amos alludes to the three annual festivals (Amos 5:21; 7:1–6; 8:10) and mentions other holidays (Amos 8:5), but the *mrzh* may have been connected with Passover. It included animals from the flock or the herd as were specified for the celebration of Passover (Amos 6:4; Deut 16:2), and it contravened the prescriptions for Passover by including leaven (Amos 5:4; Deut 16:3).

59. Hosea describes a festival of mourning for the dead that features drinking wine (Hos 9:1–4). It is a day of Yahweh (Hos 9:5), a time of death and burial (Hos 9:6) that money cannot divert (Hos 9:6). The Book of Jeremiah (Jer 16:1–9) describes a contemporary symposium and its lavish rituals for the dead. The symposia included rites of tonsure and phlebotomy that eventually were expunged (Deut 14:1; 26:14; Jer 16:6).

60. *KAI*, 26:A, III, 19; n. 49, above. The symposium that Amos described was also connected with the sun or the seasons (Amos 5:18–20; 8:5, 9–10) and was given an astronomical and meteorological interpretation by the author of the book (Amos 4:13; 5:8–9, 25–27; 8:7–8; 9:5–6). The worship of the sun was excluded by Israel's developed cosmology (e.g., Genesis 1) but continued to be both a historical problem (e.g., 2 Kgs 23:5, 11) and literary inspiration (e.g., Ps 89:37).

61. *KAI*, 13–14; 24:14–16; 26:A, III, 12—IV, 2; 30; Masson and Sznycer, *Recherches sur les Phéniciens à Chypre*, 13–20, 104–7; *CIS*, I, 5510, 5511.

62. The Sidonian onomasticon attests the worship of Astarte, Baal, Eshmun, Shamash, Reshep, Ṣid, Mulk, Tannit, and other gods; cf. A. Vanel, "Six ostraca phéniciens trouvés au temple d'Echmoun, près de Saïda," *BMB* 20 (1967) 47–95; idem, "Le septième ostracon Phénicien trouvé au temple d'Echmoun, près de Saïda," *MUSJ* 45 (1969) 345–64. An eighth-century inscription from Spain contains a dedication to Astarte and refers specifically to the Astarte worshiped in Phoenicia (ʿštrthr); cf. F. M. Cross, "The Old Phoenician Inscription from Spain Dedicated to Hurrian Astarte," *HTR* 64 (1971) 189–95. A seventh-century prayer on a gold pendant from Carthage is offered to Cyprian Astarte and her Greek paredros Pygmalion (*KAI*, 73).

63. *KAI*, 14–16. The Deuteronomistic historian mentioned that Astarte was the god of the Sidonians (1 Kgs 11:5, 33; 2 Kgs 23:13).

64. *KAI*, 13–14.

65. N. Robertson, "The Ritual Background of the Dying God in Cyprus and Syro-Palestine," *HTR* 75 (1982) 313–59; Albright, *Yahweh and the Gods of Canaan*, 129–31, 162–63, 197–98.

66. Judg 11:34–40; 2 Sam 6:16–23; 2 Kgs 9:30–37.

67. Ezek 8:14–15. The worship of Tammuz rather than Eshmun could be

explained literarily by Ezekiel's Babylonian perspective or historically as a residue of the Babylonian conquest.

68. Isa 1:29; 17:10–11; 59:10; 65:3–4; 66:17.

69. Jer 7:16–20; 44:15–30; *KAI,* 37.

70. In *KAI,* 37:A, 1, *tklt* may be Assyrian *tākultu,* a ritual meal. An inscription from 'Umm el-'Amed (*KAI,* 18) records the dedication of a gateway and doors to Ba'alšamêm that were built in 132 B.C.E. and dedicated at the *tākultu* of the god *('šl p'lt btklty bnty bšt ...). KAI,* 37:B, 1 also begins with a loan word from Babylonian *(dt).* The god Eshmun is referred to by his Greek name Adonis (*KAI,* 37:A, 14 *'dn*).

71. The date formula mentions the new moon (*KAI,* 37:A 1–3) and is separated from the ritual for Astarte by four vertical lines (*KAI,* 37:A, 4). The god of the new moon may have been *mkl,* a manifestation of Reshep/Apollo at Kition. In the Old Testament the new moon was a festival like the Sabbath (Amos 8:5; Hos 2:13; Ezek 46:1–3; 1 Kgs 4:23; Isa 1:13; 66:23) that revolved around a festal meal with invited guests (Hos 5:7; 1 Samuel 20; Psalm 81) and then was integrated into the sacrificial system (Num 10:10; 28:11–15; 29:6).

72. *KAI,* 37:A, 5 records rations for those who had built the temple for Astarte. This may have been a wooden structure that was burned in the ritual for Adonis (Robertson, "The Ritual Background," 337), and there may be a reference to such a structure in Amos 5:26 (Weinfeld, "The Worship of Molech," 149–50).

73. *KAI,* 37:A, 6 distinguishes between those who took part in the procession *(ldrkm)* and those who watched it *(wl'dmm 'š 'l sl rṣd).* Yahweh's procession in Psalm 68 has some of the same features: a parade (*hlk,* Ps 68:25; *drk, KAI,* 37A, 6) to the dwelling place of the god (*škn,* Ps 68:17; *KAI,* 37:A, 7), led by singers (*šrm,* Ps 68:26; *KAI,* 37:A, 7), and with attendants who watched its progress (*rṣd,* Ps 68:17; *KAI,* 37:A, 6).

74. *KAI,* 37A, 7 *(lšrm b'r 'š škny lmlkt qdšt bym z).*

75. *KAI,* 37:A, 9.

76. *KAI,* 37:A, 9–11 records rations for two bakers and their three assistants who baked bread *(ḥlt)* for Astarte and cakes of roasted wheat and honey *('t prmn;* Gr. *pūramous)* for the faithful. The cakes were given to those who observed the vigil of the god in Greek festivals and were prepared for the goddess in the Assyrian rituals of Adad and Ishtar (Weinfeld, "The Worship of Molech," 152–53). They were expressly forbidden in contemporary Judean rituals (Lev 2:11).

77. *KAI,* 37:A, 13 mentions barbers who officiated at the service *(lglbm p'lm 'l ml'kt).* Shaving was a sign of mourning in the Old Testament and was part of the ritual for Adonis (Robertson, "The Ritual Background," 333) and is described by Ezekiel (5:1).

78. *KAI,* 37A:14 lists twenty carpenters who made pillars for Adonis in the temple of *mkl.* Pillars belonged to the ritual for Adonis (Robertson, "The Ritual Background," 323–24) and are associated with mourning in the Old Testament (Isa 19:10; Ps 11:3).

79. Jer 7:16–34. This text uses the same expression for lighting a fire *(b'r 'š)* but uses another technical term for the bread baked for Astarte *(kawwānîm;* cf. Weinfeld, "The Worship of Molech," 150 n. 137). Sacrifice, in this version, included specifically burning their sons and daughters in the fire (Jer 7:31). This

may have been a feature of the cult of Eshmun (Robertson, "The Ritual Background," 326, 329) and might be the ritual recorded in *KAI*, 37:B.

80. Jer 44:15–30; cf. Deut 30:15–20.

81. A Dupont-Sommer, "Une inscription phénicienne archaïque récemment trouvée à Kition (Chypre)," *Mémoires de l'Academie des Inscriptions et Belles Lettres* 44/2 (1972) 271–94; V. Karageorghis, *Kition: Mycenaean and Phoenician Discoveries in Cyprus* (London: Thames & Hudson, 1976) p. 83, provides a better photograph.

82. The inscription is from the mid-seventh century. The prayer (lines 2–3) is indented and both lines are preceded by a horizontal stroke (cf. *KAI*, 37:B). The bowl is cracked, the photographs differ, and some letters are more or less doubtful (*z* and *g* in line 1, *q* in line 2, *z* and *k* in line 3, *t* in line 6). The translation assumes that the text is substantially intact. The word *ml* is related to late Heb. *mll* ("fold," "weave").

83. For instance, *qrb*, Leviticus, Numbers, Ps 65:5; *šwh*, Pss 16:8; 21:6; 89:20; cf. Gen 14:17; ʿwr, Pss 7:7; 44:24; 57:9; *šʿh*, Isa 17:7–8; 22:4; 31:1.

84. The beloved *(dd)* is mentioned most frequently in the Song of Songs (M. H. Pope, *Song of Songs* [AB 7C; Garden City, N.Y.: Doubleday & Co., 1977] 149–53) but occurs first in the song of the vineyard (Isa 5:1).

85. Num 6:1–20. The inscription mentions the cutting of his hair *(glb)*, his vow *(ndr)*, and his offering; cf. Num 6:5, 14–18. The fourth line indicates either the number of strands of hair or their weight. According to the Deuteronomistic historian, when Absalom cut his hair every three years it weighed two hundred shekels (2 Sam 14:26).

86. Deut 14:1.

87. *KAI*, 1–12; P. Bordreuil, "Une inscription phénicienne champlevée des environs de Byblos," *Semitica* 27 (1977) 23–27. In some the name of the goddess *(bʿlt)* is reconstructed from the uncertain reading *bʿl* (*KAI*, 4:4; 5:2). Two fifth-century texts include the goddess but give prominence to Baʿal ʾAddir (*KAI*, 9; F. M. Cross, "A Newly Published Phoenician Inscription of the Persian Period from Byblos," *IEJ* 29 (1979) 40–44). The latest inscription in the Byblian series invokes only Baʿal (*KAI*, 12). The colonial inscriptions mention Astarte, Anat, Osiris and Melqart (nn. 97–100, below; Masson and Sznycer, *Recherches sur les Phéniciens à Chypre*, 81–86).

88. These attitudes are clearest in the inscription of Yeḥawmilk (*KAI*, 10), who embellished the temple of Astarte (*KAI*, 10:4–6), attributed the existence and maintenance of his kingship to her (*KAI*, 10:1–3, 6–8), and invoked her protection against those who might despoil her temple and obliterate his name (*KAI*, 10:11–15).

89. In the inscription of Hiram (*KAI*, 1) the effect of good rule is the tranquillity *(nḥt)* of the city. In the fifth century, Yeḥawmilk hopes for the perpetuation of his name (*KAI*, 10:12–15) but also prays for favor in the eyes of the gods and of his people and in the eyes of the kings of the world (*KAI*, 10:10–11). In the Old Testament, Noah, Moses, and David find favor in the eyes of Yahweh (Gen 6:8; Exod 33:12; 2 Sam 15:25), and Israel finds favor in the eyes of the Egyptians (Exod 3:21), but world renown is reserved for Yahweh (e.g., Pss 8:2, 10; 68:33).

90. *KAI*, 10:9. In the Byblian colonies in Cyprus, *ṣdq* was an epithet of the

kings: *ṣmḥ ṣdq* was a title of Ptolemy II Philadelphus (A. van den Branden, "Titoli Tolemaici," *Bibbia e Oriente* 6 [1964] 60–72); a fifth-century king of Lapethos was called *ṣdqmlk* (Masson and Sznycer, *Recherches sur les Phéniciens à Chypre,* 98–100).

91. *KAI,* 4:6–7.

92. *KAI,* 1; Greenfield, "Scripture and Inscription," 254–57.

93. The Deuteronomistic evaluation of the kings consists in elaborations on whether or not the king had done what was right *(yšr)* in the eyes of Yahweh. The king's court in the city gate was used by Absalom in his attempt to usurp the throne (2 Sam 15:1–6), but the later historian gave the king's authority to decide difficult cases (e.g., 2 Kgs 3:16–28) into the hands of magistrates and priests skilled in the law (Deut 17:8–13).

94. A late inscription from Carthage (*KAI,* 89) calls Astarte *rbt ḥwt 'lt mlkt.*

95. *KAI,* 4–7, 10.

96. *KAI,* 10:8–9. The Deuteronomistic historian developed the same connection between life and justice (Deut 6:24–25) and between obedience and life (Deut 4:1; 8:1; 30:15).

97. *KAI,* 42; W. R. Lane, "The Phoenician Dialect of Larnax tes Lapethou," *BASOR* 194 (1969) 39–45. In the Old Testament the epithet *mā'oz* is applied to Yahweh (e.g., Isa 17:10; 25:4; 27:5; Jer 16:19; Neh 1:7; Pss 27:1; 31:3, 5; Prov 10:29), and life is a divine prerogative (Deut 32:39; 1 Sam 2:6; Hos 6:2; Hab 3:2; Pss 71:20; 80:19).

98. A. M. Honeyman, "Larnax tēs Lapēthou: A Third Phoenician Inscription," *Le Muséon* 51 (1938) 285–98.

99. *KAI,* 43.

100. *KAI,* 277; J. C. L. Gibson, *Textbook of Syrian Semitic Inscriptions, Vol. 3: Phoenician Inscriptions* (Oxford: Clarendon Press, 1982) 151–59. This inscription follows the Byblian chronological system by mentioning the latest event first (lines 1–5, the dedication of the shrine) and other events in sequence (lines 5–11, the construction of the shrine, and the concluding prayer). It expresses narrative sequence by *waw* + verb (line 5, *wbntw*), subordination by using conjunctions and repeating them if necessary (line 5, *k 'štrt 'rš bdy;* line 2, *'š p'l w'š ytn),* and modality by avoiding both sequence and subordination (line 9, *wšnt lm'š;* lines 9–11, *'lm bbty šnt km hkkbm 'l).* The segment *wšnt lm'š* is analyzed as *waw* + subject + precative *l* + verb *m'š* (Heb. *m'š* II = "elapse"; e.g., Job 7:5, 16) and translated, "The years may elapse, may the years of the god in his temple be like the stars of El." This sentiment, contrasting the decay of world order and the permanence of God, is also expressed of Yahweh (Isa 34:4; Ps 102:27–28).

101. *KAI,* 1, 9, 10.

102. Cross, "A Recently Published Phoenician Inscription," 40–44.

103. *KAI,* 9A, 5; Cross, "A Recently Published Phoenician Inscription," 41. The two inscriptions agree in their resemblances to texts from Sidon and differ from the other inscriptions in the Byblian series. But their exhortation not to disturb the bones of the king *(lrgz 'ṣmy)* differs from the Sidonian plea not to disturb the dead *('l trgzn).* In the Old Testament the bones of the dead were the object of filial piety (e.g., Exod 13:19; 2 Sam 21:12–14) and in Ezekiel's vision

the restoration is described as a return from the grave *(wĕhaʿălêtî 'etkem miq-qibrôtêkem)* and is illustrated by giving life to dead bones (Ezek 37:1–14).

104. *KAI*, 11.

105. Cf. nn. 98–99, above.

106. The text is constructed so that the dedication (lines 1–5) balances the prayer (lines 9–11) and together they enclose the reference to the reign of the king and the burial of the god (lines 5–9). It distinguishes between the temple (*bt*, lines 5, 10) and the shrine (*'šr qdš*, line 1), and between Astarte (lines 1, 6) and the god who was buried (lines 8) and now lives forever (lines 10–11).

107. *KAI*, 44; Gibson, *Textbook*, 144–47; E. Lipiński, "La fête de l'ensevelissement et de la résurrection de Melqart," *Actes de la XVIIe rencontre assyriologique* (Brussels, 1970) 30–58.

108. F. I. Andersen and D. N. Freedman, *Hosea* (AB 24; Garden City, N.Y.: Doubleday & Co., 1980) 49–50.

109. Hosea 1—3 progresses from the birth of the children whose names allude to the covenant traditions (Exodus 6; 34), through divorce and separation from Baʿal, to remarriage and the restoration of the covenant. An interpretation (Hos 1:5, 7; 2:1–3, 17*, 20*; 3:1–5) connects the restoration with the promise to David.

110. Hosea 4—6 describes a promiscuous relationship with the goddess (Hosea 4), exemplifies it in foreign alliances (Hosea 5), and laments the velleity enshrined in liturgies of death and resurrection (Hosea 6). The Old Testament recognizes the possibility of return from death (*ʿlh*) but rarely suggests that the dead will rise (*qwm*, Hos 6:2; Isa 26:13–19).

111. Hosea 7—8 connects the willful choice of a king with the worship of the calves, and Hosea 9—10 connects the end of the generative and productive cycles with the rejection of Yahweh their king.

112. The alternative of sonship was implicit in the opening scene (Hosea 1) and was made explicit by the author of the book (Hosea 2:1).

7

Proto-Canaanite, Archaic Greek, and the Script of the Aramaic Text on the Tell Fakhariyah Statue

JOSEPH NAVEH

In 1954 F. M. Cross published two papers that became the first of a series of excellent studies devoted to the decipherment of ancient West Semitic inscriptions and manuscripts and to the thorough investigation of the development of their scripts. These two papers also mark the beginning of a new era in the research of the origins of the alphabet.[1] After deciphering the three identical short inscriptions on the arrowheads from el-Khaḍr and dating them in the late twelfth century B.C.E., Cross drew the outlines of the evolution of the Proto-Canaanite alphabet in the second half of the second millennium B.C.E. as it appeared in the inscriptions from Serabit el-Khadem, on the Lachish bowl, the Lachish ewer, the Beth-shemesh ostracon, the el-Khaḍr arrowheads, and that from Ruweisah. Thus, building on the works of A. Gardiner and W. F. Albright, Cross laid a solid foundation for later discoveries. Whereas Cross plays a major role in West Semitic epigraphy and paleography in general, the study of the Proto-Canaanite script has become almost his personal field. In 1967 Cross reexamined the Proto-Canaanite evidence available at that time and arrived at new conclusions,[2] which could be summarized as follows:

The alphabetic writing was invented in Canaan in the first half of the second millennium B.C.E. It was a pictographic acrophonic script, meaning that the pictures of a house, the palm of the hand, water, and so on, did not stand for the respective words *bêt* (= "house"), *kaf* (= "palm"), and *mêm* (= "water") but only designated the first consonant of each word: *b, k, m*. The number of these pictographs was presumably twenty-seven (probably the same as the number of the Ugaritic alphabetic signs, without the three additional ones: *'i, 'u,* and s_2). By the thirteenth century the number of the Proto-Canaanite signs was reduced to twenty-two, but the pictographic conception still permitted the flexibility of the stances and writing in any direction: from left to right, from right to left, in vertical columns, and even in horizontal or vertical boustrophedon. Vertical writing disappeared about 1100 B.C.E. At this stage the symbols became more and more linear. Until the middle of the eleventh century they were still pictographic forms—as, for example, the ʿayin (= "eye") preserving the pupil of the eye—and the letters could have alternative stances. From the middle of the eleventh century, when all the letters were linear and most of them had stabilized stances[3] and were written only horizontally from right to left, our terminology changes: the script is no longer called Proto-Canaanite (or Canaanite) but Phoenician.

The reconstruction that Cross made in 1967 enabled the writer to conjecture in 1973 that the Greeks must have adopted the twenty-two-letter alphabet from the Canaanites at about 1100 B.C.E.[4] This was contrary to the view of classical scholars that the adoption took place in the late eighth century B.C.E.[5] The individual archaic Greek letters (partly preserving the pictographic shapes of the Proto-Canaanite ones), having lapidary features and unstabilized stances, being written horizontally in any direction or in boustrophedon, could not have been learned from an eighth-century Phoenician model but rather from a less developed twelfth- and eleventh-century Proto-Canaanite one.

Although the writer's thesis was published in a classical journal, it was generally disregarded by specialists in Greek epigraphy. Only recently has Miss L. H. Jeffery, who is one of the principal contenders of the conventional theory, mentioned the writer's work in a footnote as "an article deserving serious consideration by Greek epigraphists, though the blank on the Greek side before the eighth century remains a problem (and his argument is wrong in assuming that the tailless forms of mu and psi are early),"[6] but she did not pay any further attention to it.

Strangely enough, even some orientalists felt uneasy with the new theory. While being unable to ignore the evidence, they tried to compromise between the conventional view and the new proposition. P. K. McCarter, a student of Cross, summarized that "the Greeks, though their script did not diverge as an independent tradition before ca. 800, had experimented with the Semitic alphabet as early as ca. 1100."[7] In 1975 Cross remarked: "I am not sure that there is sufficient evidence to establish firmly either the case of Naveh or that of McCarter. At all events, the initiatives of Naveh and McCarter have brought the discussion into a new phase and complicate old problems which seemed at the point of solution."[8] A. R. Millard summarized the state of research in 1976 as follows: "Unsatisfactory though the position may be, no more precise date can be given for the adoption of the alphabet by the Greeks than the three centuries and a half, 1100 to 750 B.C."[9]

Then some newly found twelfth- and eleventh-century inscriptions were added to the corpus of the Proto-Canaanite inscriptions: The ostracon from 'Izbet Ṣarṭah,[10] the inscription on a bronze bowl from Tekke near Knossos in Crete,[11] the inscribed sherd from Qubur el-Walaydah, and two additional inscribed arrowheads from el-Khaḍr.[12] To these can be added the fragmentary inscription from Nora in Sardinia (*CIS* I, 145, known since 1840) which, according to Cross's observation, was written in boustrophedon and should be dated in the eleventh century.[13] These finds stimulated Cross to discuss anew the development of the script, which he calls now "Old Canaanite and Early Linear Phoenician," and to conclude that "these new data must be said to give added support to the thesis of Joseph Naveh for the high antiquity of the earliest use by the Greeks of the alphabet, and remove obstacles to dating their borrowing to the time of transition from Old Canaanite to Linear Phoenician toward 1100 B.C."[14]

In 1981 a bilingual (Assyrian-Aramaic) inscription was published, engraved on a life-sized statue of a king, from Tell Fakhariyah.[15] The site is about 4 km. northeast of Tell Halaf (biblical Gozan) at the headwaters of the Khabur in northern Syria and on the border with Turkey, about 350 km. east of the Mediterranean shore, viz., the bay of Alexandretta. This find is no doubt one of the most important epigraphic discoveries of the present generation. The investigation of a bilingual text is always interesting, but in this case the dating of the new find by the various disciplines is very puzzling. This problem has to be dealt with by experts in ancient art, Assyriologists, Aramaists, historians, and epigraphists. The *editio princeps* tried to examine all these criteria and to correlate their results, and thus it arrived at the conclusion that the statue and its bilingual text belong to the ninth century B.C.E. However, the script of the Aramaic text from Tell Fakhariyah is totally different from those of the other Aramaic inscriptions known so far; it is reminiscent of the Proto-Canaanite script of the eleventh century B.C.E.—that is, the script of the Canaanites at the stage of its adoption by the Arameans—rather than of the alphabetic script used in the ninth century by the Arameans or by the Phoenicians.

The authors of the *editio princeps* were wholly aware of the paleographic features of the Fakhariyah inscription.[16] However, as they preferred to base their conclusions on other criteria, they tried to attenuate the paleographic evidence by explaining that "these features imply that we are faced with a local derivative of the Phoenician alphabet, perhaps adopted as early as 1000 B.C., and which continued in use and produced its unique characteristics." Then they say: "Palaeography alone is too uncertain a means for dating the Tell Fakhariyeh inscription; its sources are too meager." They conclude as follows: "The mid-9th century date seems inescapable. Its significance for Aramaic and West Semitic epigraphy, and for theories about the date when the Greeks borrowed the alphabet (such as J. Naveh 1980 [*BA* 43, pp. 22–25]) requires additional study.[17]

Whereas Millard and P. Bordreuil still hesitate, mainly in regard to the antiquity of the Greek alphabet, S. A. Kaufman appears to provide us with conclusive solutions of all the problems.[18] He welcomes the Fakhariyah inscription, saying: "The new text's Aramaic script is a wonderful surprise. Peculiar in many respects, it should provide fuel for years of debate among Northwest Semitic palaeographers. Indeed, it has the potential of undermining many current theories about the origin of the Aramaic (and Greek!) scripts as well as the development of the Phoenician script."[19] Then he declares: "This *and other epigraphic finds of the last decade* [italics of J. N.] conclusively demonstrate that we must no longer conceive of all of the Northwest Semitic alphabetic scripts as straight-line developments from an early Phoenician ancestor. The proper view is rather similar to that associated with the wave-theory approach to linguistic change. In the 12th and 11th centuries B.C.E. the Northwest Semitic alphabet spread throughout the general area occupied by peoples speaking those closely related dialects and languages; and *local traditions and variations must have developed easily* [italics of J. N.]. . . . That the Fakhariyeh text shares the shape of its *lamed* with an 11th century (or earlier!) text from Canaan points not to the antiquity of its script—only to its peripheral position *vis-à-vis* Phoenicia."[20] In order to justify "local traditions and variations," Kaufman speaks of Byblian and non-Byblian letter forms; for example: "Tenth century Byblian [*kaf*] has only the 'palm' itself. . . . The standard, earlier, non-Byblian form of this sign must have had a tail."[21] Then in a footnote he says: "Naveh's theory *(discussed by McCarter)* [italics of J. N.] of a pre-tenth century borrowing of the alphabet still remains far-fetched, especially as one of his heretofore more convincing arguments (the antiquity of the dotted '*ayin*) is refuted by our text. I would suggest instead that the use of this *non-Phoenician* [italics of J. N.] (by the ninth century) *kap* for an additional letter supports the thesis that the creator(s) of the Greek usage of the West-Semitic alphabet knew Aramaic."[22]

In the following pages I shall discuss the characteristics of the Tell Fakhariyah script in the framework of the epigraphic material known so far and try to demonstrate that whatever conclusion one arrives at concerning its date and feature, by no means can it affect the problem of the Greek adoption of the alphabet. I shall refrain from touching on the other aspects (style of the statue, the Assyrian text, the possible historical context, and the identification of Hadad-yit'i), which belong to disciplines in which I am not competent to judge. However, I would like to mention the commonly known fact that the history of Mesopotamia and Syria in the eleventh and tenth centuries is somewhat obscure; after the death of Tiglath-pileser I in 1076 B.C.E. there is a gap in our knowledge.[23] On the other hand, the number of alphabetic epigraphs from the same period is gradually growing and the history of the alphabet at the end of the second and beginning of the first millennium is becoming ever clearer.

The main characteristics of the Proto-Canaanite script have been described above. There are two other scripts, which preserved the pictographic conception, being written either from left to right or from right to left, or in boustrophedon: the Proto-Arabian, which evolved from the Proto-Canaanite script about 1300 B.C.E.,[24] and the archaic Greek—about 1100 B.C.E. The Phoenician script is the direct offshoot (since about 1050 B.C.E.) of Proto-Canaanite. The Hebrews, after the conquest of Canaan, adopted the script used by the Canaanites and later by the Phoenicians. The adoption of this very script by the Arameans took place somewhat later than by the Hebrews. The independent Hebrew script began diverging from the Phoenician approximately about the middle of the ninth century; the Aramaic script branched off a century later, that is, in the middle of the eighth century. This means that until 850 B.C.E. Phoenician, Hebrew, and Aramaic texts were written in the same script. From 850 to 750 B.C.E., Hebrew texts were written in the Hebrew script, whereas both Phoenician and Aramaic texts were written in the script that had been developed by the Phoenicians. Only from 750 B.C.E. onward may we speak of three different national scripts: Phoenician, Hebrew, and Aramaic.[25]

This outline is based on more than fifteen late Proto-Canaanite inscriptions (from the thirteenth to the middle of the eleventh century B.C.E.), including the inscriptions on the Lachish ewer and the Lachish bowl, the Beth-shemesh ostracon, the Qubur el-Walaydah inscription, the 'Izbet Sartah sherd, five inscribed arrowheads from el-Khaḍr, and four others found in Lebanon (those of Gerba'al and Rafa as well as the recently published ones reading *ḥṣ yt'/bn zm'*[26] and *ḥṣ 'bdny / 'š 'zb'l*[27]), and the Nora fragment, written in boustrophedon.[28] It is further based on seven inscriptions from the second half of the eleventh century—including two archaic inscriptions from Byblos, the Byblos spatula, three arrowheads (from Ruweisah and Biqa' and a recently published one[29]) as well as the inscription on a bowl from Crete, on eight inscriptions from the tenth century (Aḥiram, Yeḥimilk, Abiba'al, Eliba'al, Shiftiba'al, and 'Abdo—all six from Byblos—as well as the Gezer calendar and the fragmentary Tell Halaf inscription). From the ninth century there are the Nora stele, the archaic inscription from Cyprus, and that of Kilamu—all three are considered as monumental Phoenician inscriptions; there are also six ninth-century Aramaic inscriptions: Bar Hadad, two short ivory inscriptions mentioning Hazael, two inscribed vessels from Engev and Tel Dan, and the stele of Zakkur which belongs to the end of that century; about 800 B.C.E. were also written the Hebrew inscriptions at Kuntillet ʿAjrud. Earlier Hebrew inscriptions from the ninth century are not known so far, but two Moabite inscriptions (Mesha and Kmoshyat) were written in the middle of the ninth century in the Hebrew script. There is also a ninth-century Ammonite inscription, that is, the Amman citadel inscription, written in the Aramaic script.[30]

In all of these inscriptions and in the other ones, which have not been mentioned here, the script had a one-trend development until the middle of the ninth century B.C.E. Then the Hebrew and later the Aramaic script began to separate as independent branches from the main Phoenician branch. From the eighth century onward, there is a significant increase in the number of the Phoenician, Hebrew, and Aramaic inscriptions, in which the letters continue to develop in the directions established earlier.

From the eighth and seventh centuries B.C.E. stem some inscriptions that can be labeled as Ammonite, Moabite, Edomite, or Philistine.[31] These inscriptions were written in scripts that can be called local variations of either the Aramaic script (that of the Ammonites) or the Hebrew script (that of the Philistines); there was an intrusion of Aramaic elements into the Hebrew script used by the Moabites and the Edomites.[32] Otherwise there were neither Phoenician nor Hebrew nor Aramaic local scripts. The Phoenician branch—including Punic and Neo-Punic—was a uniform script without regional variations; the same script was used both on the Phoenician mainland and in the western colonies, and the differences between the script forms are to be explained on chronological and stylistic grounds.[33] The standard Aramaic script was used in all the provinces of the Assyrian, Babylonian, and Persian empires, and the local derivations from this uniform script began only in the third century B.C.E.[34] The Hebrew script, too, evolved without local variations: in the kingdoms of Judah and Israel and later among the Jews and the Samaritans the same script was used until the first century B.C.E.[35]

The conclusions that no local scripts developed in the Phoenician, Aramaic, and Hebrew scripts were drawn independently and separately in three thorough paleographic works published in the years 1968 to 1970 (nn. 33–35), and further discoveries confirmed them. It seems to me impossible to call the trident or palm *kaf* "Byblian," when such a form occurs not only in Byblos but also on the arrowheads from Ruweisah (South Lebanon), from the Biqaʿ, on another one of unknown provenance (n. 29), and on the bowl found on Crete. In order to maintain an eighth-century date for the adoption of the alphabet by the Greeks, sensitive classicists, who were aware of so many epichoric differences in archaic Greek, proposed that there must have been Phoenician local scripts from which the Greek individuals or groups learned their epichoric scripts.[36] However, these scholars did not deal with West Semitic epigraphy. Kaufman's declaration that the Tell Fakhariyah alphabetic script "and other epigraphic finds of the last decade conclusively demonstrate" that "in the 12th and 11th centuries B.C.E. . . . local traditions must have been developed easily" (n. 20) is certainly wrong in regard to the "other epigraphic finds." As for the Tell Fakhariyah script, we shall see below.

Any anti-Phoenicio-centric view cannot deny that both the Hebrew and the Aramaic scripts branched off from the Phoenician script and that both scripts consist only of the twenty-two Phoenician letters, notwithstanding the fact that Hebrew and Aramaic had more consonants than the Phoenician language. Even the "non-Phoenician script" (in Kaufman's terminology) of the Aramaic text of the Tell Fakhariyah inscription has only twenty-two letters and it did not introduce additional ones for the consonants $\underline{d}$, $\d{d}$, $\d{z}$, and $\underline{t}$. The fact that the latter consonant, $\underline{t}$, was expressed by s and not by $\check{s}$, as in all the ninth-century B.C.E. and later Aramaic inscriptions, may indicate that the Tell Fakhariyah inscription adheres to a different tradition, unattested so far, or that it is earlier.

In the ancient Aramaic inscriptions there are final *matres lectionis*, whereas medial vowels are only rarely indicated, and then mostly in the later texts. This rule does not apply to the two eighth-century monumental inscriptions from Zinjirli dedicated to Hadad and Panamu, respectively, in the Sam'alian dialect, where medial *matres lectionis* are frequently used. Thus, unlike the script, which had a one-trend evolution (from Proto-Canaanite, through Phoenician, and then to the Aramaic branch), there were two orthographic traditions. Most ancient Aramaic inscriptions adhered to the tradition in which mainly final *matres lectionis* were indicated, but the inscription from Tell Fakhariyah, which is written in a dialect unknown so far, shares the orthography known from the Sam'alian inscriptions. This phenomenon does not necessarily testify in favor of a later date for the Fakhariyah text. The need for vowel signs in alphabetic writing was felt already at its early stage of evolution. In Ugarit, in addition to the invention of 'a, 'u, and 'i, there are certain instances of using *yod* as final and medial (!) *mater lectionis* as early as the thirteenth century B.C.E.[37]

If we compare the script of the Aramaic text on the statue from Tell Fakhariyah with those of all other inscriptions, we are inclined to date the Fakhariyah script to the eleventh century B.C.E. Most of the letters resemble those of eleventh- and tenth-century epigraphs, but some forms are known only from the twelfth- and early eleventh-century Proto-Canaanite inscriptions on the one hand and in the archaic Greek inscriptions on the other.[38] The typologically oldest forms are as follows:

The *dalet* of Fakhariyah resembles that of the 'Izbet Ṣarṭah ostracon from the twelfth century and that of the archaic Greek scripts.

Kaf in the eleventh-tenth centuries is shaped like three fingers. In the Fakhariyah *kaf* the middle finger is elongated and drawn downward, like the *kaf* of 'Izbet Ṣarṭah. In the western archaic Greek scripts both variations (which are called by Kaufman "Byblian" and "non-Byblian" or "non-Phoenician") represent *khi*.[39]

Lamed with its crook at the top does not occur in the West Semitic inscriptions after the middle of the eleventh century. However, in the archaic Greek scripts, which follow the West Semitic model at a stage when the letter stances were not stabilized, the *lambda*-forms may have their crook either at the top or at the base.[40]

The *mem* of Fakhariyah is typologically earlier than that of the Ahiram inscription from about 1000 B.C.E The similarity between *mem* and *ṣade* in Fakhariyah can be compared with the resemblance between *mu* and *san* in archaic Greek.[41]

The *'ayin* of Fakhariyah preserved the pupil of the eye. This is normal until 1050 B.C.E; its latest occurrence in West Semitic is the inscription on the bowl from Crete (probably from the second half of the eleventh century). It also survived in the archaic Greek scripts.

Pe has an unusual shape, which seems to be a reminiscence of the pictograph of *pe'ah* ("corner").[42]

These are the typologically most archaic letter forms, but all the other letters are also characteristic of the eleventh-tenth centuries B.C.E. True, lapidary and formal writings tend to preserve older forms. However, there are generally slips of the pen that disclose the real date of writing. A. Abou-Assaf and his colleagues pointed out that the *he, yod,* and *samekh* of Fakhariyah have shapes similar to their equivalents in the later inscriptions.[43] However, none of them may be considered as a clear indication for a date later than the eleventh century: the *yod* of Fakhariyah is very much like that of eleventh- and tenth-century *yod*; the slant of the *he* is not definitive evidence; as for the *samekh*, see below.

The downstroke of the *qof* crosses only the lower part of the circle. Similar forms of *qof* can be found in 'Izbet Ṣarṭah and the late-tenth-century Shiftiba'al inscription from Byblos. However, an identical *qof* occurs in the Marsiliana abecedary, which represents the archaic Greek local script used in Etruria in the middle of the seventh century B.C.E.[44]

Like the *qof*, the downstroke of the *samekh* also does not cross the horizontal bars which are above it. Such a *samekh* can be found only in the eighth-century Aramaic inscriptions. True, for many years the earliest known example of *samekh* was that of the Aḥiram inscription about 1000 B.C.E.; here the downstroke crosses all three horizontal bars. However, in the recently discovered bowl from Crete the downstroke of the *samekh* touches the middle bar and crosses only the lower one. Thus it is possible that there were analogical developments in the downstrokes of the *qof* and the *samekh*, and we cannot assume that the Fakhariyah *samekh* is late.

It is a well-known phenomenon that letters tend to develop in similar forms and even to assimilate to each other. This is the only explanation of the peculiar form of the Fakhariyah *waw*, which has a base just like the *zayin*, its neighbor in the alphabetic order.[45]

The word dividers used in the Aramaic text from Fakhariyah are a vertical stroke or two or three dots. The stroke dividing the words is characteristic of eleventh- and tenth-century West Semitic inscriptions. The three dots occur in the Lachish ewer from the thirteenth century. However, all three word dividers are well known in the archaic Greek writing.[46]

As I have tried to show above, the number of epigraphs relevant to our subject is not scant at all, and there is not even a single piece of evidence for local derivatives (except for Hebrew and Aramaic). Thus I do not believe that Millard and Bordreuil arrived at the right solution of the problem. One cannot evade the question by labeling the Aramaic script of Tell Fakhariyah either as "excentrique"[47] or as peripheral. If the non-paleographic evidence is really so unequivocal for dating this text to the ninth century, then the only possibility that can be taken into consideration is that we have here a very successful artificial archaizing script. It is so extraordinary and out of context in the ninth century that it can only be explained by assuming that its set of letters was copied without a single failure from a stele of the eleventh century. However, this is merely another excuse, because there is no indication for such imitations ever having existed in ancient West Semitic writing.

Although the script of the Aramaic text written on the statue from Fakhariyah represents the Proto-Canaanite script in the eleventh century B.C.E., it would not be legitimate to favor this evidence if it contradicts the conclusions drawn from other criteria. However, drawing conclusions without taking into consideration the paleographic evidence is equally biased. It would be wise, therefore, to ponder the problem carefully and refrain from hasty conclusions.

However, even if one believes that the Fakhariyah script represents an Aramaic local variation in the ninth century—which is a supposition that cannot be substantiated—it would be illegitimate to assume that this script (or some similar script which does not exist so far) could be the ancestor of the archaic Greek local scripts. It would be ridiculous to believe that the Greeks rejected the generally used alphabet and chose for themselves an archaic "eccentric and peripheral" set of letters employed by the inhabitants of Gozan. To assume that some other people, who lived near the Mediterranean Sea, might have written in the ninth century in the "Fakhariyah script" is merely a guess. New theories are welcomed only when they rely on a firm base. Kaufman's application of the wave theory to the development of the scripts, or his anti-Phoenicio-centric ideology cannot be based on a single find, whatever its importance. On the other hand, the supposition that the Greeks adopted the alphabet at an early stage when the pictographic conception still allowed un-stabilized stances of letters, which must have been written horizontally, but in any direction, including in boustrophedon, seems to gain additional force with new discoveries both in Canaan and in the West. I would not say that what is called "Naveh's theory" cannot be refuted. There is always a possibility that contradictory evidence will be discovered, but the Fakhariyah text alone cannot be considered as such. At any rate, it would be very unwise to base a new theory on a single and extraordinary item.[48]

NOTES

1. J. T. Milik and F. M. Cross, "Inscribed Javelin-Heads from the Period of the Judges: A Recent Discovery in Palestine," *BASOR* 134 (1954) 5–15; F. M. Cross, "The Evolution of the Proto-Canaanite Alphabet," *BASOR* 134 (1954) 15–24.

2. F. M. Cross, "The Origin and Early Evolution of the Alphabet," *EI* 8 (1967) 8*–24*.

3. In the tenth century, *gimel* could still be written as a *gamma* or as an inverted V; *waw* could have a shape resembling a Y or the numeral 4; *taw* could be written as an X or as a cross. Later these alternative forms were separated from each other and used either in the Phoenician and Aramaic scripts or in the Hebrew script.

4. J. Naveh, "Some Semitic Epigraphical Considerations on the Antiquity of the Greek Alphabet," *AJA* 77 (1973) 1–8.

5. See R. Carpenter, "The Antiquity of the Greek Alphabet," *AJA* 37 (1933) 8–29.

6. L. H. Jeffery, "Greek Alphabetic Writing," *CAH* 3/1 (1982) 823 n. 8. But see the thorough discussion of J. de Hoz, of the Seminario de Clásicas in the University of Salamanca (Spain), "Algunas consideraciones sobre los origenes del alfabeto griego," in *Estudios metodologicos sobre la lengua griega* (ed. J. A. Fernández Delgado; Cáceres: Universidad de Extremadura, 1983) 11–50.

7. P. K. McCarter, "The Early Diffusion of the Alphabet," *BA* 37 (1974) 68;

idem, *The Antiquity of the Greek Alphabet and the Early Phoenician Scripts* (HSM 9; Missoula, Mont.: Scholars Press, 1975).

8. F. M. Cross, "Early Alphabetic Scripts," *Symposia Celebrating the Seventy-fifth Anniversary of the Founding of the American Schools of Oriental Research (1900–1975)*, vol. 1: *Archaeology and Early Israelite History* (ed. F. M. Cross; Cambridge, Mass.: ASOR, 1979 [written in 1975]) 108.

9. A. R. Millard, "The Canaanite Linear Alphabet and Its Passage to the Greeks," *Kadmos* 15 (1976) 142; see also B. S. J. Isserlin, "The Earliest Alphabetic Writing," *CAH* 3/1 (1982) 816–18; idem, "The Antiquity of the Greek Alphabet," *Kadmos* 22 (1983) 151-63.

10. M. Kochavi, "An Ostracon of the Period of the Judges from ʿIzbet Ṣarṭah," *Tel Aviv* 4 (1977) 1–13; F. M. Cross, "Newly Found Inscriptions in Old Canaanite and Early Phoenician Scripts," *BASOR* 238 (1980) 8–20.

11. M. Sznycer, "L'inscription phénicienne de Tekke, près de Cnossus", *Kadmos* 18 (1979) 89–93; Cross, "Newly Found Inscriptions," 15–20.

12. Cross, "Newly Found Inscriptions," 1–20.

13. F. M. Cross, "Leaves from an Epigraphist's Notebook," *CBQ* 36 (1974) 490–93; idem, "Early Alphabetic Scripts," 103–5, fig. 8 on p. 119. See also below, n. 28.

14. Cross, "Newly Found Inscriptions," 17. See also E. Puech, "Présence phénicienne dans les îles à la fin du IIᵉ millénaire," *RB* 90 (1983) 365–95.

15. A. Abou-Assaf, "Die Statue des HDYSʿY, König von Guzana," *MDOG* 113 (1981) 3–22; P. Bordreuil, A. R. Millard, and A. Abou-Assaf, "La statue de Tell Fekheryé: La première inscription bilingue assyro-araméenne," *CRAIBL* (1981) 640–55; A. Abou-Assaf, P. Bordreuil, and A. R. Millard, *La statue de Tell Fekheryé et son inscription bilingue assyro-araméenne* (Paris: Editions Recherche sur les civilisations, 1982): A. R. Millard and P. Bordreuil, "A Statue from Syria with Assyrian and Aramaic Inscriptions," *BA* 45 (1982) 135–41.

16. Abou-Assaf et al. (*"La statue de Tell Fekheryé*, p. 97) give a dating on the basis of paleography from the beginning of the tenth century to the eighth.

17. Millard and Bordreuil, "A Statue from Syria," 140.

18. S. A. Kaufman, "Reflections on the Assyrian-Aramaic Bilingual from Tell Fakhariyeh," *Maarav* 3/2 (1982) 137–75.

19. Ibid., 142.

20. Ibid., 143.

21. Ibid., 143–44.

22. Ibid., 144 n. 18.

23. This has already been noted by Abou-Assaf et al., *La statue de Tell Fekheryé*, 98.

24. Cross, "The Origin and Early Evolution of the Alphabet," 19*.

25. J. Naveh, *Early History of the Alphabet: An Introduction to West Semitic Epigraphy and Palaeography* (Jerusalem: Magnes Press/Leiden: E. J. Brill, 1982).

26. *Sauvegarde de Tyr* (Journée internationale pour la sauvegarde de Tyr; Paris: UNESCO, 1980) 31.

27. P. Bordreuil, "Épigraphes phéniciennes sur bronze, sur pierre et sur céramique," in *Archéologie au Levant: Recuil R. Saida* (Collection de la Maison de

l'Orient Méditerranéen No. 12; Série archéologique 9; Lyon, 1982) 187–90. Bordreuil counted altogether twenty ca. eleventh-century (published and unpublished) inscribed arrowheads.

28. Cross, above (n. 13); W. Röllig ("Paläographische Beobachtungen zum ersten Auftreten der Phönizier in Sardinien," in *Antidoron Jürgen Thimme* [Karlsruhe: Verlag C. F. Müller, 1982] 120–30) vehemently argues against the boustrophedal reading and the dotted ʿayin in the Nora fragment. Should these arguments be right, the box-shaped *ḥet* is clearly earlier than the ninth century B.C.E. At any rate, Röllig's allegation cannot change the assumption that there were contacts between the Canaanites and the West as early as the late twelfth century B.C.E.

29. J. Starcky, "La flèche de Zakarbaʿal roi d'Amurru," *Archéologie au Levant*, 179–86.

30. Only the most important items have been listed here. For detailed descriptions of these inscriptions and of the unlisted ones, see the works mentioned above in nn. 1–2, 8–14, 25–29, as well as in the textbooks of H. Donner and W. Röllig, *KAI*, vols. I–III, and J. C. L. Gibson, *Textbook of Syrian Semitic Inscriptions*, (3 vols.; Oxford: Clarendon Press, 1971–82).

31. On the script used in Philistia, see J. Naveh, "Writing and Scripts in Seventh Century B.C.E. Philistia. The New Evidence from Tell Jemmeh," *IEJ* 35 (1985) 8–21.

32. See Naveh, *Early History of the Alphabet*, 100–112.

33. B. Peckham, *The Development of the Late Phoenician Scripts* (Cambridge: Harvard University Press, 1968).

34. J. Naveh, *The Development of the Aramaic Script* (Jerusalem: Israel Academy of Sciences and Humanities, 1970).

35. J. D. Purvis, *The Samaritan Pentateuch and the Origin of the Samaritan Sect* (HSM 2; Cambridge: Harvard University Press, 1968).

36. R. M. Cook and A. G. Woodhead, "The Diffusion of the Greek Alphabet," *AJA* 63 (1959) 175–78. J. A. Bundgaard ("Why Did the Art of Writing Spread to the West?—Reflections on the Alphabet of Marsiliana," *Analecta Romana Istituti Danici* 3 [1965] 56) believes that the alphabet "was transmitted from Semitic to Greek countries through contacts at many points, presumably also over quite a long period of time."

37. See *UT* 18; E. Y. Kutscher, "Reply to Prof. Loewenstamm," *Leshonenu* 32 (1968) 374; J. Blau and S. E. Loewenstamm, "Zur Frage der Scriptio plena im Ugaritischen und Verwandtes," *UF* 2 (1970) 19–33, esp. 25–30.

38. The Greek script, after branching off from the late Proto-Canaanite script about 1100 B.C.E., had an independent slow evolution: in addition to the boustrophedal writing—which continued to exist until the fifth century B.C.E.—many archaic forms survived. The development of the archaic Greek script, which was used far away from the Orient for writing non-Semitic languages, does not justify an analogous conclusion in regard to the Fakhariyah script, even if it is labeled as local or peripheral.

39. Naveh, "Some Semitic Epigraphical Considerations," 8; idem, "Some Considerations on the Ostracon from ʿIzbet Ṣarṭah," *IEJ* 28 (1978) 34.

40. Naveh, "Some Semitic Epigraphical Considerations," 3.

41. It would be worth noting that on the above-mentioned bowl from Crete, M. Sznycer ("L'inscription phénicienne de Tekke") saw the fourth letter as a *ṣade*, whereas Cross rightly read it as a *mem*: *ks šm' bn l* ["the cup of Shema son of L]."

42. Cf. the table of W. F. Albright in his *The Proto-Sinaitic Inscriptions and Their Decipherment* (Harvard Theological Studies 22; Cambridge: Harvard University Press, 1966) opposite p. 12; Naveh, *Early History of the Alphabet*, 25.

43. See the book of Abou-Assaf et al. *La statue de Tell Fekheryé*, 89, 91–93, 96–97.

44. M. Guarducci, *Epigrafia greca* (Rome: Istituto Poligrafico dello Stato, 1967) 1.228, fig. 89; Naveh, *Early History of the Alphabet*, 181, fig. 163.

45. For analogical evolutions of letters, cf. Naveh, "Some Semitic Epigraphical Considerations," 7 and n. 30. For the assimilatory tendency, cf. the shape of *bet* with its rightward base in the late-tenth-century Phoenician inscriptions (mainly from Byblos), which no doubt evolved under the influence of such a base of the *yod*.

46. Guarducci, *Epigraphia greca*, 103.

47. Abou-Assaf et al. *La statue de Tell Fekheryé*, 96.

48. My thanks are due to A. R. Millard, who kindly read the manuscript of this chapter and discussed it with me.

8

Canaanite Origins and Lineage: Reflections on the Religion of Ancient Israel

MICHAEL DAVID COOGAN

For generations, scholars have grouped together the autochthonous Semitic languages of the Levant under the rubric Northwest Semitic[1] and within this group have consistently referred to the non-Aramaic group of dialects as Canaanite.[2] Those who have investigated the latter generally include in their discussion, as a matter of course, the surviving manifestations of Hebrew (epigraphic, biblical, postbiblical, Mishnaic, etc.) with no compulsion to make Hebrew, and especially biblical Hebrew, the focus of their investigation; it is simply treated as one among the several dialects.[3]

Such scholarly objectivity has not always characterized the history of West Semitic religions. For understandable reasons, the biblical data have generally served as point of reference, "the still point of the turning world," so that scholars have spoken of "the Old Testament against its environment," the influence of Canaanite religion (especially as manifested in the texts from Ugarit) on the religion of Israel, and not infrequently of the uniqueness of the latter, its absolute difference from other ancient religions.[4] Certainly the special position of the Bible in Jewish and Christian traditions and the consequent richness of biblical evidence in contrast, for one example, to Phoenician are sufficient explanations for this tendency. But the continuing insistence on the biblical witness as central has too frequently led to misinterpretation of extrabiblical material and, more seriously, to a methodological shortcoming: the failure to describe and to analyze biblical evidence in its larger context.

The presupposition of this chapter is that for methodological purposes it is essential to consider biblical religion as a subset of Israelite religion and Israelite religion as a subset of Canaanite religion.[5] From a historical perspective it is more appropriate, then, to speak of the special development of the religion of ancient Israel, rather than of the ways in which it was influenced by other cultures, as though it was a static, fully formed reality subject only to tangential modification. To be sure, by the beginning of the first millennium B.C.E. Israel, like its neighbors Phoenicia, Ammon, Moab, Edom, and Aram, had begun to show distinctive traits in religious as well as in other aspects of its life.[6] But this was a development from a Canaanite matrix and can be understood only by the reconstruction of that matrix from all available evidence and by the analysis of parallel developments in neighboring states.

I wish to illustrate these general remarks by discussing two recent discoveries.

1. *The Deir 'Allā Text.* Although discovered in 1967 and given full publication in 1976, this difficult mural inscription, while fully discussed in several recent studies,[7] has not yet been adequately treated on the apparently simple matter of the relationship between this text and Numbers 22—24, both of which have as their protagonist Balaam the son of Beor. The Deir 'Allā text is generally agreed to date about 700 B.C.E.; many have argued that the poetic sections of the Numbers material, the "oracles of Balaam," are premonarchical in origin.[8]

There is no question of some connection between the Israelite and the Transjordanian traditions. One possibility is that both the Deir 'Allā and the biblical texts derive from a common late-second-millennium tradition of Balaam. There is certainly precedent for the continuing attribution of oracular material to prophetic figures long after their career; Isaiah 40—66 is an obvious example. It is possible, then, that a (north Mesopotamian?) seer of an earlier period could have had attributed to him oracles from a later time. Nevertheless, careful analysis of the Balaam traditions suggests otherwise.

Balaam's home is identified in Num 22:5 as "Pethor on the River [Euphrates], the land of his kinsfolk,"[9] further specified in Deut 23:5 as Aram-naharaim. Pethor is identified with Assyrian Pitru, widely attested in the Assyrian Annals as well as in earlier Egyptian sources.[10] The reference to Aram-naharaim has been called anachronistic,[11] but it is so only on the assumption that the traditions are genuinely ancient. There are thus no toponyms or other realia in the biblical traditions about Balaam that point exclusively to a second-millennium date; in fact, a first-millennium date is more congenial with the remarkably few specifics in the text.

Outside Numbers 22—24 Balaam himself occurs in relatively few passages (Num 31:8, 16 [P]; Deut 23:5–6; Josh 13:22 [Dtr²]; 24:9–10; Mic 6:5; Neh 13:2), most of which are demonstrably monarchical or later, as M. Noth observed;[12] the stories about Balaam were thus not a fixed part of earliest Israelite tradition.

The source analysis of the Balaam episode is notoriously difficult.[13] For my purposes here it is sufficient to recognize that we seem to have at least three distinguishable sets of traditions: the main narrative, which has many characteristics of E; the ass episode (Num 22:22–35), which appears to be independent of the former; and the poems.

Apart from their biblical context, the arguments for dating the Balaam oracles to premonarchic Israel are typological in nature. W. F. Albright argued that the orthography of the poems required a time of origin about 1200 B.C.E. and their fixation in writing in the tenth century.[14] Some of the evidence he cites, however, is textually suspect, and the pervasive inconsistencies in the use of supposedly archaic spellings argue strongly against his conclusion.

Albright also proposed that the poetic style of the poems was early. D. A. Robertson's careful and detailed analysis suggests rather that they "resemble early poetry in that they manifest more early forms than any standard poems, but resemble standard poetry in that they contain evidence of archaizing."[15] In other words, the presence of older elements is more likely to be due to deliberate archaizing (appropriate in the narrative context) than to genuine late-second-millennium origin.

D. N. Freedman has argued that the names of the deity in early poetry follow a discernible chronological pattern, and on the basis of his analysis he dates the Balaam oracles to the eleventh century.[16] His evidence, however, is slight, and not without exceptions which he has noted. The single instance of "Elyon" (Num 24:16; reconstructed in 24:5) is not compelling, given its wide use in poetry; even in Freedman's corpus it occurs elsewhere only in his latest group (tenth to ninth century). Similarly, "Shadday" (Num 24:4[= 16]; *not* the P designation "El Shadday"), which occurs only twice elsewhere in Freedman's corpus, is not restricted to hypothetically early poetry. Furthermore, the presence of the "Shaddayyīn" in the Deir 'Allā text makes it clear that the epithet was fully at home in eighth-century Canaanite traditions.[17]

The conclusion of these observations is that the widespread dating of the origin of the Balaam traditions to the late second millennium is mistaken. None of the typological arguments used for such dating, whether orthographic, poetic, or thematic, are convincing, and in fact several have been refuted. In what period, then, are we to locate the origin and development of the traditions? Here we return to the Deir 'Allā text, which provides a *terminus ante quem*. My own hunch is that the traditions begin in the late ninth and eighth centuries. The best parallels to the prose sections of the Numbers material with their legendary quality are the Elijah-Elisha cycles in Kings, and there are more than superficial resemblances between the content of the oracles themselves and the prophetic corpus of preexilic Israel, particularly in the oracles against the nations, whose development as a literary tradition begins in this period, and in the unexpected announcement of judgment on the solicitor of the oracle, as in the Micaiah episode (1 Kings 22) and Amos 1—2. Historically this was a period in which the Moabites (along with their sister Transjordanian states Ammon and Edom) had achieved independence of Israel and Judah, beginning with the reign of Mesha, but by the eighth century were severely threatened by the resurgence of Assyria. Balaam could then have been a court prophet in Transjordan, at the service not only of the Moabite throne but also of the Ammonites as well. (This kind of international ministry is well paralleled in Elisha's role in the rise of Hazael in Damascus [2 Kgs 8:7–15].)

The catastrophic content of the "First Combination" of the Deir ʿAllā text coincides nicely with that of the Balaam oracles in Numbers: both imply a decline of the Transjordanian states, in the latter to Israel's benefit. The development of a narrative tradition in Israel in which the Transjordanian prophet is satirized and, paradoxically, in which are embedded authentic prophetic oracles whose message is the opposite of the wishes of the Moabite king best fits into this period of decline in Transjordan. In short, the Balaam traditions, both prose and poetry, both at Deir ʿAllā and in the Bible, originate in the eighth century, and this conclusion is based and builds upon the prima facie evidence from Deir ʿAllā.[18]

2. *Kuntillet ʿAjrud and Yahweh's "Asherah."* The material from the eighth-century site of Kuntillet ʿAjrud, which as yet has been only partially published, has occasioned considerable discussion,[19] much of it centered on the highly decorated pithos A (Reg. No. 16/1) and especially its depiction of three humanoid figures over which is an inscription conveying a blessing on several individuals "by Yahweh of Samaria and by his Asherah *(lyhwh šmrn wl'šrth).*"[20]

The site itself was probably multifunctional, serving as a way station on the commercial routes through the northern Sinai peninsula, including one from the Mediterranean to the Red Sea; it also had a cultic function, as the presence of numerous inscribed votive offerings makes clear.[21] Diverse cultural strands are also in evidence at the site, including inscriptions by Judahite, Israelite, and Phoenician hands, making it a kind of microcosm of the cosmopolitan reality which Israel was at any given moment in its history.

It is not necessary here to rehearse the various interpretations of the phrase "*lyhwh šmrn wl'šrth.*"[22] Despite the grammatical difficulty, understanding the last word as "his [i.e., Yahweh's] Asherah [i.e., the goddess Asherah who was his consort]" is the most attractive of the possibilities.

The absence of biblical parallels to the precise phrasing (no matter how one interprets " 'šrth") simply underscores the highly selective character of the biblical traditions.

Like others, I am inclined to see a connection between the inscription and the drawing.[23] The simplest explanation is to take the two standing figures as representations of the two deities mentioned in the inscription, which thus serves as caption: the larger male figure is Yahweh, and the appropriately smaller female figure slightly behind him is his consort Asherah. Both figures have bovine ears, appropriate theriomorphic aspects of the "bull of Jacob" and his lady, and probably tails.[24] The posture, perspective, and general aspect of the figures are similar to "joined figurines" of the second millennium B.C.E.[25]

The attribution of a female consort to a male deity is of course no surprise, despite the best efforts of later monotheistic orthodoxy. It is methodologically questionable to label the ʿAjrud cult as syncretistic, as though the biblical sources were the accurate representation of pure and undefiled religion. Rather, what ʿAjrud gives us is a rare, although admittedly narrow, glimpse of both the texts and the iconography of actual Israelite cultic praxis.

With the Kuntillet ʿAjrud evidence in mind, the ubiquitous female figurines from Iron Age sites throughout the Levant seem even more likely than earlier thought to be representations of the divine consorts of the respective national deities.[26] This pervasive aspect of popular religion is generally not explicitly represented in biblical tradition, except perhaps in the worship of the "queen of heaven" (Jer 7:18; 44:17, 19, 25[27]). But more subtle evidence may be adduced, including the prophetic use of the marriage metaphor to describe the relationship between Yahweh and Israel, and especially the figure of Wisdom in Proverbs 8 and related later texts.

The views of R. B. Y. Scott are typical of a dominant interpretation of Proverbs 8:

> The writer may have drawn on and adapted old mythological material for his purpose, but we cannot infer from this that he was making anything more than a figurative poetic use of it.[28]

Here the depiction of Wisdom as a divine being present at creation is understood simply as a literary device, the arcane artifice of an author with antiquarian interests. I would argue that the author is not drawing directly on old mythological material but on actual Israelite belief in the consort of the deity. To be sure, this belief is continuous in Canaanite tradition, and important evidence for it is found in second-millennium sources. But I think it unlikely that the author of Proverbs 8, whenever that passage is to be dated,[29] had our Ugaritic corpus as part of his or her personal library. Rather, this passage emerges from a living Canaanite tradition in Israel, specifically the belief in the consort of the deity.[30]

Further evidence for this conclusion is found in later sources, especially Wisdom 8—9, where, as has long been observed, Wisdom cohabits with God, and Sirach 24; whether these are creative reinterpretations of the figure of Wisdom in Proverbs or independent developments rooted, like Proverbs 8, in a living tradition, or, as is most likely, a combination of both, they are testimony to the belief in the spouse of Yahweh. Even later is the remark of Philo that God is the husband of Wisdom (*sophias anēr*),[31] and although by his time the influence of Hellenistic religions in general and the worship of Isis in particular were major factors, that does not eliminate the likelihood that Philo's characterization reflected actual Israelite belief as well.[32]

The various allusions, then, to the consort of the deity in the Bible are further support for interpreting the text and iconography of the krater from Kuntillet 'Ajrud as I have done. The tradition is continuous and pervasive, a living tradition on which biblical writers drew, however subtly, not a literary construct of their own devising.

Other examples could be adduced to reinforce the argument of this chapter. Some, like the divine council, the cosmic mountain, and the divine warrior, have been thoroughly discussed.[33] Many others require primary research and synthesis of biblical evidence with extrabiblical data, both textual and artifactual, such as the cult of the dead. The remarkable continuity of an institution such as the *marzēaḥ* (in the Hebrew vocalization) in Canaanite circles from Ugarit in the second millennium B.C.E. down to Palmyra in the early first millennium C.E. and beyond is an indication of the essential unity of Canaanite culture granted the expected regional and chronological variations.[34] In fact, it may well be the case that the more private elements of Canaanite religion were less susceptible to change than those of a public, quasi-official character, for it is precisely in many such elements that we find the least variation despite wide separation in time and space.[35]

In this essay I have argued by way of example that careful consideration of extrabiblical evidence is essential for an understanding of the development of the religion of ancient Israel. Its distinctive features can be assessed only when there is full recognition of the extent of its cultural continuity with its neighbors. No matter how pejoratively he may have intended it, Ezekiel's genealogy of Jerusalem is accurate: "By origin and by birth you are of the land of the Canaanites" (Ezek 16:3).

NOTES

1. See, e.g., S. Moscati, *An Introduction to the Comparative Grammar of the Semitic Languages* (Wiesbaden: Otto Harrassowitz, 1964) 7–13; G. Garbini, *Il semitico del nord-ovest* (Naples: Istituto universitario di Napoli, 1960).

2. For the use of "dialect," see most recently W. R. Garr, *Dialect Geography of Syria-Palestine, 1000–587 B.C.E.* (Philadelphia: University of Pennsylvania Press, 1985) 2, 14 and n. 4. Notable examples of the use of the designation "Canaanite" include C. Brockelmann, *Grundriss der vergleichenden Grammatik der semitischen Sprachen* (Berlin, 1908; reprinted, Hildesheim: Georg Olms, 1961) p. 8; Z. Harris, *Development of the Canaanite Dialects* (New Haven: American Oriental Society, 1939); H. Donner and W. Röllig, *KAI* (3d ed., 1976). The use of Canaanite in this sense has been criticized as historically inaccurate (see A. F. Rainey, "The Kingdom of Ugarit," *BAR* 3, 79–80 [= *BA* 28 (1965) 105–7]), but such precision is too nice in a diachronic discussion.

3. Exceptions of course exist. An example of the tendency to make ancient Israel the focus of even a technical linguistic description is the chronological range of Garr, *Dialect Geography of Syria-Palestine*; the limits are derived from the history of Israel without comment, even though some of the data he uses do not fall within them.

4. See the remarks by F. M. Cross in the preface to *CMHE*, vii–viii as well as the detailed argument of the book itself. Useful surveys of the history of the study of the religion of Israel include G. W. Anderson, "Hebrew Religion," *The Old Testament and Modern Study* (ed. H. H. Rowley; Oxford: Clarendon Press, 1951) 282–310; H. F. Hahn, *The Old Testament in Modern Research* (expanded ed.; Philadelphia: Fortress Press, 1966) 83–118; W. Zimmerli, "The History of Israelite Religion," *Tradition and Interpretation* (ed. G. W. Anderson; London: Oxford University Press, 1979) 351–84; and most recently P. D. Miller, "Israelite Religion," *The Hebrew Bible and Its Modern Interpreters* (ed. D. A. Knight and G. M. Tucker; Chico, Calif.: Scholars Press, 1985) 201–37.

5. I deliberately use the term "Canaanite" in a broad sense, roughly equivalent to its sense in Semitic linguistics. Of interest here is the remark of Augustine that when the rural population of Carthage was asked their nationality, they called themselves Canaanites (Augustine, *Ep. ad Rom. Exp.* 13 [*Patrologia latina* 35. 2096]).

6. Heuristically it is useful to separate the religious from other elements, but I do not mean to imply a sharp distinction in antiquity between the the sacred and the secular. Clearly such realities as kingship, law, social organization, and the like all had a religious dimension to them.

7. For a summary of the discussion, see J. A. Hackett, *The Balaam Text from Deir 'Allā* (HSM 31; Chico, Calif.: Scholars Press, 1984) 1–8; see now also A. Lemaire, "Fragments from the Book of Balaam Found at Deir 'Allā," *BARev* 11/5 (Sept./Oct. 1985) 26–39.

8. See especially W. F. Albright, "The Oracles of Balaam," *JBL* 63 (1944) 207–33; D. N. Freedman, "Early Israelite Poetry and Historical Reconstructions," *Symposia Celebrating the Seventy-fifth Anniversary of the Founding of the American Schools of Oriental Research (1900–1975)* (ed. F. M. Cross; Cambridge,

Mass.: ASOR, 1979) 85–96, and elsewhere; D. M. Stuart, *Studies in Early Hebrew Meter* (HSM 13; Missoula, Mont.: Scholars Press, 1976) 109.

9. Reading *'ereṣ bĕnê 'ammôn*, with MT and G. Other textual traditions read *'ereṣ bĕnê 'ammôn*, a correction of interest in the light of the location of Deir 'Allā. W. F. Albright's suggestion ("Some Important Recent Discoveries: Alphabetic Origins and the Idrimi Statue," *BASOR* 118 [April 1950] 15 n. 13) that consonantal *'mw* is to be identified with Akkadian *a-ma-e*/Egyptian *'a-ma-w* (attested in texts of the sixteenth and fifteenth centuries B.C.E. respectively) does not explain *bĕnê*.

10. For a full review, see S. Parpola, *Neo-Assyrian Toponyms* (AOAT 6; Neukirchen-Vluyn: Neukirchener Verlag, 1970) 279; K. Kessler, *Untersuchungen zur historischen Topographie Mesopotamiens nach keilschriftlichen Quellen des 1. Jahrtausends v. Chr.* (Wiesbaden: Ludwig Reichert Verlag, 1980) 191–94.

11. A. Malamat, "The Aramaeans," *Peoples of Old Testament Times* (ed. D. J. Wiseman; Oxford: Clarendon Press, 1973) 141.

12. M. Noth, *A History of Pentateuchal Traditions* (Englewood Cliffs, N.J.: Prentice-Hall, 1972) 76.

13. See the trenchant summary of Albright, "The Oracles of Balaam," 207–8; also the animadversions of A. Rofé, *The Book of Balaam (Numbers 22:2— 24:25)* (Jerusalem: Sinor, 1979; Hebrew).

14. Albright, "The Oracles of Balaam," 209–11, 233; idem, *Yahweh and the Gods of Canaan* (London: Athlone Press, 1968) 13, 26 n. 68.

15. D. A. Robertson, *Linguistic Evidence in Dating Early Hebrew Poetry* (SBLDS 3; Missoula, Mont.: Scholars Press, 1972) 145.

16. D. N. Freedman, "Divine Names and Titles in Early Hebrew Poetry," *Magnalia Dei, The Mighty Acts of God* (ed. F. M. Cross, W. E. Lemke, and P. D. Miller; Garden City, N.Y.: Doubleday & Co., 1976) 66–68.

17. See further the discussion by Hackett, *The Balaam Text*, 85–89; and idem, "Religious Traditions in Israelite Transjordan," chap. 9 in this volume.

18. The complexity of the biblical traditions discussed above makes it clear that they have a history of their own and that they did not develop as a single nationalistic riposte to the situation in Transjordan in the late ninth and eighth centuries, but the arguments above require that this development was in the period suggested rather than considerably prior to it.

19. For a useful bibliography, see W. G. Dever, "Asherah, Consort of Yahweh? New Evidence from Kuntillet 'Ajrud," *BASOR* 255 (1984) 34–37, to which may be added Z. Meshel and C. Meyers, "The Name of God in the Wilderness of Zin," *BA* 39 (1976) 6–10; M. Weinfeld, "Kuntillet 'Ajrud Inscriptions and Their Significance," *Studi epigrafici e linguistici* 1 (1984) 121–30; A. Lemaire, "Who or What Was Yahweh's Asherah?" *BARev* 10/6 (Nov./Dec. 1984) 42–51; idem, "Date et origine des inscriptions hébraïques et phéniciennes de Kuntillet 'Ajrud," *Studi epigrafici e linguistici* 1 (1984) 131–43, with further bibliography on 140 n. 2. Cf. chap. 10 (McCarter) and chap. 11 (Tigay) in this volume.

20. See Z. Meshel, *Kuntillet 'Ajrud: A Religious Centre from the Time of the Judaean Monarchy on the Border of Sinai* (Israel Museum Catalogue 175; Jerusalem: Israel Museum, 1978), esp. ills. 12.

21. By cult I mean public ritual. More precision on the character of the cult at Kuntillet ʿAjrud will have to await full publication of the excavated material, including the faunal remains. In the article, "Of Cults and Cultures: Reflections on the Interpretation of Archaeological Evidence," *PEQ* 119 (1987), I suggest that four useful criteria in determining whether a site has a cultic function are isolation, exotic materials, continuity, and parallels. At Kuntillet ʿAjrud, the presence of exotic materials, especially the inscriptions, makes it clear that the site did have a cultic function. Thus, it was a sanctuary of some kind, perhaps used by pilgrims on their way to the southern shrine at Horeb (see 1 Kgs 19:3–8; most pilgrims would have needed more sustenance during their journey!) (= Teman? note the occurrence of "Yahweh of Teman" at ʿAjrud). But the location of the site, the evidence of Phoenician presence there, and architectural parallels all suggest that it also had a military and economic function, serving both as a protection for and as a way station on the trade routes on which it was located.

22. See the discussion by J. A. Emerton, "New Light on Israelite Religion: The Implications of the Inscriptions from Kuntillet ʿAjrud," *ZAW* 94 (1982) 13–18.

23. See especially Dever, "Asherah, Consort of Yahweh?" 30. But I am unconvinced by his suggestion that the seated figure with the lyre depicts Asherah; note that the inscription is above (and to the left) of the two standing figures, and that the seated figure is in the background (on the right), hardly a position of prominence for the "Great Goddess." Likewise I doubt the analysis of P. Beck ("The Drawings from Ḥorvat Teiman [Kuntillet ʿAjrud]," *Tel Aviv* 9 [1982] 27–31), accepted by Dever, which understands the two standing figures as depictions of Bes; Beck herself notes many "variations from the norm" of other representations of the Egyptian dwarf god, thoroughly discussed, as Beck notes, by V. Wilson, "The Iconography of Bes with Particular Reference to the Cypriot Evidence," *Levant* 7 (1975) 77–103 and pls. 15–18.

24. The larger figure to the left has both a tail and a phallus; the smaller figure on the right has breasts and, in the drawings, what appears to be something between its legs; in the photograph, however, the space between the legs seems blank.

25. See O. Negbi, *Canaanite Gods in Metal: An Archaeological Study of Ancient Syro-Palestinian Figurines* (Tel Aviv: Institute of Archaeology, Tel Aviv University, 1976) 4–7 and pls. 2–5.

26. Compare the inconclusive comments of J. B. Pritchard, *Palestinian Figurines in Relation to Certain Goddesses Known Through Literature* (New Haven: American Oriental Society, 1943) 83–87, with the remarks of K. Galling, *Biblisches Reallexikon* (HAT 1; Tübingen: J. C. B. Mohr [Paul Siebeck], 1937) 233–34, who argues that the figurines were representations of the consort of Yahweh, and that the prophetic imagery of Israel as Yahweh's wife is derived from (and is a reaction to) this element of popular religion.

27. In all four cases the Masoretic vocalization is *mĕleket*, almost certainly a *qerē* for *mĕleʾket*, a euphemizing correction showing the enduring tendency of official religion to eliminate evidence of heterodoxy even when the context called for its condemnation.

28. R. B. Y. Scott, *Proverbs, Ecclesiastes* (AB 18; Garden City, N.Y.: Doubleday & Co., 1965) 71.

29. R. J. Clifford has argued that on the basis of parallels with Ugaritic literature Proverbs 1—9 should be given an "early, pre-exilic dating... which would place these chapters in the active polemic against Canaanite religion" ("Proverbs ix: A Suggested Ugaritic Parallel," *VT* 25 [1975] 299.) The proposal has merit but is not fully convincing; its presupposition is that close similarity implies chronological proximity. If Proverbs 9 is polemical in intent, it is markedly different in tone from other preexilic attacks on the worship of Canaanite deities. I have the impression of more similarity to the use of Canaanite motifs in such sixth-century works as Second Isaiah and Job (although it should be noted that D. A. Robertson has argued for an early preexilic date for Job as well [*Linguistic Evidence*, 153–56]).

30. Earlier in Proverbs, as well as elsewhere, the figure of Wisdom is described in language appropriate for a goddess. See especially Prov 7:6, where she looks out of a window enticing young men to life; the mythological background of this depiction is suggested by the correction of the Greek version, which alters the pronoun so that the verse refers to the foreign woman rather than to Wisdom, thus avoiding what may have been too daring an image.

31. Philo, *De cherubim* XIV.49.

32. This was noted by R. Patai, *The Hebrew Goddess* (New York: KTAV Publishing House, 1967) 114.

33. See notably Cross, *CMHE*; R. J. Clifford, *The Cosmic Mountain in Canaan and the Old Testament* (HSM 4; Cambridge: Harvard University Press, 1972); P. D. Miller, *The Divine Warrior in Early Israel* (HSM 5; Cambridge: Harvard University Press, 1973); E. T. Mullen, Jr., *The Assembly of the Gods: The Divine Council in Canaanite and Early Hebrew Literature* (HSM 24; Chico, Calif.: Scholars Press, 1980).

34. The *marzēaḥ* and the events at Baal Peor (Numbers 25; Ps 106:28–31) are associated in later literary tradition, both in rabbinic sources and in the Madeba Map, as noted by M. H. Pope, "A Divine Banquet at Ugarit," *The Use of the Old Testament in the New and Other Essays* (Stinespring Volume; ed J. M. Efird; Durham, N.C.: Duke University Press, 1972) 190; see also his essay "The Cult of the Dead at Ugarit," *Ugarit in Retrospect: Fifty Years of Ugarit and Ugaritic* (ed. G. D. Young; Winona Lake, Ind.: Eisenbrauns, 1981), esp. 176–79. Other elements that need to be incorporated into a discussion of the cult of the dead include the term 'il'ib, which seems to mean the deified ancestor, the Ugaritic and Hebrew Rephaim, the use of 'elōhîm in the Bible to refer to the dead, and, from the nontextual side, the traditions of tomb architecture and furnishings throughout the Canaanite world.

35. This is all the more remarkable, given the haphazard nature of our evidence. We are relatively well informed about some areas in some periods, but by and large our knowledge of Canaanite culture is like a few spotlighted areas on an otherwise dark stage; we do not yet know precisely how the illuminated scenes fit together.

9

Religious Traditions in
Israelite Transjordan

JO ANN HACKETT

INTRODUCTION

This chapter is a review of certain pertinent sections of the biblical text as they relate to the newly discovered material from Tell Deir ʿAllā in Jordan,[1] in order to suggest new ways of looking at the religious traditions in Transjordan. The starting point is the Deir ʿAllā inscription, and a summary of my current understanding of that text is therefore in order here.

The inscription found at Tell Deir ʿAllā in the east Jordan Valley is written in black and red ink on plaster, plaster that was presumably applied to a stele that was then hung on a wall.[2] The stele came to the ground and the inscription largely burned during the earthquake that destroyed this phase at the site.[3] The text is written in what has been described as Aramaic script; following F. M. Cross, I identified it as, rather, an example of the Ammonite offshoot of that script[4] and suggested that the dialect of the text resembles South Canaanite more than Aramaic, although there are difficulties with either identification of the dialect.[5] On paleographic grounds, the inscription should date to the end of the eighth century B.C.E.

The inscription begins, after the title, with the report that the gods have come to Balaam at night, and he sees a vision. The gods give him a message, written in red ink in our text, but the message is unfortunately mangled. The next day, Balaam gets up, and fasts and cries. His people ask him why, and in response he reveals a vision he has had of a divine council meeting. The gods at the council are called in parallel lines *ʾlhn* and *šdyn*. At the assembly (*mʿd,* I, 6), they ask a goddess to cover the sky with a cloud and never to remove it. Then there is a series of phrases, identified correctly by P. K. McCarter[6] as a list of reversals: small birds terrorizing large ones; deaf people hearing; poor women mixing expensive myrrh; and so on. This is the end of what is called Combination I, an assemblage of fragments found together and placed in sequence by the editors. The title at the top *(spr bl'm)* identifies it clearly as the beginning.

Combination II, the only other large combination of fragments, consists of the beginnings of about fifteen lines, some of them more than half there and some phrases easily readable; yet nowhere can we make the connections between lines that would help us construct a narrative. I had early decided, however, as have others, to interpret one key word in the text, written *nqr*, as cognate to Hebrew *nēṣer* ("sprout" or "scion" or some such).[7] On hearing this portion of my interpretation, Cross suggested looking for evidence of child sacrifice, since the victim in some Neo-Punic inscriptions is called a *ṣmḥ*.[8] I developed that idea in my thesis and have since become even more convinced that it is the correct reading. Some of the scattered words that can fit into that interpretation, besides the suggestive *nqr*, are *mdr*, which reminds one of *mĕdūrâ* in Isa 30:33; several references to somebody's dying; and three occurrences of the root *mlk*.

In this chapter, then, I will present evidence from the Hebrew Bible that relates to Balaam, to child sacrifice, particularly in Transjordan, and to the divine name Šadday. Finally, I will suggest a combination of this material with what we know from the Deir 'Allā inscription, to determine whether there is a way to integrate all of our material into a reasonable whole.

BALAAM

There is remarkably little in the Bible that is positive about Balaam. This fact is often overlooked because we are accustomed to thinking in terms of the Numbers 22—24 Balaam stories: Balaam is presented as a worshiper of Yahweh who blesses Israel, whereas Balak is the real enemy, as well as the Moabites and the Midianites in general; they are the ones who want Israel cursed, and Balaam is a pious follower of the words of Israel's god.

There is, of course, the negative P story about Balaam that connects him with the Baal-peor incident of Numbers 25. Numbers 31:15–16 ties Balaam specifically with the Midianite version of Baal-peor, the second story in Numbers 25 (vv 6–18), which is also Priestly. In addition, the story in Numbers 31 is echoed in Josh 13:15–23, where Reuben's territory is laid out, territory that includes Beth-peor. In describing this land, the author reports that it was here that Moses defeated Sihon and the Midianite leaders and that Israel here killed Balaam son of Beor the diviner *(qōsēm)*. Interestingly, there is no mention of Peor here, even though other P material is included.

There are other places in the Hebrew Bible where the Baal-peor incident appears, but Balaam's participation either is unknown or, at least, is not mentioned: Deut 4:3–4 and Hos 9:10 (both derived from the J story of Baal-peor[9]); Josh 22:17–18 (P version; this is partly a Priestly story in Joshua[10]); Ps 106:28 (knows the combination of the J version with the P version).

Actually E (or J) also has Balaam at Peor, but there is no mention of any events like those in Numbers 25. According to Num 23:28, it is from the top of Peor, evidently a mountain, that Balaam utters his third oracle.

Deuteronomy 23:4–7; Josh 24:9–10; Neh 13:2; and Mic 6:3–5 all refer to the Numbers 22—24 Balaam stories, the more familiar blessing and cursing. The first three, however, do not necessarily reflect the final story as we have it in Numbers 22—24. Deuteronomy 23:4–5 says that no Ammonite or Moabite can come into the assembly of Yahweh, because they did not offer hospitality to Israel when they were coming from Egypt and because they hired Balaam son of Beor from Pethor to curse Israel. Then we have: but Yahweh would not listen to Balaam, and he turned the curse into a blessing (Deut. 23:6). "Would not listen to Balaam" implies that we have a remnant of a tradition where Balaam actively tried to curse Israel but was thwarted by Yahweh, something slightly, but perhaps significantly, different from Numbers 22—24, where Balaam says repeatedly that he can only say what Elohim or Yahweh puts in his mouth. Joshua 24:9–10 and Neh 13:2 are similar to Deut 23:4–6. The Micah passage is less certain but also does not necessarily refer to a pious Yahwistic Balaam.[11]

The stories in Numbers 22—24, of course, are not entirely positive about Balaam. The deity is constantly shifting around on him, happy with him one minute, angry the next, and the story of Balaam's ass makes relentless fun of this supposed seer. The really positive note is sounded only in the passages where Balaam attributes his oracles to the deity, and particularly when he says the deity is Yahweh, god of Israel (see especially Num 22:18). Without the verses where Balaam consults a deity who approves of Israel, Numbers 22—24 would resemble what must have been the tradition behind Deut 23:4–7; Josh 24:9–10; and Neh 13:2. It seems possible, especially since these chapters are notoriously difficult to divide into the usual sources, that a late hand has overlaid the original story of Balaam and Balak's attempt to curse Israel with a few mentions of Balaam's piety, in so doing turning the stories into basically positive memories of Balaam's role and integrating the Balaam tradition acceptably into Israelite tradition.[12]

Rabbinic and early Christian sources are almost uniformly negative about Balaam.[13] In rabbinic stories, Balaam is the typical gentile sorcerer and evil, greedy person. The New Testament is not at all kind to Balaam, emphasizing his willingness to do anything for money. Some early Christian sources are milder, however, because the line in Balaam's fourth oracle about a star coming forth out of Jacob was interpreted messianically, and Balaam became in the tradition the first of the Magi: through a continuous tradition from Balaam, the three wise men knew to follow the star to Bethlehem.

All of these references can be seen to come from the biblical stories of Balaam but with a good deal of expansion. There is a particularly interesting notice about Balaam in Philo, however, that does not seem to come from biblical tradition but does sound familiar when compared to the reversals passage in the Deir 'Allā inscription:

> There was a man at that time, famous for divination, living in Mesopotamia, who had been initiated into all forms of divining, but he was admired for having formulated augury especially, having shown incredible and great things many times to many people. For he foretold to some people heavy rain in high summer, to others, drought and even burning heat in mid-winter, and to still others barrenness after a good season, and, conversely, a yield after famine; to some inundations and depletions of rivers, and treatments of pestilential afflictions, and countless other things.[14]

One wonders whether it is possible that extrabiblical traditions of Balaam's oracles survived into Philo's time.

The importance of the levels of perception of Balaam is, of course, that we now know, thanks to the Deir 'Allā inscription, that there was at least this one cult on the east side of the Jordan, around 700 B.C.E., that saw Balaam as a prophet. This was not a Yahwistic cult, or at least nowhere in the extant inscription is Yahweh mentioned. The gods who are mentioned are the 'lhn; perhaps El; and the šdyn, surely the plural of the divine name Šadday. There is reference toward the end of what we can read to someone written mlk, perhaps a king, perhaps a sacrificial term, but perhaps a divine epithet. We cannot read enough of it to know.

The name of Balaam, then, was indeed involved in (probably) non-Yahwistic worship in the Jordan Valley on the east, and this during the period of the monarchy on the west. It is not surprising, therefore, to find biblical authors writing negatively about Balaam. What is surprising is to find anything positive about him, since he was apparently an honored figure in a rival cult, during the time when many of our traditions were taking shape. This positive tradition in Numbers 22—24 may, then, as was suggested earlier, be the work of a later hand, which has the effect of making Balaam acceptable to an Israelite audience in spite of the Priestly material, and perhaps even earlier epic material, about him.

REUBEN AND GAD

There are many indications in biblical texts that the Transjordanian tribes were regarded with suspicion.[15] At this time we will consider only three of those stories at length: Numbers 32; Joshua 13; and Judg 11:29–40. Although there are some less than positive stories earlier in the Pentateuch, particularly about Reuben and Reubenites, it is in Numbers 32 that we get the first clear indication of the negative feelings about the Transjordanian tribes and their willingness, or lack of it, to join with the rest of Israel in the conquest of Canaan. In Num 32:1–5, Reuben and Gad approach Moses and Eleazar and ask not to be taken across the Jordan but to be allowed to remain on the east where cattle-grazing is good. Moses is very angry at their request and accuses them of disheartening the rest of the people in the same way that the negative reports from the spies kept Israel from invading once before and left them in the wilderness for forty years. He finishes by saying that if they persist, they will ultimately destroy the whole nation. They respond, of course, that they will set up everything for their herds and their families on the east side but that they will bear arms and fight with everyone else on the west side and not return east until the conquest is finished. Moses says that as long as they do not fail to fight they can go home *něqîyîm,* "free of obligation to Yahweh and to Israel." The statement that the Transjordanian tribes will no longer have an obligation to Israel makes it clear that P does not consider the Transjordanian tribes to be full-fledged citizens.

In Joshua 22, we have the most negative story about the Transjordanian tribes. Joshua says that since Reuben, Gad, and eastern Manasseh have done all that they should for the western tribes' conquest, they can return to their families (Josh 22:1–6). They leave the rest of the people at Shiloh and start toward Gilead. They build a large altar—v 10 says on the west side of the Jordan but v 15 says, more reasonably, on the east side—in the land of Gilead. The people of Israel gather to make war on them for their apostasy, and, interestingly, Phinehas (famous for the Baal-peor incident, which also occurred in this general area of the world) and ten princes *(něśî'îm)* go to them in Gilead. In vv 16–20, they accuse the Transjordanian tribes of apostasy, compare what they have done to the incident at Peor, and say they have turned away from Yahweh and that they can move to the west if their land is unclean (i.e., if they want a tabernacle, they can move closer to the real one). Finally, they remind them of Achan (who might have been another Reubenite[16]) and his apostasy in keeping some of the devoted things that caused a defeat in battle (Joshua 7). In other words, they compare this altar-building with many of the famous preconquest apostasies.

The Transjordanian tribes answer rather ingenuously that they had no intention of making this altar a rival to the real tabernacle, that they do not intend to offer sacrifice on it, but rather that it is meant simply as a reminder for their children, so that if ever in the future the people on the west side tell them they are not part of Israel because they are across the Jordan, this altar will be proof that they are part of Yahweh's people. They call the altar "a copy" *(tabnît)* of the central altar but one not meant for sacrifice.[17] Phinehas and the others accept this explanation and everyone is pleased. The war is called off.

This chapter has been edited by a Priestly circle: the appearance of Phinehas and the concern with a sacrificial altar attest to that; the vocabulary is often typical of P as well.[18] J. Kloppenborg has pointed out, however, several old features in this story, particularly in the way sacrifices are described, which led him to posit that there was an archaic tradition behind this story.[19] So the existence of a large altar, presumably in Gilead, that is perhaps a rival of the altar in Jerusalem seems to be an element of a tradition that helps to make up the Deuteronomist's picture of the Transjordanian tribes. The story also hints at later religious divisions between east and west and may finally serve, in fact, as a later attempt to reincorporate the eastern tribes into the fold of Yahwism.

Keeping in mind the possibility that such a process may have taken place with Balaam's story, that is, it might have been expanded at a later time to make Balaam more acceptable to an Israelite audience, there is more to be said about Joshua 22. This narrative certainly does show signs of Priestly editing, but the story in its final form could not be one the Priestly circle would be entirely happy with. Phinehas and the princes are, after all, wrong in the end. The people who were so quickly ready to go to war have to accept the explanation given them by the Reubenites and the Gadites, and that explanation is, further, not flattering to those people on the west. We can conjecture, then, that there was indeed, at some period in time, a rather large altar built in the Jordan Valley on the east side. The Transjordanian tribes were criticized for performing sacrifices at this altar, as a rival to the sacrificial cult in Jerusalem. They were told that they were not proper Yahweh worshipers and apparently that people across the Jordan were not even part of Israel. When this might have happened is difficult to say. The story itself says they are afraid it will happen "in time to come." The fact that Phinehas shows up in yet another Transjordanian apostasy scene indicates Priestly handling of this story at some time (P is notorious for not accepting Transjordan as part of the promised land[20]); it may also indicate that the oppression which the Reubenites and the Gadites felt came from a Priestly group. The effect of the story as we now have it, however, is to represent the point of view of the Transjordanian tribes over against the Priestly jumping the gun, and, to reuse a phrase from above, to integrate, or reintegrate in this case, the wayward group into the fold of Yahwist Israel. Someone has perhaps brought Transjordan back into a good light, both with this story and with the Balaam traditions in Numbers 22—24. Beth-peor, after all, was in Reuben's territory, and in Joshua 22 it is precisely to this Peor apostasy that the Priestly Phinehas compares the Transjordanian tribes' building of the altar. Even in Numbers 22—24, Balaam is operating in Gadite territory. The rehabilitation of Balaam would shed a different light on the area where his traditions were centered, especially if this centering occurred because of real, although non-Yahwistic Balaam traditions in the same part of the world, as at Deir ʿAllā.[21]

In the premonarchical stories in the Book of Judges, besides the brief notice it gets in Judges 5, Gilead[22] is an integral part of the territory that is included: Jair the Gileadite is one of the "minor judges," for instance. We are told in Judges 10 that the Israelites had worshiped other gods and that Yahweh had given them, particularly those in Gilead, into the hands of the Ammonites, whereupon Jephthah was called in by the elders of Gilead. Eventually Jephthah was victorious and went home to carry out one of the few instances of child sacrifice that is patently condoned in the Bible (Judg 11:34–40). The sacrifice of Jephthah's daughter is considered sad by the narrator, but not immoral and, interestingly, not even non-Yahwistic. It was to Yahweh, after all, that the vow was made. So two of the specific instances of child sacrifice in the Bible take place in the Transjordan area, this one and Mesha's (2 Kgs 3:27), and they are the only two that are not judged sinful by the text. We might assume from Mesha's story that Moabites did not shun child sacrifice, and we might judge from Jephthah's story that Gileadites did not necessarily shy away from it either.

CHILD SACRIFICE

Almost nowhere in the biblical text is child sacrifice condoned, although there are some ambiguous passages that are surprising. Within the covenant code, in Exod 22:28b–29, is one of the texts about dedicating the firstborn to Yahweh, and there is no hint that the firstborn son is to be treated any differently from the firstborn of animals. The P material is also ambiguous in one place about this rule, Exod 13:1–2: "Consecrate to me every firstborn, whatever opens the womb, human or animal." The rest of the P material, however, either modifies this command or else condemns child sacrifice.

The E story of the binding of Isaac in Genesis 22, although usually cited for proof of negative feelings for child sacrifice in Israel, is remarkably nonjudgmental about the process, and Abraham is blessed precisely because he was willing to offer his only son (Gen 22:16–17). This blessing should make us doubt that the story is necessarily a tract forbidding child sacrifice.

D is similar to P in that child sacrifice is condemned, but always in a context of its status as foreign worship rather than as a practice that is in itself abhorrent. Twice in Deuteronomy (Deut 12:31 and 18:9–14) the Israelites are warned not to sacrifice their children by fire, because that is what "the nations" did. The Deuteronomistic material is also similar.[23] Within Dtr, of course, there is Mesha's sacrifice of his eldest son and heir apparent in 2 Kings 3. The end of the chapter is difficult to interpret, but we can see that as a result of the sacrifice, the invasion of Moab was averted. There seems to be indicated a belief in the efficacy of such a sacrifice.

In Jeremiah 7, in the middle of other types of worship that are condemned because they are not Yahweh worship, and right after a notice of "abominations" in the Temple, there is mention of child sacrifice in the Valley of Ben-hinnom, at the high place of the tophet. The reason this practice is criticized in the text is that it is something Yahweh did not command. Of the other prophets, Micah acknowledges the possibility of child sacrifice in Mic 6:7. While he is listing the kinds of sacrifice he might make, he ends his list with the question, "Shall I give my firstborn for my trespass? the fruit of my belly for my sin?" There is no hint here that the poet is suggesting something unheard of, although its position as the final sacrifice listed clearly acknowledges this child sacrifice to be more weighty than offerings of rams and calves; still the force of the list of various possible kinds of sacrifice is to make offering the firstborn look as legitimate as the others.[24]

The Book of Ezekiel, which might be expected to resemble the P material, is similarly ambivalent. Three times child sacrifice is mentioned as a bad thing, but again because it involves worship of gods other than Yahweh. The fourth mention is intriguing. In Ezek 20:25–26, because Israel had rejected Yahweh's laws, Ezekiel says, Yahweh gave them laws that were not good and defiled Israel by having them offer all their firstborn (lit. "everything that opens the womb"), in order to devastate or horrify them. Ezekiel here is perhaps simply giving his own literal reading of such commands as those in Exodus 13 or 22, that all the firstborn, human and animal, must be given to Yahweh, but this could represent a tradition of an actual period in Israel's history, past or present, when children were sacrificed as part of Israelite worship. Alternatively, this passage might indicate simply that there was a belief in Ezekiel's time that such a period had existed in Israel's history, probably based on the

Exodus passages, whether the belief was accurate or not.[25]
ing that he places this period of time in the wilderness, that
conquest of Canaan, so that it is possible he has the Transj
mind.

Psalm 106 has a number of passages pertinent to a stuc
dan. In Ps 106:28–31, there is a report of the Baal-peor ir
combines that J story of the incident with the P version, ɛ
out above. Next in Psalm 106 we have mention of the Mɛ
and, finally for now, the notice that Israel did not destroy
they encountered but mingled with them and worship
Psalm 106:37–38 says they sacrificed their sons and dɛ
šēdîm, poured out innocent blood, and sacrificed to the i
It is not completely clear which period of time the psaln
for these last verses, since there is no mention of the co
possible again that the preconquest sojourn in Transjorda
the verses that treat the Baal-peor incident.

ŠADDAY

There is one further line of argument to be put into tl
point. Several scholars have suggested that the word šēɪ
and Deut 32:17, rather than being borrowed from Akkɛ
is the etymology usually given, actually reflects the god
ʿAllā.[26] In an older orthography, the yōd that is now tɛ
in the plural ending would have been consonantal.
argument makes sense. Deuteronomy 32:16–17, in pɛ
such a meaning: "They made him [Yahweh] jealous
[reading with the Targum] and with abominable prɛ
ficed to the šdym, not Eloah, gods they had never kr
who had come in of late." For the šdym word, we woulɪ
that indicates a group of full-fledged deities, not mɪ
106:37–39 gives us an idea of just what the "abɪ
might have been to which Deut 32:16 refers: "They ɪ
and their daughters to the šdym, they poured out i
blood of their sons and daughters, whom they sacri
Canaan. The land was defiled with blood; they becɑ
they did, and prostituted themselves by their actions

COMBINATION OF BIBLICAL MATE
WITH DEIR ʿALLĀ

Finally, we need to combine what we can glean fron
we know to have been happening in the eastern Joɪ
inscription found at Deir ʿAllā was written. We kno

133

there are connections among the following: Balaam; Moab and Midian; Transjordan (Reuben and Gad); a sacrificial cult, in Reuben's territory, with sacrifices to the dead (according to Psalm 106); a large (probably sacrificial) altar, probably in Gilead; the epithet Šadday; a tradition of apostasy and rebellion, laid on Reuben, especially, but also Gad and even Manasseh; a tradition of sad but unquestioned child sacrifice, if we can interpret Jephthah and Mesha that way. The Deir ʿAllā material is related to this complex by the mention of Balaam, the *šdyn,* and perhaps because the inscription tells of a sacrificial cult, even child sacrifice, all in a Transjordanian location.

Furthermore, according to the biblical polemic, child sacrifice was said to go on now and then, performed by a couple of kings of Judah,[27] done in the Valley of Ben-hinnom,[28] and as one of the sins responsible for the Northern Kingdom's defeat by the Assyrians.[29] And if the *šēdîm* passages in Psalm 106 and Deuteronomy 32 have been correctly reread, there was a tradition that in the preconquest wandering, in the Transjordanian area, Israelites participated in a cult of Šadday gods, which included child sacrifice. Reuben and Gad might then have been looked down on because of their location in this part of the world (and perhaps because of their participation in such rites, if that is the import of Joshua 22), in a place where child sacrifice seems to have been done without the connotations of horror that we would expect, and is even reported that way by the biblical authors.

In the end, we have the following: the name Šadday connected to Balaam in Deir ʿAllā and in the Bible; that same name perhaps connected to child sacrifice at Deir ʿAllā and in Psalm 106; some evidence of a sacrificial cult, both at Deir ʿAllā and somewhere else in Transjordan, wherever Joshua 22 is meant to take place; a connection between Balaam and El in Numbers 24 and perhaps at Deir ʿAllā (the interpretation of ʾl as in I, 2, and II, 6, is not at all certain); and the refusal of the P source to take the Transjordan seriously as a part of Israel, although it is possible that someone has made an effort to smooth over some of those negative reports. (A rival cult may imply a rival priesthood, and such would not, of course, have been well received by the Jerusalem priesthood.) The information we now have that we did not have twenty years ago is that at least one such cult did exist (and we may find similar sites, of course, in future excavations). We need, therefore, to begin to make the effort to reevaluate our sources for this part of the world, and hope to make a synthesis of the old and familiar with the new and exciting.

NOTES

. The *editio princeps* is J. Hoftijzer and G. van der Kooij, *Aramaic Texts from Deir ʿAlla* (Leiden: E. J. Brill, 1976).

2. H. J. Franken and M. Ibrahim, "Two Seasons of Excavations at Tell Deir ʿAlla, 1976–1978," *ADAJ* 22 (1977–78) 65–68.

3. Hoftijzer and van der Kooij, *Aramaic Texts*, 8–10.

4. J. A. Hackett, *The Balaam Text from Deir ʿAllā* (HSM 31; Chico, Calif: Scholars Press, 1984) 9–19 (with pertinent bibliography in the footnotes).

5. Ibid., 109–24; see also J. A. Hackett, "The Dialect of the Plaster Text from Tell Deir ʿAlla," *Or* 53 (1984) 57–65.

6. P. Kyle McCarter, "The Balaam Texts from Deir ʿAllā: The First Combination," *BASOR* 239 (1980) 57–59.

7. *q* in the Deir ʿAllā plaster text can represent $*\delta > \ṣ$ in Hebrew.

8. E.g., *KAI*, 162.2 and 163.3.

9. J refers to what happened as "Israel's yoking itself to Baal-peor." P simply calls it "(the matter of) Peor." In J, Moses tells his judges to kill all the men who have yoked themselves. In P, only the man and the woman are killed directly, and several thousand others die because of a plague, not necessarily because they participated in "(the matter of) Peor." So when Deuteronomy 4 refers to what Yahweh did at Baal-peor, destroying all the men who followed Baal-peor, it is a reference to the J story, and we would not expect a mention of Balaam here. It is P who attaches Balaam to Peor.

10. See J. S. Kloppenborg, "Joshua 22: The Priestly Editing of an Ancient Tradition," *Bib* 62 (1981) 347–71. Note that the aggrandizing of Phinehas in Numbers 25, part of the anti-Midianite propaganda there (see Cross, *CMHE*, 202–3), is continued in Joshua 22 by making Phinehas again the hero in a story of Transjordanian apostasy.

11. Mic. 6:5 is part of the "mighty acts" section of the *rîb* at the beginning of Micah 6. It says, "Remember what Balak advised and what Balaam son of Beor answered him," as if approving of Balaam's answer, although here too, since the text is listing the saving acts of Yahweh for Israel, Balaam's answer is presumably perceived as an act of Yahweh rather than of Balaam. We do not know, then, whether the tradition Micah is using reported that Balaam ever tried to curse Israel.

12. Particularly suggestive in this light is the repeated Deuteronomic phrase in the assertion that Balaam can speak only what Yahweh puts into his mouth (cf. Deut 18:18), pointed out to me by R. Wilson.

13. For a good recent treatment, see J. R. Baskin, *Pharaoh's Counsellors: Job, Jethro, and Balaam in Rabbinic and Patristic Tradition* (Chico, Calif.: Scholars Press, 1983).

14. Philo, *Life of Moses* 1. 264–65.

15. See Gen 35:22a; 49:4; and 1 Chr 5:1—Reuben's reported trespass with Bilhah, his father's concubine; Numbers 16—Korah's rebellion (P), including the (J) episode of Dathan and Abiram, Reubenites (see also Num 26:9–10 and Ps 106:16–18). Particularly the tribe of Reuben fascinates people, because it seems to disappear. The 4QSam[a] material has added fuel to the fire. See F. M. Cross, "The Ammonite Oppression of the Tribes of Gad and Reuben: Missing Verses from 1 Samuel 11 Found in 4QSamuel[a]," *History, Historiography and Interpretation: Studies in Biblical and Cuneiform Literatures* (ed. H. Tadmor and M. Weinfeld; Jerusalem: Magnes Press, 1983) 148–58; A. Rofé, "The Acts of

Nahash According to 4QSam[a]," *IEJ* 32 (1982) 129–33. For an exciting recent discussion of Reuben and bibliography of the issues, see B. Halpern, *The Emergence of Israel in Canaan* (Chico, Calif.: Scholars Press, 1983) esp. 117–33.

16. In Josh 7:1, Achan is "son of Carmi, son of Zabdi, son of Zerah, of the tribe of Judah" (cf. 1 Chr 2:7; 4:1), but in Gen 46:9; Exod 6:14; Num 26:6; and 1 Chr 5:3, Carmi is a Reubenite. If these were meant to be the same character, there was presumably either some confusion in the Reuben and Judah genealogies or some mixture in tribal backgrounds.

17. "A contradiction in terms," according to Kloppenborg ("Priestly Editing," p. 366 and n. 60).

18. Ibid., 355–62.

19. Ibid., 362–71.

20. See, e.g., Num 32:7; 33:53; or even Gen 17:8.

21. I should point out here that Kloppenborg ("Priestly Editing") comes to almost the opposite conclusion in his article on Joshua 22. He says there is no resolution for Transjordan. That land is still unclean, and they still must go to the west to sacrifice legally (p. 355). Yet, as I read Joshua 22, the Transjordanian tribes have won their point in the end. Perhaps by the time this story is told in the form in which we have it, the large altar really was no longer being used, and the purpose of the narrative, as I have suggested, was to enforce the point of view that the Transjordanian Israelites were, in spite of the Priestly outlook, very much a part of Israel.

22. The names Gad and Gilead often interchange in our sources, and I have simply treated them together in this section, although realizing that they are not technically the same.

23. See the Dtr passages in nn. 27–29, below.

24. Hosea has an interesting passage in chap. 9 that is not clearly child sacrifice but may be related. After a mention of Baal-peor in Hos 9:10, the prophet says that Israel (called Ephraim here) will not reproduce, but even if they do raise children, Yahweh will take them. Hosea 9:13 says that their children will be led to the slaughterer *(hōrēg)*. The sense of this curse on Ephraim is precisely the opposite of the abundant blessings of fertility that Joseph (Ephraim and Manasseh) receives in Genesis 49, particularly v 25.

25. See M. Greenberg's treatment of these verses in *Ezekiel 1—20* (AB 22; Garden City, N.Y.: Doubleday & Co., 1983) 368–70.

26. See my discussion in *The Balaam Text,* 85–89.

27. Ahaz in 2 Kgs 16:3 and 2 Chr 28:3; Manasseh in 2 Kgs 21:6 and 2 Chr 33:6.

28. 2 Kgs 23:10; Jer 7:31; 19:1–6; 32:35; the 2 Chronicles passages cited in n. 27, above.

29. 2 Kgs 17:17.

10

Aspects of the Religion of
the Israelite Monarchy:
Biblical and Epigraphic Data

P. KYLE McCARTER, JR.

SOURCES

The Bible. When we attempt to reconstruct the religion of Israel before the destruction of Solomon's Temple, we find ourselves in a predicament. Our primary source—and almost our only source—is the Bible. It is the consensus of modern scholarship that the Hebrew Bible as we know it came into existence in the centuries following the Babylonian destruction of Jerusalem amid the crises provoked by that disaster. The present form of its various parts is the work of writers living at the time of the exile and later, and as such it is subject to many limitations as a source for the reconstruction of the religion of the earlier period.

This predicament is not ameliorated by the probability that the Bible, though a product of the exile and later periods in its present form, contains substantial preexilic material, as most scholars continue to believe. That is, there are earlier documents embedded in the present editorial framework, source materials that can be reconstructed by critical methods. Even if we attribute a high degree of credibility to the information gleaned from such materials, however, the problem of completeness remains. Early purity laws and religious regulations, for example, abound in the Bible, but it is difficult to be sure how much of the Israelite religious life can be reconstructed from them. Of the competing parties in preexilic Yahwism only one was vindicated by history, and its thought is preserved in the Bible. But the biblical writers themselves indicate that the branch of preexilic religion they are embracing was a dissenting viewpoint during much of the Israelite monarchy. It was championed by the prophetic party but excluded from the official circles of the court and Temple except during the reigns of a few kings whom the writers regard as reformers. Thus it remains the case that the Bible is a direct source for only part of the religion of the earlier period with which it is concerned.

Most often the religion supported by those in power in Jerusalem and Samaria was a kind of Yahwism different from that represented by the Bible, and it seems impossible to determine the full character of this religion on the basis of the study of the Bible alone. References to its beliefs and practices appear most of the time in prophetic or Deuteronomistic writings and thus in wholly unsympathetic contexts. And while the prophetic and Deuteronomistic writers may go on at great length about the wickedness of the religious practices they condemn, they tend to be laconic in their descriptions of those practices, relying (as they could) on their audience's familiarity with them.

There is little hope, therefore, of recovering the full diversity of the religion of the monarchy from the Bible, and our other resources are very limited. There have been no discoveries of Iron Age manuscripts on the scale of Ras Shamra or Qumran. If we want to write the history of preexilic Yahwism, therefore, we must be satisfied with filling out the biblical references to hostile religious parties on the basis of information drawn, first, from analogic comparison with what data we possess about other religious traditions and, second, from study of the small corpus of surviving First Temple inscriptions.

The Kuntillet 'Ajrud Inscriptions. For these reasons the discovery of Iron Age Hebrew texts at Kuntillet 'Ajrud, though hardly a major manuscript find, is of great importance to the study of preexilic Yahwism. This small site in the Sinai has yielded a number of inscriptions from the time of the monarchy, and their content is substantially religious.

'Ajrud is a small, isolated hill *(kuntillet)* situated near a fresh-water spring alongside the main artery from Gaza to Elath. It was excavated by Z. Meshel for the Tel Aviv Institute of Archaeology, beginning in 1976.[1] Initial pottery samples indicated that the site was exclusively Iron II— that is, it was occupied only during the time of the Israelite and Judean monarchies—and that, more specifically, it contained the remains of the two buildings dating to the eighth century B.C.E. Excavation showed that one of these buildings had eroded away almost completely. The other was a small two-story structure. On the plastered walls of an entry room, Meshel found inscriptions written with ink in Phoenician script. In a side chamber he found a number of large storage jars, or pithoi, decorated with ink drawings and writings in Hebrew script.

On the basis of paleography and an internal analysis of the texts, I would assign the Kuntillet 'Ajrud materials to the beginning of the eighth century B.C.E. and probably to the reign of Jehoash of Israel (ca. 801–786). The political situation was presumably that which prevailed after the events described in 2 Kings 14, according to which Amaziah of Judah conducted a successful campaign against Edom (v 7) shortly before his own defeat at the hands of Jehoash of Israel (vv 8–16). So at this time, roughly 790 B.C.E., the Northern Kingdom held sway over Judah and territories to the south. Edom itself seems to have remained independent,[2] but the desert west of Edom, where Kuntillet ʿAjrud was located, was probably controlled by Israel until about a decade later, when Azariah reasserted Judean authority in the region (2 Kgs 14:22).

The plaster texts are poorly preserved, and the entire corpus is fraught with interpretive difficulties. Nevertheless, because they preserve articulate records from the time of the monarchy, the ʿAjrud materials are of special importance for the reconstruction of preexilic Yahwism in all its diversity. The religion represented at the site is the religion to which the prophets objected, and it is the religion the reforms of Hezekiah and Josiah were intended, at least in part, to eliminate. In short, the inscriptions from Kuntillet ʿAjrud provide a window on some forgotten aspects of the religion of the monarchy.

I want to turn now to two of these aspects, selected from the many we might discuss. One is the localization of Yahweh. The other is Yahweh's asherah, its identity and significance. Both issues arise from consideration of the blessing formula used at ʿAjrud.

THE LOCAL CULTS OF YAHWEH

At Kuntillet ʿAjrud the divine name "Yahweh" occurs only in blessing formulas. With a single exception,[3] the form is not *yhwh* alone but *yhwh GN* ("Yahweh of GN"), where GN is a geographical name. Specifically, we find *yhwh šmrn* ("Yahweh of Samaria") and *yhwh tmn/tymn*[4] ("Yahweh of Teman"). Because in Biblical Hebrew a proper noun cannot stand in this kind of genitive relationship,[5] it has been suggested that *yhwh šmrn* should be read *yahweh šōměěrēnû* ("Yahweh, our guardian"), an interpretation that is unlikely from an orthographic viewpoint.[6] The reading *yhwh tmn/tymn* (unambiguously "Yahweh of Teman"), however, confirms the interpretation of *yhwh šmrn* as *yahweh šōměrōn* ("Yahweh of Samaria").[7] This departure from the grammar of Biblical Hebrew[8] is not surprising in the light of the presence of the same construction in other Semitic languages (see below).

These are local forms or manifestations of the national god. Because "Samaria" designated both a region and a city, "Yahweh of Samaria" might refer to Yahweh as he was worshiped in the region of Samaria or, more particularly, in the capital city of the Northern Kingdom. "Teman," however, seems always to have been a region designation.[9] In the Bible it refers to Edom or a part of Edom (Amos 1:12 [cf. 2:2]; Jer 49:7, 20; Ezek 25:13; Obadiah 9) or, perhaps more generally, to the region of Mt.

Paran, west of Edom (Hab 3:3). "Yahweh of Teman," therefore, must be Yahweh as he was worshiped in the region of Teman. This does not exclude the possibility, however, that there was a particular shrine where the Temanite Yahweh's cult was located.

As explained above, the desert region in which Kuntillet 'Ajrud is situated was probably controlled by the Northern Kingdom at the time the inscriptions were deposited. This accounts for the invocation of the Samarian Yahweh at the site. Israelites traveling from or sending messages from Samaria called upon their own god to bless other travelers or residents of 'Ajrud. The Temanite Yahweh, too, may have been the deity of a group of visitors to the site, perhaps of those who arrived from farther south. Alternatively, he may have been the local Yahweh of the region of which 'Ajrud itself was a part; in this case, this larger region must have been called "Teman" at the time.

The Divine Name Type "DN of GN." The names "Yahweh of Samaria" and "Yahweh of Teman" belong to a type well attested in non-Israelite divine names. These names take the form *DN GN,* where *DN* is the name of the national god or another major deity and *GN* is the name of a locality where *DN* was worshiped. The resulting combination, a construct chain meaning "DN of GN," identifies a local manifestation of the deity, that is, DN as worshiped in GN. In the archaic Aramaic inscription from Tell Fakhariyah (Fekherye),[10] for example, we find the divine name *hdd skn* ("Hadad of Sikan") where "Hadad" is the well-known Aramean god and "Sikan" is the name of a district in the Aramean state of Gozan in the Khabur Valley. In one sense, then, Hadad of Sikan is strictly a local deity, who, elsewhere in the inscription (lines 15–16), is called *hdd yšb skn* ("Hadad who dwells in Sikan"). At the same time, however, he is unambiguously the great cosmic Hadad "who gives pasture and watersources to all lands" (lines 2–3). Other examples of the type *DN GN* in Northwest Semitic inscriptions include the Ugaritic allusion to *'atrt ṣrm* ("Asherah of Tyre") (*CTA* 14[= *UT* KRT].4.201) and the reference to a temple of *'štrt kt* ("Ashtart of Kition") in a fifth-century Phoenician tariff from Cyprus (*KAI*, 37[= *CIS* 86] A.5).

In Biblical Hebrew the expression *DN b-GN* ("DN-in-GN") seems to be equivalent to *DN GN* at 'Ajrud.[11] In 2 Sam 15:7, for example, the divine name *yahweh běhebrôn* ("Yahweh-in-Hebron") is mentioned in the context of Absalom's temporary reconciliation with David. After four years of house arrest, he asks permission to go to Hebron, explaining the request as follows (vv 7–8): "Let me go fulfill the vow I made to Yahweh-in-Hebron *(yhwh bḥbrwn)*, for your servant made a vow when I was living in Aram-geshur, as follows: 'If Yahweh will bring me back to

Jerusalem, I shall serve Yahweh[12]!' " The "in Hebron" cannot be taken as a modifier of "I made," because the vow was made in Geshur, and it is most awkward as a modifier of "Let me go." Clearly, then, it is a modifier of "Yahweh." Although Yahweh is worshiped in Jerusalem, Absalom has to go to Hebron to fulfill his vow, because it was to the Hebronite Yahweh *(yhwh bḥbrwn)* that the vow was made.

Other likely occurrences of this construction are found in Ps 99:2,[13] where we read *yhwh bṣywn gdwl wrm hw' 'l kl 'lhym*[14] ("Yahweh-in-Zion is great! And he is exalted above all other gods!"), and in 1 Sam 5:5, where there is a reference to the Philistine god *dgwn b'šdd* ("Dagon-in-Ashdod").[15] It occurs outside the Bible in the name of a Phoenician-Carthaginian goddess called *tnt blbnn* ("Tannit-in-Lebanon")[16] and that of a Phoenician goddess on an Ammonite seal, *'št⟨rt⟩ bṣd[?]n* ("Ashtart-in-Sidon").[17]

It may prove useful to speculate on the factors that gave rise to the divine type "DN of GN" in Israel. In the era before our sources become articulate, there probably were desert centers where Yahweh was worshiped locally. These were left behind when the worshipers entered Canaan, although a few of the local manifestations may have been remembered, and the Yahweh of Teman may have been one of these. The desert shrines were replaced by new centers, some of which eventually grew to prominence. With the establishment of Yahwism in Palestine, moreover, many local deities must have been identified with the new national god. Baal-perazim *(ba'al pĕrāṣîm)* of 2 Sam 5:20, for example, seems to preserve the memory of a locally worshiped god, "the lord of [Mt.] Perazim," who was subsequently identified with Yahweh. The local shrines, then, arose in at least three ways: (1) the recollection of an ancient center of Yahweh worship in the desert, (2) the establishment of a new center in Palestine, and (3) the adoption of a Canaanite shrine where another god was previously honored. In all of these places Yahweh was invoked, but he must have been thought of and worshiped quite differently in shrines of such diverse origin. The cult of the Temanite Yahweh (category 1), for example, may have preserved archaic liturgical forms and religious concepts, while that of the Samarian Yahweh (category 2) reflected the contemporary liturgy and theology of the national god. At the usurped Canaanite shrines (category 3), pre-Yahwistic practices and ideas are likely to have survived in adapted form.

The Autonomy of Local Manifestations. At the time of the Israelite monarchy, therefore, the various local manifestations of Yahweh were often quite distinct in the manner of their conceptualization and worship. It is not surprising, then, to discover that there was a tendency (illus-

trated by the example of 2 Sam 15:7 cited above) for the local Yahwehs
to become semi-independent, almost as if they were distinct deities.

Such a development has good parallels elsewhere in the ancient Near
East, as we can illustrate by a further example of the "DN of GN"
phenomenon from non-Israelite sources. In Assyria two of the principal
centers of the cult of the goddess Ishtar were Nineveh and Arbela. Ishtar,
as worshiped in these two places, was called $^dI\check{s}tar\ \check{s}a\ ^{uru}Ninua$ ("Ishtar of
Nineveh") and $^dI\check{s}tar\ \check{s}a\ ^{uru}Arbela$ ("Ishtar of Arbela").[18] That these two
Ishtars were thought of as semi-independent goddesses is shown by the
fact that both were included in the conventional list of deities invoked as
witnesses to Neo-Assyrian treaties.[19] Simply to invoke "Ishtar," in other
words, was not regarded as sufficient.

The Reforms of Hezekiah and Josiah. With regard to the evolution of
Yahwism, one of the most important results of the religious reforms of
Iron II Judah was the elimination of the local manifestations of Yahweh,
an inevitable consequence of the removal of the local shrines and the
centralization of worship in Jerusalem. This is not to say that a purge of
the various local Yahwehs was the *purpose* of the reforms, as if Hezekiah
and Josiah recognized the tendency of the local manifestations to acquire
autonomous status and sought to check the trend. There is nothing in our
sources to suggest this. The purpose of the reforms—or one of their
several purposes—was to confine the sacrificial cult to Jerusalem. Nevertheless, the elimination of the other shrines put an end to the veneration
of the various local Yahwehs. In consequence, Yahwism was both sim-
plified and standardized in a manner inconceivable in the ninth century,
when the Israelite god was worshiped under a variety of forms and in a
variety of places.

Deuteronomy 6:4 can be cited in this context: *šěmaʿ yiśrāʾēl yhwh
ʾĕlōhênû yhwh ʾeḥad,* which might be rendered, "Hear, O Israel! Yahweh,
our god, is one Yahweh!" as if it were a polemic against the practice of
worshiping local manifestations.[20] In fact, however, the context shows
clearly that the concern of this verse is not with the unity of Yahweh
himself or even the centralization of his worship.[21] The subject is the
exclusiveness of his worship, as Deut 6:5 shows: "You shall love Yahweh,
your god, with all your heart and with all your soul and with all your
might." Israel has one god, and he is a "jealous god" (Deut 6:15),
unwilling to share his worship with other gods. Thus the worshiper must
respond to him with one heart, that is, with a wholeness of dedication.
Similarly, in Deuteronomy 12, where the centralization of worship is
called for, there is no suggestion that local shrines are to be eschewed
because they promote a disunified concept of Yahweh. The Israelite god is

to be worshiped in only one place because he so chooses. Again the operative theological principle is probably the sacral integrity of Yahweh. His oneness requires a unity of worship.

So again, there is nothing to suggest that the reforming kings viewed the existence of local shrines as a threat to the concept of the unity of Yahweh. They must have understood the several Yahwehs to be exactly what they were, namely, local forms of the national god. Still, we can see that their policies, by unifying the worship of Yahweh, had the effect of unifying the way in which he was conceived by the worshipers, thus eliminating the earlier theology of local manifestations.

YAHWEH'S ASHERAH

In the Kuntillet 'Ajrud blessing formulas, the localized divine name is followed in every instance by *wl'šrth* ("and to his/its asherah"). What we actually have, then, is *brk PN lyhwh GN wl'šrth* ("Blessed be PN to Yahweh of GN and to his/its asherah"), in which GN is either *šmrn* ("Samaria") or *tmn/tymn* ("Teman"). A similar formula may occur in the inscription from Cave II at Khirbet el-Qom,[22] the pertinent part of which seems to read *brk 'ryh lyhwh w . . . l' šrth* ("Blessed be Uriah to Yahweh and . . . to his asherah!").[23]

Who or what is the asherah invoked alongside Yahweh in these texts? Asherah was the name of a prominent goddess mentioned in Canaanite texts, such as the Ugaritic tablets, where she is the consort of the god El. A goddess Asherah also seems to be referred to in the Bible. One of the 'Ajrud blessings that mentions Yahweh and his asherah is adjacent to a drawing of two standing figures and, nearby, a seated figure playing a lyre.[24] It has been suggested that one or another of these drawings represents Yahweh's asherah and that the reference, therefore, is to Yahweh's consort.[25] Other scholars, however, have pointed out that "asherah" cannot be a proper noun in these texts, because it is modified by a possessive suffix: To say "his Asherah"—Asherah being a personal name—would violate a fundamental rule of Hebrew grammar.[26] In the Bible, moreover, "asherah" most often refers to an object of the cult, not a goddess. It was something that could be planted and chopped down—thus a wooden object, possibly a simple pole, possibly even a sacred tree. It is associated with the altar and the *maṣṣēbâ*, or "(sacred stone) pillar," as part of the standard paraphernalia of a *bāmâ*, or "high place," one of the local places of worship condemned by the prophets and the reformers. It might seem to follow from this that Yahweh's asherah at 'Ajrud is a cultic object, not a goddess.

Both of these opinions about Yahweh's asherah at 'Ajrud—that she is a goddess, that it is a wooden cult object—have already been expressed in advance of the publication of the texts. They are preliminary reactions, but each has sound reasoning behind it. We are faced with a dilemma, which cannot be resolved without reflection on the significance of the asherah as part of the Israelite cult and the relation of the object asherah to the goddess Asherah.

The Canaanite Goddess. Although there seems to be a goddess Asherah mentioned in the Bible, the existence of such a deity was doubted by many scholars[27] until confirmed by the discovery of the Ras Shamra tablets.[28] In the Ugaritic literature, where she is called *rbt 'aṭrt ym* ("Lady Asherah of the Sea"), she is the consort of El and the mother of the gods. She is described as *qnyt 'ilm* ("Creatress of the gods"),[29] who are known as *bn 'aṭrt* ("the sons of Asherah").[30] Other Late Bronze evidence for the worship of Asherah in Syria-Palestine includes (1) a reference in a fifteenth-century letter from Taanach to a certain *u-ma-an* ^{d}*A-ši-rat* ("skilled man of Asherah"), presumably a soothsayer,[31] (2) the theophorous element in Abdi-Ashirta, the name of a fourteenth-century prince of Amurra mentioned in the Amarna archive,[32] and (3) the role of the goddess Ashertu in a Canaanite myth recorded in a Hittite text from Boghazköy.[33] There is no clear attestation of a goddess Asherah in Canaanite (Phoenician and Punic) texts from the Iron Age.[34]

There are several possible or certain references in the Bible to a goddess Asherah. In 1 Kgs 15:1 (= 1 Chron 15:16) we are told that Asa removed Maacah his mother from the position of queen mother because "she made a horrible thing [i.e., an idol] for Asherah."[35] In the account of the contest between Elijah and the prophets of Baal on Mt. Carmel in 1 Kings 18 there is a reference (v 19) to "four hundred prophets of Asherah."[36] Manasseh is censured in 2 Kgs 21:7 because "he placed the image of Asherah . . . in the Temple," whereas Josiah, according to 2 Kgs 23:4, had "all the paraphernalia made for Baal and Asherah and all the Host of Heaven" taken out of the Temple and burned and, according to 2 Kgs 23:7, "tore apart the *woven garments* [?] of the holy men ["male cult prostitutes"] that were in the Temple of Yahweh where the women weaved *woven garments* [?] for Asherah."[37] In Judg 3:7 and 1 Sam 7:3 (LXX), *hā'ăšērôt* ("the Asherahs") is used alongside *habbě'ālîm* ("the Baals") as a generic term for foreign goddesses.[38]

The Cult Object. Most often in the Bible, however, *'ăšērâ* refers not to a goddess but to a cultic object or installation of some kind. It is a common noun with both *-îm* and, more rarely, *-ôt* plural forms. Along with the *maṣṣěbâ*, the asherah was associated with a shrine or temple, but its exact nature is difficult to determine. It is mentioned most often in Deuteronomistic passages, where it is an illicit cultic object installed or used by some kings, who are condemned, and destroyed by others, who are praised. Thus, for example, we are told in 1 Kgs 16:33 that Ahab, who also built "an altar to Baal" and "a temple of Baal" (v 32), made "the [?] asherah." During the reign of Jehoahaz, then, "the asherah remained in Samaria" (2 Kgs 13:16). By contrast, Hezekiah "removed the high places and shattered the pillars and cut down the asherah,"[39] according to 2 Kgs 18:14. But again, Manasseh "rebuilt the high places that his father Hezekiah had destroyed and erected altars to Baal and made an asherah,[40] as Ahab king of Israel had done" (2 Kgs 21:3).[41]

More generally, the Deuteronomistic polemic against the asherah echoes the warning against the religion of the Canaanites in Exod 34:13: "Their altars you shall demolish, their pillars you shall shatter, and their asherahs you shall cut down." Thus we read in Deut 7:5: "Their altars you shall demolish, their pillars you shall shatter, their asherahs you shall hew to pieces, and their idols you shall burn with fire" (cf. Deut 12:3). In 1 Kgs 14:15 the house of Jeroboam is threatened with exile "because they made their asherahs, provoking Yahweh," and in 1 Kgs 14:23 it is said of Rehoboam and Judah that "they, too, built high places and pillars and asherahs for themselves on every raised hill and under every green tree" (cf. Jer 17:2). Then in the Deuteronomistic retrospect at the time of the fall of Samaria we are reminded (2 Kgs 17:10) that Israel "built pillars and asherahs for themselves on every raised hill and under every green tree." But again, Josiah "smashed the pillars and cut down the asherahs and filled their place with human bones" (2 Kgs 23:14).

In Akkadian the primary meaning of the word *aširtu* is "sanctuary," "temple,"[42] a fact that raises the possibility that the Israelite-Canaanite asherah might also be a sanctuary, and there is evidence from non-Israelite sources that, taken by itself, could be interpreted in this way.[43] A third-century Phoenician text from Ma'ṣub, for example, contains the dedication *l'štrt b'šrt b'l ḥmn* ("to Ashtart in the asherah of Baal Hammon").[44] A Phoenician inscription of the early Persian period from Acco, published by M. Dothan,[45] records a tariff of goods deposited with a certain Ben-hodesh by a certain Baalsha[']alti, "who is over the asherah" *('š 'l 'šrt)*. Comparison with Hebrew titles[46] shows that Baalsha'alti was the officer in charge of the asherah at Acco. On the basis of this evidence alone it would be reasonable to conclude that the asherahs at Ma'ṣub and Acco were sanctuaries of some kind.[47]

The biblical references, however, though they do not reveal its precise character, show that the asherah was not the shrine or sanctuary itself but rather an object that constituted a part of the shrine.[48] Note in particular the way the asherah is associated with the *maṣṣēbâ* in the passages cited above and, elsewhere, with other cultic paraphernalia, such as images (Deut 7:5; etc.) or incense altars (Isa 27:9; etc.). Gideon's father's asherah, for example, was beside the altar of Baal (Judg 6:25, 28, 30), and, similarly, the asherah forbidden in Deut 16:21 would be "beside the altar of Yahweh." Apparently, then, an asherah stood beside the altar and was somehow associated with a *maṣṣēbâ*. Together these were constituent parts of a shrine or place of worship, whether a high place (Deut 18:14; etc.) or a temple (1 Kgs 16:33; etc.).

The nature of the asherah is further hinted at by the language used of its installation and destruction: It was "planted" (Deut 16:21) and then "stood upright" (2 Kgs 13:6; Isa 27:9) until "uprooted" (Mic 5:13), "cut down" (Exod 34:13; Judg 6:25–26, 28, 30; 2 Kgs 18:4; 23:14), "hewn to pieces" (Deut 7:5), or "burned" (2 Kgs 23:4, 6, 15; 1 Chron 19:3). Thus it was clearly a wooden object. In Judg 6:25, for example (cf. Judg 6:28, 30), Gideon is instructed to destroy his father's altar of Baal and "cut down the asherah that is beside it"; then (Judg 6:26) he is told to prepare a whole burnt offering to Yahweh "with the wood of the asherah you cut down." Compare Deut 16:21: "You shall not plant for yourself an asherah, any wooden thing,[49] beside the altar of Yahweh your god that you made for yourself."

In view of this information, therefore, it is not surprising that the traditional understanding of the asherah, as reflected in the Septuagint's translation *alsos*, has been that it was a sacred grove, or at least a single tree.[50] Against this view, passages suggesting that the asherah was made by human hands (1 Kgs 14:15; 16:33; 2 Kgs 17:16; 21:3)[51] have been urged by scholars who believe it was a simple wooden staff or pole,[52] or even a carved image of a goddess.[53] But if we grant the probability of this interpretation—namely, that the asherah was an upright wooden pole standing beside the altar in a temple or shrine—we will have learned nothing about its purpose or cultic function. Nor will we have any basis for explaining its apparent connection with the goddess Asherah, unless we suppose that the asherah was carved into a shape resembling the goddess. Two questions, then, must be asked. First, what was the purpose of the asherah? Second, what was its connection with the goddess?

The Personification of Yahweh's Asherah. Let us now return to the Kuntillet ʿAjrud texts. As we have noted, the formula of blessing found repeatedly there is addressed "to Yahweh of GN and his [54] asherah." In one case, where the appeal is specifically *lyhwh šmrn wlʾšrth* ("to Yahweh of Samaria and his asherah"), it is accompanied by or accidentally associated with a drawing of two standing figures with arms akimbo. The taller figure has a human torso, a bovine face with large horns, bovine hooves, and a tail hanging behind a short skirt.[55] The shorter figure is similarly human-bovine in form but also has schematically represented (human) female breasts; she stands to the left of and slightly behind the other figure in the traditional consort position in Egyptian art.[56] There can be little doubt that the two figures, with their combination of human and animal features, represent divine beings, a god and a goddess. The god is probably Yahweh, depicted with some of the features of a bull; he is, therefore, the "young bull of Samaria" (*'ēgel šōmrôn*) of Hos 8:6. The goddess, then, is Yahweh's consort.

At Kuntillet ʿAjrud, therefore, we have Yahweh depicted in the company of his consort, and we have him invoked along with his asherah. It seems to follow that Yahweh's asherah is his consort. There is no evidence, however, to suggest that the word *ʾăšērâ* could mean "consort," and, as we have noted, it is unlikely to be a name ("Asherah") in this context. Rather, in accordance with our earlier discussion, the asherah of the Yahweh of Samaria ought to be a wooden cult object associated with the worship of Yahweh in that city. We seem to have a case, therefore, of the personification of a cult object as a goddess.

The phenomenon of the personification and worship of the temple precinct and its various aspects is well attested in the ancient Near East. The best-known example is that of the Aramaic god **bayt-ʾēl* ("Bethel") worshiped in Mesopotamia and, according to Jer 48:13, in Israel.[57] This god arose from the personification of the temple (Heb. *bêt-ʾēl*) itself. Among the Jews of the Elephantine colony of the fifth century B.C.E., Bethel was worshiped alongside Yahweh—or, as they called him, Yahu—and several other deities are mentioned in the papyri. As first recognized by W. F. Albright,[58] these deities are not to be thought of as foreign gods adopted into "a polytheistic Jewish pantheon." Bethel is simply a surrogate for Yahweh,[59] and the others are hypostases. That is, they are abstract aspects of Yahweh—his sacredness, his cultically available presence, etc.—given substance (hypostasis), personified, and worshiped as semi-independent deities. They include *ḥrmbytʾl* ("the Sacredness of the Temple"), *ʾšmbytʾl* ("the Name [i.e., cultically available presence] of the Temple"), and *ʿntbytʾl* ("the Sign [of the active presence] of the Temple"). The god Herem-bethel, therefore, arose by hypostasis of the sacredness of the temple precinct. The deities Eshem-bethel and Anath-bethel are hypostases of the "name" and "sign" of Yahweh, that is, his cultically available presence in the temple. The latter also occurs in the form *ʿntyhw* ("Anath-Yahu"),[60] a name that is especially instructive for our investigation of the meaning of Yahweh's asherah.

The Divine Type "Presence of DN." Because goddesses called Asherah and Anath are known from Northwest Semitic sources, the expression *'ăšērat yahweh* ("the asherah of Yahweh"), implied by *'ăšērātô* ("his asherah") in the Kuntillet ʿAjrud texts, is precisely analogous to *ʿănat yāhû* ("the anath of Yahu") in the Elephantine papyri. We have interpreted *ʿănat yāhû* as a hypostatic form of Yahweh meaning "Sign [of the active presence] of Yahu."[61] How are we to understand it in relation to the goddess Anath, known from Ugarit and elsewhere?

It may be helpful at this point to call attention to a common pattern in Northwest Semitic religion whereby an abstract aspect of a god (a *male* deity) is hypostatized, personified, and worshiped as a goddess, who may then be thought of as the consort of the god. We can be even more specific: The abstract aspect of the god that is hypostatized is his cultically available presence. It may be called his "presence" or "face" *(pānīm)*, his "name" *(šēm* or *ʿēšem)*, his "sign" *(ʿānāt)*, and so on. There was, for example, a Punic goddess *pānē baʿl* ("the Presence of Baal)" identified with Tannit, consort of the Carthaginian Baal (Baal Hammon).[62] At Ugarit[63] the goddess Ashtart is identified by the epithet *šm bʿl* ("the Name of Baal"), an identification that persists in fifth-century Sidon.[64] This pattern suggests that the Ugaritic goddess Anath arose first as the hypostatic form of the cultic presence of a Ugaritic god, probably Baal Zaphon.[65] It also suggests that she is only analogous to—not identical to—Anath-Yahu of Elephantine Judaism.

The theological purpose of such hypostatic forms has to do with the issue of divine presence and absence, that is, immanence and transcendence. How can a being who has his existence in the divine realm be available for worship in the human realm? The god is not in the temple, but his cultically available presence is there—his "presence" or "name" or "sign." It is thus this presence that is actively worshiped. We see this, of course, in biblical Yahwism. It is Yahweh's "presence" that accompanies Israel on the journey through the wilderness (Exod 33:14; Deut 4:37). In Deuteronomistic theology it is Yahweh's "name" that dwells in the Temple. In the branch of Yahwism preserved in the Bible, however, this development goes no farther. Yahweh's "presence" and "name" are not personified and certainly not worshiped as goddesses. In the branch of Yahwism that survived in Elephantine Judaism, however, these developments do seem to have occurred.

Let us return once again to Kuntillet ʿAjrud and Yahweh's asherah. Our difficulty in understanding the term *'ăšērâ* is comparable to the problem of *ʿānāt*. We have an asherah at ʿAjrud that represents some aspect of Yahweh ("*his* asherah") and that seems to be personified, at least to the extent that it can be called upon in the invocation of a blessing. It is likely that 'ăšērâ ought to be understood as another of these terms signaling the cultically available presence of a deity.

The basic meaning of the root from which Hebrew 'ăšērâ[66] is derived ('tr) seems to be "pass along, leave a trace" and thus "influence," "affect." The Arabic noun 'atar means "track," "trace," "vestige"; "sign," "mark"; "impression," "effect," "action," "influence." Therefore, just as 'ănat yāhû means "the Sign [of the active presence] of Yahu," so 'ăšērat yahweh means "the Trace [i.e., visible token] of Yahweh," that is, "the Sign/Mark of Yahweh" or perhaps even "the Effective/Active Presence of Yahweh."[67]

This seems to resolve the dilemma of cultic object or goddess. In the cult Yahweh's 'ăšērâ, his trace, sign, or effective presence, was marked with an upright wooden pole, called an asherah, which, along with an altar, a maṣṣēbâ, and other objects, constituted his sanctuary. At the same time, the 'ăšērâ—the "trace" of Yahweh in the cult—was attributed substance, personified, and worshiped as a hypostatic personality, following the widely attested Northwest Semitic pattern we have discussed.[68] As in the other cases cited, the asherah was thought of as feminine and thus as the consort of the deity.

The religious milieu at 'Ajrud is that of the Israelite court at the beginning of the eighth century. It is the court religion from which Hosea and the other eighth-century prophets dissented. Yahweh is worshiped alongside a goddess. His asherah, the visible token of his cultic presence, is personified and probably understood as his consort. The two of them, Yahweh and his asherah, are called upon repeatedly in the 'Ajrud texts, and they are represented by the drawing of two figures standing akimbo. Yahweh's asherah is not, however, the Canaanite Asherah.[69] She is the Israelite Asherah, the personification of a hypostatic form of Yahweh. Thus the cult reflected at 'Ajrud is not syncretistic in the strictest sense. It is a form of Yahwism that derived its essential features from internal developments, but it is not the Yahwism of the prophets and reformers, and not the Yahwism we know from the Bible.

NOTES

1. The inscriptions have not been published. See provisionally Z. Meshel, *Kuntillet 'Ajrud: A Religious Centre from the Time of the Judaean Monarchy on the Border of Sinai* (Israel Museum Catalogue 175; Jerusalem: Israel Museum, 1978); idem, "Did Yahweh Have a Consort? The New Religious Inscriptions from the Sinai," *BARev* 5/2 (March/April 1979) 24–35. Preliminary treatments of the issues raised by the texts include M. Gilula, "To Yahweh Shomron and His

Asherah," *Shnaton* 3 (1978) 129–37 Hebrew; J. A. Emerton, "New Light on Israelite Religion: The Implications of the Inscriptions from Kuntillet ʿAjrud," *ZAW* 94 (1982) 2–20; P. J. King, "The Contribution of Archaeology to Biblical Studies," *CBQ* 45 (1983) 1–16, esp. 12–13; A. Lemaire, "Who or What Was Yahweh's Asherah?" *BARev* 10/6 (Nov./Dec. 1984) 42–51; idem, "Date et origine des inscriptions hébraïques et phéniciennes de Kuntillet ʿAjrud," *Studi epigrafici e linguistici* 1 (1984) 131–43; M. Weinfeld, "A Sacred Site of the Monarchic Period," *Shnaton* 4 (1980) 280–84 Hebrew; idem, "Kuntillet ʿAjrud Inscriptions and Their Significance," *Studi epigrafici e linguistici* 1 (1984) 121–30; W. G. Dever, "Asherah, Consort of Yahweh? New Evidence from Kuntillet ʿAjrud," *BASOR* 255 (1984) 21–37.

2. In the account of Edom's revolt against Judah during the reign of Jehoram son of Jehoshaphat in the mid-ninth century (2 Kgs 8:19–22), we are told that Edom remained independent "to this day," i.e., until the time of the Deuteronomistic historian.

3. A large stone bowl found in the so-called bench room reads *lʿbdyw bn ʿdnh brk hʾ lyhw[h]*, "Belonging to Obadiah son of Adnah. Blessed be he to Yahw[eh]!" Cf. Meshel, "Did Yahweh Have a Consort?" 32–33.

4. That is, *yahweh têmān* or *yahweh taymān*. The difference is dialectical, showing that speakers of both Israelite and Judean Hebrew were present at the site. In the southern dialect the diphthong *ay* remains uncontracted in all positions.

5. *GKC* §125d–g. A reconsideration of these rules in the light of the Kuntillet ʿAjrud materials has been initiated by Emerton ("New Light on Israelite Religion," 4–5).

6. We expect *šmrnw* for *šōměrēnû* ("our guardian"). The reading *yhwh šmrn* occurs in the texts found on the pithoi, which follow the standard Hebrew orthography of the period in consistently employing vowel letters to indicate final long vowels.

7. Cf. Weinfeld, "Kuntillet ʿAjrud Inscriptions," 125. The rendering "Yahweh of Samaria" seems first to have been suggested in print by Gilula ("To Yahweh Shomron and His Asherah").

8. If, indeed, it *is* a departure. In Ps 135:21, M. Dahood reads *yhwh-m ṣiyyōn* ("Yahweh [i.e., the divine name with enclitic *mem*] of Zion") for MT's awkward *yhwh miṣṣiyyōn* ("Yahweh from Zion"). See M. Dahood, *Psalms III: 101–150* (AB 17A; Garden City, N.Y.: Doubleday & Co., 1970) 262–63; cf. M. L. Barré, *The God-List in the Treaty Between Hannibal and Philip V of Macedonia: A Study in Light of the Ancient Near Eastern Treaty Tradition* (Johns Hopkins Near Eastern Studies; Baltimore and London: Johns Hopkins University Press, 1983) 186 n. 473.

9. The identification of Teman with the village of Tawilan, east of Petra, is now doubted. See R. de Vaux, "Téman, ville ou région d'Edom?" *RB* 76 (1969) 379–85.

10. A. Abou-Assaf, P. Bordreuil, and A. R. Millard, *La statue de Tell Fekheryé et son inscription bilingue assyro-araméenne* (Paris: Editions Recherche sur les civilisations, 1982).

11. Barré (*God-List,* 186 n. 472) distinguishes "four basic variations of this

construction [in Northwest Semitic]: (1) DN GN (construct chain); (2) DN *b*-GN or DN GN-*h* (with the preposition *b*-, 'in,' or the locative suffix -*h*); (3) DN *yšb/škn (b-)*GN (with the participle, 'dwelling in'); (4) DN *b'l/b'lt*, 'Lord/Lady of')."

12. One major witness to the text of Samuel (LXX[L]) reads "Yahweh-in-Hebron" here too. It is possible that the longer reading is original; see P. K. McCarter, *II Samuel: A New Translation with Introduction, Notes, and Commentary* (AB 9; Garden City, N.Y.: Doubleday & Co., 1984) 355.

13. Identified by Barré, *God-List*, 186 n. 473.

14. The original reading, *'lhym*, reflected in several witnesses, has become *h'mym* ("the people") in MT.

15. As first pointed out to me by D. N. Freedman.

16. *KAI*, 81[= *CIS* 3914].1; cited by Barré, *God-List*, 186 n. 473.

17. See N. Avigad, "Two Phoenician Votive Seals," *IEJ* 16 (1966) 247–51 and pl. 26. The reading is highly uncertain; cf. L. G. Herr (*The Scripts of Ancient Northwest Semitic Seals* [HSM 18; Missoula, Mont.: Scholars Press, 1978] 71), who follows Cross in classifying the script as Ammonite.

18. In addition to these two Ishtars, we also find the Ishtar of Bit-kitmuri, the Ishtar of Hattarina, etc.

19. See Barré, *God-List*, 113, chart 13 ("Structure of the Typical Neo-Assyrian Treaty God-List"). Barré cites treaties listing both Ishtar of Nineveh and Ishtar of Arbela (sometimes in broken form) from the reigns of Assur-nirari V, Sennacherib, Esarhaddon, and Assurbanipal.

20. This text has often been cited for evidence of "mono-Yahwism" in Israel. Cf. W. F. Bade, "Der Monojahwismus des Deuteronomiums," *ZAW* 30 (1910) 81–90.

21. Cf. E. Nielsen, " 'Weil Jahwe unser Gott ein Jahwe ist' (Dtn 6, 4f.)," *Beiträge zur alttestamentlichen Theologie. Festschrift für Walther Zimmerli zum 70. Geburtstag* (ed. H. Donner et al.; Göttingen: Vandenhoeck & Ruprecht, 1977) 288–301; M. Peter, "Dtn 6, 4—ein monotheistischer Text?" *BZ* 24 (1980) 252–62.

22. Published by W. G. Dever, "Iron Age Epigraphic Material from the Area of Khirbet el-Kôm," *HUCA* 40–41 (1969–70) 139–204. Subsequent attempts to read the text include A. Lemaire, "Les inscriptions de Khirbet el-Qom et l'ashérah de YHWH," *RB* 84 (1977) 597–608; J. Naveh, "Graffiti and Dedications," *BASOR* 235 (1979) 27–30; S. Mittmann, "Die Grabinschrift des Sängers Uriahu," *ZDPV* 97 (1981) 139–52; K. Jaroš, "Zur Inschrift Nr. 3 von Hirbet el-Qôm," *Biblische Notizen* 19 (1982) 30–41; P. D. Miller, "Psalms and Inscriptions," *Congress Volume, Vienna, 1980* (VTSup 32; Leiden: E. J. Brill, 1981) 310–32; and Z. Zevit, "The Khirbet el-Qom Inscription Mentioning a Goddess," *BASOR* 255 (1984) 39–47.

23. In fact, however, the precise sense of this part of the inscription (lines 2 and 3) has proven elusive. The difficulty is a sequence of letters in line 3 (apparently *mṣryh.*) that intervenes where the ellipsis is indicated in our transliteration and translation. This problem has been seen most clearly by Lemaire ("Les inscriptions de Khirbet el-Qom"), who believes the puzzling arrangement of the words is the result of an engraver's error. According to Lemaire (p. 598),

the word *mṣryh* ("from his enemies") belongs with what follows, *hwšʿ lh* ("he saved him"), and line 3 is to be read "et ⟨par son ashérah⟩ des ses ennemis {par son asherah} il l'a sauvé." The meaning of this part of the text, therefore, would be: "Blessed be Uriah by Yahweh and his asherah. From his enemies he saved him!"

24. P. Beck, "The Drawings from Ḥorvat Teiman (Kuntillet ʿAjrud)," *Tel Aviv* 9 (1982) 3–86.

25. Gilula ("To Yahweh Shomron and His Asherah") concludes that the smaller of the two standing figures is the goddess. Dever ("Asherah, Consort of Yahweh?") argues on the basis of parallels drawn from the visual arts of Syria and Palestine that she is represented by the seated figure.

26. This objection has force despite the putative occurrence of *krtn* ("our Keret") in Ugaritic (*CTA* 16.1.39). As we shall see, however, this does not settle the question of the presence of a divine consort at Ajrud.

27. See, e.g., B. Stade, "Zur phönischischen Epigraphik," *ZAW* 1 (1981) 345; W. R. Smith, *Lectures on the Religion of the Semites* (London: Adam & Charles Black, 1894 [1914]) 187–89; K. Budde, "The Ashera in the Old Testament," *The New World* 8 (1899) 733. These scholars and others believed that the biblical asherah was only a cult object, never a goddess. Some, including Budde, did not rule out the possibility that there might have been a Canaanite goddess by the name of Asherah, but they insisted that, even in that case, she was unknown to the biblical writers until a very late period when the cult object came erroneously to be thought of as a goddess after its proscription.

28. Even the appearance of the goddess *ʾaṯrt* ("Asherah") in the Ugaritic myths has not persuaded all scholars that biblical Hebrew *ʾăšērâ* ever refers to a goddess. E. Lipiński, e.g., insists that "no biblical passage mentions that goddess Aṯirat or her symbol" ("The Goddess Aṯirat in Ancient Arabia, in Babylon, and at Ugarit," *Orientalia Lovaniensia Periodica* 3 [1972] 116).

29. *CTA* 4.1.23; 4.3.30; 4.4.32; etc.

30. *CTA* 2.1.20–21; 4.5.63; cf. 4.1.7–9; 4.4.48–50.

31. See W. F. Albright, "A Prince of Tanaach in the Fifteenth Century B.C." *BASOR* 94 (1944) 18.

32. The name is spelled most often *¹Abdi-a-ši-ir-ta*, but also *¹Abdi-a-ši-ir-ti/te*, *¹Abdi-aš-ra-ti*, etc.; so O. Weber in J. A. Knudtzon, *Die El-Amarna Tafeln* (Leipzig: J. C. Hinrichs, 1915) 1555.

33. *Keilschrifturkunden aus Boghazköi* (Berlin: Akademie, 1921–44) xii 61; xxi 118 + xxvi 37; xxvi 34, 35. See H. Otten, "Ein kanaanäischer Mythus aus Bogazkoy," *Mitteilungen des Instituts für Orientforschung* 1 (1953) 126; translation by A. Goetze in *ANET*, 519.

34. The reading *ʾšr* on a seventh-century plaque from Arslan Tash has been interpreted as a reference to Asherah by W. F. Albright ("An Aramaean Magical Text in Hebrew from the Seventh Century B.C.," *BASOR* 76 [1939] 5–11), who restores *ʾšr[t?]*, "Asher[at?]," and F. M. Cross and R. J. Saley ("Phoenician Incantations on a Plaque from the Seventh Century B.C. from Arslan Tash in Upper Syria," *BASOR* 197 [1970] 42–49), who interpret *ʾšr* as *ʾaširô* (< *ʾaširâ*), assuming an isogloss with Hebrew and South Canaanite.

35. Hebrew *lā ʾăšērâ*, which could also be rendered, "for the asherah." Accord-

ing to Lemaire ("Who or What Was Yaweh's Asherah?" 47), the use of the definite article excludes the possibility that a name is intended. If the explanation of the meaning of the word 'ăšērâ proposed below is correct, however, this conclusion is not necessary. "When terms applying to whole classes are restricted (simply by usage) to particular individuals . . . or things," the article is employed (*GKC* §126e, cf. 125d).

36. It is possible that *wnby'y h'šrh 'rb' m'wt*, which is lacking in v 22, is secondary here.

37. Again, Hebrew *lā'ăšērâ*, which could mean "for the asherah."

38. In Judg 3:7, however, other textual witnesses reflect *hā'aštārôt* ("the Ashtarts"), which is also the reading of MT in 1 Sam 7:3 (cf. v 4).

39. MT *hā'ăšērâ*, for which the versions read *hā'ăšērôt* ("the asherahs").

40. Again the versions read the plural.

41. The synoptic passage in 2 Chron 33:3 reads, "erected altars to the baals and made asherahs."

42. *CAD* 1/2, 436–38.

43. This is the conclusions of Lipiński, "The Goddess Aṯirat."

44. *KAI*, 19.4.

45. "A Phoenician Inscription from 'Akko,' " *IEJ* 35 (1985) 81–94.

46. Such as '*šr 'l hbyt* ("who is over the house" Isa 22:15), which also occurs in a Hebrew inscription from the seventh century (*KAI*, 191.B; cf. N. Avigad, "The Epitaph of a Royal Steward from Siloam Village," *IEJ* 3 [1953] 137–52), '*šr 'l hms* ("who is over the corvée," 1 Kgs 12:18), also known from a seventh-century seal (Avigad, "The Chief of the Corvée," *IEJ* 30 [1980] 170–73), '*šr 'l h'yr* ("who is over the city," 2 Kgs 10:5), '*šr 'l hmltḥh* ("who is over the wardrobe," 2 Kgs 10:22); etc.

47. A third reference appears in Sefire I B 11: '*m 'šrthm* ("with their asherah/asherahs"). But the context is too broken to permit a confident interpretation.

48. Cf. Emerton ("New Light on Israelite Religion," 18) and Lemaire ("Who or What Was Yahweh's Consort?" 50), who explains that "the asherah is not the high place itself or the whole sanctuary but rather a cultic object which is part of the high place. In short, the asherah is more specific."

49. Although *kol-'ēṣ* ("any wooden thing") may be a gloss ["any tree"?], it corresponds to the nature of the asherah elsewhere.

50. Cf. LXX *dendra* in Isa 17:8 and 27:9. References in the Mishnaic tractate '*Aboda Zara* (3.7) show that the rabbis understood an '*ăšērâ* to be a tree worshiped by the heathen.

51. Cf. also Isa 17:8, where *wĕhā'ăšērîm wĕhāḥammānîm* ("both asherahs and incense altars") appears as a gloss on '*ăšer 'āśû 'eṣbĕ'ōtāyw* ("that which his fingers have made").

52. The modern history of the interpretation of the asherah is reviewed by W. L. Reed (*The Asherah in the Old Testament* [Fort Worth: Texas Christian University Press, 1949]) on pp.11–28.

53. Cf. Reed, *Asherah*. Noting the use of verbs of building and making with the asherah in the Bible (pp. 30–31), Reed concludes (p. 37) that "it was not a tree but it was made of wood or contained wood and could be burned." For the

argument that the asherah was carved into the shape of an idol, see generally pp. 87–96.

54. In fact, the orthography of *wl'šrth* permits us to render either "his [i.e., Yahweh's] asherah" (cf. "the asherah of Baal Hammon," in the Ma'ṣub text cited above) or "its [i.e., GN's] asherah," that is, the asherah of Samaria or Teman. To the latter possibility, which was first pointed out to me by B. A. Levine, compare the frequently suggested emendation of *bĕ'ašmat šōmrôn* ("by the guilt of Samaria") in Amos 8:14 to *bĕ'ăšērat šōmrôn* ("by the asherah of Samaria").

55. This tail, which appears on both figures, hangs *behind* the abdomen and cannot be interpreted as a phallus. There is no basis, therefore, for supposing the second figure, which has female breasts, to be hermaphroditic. Thus the akimbo posture is the only detail that supports the unlikely assumption that these figures are "two crude representations of the Egyptian ithyphallic dwarf god Bes" (Dever, "Asherah, Consort of Yahweh?" 25). On the other hand, the bovine features of both figures—the face of the larger is unmistakably that of a bull—exclude the Bes interpretation.

56. As I have already suggested, this interpretation of the two figures has not impressed itself on everyone. In his opinion that they represent Bes (cited in the previous note) Dever has many allies. But see the study of Gilula ("To Yahweh Shomron and His Asherah"), whose view of the matter agrees with that expressed in the present chapter.

57. The extensive bibliography for the god Bethel includes O. Eissfeldt, "Der Gott Bethel," *ARW* 28 (1930) 1–30 (= *Kleine Shriften*, ed. R. Sellheim and F. Maas, vol. 1 [Tübingen: J. C. B. Mohr (Paul Siebeck), 1962], 206–33); A. Vincent, *La religion des judéo-araméens d'Eléphantine* (Paris: Paul Geuthner, 1936) 562–92; and J. P. Hyatt, "The Deity Bethel and the Old Testament," *JAOS* 59 (1939) 81–98. Bethel's Aramaic origin is argued by W. F. Albright in *Archaeology and the Religion of Israel* (Baltimore: Johns Hopkins University Press, 1942) 169–71.

58. W. F. Albright, "The Evolution of the West-Semitic Divinity 'An- 'Anat- 'Atta," *AJSL* 41 (1925) 92–98; cf. idem, *From the Stone Age to Christianity* (Baltimore: Johns Hopkins University Press, 1940 [2d ed.; Garden City, N.Y.: Doubleday Anchor Books, 1957]) 373–74; idem, *Archaeology and the Religion of Israel*, 168–75.

59. See Vincent, *La religion des judéo-araméens d'Eléphantine*, 360–61, 566 n. 3; Albright, *Archaeology and the Religion of Israel*, 170–71.

60. Menahem bar Shallum swears an oath *by[hw 'lh]' bmsgd' wb'ntyhw* ("by the god Yahu, by Mesgida, and by Anath-yahu"). See A. Cowley, *Aramaic Papyri of the Fifth Century B.C.* (Oxford: Clarendon Press, 1923) no. 44, 147–48. On "Mesgida," the divinized cult place, see the literature cited by B. Porten, *Archives from Elephantine* (Berkeley and Los Angeles: University of California Press, 1968) 155 n. 15. Porten himself does not think Yahu is the first deity invoked in Menahem's oath, and he doubts that *msgd'* is personified as a god; thus he reads (p. 154) "by H[erem?] in the place of prostration and by Anathyahu." But the analogy of "Bethel" favors the assumption that the *msgd'* was deified, and (in any case) the *mesgida* was worshiped among the Nabateans, in whose language it

meant "altar" or "idol"; see J. Teixidor, *The Pagan God: Popular Religion in the Greco-Roman Near East* (Princeton: Princeton University Press, 1977) 85–87.

61. The alternative is to suppose that *'ntyhw* is a composite deity (*'anat +* *yāhû*) on the pattern of Atargatis (*'aštart + 'anat*) or Ashtar-Chemosh (*'štr + kmš*) of the Mesha stele (*KAI*, 181.17). Porten (*Archives from Elephantine*, 179) expresses considerable uncertainty on this point: "However attractive the idea may be that Anathyahu is not a composite deity, Anath plus YHW, the evidence for considering it a hypostatization is not sufficiently decisive."

62. *KAI*, 78(= *CIS* I 3778).2 (*tnt pn b'l*); 175.2 (*thinith phane bal*); 176.2–3 (*thinneith phene bal*). Phanebalos also appears on Ascalonian coins of the Roman period (G. F. Hill, *A Catalogue of the Greek Coins in the British Museum: Palestine* [London: British Museum, 1914] lix–lxi, 115–39); there she is dressed as a warrior but should not be mistaken for a male god (*pace* Teixidor, *Pagan God*, 96–97). Cross (*CMHE*, 31; cf. 28 n. 88; 30 n. 100) calls her "the war goddess of Ascalon" (cf. W. F. Albright, *Yahweh and the Gods of Canaan* [London: Athlone Press, 1968] 129 and n. 48).

63. *CTA* 16.6, 56.

64. As shown by its occurrence in the text of the Eshmunazor sarcophagus, *KAI*, 14.18.

65. Cf. *'nt ṣpn* in *CTA* 36.17.

66. The form of the noun *'ăšērâ* is distinctive. In biblical Hebrew this pattern frequently forms the participle of verbs "middle e"—i.e., the (i, a) vowel class (see GKC §§84ag, 50b)—and thus ordinarily of intransitive verbs.

67. Though it seems to have been forgotten, this etymology was proposed by G. Hoffmann nearly a century ago. See his *Über einige phönikische Inschriften* (Königliche Gesellschaft der Wissenschaften Abhandlungen 36; Historisch-philologische Klasse 1; Göttingen, 1890); cf. W. R. Smith, *Lectures on the Religion of the Semites*, 188.

68. Thus it is the "trace" or "effective presence"—not the cult object—that is hypostatized, though admittedly the distinction is a subtle one. Otherwise, our conclusion agrees closely with that of Lemaire ("Who or What Was Yahweh's Asherah?" 51): "In [the Kuntillet 'Ajrud] inscriptions, asherah is still a generic name, as shown by the pronominal . . . suffix, but it is on the way to being personified, as reflected in the way the asherah is associated with Yahweh in blessing. In a more subtle psychological or theological way, we are witnessing a kind of birth of a hypostasis in which the essence of the divine is bound to a cultic object; that is, an aspect of the divine is becoming concretized or reified."

69. This is not to say that Yahweh's asherah, once it had been personified as a goddess, was not confused with other goddesses. That a personified asherah could easily be identified with a goddess well known in the region is shown to be the case by the example of the identification of "the face of Baal" as Tanit in Carthage or "the name of Baal" as Ashtart in Ugarit and Tyre (see above). The goddess Asherah of Ugaritic mythology was originally *'atrt ym* ("the asherah of Yamm"), i.e., the hypostatized presence of the sea-god. As frequently happens with Northwest Semitic deities, her epithet, in shortened form, became her name, *'atrt*, ("Asherah"), though she continued to be called *rbt 'atrt ym* ("the lady [who is] the asherah of the Sea"). If she was worshiped widely and prominently in the Iron Age under the name Asherah, it is difficult to imagine that the Israelite goddess *'ăšērat yahweh* was not identified with her.

11

Israelite Religion: The Onomastic and Epigraphic Evidence

JEFFREY H. TIGAY

A paramount question in the history of Israelite religion has been the place of polytheism in that history. Although monotheism is recognized as an innovation of the Israelites in the biblical period, the dominant view among critical scholars has been that the Israelite populace as a whole was not monotheistic or even monolatrous until shortly before or even after the fall of the Judahite kingdom in 587/86 B.C.E. From the Bible's own viewpoint, the ancestors of the Israelites were polytheistic at least until the call of Abraham (Josh 24:1): the worship of deities other than YHWH was outlawed in the time of Moses (Exod 20:3; 22:19; etc.), but it was not effectively eliminated. Scores of biblical passages state that Israelites practiced polytheism at many stages throughout their history. The prophets warned that this apostasy would bring calamity, and when the Israelite kingdoms fell, historiographic literature cited polytheism as one of the main reasons.

In the view of biblical writers the persistence of polytheism was a deviation from an established norm, since the worship of other gods had been banned as far back as Moses. Classical criticism, on the other hand, accepted the biblical testimony about the persistence of polytheism but inferred from it that there was no monotheistic norm, but at most a minority monolatrous or monotheistic viewpoint, until late in Israelite history. For centuries after their occupation of Canaan the Israelite tribes remained polytheistic, differing little from their neighbors except in the identity of their own chief or national deity. The polytheistic worship so frequently reported by the Bible was regarded by most Israelites as normal and sensible, and that is why it was so common. Divergent as they are from each other in other respects, the biblical and the critical view share the premise that polytheistic worship *was* rampant and deeply rooted throughout the period culminating in the fall of Judah.

The most serious challenge to this premise was that of Y. Kaufmann,

who argued that true, mythological, polytheism was swiftly and effectively eradicated under Moses, from whose time onward monotheism
became the seminal idea of Israelite history and culture. What remained
of polytheism, and what the biblical writers describe as polytheism, was
mere fetishism, lacking the mythological conceptions that are at the heart
of true paganism. As for the extent of this fetishistic "polytheism,"
Kaufmann considered it restricted. He accounted for the accusations of
the prophets and the historiographers as stemming largely from prophetic hyperbole and the historiographic need to explain a catastrophe
that would otherwise seem inexplicable.[1]

Scholarly discussion of this question began in the nineteenth century,
when the only evidence available was that found within the Bible itself.
As a result, the debate has focused on the literary-historical criticism of
that evidence. To classical criticism it was the biblical claims for early
monotheism which seemed suspect; to Kaufmann it was the sweeping
charges of polytheism. Both sides agree that literary texts such as those in
the Bible cannot be used for historical research before the historian
evaluates what they are reliable for, but so long as this evaluation is based
on evidence from within the Bible itself, with no external controls, it
cannot escape its notorious subjectivity.

In the century since this debate began, a certain amount of pertinent
external evidence has been discovered by archaeologists. Figurines of
nude females, dubbed "Astarte figurines" by scholars, were taken to
confirm the biblical charges that Israelites worshiped this goddess.[2] A
few seal illustrations have been interpreted as representing alien gods and
their worship.[3] The Baalistic personal names on the Samaria ostraca have
been taken as signs of Baal worship in the Northern Kingdom, while the
preponderance of Yahwistic names on the Lachish ostraca has been
credited to the effects of Josiah's reformation.[4] However, this evidence
has never been gathered and brought to bear on the history of Israelite
religion in a focused way. The onomastic data have played only a minor
role in the debate. They have been cited in support of theories based
largely on other grounds or interpreted in the light of the biblical accusations. But only scattered details have been cited in such arguments, as
their proponents found helpful. So far as I am aware, no attempt has
been made to interpret either the pagan or the Yahwistic personal names
in the light of the total onomastic picture from Israel. Other aspects of
Hebrew inscriptions have hardly been brought to bear on our question at
all. It is to the onomastic and inscriptional data that the present study is
devoted.

THE ONOMASTIC EVIDENCE

Personal names have been studied as a source of information about religious beliefs since the nineteenth century. Ancient Semitic personal names are well designed to serve this purpose, since they often comprise construct phrases describing their bearers as servants of the god or the like, or brief sentences consisting of a name or an epithet of a deity (the theophoric element) plus a predicate, and they mean essentially: the god has done, or may the god do, such and such for the person who bears the name or for his or her parents; or they may mean: the god is king, father, great, etc. From these theophoric names one learns which deities were worshiped by various groups and about developments in the roster of deities worshiped at different times.

The use of personal names as evidence of religious belief presupposes that their meaning was understood and intended at least to some extent. This is sometimes doubted by scholars, probably because in the modern Western world names are frequently not understood because they did not originate in the language or dialect of those who use them. But in preexilic Israel most personal names were in biblical Hebrew and could be understood by any Israelite. Attention to the meaning of names is reflected in the fact that biblical characters and narrators sometimes comment on their meaning (Gen 26:36; 1 Sam 25:25; Ruth 1:20–21). That their etymologies are often paronomastic is for literary effect and does not indicate that Israelites didn't understand Hebrew names in a linguistically correct way. In fact, biblical writers often give correct explanations of names or show a correct understanding while playing on them. Cases in point are the explanations of Ishmael, Simeon, and Dan (Gen 16:11; 29:33; 30:6) and the puns on Jonathan, Isaiah, Uzziah/Azariah, and Jehoshaphat (1 Sam 14:10, 12; 2 Chr 32:22; 26:7; 19:6, 8; 20:12).[5] Even if factors extraneous to meaning—such as fashion, tradition, or aesthetics—may have influenced some parents' choice of names, what is important for present purposes is that the divine name within Hebrew personal names could not have gone unrecognized. Sensitivity to the theophoric element was so great in Israel that in later times some scribes felt compelled to change names that seemed pagan in manuscripts of Samuel, and perhaps of Chronicles as well (see below).

In studying personal names for evidence of religious belief, we must keep in mind a number of points. (1) Names express the views of those who choose them, normally parents, and not necessarily the views of those who bear the names. (2) In Northwest Semitic personal names, even those employed in polytheistic groups rarely invoke more than one deity in a single name.[6] Therefore in dealing with the question of how many deities were worshiped within a particular group we must consider the total onomastic picture of that group, not the names of a few individuals. (3) The beliefs and attitudes expressed in Northwest Semitic personal names are simple and elemental. They express thanks for the god's beneficence, hope for his blessing and protection, submission to his authority, and the like. They are not theoretical, theological statements. Thus even if the names of a particular society should reflect the predominance of a single deity to the total exclusion of all others, this would tell us only that members of that society did not expect from other gods the kinds of actions that are mentioned in personal names, and perhaps that they did not worship other gods. In itself, the absence of other gods from the onomasticon would not tell us whether that society denied the existence or divinity of those gods.

Part of the appeal of personal names to the historian of religion is the assumption that they are a relatively objective form of evidence. This is a valid assumption when names are compared to the often tendentious statements of literary texts, for the names of characters were usually not invented by the authors as part of their argument but were supplied by historical tradition. However, there are cases where names were tampered with in order to suppress their religious implications. The most celebrated example is the obliteration, during the Amarna revolution, of the name of Amon in Egyptian inscriptions where it appeared as the name of the god or as part of a personal name.[7] Something similar, though less drastic, happened to part of the onomastic evidence in the Bible. The Israelite theophoric personal names preserved in the Masoretic Text are overwhelmingly Yahwistic. According to one count, of some 466 individuals bearing theophoric names (excluding those with the elements 'ēl and 'ēlî, which are ambiguous) from the patriarchal period through the fall of Jerusalem, 413 (89 percent) bear Yahwistic names and 53 (11 percent) bear clearly or plausibly pagan names.[8] This includes eight individuals whose names contained the element ba'al, which will be discussed below. These eight—seven from the periods of the Judges and the united monarchy—are known to us from the books of Judges and Chronicles. However, as is well known, in the Masoretic Text of Samuel, the element ba'al in these names is replaced by bošet or, in one case, 'ēl.[9] There are other variants of this type. An official of David's and Solomon's is called Hadoram ("Haddu is exalted") in 2 Chr 10:18 and Adoram (either "Addu [a variant of Haddu] is exalted" or "The Father is exalted")[10] in 2 Sam 20:24 and 1 Kgs 12:18, but in 1 Kgs 4:6 he is called Adoniram ("My Lord is exalted"). In the textual tradition of Chronicles the LXX gives pagan forms for names that do not appear pagan in the MT: Jeshebeab and Jashobeam are read, respectively, as Isbaal and Iesebaal, and Abishua and Ahishammai are read as Abeisamas and Achisamas (1 Chr 24:13; 11:11; 8:4; 2:32). Whether these names were originally meant to contain pagan elements, or whether they were recognizable as such by Israelite scribes, is in some cases debatable,[11] but the drift of the evidence is clear: a certain percentage of pagan PNs has been altered in the MT to a point where they are no longer recognizable to us, and the MT cannot be automatically assumed to present us with a reliable impression of the extent of the use of pagan theophoric names in ancient Israel.

The discovery of the Samaria ostraca seemed immediately to confirm this impression. These ostraca, from approximately the first half of the eighth century, mention at least five individuals whose names contain the element *ba'al,* which indicates that *ba'al,* names remained in use longer, and may have been more popular, than the biblical evidence suggests. At the same time, these ostraca suggest a way of overcoming the uncertainty arising from the biblical evidence, for inscriptions offer us a database that has essentially not been tampered with.

THE EPIGRAPHIC ONOMASTICON

By 1979 the names of some 738 preexilic Israelites were known from Hebrew inscriptions and foreign inscriptions referring to Israel.[12] To judge from those inscriptions whose archaeological provenance is known, the vast majority of these are from the south. These inscriptions are mainly from the eighth centuries down through the fall of Judah, and the individuals seem to be quite evenly distributed throughout the period.[13] These individuals must be mostly from the upper strata of Israelite and Judahite society, though just how limited a segment of the population is involved is not clear. Those named in the Samaria ostraca are taken by many scholars to be court officials and tax collectors or owners of estates. Many of the seal owners and individuals named in the inscriptions are explicitly identified as royal officials, scribes, and the like, or are inferably so.[14] About half of the seals published in R. Hestrin and M. Dayagi-Mendels's corpus are made of precious or semiprecious stones, which points to the well-to-do.[15] The other half of the corpus is made of limestone or bone, from which the editors infer the use of seals among "wide circles"; a similar inference may be drawn from the poor workmanship on some of the seals, which is taken to indicate manufacture by the owners.[16] There is no knowing how far down the socioeconomic ladder these considerations point, and we cannot confidently suppose that the evidence we are reviewing reflects the lower strata of Israelite and Judahite society. This situation would vitiate our inquiry from the outset

note the very traditional model at work here

if we assumed that Israelite polytheism was the popular, unofficial religion and characteristic of the lower strata. However, assimilation to foreign culture is typically found among the upper strata, and many of the biblical accusations of polytheism refer explicitly to the royal court, as in the case of Manasseh whose half-century reign (698 or 687/86–642) was right in the heart of the period covered by the inscriptions.[17] If these allegations are to be taken at face value, we have every reason to expect that evidence of polytheism will appear among the upper classes and circles close to the royal court, especially in the period represented by the inscriptions.

The onomastic practices of other groups in the ancient Near East encourage this expectation. Even within a single family or city outside Israel, one often finds several deities invoked in the onomasticon. The Neo-Assyrian king Sennacherib (Sin-aḫḫē-erība), named for Sin, named his son Esarhaddon (Aššur-aḫ-iddin) for Ashur, while Esarhaddon's sons were named for Ashur, Shamash, and Sin (Aššurbanipal [Aššur-bāni-apli], Šamaš-šum-ukin, and Sin-iddin-apli). Eshmunazor, a king of Sidon in the Achaemenid period, was named for Eshmun, though his mother was a priestess of Astarte and he himself was a priest of the same goddess.[18] A list found in the temple of Eshmun near Sidon in the same period gives names compounded with the names of seven different deities (Baal, Ramman, Sism, Shamash, Eshmun, Tannit, and Astarte).[19]

In the light of these practices, and assuming the prevalence of polytheism in Israel, we should expect to find a substantial number of Israelites named for many of the gods they are said to have worshiped. These would include Baal, Ashtoreth and Asherah, Bethel (Jer 48:13; cf. Gen 31:13; 35:7), astral deities such as the sun (Shamash), the moon (Yeraḥ), and stars (such as Sakkut and Kaiwan), the "Queen of Heaven,"[20] and possibly Milkom and Kemosh[21] and names reflecting the cults of Tammuz and Moloch.[22] In the light of certain scholarly theories, one might also expect to find names compounded with the Phoenician Melqart,[23] the Assyrian Ashur,[24] and—either alone or in combination with Bethel and YHWH—Eshem, Herem, and Anath.[25]

These expectations are only minimally borne out in the epigraphic corpus of personal names. Of the 738 individuals, 351, or nearly half, bear names with YHWH as their theophoric element.[26] Forty-eight others bear names with the theophoric element 'ēl ("God/god/the deity El") or 'ēlî ("my god"). Since there is no way of telling to which deity this element refers, names with these words as their theophoric element were not included among the theophoric names in this study.

Of all the remaining names, most mention no deity at all. Only 27 seem clearly or very plausibly to refer to deities other than YHWH. These are listed in the chart on pages 164–66.[27]

These names do not include most of the theophoric elements we expected. No astral deities appear,[28] nor do Bethel, Milkom, Kemosh, Tammuz, or Moloch,[29] Ashur, Melqart, or the elements Eshem, Herem, and Anath. Remarkably, with a single apparent exception *('dt')*, no goddess appears—neither Asherah nor Ashtoreth,[30] who are said to have been worshiped alongside Baal throughout Israelite history, nor any other goddess who might be the "Queen of Heaven," whose cult is said to have been practiced by citizens and kings in Judah and Jerusalem for generations (Jeremiah 44). The absence of goddesses in the onomasticon cannot be explained on the assumption that goddesses appeared only in the names of females, while most of the names in the corpus belong to men. In West Semitic onomastica, goddesses do appear in masculine names.[31] Furthermore, some names of Israelite women are known, and while few are theophoric,[32] some are, and they contain masculine theophoric elements; *'bgyl* (D 218:62), *ḥmy'hl* (HD 34), *ḥmy'dn* (HD 63), *'mdyhw* (L. G. Herr, *Scripts*, Hebrew 143), and *yhwyšm'*.[33]

Of all the potentially pagan elements the biblical accusations led us to expect in personal names, only *b'l* appears. Five names in the Samaria ostraca clearly contain this element. In all the rest of the corpus only one further name clearly contains this element, *tṣb'l* in the seventh-century ostracon from Meṣad Hashavyahu.[34] Apart from the latter example, the *b'l* names are completely isolated in the corpus. They stem from a single region within a brief period. All the rest of the Israelite and Judahite sites of the two centuries in question together produce one additional case—a startling situation if the names reflect the cult of a deity whose cult was practiced widely throughout a good part of the period.

In fact, the *b'l* names and most, if not all, of the other names listed can just as plausibly be interpreted in a way that does not imply polytheism. It has long been recognized that *b'l* in the biblical onomasticon may have been an epithet of YHWH, synonymous with *'dwn* ("Lord").[35] The Hebrew name *b'lyh* ("YHWH is my Lord"), borne by a contemporary of David (1 Chr 12:6),[36] indicates such a use, and Hos 2:18 states this almost explicitly: "On that day . . . you will call 'My Husband' *('iši)*, and no more will you call Me 'My *b'l*.' " The latter passage dates from the approximate time and place of the Samaria ostraca and provides an apt explanation for the *b'l* names in them.[37]

The elements Gad, Bes, and Mawet may represent semidivine beings or spirits instead of full-fledged deities.[38] Gad is a common noun meaning "fortune, good fortune" in Hebrew (Gen 30:11 Qere) and cognate

KEY

b. = *ben,* not written on seal   *bn* = *ben,* written in inscription
h. = husband of   w. = wife of

Deity	Name	Provenance	Publication
Baal[a]	*'bb'l*	Samaria	SO 2:4
	b'l'	Samaria	SO 1:7
	b'lzmr	Samaria	SO 12:2–3
	b'l'zkr	Samaria	SO 37:3
	mrb'l	Samaria	SO 2:7
	tṣb'l[b]	Meṣad Ḥashavyahu	*IEJ* 12:30
Bes[c]	*bsy*	?	HD 38
Gad	*gd'(?)*	Arad	Arad 72:3
	gdy[ ][d]	Arad	Arad 71:3
Horus[e]	*pšḥr* (h. of *'dt'*)	?	HD 32
	pšḥr (bn 'dyhw)	?	M 61:28
	pšḥr	Arad	Arad 54
Isis[f]	*pṭ's*	?	HD 41
"Lady"[g]	*'dt'* (w. of *pšḥr*)	?	HD 32
Man/Min[h]	*'ḥymn*[i]	?	G 118
	ḥmn (= 'ḥymn)[j]	Megiddo	HD 42
	ḥmn (= 'ḥymn)[j]	?	*BIES* 25:242
Mawet[k]	*yrymwt* (b. *bnyhw*)	?	*Semitica* 26:46f.
	mrmwt	Arad	Arad 50
Qaus	*qws'*	Aroer (Negev)	*IEJ* 26:139
	[ ]⌜q⌝*ws*[l]	Arad	Arad 26:3
	[*qw*]⌜*s*⌝*'nl*[m]	Arad	Arad 12:3
Shalim	*ṭbšlm*[n]	Lachish	Lachish 1:2
	ṭbšln[o]	Ein Gedi	IR 139:136
	'bšlm[p]	Arad	Arad 59:4
Shamash[q]	*šwššr'ṣr*	?	*IEJ* 15:228
Yam	*ḥym (= 'hym?)*[r]	Tell Sharuhen	HD 43

NOTES TO PAGE 164

a. A few other names on the Samaria ostraca have been thought baalistic but can plausibly be explained otherwise. The view that two names on the same line are a name plus a patronym implies that there are several Baal's (see SO 1:7; 27:3; and 31a:3; and possibly 3:3 and 28:3). But this view (see G. A. Reisner, *HES* I:231; and A. Lemaire, *Inscriptions hébraïques,* 47) was rebutted by Y. Yadin, *IEJ* 9 (1959) 187. On *b'lzmr,* see Lemaire, *Inscriptions hébraïques,* 31.

b. J. Naveh (*IEJ* 12 [1962] 30) reads [*n*]*ʾʾṣbʾl,* but from the photograph and drawing on pl. 6 it seems clear that the space immediately preceding the *taw* was uninscribed.

c. Cf. the Egyptian PN *bś.y* (H. Ranke, *Die ägyptischen Personennamen* [Glückstadt: Augustin, 1935] 1:98, nos. 18, 19). Derivatives of Bes appear in biblical *bēsay,* in Egyptian Aramaic documents (*bsʾ, bsh,* W. Kornfeld, *Onomastica Aramaica aus Ägypten* [Vienna: Österreichischen Akademie der Wissenschaften, 1978] 79), and in cuneiform documents from Mesopotamia (*Bi-i(s)-sa-a,* APN, 64b).

d. The name may be incomplete and, if restored as *gdy[ʾl]* or *gdy[hw]* (Y. Aharoni, *Kĕtôvôt ʿĂrād,* 96), would not belong in this list.

e. See S. Ahituv, "Pashhur," *IEJ* 20 (1970) 95–96.

f. See I. Ben-Dor, "A Hebrew Seal from Samaria," *QDAP* 12 (1945–46) 77–83.

g. On this element, see below, p. 168.

h. If this element represents a deity (cf. B. Mazar, "A Genealogical List from Ras Shamra," *Journal of the Palestine Oriental Society* 16 [1936] 153; E. Y. Kutscher, *Hebrew and Aramaic Studies* [ed. Z. Ben-Hayyim et al.; Jerusalem: Magnes Press] 10). The element occurs in PNs at Ras Shamra, such as *ʾbmn, a-ḫi-ma-na, a-ḫi-mu-nu,* etc., where F. Gröndahl considers it to be merely a double suffix (*Personennamen,* 53, sec. 88); in the PN *ia-ri-ḫi-ma-nu* (*Personennamen,* 145), since *yrḫ* ("moon" or "moon-god") is the theophoric element, *-manu* is clearly not theophoric.

i. If the inscription is Hebrew (B. Mazar, art. "ʾḥymn," *EM* 1.218); note the uncertainty of S. Moscati, *L'epigrafia Ebraica Antica, 1935–1950,* 54, no. 7, p; K. Galling ("Beschriftete Bildsiegel," *ZDPV* 64 [1941] no. 118) considers it Aramaic.

j. See Kutscher, *Studies,* 10; Mazar, *EM* 1.219. Theoretically it is possible that *ḥmn* itself is a DN or epithet, as in the Canaanite PN *ʿbdḥmn* (F. L. Benz, *Personal Names in the Phoenician and Punic Inscriptions,* 313; cf. Gröndahl, *Personennamen,* 135). However, as Kutscher observes, hypocoristica consisting of the DN alone are rare; Benz confirms, with reference to Phoenician and Punic names, that this is the least attested type of hypocoristicon (*Personal Names,* 233).

k. See *EM* arts. "ʾḥymwt," "yrymwt," "mrmwt," and "ʿzmwt" (see also arts. "ʾlhy nkr," *EM* 1.322, sec. [1], 14, and "ḥṣrmwt," *EM* 3.279). M. Noth did not classify these and other names ending in *-mwt* as derivatives of *mwt* but as hypocoristica ending in *-ôt* and either left their meanings unexplained or resorted to Arabic rather than the known Hebrew words by which, if derived from *mwt,* they could be explained simply (*Die israelitischen Personennamen,* 39, 226, 231; cf.

W. F. Albright, "Notes on Ammonite History," in *Miscellanea Biblica B. Ubach* [Spain: Montiserrati, 1954], 134–35, on Ammonite *'nmwt).* However, each of the *-mwt* names can be paralleled by others in which a theophoric element appears in place of *-mwt,* e.g., *'ḥyh(w), yry'l, mry(b)b'l, 'zgd)* (to Ammonite *'nmwt,* R. Hestrin and M. Dayagi-Mendels, *Hôtāmôt Mîmê Bayit Ri'šôn,* 45, compare Hebrew *'nyh;* there is, however, a Safaitic-Thamudic PN *ġnmt* from *ġnm;* see G. L. Harding, *An Index and Concordance of Pre-Islamic Arabian Names and Inscriptions* (Toronto: University of Toronto Press, 1971) 458. Noth and Albright were probably reluctant to believe that a being connected with death and the netherworld would be invoked in personal names, but the comparable deities Resheph and Nergal appear in West Semitic and Akkadian names, often with meanings similar to those ending in *-mwt* (e.g., *aḫi-Nergal* [*PRU* III, 238] and *'aḫršp* [Gröndahl, *Personennamen,* 181], *mršp* [= *mr-ršp:* Gröndahl, *Personennamen,* 181], *Dannu-Nergal* [APN, 69]; cf. also *rešep* in 1 Chr 7:25). Understanding *'ḥymwt* as "my brother is Mawet" is plausible in the light of the "covenant with Mawet" in Isa 28:14–18; likewise, understanding *'zmwt* as "Mawet is strong" is plausible in the light of Cant 8:6, "love is as strong as Mawet." Lemaire (*Inscriptions hébraïques,* 53) mentions the uncertain restoration of another *mrmwt* in SO 33:3.

l. Reading dubious.

m. Reading very uncertain.

n. See Lemaire, *Inscriptions hébraïques,* 94–95.

o. The photograph in R. Hestrin et al., *Kĕtôvôt Mĕsappĕrôt,* shows clearly that the final letter is *nun;* cf. Shallun for Shallum in Neh 3:15, and cf. *EM* 7.686; Benz, *Personal Names,* 418.

p. The photograph and drawing in Aharoni, *Kĕtôvôt Ărād,* 90, show the second letter to be a *bet,* not a *mem* as Aharoni read it. *'b* is presumably an abbreviation or error for *'bd;* cf. Benz, *Personal Names,* 369 and examples on 371, sec. 3.

q. See N. Avigad, "Seals of Exiles," *IEJ* 15 (1965) 229.

r. See Kutscher, *Studies,* 9.

languages, equivalent to Greek *tyche*.[39] Like *tyche, gad* was sometimes personified and worshiped as the genius or fortune of an individual, a tribe, a city, a garden, or a well.[40] Although there are unnamed *gad*s, the term often appears as the epithet of major deities, as in the personal names *mlqrtgd* ("Melqart is (my) patron spirit") (Punic; Benz, *Personal Names,* 140), and *gdybwl* ("My patron spirit is Bol") (Palmyra; J. Stark, *Personal Names in Palmyrene Inscriptions* [Oxford: Clarendon Press, 1971] 13; see also pp. 59, 98, 144). This epithet was sometimes applied to YHWH, as in *gdyw* (SO 2:2), and possibly *gdy[hw]* (Arad 71:3), and this could be the case with other *gad* names in inscriptions and the Bible (cf. Gaddiel, Num 13:10). On the other hand, Isa 65:11 refers unfavorably to a cult of "the *gad*" (LXX: *daimoni*),[41] indicating that this *gad* was not YHWH. Whether this cult goes back to the preexilic period or not, it involves a being that, though supernatural, seems less than divine, belonging to the realm of angelology rather than polytheism. The Egyptian Bes is described as a "protective deity" who watches over sleeping people, childbirth, and newborn children; he was popular in folk religion, and it is uncertain whether he had an official cult.[42]

Mawet, too, appears to belong to the angelological realm. In biblical passages where *mwt* may be construed as a proper noun it seems to be a demonic force personifying death, plague, and destruction. Jeremiah 9:20 describes *māwet* in terms applied in cuneiform literature to the demon *lamaštu*.[43] The thinking represented in the Mawet names may be like that expressed in the covenant with Mawet in Isa 28:15: "When the sweeping flood passes through it shall not reach us." This covenant looks like an apotropaic rite,[44] and the -*mwt* names (especially biblical *'hymwt*) may have had the same purpose. Mawet thus appears to have been a supernatural demonic figure in Israel rather than a full-fledged deity.[45]

Most of the remaining names may also have nonpagan explanations. The following are worth considering.

In the names *ṭbšlm/n* and *'bšlm, šlm* could be an epithet of YHWH, as in the altar name YHWH-Shalom (Judg 6:24) and perhaps in the PN *šĕlūmî'ēl*. The epithet would mean "(Divine) Ally."[46]

Although E. Y. Kutscher was right in doubting that *hym* is the Hebrew name "Hayim," which does not appear until the Middle Ages, derivation from *hyh (hwy)* ("live") is not out of the question. Several names are derived from this root in Northwest Semitic onomastica. These include augmented derivatives of the perfect stem, such as *hy/hy', hw'* (F. L. Benz, *Personal Names,* 308) and *hyn* (F. Gröndahl, *Personennamen,* 137). Conceivably, then, *hym* could be *hy* plus the hypocoristic ending -*ām/ōm* (as in *'hzm, gršm, kmhm, mlkm,* etc.).[47] However, given the possibility that the biblical names Miriam and perhaps Abiyam derive from the DN *yām*,[48] derivation of *hym* from that DN should not be ruled out.

'dt' ("Lady") is a title of goddesses in Phoenician *(KAI, 7:4; 29:2)* and in Northwest Semitic personal names (see Gröndahl, *Personennamen*, 90), but theoretically it could be an appellative expressing the parents' hopes for its bearer.[49] Since there are no other goddesses in the Israelite onomasticon, one may doubt that in Israel this name was understood as referring to one.

Although the names containing Horus, Isis, and Shamash clearly refer to foreign deities, linguistically the Horus and Isis names are Egyptian and the Shamash name is Akkadian. Since there are no names in Hebrew (i.e., with Hebrew predicates) based on the latter two deities, and mostly uncertain ones based on Horus,[50] they are weak evidence for the worship of these deities in Israel; "naturalized" foreign cults would presumably form names in the local language.[51] Since *šwššr'ṣr* is written in Aramaic script and *pṭ's* may be in Aramaic or Phoenician script,[52] the individuals who bear these names may be foreigners. The same cannot be said of those named Pashhur, since it is borne by two priests and a priestly family in the Bible (Jer 19:14—20:6; 21:1–2; Ezra 2:38; etc.),[53] and one of these and one of the inscriptional Pashhurs have Yahwistic patronyms (Jer 21:1–2; second *pšḥr* in chart above). But one may doubt that the name was understood by Israelites who did not speak Egyptian. These two names belong to a larger group of Egyptian names found in Israel, several among priests, and since not all are theophoric (e.g., Hophni, Phinehas, *ppy* [Arad 72:2]), it is possible that the phenomenon requires a nontheological explanation (e.g., carry-over from the period of bondage in Egypt or from periods of Egyptian dominance in Canaan, or the result of later immigration from Egypt [cf. 1 Kgs 3:1; 1 Chr 2:34–35]).

If we should reject the explanations we have just weighed and consider all these names as consciously referring to deities other than YHWH, the twenty-seven individuals bearing these names would amount to 7.1 percent of those with theophoric names (excluding those whose names contain *'ēl or 'ēlî*).[54] Those with Baal names would represent 1.6 percent of the corpus, those whose names mention Shalim, Qaus, and Horus 0.8 percent, Gad and Mawet 0.5 percent, and the rest even less.

Even this low percentage may suggest more extensive conscious use of pagan PNs among Israelites than was actually the case. The figure of 7.1 percent is based on the Israelite inscriptional names published as of 1979. These do not include most of the names in two large collections from which only a few have been published. One is a collection of seventh-century bullae from an unknown site in Judah which have been studied by N. Avigad. Thirty-nine different names appear on these bullae.

Twenty-one of them are Yahwistic and one refers to a foreign deity.[55] The other is the group of names in the inscriptions found as of 1982 in the City of David excavations directed by Y. Shiloh. There are forty-six different names in these inscriptions, at least twenty-three of them Yahwistic and one possibly referring to a pagan god.[56] Since neither group of inscriptions has yet been published, it is impossible to determine how many different individuals are represented by these names, and it was therefore not possible to include them in the statistics we have cited. But a simple calculation makes the implications of these new inscriptions clear. If we should assume that each of the names in these groups represents one individual, the forty-four Yahwistic names plus the two pagan ones would raise the total number of theophoric names in the corpus to 424, and there would then be a total of twenty-nine pagan names in the corpus. The pagan names would then drop to 6.8 percent of the corpus. In fact, since the discovery of the Samaria ostraca in 1910, the percentage of pagan names in the inscriptional corpus has dropped with almost every new discovery of names.[57]

Moreover, whatever percentage of the corpus is represented by the pagan names, there were foreigners—*nokrîm* and *gērîm*—residing in Israel, and the possibility must be considered that some of those with pagan names were among them.[58] We have already noted that the seals of *šwššr'ṣr* and *pṭ's* are inscribed in foreign scripts. J. Naveh considered *tṣb'l* as possibly a gentile, partly on the basis of his dating of the inscription to the time of Josiah, since the site where it was found would have come under Judahite control only recently.[59] The names with Qaus—only one is certain—all come from sites in the Negev, where, if anywhere, one would expect an Edomite cult to make inroads. But Edomites frequently migrated into the Negev, and parts of the Negev were at times controlled by Edom.[60] It is therefore possible that the bearers of the Qaus names are Edomites. Y. Aharoni presumed that [*qw*]⌐s¬'*nl*(?) of Arad 12:3 was an Edomite since that very name had been read on Edomite seal impressions; while that fact itself is not decisive, the peculiar form -'*nl* does not seem Hebraic and may be Edomite,[61] which would strengthen Aharoni's presumption. The fact that the *b'l* names of the Samaria ostraca are virtually unique in the corpus means that they are not typical of the contemporary Israelite population; since the ostraca were found in the capital and the names are connected with the royal court and perhaps crown lands, some could represent foreigners, perhaps Phoenicians, in the service of the northern monarchy.

Finally, a certain percentage of pagan names probably represents a meaningless residue of previous onomastic practices. Onomastic habits change slowly, and the process is not necessarily expedited by religious revolutions, even zealous ones. Christians—both laity and clergy—did not begin to abandon pagan theophoric names earnestly until late in the fourth century. Before that, as A. Harnack put it, "Here was the primitive church exterminating every vestige of polytheism in her midst, tabooing pagan mythology as devilish . . . and yet freely employing the pagan names which had hitherto been in vogue!" "'The martyrs perished because they declined to sacrifice to the gods whose names they bore'!"[62] It may be assumed that a certain percentage of pagan theophoric names survived in Israel, too, simply out of inertia without their users acknowledging the deities they mention.

The statistics obtained from the corpus of inscriptional names are roughly comparable with those obtained from the Bible, especially for the periods of the divided monarchy and late Judah, to which the inscriptions belong.[63] They suggest that, at least for these periods, censorship did not significantly distort the picture given by the Masoretic Text.[64]

To appreciate the significance of these statistics we may compare the situation in unquestionably polytheistic societies. In Old Babylonian Sippar, Shamash, the chief god of that city, appeared in the names of 20 percent of people with theophoric names, Sin in 15 percent, and several other deities in decreasing percentages. In fifteenth- and fourteenth-century Assur, the chief god, Ashur, appeared in the names of 17 percent of people with theophoric names, with the two closest gods in the names of 16.6 percent and 13 percent of them. In the lists from the Eshmun temple near Sidon, Ashtart appears in 23.8 percent of the theophoric names, with all others, including Eshmun, far behind.[65] These three cases show leading deities appearing in little more than 20 percent of theophoric names; in none of them do they overwhelm their individual competitors as they do in Israel.

Our original expectation that we would find significant number of pagan theophoric names in Israel was based on the biblical accusations of polytheism. The results of our survey are puzzling in the light of those accusations. Is there any say to explain our findings without challenging those accusations? We have already noted that the corpus may reflect mostly the upper strata of Israelite society. Was polytheism in Israel perhaps largely a lower-class phenomenon? While this is conceivable, it is no answer to our problem. As noted above, the Bible records several instances of royal tolerance and patronage of pagan cults, including the half-century reign of Manasseh during the period in question. It is precisely among the upper classes and circles close to the royal court that one would expect to find pagan names, and it is hard to imagine why such names would not have appeared in those circles if the polytheism had any real following among the population. There would have been no official persecution of paganism under these circumstances, and those who believed that other gods played a role in their lives would have had no cause to fear if they expressed this belief openly.

Another possibility is that the onomasticon does not tell the whole story. It is possible that personal names reflect only one facet of the religious life of a particular society and that a deity who played a significant role might escape notice in the onomasticon. The Ammonite onomasticon is overwhelmingly dominated by El, and if one assumes that the Ammonites were polytheists, this would indicate that other important deities could go largely unmentioned in the onomasticon of their worshipers.[66] However, startling as it may be to contemplate, we do not know that the Ammonites were polytheistic, and from their onomasticon one might conclude that they were no more pluralistic in religion than were the Israelites.[67] At Ugarit one finds a lack of consistency between the pantheons of the literary texts, the cultic texts, the administrative documents, and the onomasticon.[68] The goddess Athtart was the recipient of sacrifices (*UT* 23:3) and apparently had a temple (*UT* 1088:2) and was invoked in an epistolary blessing (*UT* 2008:7), but she does not appear in any of the personal names listed in Gröndahl. Athirat, who received sacrifices (*UT* 1:6), appears in only one name (Gröndahl, *Personennamen*, 103), and Anath, who also received sacrifices (*UT* 3:16), appears in a dozen or so names (see Gröndahl, *Personennamen*, 111), "relatively infrequently" in Gröndahl's view.[69] This inconsistency may indicate that in the fourteenth and thirteenth centuries the goddesses were important in the traditional, official religion of Ugarit but not in the popular, private religion reflected in the onomasticon.[70] An analogous explanation of the onomastic evidence from Israel would be that the popular/private religion was almost exclusively Yahwistic and that other deities were worshiped only in the state religion when royal policy dictated it. In any case, in the present state of our understanding, caution demands that we recognize that onomastic evidence may not give a complete picture of the gods worshiped in a society and that to obtain a representative picture we must seek out other types of epigraphic evidence as well.

NON-ONOMASTIC INSCRIPTIONAL EVIDENCE

Other types of epigraphic evidence that reflect religious loyalties include formulas of salutation in letters, votive inscriptions and prayers for blessing, and other aspects of the inscriptions. In polytheistic societies these elements reflect the eclectic allegiances of the writers. Given sufficient documentation, a polytheistic society in the ancient Near East will yield either single texts mentioning more than one deity at a time or different but contemporary texts mentioning different deities. Israelite inscriptions of the same types are exclusively Yahwistic almost without exception.

Formulas of Salutation in Letters

Letters commonly include salutations in which the sender invokes divine blessings upon the recipient. In polytheistic societies these salutations are usually polytheistic.[71] Two groups of letters from preexilic Judah include religious salutations, those from Arad, mostly those found in level VI (605–595), and those from Lachish (shortly before the fall of Jerusalem in 587/86). Three of the salutations from Arad employ the formula, "I bless you by YHWH" (*brktk lyhwh,* nos. 16; 21, partly restored; and, from level VIII, no. 40, mostly restored). Another uses the formula, "May YHWH seek your welfare" (*yhwh yš'l lšlmk,* no. 18). In the Lachish letters the predominant salutation is, "May YHWH cause my lord to hear tidings of well-being/good (this very day)" (*yšmᶜ yhwh 't 'dny šmᶜt šlm/ṭb ('t kym),* nos. 2–5, 8, and 9). One letter employs the salutation, "May YHWH cause my lord to see this season in good health" (*yr' yhwh 't 'dny 't hᶜt hzh šlm,* no. 6). Thus all eleven religious salutations known to us in Hebrew letters are exclusively Yahwistic.[72] It is noteworthy that ten of these letters are dated after the time of Josiah, when the reforms sponsored by that king are thought by many scholars to have lapsed.

Votive Inscriptions and Prayers for Blessing

Votive objects may be donated to one deity or many, and the inscriptions on them reflect the number of deities honored by the donation. From preexilic Israelite sites we have a number of inscriptions that appear to be of votive or quasi-votive character.

The clearest case is the large stone bowl from Kuntillet ʿAjrud that has on its rim the name of its donor followed by the formula, "May he be blessed by YHWH" *(brk hʾ lyhw).*[73] In the Jewish Quarter of Jerusalem a jar was discovered with an inscription beginning with a name—presumably that of the donor—followed on the next line by [   ]*qnʾrṣ,* persuasively restored by Avigad as [*ʾl*]*qnʾrṣ,* almost certainly an epithet of YHWH in Israel.[74] A jar associated with the tombs at Khirbet el-Qom is inscribed with the word "El" *(ʾl,* probably in the meaning "God," a standard epithet of YHWH in Israel. W. G. Dever takes the inscription as implying that the bowl was "a sacred vessel, probably for libations."[75] Two other vessels, a jar fragment from Megiddo with the letters *lyw* incised on it and a bowl rim from Samaria with the incised letters *lyh,* could also be votive.[76] Since the first of these inscriptions is complete and the second probably so, they are not just the remainders of names. They are not likely to mean "belonging to" people with hypocoristic names *yh* and *yw,* since these too would be personal names of the rarest type. It is conceivable that *lyw* and *lyh* are personal names of the type *l* + DN ("belonging to DN"), such as *lâʾēl* (Num 3:24), though these are also rare.[77] But the simplest explanation is that the inscriptions characterize the vessels as devoted to YHWH.[78] The Samaria inscription uses the short form of the divine name, "Yah."[79] It is no surprise to find this form on a votive vessel, for the fact that it is used mostly in psalms indicates that its normal context was liturgical (outside psalms the form also appears in Exod 15:2; 17:16; Isa 12:2; 26:4; 38:11, and there is no reason to doubt that it is preexilic). On the other hand, *yw* does not appear elsewhere as an independent form (apart from the controversial Ugaritic *yw*), but its appearance in personal names indicates that such a usage cannot be ruled out.

Although inscriptions on non-Israelite votive objects sometimes mention several deities at once, these five mention only one at a time, and all refer to YHWH or his known appellations and epithets. Since their number is small, however, they do not by themselves confirm the unilatrous character of Israelite worship.[80]

Prayers for blessing are closely related to votive inscriptions. As in the case of the formula "May he be blessed by YHWH" on the ʿAjrud votive bowl, such prayers are often inscribed on votive objects. More often, however, they are found in graffiti, and since graffiti have less reason to restrict themselves to one deity at a time, outside Israel they are frequently polytheistic.

A few prayers for blessing have been discovered at sites in or related to the preexilic Israelite kingdoms. Unfortunately, most of these inscriptions are problematic in several ways. The difficult inscriptions in the Khirbet Beit Lei cave near Lachish include one that reads simply, "Save, O [Y]HWH" *(hwšʿ [y]hwh).*[81] Paleographically the inscription is dated broadly to the sixth century,[82] and it could be from the hand of a writer who grew up before the exile, though not necessarily. The formula "May PN be blessed" appears three times in an inscription in a cave near En-gedi, but the divine name is missing in each case.[83] The same formula appears in the longest of the inscriptions from the burial cave at Khirbet el-Qom, where line 2 reads, "May Uriahu be blessed by YHWH" *(brk. ʾryhw. lyhwh).*[84]

The Khirbet el-Qom inscription, along with others found at Kuntillet ʿAjrud, also provides evidence that is certainly heterodox and may point in the direction of paganism. Three inscriptions on large pithoi from ʿAjrud refer to YHWH and an *asherah:*[85] (1) *brkt. ʾtkm. lyhwh. šmrn. wlʾšrth* ("I bless you by YHWH of Samaria and by his [= YHWH's]/ its [= Samaria's] *asherah*");[86] (2) *brktk.lyhwh tmn wl'šrth.ybrk.wyšmrk wyhy ʿm. 'd[n]y* ... ("I bless you by YHWH of Teman and by his/its *asherah*: May he bless and protect you and may he be with my lord"); (3) ... *lyhwh htmn.wl'šrth* ("... by YHWH of Teman and by his/its *asherah*"). While the excavator, Z. Meshel, took the word *asherah* to refer to YHWH's sanctuary or symbol and A. Lemaire took it to refer to a sacred tree,[87] M. Gilula suggested that the word referred to the Canaanite goddess Asherah or her image, and that this goddess was viewed as the consort of YHWH.[88] This view construes *'šrth* as a proper noun followed by a pronominal suffix, meaning "his Asherah." However, in biblical Hebrew pronominal suffixes are never affixed to proper nouns.[89] What is more, the continuation of the third ʿAjrud inscription mentions only YHWH as acting: *wntn lh yhw klbbh* ("and may YHWH give him what his heart desires").[90] Grammar and context indicate, therefore, that *asherah* must be a common noun and not a deity, just as Meshel and Lemaire thought.[91] That a blessing should invoke a deity and a cultic object or sanctuary is not unparalleled. In Neo-Assyrian letters the salutation "May the gods bless you" is sometimes replaced by the formula "May (the city) Uruk and (the temple) Eanna bless my lord."[92] In West Semitic inscriptions we find votive objects dedicated to "Our Lord and the image of Baal (*l'dnn wlsml bʿl*): May they bless and keep him (the donor) alive" (*KAI*, 12:3–4)[93] and graffiti invoking remembrance before several deities "and all the images" (*smytʾ*, *KAI*, 251 and 256).[94] Such formulas may reflect the hypostatization of cultic objects, and Lemaire has remarked in this context the danger that such hypostatization presented to monotheism.[95] In the present passages, however, the context remains substantially monotheistic and the references to YHWH and an *asherah* represent at most the heterodoxy of one or more Yahwists at a distant site apparently frequented by others in addition to Israelites.[96]

A passage in the Khirbet el-Qom inscription has been interpreted in ways that would affect our understanding of the ʿAjrud inscriptions. The line following the blessing *brk 'ryhw lyhwh*, quoted above, is extraordinarily difficult to interpret owing to numerous scratches in the rock surface and to the writer's apparent practice of incising some of the letters twice, but not in exactly the same space. In a painstaking study of the inscription, Z. Zevit identified the following letters or apparent letters in the line *w ʿmʾ mṣrryyh/rh l'lšʾrttrh hwšʿlh*.[97] Epigraphists studying the inscription are forced to decide which signs to disregard as lexically meaningless repetitions or scratches. Lemaire read the line as *wmṣryh.l'šrth.hwšʿ lh*. By transposing *l'šrth* to the beginning of the line, following the *waw*, he obtained a passage that could be translated, "Blessed be Uriahu by Yahweh and by his *asherah*; from his enemies he saved him!'"[98] Naveh read the beginning of line 3 as *nṣry wl'šrth hwšᶜ lh,* yielding a similar formula, "Blessed be Uriahu by YHWH my guardian and by his Asherah. Save him."[99] Both of these readings yield a formula identical to that found at ʿAjrud and presume that the *heh* is a pronominal suffix connecting *'šrh* with YHWH. S. Mittmann read the line as *wmmṣr ydh l'l šrth hwšᶜ lh* ("und aus Bedrängnis preist er den Gott seines Dienstes, der ihm hilft"), which eliminates an *asherah* from the line altogether.[100] Zevit's view, however, is that the lexically significant letters in the line are *mṣryh l'šrth hwšᶜ lh,* which he translates, "and from his enemies, O Asherata, save him."[101] This interpretation sunders the *asherah* from YHWH, ruling out a construction of the final *heh* as a pronominal suffix and thus obviating the need to take *asherah* as a common noun. Instead, Asherah—in the form Asherata—can be taken as a divine name. Zevit argues that the form of Asherata is that known from certain proper names such as Jotbatha and in the poetic form of some common nouns (e.g., *'ymth,* Exod 15:16). But it is doubtful that these two phenomena should be grouped together or understood as cases of "double feminization," as Zevit suggests. The termination *-ah* in these forms is toneless in the Masoretic Text, indicating that it is not the feminine ending. The proper nouns in which the termination appears are all place-names,[102] which supports the old view that it is a *heh*-locale which became fused to the name and is now otiose.[103] It is most improbable that the name of a goddess would take the same form. If Zevit's reading of the line is correct, perhaps a better interpretation is suggested by his suggestion that the *lamed* preceding *'šrth* means "for" or "for the sake of"; conceivably the prayer means, "Save him from his enemies for the sake of his *asherah*" (i.e., a cultic symbol in the sanctuary where he worships). In any case, the fact that the inscription continues with a singular verb *hwšᶜ lw* ("save him") indicates that this inscription too expects only one deity to be active;[104] that the inscription should mention two deities but ask only one of them to save Uriahu seems unlikely.

Finally there is an ostracon found on the surface at Tell Qasile with the ambiguous inscription, *ᶜzᵓhb. 'pr.lbyt.ḥrn,* followed by the sum "30 shekels."[105] The inscription can be taken to refer to a shipment of ophir gold to, or belonging to, the town of Beth-horon. In that case, Beth-horon is merely the surviving pre-Israelite name of the town and has no significance for Israelite belief. But it is also possible to understand the inscription to indicate a shipment of gold to a temple of the deity Horon, possibly in Tell Qasile or Yabneh. B. Mazar, who first published the inscription, mentioned both possibilities and ultimately inclined toward the second.[106] Even if this interpretation should be the correct one, what it shows about Israelite practice is uncertain. While the script of the ostracon is Hebrew, the number 30 is written anomalously with a Phoenician numeral; Egyptian numerals are normally used for the tens in Hebrew inscriptions. As Aharoni observed in this connection, "At a harbor town like Tell Qasile Phoenician influence is not surprising,"[107] and what he said in connection with numerals may hold good for a possible donation to a temple of Horon. In other words, the ostracon may represent local Phoenician influence on a coastal Israelite, not a cult that had made inroads in the Israelite heartland. One may even wonder whether the Hebrew script necessarily implies that this inscription was written by an Israelite. The Moabites used Hebrew script (witness the Mesha inscription), and perhaps it was used in Philistia too. A fragmentary inscription in Hebrew letters was found incised before firing on a fragment of an eighth-century jar at Ashdod, from which M. Dothan inferred that "by the eighth century B.C.E., if not earlier, the Ashdodites shared a common script and language with their neighbors, the Phoenicians, and with the people of Israel and Judah."[108]

Of the inscriptions surveyed up to this point, eleven letters with religious salutations are exclusively Yahwistic, five inscriptions that are arguably votive use forms of YHWH or his epithets, and a prayer on the wall of a cave mentions only YHWH. Almost all of these inscriptions are from sites near Israelite population centers—Lachish, Arad, Khirbet el-Qom, Megiddo, Samaria, and Khirbet Beit Lei; only the votive bowl from ʿAjrud is from a peripheral site. Inscriptions that arguably refer to another deity include three from ʿAjrud, one from Khirbet el-Qom, and one from Tell Qasile. We have argued that grammatical and contextual evidence militate against such interpretations of the ʿAjrud and el-Qom inscriptions. In any case, only the el-Qom inscription is from the heartland of Israelite settlement, whereas the ʿAjrud and Tell Qasile inscriptions are from peripheral sites exposed to foreign influence.

Miscellaneous Aspects of the Inscriptions

Various other aspects of the inscriptions also carry religious implications.

Oaths. In polytheistic societies, oaths may name several deities at a time. In the Bible it is considered a test of loyalty to YHWH that the Israelite swear only by him (Deut 6:13–14; 10:20; 23:7 [cf. Exod 23:13]; Isa 45:23; Jer 12:16; Amos 8:14). Although we have no Israelite legal inscriptions, the genre in which oaths are normally found, two or three of the Lachish letters contain oaths, and they are all Yahwistic, each containing the formula *ḥy yhwh* ("by the life of YHWH") (Lachish 6:12; 3:9 [written *ḥyhwh*]; 12:3).[109] Although the number of examples is small, these oaths undoubtedly reflect the beliefs of the authors of the letters, for oaths are not conventional parts of letters which might represent the beliefs or habits of scribes.

Cave graffiti. Although Khirbet Beit Lei inscriptions A and B are difficult to read, it is clear that their content is religious. Epigraphists agree that each of these inscriptions mentions YHWH, and none finds any other deity in them.[110]

Temples, temple vessels, and cultic personnel. Arad 18:9 refers to the temple of YHWH *(byt.yhwh)*. Another sanctuary of YHWH, in the days of Omri and Ahab, is implied by the Mesha inscription, which mentions that Mesha took vessels of YHWH *([k]ly yhwh)* as booty from Nebo, in Reubenite territory in Transjordan (lines 17–18).[111] There is one possible reference to a temple of a foreign god, *byt.ḥrn*, in the Tell Qasile inscription; as noted above, it is not certain that this inscription is Israelite or that it reflects practices in Israelite population centers. One or two seals belonging to cultic personnel are known. The priest of Dor *(khn d'r)* bears the Yahwistic name *[z]kryw*,[112] though this does not necessarily mean that he was a priest of YHWH. The seal of *mqnyw* identifies him as "servant of YHWH" *('bd.yhwh)*.[113] Cross speculates that the title may imply that *mqnyw* was a cultic functionary. Even if this should not be the case, this is the only Israelite inscription to identify a person as the servant of a deity, and the deity is YHWH.

An amulet. An inscription on a small piece of rolled silver—presumably an amulet—was found in excavations in Jerusalem.[114] Even a person who might have feared to express allegiance to foreign gods openly, for fear of persecution, could have felt free to carry an amulet mentioning such a god, since the amulet was small enough to conceal. As of the time of initial publication only one word of this inscription had been identified: the divine name YHWH.

Other inscriptions. There are some inscriptions at 'Ajrud that mention Baal and *'šrt*. For the present, it seems that these are not Israelite. They are part of the group whose script Meshel terms "Phoenician."[115]

CONCLUSIONS

The religious aspects of the inscriptions duplicate the picture emerging from the onomastic evidence. Despite the relatively small number of examples in each category, the cumulative effect of the whole is unmistakable. In every respect the inscriptions suggest an overwhelmingly Yahwistic society in the heartland of Israelite settlement, especially in

Judah. If we had only the inscriptional evidence, I doubt that we would ever imagine that there existed a significant amount of polytheistic practice in Israel during the period in question.[116]

That we do think there was significant polytheism in Israel is due to the biblical evidence cited at the beginning of this chapter. So long as reservations about this evidence were based on literary-historical criticism of biblical literature, it was easy to dismiss them as apologetic and inconclusive. But the extrabiblical evidence we have reviewed seems now to lend substance to those reservations. Since personal names, salutations, votives, prayers, and oaths express thanks for the gods' beneficence, hope for their blessing and protection, and the expectation that they will punish deception, the low representation of pagan deities in the names and inscriptions indicates that deities other than YHWH were not widely regarded by Israelites as sources of beneficence, blessing, protection, and justice.

It is not entirely surprising to find that Israelites did not look to the "national" gods of foreign nations, such as Kemosh, Milkom, Dagon, or Ashur, for these benefits. It could be argued that the Israelites viewed those gods as doing only for foreigners what YHWH does for Israel (see Judg 11:24). What is more surprising is to find similar indifference to nature gods whose spheres were not limited to specific nations, for the Israelites surely recognized that they were as dependent on the sun and rain and fertility as their neighbors were. If the bulk of the Israelites ignored the gods of these phenomena, they must not have considered these phenomena divine or independently effective. In other words, a unilatry which ignores the gods of other *nations* can be classified as monolatry. But a unilatry that ignores phenomena on which *all* nations depend looks like monotheism.

The evidence we have reviewed does not require us to deny that any polytheism existed. One cannot dismiss out of hand such circumstantial statements as Jeremiah's charge that some Israelites would "say to a block of wood, 'You are my father,' and to a stone, 'You gave birth to me' " (Jer 2:27). A statement like this, implying that the statue is more than a fetish, may even imply mythological polytheism. Entitling a celestial goddess "Queen of Heaven" may also imply that the goddess had a mythology, though the title could be simply vestigial. But in any case, our evidence implies that there was not much polytheism of any kind, mythological or fetishistic.

What, then, of the biblical indictments of the Israelites for centuries of polytheism? Much of the polytheism described by Kings was sponsored by the royal court: the chapels that Solomon built for his foreign wives, Ahab's tolerance of Jezebel's zeal for Baal, and Manasseh's paganizing.

The inscriptional evidence, part of which reflects the upper classes in the time of Manasseh, does not contradict these charges against the kings,[117] but it indicates that this polytheism must have attracted few adherents even among the circles connected with the court. In the case of Solomon and Ahab, tolerance of polytheism must have been motivated by the same political considerations that led to their marriages with foreign princesses. In the case of Manasseh, the polytheism must have been the king's idiosyncrasy. To the extent that the prophets and the historiographers indict the public at large, some of their ire may have been directed at the cult of certain spirits and demons reflected in a few of the personal names surveyed above. While the worship of semidivine beings is not inherently incompatible with monotheism, biblical dogma defined it as such and the prophets and historiographers accepted this dogma. The critical historian needs to recognize the difference.[118]

The testimony of these witnesses must also be interpreted in the light of their tasks and their world view. Exaggeration is a characteristic of orators everywhere, and the prophets were no exception; "every one knows that scholastic precision is not to be looked for in what is said for impression."[119] The authors of Kings were confronted with the task of explaining the fall of Judah in accordance with the axiom that had always dominated Israelite historiosophy: National calamity is the result of sin (see already Judg 5:8a). The doctrine of collective responsibility led prophets and historiographers alike to generalize the guilt of individuals or groups to the entire people. One man, Achan, violated the ban on booty at Jericho and God told Joshua, "Israel has sinned! They have broken the covenant . . . they have taken of the proscribed . . . they have stolen . . . they have broken faith!" (Josh 7:11; cf. v 1); thirty-six Israelites died for the sin. Similarly the sins of the Golden Calf and Baal-peor were attributed to "the people," though Moses' commands to execute the guilty make it clear that only some of the people were involved (Exodus 32; Numbers 25).[120] The sweeping biblical indictments, in sum, are based more on theological axioms than on historical data. The epigraphic evidence, with its lack of a comparable *Tendenz,* argues against attributing any statistical significance to those indictments.

Combining the evidence of the inscriptions and the more circumstantial statements of the biblical writers, we may suppose that there existed some superficial, fetishistic polytheism and a limited amount of more profound polytheism in Israel, though neither can be quantified. Since the inscriptional evidence sets in for the most part in the eighth century, these conclusions apply directly only to the period beginning then. They do not directly argue against the greater prevalence of polytheism earlier. It remains theoretically possible that the prophets and late historiographers imputed to the eighth through the early sixth century actual sins of earlier generations.[121] But since the epigraphic evidence about the onomasticon suggests that personal names in the biblical text were not extensively censored (see above), this implies that the essentially non-polytheistic onomastic picture given by the Bible all the way back to the beginning of the divided monarchy is realistic. Furthermore, the evidence for polytheism before the eighth century comes from the same type of historiographic literature that has proven so hard to follow for the eighth century and following. If it is difficult to take those sources literally for the religious situation in and near their own times, it is hard to do so for earlier times. After the united monarchy, perhaps even earlier, the evidence currently available makes it very difficult to suppose that many Israelites worshiped gods other than YHWH.[122]

NOTES

1. Y. Kaufmann, *The Religion of Israel* (trans. from the Hebrew and abridged by M. Greenberg; Chicago: University of Chicago Press, 1960) esp. 122–49. The *Oxford English Dictionary* defines fetish as "an inanimate object worshipped . . . on account of its supposed inherent magical powers, or as being animated by a spirit." The former meaning is that used by Kaufmann: "If the god is not understood to be a living, natural power, or a mythological person who dwells in, or is symbolized by, the image, it is evident that the image worship is conceived to be nothing but fetishism." (Kaufmann, *Religion,* 9; cf. 14; on 9–10 and 131 n. 2, Kaufmann discusses some exceptions to this belief).

2. M. Burrows, *What Mean Those Stones?* (New Haven: ASOR, 1941) 218–21; further sources cited by J. B. Pritchard, *Palestinian Figurines in Relation to Certain Goddesses Known Through Literature* (New Haven: American Oriental Society, 1943) 2–3, nn. 5–6.

3. M. Smith, *Palestinian Parties and Politics That Shaped the Old Testament* (New York: Columbia University Press, 1971) 25.

4. On the Baal names, see M. Noth, *Die israelitischen Personennamen im Rahmen der gemeinsemitischen Namengebung* (BWANT 3/10; Stuttgart: W. Kohlhammer, 1928) 119–22; J. Bright, *A History of Israel* (3d ed; Philadelphia: Westminster Press, 1981) 260–61; W. F. Albright, *Archaeology and the Religion of Israel* (4th ed; Baltimore: Johns Hopkins University Press, 1956) 160–61; T. Meek, *Hebrew Origins* (New York: Harper & Brothers, 1960) 223. On Lachish, see H. Torczyner, *Tĕʿûdôt Lākîš* [*The Lachish Ostraca*] (Library of Palestinology of the Jewish Palestine Exploration Society 15–17; Jerusalem: Jewish Palestine Exploration Society, 1940) xxxvii, 2–7 (in fact, most of the fathers named in the Lachish ostraca, who must have been born before Josiah's reformation, also have Yahwistic names).

5. See Y. Zakovitch, *Kĕfel Midrĕšê Šem* (M.A. thesis, Hebrew University, 1971) index, 271–85, on these names.

6. Exceptions mostly mention gods in the plural, such as Phoenician/Punic

'bd'lm. See F. L. Benz, *Personal Names in the Phoenician and Punic Inscriptions* (Studia Pohl 8; Rome: Biblical Institute Press, 1972) 149.

7. J. A. Wilson, *The Culture of Ancient Egypt* (Chicago: University of Chicago Press, 1959) 221.

8. These statistics are based on data collected by my student, Dana M. Pike, in an unpublished seminar paper, "Israelite Theophoric Personal Names in the Bible: A Statistical Analysis" (1983). Pike's own statistical conclusions differ from those presented above, in part because he does not count names containing *b'l* and certain other elements among the pagan names. While I agree that many of these names are not pagan (see below), for the purposes of the present study I have counted them as plausibly pagan in my statistics, since many scholars view them that way and I wanted to give the case for pagan names every reasonable benefit of the doubt. After recomputing Pike's statistics to include *b'l* names and to exclude individuals likely to have been born and named after the fall of Jerusalem, the breakdown of theophoric names in the Bible by period is roughly as follows:

Period	Theophoric Names	Yahwistic	Probably Pagan
Patriarchal	3	0 (0%)	3 (100%)
Exodus-conquest	6	3 (50%)	3 (50%)
Judges-united monarchy	163	140 (86%)	23 (14%)
Divided monarchy	127	123 (97%)	4 (3%)
Late Judah	97	92 (95%)	5 (5%)
Uncertain but not postexilic	70	55 (79%)	15 (21%)
TOTAL	466	413 (89%)	53 (11%)

9. Lists in G. B. Gray, *Studies in Hebrew Proper Names* (London: Adam & Charles Black, 1896) 121–22; Noth, *Die israelitischen Personennamen,* 119. (I do not include among the *ba'al* names those which are only conjectured to include *ba'al,* since they can be explained plausibly in their present forms.) In "Ishbosheth and Congeners," *HUCA* 46 (1975) 71–87, M. Tsevat suggests that *bōšet* is not a *"dysphemism"* for *ba'al* in these names but rather a legitimate element of personal names, cognate to *baštu* in Akkadian personal names, where it means "dignity, pride, vigor, guardian angel, patron saint"; he holds that the people who bore these names were known by two different names. If this were so, however, one would expect to find this element appearing randomly in Hebrew names, not only in the names of individuals who are known to have had *ba'al* names. (Yashabeam, which appears for *yōšēb baššebet* [1 Sam 23:8] in 1 Chr 11:11, is read as Iesebaal in the LXX.) That Baal was sometimes referred to derogatorily as *bōšet* is clear from Hos 9:10 and Jer 11:13.

10. See B. Maisler (Mazer), "'*drm,*" *EM,* 1.116–17.

11. Ibid.

12. Limitations of space preclude a full listing; I hope to present such a list

181

elsewhere. In preparing the list, I relied mainly on the following: Y. Aharoni, *Kĕtôvôt ʿĀrād* (Jerusalem: Bialik Institute and Israel Exploration Society, 1975); N. Avigad, "New Names on Hebrew Seals," *EI* 12 (1975) 66–71; P. Bordreuil and A. Lemaire, "Nouveaux sceaux Hébreux, Araméens, et Ammonites," *Semitica* 26 (1976) 45–53; D. Diringer, *Le iscrizioni antico-ebraiche palestinesi* (Florence: Felice le Monnier, 1934). L. G. Herr, *The Scripts of Ancient Northwest Semitic Seals* (HSM 18; Missoula, Mont.: Scholars Press, 1978); R. Hestrin and M. Dayagi-Mendels, *Ḥôtāmôt Mîmê Bayit Ri'šôn* (Jerusalem: Israel Museum, 1978); Z. Meshel, *Kuntillet ʿAjrud: A Religious Centre from the Time of the Judaean Monarchy on the Border of Sinai* (Israel Museum Catalogue 175; Jerusalem: Israel Museum, 1978); A. Lemaire, *Inscriptions hébräiques 1: Les ostraca* (Littératures anciennes du Proche Orient; Paris: Editions du Cerf, 1977); S. Moscati, *L'epigrafia Ebraica Antica, 1935–1950* (BibOr 15; Rome: Pontifical Biblical Institute, 1951); Torczyner, *Tĕʿûdût Lāḵîš;* F. Vattioni, "I sigilli ebraici," *Bib* 50 (1969) 357–88; idem, "I sigilli ebraici II," *Augustanianum* 11 (1971) 447–54; idem, "I sigilli ebraici III," *AION* 38 (1978) 227–54; and R. B. Lawton, *Israelite Personal Names on Pre-Exilic Hebrew Inscriptions Antedating 500 B.C.E.* (Ph.D. thesis, Harvard University, 1977): the substance of this thesis has since been published in *Bib* 65 (1984) 330–46. Where names are preserved only partially, they are included if enough of the name is preserved to recognize its theophoric element.

13. The main collections of inscriptions are from eighth-century Samaria, late-seventh- to early-sixth-century Arad, and early sixth-century Lachish. The chronological distribution of the seals is charted by Herr, *Scripts,* 212–13, though the paleographic basis of the dating is not always exact; see J. Naveh's review of Herr in *BASOR* 239 (1980) 75 (last par.).

14. See, e.g., Hestrin and Dayagi-Mendels, *Ḥôtāmôt,* nos. 1–27, for some of the men named in the Lachish and Arad ostraca (R. Hestrin et al., *Kĕtôvôt Mĕsapperôt* [*Inscriptions Reveal*] [Israel Museum Catalogue 100; 2d ed.; Jerusalem: Israel Museum, 1973] 26, no. 14); and the seals listed in N. Avigad, "Hebrew Epigraphic Sources," *WHJP* 4 (1979) 37–38.

15. The precious character of seals is also implied by their use in biblical imagery for something precious (Cant 8:6; Jer 22:24; Hag 2:23).

16. Hestrin and Dayagi-Mendels, *Ḥôtāmôt,* 7, 8.

17. See, e.g., 1 Kgs 11:4–10; 15:13; 16:31–33; 18:19; 2 Kgs 1:2; 21:3–7; 23:11; Jer 44:17.

18. *ANET,* 662.

19. Ostracon A in A. Vanel, "Six ostraca phéniciens trouvés au temple d'Echmoun, près de Saïda," *BMB* 20 (1967) 45–95; cf. ostracon G in idem, "Le septième ostracon phénicien trouvé au temple d'Echmoun, près de Saïda," *Mélanges de l'Université Saint-Joseph* 45 (1969) 343–64.

20. Ishtar or Anath; see I. Ephʿal, "*mlkt hšmym,*" *EM* 4.1158–59; B. Porten, *Archives from Elephantine* (Berkeley and Los Angeles: University of California Press, 1968) 165, 176–78.

21. See 1 Kgs 11:7; 2 Kgs 23:17. Though the sanctuaries of these deities stood outside Jerusalem, one may assume that they had some contact with the population of the city (cf. M. Smith, *Palestinian Parties,* 17).

22. Tammuz or Tammuz-like figures may have been known by the names Adon (whence Adonis; cf. Jer 22:18), Naaman (cf. Isa 17:17), Hadadrimmon (cf. Zech 12:11), Baal or Hadad/Haddu. See J. C. Greenfield, *"tmwz,"* EM 8.587–92, secs. 5–6. Whether we should expect personal names based on the dying and rising god figure is uncertain; though common in Sumerian texts, names with Tammuz/ Dumuzi (or Dammu) are virtually nonexistent in the Akkadian onomasticon. Whether Moloch represents the name of a deity is debated; see M. Weinfeld, "The Worship of Molech and of the Queen of Heaven and Its Background," *UF* 4 (1972) 133–54 for discussion and bibliography.

23. If Jezebel's Baal was Melqart; see Albright, *Archaeology and the Religion of Israel,* 156–57; R. de Vaux, *The Bible and the Ancient Near East* (Garden City, N.Y.: Doubleday & Co., 1971) 238–51.

24. Assuming the old view that the Assyrians imposed the cult of Ashur on conquered peoples. But this view is now discredited; see J. McKay, *Religion in Assyria Under the Assyrians* (SBT, Second Series, 26; Naperville, Ill.: Alec R. Allenson, 1973); M. Cogan, *Imperialism and Religion* (SBLMS 19; Missoula, Mont.: Society of Biblical Literature and Scholars Press, 1974).

25. Assuming that the mention of these deities in the Elephantine papyri reflects preexilic Israelite religion; see A. Cowley, *Aramaic Papyri of the Fifth Century B.C.* (Oxford: Clarendon Press, 1923) xviii–xx; contrast Porten, *Archives,* 165–79, 328–33; M. Silverman, "Aramean Name-Types in the Elephantine Documents," *JAOS* 89 (1969) 691–709.

26. Since we cannot exclude the possibility that some of the inscriptions are forgeries, each set of statistics in the present study was calculated in two ways. The first is restricted to names that appear in inscriptions on objects acquired in controlled archaeological excavations in Israel or, if the names are explicitly identified as Israelite, abroad. The second consists of all Israelites whose names are preserved in epigraphic sources, including those found on the surface and those acquired in the antiquities market and identified as Israelite by paleographic evidence; even in this case, names from inscriptions found outside Israel are excluded if they are not explicitly identified as Israelite (i.e., if scholars have considered them Israelite because the names or the script seemed Hebrew). These two sets of statistics do not differ from each other significantly, which means that even if there are some forged inscriptions in the larger corpus, they have not skewed the evidence we are considering. Therefore we may confidently cite the statistics from the larger corpus in the body of this study.

27. Excluded from the list are names that are conceivably pagan but not likely so. Several of these are names that could be construed as unaugmented DNs, such as *šlm* and *šḥr.* However, as Benz observes with reference to Phoenician and Punic names, a hypocoristicon consisting of the DN alone is the least attested type of hypocoristicon (Benz, *Personal Names,* 233). It is preferable to understand these names as belonging to more common types, such as hypocoristica consisting of the verbal element (e.g., *šlm* and *šḥr* as in *šlmyhw* and *šḥryh;* note also Ammonite *šwḥr,* Hestrin and Dayagi-Mendels, *Ḥôtāmôt)* no. 101. Also excluded are names based on very dubious readings.

28. The single exception is the Akkadian name *šwššr'ṣr,* "May Shawash (= Shamash) guard the king," written on a seal in Aramaic script. This man is

likely to be a foreigner, despite the fact that his daughter bears a Yahwistic name. The name *ks'* (Moscati, *L'epigrafia*, 75, no. 8) has been connected with the deified full moon (Vattioni, "I sigilli ebraici," 370, no. 107; idem, "I sigilli ebraici II," 382–83), but, as noted in n. 27 above, personal names consisting of the divine name alone are the rarest types of theophoric name, and *ks'* is more simply interpreted as a calendar name referring to the bearer's day of birth (see J. J. Stamm, *Die akkadische Namengebung* [MVAG 44; Leipzig: J. C. Hinrichs, 1939]; cf. Noth, *Die israelitischen Personennamen*, 223 n. 5). On *šḥr*, see n. 27.

29. Theoretically, names containing *'d(w)n* or *n'm* could refer to Tammuz (Adonis), *b'l* could refer to Tammuz or Moloch, and *mlk* could refer to Moloch (see above, n. 22). However, names like *'d(w)ny(h)w* (biblical and SO 42:3) and *mlkyhw* (biblical and frequently in inscriptions, e.g., Aharoni, *Kĕtôvôt 'Ărād* 24:14) show the use of two of these epithets for YHWH (on *b'l*, see above), and there are no Israelite names in which these elements likely refer to other gods.

30. The PNs *'bdlb't* ("servant of the Lion-Lady") and *bn 'nt* ("son of Anat"), inscribed on arrowheads found at El-Khadr near Bethlehem, are too early for the present study (see most recently F. M. Cross, "Newly Found Inscriptions in Old Canaanite and Early Phoenician Scripts," *BASOR* 238 [1980] 4–7). Given the connection of these names with archers at Ugarit and with other Canaanite military personnel, it is probable that they refer to Canaanites. Goddesses are virtually absent in the biblical onomasticon as well, except for a few names possibly based on Anat (mainly Anath [or Ben Anath], father of Shamgar; the PNs Anathoth and Anathothiah may personify the town of Anathoth or be based on it and not directly on the DN).

31. E.g., Phoenician Bodashtart (Benz, *Personal Names*, 82–88), Abdi-Ash-irta of the Amarna letters (EA 60:2, etc.), and Anathi at Elephantine (AP 22:108).

32. See J. J. Stamm, "Hebräische Frauennamen," VTSup 16 (1967) 301–39; contrast B. Porten, *"šm, šmwt 'sm prtyym byśr'l,"* EM 8.44.

33. For the last name, see N. Avigad, "Seals of Exiles," *IEJ* 15 (1965) 228. For masculine theophoric elements in Jewish names at Elephantine, see Torczyner, *Tĕ'ûdôt*, 15 n. 2; Porten, *"šm, šmwt."*

34. Conceivably *yrb'*[ ] in an eighth-century inscription from Hazor (Hestrin, *Inscriptions Reveal*, 122:112) could be *yrb'l*, though the restoration *yrb'm* is also plausible; an eighth-century Israelite king bore that name.

35. J. Wellhausen, *Der Text der Bücher Samuelis* (Göttingen: Vandenhoeck & Ruprecht, 1871) 95; Gray, *Studies in Hebrew Proper Names*, 141–46; S. R. Driver, *Notes on the Hebrew Text and the Topography of the Books of Samuel* (2d ed.; Oxford: Clarendon Press, 1960) 253–55; cf. Noth, *Die israelitischen Per-sonennamen*, 120–21, where this view is rejected.

36. The name resurfaces much later in the Murashu archives of fifth-century B.C.E. Babylonia; see M. D. Coogan, *West Semitic Personal Names in the Murašu Documents* (HSM 7; Missoula, Mont.: Scholars Press, 1976) 15, 69.

37. If Hosea 1—3 is earlier than the rest of the book (see Kaufmann, *The Religion of Israel*, 368–71; H. L. Ginsberg, *EncJud* 8:1014–16), then the Samaria ostraca reflect the *continuation* of the practice reflected in Hos 2:18.

38. What Greeks termed *daimónia* as distinct from *theoí* (Plato, *Symposium* 202E).

39. See BDB and KBL, s.v. *"gd"*; O. Eissfeldt, "Gut Glück in semitischer Namengebung," *JBL* 82 (1963) 195–200. Note *hgd* with the definite article in *KAI*, 72B:4. For the equivalence with *tyche*, see LXX at Gen 30:11 (cf. *Tg. Pseudo-Jonathan, mazzālāʾ ṭābāʾ*) and G. A. Cooke, *A Text-Book of North Semitic Inscriptions* (Oxford: Clarendon Press, 1903) no. 112, 4.

40. M. Höfner, "Gad," *Wörterbuch der Mythologie* (ed. H. W. Haussig; Stuttgart: Klett, 1965) 438–39; cf. J. Teixidor, *The Pagan God: Popular Religion in the Greco-Roman Near East* (Princeton: Princeton University Press, 1977) 159–60; on *tyche*, see N. Robertson, *"Tyche," Oxford Classical Dictionary* (2d ed.; ed. N. G. L. Hammond and H. H. Scullard; Oxford: Clarendon Press, 1978) 1100–1101. The comparable Mesopotamian phenomena are *šēdu* and *lamassu;* see A. L. Oppenheim, *Ancient Mesopotamia: Portrait of a Dead Civilization* (Chicago: University of Chicago Press, 1964) 198–206.

41. See T. H. Gaster, *Myth, Legend, and Custom in the Old Testament* (New York: Harper & Row, 1969) 584–85.

42. H. Altenmüller, "Bes," *Lexikon der Ägyptologie* 1/5 (ed. W. Helck; Wiesbaden: Otto Harrassowitz, 1975) cols. 721–22. Cf. H. Bonnet, *Reallexikon der ägyptischen Religionsgeschichte* (Berlin: Walter de Gruyter, 1952) 108 ("apotropäischer Dämon").

43. See S. Paul, "Cuneiform Light on Jer. 9:20," *Bib* 49 (1969) 373–76, and S. Talmon, "On the Emendation of Biblical Texts on the Basis of Ugaritic Parallels," *EI* 14 (1978) 122–24.

44. For an apotropaic use of a covenant, cf. the first Arslan Tash amulet, *KAI*, 27, lines 8ff., and Hos 2:20; Job 5:23.

45. See S. E. Loewenstamm, *"mwt," EM* 4.755–57; D. R. Hillers, "Demons, Demonology," *EncJud* 5.1521–26.

46. For *šālôm* and *šôlēm* meaning "ally," cf. Pss. 7:5 and 55:21, and note the use of Akkadian *šalāmu* as the antonym of *nakru* ("enemy") in treaty texts from Ugarit (e.g., *PRU* IV, p. 49:12f.; see further literature cited in J. H. Tigay, "Psalm 7:5 and Ancient Near Eastern Treaties," *JBL* 89 [1970] 182–83). For *ʿb(d)šlm* and biblical *ʾbšlwm,* meaning respectively "servant of the (Divine) Ally," and "(My) father is the (Divine) Ally," one may note that in a *salīmum* treaty the sovereign might be addressed as "father," while the vassal might be addressed as "slave." See H. Tadmor, "Treaty and Oath in the Ancient Near East: A Historian's Approach," *Humanizing America's Iconic Book: SBL Centennial Addresses 1980* (ed. G. M. Tucker and D. A. Knight; SBL Centennial Publications, Chico, Calif.: Scholars Press, 1982) 131. On the other hand, YHWH-Shalom could mean "YHWH is (the source of) well-being."

47. See Noth, *Die israelitischen Personennamen,* 38; Zadok in *EM* 8.59; Benz, *Personal Names,* 243; F. Gröndahl, *Die Personennamen der Texte aus Ugarit* (Rome: Pontifical Biblical Institute, 1967) 53, sec. 87.

48. See J. Urman, *"ʾbyh, ʾbyhw, ʾbym," EM* 1.24; S. Ahituv, *"mrym," EM* 5.461.

49. Cf. Noth, *Die israelitischen Personennamen,* 231.

50. *ʾašḥûr* and *ʿammiḥûr* look as if they could be based on Horus, but the first

could be from *šāḥôr* ("black") and the second is textually uncertain (see Gray, *Studies in Hebrew Proper Names*, 43 n. 1; for another suggestion regarding *'ašḥûr*, see S. E. Loewenstamm, "'šḥwr," *EM* 1.761). The PNs *ḥûr, ḥûrî, ḥûray, ḥûrām* (the latter two textually uncertain), and *ben ḥûr*, could be based on the DN Horus or the common noun *ḥōr* ("nobleman") (cf. the PN *šûa'* with the same meaning; see J. C. Greenfield, "Some Glosses on the Keret Epic," *EI* 9 [1969] 60–61). The names *ḥarnefer* and *ṣiḥā'* are linguistically Egyptian (see the articles on these names by S. E. Loewenstamm, *EM* 3.303, and S. Ahituv, *EM* 6.708–9).

51. For Northwest Semitic deities in Egyptian PNs, see J. A. Wilson, "The Egyptians and the Gods of Asia," *ANET*, 250. Note also the Egyptian DNs in Phoenician PNs from fourth- to third-century Cyprus ('bd's, 'bd'sr, 'bd'bst, 'bdḥr; see *CIS*, I, 50:1; 46:1; 86B:6; 53), and the Edomite DN Qaus in Aramaic and Arabic PNs in fourth-century documents from Beer-sheba (J. Naveh, "The Aramaic Ostraca from Tel Beer-Sheba [Seasons 1971–1976]," *Tel Aviv* 6 [1979] 194–95).

52. On the first, see N. Avigad, "Seals of Exiles," 228. The seal of *pṭ's* was said to have been found by a peasant in the fields of Samaria (I. Ben-Dor, *QDAP* 12 [1945–46] 77). Its script is classified as Aramaic by Herr (30, no. 48); Naveh considers the script and orthography possibly more Phoenician than Aramaic (the absence of final *yod* is paralleled in the Phoenician inscription *KAI*, 29.1; in Aramaic inscriptions Isis in PNs is always spelled 'sy), but more likely either of these than Hebrew (private communication).

53. Aharoni, *Kĕtôvôt 'Ărād*, 88, notes that the sherd containing the name of Pashhur at Arad was found near the sanctuary.

54. In the corpus of names found in controlled archaeological excavations there are 167 Yahwistic PNs and 18 likely pagan PNs; these constitute, respectively, 90.3 and 9.7 percent of the theophoric PNs.

55. The collection was received by the Israel Museum in 1979. Three of them have been published by N. Avigad, "The Governor of the City," *IEJ* 26 (1976) 178–82; idem, "Baruch the Scribe and Jerahmeel the King's Son," *IEJ* 28 (1978) 52–56. The statistics cited above are based on a list of the names in the entire collection which Avigad kindly sent to me.

56. A few of the City of David names are mentioned by Y. Shiloh, "The City of David Archaeological Project. The Third Season—1980," *BA* 44 (1981) 165–66. I was able to see a list of the names through the courtesy of Shiloh and Naveh.

57. As this article was nearing completion, Avigad kindly sent me a reprint of his article "A Group of Hebrew Seals from the Hecht Collection," *Festschrift Rëuben R. Hecht* (Jerusalem: Koren Publishers, 1979) 119–26. These seals name from eight to ten individuals with Yahwistic PNs and none with pagan PNs.

58. Since seal owners and many others mentioned in the inscriptions were often among the upper economic strata, it is well to recall that foreigners in Israel were often there for purpose of trade and that even *gērîm* sometimes became financially successful (see Lev 25:47).

59. J. Naveh, "More Hebrew Inscriptions from Meṣad Ḥashavyahu," *IEJ* 12 (1962) 30–31.

60. See Num 20:16; Deut 1:44; on Seir west of the Arabah, see the evidence summarized by H. Liver, "š'yr," *EM* 8.324–25.

61. See Maisler (Mazar), cited by Albright in *BASOR* 72 (1938) 13 n. 45.

62. A. Harnack, *The Mission and Expansion of Christianity in the First Three Centuries* (New York: Harper Torchbooks, 1961) 422–30.

63. See above, n. 8. Yahwistic PNs become prevalent in Israel only under the united monarchy. This is probably due to the same inertia in onomastic habits that we have noted above.

64. In fact, these statistics underscore the fact that demonstrable censorship of PNs does not pervade the entire Bible. It is limited to the MT of Samuel and possibly, to a lesser extent, of Chronicles.

65. For Sippar, see R. Harris, "Notes on the Nomenclature of Old Babylonian Sippar," *JCS* 24 (1972) 102–4; for Sidon, see above, n. 19; for Assur, see H. Fine, "Studies in Middle-Assyrian Chronology and Religion," *HUCA* 25 (1954) 116–24. The "overwhelming predominance" of Ashur in the Old Assyrian onomasticon from Cappadocia, to which Fine refers (p. 120), amounts at most to 44.8 percent of the theophoric names there; Adad, Ishtar, and Sin appear in 13.7 percent, 13.7 percent, and 12.3 percent respectively (based on statistics cited by Stamm, *Namengebung,* 68–69).

66. Since *'el* is by far the main theophoric element in Ammonite PNs and Milkom appears at best only once, I assume that El was the chief god of the Ammonites and that Milkom was merely a title of El. (See the list of Ammonite PNs in K. P. Jackson, *The Ammonite Language of the Iron Age* [HSM 27; Chico, Calif.: Scholars Press, 1983] 95–98). The possible occurrence of Milkom in PN is in the seal *CIS* II, 94; (see Avigad, "Seals of Exiles," 225 n. 12; F. M. Cross, "Heshbon Ostracon II," *Andrews University Seminary Studies* 11 (1973) 128 n. 6; Cross, "The Seal of Miqnêyaw, Servant of Yahweh," *Ancient Seals and the Bible* [ed. L. Gorelick and E. Williams-Forte; Malibu, Calif.: Undena Publications, 1984] 55–63). Having inspected the seal at the British Museum, I believe there was never an *'ayin* at the beginning of the last line and that the line must therefore be read *bdmlkm* or *br mlkm.*

67. Apart from PNs, there is very little epigraphic evidence about Ammonite religion; nothing suggests that any other deity was worshiped by many Ammonites.

68. This inconsistency is graphically illustrated by the charts in J. C. de Moor, "The Semitic Pantheon of Ugarit," *UF* 2 (1970) 187–228.

69. Gröndahl, *Die Personennamen,* 83.

70. For the distinction between official and popular religion, see R. Albertz, *Persönliche Frömmigkeit und offizielle Religion* (Stuttgart: Calwer Verlag, 1978), and the symposium *Études sur le panthéon systématique et les panthéons locaux* (*Or* 21/1–2 [1976]) 1–226.

71. See E. Salonen, *Die Grüss- und Höflichkeitsformeln in babylonisch-assyrischen Briefen* (StudOr 38; Helsinki: Societas Orientalia Fennica, 1967) 17–19, 83–85; H. Schmökel, "Hammurabi and Marduk," *RA* 53 (1959) 188–92; W. F. Albright, "A Prince of Taanach in the Fifteenth Century B.C.," *BASOR* 94 (1944) 17; *ANET*, 485; Kaiser, *ZDPV* 86 (1970) 15–19; *KAI*, 50:2–3; Porten, *Archives*, 159–60, 173–79 (cf. H. L. Ginsberg, *ANET*, 491 n. 3); *KAI*, 266:1–2 (on the latter, see B. Porten, "The Identity of King Adon," *BA* 44 [1981] 36–52).

72. Three other passages in these letters also express wishes that YHWH act in a certain way. Arad 21:4 asks, "May YHWH recompense [my] lord ... (*yšlm yhwh l'dn*[y]); in Lachish 5:7–8 the writer prays *yr'k yhwh hqṣr bṭb hym*, "May YHWH allow my lord to witness a good harvest today" (thus D. Pardee, *Handbook of Ancient Hebrew Letters: A Study Edition* (Chico, Calif.: Scholars Press, 1982) 96–97, following Lemaire, *Inscriptions,* 117). On Lachish 2:5, see Lemaire, *Inscriptions,* 99–100; Pardee, *Handbook,* 80.

73. Meshel, *Kuntillet 'Ajrud,* pl. 10. On the votive character of the formula, see J. Naveh, "Graffiti and Dedications," *BASOR* 235 (1979) 27–30.

74. See N. Avigad, "Excavations in the Jewish Quarter of the Old City of Jerusalem, 1971 (Third Preliminary Report)," *IEJ* 22 (1972) 195–96; P. D. Miller, "El, the Creator of Earth," *BASOR* 239 (1980) 43–46; N. Habel, " 'Yahweh, Maker of Heaven and Earth': A Study in Tradition Criticism," *JBL* 91 (1972) 321–37.

75. See W. G. Dever, "Iron Age Epigraphic Material from the Area of Khirbet el-Kôm," *HUCA* 40–41 (1969–70) 173. Dever (p. 169) is certain that the bowl comes from the Khirbet el-Qom tombs. As a parallel to this inscription, one may cite a Sumerian vase from Lagash with the votive inscription ᵈBa-ú, "(for) Ba'u" (V. Donbaz and W. W. Hallo, "Monumental Texts from Pre-Sargonic Lagash," *OrAnt* 15 [1976] 4, no. VII).

76. H. G. May, "An Inscribed Jar from Megiddo," *AJSL* 50 (1933–34) 10–14 (Moscati, *L'epigrafia,* pl. 29, no. 1; *lyh* on p. 111 is an error); G. A. Reisner, *HES* I, 238; II, 55b (cf. Diringer, *Le iscrizioni,* 69f.).

77. Cf. the inscription *l'l* on a seal published by L. Y. Rahmani "Two Syrian Seals," *IEJ* 14 (1964) 180–84; cf. J. Naveh, *Leshonenu* 29 (1965) 184. For other names of this type, see Noth, *Die israelitischen Personennamen,* 153; T. Nöldeke, "Kleinigkeiten zur semitischen Onomatologie," *WZKM* 6 (1892) 314–16.

78. A tannaitic source quoted in the Talmud refers to vessels with God's name inscribed on the handle (*b. Šabb.* 61b; *'Arak.* 6a; in *m. Yoma* 4.1, Lev 16:8 is understood to mean that the lots were inscribed *lyhwh* and *l'z'zl*). Inscriptions of this type, reading simply "for DN," appear on vases found on Malta (*l'štrt* and *ltnt* in full and abbreviated forms). See M. Cagiano de Azevedo et al., *Missione Archeologica Italiana a Malta. Rapport preliminare della campagna 1964* (Rome: Universita di Roma, Centro di Studi Semitica, 1965) 81–83. Cf. F. M. Cross, *CMHE,* 29.

79. In the Khirbet Beit Lei inscription B, *yh* appears, though Cross does not take it as the divine name (see J. Naveh, "Old Hebrew Inscriptions in a Burial Cave," *IEJ* 13 [1963] 85–86; Cross, "The Cave Inscriptions from Khirbet Beit Lei," *Near Eastern Archaeology in the Twentieth Century: Essays in Honor of Nelson Glueck* [ed. J. A. Sanders; Garden City, N.Y.: Doubleday & Co., 1970] 302, 306 n. 17 [contrast Naveh, 86 n. 25]; Lemaire, "Prières en temps de crise: Les inscriptions de Khirbet Beit Lei," *RB* 83 [1976] 560; P. D. Miller, "Psalms and Inscriptions," *Congress Volume, Vienna 1980* [VTSup 32; Leiden: E. J. Brill, 1981] 329).

80. By "unilatry" and "unilatrous" I refer to the worship of a single god where scholars are uncertain whether the worshipers are monotheistic or monolatrous.

81. Naveh, "Old Hebrew Inscriptions," 86, Inscription C; Cross, "Cave Inscriptions," 302; Lemaire, "Prières," 561.

82. Cross, "Cave Inscriptions," 302–4; the revised date is accepted by J. Naveh, "A Paleographic Note on the Distribution of the Hebrew Script," *HTR* 61 (1968) 74. Lemaire ("Prières," 563–65) holds that the paleography favors the end of the eighth century.

83. P. Bar-Adon, "An Early Hebrew Inscription in a Judean Desert Cave," *IEJ* 25 (1975) 226–32. Bar-Adon believes that the traces of line 4 support a reading "blessed by YHW⌈H⌉" 230).

84. Dever, "Iron Age Epigraphic Material," 159–69. Z. Zevit reads, *brkt 'ryhw lyhwh*. ("I blessed Uryahu to YHWH") ("The Khirbet el-Qom Inscription Mentioning a Goddess," *BASOR* 255 [1984] 43).

85. The first two inscriptions are transcribed in Meshel, Hebrew section, 20 (page facing pl. 10), English section, 13. The revised reading of the second inscription and the text of the third is given, on the basis of information provided by Meshel, by M. Weinfeld, "Further Remarks on the 'Ajrud Inscriptions," *Shnaton* 5–6 (1978–79) 233 (Hebrew). A drawing of the third was published in the Jerusalem *Post* of 13 March, 1979, p. 3.

86. The second possibility, "by YHWH of Samaria and by its *asherah*," was first suggested to me by B. A. Levine in November of 1980. For the syntax, cf. *rkb yśr'l wpršyw* (2 Kgs 2:12), etc. (see *GKC* 128a); (P. Joüon, *Grammaire de l'Hébreu biblique* (Rome: Pontifical Biblical Institute, 1923) sec. 129a).

87. Meshel, *Kuntillet 'Ajrud*, 20 (English section, p. 13); Lemaire, "Les inscription de Khirbet el-Qom et l'ashérah de YHWH," *RB* 84 (1977) 603–8. Asherah as a sacred tree or pole is well attested in the Bible (see Deut 16:21). The view that *asherah* refers to a sanctuary is based on the meaning of the word and its cognates in Phoenician, Aramaic, and Akkadian (see E. Lipiński, "The Goddess Atirat in Ancient Arabia, in Babylon and in Ugarit," *Orientalia Lovaniensia Periodica* 3 [1972] 101–19), but there are no certain attestations of this meaning in the Bible. See J. A. Emerton, "New Light on Israelite Religion: The Implications of the Inscriptions from Kuntillet 'Ajrud," *ZAW* 94 (1982) 16–18 (Emerton concedes the possibility that at 'Ajrud the word could have the meaning it has in Phoenician, especially given the "Phoenician" inscriptions found there [see below]).

88. M. Gilula, "To Yahweh Shomron and His Asherah," *Shnaton* 3 (1978–79) 134–37 (Hebrew; English summary, pp. XV–XVI).

89. Lemaire, "Les inscriptions de Khirbet el-Qom et l'ashérah de YHWH," 607; Meshel, "Did Yahweh Have a Consort? The New Religious Inscriptions from the Sinai," *BARev* 5/2 (March/April 1979) 31; Emerton, "New Light on Israelite Religion," 14; A. Lemaire, "Who or What Was Yahweh's Asherah?" *BARev* 10/6 (Nov./Dec. 1984) 47–79. In other *ancient* Semitic languages such a usage is found only where a speaker attached a first person suffix to the name of a person or deity as a way of expressing affection (G. R. Driver, "Reflections on Recent Articles," *JBL* 73 [1954] 125; M. Tsevat, "Studies in the Book of Samuel, IV," *HUCA* 36 [1965] 53–54; third person suffixes are cited by Driver only from Arabic and Ethiopic). Stylistically, too, such a construction of the passage is anomalous. In the Ugaritic myths, where Asherah is El's consort, she is never

termed "El's Asherah." Passages mentioning El and Asherah together treat them independently, e.g., "Loudly doth El cry to Lady Asherah of the Sea"—not "to *his* Asherah" (I AB i, 43–44 [*UT* 49, i, 15–16; *ANET*, 140a]).

As Meshel notes ("Did Yahweh Have a Consort?" 31), one might attempt to circumvent this grammatical problem by construing *asherah* as a common noun meaning goddess, as the plurals *'šrym* and *'šrwt* have sometimes been taken (U. Cassuto, *"'šrh," EM* 1.787). "The *asherah*" in a few verses certainly refers to a goddess (in 1 Kgs 18:19 the *asherah* has prophets like Baal, and the *asherah* is paired with the Baal in 2 Kgs 23:4). But a passage meaning "YHWH and his goddess" would also be implausible, for words and phrases meaning "deity of so-and-so" usually refer to the deity of a person (see *CAD* I/J, 89–90, 94–97, 271, and 273–74, s. vv. *"iltu,"* A, secs. b and d; *"ilu,"* sec. b; *"ištartu"* and *"ištaru,"* sec. 2). The few cases where one deity is described as the deity of other deities are not epithets of unnamed deities (as would be the case *ex hypothesi* at ʿAjrud) but indicative clauses praising the status of one deity as being preeminent among the others (always plural). For example, Ishtar is called *ilti ᵈIgigi,* "the goddess among the Igigi gods" (quoted in *CAD* I/J, 89, s.v. *"iltu,"* A, sec. a, end).

90. For the text, see Meshel apud Weinfeld, "Further Remarks on the ʿAjrud Inscriptions," 237. The inscription from Khirbet el-Qom to be discussed below also goes on to mention only one deity acting on behalf of the party who is blessed. *hwšʿ lh* at the end of line 3 there is singular; since that inscription regularly uses *matres lectionis* to indicate final long vowels, the plural would have been written *hwšʿw lh*. The continuation of the second of our ʿAjrud inscriptions also appears to regard only YHWH as blessing and protecting the addressee, since the verbs are written *ybrk wyšmrk wyhy ʿm 'dny*. Since a final accented vowel is indicated orthographically in *'dny* (line 2), it is reasonable to assume that *wyhy* would have been written *wyhyw* if it were plural (the defective writing *brkt* for *bēraktî* in the first inscription does not necessarily argue against this, since unaccented final vowels may have been treated differently from accented ones). The same argument may apply to *ybrk*, unless this is taken as elliptical or haplographic for *ybrkk*, parallel to the following *wyšmrk*, in which case a third person plural suffix *-u* would become medial and would not be represented by a vowel letter.

91. Dever notes the linguistic problem in taking *asherah* as a divine name but argues that the female lyre player drawn on Pithos A near one of the inscriptions is a goddess—in his view, Asherah—and that therefore the inscription must refer to her (W. G. Dever, "Asherah, Consort of Yahweh? New Evidence from Kuntillet ʿAjrud," *BASOR* 255 [1984] 21–37). To me this is not persuasive. If on linguistic grounds *asherah* in this inscription cannot be the name of a goddess, then the picture, if it is of a goddess, must not be related to the inscription. There are more than twenty different motifs in the drawings on the two pithoi, and they cannot all be connected with the inscriptions. Beck's study of the drawings mentions several considerations that make it questionable whether the lyre player in particular is related to the inscription mentioning *asherah*. On the whole, Beck's general impression is that the drawings are by different hands and from different times than the inscriptions. See P. Beck, "The Drawings from Ḥorvat Teiman (Kuntillet ʿAjrud)," *Tel Aviv* 9 (1982) 4, 43–47; cf. Gilula, "To Yahweh Shomron

and His Asherah," 136. If the painters were not the writers of the Hebrew inscriptions (Beck [p. 62] thinks they may have been itinerant craftsmen), it is possible that they were not Israelites. The non-Hebrew inscriptions at the site, its location at a desert crossroads, and other evidence confirm that it was frequented by others in addition to Israelites. See Meshel's section, "The Nature of the Site and Its Date," between pls. 17 and 18 in the Hebrew section and on 20–21 in the English section of *Kuntillet 'Ajrud;* cf. Dever, "Asherah, Consort of Yahweh?" 31 top with n. 45.

92. ABL 274:2–5; 268:2–7, in A. L. Oppenheim, *Letters from Mesopotamia* (Chicago: University of Chicago Press, 1967) 156–57, nos. 93–94; further examples are listed by Salonen, *Die Grüss- und Höflichkeitsformeln*; cf. also the prayer for blessing by the temple Etemenanki cited in *CAD* K, 193d.

93. The dedication to the *sml* of Baal is reminiscent of 2 Chron 33:7, where *sml* replaces *'šrh* of the parallel passage 2 Kgs 21:7.

94. Note also oaths invoking temples and sacred objects, cited by Porten, *Archives*, 154–56; cf. *ANET*, 544b, end.

95. Lemaire, "Les inscriptions de Khirbet el-Qom," 608; "Who or What Was Yahweh's Asherah?" 51. On hypostatization, see Albright, *Archaeology and the Religion of Israel*, 174; idem, *From the Stone Age to Christianity* (2d ed. Garden City, N.Y.: Doubleday Anchor Books, 1957), 373; J. Teixidor, *Pagan God*, 31, 86; Silverman, "Aramean Name-Types in the Elephantine Documents," 708–9.

96. For the distinction between heterodoxy and paganism/polytheism, see Kaufmann, *The Religion of Israel*, 135–38; a similar distinction was made earlier by E. Kautzsch, "Religion of Israel," *A Dictionary of the Bible* (ed. J. Hastings; Edinburgh: T. & T. Clark, 1898–1904), Extra Volume, 690, 702. For non-Israelites at Ajrud, see above, n. 91.

97. Zevit, "The Khirbet el-Qom Inscription," 39–47.

98. Lemaire, "Les inscriptions de Khirbet el-Qom et l'ashérah de YHWH," 595–608; idem, "Who or What Was Yahweh's Asherah?" 42–51.

99. Naveh, "Graffiti and Dedications," 28–29, including n. 10.

100. S. Mittmann, "Die Grabinschrift des Sängers Uriahu," *ZDPV* 97 (1981) 144.

101. Zevit, "The Khirbet el-Qom Inscription," 39–47.

102. Examples are Timnatha, Ephratha, Gudgoda, Kehelatha, Jotbatha, and Berotha. Ephrata, the wife of Caleb in 1 Chr 2:50 (cf. v 19); 4:4, is no exception, since she is identified with Ephrat(a) = Bethlehem (see E. L. Curtis, *A Critical and Exegetical Commentary on the Books of Chronicles* [ICC; Edinburgh: T. & T. Clark, 1965] 90, and especially U. Cassuto, "'prt, 'prth," *EM* 1.515–16.

103. See *GKC* 90g; Joüon, *Grammaire*, sec. 93f; A. F. Rainey, "*šm, šmwt, mqwmwt,*" *EM* 8.14. On the common nouns with this termination in poetry, see *GKC* 90g; Joüon, *Grammaire*, sec. 93i–k.

104. P. D. Miller, "Psalms and Inscriptions," 319 n. 18.

105. B. Maisler (Mazar), "Two Hebrew Ostraca from Tell Qasile," *JNES* 10 (1951) 265–67.

106. Maisler's preference was based on the apparent word divider between *byt* and *ḥrn*. Note that *byt.yhwh* ("the Temple of YHWH") is written with a word divider in Arad 18:9. A cursory survey suggests that compound place-names are

generally written as one word; note (though not all the photographs are clear enough to be certain that there is no word divider): *b'ršb'* (Arad 3:3–4), *rmtngb* (Arad 24:13, 16), *bythrpd* (Lachish 4:5), *ḥṣr'sm* (Meṣad Hashavyahu, lines 3–4 [J. Naveh, "A Hebrew Letter from the Seventh Century B.C.", *IEJ* 10 (1960) 131]), *byt⌐š⌐['n]* (N. Tzori, "A Hebrew Ostracon from Beth-Shean," *BIES* 25 [1961] 145–46; see J. Naveh, "Canaanite and Hebrew Inscriptions [1960–1964]" [in Hebrew], *Leshonenu* 30 [1966] 72 no. 9). In the Mesha inscription, on the other hand, compound place-names beginning with *byt* are written with word dividers (Mesha, lines 27, 30). If the following were considered place-names (they appear in the slot used for names of places and clans or districts), they would attest to this practice in Hebrew inscriptions too: *gt.pr'n* (Samaria 14:1–2 [see Lemaire, *Inscriptions*, 31]), *krm.htl* (Samaria 53:2, etc.), *krm.yhw'ly* (Samaria 55:2, etc.).

107. Y. Aharoni, "The Use of Hieratic Numerals in Hebrew Ostraca and the Shekel Weights," *BASOR* 184 (1966) 19.

108. M. Dothan, "Ashdod of the Philistines," *New Directions in Biblical Archaeology* (ed. D. N. Freedman and J. C. Greenfield; Garden City, N.Y.: Doubleday Anchor Books, 1971) 24 and fig. 29. This inscription is earlier than the reign of Josiah when Dothan thinks it conceivable that Ashdod was conquered by Judah (M. Dothan, "Ashdod—Seven Seasons of Excavation," *Qadmoniot* 5/1 [1972] 11–12).

109. In 12:3 the *ḥet* is restored. Aharoni considered this formula possibly present in Arad 21:5, *ḥyh[wh?]*; the restoration is not accepted by Lemaire, *Inscriptions*, 186.

110. See Naveh, "Old Hebrew Inscriptions," 81–86; Cross, "Cave Inscriptions," 299–302; Lemaire, "Prières," 558–67.

111. An inscribed temple artifact—the ivory head of a priestly scepter—was published by Lemaire in 1981. The inscription, with Lemaire's plausible restorations, reads: *lb⌐y⌐[t yhw]⌐h⌐qdš khnm* ("belonging to the tem[ple of YHW]H, holy to the priests"). See A. Lemaire, "Une inscription paleo-hébraïque sur grenade en ivoire," *RB* 88 (1981) 236–39; idem, "Probable Head of Priestly Scepter from Solomon's Temple Surfaces in Jerusalem," *BARev* 10/1 (Jan./Feb. 1981) 24–29.

112. N. Avigad, "The Priest of Dor," *IEJ* 25 (1975) 101–5.

113. Cross, "The Seal of Miqnêyaw, Servant of Yahweh," 55–63.

114. G. Barkai, "The Divine Name Found in Jerusalem," *BARev* 9/2 (March/April 1983) 14–19.

115. Meshel, *Kuntillet 'Ajrud*, 19; English section, 12–13. YHWH is mentioned in this group too. Though these are not in Hebrew script, it is questionable whether these inscriptions are Phoenician, since they use *matres lectionis* (note such spellings as *wyšb'w, yhwh, ytnw*).

116. I do not believe that the iconographic evidence from Israel modifies this picture to any extent. The evidence most often cited in this connection, the so-called Astarte figurines and plaques, is more plausibly interpreted otherwise. From Pritchard's study of Palestinian figurines it emerges that, with few exceptions, Israelite sites have yielded only figurines of types VI and VII, which have large breasts, pregnant bellies, or are accompanied by children, and which lack the symbols of divinity found in other types. Pritchard concluded that there is no

direct evidence connecting these figurines with any of the prominent goddesses and debated whether these represented a goddess or a cultic prostitute or were talismans "used in sympathetic magic to stimulate the reproductive processes" (Pritchard, *Palestinian Figurines*, 86–87). With their emphasis on full breasts and childbearing, these figurines represent what women in particular most wanted, that is, what they would have been most likely to try to obtain by magical means (note the frequency of infertility and dry breasts in curses: Exod 23:26; Hos 9:14; D. R. Hillers, *Treaty Curses and the Old Testament Prophets* [BibOr 16; Rome: Pontifical Biblical Institute, 1964] 61–62; *ANET*, 441c; note also the contrasting reference to "blessings of the breasts and womb," Gen 49:25). The prehistoric "Venus" figurines are interpreted similarly in A. de Waal Malefijt, *Religion and Culture* (New York: Macmillan & Co., 1968) 119–23 (reference courtesy of Prof. Harvey Goldberg). See, further, Albright, *Archaeology and the Religion of Israel*; M. Tadmor, "Female Cult Figurines in Late Canaan and Early Israel: Archaeological Evidence," *Studies in the Period of David and Solomon and Other Essays* (ed. T. Ishida; Winona Lake, Ind.: Eisenbrauns 1982) 139–73. The likelihood that these figurines represent goddesses is further diminished by the absence of Israelite PNs mentioning goddesses; people who kept such figurines but did not think to give their children names like the Phoenician *'m'štrt* ("Ashtoreth is his/her mother"), *'štrtytn* ("Ashtoreth gave"), or *p'l'štrt* ("Ashtoreth made"), nor to invoke the blessings of a goddess or devote an offering to her, are not likely to have worshiped fertility goddesses.

Another type of evidence that might point to paganism is a seal illustration showing the adoration of a scarab beneath the solar disk (see M. Smith, *Palestinian Parties*, 25 with n. 78), but such scenes are rare in Israel.

Although Dever has shown that one of the illustrations on a pithos of 'Ajrud may represent a goddess, we do not know that it was drawn by an Israelite artist, and the bearing of evidence from 'Ajrud on Israelite practice is uncertain; see above, n. 91.

117. As observed by M. Cogan, descriptions of Judahite idolatry in the Neo-Assyrian age in the Books of Kings are not all "schematic and nonhistorical rhetoric, the product of Deuteronomistic historiography" (M. Cogan, *Imperialism and Religion*, 72).

118. See M. Smith, *Palestinian Parties*, 218 n. 111; Kaufmann, *The Religion of Israel*, 135–38; M. Greenberg, "Religion: Stability and Ferment," in *WHJP* 4/2, 104.

119. G. F. Moore, *Judaism* (Cambridge: Harvard University Press, 1958) 1:357; cf. A. J. Heschel, *The Prophets* (New York: Harper & Row, 1962) 13–14 ("in terms of statistics the prophets' statements are grossly inaccurate"); Kaufmann, *The Religion of Israel*, 419–20. Isocrates described rhetoric as "the art of making great matters small, and small things great" (C. H. Holman, *A Handbook to Literature* [4th ed.; Indianapolis: Bobbs-Merrill Co.], 380).

120. Cf. W. Eichrodt, *Theology of the Old Testament* (OTL; 2 vols.; Philadelphia: Westminster Press, 1961–67) 2.231–40, 435–37; Kaufmann, *The Religion of Israel*, 135, 229–30, 270.

121. As did Ezekiel; see Kaufmann, *The Religion of Israel*, 405–8, 430–32; M. Greenberg, "Prolegomenon," in C. C. Torrey, *Pseudo Ezekiel and the Original*

Prophecy, and *Critical Articles by S. Spiegel and C. C. Torrey* (N.Y.: Ktav, 1970) xx–xxv; contrast M. Smith, "The Veracity of Ezekiel, the Sins of Manasseh, and Jeremiah 44:18," *ZAW* 87 (1975): 11–16.

122. The artificiality of Judges' evidence for polytheism has long been recognized; see J. Wellhausen, *Prolegomena to the History of Ancient Israel* (New York: Meridian Books, 1957), 231, 234–35; Kaufmann, *The Religion of Israel,* 138–39, 260; M. Smith, *Palestinian Parties,* 20. In contrast to the recurrent national polytheism of the framework, the older parts of Judges mention the worship of other gods only in 5:18a; 6:25–32 (the latter limited to one town); and perhaps 9:4, 46 (in Shechem).

[Author's Note: In the present study, based on inscriptions known as of 1979, individuals with Yahwistic names outnumber those whose names are plausibly pagan by 351 to 27, or 92.9 percent to 7.1 percent. Since the completion of the manuscript, the full-length version of this study has appeared under the title *You Shall Have No Other Gods. Israelite Religion in the Light of Hebrew Inscriptions* (HSM 31. Atlanta: Scholars Press, 1986). There the statistics are based on inscriptions known as of 1986, resulting in a slight increase in the ratio of individuals with Yahwistic names to those with plausibly pagan names: 557 (94.1 percent) have Yahwistic names and 35 (5.9 percent) have names that are plausibly pagan.]

12

The Contribution of Hebrew Seals to an Understanding of Israelite Religion and Society

N. AVIGAD

Ancient Hebrew seal inscriptions consist in the main of personal names, that is, the name of the seal owner and his patronymic. At times the title of the seal owner and the name of his superior are added. These data, slight as they are, are nevertheless of great significance for the study of the onomasticon, script, and language and throw light on matters of religious and social interest.

The main source of Hebrew personal names is, of course, the Bible. But other sources such as the Samaria ostraca, the Lachish letters, and the Arad ostraca furnish most valuable additions. However, by far the largest and most important extrabiblical source of this purpose are the Hebrew seals.

Hebrew seals have much in common with other West Semitic seals and sometimes it is difficult to distinguish between them. We identify seals as Hebrew by the following criteria: (1) names compounded with an Israelite divine element; (2) other names that appear in context with Israelite theophorous names; and (3) typical Hebrew script.

As a result, we counted a total number of approximately 328 published Hebrew seals and 57 seal impressions. These 385 seal inscriptions contain 305 diverse personal names. The bulk of these seals are preexilic, dating to the eighth to sixth centuries. Only a small number of seals can be assigned to the exilic or postexilic periods.

In addition, a hoard of approximately 220 Hebrew inscribed clay bullae dating to the end of the preexilic period has been found, which has not yet been published in full. In these bullae mention is made of about 238 individual persons who bore 124 diverse names.

Hebrew personal names, in common with other West Semitic names, very often express religious ideas and beliefs. They are sentence names compounded with the divine name of Yahweh or El, or their appellatives *'ab, 'ah,* and *'am* plus a verb or a noun, expressing feelings of gratitude, devotion, hope, or prayer. These theophorous names are sometimes abbreviated by omitting the divine element. Other names are of a secular character.[1]

The onomasticon of the seals, representing various classes of the population, comprises names of various kinds. Of the 305 diverse personal names that appear on the Hebrew seals, 146 names, or 45 percent, are of the Yahwistic type, that is, they are compounded with the divine name of Yahweh in its three syncopated forms: -*yhw,* -*yw,* and -*yh.* Only 17 names contain the element El which became a virtual equivalent of Yahweh. The rest are either hypocoristica of theophorous names or secular names. Similar statistics may be observed among the yet unpublished hoard of bullae mentioned above, which contains about 124 personal names. Fifty-six of them, or 46 percent, are Yahwistic; all of them are compounded with -*yhw.* Nine names contain the element El.

The onomasticon of the Hebrew seals comprises more or less names current in the Hebrew Bible. However, many names are new. The theophorous names reveal new expressions of piety and praise to Yahweh that frequently have their roots in some passages of the Scriptures.[2]

'bryhw	"Yahweh is mighty" (cf. Gen 49:24; Isa 1:24).
gmlyhw	"Yahweh has rewarded."
dltyhw	"Thou hast delivered, O Yahweh (cf. Ps 30:2).
dmlyhw	And *dml'l* provide a correct reading of the biblical *rmlyhw* (2 Kgs 15:25)
hglnyhw	To be vocalized *higgale-na-ya,* "Be revealed, O Yah."
ḥṣlyhw	"Yahweh has rescued."
yḥmlyhw	"May Yahweh be compassionate."
ntbyhw[3]	"The path of Yahweh" (cf. Ps 119:35).
'mdyhw	"Yahweh is with me" (comp. *'mnw'l* in Isa 7:14).

Other names are complementary to their hypocoristica known from the Bible.

klklyhw "Yahweh has sustained" (Gen 50:21; 45:11) explains the previously obscure *klkl* (1 Kgs 5:11).

'nyhw[4] > *'wn, g'lyhw* > *yg'l, zmryhw* > *zmry, ḥlṣyhw* > *ḥlṣ,* *yhw'l* > *yw'l, yhw'ly* > *'ly, 'mlyhw* > *'ml*

This overwhelming popularity of the Yahweh names attests to the worship of one god—Yahweh. The worship of foreign gods, of which the

196

Israelite people were so often accused by the prophets, was apparently not so deeply rooted and widespread as to affect their personal names. This applies at least to the divided monarchy of Judah. In the early times of David, names compounded with the divine element Baal were rather common, for example, biblical Eshbaal, Jerubaal, Meribbaal, Baalhanan, and the like. They reflect Canaanite influence, and Baal is generally explained here as meaning lord and standing for Yahweh. But such names still continued to be used in Samaria, which was notorious for its cult of the Baal as attested in the Samaria ostraca of the early eighth century which contain names such as *b'l'*, *'bb'l*, *mrb'l*, *b'lzmr*, etc.[5]

In the entire corpus of Hebrew seals we find only one seal bearing a Baal- name: *l'z' bn b'lḥnn*.[6] It has a typical Hebrew script of the eighth century and comes perhaps from the same background as the ostraca. One Baalhanan mentioned in the Hebrew Bible was king of Edom (Gen 36:38), and another was an official under King David, a native of Gederah (1 Chr 27:28).

Another pagan name may be found on the sixth-century seal of "Yehoyishma daughter of *Šawaš-šar-uṣur*."[7] The owner of the seal had a Yahwistic name, whereas her father bore a Neo-Babylonian name meaning "Shamash protect the king." Jews adapted Babylonian names only in exile. Thus it may be assumed that *Šawaš-šar-uṣur* was one of the early Judean exiles to Babylon who gave his daughter the Yahwistic name *yhwyšm'*, "Yahweh will hear (the prayer)," thus expressing the hope for redemption with divine help.

Two seals of cultic funtionaries have a direct bearing on our issue. The first, and one that is outstanding among them, is a unique seal bearing the legend, *lmqnyw 'bd yhwh*, "(Belonging) to Miqnêyaw servant of Yahweh." This seal, said to have been found in Jerusalem, has been published quite recently and exhaustively treated by F. M. Cross and there is only little for us to add.[8]

The legend repeats itself on both sides of the seal: once in positive (without the *lamed*) and once in negative writing for sealing (Fig. 1). A paleographic analysis would suggest a date of the first half of the eighth century B.C.E. for the seal.

The owner's name Miqnêyaw is shortened from Miqneyahu (1 Chr 15:18, 21) and may be taken to mean "the creature of Yahweh." The syncopated form of the divine name *-yw* (to be pronounced as a diphthong *yaw*) is characteristic to northern Israel, but it was current also in Judah in the eighth century.[9] Compare also the very similar name *qnyw*, meaning "Yahweh has created," which appears on another seal.[10]

The most important feature of this unique seal is the epithet *'bd yhwh*, "servant of Yahweh," which has never been found before on a Hebrew seal or in any other Hebrew inscription. Here it is obviously a *terminus technicus,* an official title, the ecclesiastic equivalent of the secular title *'bd hmlk,* "servant of the king."

In the Hebrew Bible various persons who performed faithfully the will of God are called by him "my servant," as *'bdy yš'yhw, dwd 'bdy, 'bdy y'qb, 'brhm 'bdy.* But the formula "PN + *'ebed* + *Yahweh,*" as on the seal, is peculiar to two persons only: *mōšeh 'ebed yhwh,* "Moses, the servant of Yahweh," and *yĕhôšua' ben nûn 'ebed yhwh,* "Joshua bin Nun, the servant of Yahweh." Yet here too *'ebed yhwh* is no more than an expression of devotion and faithfulness, and not a *terminus technicus.* In Mesopotamia the formula "servant of DN" is widely used in cuneiform documents and on cylinder seals both in general terms and as a cultic title.[11] Some West Semitic seals seem also to contain this formula. Punic inscriptions mention cultic functionaries with the title "servant of the temple of DN."[12]

The seal of Miqnêyaw seems to prove that certain functionaries in the Temple of Jerusalem bore ex officio the cultic title *'ebed yhwh.* This title would fit foremost for priests, but, as the seal discussed below will show, priests utilized the title "priest."

Among other possible temple functionaries, Cross favors the temple musician. In this he seems to be influenced by the fact that the only person by the name of Miqneyahu mentioned in the Bible was one of early Israel's famous singers and musicians. In the psalms (Ps 135:1–2), the term *'abdê yhwh* seems to connote the temple choir. Cross suggests, therefore, that Miqnêyaw the servant of Yahweh was perhaps a temple singer of stature, a namesake of biblical Miqneyahu. This remains, of course, open to other interpretations, but I know of no better one than that suggested by Cross.

The second seal related to a temple functionary is also inscribed on both sides.[13] One inscription reads, *lṣdq bn mk',* "(Belonging) to Ṣadoq son of Mika' "; and the second side bears the inscription, *lzkryw khn d'r,* "(Belonging) to Zekaryaw priest of Dor" (Fig. 5). We assume that Ṣadoq was the first seal owner and the father of Zekaryaw. The seal passed apparently as an heirloom to his son the priest, who had his name and title engraved on the other side, omitting the patronymic.

The script suggests a date of the eighth century B.C.E. Dor at that time was a harbor town in the Northern Kingdom of Israel (1 Kgs 4:11). The divine element *yw* of the priest's name is typical of names in Israel and fitting for a resident of Dor. *Khn d'r* is in the construct state meaning "priest of Dor."[14] Obviously he served in a sanctuary located at Dor.[15] It stands also to reason that a priest with a Yahwistic name served in a Yahwistic sanctuary. The Bible makes no mention of a sanctuary at Dor.

In the period of the Judges, places of worship were scattered throughout the country. After the establishment of the Temple in Jerusalem attempts were made to centralize the cult in this Temple. However, the political division of the monarchy after Solomon's death was followed by a religious schism. Jeroboam, the first king of the Northern Kingdom of Israel, set up rival sanctuaries to Jerusalem.

Such official sanctuaries are known to have been at Dan in the north and at Bethel in the south of Israel; both were earlier places of worship. The Bible mentions one of the priests, 'ămaṣyâh kōhēn bêt-'ēl, "Amaziah the priest of Bethel" (Amos 7:10), a formula that closely parallels our zkryw khn d'r. The sanctuaries at Dan and Bethel were denounced by the prophet Amos for the idolatries, along with the sanctuaries at Gilgal and Beer-sheba in Judah (Amos 5:5; 8:14). Various other places of worship that are not mentioned in the Bible seem to have existed in Israel and Judah.[16] Remains of such a sanctuary dating to the Israelite period were uncovered at Arad in Judah.[17] Our seal attests to the function of another undocumented Israelite sanctuary at Dor on the western extremity of the Northern Kingdom. It probably came to an end with the Assyrian conquest of Israel in 722 B.C.E. In recent years, archaeological excavations have been conducted at Dor. By a lucky stroke of the spade this sanctuary may come to light one day.[18]

Two bullae are related to the time of Jeremiah, before the fall of Jerusalem. They were found together with a large hoard of bullae, the remainders of an archive of papyrus documents that was destroyed by fire.[19]

One bulla is inscribed, lbrkyhw bn nryhw hspr, "(Belonging) to Berekyahu son of Neriyahu the scribe" (Fig. 6). The other bulla bears the inscription, lyrḥm'l bn hmlk, "(Belonging) to Yerahmeel son of the king." Both seal owners can be identified with two persons mentioned in Jeremiah 36. The first is known by his hypocoristic name "Baruch son of Neriah the scribe."

Baruch was the secretary of the prophet Jeremiah and his devoted friend and disciple. He served him faithfully in his struggle against the religious offenses of the people and against the foreign policy of the kings, which was about to result in the destruction of Jerusalem. Some scholars maintain that Baruch the scribe was the biographer of the prophet and that his writings were actually one of the main sources of the Book of Jeremiah.

The Bible relates that in the fourth year of Jehoiakim king of Judah (605/604 B.C.E.), Baruch the scribe wrote down from dictation a scroll containing the oracle of Jeremiah against the foreign nations and the predictions concerning the fall of Judah and Jerusalem. Baruch read these

Fig. 1.   *lmqnyw ʿbd yhwh*   **Fig. 2.**   *l ʿlyw*

Fig. 3.   *l ʿzryw hgbh*   **Fig. 4.**   *l ʿlqnh*

Fig. 5.   *[l] zkryw khn dʿr*   **Fig. 6.**   *lbrkyhw bn nryhw hspr*

Fig. 7.   *lmnšh bn hmlk*

Fig. 8.   *lnryhw bn hmlk*

Fig. 9.   *[l] ydw ʿšr ʿl hbyt*

Fig. 10.   *lntn ʿšr ʿl hbyt*

Fig. 11.   *lplʿyhw ʿšr ʿl hms*

Fig. 12.   *lntbyhw nʿr mtn*

Fig. 13.   *lyhwʿdn bt ʿryhw*

Fig. 14.   *lmšwlmt*

prophecies publicly in the Temple. The enraged king burned the scroll and ordered the seizure of the prophet and the scribe. This mission was entrusted to three officials, one of them being Jerahmeel son of the king, the owner of our second bulla.

Baruch is involved in a unique and most important biblical account of a legal procedure in transferring property. In Jer 32:1–15 we are told how Jeremiah, kept in custody by King Zedekiah, purchased a field from his cousin Hanameel in Anathoth. The contract is drawn up in duplicate, signed by witnesses according to law and custom, and sealed. The deed of purchase is entrusted to Baruch ben Neriah for safekeeping in an earthen jar.

We may assume that according to the common practice the scribe signed and sealed the deed. This sealing of Baruch must have been similar to our present bulla, and the document sealed by this bulla was most probably also kept in an earthenware jar. We are unable, of course, to say what the content of the document was, legal or administrative. The bulla that Baruch left behind is a personal belonging of his, a uniquely tangible testimony of the life and deeds of a prominent personage who left a deep imprint on our biblical heritage.

It is noteworthy that the seal inscriptions are the only Hebrew epigraphic source that mentions contemporary persons known from the Bible. None of the ostraca from Samaria, Lachish, and Arad, nor any other Hebrew inscription, do contain such names. Except for the two instances mentioned above (Baruch ben Neriah and Jerahmeel), names of four kings of Israel and Judah appear on the seals of their officials:[20] *šmʿ ʿbd yrbʿm, ʾbyw ʿbd ʿzyw,* and *ʾšnʾ ʿbd ʾḥz, yhwzrḥ bn ḥlqyhw ʿbd ḥzqyhw.* The officials are unknown, but their superiors are known kings. These well-dated seals are of invaluable chronological importance. More often seals use the general title *ʿbd hmlk* without mentioning the king's name, as *yʾznyhw ʿbd hmlk, ʿbdyhw ʿbd hmlk, gʾlyhw ʿbd hmlk,* and others.

Some members of the royal family were apparently employed as officials in the king's service. Their seals were found to be inscribed with the legend, "PN, the son of the king." Some of these title bearers may have been proper sons of kings, as for instance *yhwʾḥz bn hmlk,* who could be the son of Jehoram king of Judah, and *mnšh bn hmlk,* who was perhaps the son of Hezekiah king of Judah. The latter seal is published here for the first time (Fig. 7).[21] The problem with Manasseh is that he ascended the throne when he was only twelve years old and it is questionable whether he had a seal before that age. However, as a crown prince, Manasseh perhaps possessed property of his own in spite of his young age, and the seal was used by the custodian of this property. Alternately it may be assumed, however, that Manasseh of the seal was not Hezekiah's son but rather one of the many members of the royal family who held positions in the service of the king.

Presumably such was the case with a number of other officials whose seals and bullae were found, such as *'lšmˁ bn hmlk, g'lyhw bn hmlk, nryhw bn hmlk,* and others. The last-mentioned seal of Neriyahu is published here for the first time (Fig. 8). It is adorned with a nicely executed proto-Aeolic capital. No princes with these names are known from the Bible, but several officials with the title "son of the king" are known to have fulfilled duties connected with matters of security, among them the above-mentioned Jerahmeel who was sent to arrest Baruch and Jeremiah. This had led some scholars to hold the view that these title bearers were ordinary officials, not of royal stock.[22]

The highest official in rank at the royal court bore the title *'šr 'l hbyt,* "He who is (in charge) over the (royal) house."[23] Seven such "governors of the palace," or major-domos, are known from the Bible. Of these we shall mention here only two, Shebna and Eliakim, who served under Hezekiah king of Judah. Shebna was the chief minister of the state, occupying a powerful position at the royal court. Eliakim son of Hilkiah was the head of the delegation whom the king sent to negotiate with the Assyrians (2 Kgs 18:18; Isa 36:3). The dignity of this status is signified by the allusion to the symbolic acts of investiture to this office of Eliakim when the prophet Isaiah called him "a father to the inhabitants of Jerusalem and to the house of Judah" (Isa 22:21).

So far only one seal of such a top-ranking officer was found (Fig. 9). It is inscribed, *[l]ydw 'šr 'l hbyt,* "(Belonging) [to] Iddo who is over the house."[24] No minister by this name is mentioned in the Bible. The same is true of *ntn 'šr 'l hbyt,* "Natan who is over (the) house," whose bulla was found together with that of Berekyahu the scribe mentioned above (Fig. 10).[25] On the other hand, Gedalyahu *'ăšer ˁal habbayit,* whose bulla was found at Lachish, is tentatively identified with Gedaliah son of Ahikam, who was appointed governor of Judah by the Babylonians and subsequently assassinated (2 Kgs 25:22–25).

A unique seal of a high-ranking official brings into focus a subject of social interest, namely, the use of forced labor in ancient Israel. The Israelites, who were themselves subjected to labor during their sojourn in Egypt, adopted later the corvée system from the indigenous Canaanites and imposed it on them after the conquest. This was the practice of the day. With the establishment of the monarchy, the corvée became a state-organized institution in Israel. David appointed a high-ranking officer in charge of the corvée: *'ădōrām ˁal hammas,* "Adoram who is (in charge) over the corvée" (2 Sam 20:24; 1 Kgs 4:6; 5:28).

Under Solomon the practice of corvée reached its peak. His great building projects, such as the Temple and the palace, required large contingents of laborers and a special administration to manage them. Laborers were also conscripted from the Israelite population (1 Kgs 5:27). The officer in charge of this conscription was Adoniram, [*'ašer*] *'al hammas*, who is identical with Adoram the former functionary of David. The burden of forced labor imposed by Solomon in the Israelite population was one of the causes of the split of the united monarchy.

There is no mention in the Scriptures of any chief of corvée after Adoram, and no clear-cut evidence of official corvée in the Judean monarchy. Many scholars held that it was abolished.

The next seal to be discussed provides the clue in this matter. The seal is inscribed on both sides.[26] One inscription contains the owner's name and his patronymic, *lpl'yhw mttyhw*, "(Belonging) to Pela'yahu (son of) Mattityahu." The other side is inscribed with the legend, *lpl'yhw 'šr 'l hms*, "(Belonging) to Pela'yahu who is (in charge) over the corvée" (Fig. 11). In biblical Hebrew *ms* is the equivalent of *ms 'bdh*, "forced labor," and compares to Akkadian *massu*. The name Pelaiah appears in the Bible in late contexts only. Paleography also points to a date in the seventh century B.C.E.

The seal proves that the corvée continued to be practiced in Judah as a state-organized institution administered by top-ranking officers. Pela'yahu the seal owner was one of these officers. Conscripted labor seems to have been used in Judah whenever required for large building programs. One particular case of forced labor is echoed in the oracle of Jeremiah denouncing King Jehoiakim for building his palace with no regard for justice, making men work without pay (Jer 22:13).

The practice of compulsory labor is apparently reflected in a Hebrew letter of the late seventh century found at Mesad Hashabyahu near Yavneh-Yam.[27] In this ostracon, a reaper complains that his cloak was confiscated by the overseer Hosha'yahu, who falsely accused him of not fulfilling the prescribed quota of work. The letter is addressed to an anonymous *śar* who was apparently the officer in charge of the corvée (cf. *śārê missîm* in Exod 1:11).

Another clay bulla found together with the previous ones bears the inscription *śr h'r* ("governor of the City").[28] The name of the officeholder is omitted. The iconography of the seal represents a royal personage in Assyrianizing form and his courtier, a unique motif on Hebrew seals. It is most probable that "City" stands here for Jerusalem and that the seal belonged to the "mayor" of Jerusalem who functioned in the time of Jeremiah.

Here again this official post is well attested in the Bible. In the premonarchic period Zebul of Shechem is mentioned bearing this title (Judg

9:28–30). Amon, the *śar-hā'îr* or governor of Samaria was ordered by Ahab king of Israel to put the prophet Micaiah in prison (1 Kgs 22:26). Maaseiah, a governor of the city (Jerusalem), was commissioned by Josiah king of Judah to repair the house of the Lord (2 Chr 34:8). Under the same king, there was a gate in Jerusalem that was named after Joshua, the governor of the city (2 Kgs 33:8).

One group of seals belongs to functionaries who bore the title *n'r (na'ar)*. Meaning "youth" or "boy," this term designated originally young servants, juvenile attendants, youthful squires such as the *na'ar* of the priest Eli (1 Sam 2:13, 15), of the prophet Elisha (1 Kgs 18:43), of Jonathan (1 Sam 14:1) the *na'ar* of Boaz (Ruth 2:5–6), and others.[29] But Ziba, the *na'ar* of Saul (2 Sam 9:9–10) and of the house of Saul (2 Sam 19:9), was no longer a youngster. He held the important position of custodian of the personal property of Saul and his family.

In the later period of the monarchy the title *na'ar* came to signify an established class of officials. This information we gather not from the Bible but from the seals. Three such seals bear the following legends: *lbnyhw n'r ḥgy, lmlkyhw n'r špṭ*,[30] and *lntbyhw n'r mtn*[31] (Fig. 12); four seal impressions are inscribed with the identical legend: *l'lyqm n'r ywkn*. In addition, two *nĕ'ārîm* are mentioned in one of the inscribed sherds from Arad (no. 110): *šmyh (bn) mšlm n'r 'lntn* and *mky n'r gdlyh*.[32]

We do not know the exact function of these *nĕ'ārîm*. Following the prototype of Ziba the *na'ar* of Saul, we may assume that they were also custodians of property, administrators of estates and the like, whom we may term "stewards." But unlike Ziba, our present stewards were in the service of private persons and not of kings. None of their masters and employers are known to have been kings. The name *ywkn* in the above-mentioned seal impressions was previously believed to be that of Joiachin the king of Judah, but scholars of late are inclined to drop this interpretation.

Whatever the exact function of the *nĕ'ārîm* was, their seals attest to the fact that beside the well-known royal civil service that is represented in some of the above-mentioned seals, there existed in the Israelite society a class of private officials who were in the service of wealthy or prominent persons.

Last but not least, a group of Hebrew seals that belonged to women should be mentioned. These seals throw light on the social status of the Israelite women and of their legal right in matters of signing contracts and the like. In this respect we have no information from the biblical sources. The fact that the Israelite woman was subordinate to her husband would seem to contradict such a right. However, the fact that she possessed a seal of her own indicates that she had the right to use it and to sign legal documents. Admittedly no bulla of a woman's seal has yet been found.

So far we know of thirteen such seals. The women noted on the seals are denoted according to their father "X daughter *(bt)* of Y," or according to their husband "X wife *('št)* of Y." Some of the female names occur in the Bible *('bgyl, rḥl)*; others are new *(ḥmy'dn,ḥmy'hl, n'hbt)*.[33] Of interest are Yahwistic names, which are rare in the feminine onomasticon, such as *'mdyhw, yhwyšm'*, and *yhw'dn*. The last-mentioned seal reads *lyhw'dn bt 'ryhw* and is published here for the first time (Fig. 13). It is a faience scaraboid, and for technical reasons only a facsimile could be prepared of it. Jeho'addan from Jerusalem was the name of the mother of King Amaziah (2 Kgs 14:2; 2 Chr 25:1). She lived in the eighth century, whereas our seal seems to date to the seventh century B.C.E. Another unpublished seal is that of *mšwlmt*, "Meshulemet" (Fig. 14), which is the name of the wife of King Manasseh and mother of King Amon (2 Kgs 21:19). Any attempt to identify the owners of the last two seals with the royal mothers mentioned in the Bible will be highly speculative.

Special mention should be made of two other seals of this category. One belongs to *m'dnh bt hmlk*, "Ma'adana daughter of the king," which is decorated with a beautiful design of a lyre.[34] Unfortunately, the princess did not disclose the name of her royal father. The other seal bears the inscription, *lšlmyt 'mt 'lntn pḥw'*, "(Belonging) to Shelomith maidservant of Elnathan the governor," and dates to the postexilic period of the return of the exiles from Babylon (late sixth century B.C.E.).[35] The seal was found together with a hoard of bullae from the early Persian period, containing, among others, a bulla of Elnathan the governor and official bullae bearing the name of the province of Yehud.

Whatever the correct interpretation of "maidservant" in this context may be, either a subordinate of the governor, the female equivalent of *'ebed* ("servant") designating a high official, or, alternatively, the governor's wife,[36] it is clear that Shelomith, the owner of the seal found amid official seals and bullae, held an important position in the administration of the province of Judah. She was perhaps in charge of the official archive where the sealed documents were kept. It is a remarkable fact that a woman held such an office in the administration. It should be remembered that under the Persian regime women are known to have enjoyed increased legal rights.

NOTES

1. G. B. Gray, *Studies in Hebrew Proper Names* (London: Adam & Charles Black, 1896); M. Noth, *Die israelitischen Personennamen im Rahmen der ge-*

meinsemitischen Namengebung (BWANT 3/10; Stuttgart: W. Kohlhammer, 1928); *Encyclopedia Biblica* 8 (Jerusalem: Bialik Institute, 1982) cols. 29–65 (Hebrew).

2. For a catalogue of published Hebrew seals (which includes also many non-Hebrew seals), see F. Vattioni, "I sigilli ebraici I," *Bib* 50 (1969) 357–88; II, *Augustanianum* 11 (1971) 447–54; III, *AION* 38 (1978) 227–54.

3. N. Avigad, *EI* 15 (1981) 303.

4. N. Avigad, *BASOR* 246 (1982) 59–61.

5. D. Diringer, *Le iscrizioni antico-ebraiche palestinesi* (Florence: Felice le Monnier, 1934) 23–31; B. Mazar (Maisler), "The Historical Background of the Samaria Ostraca," *Journal of the Palestine Oriental Society* 21 (1948) 117–33.

6. Diringer, *"Le Iscrizioni"*, p. 195:36.

7. N. Avigad, "Seals of Exiles," *IEJ* 15 (1965) 222–32.

8. F. M. Cross, "The Seal of Miqnêyaw, Servant of Yahweh," *Ancient Seals and the Bible* (ed. L. Gorelick and E. Williams-Forte; Malibu, Calif.: Undena Publications, 1984) 55–63.

9. This subject is discussed in detail by Cross in "The Seal of Miqnêyaw," 57–58. I should like to add to his list of *-yw* names an unpublished seal inscribed: *l'lyw*, "(Belonging) to 'Alyaw" (Fig. 2). It is decorated with the figure of a locust and looks very much like the seal of *'zryw hgbh* (Fig. 3), published by N. Avigad, *IEJ* 16 (1966) 50–53. (The new seal has been acquired by D. J. Content of New York, to whom I am indebted for permission to publish it.) I might add here still another unpublished seal bearing a name with the root *qny: 'lqnh,* "God has created." It is decorated with the figure of an ibex (Fig. 4).

10. Diringer, *Le iscrizioni,* 174:13.

11. Cross, "The Seal of Miqnêyaw," 61.

12. Ibid., 62.

13. N. Avigad, "The Priest of Dor," *IEJ* 25 (1975) 101–5.

14. Compare: *khn 'n*, "priest of On" (Gen 41:45); *khn mdyn*, "priest of Midian" (Exod 3:1); *khn byt'l*, "priest of Bethel" (Amos 7:10).

15. In an unconvincing attempt to prove that there was no sanctuary at Dor, M. Haran ("A Temple at Dor?" *IEJ* 27 [1977] 12–15) argued that Zekaryaw was not necessarily the priest of Dor but rather a resident of this town serving as a priest at a sanctuary in some other place.

16. For convenient summaries on this subject, see R. de Vaux, *Ancient Israel: Its Life and Institutions* (trans. J. McHugh; New York: McGraw-Hill Book Co., 1961) 289–308, 331–39; and M. Haran, *Temples and Temple Service in Ancient Israel: An Inquiry Into the Character of Cult Phenomena and the Historical Setting of the Priestly School* (Oxford: Oxford University Press, 1978).

17. Y. Aharoni, "The Israelite Sanctuary at Arad," *New Directions in Biblical Archaeology* (ed. D. N. Freedman and J. C. Greenfield; Garden City, N.Y.: Doubleday & Co., 1969) 25–39.

18. Recently G. Garbini (*Or Ant* 21 [1982] 170–71) declared the seal of the Priest of Dor (Fig. 5) as well as that of *'zryw hgbh* (Fig. 3) to be forgeries (together with some other authentic seals). He argues that these seals are engraved in a horizontal position and not vertical as was, to his view, the practice in northern Israel; that the locust occupies the length of the seal and not its width as

on other seals; that the dividing lines between the two lines of the inscriptions are missing; that the letter *qof* on the Dor seal is clumsy and the two *nuns* are unequal in shape; and, above all, that the script of the *'zryw* seal is schematic, scholastic, and rigid *(sic!)*. To say the least, these arguments are extremely unconvincing. Now it is to be expected that the new and beautiful seal of *'Alyaw*, which is published here (Fig. 2), will be the next victim to be declared a fake. In contrast, see A. Lemaire "Date et origine des inscriptions paléo-hébraîques et phéniciennes de Kuntillet 'Ajrud," in *Studi epigrafici linguistici* 1 (1984) 141 n.19.

19. N. Avigad, "Baruch the Scribe and Jerahmeel the King's Son," *IEJ* 28 (1978) 52–56.

20. For the following seals, see Vattioni, above, n. 2, Index.

21. Another seal with the same legend was published by the present writer twenty years ago (*IEJ* 13 [1963] 133–36) as being Hebrew, but it was later determined to be Moabite. The appearance now of a Hebrew seal with the same name and title is a unique accident, but it is surely authentic.

22. For recent treatments of this subject, see A. Lemaire, "Note sur le titre *bn hmlk* dans l'ancien Israël," *Semitica* 29 (1979) 59–65; N. Avigad, "Titles and Symbols on Hebrew Seals," *EI* 15 (1981), 304.

23. Cf. T. N. D. Mettinger, *Solomonic State Officials: A Study of the Civil Government Officials of the Israelite Monarchy* (Lund: Gleerup, 1971).

24. N. Avigad, "A Group of Hebrew Seals from the Hecht Collection," *Festschrift Rëuben R. Hecht* (Jerusalem: Koren Publishers, 1979) 119–26, no. 1.

25. This bulla is published here for the first time.

26. N. Avigad, "The Chief of the Corvée," *IEJ* 30 (1980) 170–73.

27. J. Naveh, "A Hebrew Letter from the Seventh Century B.C.," *IEJ* 10 (1960) 129–31; *IEJ* 14 (1964) 158–59.

28. N. Avigad, "The Governor of the City," *IEJ* 26 (1976) 178–82.

29. J. MacDonald, "The Status and Role of the *Na'ar* in Israelite Society," *JNES* 35 (1976) 147–70; H. P. Stähli, *Knabe—Jüngling—Knecht. Untersuchungen zum Begriff na'ar im Alten Testament* (Frankfurt am Main: Peter Lang, 1978).

30. N. Avigad, "New Light on the Na'ar-Seals," *Magnelia Dei, The Mighty Acts of God* (ed. F. M. Cross, W. E. Lemke, and P. D. Miller; Garden City, N.Y.: Doubleday & Co., 1976) 294–300.

31. N. Avigad, "Titles and Symbols on Hebrew Seals," *EI* 15 (1981) 303.

32. A. F. Rainey, "Three Additional Texts," apud Y. Aharoni, *Arad Inscriptions* (Jerusalem: Israel Exploration Society, 1981) 122–23, no. 110.

33. Vattioni, 324, 412, 60, 61, 226.

34. N. Avigad, "The King's Daughter and the Lyre," *IEJ* 28 (1978) 146–51.

35. N. Avigad, *Bullae and Seals from a Post-exilic Judean Archive* (Qedem 4; Monographs of the Institute of Archaeology, Hebrew University; Jerusalem: Hebrew University, 1976) 11:14.

36. A striking parallel mentioning a maidservant *('āmāh)* of a high-ranking official occurs in a preexilic tomb inscription from Jerusalem (N. Avigad, *IEJ* 3 [1953] 137–52). The status of the *'āmāh* who is buried together with her master represents a problem of highly social interest which has not yet been satisfactorily solved. (Cf. Avigad, *Bullae and Seals,* 31–32).

13

The Contribution of Archaeology to the Study of Canaanite and Early Israelite Religion

WILLIAM G. DEVER

The rationale for undertaking a topic as daunting as the present one is simply that most previous studies of the archaeological and historical background of early Israelite religion (below) appear to have suffered from two fundamental methodological deficiencies. (1) These studies have pursued the analysis of the two classes of pertinent data—textual and artifactual—in isolation from each other. Moreover, the exclusion or misapplication of the archaeological evidence and the overinterpretation of the literary evidence have produced a distorted picture. Thus we may have many "Old Testament theologies" but no comprehensive "history of the religion of ancient Israel" that does justice to what we can know today through the interdisciplinary inquiry of textual and theological studies coupled with archaeology, ethnology, and comparative religion. (2) Previous studies have stressed the uniqueness of Israelite religion at the expense of those features it had in common with ancient oriental religions in general and with Late Bronze Age Canaanite religion in particular. The resultant reconstruction has been arbitrary and ultimately unpersuasive.

The approach here will seek to redress the balance in two ways: (1) by giving precedence to the contribution of archaeology, especially when conceived as a newer and independent, yet interrelated, discipline that has unique explanatory potential; and (2) by adopting a phenomenological or "functionalist" approach to the study of religion, one that relies more on sociological and anthropological than on theological method, and more on material remains of the cult than on ideology (see further below).

The specific questions to be addressed here, using the above methodology, are the following. (1) What was the actual nature of early Israelite religious *practice?* (2) What was the *social milieu* in Late Bronze–Iron I Palestine in which it flourished? (3) What were the *specific factors* in continuity with the Canaanite cultural sphere that may have played a formative role in shaping the early Israelite cult? (4) Finally, what was distinctively *Israelite* in this religion?

Two preliminary observations are necessary. First, the particular approach and methodology adopted here require us to define certain basic terms that will be presumed throughout. Thus, for our purposes, we shall regard one referent in the discussion, religion, as a set of symbolic thought forms and acts that relate human beings to the ultimate conditions of existence, perceived as the Holy.[1] Consequently, religion will be considered here in two aspects, thought and action, that is: (1) *theology,* this being the intellectual and moral systematization of religious belief; and (2) *cult,* this being the individual and communal acting out of religious beliefs in worship and ritual (i.e., the *practice* of religion, our primary concern here). The other referent in our discussion, archaeology, will be considered, in common with most current understandings, as simply the science of material culture (below). More precisely, we may define archaeology as the systematic analysis of extinct cultures through their material remains.

Second, it is necessary, given so vast a topic, to delimit our inquiry quite narrowly. We shall confine our survey of the archaeological evidence to the cultural-geographical entity commonly known as Syria-Palestine (i.e., approximately the area of modern Israel, Jordan, Lebanon, and coastal-central Syria), the immediate world of which ancient Israel was a part. The chronological limits are imposed largely by the topic itself. While the "Canaanite" civilization in Palestine could be traced from the Early–Middle Bronze Age (ca. 3100 B.C.E. onward), the direct and best-documented cultural precursors of ancient Israel lie in the Late Bronze I-II period, about 1500–1200 B.C.E. At the other end, a focus on early Israelite religion presumes a treatment of only the premonarchical period, from the emergence of Israel down to about 1000 B.C.E. (see further J. S. Holladay, chapter 14 in this volume).

PROLEGOMENON:
METHODOLOGICAL CONSIDERATIONS

Previous Scholarship on
Archaeology and Religion:
Disciplines in Isolation

Before setting forth our own methodological principles on the relationship of archaeology to studies of Israelite religion, we need to see how this relationship has been conceived in the past. We may begin with a brief résumé of several typical, landmark studies, both of Israelite religion and of its possible predecessors in Canaanite religion and culture, showing that their conception and use of archaeological evidence are minimal.

Histories of the Religion of Israel

The older history of religion school, which flourished before the advent of modern archaeology, is generally exempt from criticism here. Yet it should be observed that R. Kittel's *A History of the Hebrews* (1895) and his *Geschichte des Volkes Israel* I–II (1909–12), along with E. Sellin's *Alttestamentliche Religion in Rahmen der andern altorientalischen* (1908), had already employed textual discoveries from Egypt and Mesopotamia to push Israel's origins back farther in time than J. Wellhausen would have allowed. S. A. Cook's *The Religion of Ancient Palestine in the Second Millennium* (1908) made more direct use of artifactual discoveries from Syria-Palestine to place early Israel in the general setting of Canaanite culture. This school continued to produce numerous works on ancient Israel throughout the twentieth century. Most, however, were based on increasingly refined methods of literary criticism and made little or no use of archaeology, despite its sometimes spectacular progress during this period. Examples of a late reflex of the history of religion school would be R. H. Pfeiffer's *Religion in the Old Testament* (1960), which scarcely refers once to archaeological data, apart from brief mention of the Ugaritic texts. H. H. Rowley's *Worship in Ancient Israel: Its Forms and Meaning* (1967), despite its author's well-known encyclopedic range, does little more than cite some of the standard archaeological references of the period; there is virtually no hint of the Canaanite socioeconomic world in which early Israel emerged.

More recent treatments of Israelite religion are difficult to assign to any particular school, since they combine literary criticism, form and redaction criticism, *Heilsgeschichte,* and many other methods. Most of these works move closer to our concern, however, in that they reflect the results of a generation of studies on the Israelite cult (below). H. Ringgren's *Israelite Religion* (1966) focuses extensively on aspects of the cult, albeit with a modification of some of the more extreme earlier positions of the Scandinavian school (below), especially on divine kingship, but gives scant attention to premonarchic Israel or to the possible contribution of archaeology. H. J. Kraus's *Worship in Israel: A Cultic History of the Old Testament* (1966) is similar, more strictly form critical but somewhat better balanced overall. It even includes a brief section on "The Influence of Archaeological Discoveries on the Study of Old Testament Worship," although this turns out to be only a discussion of the impact of Mesopotamian textual discoveries on early figures like P. Volz and S. Mowinckel. Kraus does, however, call for the replacement of the phenomenological approach of the Scandinavian and British myth and ritual schools (below) by a history of the cult more derived from the primary sources (although in speaking of sources Kraus obviously has in mind almost exclusively the Old Testament).

Other recent works, purportedly histories of Israelite religion and cult, are in fact Old Testament theologies or works of Christian apologetic (see further below). These would include R. E. Clements's *Prophecy and Covenant* (1965); Th. C. Vriezen's *The Religion of Ancient Israel* (1967); and W. H. Schmidt's *The Faith of the Old Testament: A History* (1983), which the author regards as standing midway between a history of Israelite religion and a theology of the Old Testament. The most ambitious of the modern treatments within our scope is no doubt G. Fohrer's *History of Israelite Religion* (1973).[2] Yet none of the above works betray any real awareness of the potentially revolutionary impact of archaeology in the last thirty years.

In a class by themselves, yet perhaps typifying an emerging Israeli school, are two pertinent works. Y. Kaufmann's monumental *History of Israelite Religion,* eight volumes in Hebrew (1937–), has appeared as a one-volume abridgment, edited by M. Greenberg as *The Religion of Israel* (1960). Kaufmann's presuppositions are clear in such statements as: "Israelite religion was an original creation of the people of Israel. It was absolutely different from anything the pagan world ever knew"; or, "The Bible is utterly unaware of the nature and meaning of pagan religion."[3] Much more sophisticated is *Temples and Temple Service in Ancient Israel: An Inquiry Into the Character of Cult Phenomena and the Historical Setting of the Priestly School* (1978), by M. Haran, Kaufmann's successor at the Hebrew University of Jerusalem. It deals, however, only with the monarchical period, beyond our purview here. Furthermore, the treatment of early Israelite religion in general rests almost entirely on literary analysis of the contents of the P material, which most other scholars would regard as postexilic. A commendable attempt is made to utilize the results of recent archaeology, especially Israeli, but in what must be regarded as an inadequate fashion.[4]

The Socioanthropological Schools

The earlier patternist approach of the Scandinavian school, as well as that of the British myth and ritual school, is too well known to need summarizing here. The same is true of the works of certain precursors of form criticism, such as Mowinckel and J. Pedersen. Today it is all too easy to document the charge that these schools indulged in "parallelomania," that they imposed a rigid and largely idealistic structure on ancient Israelite religion, and that even at best they exaggerated the role of the cult.[5] Yet it should be recalled that the works of several of these scholars from the 1930s to the 1950s were the first to employ modern fieldwork and research in anthropology and comparative religion, as well as making the first, albeit uncritical, attempts to utilize excavated remains—especially, of course, the Ugaritic texts, from 1929 onward (below). More pertinent to our inquiry, these schools challenged the increasingly artificial and one-sided analyses of literary criticism by restoring an emphasis on cult, that is, on actual *ritual and practice* in early Israelite religion.

Two works defy simple classification. One is the first volume of E. Vogelin's massive *Order and History,* vol. 1, *Israel and Revelation* (1956), which is a grandiose attempt to place ancient Israel on the stage of world history. Vogelin's idealistic philosophical orientation, however, gives his treatment a somewhat lofty perspective that has little patience with the more mundane details of material culture that archaeology provides. Much more satisfactory is the treatment of ancient Israelite belief *and practice* in the exhaustively documented, sensitive, well-balanced *magnum opus* of the late R. de Vaux, *Ancient Israel: Its Life and Institutions* (1961; French ed. 1958–60). The major portion of this work is a long section (pp. 271–517) on religious institutions, in which abundant and expert reference is made to the latest archaeological discoveries, both texts and artifactual evidence. Indeed, de Vaux's treatment of ancient Israelite religion is almost ideal and will likely not be surpassed for a generation. It is no coincidence that its author was one of the few modern scholars besides W. F. Albright (below) who could control the ancient Near Eastern, archaeological, and biblical data.[6]

We turn now to a more recent, characteristically American offshoot of the socioanthropological approach to Israelite religion, attempting to embrace archaeology's contribution. This approach may actually be traced back to W. C. Graham and H. G. May's pioneering work *Culture and Conscience: An Archaeological Study of the New Religious Past in Ancient Palestine* (1936). Their work is regarded now largely as a historical curiosity because of its overriding evolutionary framework, expressed in the classic form of Protestant liberalism of the 1930s. Graham and May were the first, however, to take archaeology seriously as a discipline capable of providing the *material basis* for an understanding of Israelite and ancient oriental religion.[7]

Passing over the intervening years when the socioanthropological approach was eclipsed by newer literary methods, we come now to a recent resurgence of this school that concentrates on early Israelite origins, with the application of newer and more sophisticated interdisciplinary methods and research objectives as well as many fresh (although still controversial) insights. This appears promising, particularly in the openness of several of the works cited below to the contribution of archaeology. The trend began with G. E. Mendenhall's seminal essay "The Hebrew Conquest of Palestine" (1962), the classic formulation of the "peasants' revolt" model (see below). Many of the responses, however, concentrated less on sociological factors and more on older conquest or nomadic infiltration models, critiques of M. Noth's notion of amphictyony, and the like.[8] A symposium celebrating the seventy-fifth anniversary of the American Schools of Oriental Research in Jerusalem in 1975 was given over entirely to early Israelite history and included what was at that time the best survey of Iron Age sanctuaries and cult elements in Palestine.[9]

Undoubtedly the most provocative recent work is N. K. Gottwald's massive *The Tribes of Yahweh: A Sociology of the Religion of Liberated Israel, 1250–1050 B.C.E.* (1979), which may be said at the very least to have inaugurated a new era in our investigation. Gottwald's "historical cultural–material" paradigm will strike many as uncomfortably close to Marxist (or other) theories of economic determinism. But it is to Gottwald's credit that he grappled earnestly (and almost alone among biblical historians) with the theory of "the new archaeology" and the evidence at the time (ca. 1976),[10] despite the still amateurish state of our discipline and the lamentable lack of synthesis or even publication of raw data by Syro-Palestinian archaeologists. Particularly stimulating is Gottwald's deliberate, systematic agenda for future research into Israelite origins, whatever explanatory models are to be employed. One need not approve of all that Gottwald says to agree that "only as the full *materiality* of ancient Israel is more securely grasped will we be able to make proper sense of its *spirituality.*"[11]

Two works that appeared almost simultaneously in 1983 are partly discussions with and reactions to Mendenhall and Gottwald, but they also advance our investigation somewhat further. D. N. Freedman and D. F. Graf's edited volume of essays, *Palestine in Transition: The Emergence of Ancient Israel* (1983), comes out of the Society of Biblical Literature's "Social World of Biblical Antiquity" colloquium (itself a significant departure). Here the most relevant essay is M. L. Chaney's long piece on ancient Palestinian peasant movements. Chaney adduces some recent archaeological data, but largely as a basis for refuting both the conquest and the nomadic infiltration models for the Israelite settlement of Palestine, in favor of a modified peasants' revolt model. Unfortunately, Chaney is not *au courant* enough to give even a sufficient impression of Syro-Palestinian archaeology's recent results or its explanatory potential today.[12]

B. Halpern's *The Emergence of Israel in Canaan* (1983) also challenges the original peasants' revolt model but is a rather elegant, much more ambitious attempt to understand early Israel as a successor state in the period of international fragmentation and decline at the end of the Late Bronze Age. Halpern begins by asking: "Was there anything that could be called a common cult, beyond subscription to Yahweh? What were the dominant, what were the peripheral, trajectories of religious practice and symbolism in the early eras? Can one discern in the historical developments the origins of some of these (pentateuchal—W.G.D.) materials? Is it possible to recover a residue of Israel's self-conception before kingship in the nation's birth narratives?"[13]

Halpern's pursuit of these fundamental questions is admittedly inconclusive; and of archaeology he says only that "the present state of knowledge and current archaeology offer no real hope to the historian."[14] His own original and provocative search for Israelite ethnicity, however, leads him to stress continuity with Late Bronze Age Canaanite culture—so much so that his conclusions anticipate ours (below):

> Scholars sometimes speak of the "introduction" of the cult of Baal into Israel in the ninth century B.C.E., of Canaanite influence on Israel's religion. . . . But Israelite religion did not import Canaanite. Israel's religion was a Canaanite religion. . . . Israel's religion—the practice of the people—did not develop along the lines of the expurgated fragments the Zadokite clerisy enshrined.[15]

The American Archaeological School

Particularly relevant to our inquiry is the work of several scholars, mostly American, who either have been archaeologists themselves or have been rather heavily influenced by archaeologists. Preeminent among them, of course, would be W. F. Albright. It is impossible to do justice to his achievements in this brief review, but we must at least note his contributions to our specific inquiry. Already in his obscure work *The Archaeology of Palestine and the Bible* (1935; reprint, 1974), Albright had mounted his well-known attack, in the name of archaeology, on the hypothetical reconstruction of Israelite religion in Wellhausen and his successors. The most impressive and most lasting formulation of his lifelong position was in his magisterial *From the Stone Age to Christianity: Monotheism and the Historical Process* (1940). Yet the most specific treatment of Israelite religion was in *Archaeology and the Religion of Israel* (1942). In retrospect, this work, despite its "positivist" leanings and many interpretations that must now be reworked, constitutes the first really adequate historical description of Canaanite and Israelite religion that employs both texts and the whole range of available archaeological evidence. Later works, especially Albright's chapter in *The Old Testament and Modern Study* (1951) and *Yahweh and the Gods of Canaan* (1968), followed the same lines, bringing the discussion up to date.[16] Albright's long-anticipated history of the religion of Israel never materialized, and in any case his notion of Israel's "radical empiricism" would be contested today. But Albright's lasting contribution to our inquiry was the archaeological revolution he launched—which is in fact only now gaining momentum (below).

Another prominent American scholar in our field, G. E. Wright, combined Syro-Palestinian archaeology and biblical studies in an even more deliberate, self-conscious manner. Yet it appears that Wright's distinctive program of "biblical archaeology" yielded relatively few direct results for the history of Israelite religion, apart from his controversial treatment of Shechem and the premonarchic traditions in Joshua 24 and Judges 9. The reasons for this are not difficult to analyze. Throughout much of his productive career, Wright was preoccupied rather with Old Testament *theology,* where his emphasis on the uniqueness of ancient Israel and on the historicity of Israelite faith not only distracted him from archaeology but may have prevented him from fully appreciating Israel's continuity with Late Bronze Age Canaan.[17]

Modern Comparative Linguistic and
Religiohistorical Studies
on Canaan and Israel

A final category of recent literature embraces more specific, descriptive treatments of Canaanite and Israelite religion. We refer not to such works as T. H. Gaster's *Thespis: Ritual, Myth, and Drama in the Ancient Near East* (1961), since these really belong with the earlier myth and ritual approaches. J. Gray's *The Legacy of Canaan: The Ras Shamra Texts and Their Relevance to the Old Testament* (1965), however, is a standard, useful summary of the evidence. Yet despite its commendable survey of the Ugaritic texts, Gray's *Legacy of Canaan* makes virtually no references to the archaeology of the site, much less to the actual physical remains of Canaanite religion at Ugarit or anywhere else in Syria-Palestine. The result is that the rich liturgical texts are treated like cult libretti with neither stage, sets, nor actors.

More recently, J.-M. de Tarragon's *La culte à Ugarit d'après les textes de la pratique en cunéiformes alphabétiques* (1980) focuses specifically, and very ably, on the cult itself (below). But here too the archaeological context of the texts is almost totally ignored. Only two pages are devoted to archaeology, where mention is made of the Ras Shamra temples and their furnishings, tombs, votives, the mysterious stone anchors, and glyptic art. Tarragon concludes only that "the archaeological data would have to be evaluated in a complex comparison with other Syrian rites of the same period as well as with external influences."[18]

Easily the most authoritative study is F. M. Cross's *Canaanite Myth and Hebrew Epic: Essays in the History of the Religion of Israel.*[19] Here both the Ugaritic and the biblical texts are treated in masterly fashion. Furthermore, Cross attempts a new and in many ways revolutionary synthesis, eschewing the idealistic and romantic views of earlier schools in favor of the mass of new historical and textual data, most of it, as he observes, stemming from the progress of archaeological discoveries. Cross stresses throughout the "continuities between the early religion of Israel and the Canaanite (or Northwest Semitic) culture from which it emerged" (p. vii). He also emphasizes the central role of the cult and of cult myth in the period of the tribal league, arguing, however, that the innovative Israelite feature here was largely the coupling of myth *and* history in tension, in what he terms "epic form." This epic, in which the old Canaanite high god El is merged with the figure of Yahweh, the god of Israel's deliverance, becomes the essence of the cultic recitation, enactment in ritual drama, and covenant renewal. Yet Cross's collection of seminal essays, although in a class by itself, is obviously only a prolegomenon to a full-scale history of Israelite religion, as he himself states in his preface. And, it must be confessed, archaeology in Cross's usage refers almost exclusively to *texts,* not material culture, much less what we shall show archaeology can contribute today toward an understanding of the socioeconomic setting of early Israelite religion.[20]

The "Revolution" That Failed to Materialize

Beginning in the 1930s and continuing through the 1960s, contemporary with the *floruit* of the "biblical archaeology" movement, Albright and others had sought to characterize an archaeological revolution that would radically change the way ancient Israel was viewed by modern scholarship.[21] There is no doubt that archaeological discoveries—especially the textual evidence brought to light in the past fifty years—have enormously expanded our knowledge of the biblical milieu in general. But, as I have noted elsewhere, "while the 'external evidence' of archaeology may have enhanced our appreciation of the value of the Biblical sources for understanding both Israelite history and theology, it has not proportionately given us an independent and direct witness to the ancient *cult.*"[22] Even a cursory review of the literature (above) will show that no revolution has in fact occurred; on the contrary, there is a tendency among biblical scholars, perhaps growing, to ignore most categories of data that modern archaeology produces.

Reasons for the Disenchantment
with Archaeology

Earlier in this century (until the 1960s, one may argue) Syro-Palestinian archaeology was still such an amateur discipline that it produced few truly useful data for the social historian, and even today the sad state of publication means that improved data are still largely inaccessible to the generalist. Moreover, since nearly all biblical scholars have been linguistically and historically trained, they have tended quite naturally to concentrate on texts rather than on artifactual evidence. The result of biblical scholarship's focus on literary criticism, as we have seen, was largely a history of the literature *about* the religion of ancient Israel rather than a description of actual religious practice. There seems little doubt, furthermore, that the enthusiasm of the last generation for *theology* has been to the detriment of all phenomenological studies. Even "biblical archaeology," in our opinion, became so enamored with theology that its agenda often consisted largely of issues such as the historicity of the patriarchs, Mosaic monotheism, and the like (i.e., questions of faith, or faith and history). For the period of our inquiry, "biblical archaeology" focused largely on the Israelite conquest of Palestine; but it gave little attention to the complex process of socioeconomic change in the era of the Judges and thus failed to elucidate the actual background against which the early Israelite cult emerged. Indeed, throughout its history the "biblical archaeology" movement has been preoccupied with political history rather than with either religious or social history.[23]

In the past two decades, other factors have militated against archaeology's use by biblical historians, especially in the study of Israelite religion. One has been an inevitable reaction against the extreme emphasis on cult in the myth and ritual school—often based, to be sure, on distortions of the archaeological record. Thus Wright went so far as to suggest dropping the term "cult" altogether, as no longer useful to the discussion.[24] But something else was evidently operative here, not simply the downplaying of the Israelite cult but what may be termed an anti-materialist bias in the interpretation of the nature of religion in general. This may have been simply another legacy of Albright's positivism. But there was a broader tendency, a preference for theology over cult that seems to be a typically Protestant problem, a characteristic not only of Pietistic but of most Reformation and restorationist thought. There has thus been a temptation among biblical theologians to "idealize" or "spiritualize" ancient Israelite religion, or at best to emphasize cultic proclamation *(Heilsgeschichte)* rather than actual cultic practice (much less folk religion; below). In this view, archaeology is naturally seen as having little relevance.

Still more recently, we have witnessed biblical scholars not only ignoring archaeology but actually opposing it. This has come about in the past decade or so, as "biblical archaeology" of the classic style has waned and Syro-Palestinian archaeology has begun to come of age as a separate professional and academic discipline. It is now less dependent on biblical studies (especially theology) and more dependent on other disciplines: cultural anthropology, for its theory and methodology; and the natural sciences, for their analytical techniques.[25] Some biblical scholars have mistakenly assumed that the professionalization of Syro-Palestinian archaeologists means that the latter have inevitably become mere technicians, with little concern for broad humanistic scholarship. Others fear that overspecialization will result in the isolation of archaeology from the field of biblical studies. It is significant that the negative reactions have come almost exclusively from nonarchaeologists, *not* from former "biblical archaeologists," most of whom have made the transition relatively painlessly. The objections stem largely from a failure to understand either the motivation or the agenda of the "new archaeology" of the 1970s and 1980s. What we are calling for is more, not less, dialogue with biblical scholars. And Syro-Palestinian archaeology can now play for the first time an independent and therefore productive role—precisely because of its secularization, which has liberated it to develop its own appropriate research methods and objectives. Ironically, our branch of archaeology, freed of its positivist notions, now begins to have both the analytical and the conceptual tools to contribute toward a *truly* positive view of ancient Israelite religion (below).

Another aspect of the minimization of archaeology and its focus on the material basis of the cult has been the predisposition of biblical historians against certain philosophical positions derived from sociology, economics, and cultural anthropology—all disciplines from which both archaeology and biblical studies have increasingly borrowed. Thus Gottwald's *Tribes of Yahweh,* whose reconstruction of early Israel makes a tentative but commendable use of the "new archaeology" to document social structure and material culture (above), has been dismissed as simply Marxist economic determinism projected upon the biblical texts. (Mendenhall; but see further below on archaeology as the science of material culture.) This largely emotional reaction is little more than a comment on the lingering provincialism of some American biblical scholarship in the late twentieth century. Like archaeology, biblical scholarship needs to venture outside the cloister.

A New Program for Relating Archaeology to the Study of Israelite History and Religion

Having documented the overall failure of biblical scholars to take archaeology seriously as a parallel way of viewing the cult, let us turn now to a more optimistic assessment for the future, with special reference to early Israelite history and religion.

General Observations

At the outset we should note that much of the polemical and unproductive controversy over "biblical archaeology" in recent discussions might have been avoided if we had considered history and archaeology as merely two *aspects* of the attempt to elucidate the human past. History focuses primarily on textual facts, archaeology on artifacts. And today both disciplines, taking a cue from anthropology (as well as cultural and economic geography), pay considerable attention also to "ecofacts"—the contextual factors, both natural setting and social environment (ecology), that help to shape culture. But although both disciplines are increasingly influenced by anthropology, the former continues to be more particularizing (cultural history) and the latter traditionally more generalizing (culture). Here we shall proceed by assuming that the distinctions between all three disciplines are more matters of emphasis, specialized techniques, academic accommodation, and, above all, materials chosen for analysis than they are irreconcilable differences in theory and method, much less in ultimate objectives.

The Task at Hand

When we turn, however, to the specific problem before us—an adequate conception of early Israelite religion—further precision is necessary on the relationship of two of these disciplines, Syro-Palestinian archaeology and biblical history. Let us begin by observing that our twofold task is to reconstruct ancient Israelite religion on the basis of its extant remains: belief through texts, cult through material culture. The former should be the province of biblical history and theology, the second of archaeology. We regard the division of the inquiry into two aspects as justifiable, indeed necessary, on the grounds that belief and practice, while obviously complementary, are not the same, nor can one necessarily be extrapolated from the other. To put it another way, a true phenomenology of religion will consider not only normative religion, or what the texts produced by the establishment insisted *should* have prevailed, but also popular or folk religion, what the majority of adherents actually *practiced.* One of the difficulties with most histories of the religion of Israel is that they are based on texts that are both late and elitist.[26] Only through the corrective of archaeology and its inquiry into the actual contemporary remains and the behavior they reflect, can we hope to penetrate behind these texts to gain a more balanced picture of early Israelite religion in all of its variety.

Methodological Principles

We must not press the above practical division of labor too far, however, since the two aspects of the task are interrelated. Indeed, we may argue that texts, as well as the more typical categories of material remains, are also archaeological artifacts. Thus biblical texts can be legitimately viewed as simply inscribed artifacts, that is, the fossilized results of human thought and action, which require interpretation no less (and perhaps methodologically no differently?) than any other artifacts before they constitute data, that is, possess power to communicate anything meaningful to us concerning the past. The only difference in this case would be that the Hebrew Bible is a "curated" artifact, not rediscovered in archaeological context but always preserved and interpreted in a living community. It is thus an ancient artifact but one that represents a continuous, changing tradition. Here the challenge is for the interpreter, Jewish or Christian, to stand sufficiently far outside the tradition to gain proper perspective. By contrast, the other artifacts with which we must deal (including, of course, nonbiblical texts) were long lost and thus when recovered represent a "broken traditon."[27] Yet neither "continuous" nor "broken" traditions can be taken simply at face value by the historian: both require critical interpretation.

It is commonplace for textual specialists to assert (1) that texts constitute the only primary historical evidence, since they provide a direct, reliable, comprehensive witness to human thought and action; and (2) that the interpretation of texts is both more obvious and more "objective" than that of artifacts. The assumption seems to be that texts are eloquent but artifacts are mute.[28] Nothing could be farther from the truth, as the whole enterprise of modern archaeology shows (below). Here a distinction made by earlier "biblical archaeologists," although perhaps overly optimistic, can still be helpful: The biblical texts constitute internal (and therefore more subjective) evidence, while archaeology is capable of providing external (and therefore more independent) evidence. What is obviously essential is that *both* categories of evidence are taken into account and that both are subjected to rigid and *similar* scrutiny— neither controlling the other but each supplementing and correcting the other—so that both come to be true data.

This leads us to a final consideration of what constitutes primary evidence and thus to the unique (although related) role of archaeology in illuminating the Israelite cult. It is self-evident that archaeology can produce useful realia for the historian of religion, that is, material remains of the ancient cult such as temples, shrines, and religious paraphernalia (although today this list could be considerably expanded).[29] We would encourage and expect more use of these neglected resources, especially as archaeological data become more proficiently excavated, interpreted, and published. Yet almost no historian of Israelite religion seems to have realized that archaeology's most useful contribution to biblical studies in the future may lie in another direction, in its *increasing capacity for writing social and economic history* and thus providing a setting in which events described in biblical accounts may become credible.[30]

The new agenda is unabashedly materialistic, in the sense that the study of material culture is one of our best clues to culture. Thus in the future we hope, through archaeology as a discipline *and* an interdisciplinary inquiry, to reconstruct a context in the early Iron Age in Palestine in which Israelite religion can be understood in the light not only of texts but also of settlement patterns, demography, subsistence systems, social structure, political organization, level of technology, artistic production, and even possibly ethnicity in the archaeological record (below). This, rather than *Kulturgeschichte* or "political history," is what I think Syro-Palestinian and "biblical" archaeology finally has the theoretical tools to do. Data comprise not simply facts but facts in context, facts interpreted, that is, *meaningful* facts. Today's interdisciplinary archaeology begins to have the potential for providing such data on many aspects of ancient Israelite culture—including religious belief and practice, even though this is a difficult and neglected area. The social world of ancient Israel is already a growing field of investigation for younger biblical scholars; and I predict that this trend will only be enhanced by the concomitant (though largely independent) growth of the new archaeology. Yet this is for the most part an admittedly programmatic approach.[31] The remainder of this paper must be devoted to suggestions of what archaeology, even in its present immature state, can contribute specifically to the study of early Israelite religion and cult and their antecedents.

A SURVEY OF THE ARCHAEOLOGICAL EVIDENCE FOR RELIGION AND CULT IN LATE BRONZE–IRON I SYRIA-PALESTINE

The Late Bronze Age, ca. 1500–1200 B.C.E.

We begin our survey, as stated in the introduction to this chapter, with the Late Bronze Age Canaanite milieu, which we regard as essential background.

Physical Remains of the Cult

Temples. We now possess nearly thirty LB I–II temples from Syria-Palestine, many published only in the last decade but a number known since the 1940s and 1950s. In Syria, we can cite (by date of first adequate publication) the temples of "Baal" and "Dagan" at Ugarit (1931); of Carchemish (1952); of Ebenda II–I (1950); of Kamid el-Lôz (1972); of Mumbaqat (1974); and of Meskene (1974–1975).[32] These temples are mostly of the *Langbau* type (below) with either three or, more commonly, two rooms along the central axis. This type, which first appears toward the beginning of the Middle Bronze Age in both Syria and Palestine, seems to represent a local Canaanite temple form, with a history extending well into the Iron II period.

In Palestine, at least twenty LB I–II temples have now been published in some detail (Fig. 15). To the previously known Stratum VIIA Temple 2048 at Megiddo (1948); the Strata IX (Mekal), VIII, and VII temples at Beth-shan (1940); Fosse Temples I–III at Lachish (1940); and the Area C Stele, Area H Orthostat, Area A Longroom, and Area F Square temples at Hazor (1958, 1959, 1972),[33] we can add nearly a dozen others. Fortunately, in addition to improved excavation and publication of these more recent temples, we now have several useful comparative and synthetic studies, to which we shall refer for details (below).

The remaining LB I–II temples in Palestine are the Field V Migdal Temple 2 at Shechem (1965); the "Airport Temple" at Amman (1966); the Mt. Gerazim/Tananir temple (1969); the Deir ʿAllā Sanctuary (1969); the Timnah Temple (1972); the Jaffa "Lion Temple" (1974); the temples at Shiqmonah, at Tel Kittan III, and at Tel Mevorakh XI–IX (1977); and the Level VII "Summit Temple" at Lachish (1978).[34]

Both A. Mazar and E. Stern, in the course of publishing their own exceedingly important temples from Tell Qasile XII–X and Tel Mevorakh XI–IX, respectively, have provided up-to-date comparative studies of LB–Iron I temples in Syria-Palestine, with bibliography and illustrations (to which we refer for convenience sake).[35] In addition, A. Kuschke has surveyed similar ground in the second edition of the *Biblisches Reallexikon.*[36]

All three commentators attempt a typological classification of the LB II temples. Kuschke suggests a fourfold division, (see p. 225), principally on overall plan and orientation of the entrance. Mazar regards the extant Palestinian LB I—II temples as simply either "symmetric," mostly bipartite longroom, with direct access; or "irregular" like the Lachish Fosse Temples. He regards the former as going back to local, Canaanite traditions in the Middle or even the Early Bronze Age in Palestine, whereas the latter are more "foreign," perhaps of Cypro-Aegean derivation. Stern is even less sanguine about any generalizations on the basis of ground plan. He nevertheless suggests several very general categories, of which the most common is the "bench temple," the predominant local Palestinian type, going back to the Chalcolithic period. Subtypes can be distinguished on the basis of whether or not the cella is raised or not, Subtype 1 being probably of Egyptian origin.[37]

Few archaeologists in reporting their own temples have gone beyond

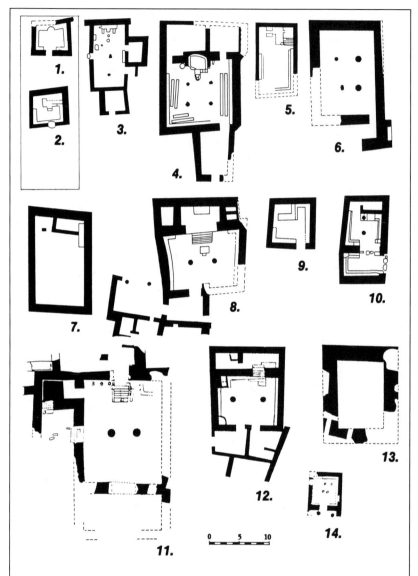

Fig. 15. Late Bronze and Iron I temples from Palestine.

1. Hazor, Area C temple; **2.** Tell Qasile, Str. XII; **3.** Lachish, Fosse Temple I; **4.** Lachish, Fosse Temple III; **5.** Tel Mevorakh, Str. XI; **6.** Beth-shan, North Temple, Str. V; **7.** Tell Abu Hawam, Str. IVa; **8.** Beth-shan, Str. VI; **9.** Tell Qasile, Str. XI; **10.** Tell Qasile, Str. X; **11.** Lachish, the Summit Temple, Str. VII; **12.** Beth-shan, Str. VII; **13.** Tell Kittan, Str. IV; **14.** Tell Kittan, Str. V. (Nos. 1–10, after A. Mazar, *Tell Qasile* I, fig. 15:A–J; nos. 11–14, after E. Stern, *Tel Mevorakh* II, fig. IVa:1, 2; IVb:1, 2. Scale approximate.)

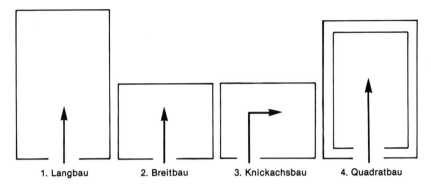

1. Langbau   2. Breitbau   3. Knickachsbau   4. Quadratbau

rather elementary architectural typologies to a consideration of either temple ideology or function. The only larger-scale synthetic work attempted recently, M. Ottosson's *Temple and Cult Places in Palestine* (1980), is by a nonspecialist; it is useful for general description but cannot be relied upon for either detail or critical judgment.[38] The symposium edited by A. Biran, *Temples and High Places in Biblical Times* (1981), features essays by a number of prominent archaeologists, but many are irrelevant to our topic, and none is really synthetic.[39] Among recent excavators who have published their own, very pertinent material, the approach of Stern may be taken as typical. In presenting what is surely one of the largest and most significant collections of *in situ* cult paraphernalia, from the Strata XI–X temple at Tel Mevorakh, Stern gives a thorough comparative discussion of both the structure and its contents. He devotes just three sentences of interpretation, however, to "the cult," speculating not at all on the function of the temple and suggesting only that the gods identified with it may have been Baal and and 'Ashtoret.[40]

Temple paraphernalia. The first, and perhaps most important, category of evidence consists of temple architectural furnishings. The most prominent features are certainly central platforms or arches in nearly all the known temples, and, in Palestine especially, low front and side benches. The altars and benches show that the presentation of votives and sacrifices was a central activity in the cult (below).

A second category consists of movable objects. In Syria, excavations until recently have been rather poorly carried out. Yet from the "Baal" and "Dagan" temples at Ugarit, for instance, we have an abundance of material.[41] At Alalakh, the temples in Levels IV and I produced bronze weapons, beads, bullae, scarabs, seals, basalt altars, terra-cotta stands, and statuettes of a goddess and of King Idri-mi.[42]

Even in "poor Palestine" we have ample evidence. Tel Mevorakh is not alone in producing a rich trove of cult objects, including a large assemblage of pottery and ceramic votive vessels; stone vessels; bronze knives, arrows, jewelry, cymbals, and a serpent; glass pendants; and cylinder seals and beads. The Area H temple at Hazor produced a hoard of ceramic votives and vessels, together with a potter's workshop in the temple forecourt (below); a terra-cotta house/temple model and a liver model with a cuneiform text; magnificent stone votive figures and other vessels, basins, and altars; quantities of cylinder seals and beads; and several bronzes, including a bull, a snake, male and female figurines, and a fine plaque of a priest or other dignitary.[43] The Amman "Airport Temple" was incredibly rich in precious materials, including imported pottery, gold jewelry, scarabs, and cylinder seals.[44] The Lachish Fosse Temples, known since the 1930s, yielded great quantities of votives, some inscribed, from numerous *favissae* in the temple precincts.[45] And the "Summit Temple" found recently produced, among other things, a splendid gold relief of a nude goddess on horseback (below). Finally, at many sites, too numerous to mention, we have ceramic votive vessels of several types, in addition to terra-cotta cult stands (below). Given these actual objects from temple contexts, can we say *nothing* regarding the Canaanite deities or how they were worshiped?

Other cultic objects. The only definitely cultic items found outside temple precincts in LB Syria-Palestine are figurines (Fig. 16). There are numerous examples of bronze figurines, of both male and female deities. The most common are rather standardized representations of a warlike Baal, often brandishing in his upraised arm a bundle of thunderbolts, recalling Baal's storm-god imagery ("Cloud Rider") at Ugarit. There are other seated statuettes, however, that more likely represent El on his throne, as do several small steles.[46] The female deities are occasionally represented in bronze or gold plaques or pendants, in the older MB II style; but they appear more often in the ubiquitous terra-cotta "Mother Goddess" figurines. Often mold-made, these portray the Lady—probably Elat/Asherah or ʿAnat—nude *en face*. There appear to be two principal types of the female figurines: (1) standing goddesses, usually wearing the Egyptian "Hathor headdress," sometimes with very exaggerated pubic triangles, often clutching serpents or lotus/lily blossoms in their outstretched hands; and (2) reclining "couch" figurines, also nude, but with arms extended at their sides, possibly not deities but "mourning figures" connected with funeral rites.[47] It should be stressed that most of these male and female figurines have not been found *in situ*, so we cannot be sure whether they were votives for either temples or house shrines, nor can we do more than speculate on how they were actually used in religious rites. All that is clear is that many represent various deities.

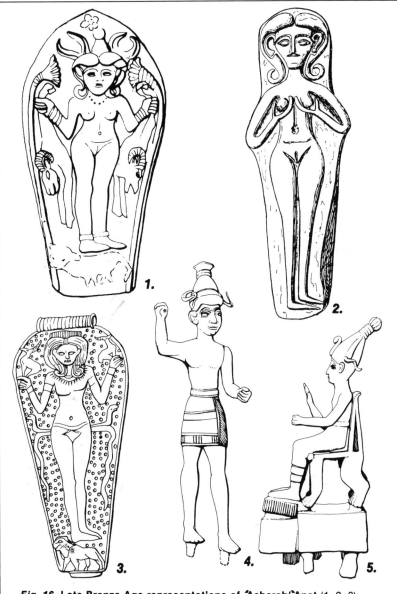

Fig. 16. Late Bronze Age representations of ʿAsherah/ʿAnat (1, 2, 3) and El (4, 5).

1, 3. Gold pendants from Minet el-Beida (Negbi, *Canaanite Gods in Metal*, figs. 118, 119);
2. Terra-cotta mold-made plaque from Gezer (Macalister, *Gezer* II, fig. 500); 4, 5. Bronze striding and seated figures, from Ugarit, *niveau* I, and Byblos (Negbi, *Canaanite Gods in Metal*, figs. 43, 55).

227

Tombs, mortuary installations, and burial deposits. It would be obvious to any ethnographer or cultural anthropologist that burial rites in almost any period should be rich in implications for religious belief and practice. yet the numerous tombs of LB Syria-Palestine have scarcely been investigated from this aspect. We cannot survey the extensive evidence here but must be content to point to a resource for future research. In particular, an archaeological context should be sought for the "*kispu* festival" known from the Ugaritic texts, in which libations or drink offerings for the dead are poured into underground tombs through a channel from the surface.[48] In addition, closer attention should obviously be paid to tomb deposits, many of which may be best understood in symbolic terms as votives to the gods or food offerings for the deceased. Even the style of the tomb architecture itself may suggest conceptions of life after death. Yet virtually *all* of this possible evidence for cult has been neglected to date, by both historians and archaeologists.[49]

Textual Evidence

Here we need not survey the evidence except in the briefest compass, since there now exist several authoritative, up-to-date treatments by textual specialists. The best and fullest discussion is that of J.-M. de Tarragon, *Le culte à Ugarit* (1980). He gives an extensive treatment not simply of the well-known Canaanite mythology so dramatically revealed in the Ugaritic texts but also of actual *cult practice* as revealed in these texts. The principal features, according to Tarragon, are (1) frequent offerings, principally of food and drink for the gods; (2) animal sacrifices of various kinds; and (3) periodic rituals (perhaps at the new year and other times) such as the "enthronement of Baal," the "sacred marriage," the *marzeaḥ* banquet, the *kispu* festival, and the like. It is possible also to reconstruct a rather elaborate cadre of cult personnel, including, of course, the participation of the king and queen but also involving priests, cult devotees ("sacred prostitutes"?), singers, sculptors, garment makers, and many other officials attached to the temple precincts. Yet, as we have seen (above), Tarragon does not speculate whatsoever on the relationship of the elaborate cult he has reconstructed from the texts to the actual archaeological context at Ugarit, which surely provides in large part the physical *setting* for the cult.

Interpreting the Finds

This résumé of the rich but neglected archaeological evidence is too cursory to be more than suggestive. Yet even on the basis of this limited survey, plus little more than intuition, we can easily extrapolate something of the nature of the cult from its physical remains and from there move toward a comparison of the archaeological and textual data concerning Canaanite religion.

The temples. The relatively small size of the LB temples, their simple bipartite/tripartite or "irregular" floor plan, the generally spartan furnishings, the prominence of the altar and/or low benches in the main room, and the *favissae*—all leave no doubt that presentations of votives, of food and drink offerings, and of animal sacrifices were the main aspects of Canaanite temple worship.

Temple offerings. We can specify what many of the votives were, and these represent not only everyday items but also exotic, imported, or very expensive gifts (above). The many ceramic vessels, cult stands, and small altars indicate food and drink offerings, various libations, animal sacrifices, and possible incense offerings. Unfortunately the lack of careful excavation and sieving or flotation of paleo-botanical/zoological remains precludes our saying very much about which foodstuffs or animals were offered in these temples or how the offerings were presented (i.e., whole, burnt, consumed on the premises, etc.).[50]

Yet there are more data than commonly supposed. For instance, the LB I Area H Orthostat temple at Hazor features both a large rectangular stone altar and a semicircular sacrificial basin in the forecourt, with a drain channel made of discarded cult stands leading away from the area. This is almost certainly to be understood as evidence for blood sacrifice. In the same temple forecourt is a potter's workshop, complete with kiln and several stacks of miniature standardized bowls, clear evidence for the production and sale of votives in the *temenos* area.[51] Finally, we should note that small steles found *in situ* at several sites indicate that representations of the gods themselves could be erected by temple functionaries or possibly offered as votives by worshipers. These finds include a stele of Mekal (= El or Baal) from the Stratum IX "Thutmosis III" temple at Beth-shan; the Tanit stele from the Area C stele-temple at Hazor; and the gold foil representation of Qudshu-Asherah-'Anat from the "Summit Temple" at Lachish.[52]

Temple and other rituals. Here the evidence, although scant, may be interpreted both in positive and in negative aspects. The small size and simple architectural layout of the temples—and especially the general lack of any associated structures except a small open forecourt—all point, as we have suggested above, to little ritual beyond the presentation of individual gifts. It is significant that there is no evidence whatsoever for a setting for any large-scale, much less public, rituals or "cult drama," such as presupposed by most readings of the Ugaritic texts. If large public celebrations, banquets, or the like were part of cult observance, they must have taken place elsewhere—either in the open, perhaps in the palaces, or in large public buildings that have not yet been clearly identified. There is some suggestive evidence for music in temple service, such as the bronze cymbals from Tel Mevorakh; but there is neither room nor architectural planning that would indicate anything like the antiphonal choirs that scholars have postulated for the recitation of some of the Ugaritic mythological texts. There is certainly no archaeological confirmation of the supposed practice of temple "sacred prostitution." Perhaps the only evidence for cult drama at all is the mask from the Area H Orthostat temple at Hazor (above), which suggests that priests or others may have acted out certain roles publicly. By and large, however, what temple ritual for which we do have archaeological evidence is individual, simple, and mostly private. Temple worship consisted apparently of adoring and serving the deities (possibly also their representatives, the priest-king or priests) by the bringing of gifts into the "house of the god/gods." The common occurrence of the LB figurines in domestic contexts would seem to corroborate the prevalence of individual rites of worship (possibly in unrecognized house shrines). Other aspects of individual worship are, of course, rarely attested in the archaeological record, but we see them reflected no doubt in the art of the period. For instance, the "sacred tree of life" is one of the most common elements and also reflects a concern with fertility.

The identification of individual deities. Here there is some archaeological evidence, although partly circumstantial (and again largely ignored). We have already noted the possibility of recognizing Mekal at Beth-shan, Tanit (Asherah) at Hazor, and Qudshu-Asherah-'Anat at Lachish. The two principal temples at Ugarit were designated "Baal" and "Dagan," although without any foundation in the archaeological material. We may note, however, that the famous Lachish ewer, mentioning "a gift, a lamb for my Lady Elat" (= Asherah), was found in debris of Fosse Temple III.[53] It is seldom recalled that on the altar of the "Lion Temple" at Jaffa (LB–Iron I) there was found the perfectly preserved skull of a lioness. A mass of recent archaeological and textual data confirms that one of the principal epithets of Asherah in LB–Iron I was "the Lion Lady," and she is often associated with lion imagery.[54] Finally, the occurrence of bronze snakes in sacred contexts at Megiddo, Gezer, Hazor, Tel Mevorakh, and Timnah[55] may suggest that the "snake-goddess" (probably Asherah-'Anat, often depicted holding snakes) was worshiped there.

As noted above, several bronze figurines probably to be identified as El and Baal appear in temple as well as in domestic contexts.

Conclusions. Several general observations should be stressed. (1) First, both the LB temples themselves and the artifactual evidence belong in direct continuity with the earlier Canaanite Middle Bronze Age culture in Syria-Palestine (ca. 2000–1500 B.C.E.). (2) Second, the known temples at individual sites are both numerous and varied in type. Even in the very small areas typically excavated, we have no fewer than four contemporary LB temples at Hazor and at Lachish. To judge from this, at many sites in Syria-Palestine there must have been a dozen or more temples, suggesting a multiplicity of deities. Either each had his or her own temple and following, or possibly any and all deities could be worshiped at a typical temple. (3) Third, all of the elements of Canaanite religion that we have been able to isolate through their archaeological remains witness unanimously to the vitality of a "fertility cult." The votives are propitiatory offerings. The food offerings and animal sacrifices represent symbolically the two principal elements of the Canaanite Late Bronze Age economy, agriculture and pastoralism. And the ubiquitous "Mother Goddess" fertility figurines, even on a minimalist interpretation, underline the centrality of the theme of reproduction.

These general observations, of course, tend to corroborate what is already known from the texts at Ugarit concerning the Canaanite pantheon and the nature of religion in the Late Bronze Age in Syria-Palestine. This cult undoubtedly developed from a long local tradition, stretching back at least to the beginning of the Middle Bronze period, in which fertility motifs naturally predominated in a marginal-zone society and economy that depended on precarious rainfall agriculture. Both theology and ritual were intrinsically related to nature—that is, to the very conditions of existence—and were designed to enhance and to ensure its regenerative powers.[56]

The Iron I Period, ca. 1200–1000 B.C.E.

When we come to the early Israelite society, one of several that emerged in the wake of the collapse of the Late Bronze Age culture, we shall confine ourselves to its proper geographical and cultural sphere, ancient Palestine. (In any case, Syria is poorly documented in the early Iron I period). Our survey will cover the archaeological horizon known generally as Iron I, or, historically, the period prior to the Israelite monarchy.[57]

Physical Remains of the Cult in Iron I

Canaanite temples. Despite the general breakup of Canaanite cultural hegemony at the close of the Late Bronze Age, with the destruction or disruption of many sites in Palestine, Canaanite influence continued, especially at sites that did not become "Israelite" (below). Thus we can properly speak of the Canaanite temples at Beth-shan VI ("Seti I," almost certainly Egyptianizing) and possibly also of Tell Abu-Hawam IVa.[58] Here the continuity with the LB temples that we surveyed above is, not surprisingly, quite striking. Yet these temples and their contents—especially the elaborate and well-preserved ones at Beth-shan—although exactly contemporary with the rise of the Israelite tribal league, are seldom considered as reflecting the general cultural milieu.

Philistine temples. One of the more dramatic stories of modern archaeology has been the recovery of the rich material culture of the Philistines, formerly only shadowy actors on the stage of early Israelite history.[59] We now have a small "Lion Temple" at Jaffa, reused from LB II (above). Much more significant, however, are the Philistine temples of Tell Qasile XII (319), XI (200), and X (131), splendidly excavated and lavishly published recently by A. Mazar. This series of temples with their exotic and well-preserved furnishings and contents gives us our first real glimpse of the Philistine cult. Without going into details of interpretation,[60] we may note that what is striking is the degree to which Philistine religion had quickly assimilated to the old Canaanite fertility cults, still evidently vital in Palestine in the twelfth and eleventh centuries B.C.E.

Early Israelite shrines. As is well known, we possess no real Israelite temples earlier then the Arad Stratum XI temple (tenth or ninth century B.C.E.). Generally overlooked (or dismissed as too controversial in interpretation), however, is what appears to be an early Israelite alteration and reuse of an LB Canaanite temple; we refer to Migdal Temple 1 at Shechem, probably the "house of El-berith" of Judges 9:46.[61] Moreover, there is a growing corpus of twelfth to tenth century B.C.E. shrines or cult places at sites in central Palestine that are, without doubt, Israelite. Some of these have long been known, such as the house shrine in Building 2081 of Megiddo Stratum VA; the Tell el-Far'ah (N) *niveau* 3 shrine near the city gate; the Taanach "Cultic Structure"; and the Hazor Stratum XI cult structure in Area B.[62] These have been surveyed several times, but they have received nothing like the attention they deserve as *actual Israelite cult places.*

More recently, another small shrine, with a large number of ceramic vessels and stands and several horned altars, "Cult Room 49" at Lachish, has been published by Y. Aharoni.[63] A much larger cultic structure is Biran's tenth to ninth century B.C.E. "high place" at Dan, perhaps a Canaanite style *bêt bāmôth*, but certainly Israelite.[64] Still more fascinating and more pertinent is the recent publication by A. Mazar of a twelfth-century B.C.E. open-air hilltop shrine about five miles due east of Dothan, in the heartland of Israelite tribal territory.[65] The most spectacular find from the low stone *bāmāh* is a superbly modeled bronze bull, which is difficult not to connect with the worship of El, the bull figure par excellence at Ugarit. Recently another isolated early Israelite hilltop shrine has been reported by A. Zertal, located high on Mt. Ebal, in the territory of ancient Manasseh. This installation features a large altar with quantities of animal bones. The pottery is said to be twelfth to eleventh century B.C.E., but few details are known.[66]

Archaeology and the Early Israelite Cult

Interpretation of the finds. Although the actual physical remains of the early Israelite cult to date may seem relatively meager, they nevertheless permit a tentative interpretation and one that, moreover, is quite independent, let us say, of the narratives in Joshua-Samuel. (1) It is perhaps significant that no pre-tenth century B.C.E. temples have yet been found, only household shrines and small open-air sanctuaries. The early Israelite cult seems to reflect a simple, agrarian, nonurban society. In any case, religious practice appears to have required neither elaborate cultus nor ritual. (2) The cult paraphernalia at the few known sites consists largely of ceramic vessels, cult stands, and the like, evidence of food offerings and animal sacrifices, that is, agricultural produce similar to that presented in the Canaanite LB fertility cults. A further reflection of the agricultural basis of this new society and religion is the recent evidence for production of olive oil in the immediate vicinity of several of these Israelite shrines.[67] (3) The only innovation in the Iron I remains that cannot be derived from LB is the small four-cornered or "horned" altar, which may perhaps be considered as evidence for the introduction of incense offerings by the Israelite cult.[68] Otherwise, the material basis of the early Israelite cult can hardly be distinguished from that of the Canaanite cult of the Late Bronze Age in any significant detail. It must be stressed that whatever socioeconomic differences in the two cultures may be discerned, there is nothing in the archaeological record per se that reflects "Yahwism"—or, indeed, any distinctive new Iron I ideology (below).

The socioeconomic setting. If the results of our archaeological inquiry thus far are thought to be somewhat disappointing, the "silence" may be due simply to the present state of our knowledge or, more likely, to the limitations of traditional archaeology. There is another and more realistic avenue of approach, however, one that makes use of the growing potential of today's interdisciplinary archaeology. This approach seeks not simply isolated "finds" of the period to illustrate religion. It attempts to reconstruct the entire social and economic setting of Iron I Palestine, so as to place Israelite religion and cult in a broad enough *context* to make them more readily understandable. It is this general approach in the recent work of Gottwald, Chaney, Halpern, and others (above) that is congenial to the modern archaeologist's perspective. But the conclusions these scholars reached, mostly on other grounds, can now be supported by much more archaeological evidence than they were able to adduce even a few years ago.

In the past fifteen years, there has been a virtual explosion of discoveries relating to Israel's emergence in Palestine—most of the data, however, just beginning to be accessible to the historian and the biblical scholar. After years of concentrating on large tell sites and failing to isolate clear early Israelite remains, archaeologists have finally begun to turn to a much more promising problem-solving approach that focuses largely on one-period sites and regional surveys.[69] Consequently, we can now claim to have identified a half dozen or more distinctive early Iron I villages and village cultures that may tentatively be identified as "Israelite" (see further below on "ethnicity"). Among them would be ʿAi and Khirbet Radannah (1969, 1971); Tel Masos (= Hormah?; 1974, 1975, 1978, 1983); ʿIzbet Ṣarṭah (= Ebenezer?; 1977); Giloh (1981); and Shiloh (1983).[70] In addition, extensive surveys have been carried out in lower Galilee, in the northern West Bank, and in the hill country north of Jerusalem by I. Finkelstein, Z. Gal, and A. Zertal. Here, in the ancient heartland of the Israelite settlement in central Palestine, we can now document for the first time the establishment of dozens of new early-twelfth-century B.C.E. villages, their gradual growth and spread in the twelfth and eleventh centuries B.C.E., and their decline by the early tenth century B.C.E. as urbanism increased toward the founding of the monarchy.[71] When published, these surveys—together with the older work of Aharoni in upper Galilee and the regional surveys of the Tel Aviv Institute of Archaeology along the coastal plain and in the northern Negev—will truly "revolutionalize" (at last) our knowledge of the process of early Israelite settlement in Palestine.

Already we can draw a provisional picture of the distinguishing characteristics of what may be termed early "Israelite" society, based on recent research that combines the insights of the newer interdisciplinary archaeology. (1) The sites are mostly in the central regions of Palestine, not on destroyed or deserted LB II sites (where they had been sought previously) but founded *de novo* in the early twelfth century B.C.E. (2) Nearly all are small, unwalled villages, characterized by early "four-room" courtyard houses, rock-hewn cisterns, and silos—typical characteristics of the material culture of agrarian or peasant societies. (3) The subsistence system is based on small-scale terrace farming, with some herding of livestock and primitive "cottage industries," but also with scant evidence for trade with more distant urban centers. (4) The social structure, compared with that of the urban Late Bronze Age, appears to be less rigidly stratified, although there is already evidence for fairly widespread literacy.[72] (5) The pottery, however—in contrast to the newly introduced house forms, distinctive socioeconomic structure, and the new settlement patterns—is solidly in the LB IIB Canaanite tradition. Nearly all forms exhibit only the expected, normal development from the thirteenth into the twelfth (and even eleventh) century B.C.E.[73] (6) Most of these early Iron I sites are abandoned by the end of the eleventh century B.C.E. or before, with the growth of a more concentrated urban population in the monarchy.

The above picture, provisional and partly intuitive, rests largely on still unpublished material. But several recent studies or works in progress have already begun to move toward a similar synthesis. The most promising is a review by L. E. Stager of early highland villages in ancient Israel, based on archaeology, ethnography, ecology, and demography as well as on textual and historical sources.[74] This new approach, just beginning, will be, in my opinion, *much* more productive than searching for "Israelite destruction layers" at the major tell sites of Palestine; and in due time it may be expected to inform us not only on socioeconomic structure in Iron I but also on early Israelite religious thought and practice.

Related research has shown at the same time that most of the elements that scholars had utilized until recently as diagnostic traits for distinguishing Israelite remains belong either to the common Canaanite heritage of Iron I Palestine or in some cases were introduced from the Aegean world by the Sea Peoples. These elements would include the "four-room house," the collar-rim storage jar, and the bench tomb.[75] Even the silos, plastered cisterns, and hillside terraces, which Albright and others had thought to be Israelite innovations, are now known to have originated, at least on some scale, in the Late Bronze Age and even earlier.

CONCLUSION

What model, then, does archaeology support in the current debate over Israelite origins? And what do recent archaeological data say specifically about the sources of Israelite religion? Indeed, archaeologically speaking, can we define Israelite "ethnicity" itself, or must we be content simply to describe Israelite religious *practice*?

1. First, and most important, the inescapable conclusion—only likely to be enhanced by future archaeological research—is that the Israelite settlement of Palestine (in archaeological terms, the transition from the Late Bronze to the Iron Age) was a gradual, exceedingly complex process. It involved social, economic, and political—as well as religious—change, with many regional variations. Recent archaeological discoveries are thus at least *compatible with* the "peasants' revolt" model. Archaeology cannot, however, be construed any longer as supporting "nomadic infiltration," much less "conquest" models, as previous scholars had maintained.[76] It must be stressed that in the light of archaeology today, it is the LB–Iron I *continuity*—not the discontinuity—that is striking, and the more so as research progresses. In other words, of the two biblical accounts, Joshua and Judges, the latter is by far the more realistic and thus more historically reliable. And for the purposes of the present inquiry into religion and cult, it is the latter's frank recognition of syncretism in early Israelite religion[77]—of the pervasive influence of the old fertility cults of Canaan—that instills further confidence in this account.

2. Archaeology, however, does not yet, and probably cannot, comment on the political or religious ideology behind the emergence of ancient Israel. We may tend to agree that Yahwism, whether a revolutionary social movement or not, was probably the driving force. But *archaeologically* we can say only that in the cultural vacuum following the collapse of Canaanite society about 1200 B.C.E., there arose in central Palestine a new ethnic consciousness and solidarity. The emergence of this ethnicity need not have been accompanied by a revolt at all; it may be viewed rather as simply a normal and even predictable historical development in the evolution of society. Insofar as the ideology of the Israelite movement found concrete expression in the new economic, social, and religious forms, however, we can hope to trace these forms in the archaeological record, since this comprises the "material correlates" of human behavior.[78]

But archaeology cannot penetrate behind action to the wellsprings of thought and emotion. It must constantly struggle to comprehend the relics of a past religion—a lost symbolic system—but it cannot explain their ultimate derivation. What archaeology *can* contribute is a better understanding of the ecology of socioeconomic change as well as a more empirical material basis on which we can at least begin to distinguish Israelite "ethnicity"[79]—not the least characteristic of which was a distinctive religious consciousness and cult. Above all, archaeology, with its focus on actual religious practice, offers an invaluable counterbalance to all idealistic systems that rob ancient Israelite religion of its diversity and vitality.[80] The textual and historical analysis of F. M. Cross and his many students on the Canaanite background of early Israelite religion constitute a truly revolutionary prolegomenon. Now it is time for Syro-Palestinian archaeology to demonstrate how radical that revolution is by illuminating the actual cult.

NOTES

1. I am aware, of course, of the near-impossibility of satisfactorily defining "religion." My conception here seeks to avoid such methodologically meaningless definitions as "the numinous" by laying stress throughout on the *material consequences* of religious thoughts and acts—at least a testable proposition. On the defense of such a concept against the charge of "reductionism," see H. H. Penner and E. A. Yonan, "Is a Science of Religion Possible?" *JR* 52 (1972) 107–33. Note also that the phenomenological or "functionalist" approach advocated here is purely pragmatic and is not to be confused with certain philosophical schools similarly named; cf. M. Harris, *The Rise of Anthropological Theory: A History of Theories of Culture* (New York: Thomas Y. Crowell Co., 1968) 423–25, 514–28. On "phenomenology" or "the science of religion" as an *empirical* discipline, see M. Eliade, "Methodological Remarks on the Study of Religious Symbolism," *The History of Religions: Essays in Methodology* (ed. M. Eliade and J. M. Kitagawa; Chicago: University of Chicago Press, 1959) 86–107.

2. On "the failure of sociological nerve," in Fohrer's approach, however, see the critique of N. K. Gottwald, *The Tribes of Yahweh: A Sociology of the Religion of Liberated Israel 1250–1050 B.C.E.* (Maryknoll, N.Y.: Orbis Books, 1979) 602–08. Fohrer's *History of Israelite Religion* represents largely a renewed application of literary criticism, not a new approach.

3. Y. Kaufmann, *The Religion of Israel* (Chicago: University of Chicago Press, 1960), 2, 7.

4. See further my critique of Haran's use in W. G. Dever, "Material Remains and the Cult in Ancient Israel: An Essay in Archaeological Systematics," *The Word of the Lord Shall Go Forth: Essays in Honor of David Noel Freedman in Celebration of His Sixtieth Birthday* (ed. C. L. Meyers and M. O'Connor; Winona Lake, Ind.: Eisenbrauns, 1983) 575. See also below on my reservation that *many* of the biblical texts are both late and elitist—and thus may constitute less direct evidence of the actual early cult than archaeological discoveries.

5. A detailed critique from the viewpoint of archaeology would be relevant but beyond our scope here. See, generally, the standard histories of Old Testament scholarship. Cf. H. F. Hahn, *The Old Testament in Modern Research* (expanded ed.; Philadelphia: Fortress Press, 1966) 64–74.

6. Pertinent also are R. de Vaux's eminently sensible "Method in the Study of Early Hebrew History," *The Bible in Modern Scholarship* (ed. J. P. Hyatt; New York: Abingdon Press, 1965) 15–29; and idem, "On Right and Wrong Uses of Archaeology," *Near Eastern Archaeology in the Twentieth Century: Essays in*

Honor of Nelson Glueck (ed. J. A. Sanders; Garden City, N.Y.: Doubleday & Co., 1970) 64–80.

7. See the critique of W. C. Graham and H. G. May in Hahn, *Modern Research*, 209–12. Note also that May was, in fact, a practicing archaeologist, a member of the field staff of the Oriental Institute's excavations at Megiddo. His *Material Remains of the Megiddo Cult* (ed. H. G. May and R. Engberg; Chicago: University of Chicago Press, 1935) was a pioneering work very much in line with what is being advocated here for the study of Israelite religion.

8. The discussion can be brought up to date by comparing G. E. Mendenhall, *The Tenth Generation: The Origins of the Biblical Tradition* (Baltimore: Johns Hopkins University Press, 1973); idem, "Ancient Israel's Truncated History," *Palestine in Transition: The Emergence of Ancient Israel* (ed. D. N. Freedman and D. F. Graf; Sheffield: Almond Press, 1983) 91–103; M. Weippert, *The Settlement of the Israelite Tribes in Palestine: A Critical Survey of Recent Debate* (London: SCM Press, 1971); C. H. J. de Geus, *The Tribes of Israel: An Investigation Into Some of the Presuppositions of Martin Noth's Amphictyony Hypothesis* (Assen: Van Gorcum, 1976); J. M. Miller, "The Israelite Occupation of Canaan," *Israelite and Judaean History* (ed. J. H. Hayes and J. M. Miller; Philadelphia: Westminster Press, 1977) 213–84; Gottwald, *Tribes of Yahweh;* M. L. Chaney, "Ancient Palestinian Peasant Movements and the Formation of Premonarchic Israel," *Palestine in Transition,* 39–90; B. Halpern, *The Emergence of Israel in Canaan* (Chico, Calif.: Scholars Press, 1983); and literature cited in these works. See also the debates between Gottwald, Hauser, Mendenhall, and Thompson in *JSOT* 7 (1978); and J. M. Sasson, "On Choosing Models for Recreating Israelite Pre-Monarchic History," *JSOT* 21 (1981) 3–24.

9. Y. Shiloh, "Iron Age Sanctuaries and Cult Elements in Palestine," *Symposia Celebrating the Seventy-fifth Anniversary of the Founding of the American Schools of Oriental Research (1900–1975)* (ed. F. M. Cross; Cambridge, Mass.: American Schools of Oriental Research, 1979) 147–57. See also the essays by Tadmor on history and chronology ca. 1200 B.C.E.; by Weippert, updating his 1971 treatment; and by Yadin, on the "conquest" model.

10. Gottwald, *Tribes of Yahweh,* esp. 193–203, 732–35, 787–93. While Gottwald generously credits me as an informant and spokesman for the "new archaeology," he wrote having seen only my brief 1976 treatment in the *IBDSup.* Gottwald's intuitive use of the "new archaeology" when he wrote ca. 1976 would, I believe, only be confirmed by subsequent developments in our discipline, on which see W. G. Dever, *Archaeology and Biblical Studies: Retrospects and Prospects* (Evanston: Seabury-Western Theological Seminary, 1974); idem, "Archaeological Method in Israel: A Continuing Revolution," *BA* 43 (1980) 41–48; idem, "Biblical Theology and Biblical Archaeology: An Appreciation of G. Ernest Wright," *HTR* 73 (1980) 1–15; idem, "The Impact of the 'New Archaeology' on Syro-Palestinian Archaeology," *BASOR* 242 (1981) 15–19; idem, "Retrospects and Prospects in Biblical and Syro-Palestinian Archaeology," *BA* 45 (1981) 103–7; idem, "Material Remains and the Cult" (1984); and see further idem, "The 'Fourth Revolution': Rhetoric or Reality?" (forthcoming in the J. A. Callaway Festschrift); and idem, "Syro-Palestinian and Biblical Archaeology," *The Hebrew Bible and Its Modern Interpreters* (ed. D. A. Knight and G. M. Tucker; Philadel-

phia: Fortress Press, 1985). It should be noted that *most* of the literature on the theory and method of the "new archaeology" and its impact on biblical and Syro-Palestinian archaeology is too recent to have found as yet much published response from biblical scholars.

11. Gottwald, *Tribes of Yahweh*, xxv (italics NKG); see the agenda for future research, 650–75. Related to Gottwald's treatment, but largely independent and principally a critique of Noth's "amphictyony," is de Geus, *Tribes of Israel.* His partly socioeconomic approach to early Israel also employs the notion of ethnicity; but his use of archaeology is somewhat negative and confined to evidence for technology, such as terrace farming and plastered cisterns. See *Tribes of Israel,* 48–53, 65–74, 156–64, passim; and, further, the response in Gottwald's epilogue (*Tribes of Yahweh,* 894–99).

12. See n. 8, above. In all fairness, it should be noted that Chaney—whose efforts to use the "new archaeology," like Gottwald's, are commendable—apparently wrote the 1984 essay about 1976–78. (Gottwald [*Tribes of Yahweh,* 914] already refers to the essay in early form.) For instance, in rightly rejecting the conquest model, Chaney is able to use only Lapp's obsolete 1967 treatment of the archaeological evidence, with some reference to Miller's more recent survey in 1977. Cf. my remarks in n. 10, above.

13. Halpern, *Emergence of Israel,* 5.

14. Ibid., 212; here Halpern refers to my "Continuing Revolution" (1980), but finds it too "optimistic." Halpern's independent stress, however, on Israelite religion as cult, not theology, and on its continuity with Canaanite religion, from an entirely different perspective, is remarkably similar to mine here. See further his trenchant comments in *Emergence of Israel,* 239–61, and P. D. Miller, "Israelite Religion," *The Hebrew Bible and Its Modern Interpreters,* 201–37.

15. Halpern, *Emergence of Israel,* 246, 247.

16. See further "The Impact of Archaeology on Biblical Research," *New Directions in Biblical Archaeology* (ed. D. N. Freedman and J. C. Greenfield; Garden City, N.Y.: Doubleday & Co., 1969) 1–14. This was the last of Albright's periodic surveys of archaeology and Old Testament studies. I have offered a brief critique of Albright's "biblical archaeology" in "The Impact of the 'New Archaeology,'" 24 n. 22; see at much greater length "Syro-Palestinian and Biblical Archaeology," 53–54.

17. For Shechem, see G. E. Wright, *Shechem: The Biography of a Biblical City* (Garden City, N.Y.: Doubleday & Co., 1965) 123–38. For the response of critics, together with an overall critique of Wright as a "biblical archaeologist," see Dever, "Biblical Theology and Biblical Archaeology." Wright's basic faith against culture motif, which led him to theological evaluations of Israelite historical Yahwism over naturalist Canaanite religion, was in many ways in sharp contradiction to his fundamental approach as historian and archaeologist—as critics like Barr, Stendahl, and others pointed out. See, more recently, Gottwald, *Tribes of Yahweh,* 903–9, with reference also to L. Clapham in *Magnalia Dei, The Mighty Acts of God* (ed. F. M. Cross, W. E. Lemke, and P. D. Miller; Garden City, N.Y.: Doubleday & Co., 1976).

18. J. M. de Tarragon, *La culte à Ugarit d'après les tertes de la pratique en cunéiformes alphabétiques* (Paris: Gabalda, 1980); cf. 182.

19. F. M. Cross, *CMHE* (Cambridge: Harvard University Press, 1973).

20. On our differing views of "biblical archaeology" and the recent professionalization of Syro-Palestinian archaeology, see the exchange in F. M. Cross, "W. F. Albright's View of Biblical Archaeology and Its Methodology," *BA* 36 (1973) 2–5; and Dever, "Retrospects and Prospects."

21. See, e.g., the very early statement about archaeology's having "completely transformed our knowledge of the historical and literary background of the Bible," in Albright's 1935 *The Archaeology of Palestine and the Bible* (Cambridge, Mass.: ASOR, reprinted 1974) 127. This statement, in one form or another, was repeated and reemphasized even in Albright's last works. Similar optimistic statements concerning an archaeology "revolution—just beginning" can be found in virtually every survey of the field in relation to biblical studies from the 1930s to the 1960s, such as G. A. Barton, "The Present State of Old Testament Studies," *The Haverford Symposium on Archaeology and the Bible* (ed. E. Grant; Haverford, Pa.: Haverford College, 1938) 74; G. E. Wright, "The Present State of Biblical Archaeology," *The Study of the Bible Today and Tomorrow* (ed. H. R. Willoughby; Chicago: University of Chicago Press, 1947) 74–97; W. F. Albright, "The Old Testament and the Archaeology of Palestine," *The Old Testament and Modern Study* (ed. H. H. Rowley; London: Oxford University Press, 1951) 1–26; J. B. Pritchard, "Culture and History," in Hyatt, *The Bible in Modern Scholarship,* 313–24; W. F. Albright, "The Impact of Archaeology on Biblical Research," in Freedman and Greenfield, *New Directions,* 1–14; G. E. Wright, "Biblical Archaeology Today," in *New Directions,* 149–65; Hahn, *Modern Research,* 205–25 (and also H. D. Hummel, 291–95). By contrast, in 1976 R. E. Clements (*A Century of Old Testament Research* [London: Lutterworth, Press, 1976]) makes virtually no reference to archaeology. The latest survey, by J. Gray ("Recent Archaeological Discoveries and Their Bearing on the Old Testament," *Tradition and Interpretation* [ed. G. W. Anderson; London: Oxford University Press, 1979]), 65–95, simply demonstrates how difficult it is for a nonspecialist to cope with the archaeological data. A practical aspect of the difficulty is, of course, simply the sheer bulk of the accumulating archaeological material. But there are far more significant philosophical issues—especially as Syro-Palestinian archaeology and biblical studies inevitably diverge as *two disciplines.* I have treated these problems in some detail in *Archaeology and Biblical Studies,* calling for a *new dialogue* between these two increasingly distant but related disciplines. More recently, my graduate students and I at Arizona have been exploring a new style of "biblical archaeology." Two forthcoming doctoral dissertations, by Thomas Davis and Bonnie Wisthoff, on a critique of "biblical archaeology" and a new study of archaeology and cult will mark the departure. For a recent, in my view unduly pessimistic, appraisal of the prospects of archaeology's contribution—by a prominent heretofore promoter of Albrightian-style "biblical archaeology" (!)—see D. N. Freedman, in *BAR* 11/1(1985), "BAR lines: The Relationship of Archaeology to the Bible," 6, 7.

22. Dever, "Material Remains and the Cult," 582 n. 2.

23. See the works cited in n. 10, above.

24. See, e.g., G. E. Wright, "Cult and History," *Interpretation* 16 (1962) 3–20. One cannot help thinking that the somewhat jaundiced view of the cult in

Wright and many other Old Testament theologians was somehow related to their low-church Protestant heritage, that is, a function of their overriding preoccupation with theology and "the proclamation of the Word." Cross has made a similar observation concerning Lutheran presuppositions in certain European schools in *CMHE*, 83 n. 13.

25. See my treatments cited in n. 10 above, with full references to the literature.

26. So, e.g., Haran (n. 4, above). The point seems obvious, but this very caution has had to be raised again and again; see, most recently, Halpern, *Emergence of Israel*, 3–6, 241, 246, 261. See also M. Buss, ed., *Encounter with the Text: Form and History in the Hebrew Bible* (Philadelphia: Fortress Press, 1979), and especially J. T. Willis, "Redaction Criticism and Historical Reconstruction," 83–89.

27. The analogy is taken from an unpublished 1981 paper of G. Buccellati, "Archaeology and 'Biblical' Archaeology," which I have seen through the author's courtesy.

28. The concomitant assumption of many textual and biblical scholars is that it takes a trained specialist to interpret texts, but *anyone* can be an archaeologist (i.e., the latter has no methodology, nor is it really a discipline). Nothing has hindered the progress of modern archaeology more than this perverse defense of amateurism.

29. See further my programmatic essay, "Archaeology and the Cult."

30. Gottwald *(Tribes of Yahweh)* comes closest; cf. n. 10, above. Chaney's work, "Ancient Palestinian Peasant Movements," also moves in this direction; cf. n. 12.

31. See my perhaps overly optimistic predictions in several of the works cited in n. 10, above; but note the cautions in "The 'Fourth Revolution': Rhetoric or Reality?" (forthcoming).

32. These and succeeding temples/shrines are cited in the text simply by date of *first general* publication, with fuller (although still not exhaustive) citation in the notes as required. See C. F. A. Schaeffer, *Syria* 12 (1931) 9, fig. 2; idem, *Syria* 14 (1933) 122, fig. 14; idem, *Syria* 16 (1935) 154–56, pl. 36; C. L. Woolley, *Alalakh: An Account of the Excavations at Tell Atchana in the Hatay, 1937–1949* (London: Oxford University Press, 1955) 71–73, 82–96, figs. 30, 34a–c; idem, *Carchemish* III (London: Oxford University Press, 1952) 167–71, pl. 29; R. Naumann, *Architektur Kleinasiens* (Tübingen: Wasmuth, 1971) 464, fig. 600 (Ebenda); *Bericht über die Ergebnisse der Ausgrabungen in Kāmid el-Lōz in den Jahren 1971 bis 1974* (ed. R. Hachmann; Saarbrücken: University of Saarbrücken, 1982) 17–29, figs. 3–4; E. Heinrich et al., "Vierter vorläufiger Bericht über die von Deutschen Orient Gesellschaft mit Mitteln der Stiftung Volkswagenwerk in Habuba Kabira (Habuba Kabria, Herbstkompagnen 1971 und 1972 sowie Testgrabung Frühjahr 1973) und in Mumbaqat (Tall Munbaqa, Herbstkampagne 1971) unternommen archäologischen Untersuchungen (Fortsetzung)," *MDOG* 106 (1974) 53–97; W. Orthmann and H. Kuhne, "Mumbaqat 1973. Vorläufiger Bericht über die von der Deutschen Orient Gesellschaft mit Mitteln der Stiftung Volkswagenwerk unternommenen Ausgrabungen," *MDOG*

106 (1974) 53–97; J. Cl. Margueron, "Quatre campagnes de fouilles à Emar (1972–74): Un bilan provisoire," *Syria* 52 (1975) 53–85.

33. See G. Loud, *Megiddo II: Seasons of 1935–39, Text and Plates* (Chicago: University of Chicago Press, 1948) 105, fig. 347; A. Rowe, *The Four Canaanite Temples of Beth-Shan*, Part I: *The Temples and Cult Objects* (Philadelphia: University Museum, University of Pennsylvania, 1940) 6–12, fig. 3; O. Tufnell, *Lachish II: The Fosse Temple* (London: Oxford University Press, 1940); Y. Yadin, *Hazor, the Head of All Those Kingdoms* (London: Oxford University Press, 1972) 67–105; idem, *Hazor, the Rediscovery of a Great Citadel of the Bible* (London: Weidenfeld & Nicolson, 1975) 43–119.

34. See Wright, *Shechem*, 95–102; J. B. Hennessey, "Excavation of a Late Bronze Age Temple at Amman," *PEQ* 98 (1966) 155–62, and V. Hankey, "A Late Bronze Age Temple at Amman," *Levant* 6 (1974) 131–78; add now L. G. Herr, ed., *The Amman Airport Excavations, 1976, BASOR* 48 (Philadelphia: ASOR, 1984); R. G. Boling, *Report on Archaeological Work of Suwānnet eth-Thanīya, Tananir, and Khirbet Minha (Munhata), BASOR* Supplements 21 (ed. G. M. Landes; Missoula, Mont.: Scholars Press, 1975) 33–85; H. J. Franken, *Excavation at Tell Deir 'Allā* I (Leiden: E. J. Brill, 1969) 19–22; idem, "The Excavations at Deir 'Allā in Jordan," *VT* 12 (1962) 378–82; B. Rothenberg, *Timna, Valley of the Biblical Copper Mines* (London: Thames & Hudson, 1972) 125–79, figs. 39, 41; J. Kaplan, "Jaffa 1972–1973," *IEJ* 24 (1974) 135, 136; J. Elgavish, "Shiqmona," *IEJ* 27 (1977) 122, 123; E. Eisenberg, "The Temples at Tell Kittan," *BA* 40 (1977) 77–81; E. Stern, *Excavations at Tel Mevorakh (1973–1978), Part II: The Bronze Age* (*Qedem* 18; Jerusalem: Hebrew University of Jerusalem, 1984), fig. II; D. Ussishkin et al., *Excavations at Tel Lachish, 1973–1977. Preliminary Report* (= *Tel Aviv* 5 [1978] 1–97; Tel Aviv: Institute of Archaeology, 1978) 10–25, fig. 3.

35. See A. Mazar, *Excavations at Tell Qasile, Part I: The Philistine Sanctuary: Architecture and Cult Objects* (*Qedem* 12; Jerusalem: Hebrew University of Jerusalem, 1980); E. Stern, *Excavations at Tel Mevorakh*.

36. A Kuschke, "Temple," *Biblisches Reallexikon* (2d ed.; ed. K. Galling; Tübingen: J. C. B. Mohr [Paul Siebeck], 1977) 333–42.

37. On the above, see Kuschke, "Temple," 333; A. Mazar, *Excavations at Tell Qasile*, 62–68; Stern, *Excavations at Tel Mevorakh*, 32–36. An older attempt at temple typology is G. R. H. Wright, "Pre-Israelite Temples in the Land of Canaan," *PEQ* 103 (1971) 17–32; add now J. M. Lundquist, "What Is a Temple? A Preliminary Typology," *The Quest for the Kingdom of God: Essays in Honor of George E. Mendenhall* (ed. H. B. Huffmon, F. A. Spina, and A. R. W. Green; Winona Lake, Ind.: Eisenbrauns, 1983) 205–19. What is needed, however, is not so much temple typology as temple *theology*, i.e., a functionalist approach.

38. M. Ottosson, *Temples and Cult Places in Palestine* (Uppsala: University of Uppsala, 1980.) As a single example of Ottosson's idiosyncratic views, he regards the well-known Fosse Temple at Lachish as simply a potters' workshop; see *Temples and Cult Places,* 90–93.

39. See further my critique in "Archaeology and the Cult," 575.

40. Stern, *Excavations at Tel Mevorakh*, 22–39. There is, of course, no goddess "Ashtoret" at Ugarit; the name first occurs in the Hebrew Bible as a

deliberate corruption of Canaanite "Ashtart" with the vowels of the Hebrew *bōšet* ("shame"). Baal's consort at Ugarit is ʿAnat; the other two female deities are Asherah, El's consort, and the androgynous deity Ashtart (Astarte).

41. See conveniently G. Saadé, *Ougarit* (Beirut: Imprimerie Catholique, 1979) 133–43 and references there.

42. See references in n. 32, above.

43. For illustrations of all four Hazor LB temples, see conveniently Yadin, *Hazor, the Rediscovery of a Great Citadel of the Bible,* 43–119; and idem, *Hazor, the Head of All Those Kingdoms,* 67–105.

44. Cf. n. 34, above.

45. See Tufnell, *Lachish II,* 43, 44, 59–91. The votives include ivory, bone, glass, beads, scarabs, seals, stone vases, gold jewelry, and bronze figurines—in addition to the many ceramic objects and vessels.

46. On the bronze figurines, see now the convenient summary, with illustrations, by O. Negbi, *Canaanite Gods in Metal: An Archaeological Study of Ancient Syro-Palestinian Figurines* (Tel Aviv: Institute of Archaeology, Tel Aviv University, 1976). But note that this work must be used with great caution; see my review in *JBL* 98 (1979) 101–3.

47. The distinction between the two types follows M. Tadmor; see "Female Relief Figurines of Late Bronze Age Canaan," *EI* 15 (1981) 79–84 (Hebrew); idem, "Female Cult Figurines in Late Canaan and Early Israel: Archaeological Evidence," *Studies in the Period of David and Solomon and Other Essays* (ed. T. Ishida; Winona Lake, Ind.: Eisenbrauns, 1982) 139–73. Tadmor, however, follows earlier studies such as Pritchard's (1940) and their "minimalist" interpretation. For the notion that the female figurines represent the *composite* Canaanite deities Asherah-ʿAnat-Astarte, see W. G. Dever, "Asherah, Consort of Yahweh? New Evidence from Kuntillet ʿAjrud" *BASOR* 255 (1984) 28–29 and references there.

48. See J. Cl. Courtois, "La maison du prêtre aux modèles de poumon et de foies d'Ugarit," *Ugaritica* VI (1969) 91–119 (a libation tube, decorated on the sides, according to Courtois, with representations of Baal). Cf. W. T. Pitard, "The Ugaritic Funerary Text RS 34.126," *BASOR* 232 (1978) 65–75; M. H. Pope, "The Cult of the Dead at Ugarit," *Ugarit in Retrospect: Fifty Years of Ugarit and Ugaritic* (ed. G. D. Young; Winona Lake, Ind.: Eisenbrauns, 1981) 159–79.

49. See, e.g., A. Tainter, "Mortuary Practices and the Study of Prehistoric Social Systems," *Advances in Archaeological Method and Theory* (ed. M. B. Schiffer; New York: Academic, 1976) 1. 105–41. We have noted the failure of historians and biblical scholars above. No less culpable, however, are archaeologists, who in publishing their material have *rarely* drawn sufficient attention to the related textual data. Unfortunately our plea for broad, comparative, interdisciplinary studies is likely to go unheeded as scholars in both disciplines become more and more highly specialized. It is a high price to pay, and it can perhaps be offset only by more cooperative, teamwork projects.

50. As far as I know, despite the advent of modern interdisciplinary *theory,* few temples or shrines have yet been excavated properly in this regard. At Gezer, when the MB-LB "High Place" was reexcavated with these techniques, quantities of burnt sheep/goat remains were recovered.

51. See references in n. 43, above.

52. A. Rowe, *The History and Topography of Beth-Shan* (Philadelphia: University Museum, University of Pennsylvania, 1930) 1, 14, 15, pl. 33; Yadin, *Hazor, the Rediscovery of a Great Citadel,* 45–57; idem, "Symbols of Deities at Zinjirli, Carthage, and Hazor," *Near Eastern Archaeology in the Twentieth Century,* 199–231; C. Clamer, "A Gold Plaque from Tel Lachish," *Tel Aviv* 7 (1980) 152–62.

53. See Tufnell, *Lachish II,* 47–54, Frontispiece, pl. 60; and further F. M. Cross, "The Evolution of the Proto-Canaanite Alphabet," *BASOR* 134 (1954) 20, 21.

54. For references, see Dever, "Asherah, Consort of Yahweh?" 28, 29 nn. 29, 36.

55. See the references in Stern, *Excavations at Tel Mevorakh,* 22 nn. 1–6. Add now the fine bronze Gezer serpent, from an LB IIA context in Field VI (*Gezer* IV, in press).

56. One of the major flaws in most treatments of Canaanite religion is the absence of the "sympathy" so fundamental to insight into any religion; on this, see W. C. Smith, "Comparative Religion: Whither—and Why?" *The History of Religions,* 31–58. J. Bright (*A History of Israel* [Philadelphia: Westminster Press, 1975] 116, 117) describes Canaanite religion as "an extraordinary debasing form of paganism." Albright is, somewhat reluctantly, a bit less negative; Cross is a refreshing exception to the general judgmental trend. The fact is that if a religion is to be evaluated by its ability to relate the individual symbolically to the *actual* conditions of existence—its integrative power—then we may judge Canaanite religion to have been perhaps more profound, more "authentic," than the rather austere Yahwism of their period; and apparently many Israelites agreed.

57. For the united monarchy in the tenth century B.C.E., see my survey of the archaeological material, including cultic, in "Monumental Architecture in Ancient Israel in the Period of the United Monarchy," *Studies in the Period of David and Solomon,* ed. Ishida, 269–306. See also J. S. Holladay, chap. 14 in this volume, for Iron II (ninth to seventh centuries B.C.E.). My views on the cult in Iron II will be found in "Archaeology and the Cult"; and add now "Asherah, Consort of Yahweh?" and observations there.

58. See Rowe, *Four Canaanite Temples,* 6–35, figs. 3, 4, 5, 9; E. Anati, "Tell Abu Hawam," *EAEHL* 1. 9–12 (and references there).

59. See now the authoritative summary by T. Dothan, *The Philistines and Their Material Culture* (Jerusalem: Israel Exploration Society, 1982).

60. See A. Mazar, *Excavations at Tell Qasile.*

61. Wright, *Shechem,* 123–38.

62. See references in Shiloh, "Iron Age Sanctuaries," 149–53.

63. Y. Aharoni, *Investigations at Lachish: The Sanctuary and the Residency (Lachish V)* (Tel Aviv: Institute of Archaeology, Tel Aviv University, 1975) 26–32, figs. 6, 7.

64. A. Biran, "Tel Dan," *BA* (1974) 26–51; idem, "An Israelite Horned Altar at Dan," *BA* 37 (1974) 106, 107; idem, "Two Discoveries at Tel Dan," *IEJ* 3 (1980) 89–98; L. E. Stager and S. R. Wolff, "Production and Commerce in Temple Courtyards: An Olive Press in the Sacred Precinct at Tel Dan," *BASOR* 243 (1981) 95–102.

65. A. Mazar, "The 'Bull Site'—An Iron Age I Open Cultic Place," *BASOR* 247 (1982) 27–42.

66. See, provisionally, A. Zertal, "Has Joshua's Altar Been Found on Mt. Ebal?" *BAR* 11/1 (1985) 26–43. I have discussed the Mt. Ebal installation with Zertal, and also with other Israeli archaeologists who have seen the site and the material; opinion remains divided over exact interpretations, but the date of the twelfth to eleventh century seems firm.

67. See n. 64, above.

68. M. Haran has dealt extensively with this question in *Temples and Temple Service in Ancient Israel: An Inquiry Into the Character of Cult Phenomena and the Historical Setting of the Priestly School* (Oxford: Oxford University Press, 1978) (230–38); but he concluded, despite a survey of these tenth-century B.C.E. horned altars, that incense was introduced into the Israelite cult only about the seventh century B.C.E. (Haran's distinction of "everyday ritual" from "cult" seems forced to me.) On the possibly related cult stands, or "incense stands" (?), see C. L. Meyers, *The Tabernacle Menorah: A Synthetic Study of a Symbol from the Biblical Cult* (Missoula, Mont.: Scholars Press, 1976). Meyers's suggestive study is one of the very few attempts by either biblical scholars or archaeologists to deal with actual Israelite cultic material.

69. I have advocated such an approach for some time; see Dever, "Retrospects and Prospects," 106.

70. J. A. Callaway, "The 1966 'Ai (Et-Tell) Excavations," *BASOR* 196 (1969) 2–16; J. A. Callaway and R. E. Cooley, "A Salvage Excavation at Radannah, in Bireh," *BASOR* 201 (1971) 9–19; R. E. Cooley, *The Bulletin Series of the Near East Archaeological Society* 5 (1975) 16, fig. 5; cf. J. A. Callaway, "A Visit with Ahilud," *BAR* 9/5 (1983) 42–53; Y. Aharoni, V. Fritz, and A. Kempinski, "Excavation at Tel Masos (Khirbet el-Meshâsh), Preliminary Report on the Second Season, 1974," *Tel Aviv* 2 (1975) 97–124; A. Kempinski and V. Fritz, "Excavations at Tel Masos (Khirbet el-Meshâsh), Preliminary Report on the Third Season, 1975," *Tel Aviv* 4 (1977) 136–58; add now V. Fritz and A. Kempinski, *Ergebnisse der Ausgrabungen auf der Ḥirbet el Mšāš (Tēl Māśōś)* (Wiesbaden: Otto Harrassowitz, 1983); M. Kochavi, "An Ostracon of the Period of the Judges from 'Izbet Ṣarṭah," *Tel Aviv* 4 (1977) 1–13; A. Mazar, "An Early Israelite Settlement Site Near Jerusalem," *IEJ* 31 (1981) 1–36; I Finkelstein, S. Bonimowitz, and Z. Lederman, "Shiloh, 1982," *IEJ* 33 (1983) 123–26; idem, "Shiloh, 1983," *IEJ* 33 (1983) 267–68. Mazar's article is an extremely well balanced, useful survey, typical of the newer archaeological approaches to the Israelite "conquest."

71. These surveys are published only in preliminary notices. Z. Gal's Hebrew dissertation, however, is scheduled to appear soon in English. See also I. Finkelstein, *The 'Izbet Ṣarṭah Excavations and the Israelite Settlement in the Hill Country* (unpublished doctoral diss., Tel Aviv University, 1983; Hebrew). Finklestein's conclusion, however, that the "new" styles of pottery in the twelfth-century B.C.E. hill country settlements imply newcomers *ethnically* is belied by his own Iron I pottery from 'Izbet Ṣarṭah which is virtually identical to twelfth- to eleventh-century B.C.E. Gezer—which no one would argue is "Israelite." I owe my knowledge of these surveys largely to presentations the authors made at the Tenth

Archaeological Conference in Israel, in Jerusalem in the spring of 1982; see *IEJ* 33 (1983) 274, 275. This entire conference was devoted to regional survey and research—a good indication of the trend noted above in n. 69.

72. Note the inscribed jar handle from Khirbet Raddannah, and especially the abecedary from 'Izbet Ṣarṭah; see n. 71, above, and on Khirbet Raddannah add F. M. Cross, and D. N. Freedman, "An Inscribed Jar Handle from Raddanna," *BASOR* 201 (1971) 19–22. These inscriptions are in Old Canaanite script; see F. M. Cross, "Newly Found Inscriptions in Old Canaanite and Early Phoenician Scripts," *BASOR* 238 (1980) 1–20.

73. See, provisionally, the exemplary treatment of A. Mazar, "An Early Israelite Settlement Site," the best analysis of transitional late LB/early Iron I pottery to date. *Gezer* IV, in press (1987), will fully confirm the continuity of LB II ceramic forms into the twelfth, and even the eleventh century B.C.E., on the basis of well-stratified material.

74. See L. E. Stager, "The Archaeology of the Family in Early Israel" (*BASOR* 262, 1985). Stager documents the jump from 23 LB II settlements in the Central Hills to 114 in early Iron I—mostly agrarian villages of about 100–200 population, which Stager regards as "multi-family compounds" and connects with serveral Hebrew terms for "nuclear family." Stager does not, however, specify what is "early Israelite" in the material culture of these villages. I owe knowledge of Stager's work to personal conversations and also to his Kalish Lectures at the University of Arizona in 1979. Another recent indication of the more sociological and ecological approach is C. L. Meyers, "Of Seasons and Soldiers: A Topological Appraisal of the Premonarchic Tribes of Galilee," *BASOR* 252 (1983) 47–59.

75. The evidence for these observations, shared by several other archaeologists, is as yet largely unpublished. Provisionally, see A. Mazar, "Early Israelite Settlement," 10, 11, nn. 8–14 and references there (the "four-room house"); idem, 28–31, and M. Ibrahim, "The Collared Rim Jar of the Early Iron Age," *Archaeology in the Levant: Essays for Kathleen Kenyon* (eds. P. R. S. Moorey and P. J. Parr; Warminster, England: Aris & Phillips, 1978) 116–27. My inclusion of the bench tomb in this category of "early Iron I" (not "Israelite") type fossils is based on such finds as the twelfth-century B.C.E. classic bench tomb, with Philistine pottery, at Tel 'Eitun; see G. Edelstein et al., "The Necropolis at Tell 'Aitun," *Qadmoniot* 4/3 (1971) 86–96, fig. 1 (Hebrew).

76. Again, I cannot present the full evidence here, but there is without doubt a general consensus among archaeologists. This is seen, e.g., in A. Mazar, "Early Israelite Settlement," as well as in several recent presentations of Kochavi on "models" for the Israelite settlement in Palestine. The current archaeological opinion would support even *more* strongly the conclusions of such biblical scholars as Gottwald and Chaney; cf. above and nn. 2, 8. See further my chapter "The Israelite Settlement in Canaan: New Archaeological Models," forthcoming in the 1985 Stroum Lecture Series, the University of Washington.

77. For an earlier stress on syncretism (although not defended archaeologically), see G. W. Ahlström, *Aspects of Israelite Syncretism in Israelite Religion* (Lund: Gleerup, 1963); N. Habel, *Yahweh Versus Baal: A Conflict of Religious Cultures* (New York: Bookman Associates, 1964); J. Gray, *The Legacy of Canaan: The Ras Shamra Texts and Their Relevance to the Old Testament*

(VTSup 5; Leiden: E. J. Brill, 1965); W. Dietrich, *Israel und Kanaan. Vom Ringen zweier Gesellschaftssysteme* (Stuttgart: Schweizerisches katholisches Bibelwerk, 1979); O. Keel, ed., *Monotheismus in Alten Israel und seiner Umwelt* (Stuttgart: Schweizerisches katholisches Bibelwerk, 1980).

78. By this stress on *behavior* I do not mean necessarily to identify myself with the "behavioralist" or "processualist" schools of current American archaeology. I do mean to side with L. R. Binford (*Pursuit of the Past: Decoding the Archaeological Record* [New York: Thames & Hudson, 1983] 31, 32), who regards ideas as often beyond the limits of archaeological inquiry. He states: "Sometimes our questions about how it was in the past involve finding out the roles which our ancestors played in their environment: The information required will therefore be behavioral and ecological, not ideological."

79. On the theoretical problems of identifying ethnic groups in general in the archaeological record, see K. A. Kamp and N. Yoffee, "Ethnicity in Ancient Western Asia During the Early Second Millennium B.C.: Archaeological Assessments and Ethnoarchaeological Prospectives," *BASOR* 243 (1980) 85–104, and references there. Kamp and Yoffee's proposals for fieldwork, however, will strike most as unrealistic. We have spoken *much* too confidently of "Israelite" material culture, and we must now begin to explore more systematically the archaeological components of the designation.

80. Obviously archaeology, despite its welcome emphasis on "folk religion," cannot really get at many aspects of *individual* religious practice, where we are still almost wholly dependent on the biblical texts. See, e.g., the perceptive essay of M. Greenberg, *Biblical Prose Prayer as a Window to the Popular Religion of Ancient Israel* (Berkeley and Los Angeles: University of California Press, 1983).

14

Religion in Israel and Judah Under the Monarchy: An Explicitly Archaeological Approach

JOHN S. HOLLADAY, JR.

INTRODUCTION

It has long been noted that the biblical tradition, however polyvalent it may seem, is the continuously edited, consciously selected, generally prescriptive literary tradition of a very small hierarchy. Similarly, the literary archives of Ugarit, Mesopotamia, and ancient Egypt are also, for the most part, collections, preselected documents reflecting specialized theological perspectives. It is a tremendously long step from these didactic, literary, and theological documents to actual religious organization and practice, even when, as in the more prescriptive portions of the Pentateuch or the rubricized portions of ancient myths or incantations, the essentials of various rituals are seemingly spelled out in detail. The uneasy thought that actual religious practice in ancient Israel might not have mirrored our texts in any recognizable fashion has disturbed many a scholar's ponderings. Yet, it must be admitted, little seems to have been done about the problem except to strive to mine the biblical mother lode yet deeper.

Certainly, from the perspective of an archaeologist, biblical prescription does not literally translate into what we seem to be seeing in the dirt. Yet what we do see archaeologically are the unedited fossil records of past human activity on a very wide scale. This is particularly true for *patterned* activities, that is, events taking place at the same place time after time in the same fashion. And few human activities are more "patterned" than those connected with religious observances. Given the scale of excavation in the Iron II period and the importance of religious observances in the premodern era, it seems more than reasonable to suggest that by now we should be able to say something useful about the actual organization and practice of religion in ancient Israel and Judah purely on the basis of the archaeological record. That such an analysis might have considerable value as an independent check on historical reconstruction seems obvious enough to make the effort not only worthwhile but worthy of inclusion in a body of essays bearing on the general problem of Israelite religion.

The present investigation had only one simple ground rule: The study had to be purely archaeological. That is to say, it had to operate under the same guidelines and on the same basis as archaeological work anywhere else. It could have no access to special information or regard for special considerations, such as the notion that monotheistic principles rule out certain interpretations—for example, that figurines frequently found on archaeological sites of the late Judean kingdom might have religious significance.

In the sense used in this study, archaeology could be characterized as an increasingly "scientific" subspecialization uncomfortably straddling the intellectual void between anthropology and history. We use the word "scientific" to indicate that archaeology increasingly makes use of the hypothetico-deductive approach, utilizes models in theory building, deals with inherently falsifiable hypothetical propositions, and depends, in the final analysis, upon quantifiable data sets and empirical observations. As a subdiscipline, archaeology deals exclusively with the patterning of physical objects or traces of objects in space, time commonly being inferred from differential spatial patterning, for example, stratigraphic superimposition or presence-absence patterns at complementary sites. All archaeological interpretation necessarily proceeds, in one manner or another, on the basis of ethnographic analogy. In other words, a "wall" (or a "shrine") is so defined because it looks like the remains of something identifiable yet today as a "wall" (or a "shrine"). The most powerful arguments used by archaeologists, in common with most scientists, are those which are statistically based, although this does not necessarily mean that formal statistical procedures must be invoked at all times. It does mean, however, that whenever the data permit, they are best dealt with in quantified fashion and in tables, charts, and graphs. This is a desideratum often honored in the present chapter, as elsewhere, in the breach, in part due to restrictions upon length and space and in part to weaknesses in the database occasioned by selective publication of the original data. Finally, it was essential that the scale of investigation and data collection be compatible with the scale of the smallest phenomenon under study. Thus, if we were to be interested in the possibility of analyzing certain aspects of domestic religious practice, we could profitably utilize only site reports that permitted the localizing of data to individual building units (preferably to rooms within building units), that reported data in a reasonably consistent fashion, and that contained enough building units to make the study viable.

In terms of the research history of the project, work has proceeded in a stepwise fashion, alternating between inductive reasoning and hypothetico-deductive reasoning. The first step was the inductive identification of various categories of "religious artifacts" and "possibly religious artifacts" on the basis of a cursory overview of known or supposed cult sites and sacred areas, both within and outside Israel and Judah proper. The second step was an equally rapid overview of the find spots of similar artifacts right across several well-published sites and across all known or supposed cult sites, not only Israelite and Judahite but also Philistine, Phoenician, and Syrian. This resulted in the inductive inference (hardly new) that some of these items (figurines, model furniture, and miniature altars) seemed more at home, as it were, in domestic settings than in a more formal cultic setting, while others—for example, tall limestone altars and so-called cult stands—seemed far more likely to be found in settings identifiable in other respects as cult centers. Complicating this, however, was the discovery that every Israelite and Judean cult center so far identified (whether correctly or not is another story) seemed to represent a different tradition. On the one side we had two full-fledged, but wholly different and quite disparate in size, sanctuaries with precincts (Arad, Dan), while on the other side we had a one-room shrine too small to accommodate more than a few worshipers at a time (Lachish Stratum V, Building 49). To the extreme south we had a desert way station with unparalleled artistic and epigraphic material (Kuntillet ʿAjrud), and on the edge of the Plain of Esdraelon we had two storerooms, a possible olive press, and a cistern (Taʿanach), obviously part of something, but what? Outside the two major capitals of the divided kingdom there was a cave (Jerusalem) and a moated island of rock (Samaria E 207), while at least thirty tumuli—open-air sites covered under enormous piles of loose rock—stood on the hilltops and ridges west of Jerusalem. What, if anything, bound these together?

Once the material culture complements of these cult centers had been added to the data under consideration, we found ourselves faced with such a bewildering array of options that every attempt at synthesis seemed doomed by the impossibility of demonstrating that it, and not some other, was the simplest and most adequate covering hypothesis (the test of "Ockham's razor"). So we began at the other end and developed a historically informed hypothetical model of religious organization in a typical Syro-Palestinian national state of the Iron II period. Localized concentrations of religiously significant material culture remains were then examined in detail and progressively related to the hypothetical model, fleshing out the theoretical framework with archaeologically derived data assemblages and relationships. In that sanctuaries or shrines

251

relating to corporate religious practice at different levels of political organization could be identified for a reasonable number of slots in the overall model, with these shrines corresponding well to theoretical expectations at those levels in the structure of the hypothetical model, the model tended to be supported—or at least not disallowed—by the data. Finally, items deemed religiously significant but not related to any known localized concentration (= sanctuary, shrine, or cult area)[1] were analyzed in the light of the fleshed-out model and its apparent historical development, yielding a provisional model for domestic religious activity—and the relationship of this activity to known cult areas, sanctuaries, or shrines—during the period of the monarchy.

A CAPSULE REVIEW OF DATA RELEVANT TO THE HISTORY OF THE RELIGION OF ISRAEL AND JUDAH DURING THE UNITED AND DIVIDED MONARCHIES

Four major classes of archaeological data are available for the reconstruction of the religion or religions of Israel and Judah: architectural, artifactual, artistic, and epigraphic. In this study we will deal primarily with the first two, and touch upon the third and fourth only tangentially, since each forms a specialized study in itself.[2] For similar reasons, we will also bypass funerary practices.[3]

Architecture

Recent discoveries of a wide variety of sanctuaries, shrines, and cult areas both in and outside the lands of Israel and Judah have opened new doors for the study of the material aspects of Israelite religions. We will begin, however, with two clusters of artifactual evidence that have long been known. Both are from the last half of the period of the united monarchy.

Megiddo Stratum VA, Locus 2081.[4] Tucked into the front corner of a large packed-chalk courtyard fronting onto an unusually strongly built building with porticoed entrance was a particularly fine collection of cultic furniture, apparently a small shrine largely *in situ*. The finds included horned limestone altars, a steleform stone, limestone and pottery cult stands, chalices, and a small selection of bowls and juglets. Burned grain came from the surface by the altars and a bowl full of burned sheep/goat astragali came from somewhere (exact location unspecified) in the general area of the courtyard. A raised stone slab in the northwest corner may have served as a podium. As best as can be determined, the setting is a semipublic space probably involved with the residence of an important government official.

Megiddo Stratum VA, Building 10.[5] Building 10 has the appearance of a store building[6] or a special-purpose building, possibly a barracks, but none of the characteristics of a typical sanctuary (cf. Table 2, below). Three horned altars and two model shrines were found in the vicinity, while from the building and its northern extensions (?) came a pierced censor (?), two plaque-type female figurines, and a spouted vessel in the shape of a quadruped. The important Building 338 stood immediately to the north, surrounded on two sides by a walled courtyard. This structure, originally taken to be a "temple," probably was a palace. To the south stood an early "four-room" house with monolithic columns, also taken to be a cultic structure because of its "standing stones." It seems likely that the altars came from a shrine, probably similar to Locus 2081 (above) which once existed in the general neighborhood but was destroyed (by G. Schumacher?) before the Chicago expedition commenced its work. The other materials from the area probably should be counted toward domestic contexts.

Ta'anach "Cult Structure."[7] Initially, this location seems to have been identified as "cultic" primarily because R. Sellin had earlier found an elaborate cult stand *(Räucheraltar)* in the vicinity. During the first season of the Joint Concordia–ASOR Excavations, P. W. Lapp found what presently appear to be two storerooms, dated to the end of the united monarchy, cornering on a court with an olive press.[8] A mold for female plaque-type figurines and three lots of sheep/goat astragali[9] were the only cultic artifacts in a very large body of domestic (?) goods.[10] From the third season's excavations, however, in a cistern only meters away, came a second, even more elaborate, cult stand, some chalices, and a tall cylindrical cult stand with rows of tab-like pendant "leaves," apparently confirming the cultic nature of the area.[11] These rooms could be the storerooms of a sanctuary, like those very briefly mentioned for the Dan *temenos;* the storerooms of a rather devout household (at Sarepta and in early monarchical Jerusalem model shrines seem to be associated with domestic debris, rather than sanctuaries); or the storerooms of someone closely connected, perhaps in a commercial sense, with a nearby sanctuary.[12] Whatever the decision on this count, the structure helps very little with our determination of sanctuary architecture, operation, or fittings, except, if the rooms are connected with a sanctuary, in the sense that they illustrate the auxiliary buildings and commercial activity of a medium-sized urban sanctuary.

Lachish Stratum VA Shrine (Building 48).[13] Pending publication of the Arad sanctuary, this is presently our best-preserved and published Judean shrine or sanctuary. Dating to the late tenth century, it is a small room (7.6 sq. m.) built against a long terrace wall and entered directly from the street. The room is lined with benches, with a raised section of one bench serving as a podium in the northwestern corner of the room, directly west of the presumed doorway. Scattered upon the benches, podium, and floor were a limestone altar, 4 tall stands (2 fenestrated), 2 chalice-like "incense burners" (interiors burned) with peg-like bases for fitting into the tall stands, 7 chalices, 3 lamps, 2 juglets, 5 jugs, 1 small cooking pot, and some 7 bowls. What would appear to be a broken piece of basalt saddle-quern is termed a *maṣṣebah,* which seems to be pressing the evidence somewhat.[14] About 12 m. southeast of the sanctuary, however (but lacking any direct stratigraphic connection), stood a tall plano-convex limestone stele (?) with a pile of black ashes some 50 cm. in diameter to the south, "likely remnants of an olive tree," according to Waisel and Liphschitz.[15] Three to 4 m. west in the same street was a pit filled with various broken and unbroken *maṣṣeboth,* one dressed with a chipped (*not* toothed!) chisel and a stone with 7 shallow "cupmarks."[16] The evidentiary value of these latter materials is not entirely clear and is somewhat compromised by the inclusion in the discussion of another pit from Level III (!) (either late eighth or seventh-sixth centuries B.C.E.), also described as "farther south in the street" and termed a *favissa* of a presumed long-lived, but unexcavated, "high place" attributed to the raised area above the terrace wall against which the small shrine was built.[17]

"Temenos" at Tel Dan.[18] The sanctuary area in the northwest corner of Tel Dan is the largest (more than a half acre) yet known from Israel or Judah. Two successive large platforms (or *"Bamoth,"* as A. Biran terms them), the more recent reached by a monumental staircase (still later in its present configuration), stood in the northern part of a packed limestone courtyard, whose entrance in Hellenistic times was in the middle of the southern *temenos* wall. To the west of this entrance was an olive press,[19] while somewhere between the platform and the entry gate was a partially ruined pavement of flat ashlar stones bearing the impressions in plaster of two round column bases. Various buildings seem to have flanked the platform to the east and west, though this is not entirely clear from the publications. The complex apparently originated with the beginnings of the divided monarchy, and, according to the excavator, continued in use into the Roman period. A very few small finds have been mentioned in the publications: one limestone altar, unusually short, with

heavily calcined upper surface; decorated tall stands ("incense burners"); three Egyptianizing male figurines in faience, one with Syrian-style beard and quilted headdress, came from the area of the olive press; and a fragmentary bearded terra-cotta head came from another area. A seven-spouted lamp on a tall foot and the head of an eighth- to seventh-century female figurine came from unspecified locations. Large quantities of "domestic" pottery and sheep, goat, and gazelle bones—unburnt—were briefly described from several locations. Finally, a single corner horn of a large ashlar-built stone altar, apparently very much like the well-known Beer-sheba altar, has recently appeared. The platform, 7 x 18 m. in its early phase and 18 x 19 m. in its later phase, may once have carried a major building,[20] a "tabernacle,"[21] or no structure. The latter is the excavator's interpretation and one possibly supported by R. J. Bull's interpretation of the strikingly similar (although higher) Samaritan platform (ca. 21 x 18 m. square x 8 m. high) on Tell er-Ras as an altar of sacrifice.[22] G. Ahlström cites later Phoenician *temenos* platforms appearing on Phoenician coins.[23]

Whatever the situation with the large platform, the very size and dominant position of the Dan *temenos* identifies it as one of the major sacred complexes of the Northern Kingdom, following the breakup of the united monarchy. Given the large area and extent of excavation, one female head of a common type seems insignificant and probably should be seen as intrusive in fill or mud-brick. Clearly, unless the preliminary reports have been misleading, female figurines were not a dominant part of the cultic assemblage. On the other hand, the faience male figurines are closely associated with the olive press, and the bearded male terra-cotta head is without parallel in ancient Israel, though not dissimilar to a recently published Phoenician mask.[24] At first glance, the trident-incised bar-handled bowl[25] found with the fragmentary head looks to be late eighth century and might point to the period of Assyrian domination, though this would require much better data to be of real assistance in interpretation. The tall stands are normal for a sanctuary area, although at least one was unusually well decorated, as might befit a major sanctuary.[26] Finally, one hesitates to make too much of an omission, but the citation of sheep, goat, and gazelle bones at more than one location raises the question of whether or not large cattle were involved in sacrifices at the site (assuming that the small cattle and gazelle bones were, in one way or another, sacrificial), and if not, why not?[27]

Beer-sheba.[28] Aside from noting that fragments, some soot-stained,[29] of a large, ashlar-built horned altar were found sealed under the Stratum II Rampart and incorporated into a rebuild of the Stratum II Pillared

Buildings, we can say very little about the presumed location of a sanctuary at Beer-sheba.[30] An unusual cylindrical limestone altar, only 23.5 cm. high, was found just outside a late phase of the site's gateway. It may, however, be later than Beer-sheba Stratum II. Fragments of chalices came from Stratum V stratification in the northeastern sector of the tell.[31] Given the materials and techniques of construction, it may be inferred that the large Beer-sheba altar is more closely associated with the Tel Dan fragment than with the spatially nearer Tel Arad altar, but whether this relates to dating or policy is not certain. If the Arad altar were indeed somewhat later than the excavator's claims would allow, and if the erection of the altar at Beer-sheba were to be dated to the late tenth-early ninth centuries, then a claim could be forwarded for the existence of ashlar altars in both the Southern and the Northern Kingdom around either the close of the Solomonic monarchy or the opening years of the divided monarchy, followed by a change, in the Southern Kingdom, to altars built of fieldstone. In such a case, the location of numerous chalices in Stratum V deposits in the northeast quarter of the tell at Beer-sheba is suggestive, though hardly more, of a possible original location for this altar.

Arad "Temple."[32] The single most important Judean sanctuary yet discovered, the long-lived "temple" at Arad is still basically unpublished, and little can be done with the small finds. The sanctuary itself occupied the entire northwest corner of the fortress at Arad (more than 10 percent of the available building space) and was comprised of a large 10 × 10 m. courtyard letting into a narrow broad room (9 × 2.7 m.) with benches along the western and (probably) southern walls. The central axis of the complex culminated in an elevated niche (1.2 × 1.2 m.), approached by stairs, in the rear wall of the broad room directly opposite the doorway. In the niche, lying on its face, was a well-dressed curved-top stele about 1 m. high, with traces of red paint still adhering. Two other, more roughly formed, flint slabs were found in the back wall of the niche, covered over by the plaster. On the steps leading to the niche, lying on their sides under a heavy plaster coating, were two limestone altars, obviously originally flanking the stairs. Burnt organic residue was found in the depression on the top of each altar. In the courtyard, along the central axis of the complex, was a large altar built of fieldstones and mud mortar, topped in its second phase with a flint slab surrounded by runnels in the mud mortar. In later phases secondary chambers were built in the courtyard, the broad room was widened, and a stone-lined "basin" was installed in the courtyard. From these chambers came fragments of a small tall stand or elaborate large chalice ("incense burner") and an "exceptionally large oil lamp."[33] Near the altar, in stratigraphy assigned to Stratum IX, was found a bronze weight in the form of a recumbent lion, and in stratigraphy assigned to Stratum X were found 2 shallow burnished plates with *qoph* and either *kaph* or Phoenician *shin* incised on the rims.[34] Ostraca attributed to the side rooms of the complex include priestly names known from the Bible (Meremoth, Pashhur, and "the sons of Korach").[35] A chalk stamp-seal, possibly depicting the plan of the fortress and indicating the site of the sanctuary by a raised bump, is attributed to courtyard deposits of Stratum IX.[36] Two stone blocks with depressions carved in their surfaces are taken to be "offering tables" and two kilns "near the entrance to the temple" may witness to a potter's industry connected with the sanctuary: "From the vessels found beside them, it seems that mainly vessels for use in the temple were fired here."[37] Unfortunately, we are never informed about what sorts of pottery vessels were found in the temple complex.

In the absence of tightly controlled stratigraphic evidence or even published groups of pottery from known loci, accurate dating of this sanctuary, let alone its detailed phasing, is problematic. Ze'ev Herzog et al. attribute its inception to the Solomonic period, with terminations of the altar phase at the end of the eighth century (Stratum VIII) and of the sanctuary itself in the seventh century (Stratum VII).[38] Unfortunately for simplicity, these dates and stratigraphic interpretations are not generally accepted,[39] although we would probably be on safe ground if we attributed the founding of the sanctuary to the tenth to ninth centuries and its end to the seventh to sixth centuries, that is, roughly the life span of the Judean monarchy.[40]

Samaria Locus E 207.[41] This is the most neglected sacral area in either the Northern or the Southern Kingdom. Excavated by E. L. Sukenik for the Joint Expedition (1931–33), the site was not properly published until 1957, when it was overshadowed by K. M. Kenyon's publication of the stratified pottery. Nonetheless it is an impressive site. Some 635 m. east-southeast of the easternmost extension of the Israelite fortifications a large trench, averaging 3.5 m. deep and 6 m. wide at the top (narrowing down to 4 m. at the bottom), was dug out of the bedrock, all but encircling a trapezoidal island of rock 30 × 26 × 26 m. in plan. A narrow (2.4 m. wide) causeway connected the "island" to the surrounding territory on the west. Only a small sector of space inside the trench "was cleared. The rock here was close to the surface and the ground had been used in later times as a burial place or quarry, several rock-cuttings and empty troughs or shafts coming to light. In one place...a dromos...led to a cave..., but the latter was found empty though the stone blocking was still in place."[42] The trench, which was about three-quarters excavated, was "found to be packed with broken Israelite pottery.... The filling was remarkably homogeneous. None resembled any of the wares peculiar to Periods I, II or III. [The ware of] some pieces [was] ... like that of Periods IV and V, but for the most part the ware was pale and well-levigated like that found in Period VI.... The variety of the forms is remarkable.... Out of 251 objects figured [in Figs. 13–31] 155 come from E 207 and 33 others ... were also represented there."[43] Amid this mass of pottery, covering virtually all of the common shapes, was an Egyptian-style oven lid,[44] two fragments of a mold for making an Egyptianizing plaque portraying a seated Isis and the infant Horus, together with 26 other female figurines, 2 male figurines ("riders"), and 120 animals ("horse, 34, bovine, 83, camel, 1, sheep, 1, donkey, 1"),[45] 1 model couch, 1 model chariot wheel, 15 chalices of later style, 1 fenestrated stand, about 143 "cups-and-saucers," and 3 rattles. Analysis of the pottery suggests that food preparation, eating, and drinking were important aspects of the activities accounting for the pottery deposits. The fact that "several baskets-full" of lamps[46] came from the trench must say something about the timing of at least some cultic activities. The lamps were mostly of normal "shell"-lamp style, including one with at least 2 spouts (and possibly 7), but there was one high-based "Lachish II"-style lamp and one, possibly also multiple-spouted, on a tall pedestal base.

Kuntillet ʿAjrud.[47] Maximally, this is a full-fledged desert sanctuary decorated with frescoes and religious texts, collecting tithes from nonsedentary populations, travelers and caravaneers, with an improbably hypothesized full-blown weaving industry specializing in priestly vestments made of fine linen ornamented with richly dyed wool and possibly offering a brisk trade in baked goods as well. It received *ex voto* offerings of massive stone bowls sometimes inscribed in Hebrew from people with Judean (?) names ending in -*yw* and had, in the "Bench Room," taken to be the ritual center, a large pithos—perhaps originally two—elaborately decorated with religious scenes and supplications.[48] Minimally, Kuntillet ʿAjrud is a caravanserai with some fascinating murals (mostly, however, in the ruinously preserved "Building B"), religiously inspired graffiti and inscriptions picturing mythological beings and religious symbols and invoking or mentioning Yahweh, El, Baal, and Asherah. Pending more adequate publication, it would seem that these graffiti and inscriptions probably involved more than one population group. This seems clearly the case for the well-studied paintings.[49] Nor is it all that clear that the art motifs parallel already known artistic motifs current in Judah.[50] Moreover, it is difficult, if not impossible, to connect any one text with any one depiction.[51] Certainly, from our own peculiar interest in the present study, it seems necessary to point out that wall decorations and religiously inspired drawings and graffiti on a couple of pithoi do not, in themselves, signify a major Judean sanctuary or, in this out-of-the-way setting and multicultural environment, even testify in any totally unambiguous way to major trends of Judean or Israelite thinking. On the other hand, they unquestionably illuminate the sorts of syncretistic speculation that must have occurred to persons bridging cultures in the long-distance trading networks that tied Israel, Judah, Phoenicia, Philistia, and the South Arabian kingdoms one to another, and thus, to the degree that Judean citizens were involved in this commerce, these artistic and epigraphic remains testify to the religious tensions that might exist between a state-dominated religion (see below) and the wider world of Mediterranean polyculturalism.

From an architectural point of view, the "Bench Room" sufficiently replicates the entry rooms of the Tel Arad gateway, except for the rear rooms and absolute scale, so that it probably is better taken as an example of fortress gateway planning than religious architecture.[52] No specifically "religious" artifact (as opposed to inscribed artifacts) was found at Kuntillet ʿAjrud.[53] Despite its unquestionable significance for the wider study of Israelite religion in general, Kuntillet ʿAjrud fails to illuminate the specific area of *corporate* religious activity in Israel or Judah during the united monarchy. It *may,* however, provide some of the mythopoeic backdrop for some of the items closely associated with the *"distributed"* cultus (see below).

Jerusalem Cave 1.[54] Remarkably similar in its contents, as well as its extramural location, to Samaria E 207, this cave, some 8.12 m. deep and with a maximum width of 4.2 m., contained more than 1,200 pottery vessels, many complete or restorable,[55] 16 female figurines (13 solid, 3 hollow-bodied), 2 anthropomorphic vessels, 38 figurines of quadrupeds, 21 "horse-and-rider" figurines, 7 figurines of birds, 3 model couches, 1 model shrine, 2 miniature "cuboidal" limestone altars, 1 rattle, and 1 fenestrated stand. All told, about one object in fourteen in this deposit has an overtly "cultic" or "religious" aspect.[56] Further, T. A. Holland notes that "many vessels . . . near the entrance of the cave . . . had been left *in situ* unbroken. . . . Some of the complete bowls still had the remains of animal bones within them which is further proof that the cave was a repository of ritual gifts."[57]

The cave was man-made, with two lobes partly divided by a wall extending back from a central pillar left in the bedrock. The rear of the southern lobe (the cave entrance was to the east) was walled off, creating a podium or raised bench in a domed alcove, which could also be accessed from the deeper northern chamber by means of a "window" in the dividing wall. Despite formal similarities with late Iron II tombs, "there was no trace of burials."[58] Two lamp (?) niches flank either side of the cave, some 1.5 m. back from the entrance. In front of the southern niche four large stones and a couple of smaller ones appear on plan, possibly forming either a step or a small platform against the side wall of the cave. Apart from the stone wall, these are the only stones shown on plan. In front of these stones is a large scatter of pottery, most of it apparently intact. This scatter is densest nearest the stones and thins out toward the stone pillar (located 3.4 m. into the cave) and the northern side of the cave. In the deeper northern lobe a second "large pottery heap" is indicated on the plan, with no attempt at drawing individual pots, and with 7 or 8 individual pots being indicated immediately to the west and northwest of the heap. The cave floor was reached by way of a passage between two house rooms (?; see n. 59, below). One of these rooms was paved, the other apparently not. The cave entrance was below grade, with entrance wash indicated on the plan. Various vessels, including a lamp and some juglets, are figured on plan along the sides of the entryway.[59] The only 2 complete female figurine heads found in the cave came from these entrance wash levels.

The Tumuli West of Jerusalem.[60] An unknown number of tumuli of various sizes top the hills and ridges west of Jerusalem. Inconclusively excavated by W. F. Albright in 1923, they were reinvestigated by R. Amiran in 1953. Twenty tumuli were mapped, one was totally excavated, and two more were sounded. Basically, the general form appears to be that of a truncated cone formed of loose stones contained within a series of thin stone wall segments, perhaps originally one continuous wall. Tumulus 5, the only one completely excavated, stood 6 m. high and was 32 m. in diameter. Covered over by this large heap of stones was an area surrounded by a carefully constructed perimeter wall made up of 17 straight sections, with stepped entranceways leading through the wall on the east and the west.[61] Asymmetrically disposed within this circular area was a platform some 6 m. wide (east to west) and 10 m. long, built up on the downhill side by a small terrace wall supporting an earthen fill. On this leveled platform was built "an elongated rampart," a heap of red earth and stones .5 m. high, 1.75 m. wide, and 5 m. long. This was bordered on the eastern (downslope) side by a flagged pavement made up of 2 rows of local chalky stone. The pavement lay some .3 to .35 m. below the top of the "rampart" and curved eastward about 3 m. into its southward run, then continued south for another 2 m. At the point of curvature, lying between the "rampart" and the pavement, was a flagstone-lined hexagonal pit roughly 1 m. long by .75 m. wide cut into the earthen fill of the platform. The pit was filled with "well-silted earth, without any sherds or bones, only very small pieces of charcoal could be distinguished in it."[62] Downslope within the enclosure (to the east) "was found an area full of burnt debris, charcoal pieces, burnt animal bones, and black earth saturated with fat; even the stones found there were blackened. Most of the sherds collected from this tumulus were found around here. The fragments of [a] cooking pot . . . were found on the sloping rock, immediately below the burnt spot."[63] At the southernmost part of the ring-wall was a right-angled "fence . . . made of large field-stones planted into the shallow surface soil" surrounding a semicircular platform (or stone heap?) extending inward from the ring-wall.[64]

Small finds from the three tumuli excavated were exclusively pottery of "domestic" character, all of it generally datable to the period ending either in the Lachish III or II horizons.[65] Most common were the large strap-handled bowls with folded rim and ring-burnished interiors (13 exx. published) followed by small to large bowls (10 exx., including 2 "degenerate" bar-handled bowls), various forms of the deep "Judean" cooking pot (5 exx., including one with a *taw*-marked handle), 3 wide-mouthed and 2 narrow-mouthed jugs and 1 jug body, 6 store jars and 2 store jar handles marked with *taw*, 1 wide-rimmed holemouth jar, 1 ring-stand, and one characteristically "Lachish II" high-based lamp.

Given the general configuration of the data, and assuming that they also apply to most of the other tumuli, we probably are justified in seeing the tumuli as "cultic" in one manner or another, but not operative in the same manner or with the same symbols as the other sites discussed in this section. Given, further, the widespread use of tumuli as burial sites in Anatolia and as the means of safeguarding cremation sites in Cyprus,[66] some sort of association with funerary practices seems warranted,[67] but to go past this would have to involve, as a first step, more certain knowledge about osteology and wet-sieved fractions than we now possess.

Ashdod, Sanctuary in Area D.[68] The excavations at Ashdod provide three valuable clues in our study of Israelite and Judean religious practice during the period of the divided monarchy. (1) More than any other single site, they provide a ratio between the numbers of religiously affective small finds in "normal" neighborhoods and those in the immediate vicinity of sanctuaries, even if the sanctuary is, as in the present case, relatively small. (2) Ashdod, together with Shrine 1 at Sarepta, furnishes us with an example of a functioning non-Israelite or Judean sanctuary, against which Israelite and Judean shrines and sanctuaries of the same or similar date can be seen in greater perspective. (3) Together with Sarepta, Ashdod provides the corporate cultic setting for classes of artifacts whose cultic associations in Israel or Judah have been questioned. We will deal with each of these points in turn.

1. Ashdod is so rich in figurative materials and presumptive cultic vessels that virtually any excavation area of the Iron II period could be mistaken, in isolation, for a cultic area. How, then, can one be confident that any one area exhibiting quantities of religious artifacts was indeed some sort of cult center? Fortunately the answer is quite straightforward. In the first place, the sanctuary in local Stratum 4 of Area D is architecturally distinguishable (see par. 2 below). In the second place, all excavation areas of the townsite are *not* equal in numbers of religiously affective artifacts. Although the statistic is admittedly rough, involving as it does varying numbers of strata, unequally excavated and impossible to quantify with precision in terms of cubic meters of earth excavated, a comparison of the average number of religiously affective artifacts in each excavation area in terms of the overall square meterage of that area (in itself not always an easy thing to measure) is more than usually rewarding (see Table 1).

2. The sanctuary in Area D was distinguished in excavation by *(a)* having whitewashed walls, *(b)* having a whitewashed podium or "altar" (Locus 1022) and a bench (Locus 1046), and *(c)* by the quantity of "fragments of cult vessels" that lay on the floor of the main room, sealed under fallen bricky detritus.[69] The room exhibited a modified indirect access plan, with approach being through a 3.5 m. long hall, although, surprisingly, the podium was immediately upon the right once one got into the L-shaped room itself, which was roughly at the midpoint of the bottom leg of the (backwards) "L." Judging from the preserved plans, the building had no provisions for an outside door. Entry was upon a raised walk or bench, running along the southern side of the building, some 30 cm. above the first-phase floor but only 15 cm. above that of the second phase. This was the only bench in the room. Two rooms, apparently storerooms, could be reached from the main room. In them were cult furniture, including a fenestrated "incense stand" and "offering vessels" so far peculiar to Ashdod,[70] together with 3 drinking bowls, 3 large bowls, 2 jugs, a juglet and a oenochoe, 2 kraters, a store jar (wine jar?), a cooking pot, a foot bath, and a stone spindle whorl.[71] From the main room are published two dipper juglets, a Cypro-Phoenician painted bowl, a cooking jug (?), and a model couch or chair. North of the western storeroom, in what is termed "Room 1001" but which might be an outdoor cul-de-sac, was a large, partly stone lined pit, taken by the

TABLE 1

Excavated Areas	A	B	C	D	G	H	K	C1	T. = 8
Religious Objects	14	17	11	163	6	17	8	4	T. = 240
Approx. Sq. m./Area	450	400	140	900	320	187	116	171	T. = 2684 sq. m.
Av. Sq. m./Obj.	32	23.5	12.7	5.5	53.3	11	14.5	42.75	Mean = 11.18 sq. m.

Comments: 240 objects considered religiously affective in terms of criteria utilized by the present study were published from 8 excavation areas at Ashdod (*Ashdod I, II*). The average density of cultic artifacts per square meter of surface area for the site as a whole was 11.18 square meters per "religious object." Leaving aside Area D, the site of a sanctuary, the average density was 1 for each 23.17 square meters. For the area of the sanctuary (Area D), the population density is 1 for each 5.52 square meters. Thus, Area D had roughly 4.2 times the "religious artifact density" of the average of the rest of the excavation areas, 2.0 times the density of the next closest area, Area H, and 2.3 times that of the next, Area C.

263

excavators to be a *favissa*. From this pit were published 6 kraters, 2 jugs, 2 bowls, a lamp, a pilgrim flask, a female plaque-type figurine with her right hand at her side and her left hand supporting her left breast, a model chair, and three zoomorphic heads from kernos rings.[72]

3. While the finds in the rooms and the putative *favissa* of the sanctuary were not as rich as the immediate neighborhood (see par. 1, above), the presence of model chairs, a female plaque type of figurine, and the zoomorphic kernos heads together with recognizable cult furniture points to a kind of association of items of this general class with a center for corporate worship not witnessed in Israel or Judah *except at Samaria E 207 and in Jerusalem Cave 1*. We will deal further with the implications of this observation below under "Artifacts" and in later sections of the chapter.

Sarepta, Shrine 1.[73] This small one-room shrine, only some 16 sq. m. in area, was a long-room structure apparently built up against a larger building.[74] It was architecturally distinguished by a cement floor, an entryway that changed from indirect access to direct access in the course of the shrine's life, a podium centered on the back wall, benches running along all four sides of the building, and a broken-out rectangle in the floor in front of the podium where something (a "betyl" or an incense altar?) had forcibly been removed. A dark ash deposit surrounding this area and the podium suggests that either the podium or the removed object was an altar. In opposition to the sanctuary at Ashdod and most presumptive Israelite and Judean sanctuaries, "there was a noticeable lack of the most common kinds of artifacts found elsewhere in the excavated area, the common everyday ceramic ware."[75] Instead, there were 9 or 10 female figurines, mostly completely clothed and either holding an object (dove or tambourine) or sitting or standing with hands or a hand over an obviously pregnant abdomen,[76] 1 bearded head of a male figurine twice the size of the female figurines, two carved ivory figurines of women, a cultic mask, 25 faience amulets of Egyptian design, a model sphinx (or cherub) throne, a tall red-burnished stand, 12 ordinary lamps and a miniature lamp, 12 round pottery disks made from potsherds, a small alabaster jar, a faience jar or box lid, and 95 beads.[77] Apparently from another season was an ivory label reading, "The statue(m) which Shillem, son of Mapaʿal, son of ʾIzai made for Tanit ʿAshtart."[78] J. B. Pritchard plausibly argues for a now-vanished wooden (male) cult statue.[79] This discovery is given added importance by a small glass inset, found close to the shrine, decorated with the " 'Sign of Tanit,' . . . a triangle and a circle separated by a horizontal bar with upturned ends."[80] The shrine is dated to the eighth-seventh centuries

B.C.E., and its poorly preserved successor (Shrine 2), to the sixth-fifth centuries).[81]

Tell Ta'yinat.[82] The small but well-built eighth-century temple at Tell Ta'yinat, generally cited as the nearest contemporary evidence for the plan, siting, and construction of the Solomonic Temple at Jerusalem, is too well known to require extensive comment.[83] Nor is it sufficiently well published to enable us to compare the artifactual evidence with known Judean and Israelite shrines. What is useful here, in terms of our hypothetical model of state religious organization (below), is to placard it as a probable example of a "national" shrine and, in this connection, to note *(a)* its central location, *(b)* its use of appropriate local iconographic motifs, *(c)* its direct access plan, and *(d)* its close association with the large *Bit Hilani*-style palace, almost surely the seat of a minor Syrian king (as opposed to a governor's palace), witnessing clearly to the role of the official cultus in promoting national unity under the monarchy.

Artifacts[84]

We can be brief. For most presumptive Judean and Israelite cult places, the distinguishing *mobilia* seem to be the tall, generally "horned," limestone "incense altars" (see Table 2, below) found from Dan (an unusual short one, probably originally on a separate stand) to Beer-sheba (an unusual cylindrical form);[85] tall "cult" stands, often fenestrated and/or decorated with red burnish and/or pendant tab-like leaves;[86] and "incense bowls" fitting onto the above, with the same types of attributes.[87] Chalices are, in general, found only in the earlier periods and are not generally characteristic of the Lachish III or II horizons.[88] They were often ornamented like the tall "cult" stands.[89] Lamps, which are hardly unique to sanctuaries, nevertheless appear consistently in these sacred assembly areas, sometimes in elaborated 7-spouted form and/or on pedestal bases. Steleform stones appear at a significant number of sites (see Table 2, below), and at most sites ordinary pottery vessels connected with eating and drinking play a significant role. Among the *immobilia* we regularly note benches, podia, and, now at three sites, large altars of burnt offerings.

Cult areas Jerusalem Cave 1 and Samaria E 207 stand significantly apart from all the other Judean and Israelite activity areas considered above. Both are characterized by a great number of figurines of women, "horses-and-riders," and animals/birds, items lacking in statistically significant numbers from any of the other secure Judean or Israelite cult areas, shrines, or sanctuaries. At Samaria E 207 and in Cave 1 at Jerusalem, cult stands play a diminished role (one each) and the tall limestone altars simply do not appear. Neither site gave evidence for a large altar of burnt offerings. Vessels for eating and drinking are, at these two sites, even more in evidence than they are at the other sites. Among the more usual sort of sanctuaries and shrines, Tel Dan stands out as having more figurative materials than any other: 5 published to date, of which 4 are apparently male and one (a head only) is female. It should be noted, however, that the three faience figurines all came from the vicinity of the olive press, and may represent some sort of special event or circumstances unrelated to the normal operation of the sanctuary. Nevertheless, the prominence attained by male figurines at this site, however they are to be explained, is clearly noteworthy. Finally, a special class of cult vessel, rather like a slender ginger jar with pendant (?) denticulate moldings (the vessel's orientation is not certain), occurs in quantity in association with the Ashdod Area D sanctuary but has not yet, to my knowledge, been identified in Judean settings.

TOWARD AN INTERPRETATION OF CLUSTERED PHENOMENA: LOCALIZED SETTINGS FOR CORPORATE WORSHIP (CULT AREAS, SHRINES, SANCTUARIES)

Theory

The dominant religious structure within any nation-state of the Iron II period in the general Syro-Palestinian setting almost certainly paralleled the political structure of the state, confirming and complementing the overtly political state government with the stipulations, sanctions, and blessings of the true ruler or rulers of the universe.[90] As a parallel apparatus to the purely political organization, such a religious structure could no more suffer "political," that is to say, religious, heterodoxy than could the political apparatus.[91] While we should assume, on the basis of ethnographic analogy, that various shrines and sanctuaries would have special traditions and characteristics that would distinguish them from others under the same jurisdiction (the national sanctuary, or, differently put, the sanctuary associated with the palace complex), this should not obscure the requirement that, in all matters considered essential to the religious establishment (at that particular point in time), the lower levels of the organization must either have been obedient or have placed their careers and positions at jeopardy. At the same time, it is inevitable in any complex society that individuals and groups of individuals may find themselves, for good and sufficient reasons, at odds with the religious establishment or status quo, giving rise to alternative forms of religious expression. In a culture in which priesthood was a hereditary occupation, it is possible to see how such divisions might have led to the formation of genuine nonconformist sects, although it is more probable that such divisions would at first give rise to rival political parties within the same cultus, with a "Nonconformist" religion possibly emerging from irreconcilable differences over either content of religious thought or form of religious expression.

Given a hierarchically ordered form of state religion, and it is hard to conceive of any other for this time and place,[92] it is reasonable to suppose that the outward physical expression of the corporate life of any prominent dissenting groups, that is, their places of corporate worship and the modes of worship conducted in these places, would "shadow" the politically dominant religious institutions, at least for the less radical of these communities. While it is inherently improbable that there was a state-wide—or even regionally—hierarchically organized priesthood for any but the officially recognized cultus, it is reasonably sure that each political entity, from capital city to village, had its own consenting nonconformist communities, whether large or small is immaterial, and, in the nature of things religious, it is equally sure that each community had its own acts of corporate worship. Thus, at a minimum, *we should expect to find archaeologically recoverable evidence for more than one community of believers at each level of political organization.*[93] This holds true whether we are dealing with a state temple or a conventicle meeting in a private household, the chief problem being whether or not we could identify and characterize the depositional patternings of conventicles. State temples are another thing entirely. It would be hard to miss one of these unless it were so thoroughly destroyed and its foundations quarried out as to leave no trace upon the land.[94] Nor should we imagine that dissenting groups were entirely divorced from the dominant state religion. It is more reasonable to suppose that a great many people took care to propitiate and supplicate the powers of the universe on more than one level, convening with their fellow citizens at the great national festivals, offering their tithes at the local "Establishment" sanctuaries, and, in some other forum, ensuring that matters overlooked or downplayed by the official cultus were not neglected by them and their families.[95]

From this analysis we can derive a general theorem: "Corporate religious expression in a typical Iron II Syro-Palestinian nation-state should have operated on several different levels, each with its own place in the social order and each with its own set of material affects." On the basis of this theorem, and with due regard for what is generally known about the culture and archaeology of the region, it then becomes possible to construct a simple model of religious organization in Judah and Israel that should prove to be of material assistance in "decoding" the fragmentary and dispersed fragments of the archaeological record that are currently at our disposal.[96]

A Preliminary Model of Religious Organization in Typical Syro-Palestinian Nation-States of the Iron II Period

Established Worship

Given the operative hypothesis that one of the major goals of the religious establishment is to promote national unity and a feeling of distinctiveness vis-à-vis neighboring states, it is apparent that the *established* religious tradition should be national in scope.

At the town or national level, religious structures of this "Establishment" cultus, as we shall term it, should be archaeologically distinguishable by, in this order, *(a)* a concentration of cultic apparatus and *(b)* distinctive architectural traits suited to the functions of the cultus.[97] In the truest sense of the term, these are "public buildings." As such, they should be a key part of the overall town planning. Since they are designed to serve as symbols of the divine authority behind the state, it seems reasonable that they should have a direct-access plan.[98] As an important official building and divine correlate to the palace of the king, governor, or appointed official, the shrine of the deity should exhibit traces of monumental architecture appropriate to the level of political organization (e.g., Beer-sheba altar, ashlar masonry at Dan, columns [?] at Arad). In an independent nation-state, cult symbolism and artifacts should, in largest measure, either be *(a)* local/appropriate to the region, but clearly distinct, at least in the aggregate, from those of rival polities or *(b)* reflective of the ruling imperial culture (applicable in a client state). Town shrines should contain a subset of the cult apparatus at the state level. It is uncertain whether or not we should expect shrines of the "Establishment" variety at a level lower than that of the lowest appointed governing official, but the tentative conclusion that these functions should be seen as parallel on all levels suggests not. If true, this may rule out independent shrines in small villages, but it need not rule out neighborhood shrines within urban communities large enough to accommodate them.

At the neighborhood level, shrines should (again) be archaeologically distinguishable by *(a)* concentration of cultic apparatus and *(b)* architectural traits. Local shrines should be "public" and favorably sited in the local portion of the town plan, although not necessarily very large. They might well have a direct-access plan for the same reasons as given above. The cultic apparatus should be a subset of the cult apparatus at the town

268

level. Foreign materials should either be wanting or of marginal importance. (This could be reversed in a heavily mercantile setting.)

Tolerated Nonconformist Worship

Hypothesis. The social function of "Nonconformist" religion (as we shall term it) in a society can be seen as an attempt on the part of individuals or groups of individuals to remedy perceived deficiencies in the established religion. Examples are: *(a)* restricted access to significant aspects of the cultus for women, "unclean" individuals, resident aliens, or the like, or *(b)* misdirected or inadequate religious or social objectives (e.g., failure properly to recognize or worship certain aspects of the divine world), and so on.

Locations of tolerated "Nonconformist" worship. These should be archaeologically distinguishable *(a)* by localized concentrations of material correlates of cultic activity and *(b)* by distinctive architectural traits vis-à-vis the "Established" sanctuaries. We would not expect a state or national-level "Nonconformist" shrine in a state with an established religion. Since nonconformist religion may, indeed *should*, only be "tolerated" (if that) by the secular and religious governing authorities, the cult place should not compete for attention with "Establishment" sanctuaries. Since it is outside the official governing structure of the community, such a cult place might well be outside the fortified town site, for example, the extramural location of Samaria E 207 as over against the siting of the Arad sanctuary in the favored northwest corner of the fortress at Arad. Such an extramural location might particularly apply if core members of the nonconformist religious group were foreigners. Political considerations, if nothing else, would dictate that any "Tolerated Nonconformist" shrine should be smaller scale than the "Establishment" shrines at the same level of political organization. Since they would lie outside the area of direct governmental sponsorship and control, they would not form a key part of the town plan and would not be expected to be sited on particularly good ground. Especially within built-up town sites it might be anticipated that they would exhibit an indirect access plan. In fact, from outward appearances, particularly in plain view, publicly visible cult places might appear "private." As a conscious or unconscious attempt at modification of the "Establishment" cultus, "Nonconformist" cult apparatus probably would not be a direct subset of the state cultus, although it seems reasonable to suppose that there might be a possible tendency toward mutual accommodation through time. In a small nation-state with culturally significant neighbors, a nonconformist cult or group might be expected to exhibit explicit signs of "foreign" influence, although this would vary depending upon what perceived weaknesses of the official cultus were at issue. That is to say, from the material culture viewpoint we might expect to find, in such a sanctuary, cult symbols from foreign cultures, amulets from foreign cultures, and possibly even specialized cultic apparatus more favored outside the nation-state than within it. But these symbols should—except in explicitly "foreign" shrines—be "in bounds."[99]

Since nonconformist religion in a tightly governed national state lies outside the official bounds of organized society, such a religious movement (or, from the archaeological viewpoint, such patterning of material cultural affects) might well be hypothesized to be *regional* in scope, with variability between neighboring regions of the same national state. Such divisions should reasonably be conceived of as following natural lines of communication[100] or lying within natural boundaries or geopolitical subentities in the larger nation-state.[101] That is, they should follow the contours of a particular territory in which personal reputations of individuals could be known on, perhaps, no more than a secondhand or thirdhand basis.

"ESTABLISHMENT" AND "NONCONFORMIST" SANCTUARIES, SHRINES, AND CULT AREAS IN ISRAEL AND JUDAH DURING THE PERIODS OF THE UNITED AND DIVIDED MONARCHIES

Table 2 presents an analysis of the archaeological data just reviewed, enabling the direct comparison of features of locations characterized by the clustering of artifacts or other features generally considered indicative of patterned religious activity on the part of population groups above the household level. These locations have been arranged in rough chronological order and grouped as follows: premonarchical, monarchical, non-Israelite sites, and sites that either are *not* cult areas or that cannot contribute significantly to our understanding of cultic artifacts or architecture.

In the main group, three sites stand out as substantively different from the other five: Samaria E 207, Jerusalem Cave 1, and the tumuli west of Jerusalem. The tumuli, in turn, are distinguished from the other two by the absence (to date, at any rate) in the latter of figurative images as well as by their totally different sitings and their apparent one-time usage. Siting, the absence of large altars for burnt offerings (a characteristic shared with the small shrines Megiddo Locus 2081 and Lachish Stratum V Building 49), the absence of tall limestone incense altars, foreign influence (not clearly attested to date for Jerusalem Cave 1), and particularly the presence of statistically significant quantities of figurines absolutely set off Jerusalem Cave 1 and Samaria E 207 from the remaining five.[102]

In terms of our model, identifiable "Establishment" shrines and sanctuaries should outnumber "Nonconformist" shrines and sanctuaries, though this is not absolutely demanded by the model. From another perspective of the model, however, the mere "obviousness" of the Dan and Arad sanctuaries marks them off as "Establishment," while the other three conform in so many ways that they are clearly of the same tradition.

Within the five presumptively "Establishment" units, two are clearly "shrines" (Megiddo Locus 2081 and Lachish Stratum V Building 49) and one is of unknown size (Beer-sheba) but is presumably a sanctuary, since there is an altar for burnt offerings. Arad is clearly a sanctuary, in terms of our classification, and probably coordinate with Beer-sheba. Dan is outsized with reference to the others, although, in terms of our classification, clearly a sanctuary. Together, these make up a ranked hierarchy, as predicted by the model. Not only are our expectations fulfilled in this respect but we may also note that the consistent use of direct-access plans and the prime locations of Dan, Arad, and Megiddo Locus 2081 also fit the predictions. Finally, we observe that the two shrines do indeed seem to have a subset (lacking the altar of burnt offerings) of the cult apparatus of the larger sanctuaries but add nothing that would be inappropriate in the higher members of the series. Despite the limited sample size, this is not only a remarkably good "fit" of actual data to the hypothetical model but also a good example of the power of a well-constructed model to assist in the interpretation of complex configurations of archaeological data.

On the basis of currently available data, it now becomes possible to assign these sanctuaries and shrines to specific niches and roles in the overall structure of the ancient nation-states. The Ta'yinat temple is clearly an example of a "State Sanctuary" sharing pride of location with the royal palace. The sanctuary at Dan is unquestionably at a higher level of importance (whether national or provincial) than those at Arad and Beer-sheba, while the latter reasonably stand out as "regional" centers of worship coordinate with governmental centers obviously built to extend the influence of the central government into economically important peripheral areas, a classic illustration of A. L. Oppenheim's "Forced Urbanization" hypothesis as modified and developed for the Palestinian landscape by Ahlström.[103] Megiddo Locus 2081, probably located in the courtyard of an important government official, Lachish Stratum V Building 49, and possibly also the original siting for the tall limestone altars found near Building 10 at Megiddo, neatly fit into the "local" or "neighborhood" shrine category, with Megiddo Locus 2081 and probably the

TABLE 2
FEATURES OF IRON I AND IRON II CULT SITES

Site name	Siting* 1/2/E	Size l/m/s	Multiple rooms ?	Dir/ind access	Podium ?	Benches ?	Incense altar(s)	Altar for burnt offerings	Favissae ?	Stelae ?	Foreign influence	Figurines ?
Hazor	1?	m?	yes?	ind?	no	yes	no	no	yes?	no	no	AE male
Bull site	ext	m	no	n/a	yes(?)	no	no	poss.	no	yes	no	AE bull
Megiddo L.2081	1	s	no	dir	yes	no	yes	no	no	yes	no	no
Dan—Temenos	1	vl	yes?	dir	bamah(?)	no(?)	yes	yes	no(?)	no(?)	yes	4m, 1f
Lachish—Str. V	2(?)	s	no	dir(?)	yes	yes	yes	no(?)	no(?)	yes	no	no
Arad XI–	1	1	yes	dir	yes(?)	yes	prob.	yes	no(?)	yes	no	no
Arad X–	1	1	yes	dir	yes(?)	yes	prob.	yes	no(?)	yes	no	no
Arad IX–	1	1	yes	dir	yes(?)	no(?)	yes	yes	no(?)	yes	?	no
Arad VIII–	1	1	yes	dir	yes(?)	yes	no(?)	no(?)	no(?)	yes(?)	no	lion wt.
Beer-Sheba	?	?	?	?	?	?	at gate (?)	yes	?	?	no	?
Samaria—E 207	ext	1	?	?	?	?	no	no(?)	yes(?)	no(?)	yes	165
Jerusalem—Cave 1	ext	m	yes	ind(?)	yes(?)	no	no**	no	no	no	no(?)	84
Tumuli	ext	1	no	dir	rampart?	no	no	no?***	no	no	no(?)	no
Ashdod D Sanct.	2	m	yes	ind	yes	yes	no	no	yes(?)	no	yes(?)	9
Sarepta Shrine 1	2	s	no	i > d	yes	yes	yes#	no	no	no	yes	12
Ta'yinat Sanct.	1	1	yes	dir	yes	yes(?)	poss	no(?)	no(?)	no(?)	plan(?)	no(?)
Ta'anach—Cult Str.	?	m	yes	?	?	?	yes(?)	?	no(?)	yes(?)	no	1 mold
Megiddo—Bldg. 10	1	m	yes	ind(?)	no	no	near	no	no	no	no	yes
Kuntillet 'Ajrud**	1	s	yes(?)	dir	no	yes	no	no	no(?)	no	yes	no

NOTES TO TABLE 2

* Siting: "1" = prestigious location; "2" = nondescript location; "E/EXT" = extramural location.

** Two cuboidal altars, but no tall limestone altars or substitutes.

*** "Burning Area." Perhaps only an area for roasting sheep, goats or cattle, but possibly a funeral pyre (Karageorghis 1969: 151–64).

\# Assuming the missing "Betyl" was really an incense altar.

N.B. Kuntillet 'Ajrud and Megiddo Building 10 are not here considered shrines or sanctuaries in any technical sense, but are included for comparison. On balance, the "Cult Structure" at Ta'anach appears to be the storerooms to a wealthy household, although it is not impossible that it houses some of the paraphernalia of a household shrine. A less likely possibility, from the present perspective, would be that it was part of the storeroom facilities of a sanctuary.

shrine materials (as opposed to "domestic" religious materials) found near Building 10 demonstrating both the primary location and the close connection between civil and religious authority.[104]

Whether the tumuli west of Jerusalem represent special-function sites associated with the "Establishment" cultus is uncertain but, to my mind, improbable. Whatever their status, however, nothing presently links them with the "Nonconformist" cultus represented by Samaria E 207 and Jerusalem Cave 1. In terms of "Nonconformist" cultic activity under the model, we would expect significant regional differences between two such widely separated sites from different regions, although these differences would be by virtue of "social distance" and not because of state policies, as in the case of Judean and Israelite sanctuaries. There are, however, a significant number of shared features between Jerusalem Cave 1 and Samaria E 207. (1) In opposition to the "Establishment" sanctuaries and shrines, these cult areas are characterized by the presence, as we have already noted, of a statistically significant quantity of small figurines, symbolically dominated by female figurines (and presumably associated symbols such as model birds [at Jerusalem only], model furniture, and miniature lamps) and horse-and-rider figurines (possibly associated with a chariot wheel at Samaria), but numerically dominated by small statuettes of animals.[105] (2) Each area had large numbers (about 1,200 for Jerusalem and in excess of that for Samaria) of vessels associated with food and drink service. At the risk of stating the obvious, the size and character of most of these vessels is in excess of the requirements for token food and drink offerings. In fact, small saucers and miniature bowls suited to this role are conspicuously absent from the better-documented Samaria assemblage. (3) Each area had one tall fenestrated stand of the sort generally associated with "Establishment" shrines and sanctuaries. (4) Neither area had the sorts of tall limestone altars that define every "Establishment" shrine or sanctuary yet found, although Jerusalem Cave 1 did have two miniature cuboidal altars of the sort commonly found in household clusters at sites along the caravan route passing through the Beer-sheba–Zered Depression. (5) Lamps form an important part of the material culture assemblages, for obvious reasons in Cave 1 at Jerusalem but not for the same obvious reason at Samaria. (6) Both areas are extramural, confirming more forcibly than anticipated the model's "second-class" status for site-selection of "Nonconformist" centers for group rituals.

Two other possible cult areas, of severely restricted compass, were revealed by the writer's unpublished object-by-object review of the find spots of all possibly "religious" objects from the four sites of Hazor, Tell en-Nasbeh, Tell Beit Mirsim, and Beer-sheba.[106] (1) The extramural Cave

193 at Tell en-Nasbeh, outside which were found 2 pillar-based figurines, a model chair, and a horse-and-rider figurine and inside which was found a miniature chalice. (2) Tell Beit Mirsim Courtyard NW 32–12, an open courtyard with 2 stone-lined basins (wine presses?). Into this courtyard a cave opened. Two pillar-based figurines and 2 animal figurines came from the courtyard proper and 1 zoomorphic vessel came from the courtyard's cistern. That these are not "domestic" groups is evident not only from the find spots (although it is possible that each cave served as poor-quality housing) but from the fact that, in general, an individual house had only 1 female figurine, while each of these locations had 2.

Thus, from an examination of the evidence for patterned group activities of the sort connected with various kinds of figurines in both Israel and Judah we now have two major cult areas, both extramural, and two minor cult areas, one extramural. The three Judean cult areas are all located near or in caves, and Cult Area E 207 at Samaria *may* have been associated with an unused, but sealed, tomb.[107] Given this shape to the emerging data, one might be inclined to seek for other extramural locations, characterized by sherd scatters of late eighth- to seventh-century pottery,[108] within, say, a kilometer radius of other sites. In the Judean hill country, it seems plausible to suggest that these might all be caves, and a reexamination of the data relating to the *funerary* use of these figurines and associated materials seems warranted.

THE "DISTRIBUTED" CULTUS: CULTIC MATERIALS GENERALLY FOUND IN DOMESTIC CONTEXTS IN ISRAEL AND JUDAH

A wide variety of artifacts that would generally be regarded as "religious" in intent and function if found in, say, Anatolia, appear with great regularity in Judean and Israelite *domestic* stratigraphy, particularly that of the last years of both the Israelite and Judean states (Hazor Stratum V in the north and the Lachish Level III and II horizons in the south). This variety includes most of the types of artifacts already noted above in connection with Philistine and Phoenician shrines or sanctuaries and in connection with the presumptively "Nonconformist" cult areas in Israel and Judah: female figurines of various regionally dependent varieties, horse-and-rider figurines, various sorts of zoomorphic figurines, anthropomorphic and zoomorphic vessels, model furniture and chariot wheels, rattles, model lamps, cup-and-saucer vessels, cuboidal limestone altars, and others.[109]

In spite of its obvious importance in the religious life of ancient Israel and Judah, space limitations allow us merely to open the door to this subject. A careful study of the find spots and associations of these items in domestic stratification of the best-published Judean and Israelite sites—Beer-sheba, Tell Beit Mirsim, Tell en-Nasbeh, and Hazor—reveals that these items occur in small clusters, regularly but discontinuously distributed throughout the domestic quarters of the final Israelite or Judean strata of these sites.[110] To illustrate some of the larger groups: head and base of a pillar-based figurine, miniature lamp on a stand, zoomorphic vessel in animal shape (house at Tell Beit Mirsim [TBM] including Loci NW 22–13, –4, –5); pillar-based figurine head, rattle, hollow head of an ape, head of a zoomorphic quadruped (TBM NW 31– 10, –11); pillar-based figurine, miniature lamp on a stand, model chair, "fragment of a figurine" (house at Beer-sheba [BS] including Loci 48, 46, 25, 22); zoomorphic vessel of a bird, model chair (BS Locus 808); pillar-based figurine, 2 cuboidal limestone altars, model chair (BS Loci 430, 443, 442); 3 torsos of horse-and-rider figurines, a jug (?) fragment with a human arm appliqué, carved ivory pyxis with man adoring sacred tree guarded by cherub, cup-and-saucer vessel, fragmentary torso of a woman holding a child (?), cup from a kernos ring (Hazor Area B House 3067a and open space before house). Shape and contour are introduced into what is otherwise simply a chaos of individual items by the application of elementary descriptive statistics. About 45 percent of all houses in Level A at Tell Beit Mirsim exhibited signs of cultic activity.[111] Conversely, and this seems significant, some 55 percent did not. There were no "neighborhood" characteristics to the data, although, given the percentages, neighboring houses often shared characteristics. Of 22 houses with religiously affective artifacts, not including miniature vessels, 10 had only one artifact (6 pillar-based figurines; 2 "horses," probably from horse-and-rider figurines; 1 animal figurine; 1 animal vessel). Of the 12 houses with more than one artifact, only one lacked a pillar-based figurine, that one having 1 animal figurine and 1 rattle. Two "houses" had 2 pillar-based figurines, but one of these probably was in reality fragments of 2 houses, so that only one house (NW 22–5, –4, –13), apart from the generalized debris of the "West Tower" (2 pillar-based figurines), had 2 pillar-based figurines. The statistics are similar for the published data from Strata III–II houses at Beer-sheba.[112] No house had 2 pillar-based figurines. Of 4 houses with multiple items, 3 had pillar-based figurines, 1 had only a bird-shaped vessel and a miniature chair. Of 6 houses having only 1 artifact of these general classes, 2 had pillar-based figurines, 1 had a "fragment of a figurine," 1 had an animal figurine, 1 had a tall fenestrated stand, and 1 had an animal vessel. (See Table 3.)

Given the fragmentary and incomplete nature of artifactual recovery, to say nothing of the vagaries of archaeological reporting, the dominance of the pillar-based figurine in the above statistics is impressive and surely

TABLE 3

Site	No. of houses	Houses w/o cultic art.	Houses w/ cultic art.	Houses w/ > 1 art.	Houses w/o P-B fig.	Houses w/ P-B fig.	Houses w/ 2 P-B figs	Items present in houses w/o P-B fig.
T.B.M.	c.50	27	22	12	5	18	1 (?)	anim fig, rattle/horse/horse//anim fig//
Beer-sheba*	c.21	11	10	4	5 (4?)	5 (6?)	0	bird ves, mod chair//frag fig//anim fig//anim ves//fenstr stand

"Distributed" cultic elements at Tell Beit Mirsim and Beer-sheba. Numbers of houses without (w/o) and with (w/) cultic artifacts, houses with more than (>) 1 cultic artifact, artifact-containing houses without and with pillar-based figurines, houses with 2 pillar-based figurines and cultic artifacts or groups of artifacts present in houses lacking pillar-based figurines.

*Based upon data presented in *Beer-sheba I*.

signifies the central figure of the domestic shrines represented by these remains.[113] But who is this figure? It is inconceivable that the occupants of these houses could not have given her a name. And if they named her, surely that name would have had some currency, since nearly half of all households at Tell Beit Mirsim were involved. Given what little we know from epigraphic remains, largely the Khirbet el-Qom tomb inscription[114] and the Kuntillet 'Ajrud materials,[115] there is only one major goddess known to Judah during the later part of the Iron II period: the goddess Asherah/Asherata, possibly syncretized with, assuming, or confused with attributes of both 'Anat and 'Astarte.[116] Given the only epigraphic evidence connected with the female figurines at Sarepta (see above), we may go further and suggest that the figure of Tannit, apparently the Punic/Phoenician designation for Asherah/'Ashtarte as the Mother Goddess,[117] may also lie behind the symbolism of goddesses seated upon thrones,[118] including a cherub throne at Sarepta, bearing children, offering divine milk, and playing upon the lyre and the tambourine—not to mention being associated with lion and serpent iconography as *Labi't* ("Lady of the Lion") and *Tannit* ("Lady of the Serpent").[119] The similarity of the "Sign of Tannit" to the bell-shaped figurines of Sarepta and their wheel-made sisters from Samaria and Tell Jemmeh would probably not come as any great surprise to those devotees who visited the cave just outside Jerusalem or the highly visible cult area outside the gates of Samaria.[120]

Finally, we come to the question of chronology. There is every indication that what we have termed the "distributed" cultus was not at every time and in every place a constant high-level phenomenon in either Judah or Israel. The evidence from pre-Lachish III/II Judah is virtually nonexistent, but what evidence we have from Tell Beit Mirsim suggests that so much of the evidence is in the actual destruction debris of the houses themselves and so little is in lower street accumulations or subfloor buildup that it would appear as if the cult of the *dea nutrix* was active, to the extent and in the form we have sketched above, only during the last years of the site's life, say, from about 720 to 587 B.C.E. (dating Lachish III to 701 B.C.E.) or from about 610 to 587 B.C.E. (dating Lachish III to 597 B.C.E.).[121]

The evidence from Hazor, where we have the best stratigraphic sequence yet published for the entire Iron II period, is very much in the same vein; surprisingly so, given the different locale, considerable variance in material culture affects and different absolute dates (less different if Lachish III is dated to 701 B.C.E., as opposed to 597 B.C.E. or sometime toward the end of the seventh century). While it should be noted that the figures in part reflect a somewhat broader areal exposure in Stratum V, it seems clear that what was a relatively stable low-level pattern of distributed cultic activity for Strata XI–VI (mean = 7.33 cultic artifacts/ stratum with a standard deviation [S.D.] of +/– 3.5), and, in fact, for Strata XI–VI and continuing through Strata IV–III (mean = 7.0 cultic artifacts/stratum, S.D. = +/– 3.42), suddenly took a 500 percent jump in Stratum V (36 cultic artifacts). Put another way: for 8 out of 9 strata we were able to identify 56 possible religiously affective artifacts, for an average of 7 artifacts per stratum, with a standard deviation from that number of only +/– 3.42 artifacts per stratum. But for Stratum V alone there were 36 possible religiously affective artifacts, selected according to the same criteria. See the graph below, where the absolute numbers of artifacts are plotted by strata against time.

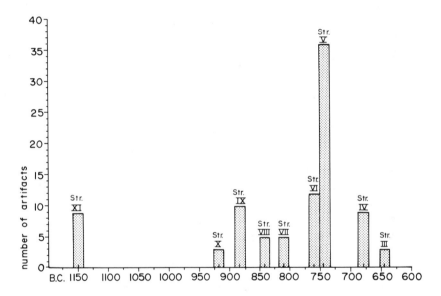

Religiously affective artifacts at Hazor plotted against time.
(Graph by J. E. Pfaff.)

That these sudden bursts of popular piety were inspired by the events of the day seems a reasonable assumption. What we are presently unable to determine with any degree of accuracy is just when (and why) the changeover is made from the earlier form of plaque-type figurines to the fully modeled figurines and exactly what were the other components to the distributed/"Nonconformist" cultus prior to the explosive "last years." Plaque-type figurines seem to be found in what might pass for domestic *favissae* in either Hazor Stratum IX or VIII (the data are unclear), and plaque-type figurines are present in extrahousehold second-ary locations in Tell Beit Mirsim Level B contexts characterized by red-burnished pottery, that is, in Solomonic or post-Solomonic contexts,[122] but we lack sufficient stratified data bridging the gap between these dates and the last years of both Israelite and Judean cities to document the period of transition, if indeed there was one. At present, it seems valid to suggest that the plaque-type figurines went into eclipse both in Israel and in Judah somewhere in the ninth century B.C.E. and that more fully formed figurines came into vogue at some time in the eighth century in the north and either the later eighth century or the middle years of the seventh century in the south (the absolute date being dependent upon the absolute dating of Lachish Level III). It is important to note, in this regard, the congruence of relative dating between the evidence we have been examining and that afforded by the pottery complements of Jerusa-lem Cave 1 and Samaria E 207 (see above), which independently witness to surprisingly short periods of intense active use of each of these cult areas.

SUMMARY CONCLUSIONS

An archaeological examination of the material culture data relating to religious activity in Israel and Judah during the period of the monarchy yields the following data:

1. During the period of the united monarchy, local or neighborhood shrines, identifiably connected in one or two instances with the resi-dences of important government (presumptively) officials and exhibiting similar configurations of material culture remains, existed in both halves of the united kingdom.

2. Following the breakup of the united monarchy, the only major Israelite sanctuary presently known to us (Dan) seems to have been "differenced" from the continuing putatively "Jerusalemite" tradition represented by the Judean sanctuary at Arad. The basic material culture complements of both sanctuaries, however, show continuity with the past and are, as best as can be determined in the face of inadequate publica-tion, reasonably congruent. The material culture complements of these and other sites of the period of the Hebrew monarchy may be described as largely concerned with formal sacrificial ritual, probably including the eating of ritual meals, and are, as far as our present data go, essentially aniconic, if we exclude the possible serpent motif[123] on a block of the Beer-sheba altar and the floral motifs on early chalices and tall stands with bowls. This aniconic tendency of the data not only contrasts strongly with other finds of the period of the early monarchy but appears to come into direct conflict with biblical descriptions of the Solomonic Temple

and may be presumed to be one of the factors in the present (inductive) reconstruction most susceptible to modification by new evidence.[124] In this connection it is important to note that our hypothetical model is more or less neutral with regard to appropriate iconographic motifs.

Both sanctuaries are, as were the earlier shrines, optimally sited and witness direct-access approaches, characteristics indicative of their direct association with the ruling authority and of their intended importance to the life of the community. The Beer-sheba altar and bronze tall stands with bowls pictured in the Lachish Reliefs are witnesses to other sanctuaries or shrines distributed throughout Judah and, at least in the case of Lachish, still extant at 701 B.C.E.[125] Monumental altars of burnt offerings presently seem to be restricted to multicomponent "sanctuaries," as opposed to unitary "shrines," but both levels share the use of tall limestone horned altars and/or tall cult stands with attached or demountable bowls, each identifiably connected with burning in at least some instances.

3. A totally different form of religious expression is witnessed, both north and south, by small clusters of cultic artifacts, heavily biased toward the iconographic, discontinuously distributed (both spatially and temporally) throughout domestic quarters and by larger clusters of restricted chronological span centered on extramural locations near major cities (Jerusalem Cave 1 and Samaria E 207). Smaller Judean ("local" or "neighborhood") cult areas, featuring modest supersets of the domestic clusters, seem to be attested near cave mouths.[126] The larger cult areas are further characterized by large numbers of lamps and ordinary vessels associated with food preparation and eating and drinking. Smaller vessels attributable to token food offerings are not characteristic of these assemblages.

4. There is sufficient evidence to indicate that commercial activity, probably connected with sacramentals and votives, was part of the cultic activity of both types of major cult areas.

The most economical hypothesis covering the above data seems to be to assign the aniconic shrine- and sanctuary-centered worship to an officially established, hierarchically organized state religion (or religions, in the case of the divided monarchy), operative in close coordination with the state's political apparatus.[127] The "distributed" cultic remains and iconographic "clustered" phenomena, both of which seem totally isolated from the life of the official shrines and sanctuaries, are probably best explained as popular phenomena, probably dependent upon traditions of folk religion stretching back into the Bronze ages, but revitalized by foreign contacts—particularly with Phoenicia (e.g., Kuntillet ʿAjrud)— during the great age of mercantile activity which immediately preceded, and probably occasioned, the Assyrian and Babylonian takeovers of the two kingdoms.[128, 129]

NOTES

1. For purposes of the present study I will generally employ the term "cult area" or some variant to designate an architecturally undistinguished or undefinable area where concentrations of religiously affective artifacts have been found. I take the term "sanctuary" to refer to a larger, multicomponent or presumably multicomponent structure generally incorporating exterior space (courtyard or *temenos*) into the overall design. A "shrine," as the term is used here, is smaller and simpler than a sanctuary, ideally being a unitary structure such as a single room or a cult room with attached storerooms. "Shrines" tend to be integrated into their surrounding neighborhoods. "Sanctuaries" dominate and define their neighborhoods. It is unclear from the literature exactly what most investigators understand by the use of the term "temple," and I have avoided its use here except in reference to excavators' terminology and with reference to the Tell Ta 'yinat and Jerusalem buildings, where it is common usage. The term would be a convenient designator for the/a major sanctuary of a given nation-state. Given the character of excavated data, precision in the use of even these very loose definitions is difficult. For example, is the Ashdod complex a "sanctuary" dominating the neighborhood? (probably)—or simply a shrine with a couple of convenient storerooms? (possibly).

2. The epigraphic data are dealt with elsewhere in the present volume: see esp. chap. 8 (Coogan), chap. 9 (Hackett), chap. 10 (McCarter), chap. 11 (Tigay), and chap. 12 (Avigad).

3. It may be observed that, in general, funeral rituals have their own logic, not always in total accord with the group religious practices of a population. That is to say, funerary assemblages may more reasonably be expected to conform to the needs and desires of a restricted segment of the population at a particularly stressful time in the lives of unique individuals and their close associates than to the general dictates of the wider society. Thus, they may more reasonably be expected to conform to the contours of what we will here term "distributed" materials (interpreted as materials relating primarily to domestic religious expression) than to "clustered" assemblages of religiously affective material culture items (interpreted as materials relating to settings of corporate worship). Given a large, well-dated, statistical sample, the utility of such evidence for determining the degree of conformity to various societal norms at various stages of a society's development is obvious, but it may be doubted that data presently in hand allow for such determinations. For one of the few cross-cultural studies of funerary practices and their implications for archaeological analysis, see L. R. Binford's "Mortuary Practices: Their Study and Potential" in his *An Archaeological Perspective* (New York: Seminar Press, 1972) 208–43. For an analysis of the implications of Chalcolithic mortuary practices in regard to the question of rank status groups in Chalcolithic society, with an excellent review of the literature, cf. T. E. Levy and D. Alon, "The Chalcolithic Mortuary Site near Mezad Aluf, Northern Negev Desert: A Preliminary Study," *BASOR* 248 (1982) 37–59.

4. G. Loud, *Megiddo II: Seasons of 1935–39, Text and Plates* (Chicago: University of Chicago Press, 1948) 45–46, figs. 101–2, 388, pp. 161–62.

5. R. S. Lamon and G. M. Shipton, *Megiddo I: Seasons of 1925–34, Strata I–V* (Chicago: University of Chicago Press, 1937) 4–11.

6. A good deal of charred grain was found in jars in rooms 6 and 7.

7. Cf. P. W. Lapp, "The 1963 Excavations at Ta'anek," *BASOR* 173 (1964) 4–44; idem, "Ta'anach by the Waters of Megiddo," *BA* 30 (1967) 2–27; idem, "The 1969 Excavations at Tell Ta'anek," *BASOR* 195 (1969) 2–49; and A. E. Glock, "Taanach," *EAEHL,* 1138–47.

8. Cf. L. E. Stager and S. R. Wolff, "Production and Commerce in Temple Courtyards: An Olive Press in the Sacred Precinct at Tel Dan," *BASOR* 243 (1981) 95–102, esp. 99.

9. Ibid., 98 n. 7; cf. B. Hesse, "Ancient Flocks and Barnyards," *American Schools of Oriental Research Newsletter* 37 (1985) 10–11, esp. 11.

10. Lapp, "The 1963 Excavations at Ta'anek," 26–32.

11. Lapp, "The 1969 Excavations at Tell Ta'anek," 42–44.

12. Cf. Stager and Wolff, "Production and Commerce in Temple Courtyards," 99–100.

13. Y. Aharoni, *Investigations at Lachish: The Sanctuary and the Residency (Lachish V)* (Tel Aviv: Institute of Archaeology, Tel Aviv University, 1975) 26–32 (hereafter cited as *Lachish V*).

14. Ibid., pl. 34 descr., p. 32

15. Ibid., 29–30.

16. Ibid, 31.

17. Ibid.

18. Cf. A. Biran, "Tel Dan," *BA* 37 (1974) 26–51; idem, "An Israelite Horned Altar at Dan," *BA* 37 (1974) 106–7; idem, "Notes and News: Tel Dan 1975," *IEJ* 26 (1976) 54–55; idem, "Notes and News: Tel Dan 1976," *IEJ* 26 (1976) 202–6; idem, "Notes and News: Tel Dan 1978," *IEJ* 28 (1978) 268–71; idem, "Two Discoveries at Tel Dan," *IEJ* 30 (1980) 89–98; idem, "Tell Dan Five Years Later," *BA* 43 (1980) 168–82; idem, "Notes and News: Tel Dan 1979, 1980," *IEJ* 31 (1981) 103–5; idem, "Notes and News: Tel Dan 1981," *IEJ* 32 (1982) 138–39. We will not deal with the canopied (?) structure at the entrance to the Israelite gateway (cf. Biran "Tel Dan," 43–47), since no evidence has been forwarded for its specifically cultic function. The supposed parallel with the gateway installation at Tell el-Far'ah (N), cited by Lapp and Shiloh (Lapp, "The 1963 Excavations at Ta'anek," 32; Y. Shiloh, "Iron Age Sanctuaries and Cult Elements in Palestine," *Symposia Celebrating the Seventy-fifth Anniversary of the American Schools of Oriental Research* (1900–1975) [ed. F. M. Cross; Cambridge, Mass.: ASOR, 1979] 147–57, esp. 152), has lost most of its convictional power since the publication of Stager and Wolff arguing that both the Tell el-Far'ah (N) and Ta'anach installations were olive presses ("Production and Commerce in Temple Courtyards"). It is not impossible, however, that each of these three installations did involve a steleform standing stone; cf. Shiloh, "Iron Age Sanctuaries and Cult Elements in Palestine," 152 n. 29.

19. Stager and Wolff, "Production and Commerce in Temple Courtyards," 95–96.

20. Cf. Shiloh, "Iron Age Sanctuaries," 153.

21. With reference to the Tell er-Ras structure, which may be seen as a parallel to the *"Bamoth"* at Tel Dan, cf. F. M. Cross, "The Priestly Tabernacle in the Light of Recent Research," *Temples and High Places in Biblical Times* (ed. A. Biran; Jerusalem: Hebrew Union College, 1981) 169–78; and E. F. Campbell, Jr., "Jewish Shrines of the Hellenistic and Persian Periods," *Symposia,* 159–67, esp. 161–62.

22. R. J. Bull, "An Archaeological Context for Understanding John 4:20," *BA* 38 (1975) 54–59.

23. G. W. Ahlström, "An Archaeological Picture of Iron Age Religions in Ancient Palestine," *StudOr* 56 (1984) 117–45, 15 n. 64. The simplest solution does seem to be to regard the *"Bamoth"* as platforms for major buildings, with the nearest parallel being the platform for the Lachish palace (cf. O. Tufnell, *Lachish III: The Iron Age. Text and Plates. The Wellcome-Marston Archaeological Research Expedition to the Near East* [London: Oxford University Press, 1953] 78–86). This much larger platform is actually a series of successive phases, Palace A being 32 m. square x 7 m. high, Palace B being a 32 x 46 m. southward extension of Palace A, and Palace C involving the addition of a monumental stairway and a strip about 3.5 m. wide running along the western side of Palaces A and B (ibid.). This solution has the drawback, however, that the interior structure of the Dan platform seems not to be casemated (according to the published reports), whereas all the presumed parallels are.

24. Cf. Biran, "Tell Dan Five Years Later," with J. B. Pritchard, *Recovering Sarepta, A Phoenician City* (Princeton: Princeton University Press, 1978) 93, fig. 88.

25. Biran, "Tell Dan Five Years Later," 179.

26. Ibid.

27. P. Wapnish, B. Hesse, and A. Ogilvy deal only with "Hellenistic or Roman refuse from a non-residential area" (p. 35) in their analysis of 1974 faunal remains from Area T, the sanctuary area ("The 1974 Collection of Faunal Remains from Tel Dan," *BASOR* 227 [1977] 35–62).

28. *Beer-sheba I: Excavations at Tel Beer-sheba, 1969–1971 Seasons* (ed. Y. Aharoni; Tel Aviv: Institute of Archaeology, Tel Aviv University, 1973); Y. Aharoni, "Excavations at Tel Beer-sheba, Preliminary Report of the Fourth Season 1972," *Tel Aviv* 1 (1974) 34–42; idem, "Tel Beersheba," *EAEHL,* 160–68; idem, "Excavations at Tel Beer-sheba, Preliminary Report of the Fifth and Sixth Seasons, 1973–1974," *Tel Aviv* 2 (1975) 154–56; Y. Yadin, "Beer-sheba: The High Place Destroyed by King Josiah," *BASOR* 222 (1976) 1–17; Z. Herzog, A. F. Rainey, and S. Moshkovitz, "The Stratigraphy at Beer-sheba and the Location of the Sanctuary," *BASOR* 225 (1977) 49–58.

29. Cf. Z. Herzog et al., "The Israelite Fortress at Arad," *BASOR* 254 (1984) 1–34, esp. 11.

30. Despite the arguments of Yadin, "Beer-sheba: The High Place Destroyed by King Josiah," and Herzog et al., "The Stratigraphy at Beer-sheba and the Location of the Sanctuary."

31. For the small cylindrical altar, see Aharoni, "Excavations at Tel Beer-sheba, Fourth Season 1972," 38. For the chalices, cf. Aharoni, *Beer-sheba I,* pl. 54: 4(?),

6–9, cf. pl. 87. Fragments of 4 to 5 chalices came from this general area. Note also the presence of 9 jugs (possibly deep one-handled cooking pots [?], note the pattern of smoke-smudging on pl. 40:3, cf. 40:1), 4 bowls, and 2 cooking pots.

32. Y. Aharoni, "Arad: Its Inscriptions and Temple," *BA* 31 (1968) 2–32; idem, "Arad: The Upper Mound," *EAEHL*, 82–89; Herzog et al., "The Israelite Fortress at Arad," 1–34; M. Aharoni and A. F. Rainey, "On the Israelite Fortress at Arad," *BASOR* 258 (1985) 73–74.

33. Herzog et al., "The Israelite Fortress at Arad," 22, fig. 15.

34. Ibid., 12, 32; cf. F. M. Cross, "Two Offering Dishes with Phoenician Inscriptions from the Sanctuary of ʿArad," *BASOR* 235 (1979) 75–78.

35. Cf. Aharoni, "Arad: Its Inscriptions and Temple," 11.

36. Ibid.

37. Ibid., 11. These kilns, however, are not mentioned in Herzog et al., "The Israelite Fortress at Arad," 1–34. They may have been stratigraphically misattributed.

38. Aharoni, "The Israelite Fortress at Arad," 1–34.

39. Cf., e.g., Y. Yadin, "A Note on the Stratigraphy at Arad," *IEJ* 15 (1965) 180; C. Nylander, "A Note on the Stonecutting and Masonry of Tel Arad," *IEJ* 17 (1967) 56–59; J. S. Holladay, "Of Sherds and Strata: Contributions Toward an Understanding of the Archaeology of the Divided Monarchy," *Magnalia Dei, The Mighty Acts of God* (ed. F. M. Cross, W. E. Lemke, and P. D. Miller; Garden City, N.Y.: Doubleday & Co., 1976) 253–93, chart 3, p. 275; W. G. Dever, "Material Remains and the Cult in Ancient Israel: An Essay in Archaeological Systematics," *The Word of the Lord Shall Go Forth: Essays in Honor of David Noel Freedman in Celebration of His Sixtieth Birthday* (ed. C. L. Meyers and M. O'Connor; Winona Lake, Ind.: Eisenbrauns, 1983) 571–87, esp. 573; M. Aharoni and A. Rainey, "On the Israelite Fortress at Arad," 73–74.

40. Materials attributed to the Stratum XI destruction could, in my opinion, be dated as late as the second half of the eighth century (!) (which would not rule out a much earlier founding date), but we have too few published data to be secure in this judgment.

41. J. W. Crowfoot, K. M. Kenyon, and E. L. Sukenik, *Samaria-Sebaste I: The Buildings at Samaria* (London: Palestine Exploration Fund, 1942) 23–24; J. W. Crowfoot, G. M. Crowfoot, and K. M. Kenyon, *Samaria-Sebaste III: The Objects from Samaria* (London: Palestine Exploration Fund, 1957) 76–84, 137–96.

42. E. L. Sukenik in J. W. Crowfoot, Kenyon, and Sukenik, *Samaria-Sebaste I*, 23–24.

43. G. M. Crowfoot in J. W. Crowfoot, G. M. Crowfoot, and K. M. Kenyon, *Samaria-Sebaste III*, 137. Given the perspective of time, it may be suggested that a few items, e.g., the high-based lamp, four-handled bowls, burnished red-slipped saucers, and the more "Assyrianizing" thinware drinking bowls, post-date Period VI (ibid., figs. 27:4, 20:1, 13:12–13, and 18:9–10 respectively).

44. Ibid., fig. 28:3.

45. Ibid., 76–82.

46. Ibid., 181.

47. Z. Meshel, *Kuntillet ʿAjrud: A Religious Center from the Time of the Judaean Monarchy on the Border of Sinai* (Israel Museum Catalogue 175;

Jerusalem: Israel Museum, 1978); Z. Meshel and C. Meyers, "The Name of God in the Wilderness of Zin," *BA* 39 (1976) 6–10.

48. Stager and Wolff, "Production and Commerce in Temple Courtyards," 98; P. Beck, "The Drawings from Ḥorvat Teiman (Kuntillet ʿAjrud)," *Tel Aviv* 9 (1982) 3–4; Dever, "Material Remains and the Cult," 576; Ahlström, "An Archaeological Picture of Iron Age Religions in Ancient Palestine," 132–35.

49. Beck, "The Drawings from Ḥorvat Teiman (Kuntillet ʿAjrud)," 43–45.

50. Ibid., 44.

51. Ibid., 46–47.

52. Herzog et al., "The Israelite Fortress at Arad," figs. 10, 16, 21. It should be remembered that there were 3 "bench rooms," according to this way of counting, in each of three phases of the Solomonic gateway at Gezer (J. S. Holladay in W. G. Dever et al., "Further Excavations at Gezer," *BA* 34 [1971] 115–16), and benches have also been found associated with several other Israelite and Judean gateways, including those at Tel Dan, Tell en-Nasbeh, and Khirbet el-Qom.

53. Meshel, *Kuntillet ʿAjrud,* 19.

54. K. M. Kenyon, *Jerusalem: Excavating 3000 Years of History* (London: Thames & Hudson, 1967); idem, "Excavations in Jerusalem 1967," *PEQ* (1968) 97–109; idem, *Digging Up Jerusalem* (New York: Praeger Publishers, 1974); T. A. Holland, "A Study of Palestinian Iron Age Baked Clay Figurines, with Special Reference to Jerusalem: Cave 1," *Levant* 9 (1977) 121–55.

55. Holland, "A Study of Palestinian Iron Age Baked Clay Figurines," 136.

56. Put another way, some 7.08 percent of the objects found fell into the categories treated here in this chapter as witnessing to "religious" behavior.

57. Holland, "A Study of Palestinian Iron Age Baked Clay Figurines," 151–52.

58. Ibid., 136.

59. Ibid., fig. 6. For more evidence concerning the domestic nature of the outer rooms, cf. Y. Shiloh, *Excavations at the City of David I* (*Qedem* 19; Jerusalem: Institute of Archaeology, Hebrew University, 1984) 28. In connection with our general topic, note also Shiloh's evidence for a "10th century B.C.E. ... cultic corner" in Area E1 (ibid., p. 27) and, among other cultic and possibly cultic artifacts cited, "a fill which contained fragments of some 58 ceramic fertility and anthropomorphic figurines," also from E1. This latter group is mentioned in connection with Stratum 12 remains, which might fit in with Kenyon's date ("+/− 700 B.C."; cf. Kenyon, "Excavations in Jerusalem 1967," 108–9) for the pottery from Cave 1, although it is not entirely clear, on the basis of Shiloh's published report, that the fill derives from this period (Shiloh, *Excavations at the City of David I,* 13). It should be noted that 4 vessels from Cave 1 bore graffiti (Kenyon, "Excavations in Jerusalem 1967," 109).

60. R. Amiran, "The Tumuli West of Jerusalem: Survey and Excavations, 1953," *IEJ* 8 (1958) 205–27.

61. Prior to heaping up rocks over the tumulus, these entrances, certainly the western one, were carefully blocked with laid-in courses of stone.

62. The description reads like either wind-sorted or worm-laid earth.

63. Amiran, "The Tumuli West of Jerusalem," 213–15.

64. Ibid., 216.

65. Amiran, in 1958, opted for "the second half of the eighth and the seventh

century B.C." (ibid., p. 222). A reasonable guess might be that we are, in the three tumuli, at differing dates intermediate between the Lachish III and II horizons.

66. V. Karageorghis, *Salamis in Cyprus: Homeric, Hellenistic and Roman* (London: Thames & Hudson, 1969) 151–64.

67. So Amiran, "The Tumuli West of Jerusalem," 226–27.

68. M. Dothan and D. N. Freedman, *Ashdod I: The First Season of Excavations, 1962* ('Atiqot, English Series 7; Jerusalem: Department of Antiquities and Museums, 1967) 571–87. Sources for Table 1 (below) include the preceding volume and M. Dothan, *Ashdod II–III: The Second and Third Seasons of Excavations, 1963, 1965, Soundings in 1967* (Text, Figures, and Plates: 'Atiqot, English Series 9–10; Jerusalem: Department of Antiquities and Museums, 1971).

69. Dothan and Freedman, *Ashdod I,* 132–33.

70. Ibid., fig. 38: 6–8.

71. Judging from the text, a good deal of the material found was not published.

72. Comparison of levels suggests that the pit was cut from local Stratum 3a levels and does not belong to Stratum 4, but it also seems likely that the sanctuary tradition persisted in the area following the destruction of the Stratum 4 sanctuary, so the inference that the pit was a *favissa* still seems a reasonable one.

73. J. B. Pritchard, *Sarepta: A Preliminary Report on the Iron Age, Excavations of the University Museum of the University of Pennsylvania, 1970–72* (Philadelphia: University Museum, University of Pennsylvania, 1975); idem, *Recovering Sarepta, A Phoenician City.*

74. Pritchard (*Recovering Sarepta, A Phoenician City,* 134) presents a less convincing reassessment, suggesting that the shrine was directly connected to "possible . . . living quarters for the shrine's custodian or priest." It is my impression that such an arrangement would be unique in the Middle East, at least for the period involved.

75. Pritchard, *Sarepta: A Preliminary Report,* 22.

76. Even the one supposedly nude figurine supporting both breasts with her hands seems to be wearing a clinging long flowing garment (ibid., fig. 46:3). For the seated pregnant woman, see W. Culican, "Dea Tyria Gravida," *AJBA* 1 (1969) 35–50; and H. Seedan, "Peace Figurines from the Levant," *Archéologie au Levant: Recueil à la mémoire de Roger Boccard* (Lyon: Maison de l'Orient, 1984) 107–21. (I owe these references to Michèle Daviau.)

77. Pritchard, *Sarepta: A Preliminary Report,* 22–37.

78. Pritchard, *Recovering Sarepta, A Phoenician City,* 104–5.

79. Ibid.

80. Ibid., 107–8.

81. Pritchard, *Sarepta: A Preliminary Report,* 40.

82. R. C. Haines, *Excavations in the Plain of Antioch II* (OIP 95; Chicago: University of Chicago Press, 1971) 53–55.

83. Five features of the complex may be less than familiar: (1) The excavators identified a short "bench" in the northwestern corner of the "cella," or center room of the temple. An unpaved section along the northern wall in the "sanctuary," equivalent to the Solomonic Temple's *"debir"* or "Holy of Holies," looks on plan as if it could have been the location of a similar "bench," perhaps removed in a later phase (cf. item 5, below), though this is certainly not the only possible

287

JOHN S. HOLLADAY, JR.

interpretation. (2) A tall stand with a rectangular "basin" on top, in appearance not all that far removed from an Israelite "horned altar," flanked the entrance steps to the right, rather like the supposed original positioning of the incense altars upon the steps of the Arad sanctuary. (3) The interior walls of the "cella" were coated with a thin white plaster, not unlike the interior whitewash treatment of the Ashdod sanctuary (bits of red- and blue-painted plaster were found in the innermost room of the Taʿyinat temple in association with the "altar"). (4) A double basin (?), built of ashlar stones set so that they formed a curb wall rising above the paved surface of the forecourt of the temple, stood some 17 m. east of the temple entrance. This must be compared with the stone-lined "basin" in the courtyard of the Arad sanctuary, supposedly a later addition to the sanctuary (see above) and, possibly, to the stone-lined pit at Ashdod, which, however, was not in front of the sanctuary proper. (5) Some sort of small mud-brick "table" or altar, probably rebuilt, to judge from the indications of an unpaved rectangle in the floor of the "sanctuary" which was only partially overlapped by the "table," stood immediately before the "altar" or podium, immediately reminiscent of the location of the "betyl" or possible incense altar in the Sarepta shrine.

84. Artifacts from "distributed" locations, i.e., scattered throughout occupational or other areas, will be dealt with in the section "The 'Distributed' Cultus," below. In the present section, we will be discussing only objects from "clustered" locations, i.e., from areas characterized by a high density of religiously affective artifacts. In the absence of counterindications, these areas may be interpreted as presumptive locations for corporate worship or other religiously motivated group activity.

85. The various styles do seem to be chronologically significant, and, as noted above, the Beer-sheba altar may be later than the period of the Judean monarchy.

86. A limited number of these stands have come from domestic contexts. Note that examples of the presumptive copper or bronze prototypes for these red-burnished stands, with attached bowls, appear in the Lachish Reliefs as part of the booty being taken from the despoiled city.

87. It seems reasonable to suppose that these are simply large-scale "chalices" for formal institutional use. Note that the examples from Lachish Stratum V Building 48 were described as burned on the interior. Cf. Aharoni, *Lachish V,* 26.

88. An unpublished slide in the collection of the Department of Near Eastern Studies at the University of Toronto shows a chalice in materials from Jerusalem Cave 1. (My attention was drawn to this slide by Michèle Daviau.)

89. Chalices are frequently found in earlier Iron II tombs and also, in reduced numbers, in domestic stratification. They are among the most often painted or otherwise elaborated forms in the early Iron II, even down to the time of the fall of Samaria; cf. fig. 25 in J. W. Crowfoot, G. M. Crowfoot, and Kenyon, *Samaria-Sebaste III.* It would not be amiss to note here that their cultic associations are firmly rooted in Canaanite rituals of the Late Bronze II (cf. W. Wreszinski, *Atlas zur altägyptischen Kulturgeschichte* (Part II; Leipzig: J. C. Hinrichs, 1935) pls. 36, 53, 54a, 55a, 56–58, 71, 78, 79, 107–9, 145–47, 183; A. J. Spalinger, "A Canaanite Ritual Found in Egyptian Military Reliefs," *Journal of the Society for the Study of Egyptian Antiquities* 8 (1978) 47–60.

90. Cf. the central thesis (which to my mind is undoubtedly correct) of G. W.

Ahlström's stimulating monograph *Royal Administration and National Religion in Ancient Palestine* (Leiden: E. J. Brill, 1982), a book that came into my hands after the structure of the present study was completed.

91. This is not to say that either the governor or the principal priest of a Shephela town acted totally in accord with his co-appointee in the Judean hill country. But each was ultimately to be true to the dictates of the Jerusalem court in all matters of importance or to be considered a rebel.

92. Among other reasons, the mere fact that the state religion was in the business of collecting tithes and gifts on a large scale mandated its close control by the same general authority responsible for levying other sorts of taxes. Cf. Ahlström, *Royal Administration*, 2, 8, 44ff.

93. Absence of such evidence would be taken as a sign of an extraordinarily united religious polity.

94. The Jerusalem Temple probably is a case in point. For the difficulty of missing a major structure, cf. Tel Dan, above.

95. The religious ambivalence of the typical Japanese citizen comes to mind. At various points in time a family may participate in a Shinto wedding or infant presentation ceremony, make pilgrimages to Buddhist temples and Shinto shrines, have their fortune told by Tao popular diviners, meet in each other's houses in voluntary devotional cults to individual bodhisattvas (Buddhist divinities), celebrate Christmases in addition to periodic Buddhist and Shinto festivals, be buried following funeral masses in a Buddhist temple, memorialized in Buddhist ceremonies, and throughout all be maintaining both a Shinto shrine and a Buddhist altar in the home (H. B. Earhart, *Japanese Religion: Unity and Diversity* [3d ed.; Belmont, Calif.: Wadsworth Publishing Co., 1982] 7–16). In a recent poll, 82 percent of Japanese men surveyed denied having any religious belief. In another survey, 70 percent of the respondents "stated that they had no personal religion and were not affiliated directly with any religious group. Yet over 80 percent thought it was desirable to have a religion! . . . [Finally,] official statistics . . . report that over 160 million persons are related to Japanese religious organizations in a country with a population of some 110 millions!" Cf. E. E. Best, "The Definition of Religion and the Interpretation of Evidence: The Role of Religion in Contemporary Japanese Society," *Studies in Religion* 6 (1977) 14; Earhart, *Japanese Religion*, 3–4; R. S. Ellwood and R. Pilgrim, *Japanese Religion* (Englewood Cliffs, N.J.: Prentice-Hall, 1985) 126–44. I owe the insight and references to my daughter, Karen Holladay.

96. Without making a big thing of it, we probably should call attention to the fact that the hypothetico-deductive approach is far better than induction for interpreting dispersed fragments of an ancient whole. One can all too easily construct chimeras, as, I would argue, has generally been done in the past by students seeking inductively to interpret the very topic under discussion.

97. Item *a* is too basic to require extensive comment. In the absence of distinctively "religious" artifacts, at a minimum in buildings architecturally analogous to the buildings in question (the function of these religious artifacts being inferred on the basis of ethnographic analogy), we could have no particular warrant for terming any particular structure "religious."

98. I.e., since the temple, sanctuary, or shrine is intended to be an important

part of the general cultural milieu of the populace, the building should not be a "closed box." A significant part of the sanctuary might reasonably be expected to be open to public view, even if access to certain more sacred portions of the structure were reserved to priests.

99. In a sovereign nation-state of the period it is hard to see the possibility of genuinely "foreign" shrines except, possibly, in totally domestic situations or within officially sanctioned "Karum-"like trading colonies or military garrisons. An excellent example of the latter, as Paul Dion reminds me, is the Jewish "temple" at Elephantine. An example of the former might be the apparent private shrine, featuring a fenestrated stand decorated in "Cypro-Phoenician" fashion and Phoenician-style cult mask, in Room 44 of the anomalous one-story House 14 in Stratum V at Hazor. Cf. Y. Yadin et al., *Hazor I: An Account of the First Season of Excavations, 1955* (Jerusalem: Hebrew University, 1958) pls. 57:22, 60:10. For the building plan, cf. Y. Yadin et al., *Hazor II: An Account of the Second Season of Excavations, 1956* (Jerusalem: Hebrew University, 1960) pl. 203. Given the practice of binding treaties through royal marriages, it seems reasonable to hypothesize that a major foreign wife's palace or palace quarter might have a shrine, with officiating priests, suitable for her private worship and that of her attending ladies.

100. The patterning of miniature "cuboidal" limestone altars in the Judean setting seems to be a case in point.

101. The patterning throughout both Israel and Judah of various styles and substyles of female figurines probably provides several sets of cases in point.

102. Were Samaria E 207 architecturally recoverable, it would probably show differences in this area as well.

103. A. L. Oppenheim, *Ancient Mesopotamia: Portrait of a Dead Civilization* (Chicago: University of Chicago Press, 1964) 118; Ahlström, *Royal Administration, 1–2,* 10ff..

104. These examples are all pre-Shishak. If this situation persists, it may become important to inquire into the reasons for there being no equivalent shrines of the post-Solomonic period. At the present, I am inclined to regard this as a statistical eccentricity and would regard some of the chalices and other cultic implements from the Area B "Citadel" at Hazor and its immediate vicinity as witnessing to some sort of semipublic shrine in that building. Note also the evidence for either a well-outfitted shrine or a sanctuary, probably the latter, from late-eighth-century Lachish (cf. n. 86, above).

105. In Jerusalem Cave 1 there were 16 female figurines, 21 horse-and-rider figurines, 7 model birds, and 38 model animals. At Samaria E207, there were 23 female figurines, 2 heads from "riders," 0 birds, 120 model animals (including horses from "horse-and-rider" figurines). The ratio of animals, including birds, to female figurines in Jerusalem Cave 1 is 2.8 to 1 (or 4.1 to 1, if horse-and-rider figurines are included with the animals). At Samaria the equivalent figures are 5.2 to 1 (or 5.3 to 1 if the riders' heads are added to the group of animal figurines).

106. J. S. Holladay, "Archaeology and the Religion of Israel," manuscript in progress.

107. J. W. Crowfoot, Kenyon, and Sukenik, *Samaria-Sebaste I,* 24–25, cf. fig. 11 and sects. 5–5, 6–6. Probably not too much should be made of this last point,

however, since the tomb probably is much later (as suggested by its typology) than the date of the cultic use of the area.

108. Ibid., 24.

109. This is not to say that either Philistine or Phoenician cultic practices—as witnessed by their material culture complements—are being imported wholesale into either Israel or Judah. We have noted one case of possible direct importation in n. 99, above, probably the private shrine of a Phoenician individual living at Hazor, but this is not what we are witnessing on the broader scale. Cultural diffusion—if that is what is involved—and direct importation are two completely different processes. Both Israel and Judah have their own characteristic assemblages of these materials and therefore presumably their own characteristic domestic cultus, which must be presumed to have been thought suitably "Israelite" or "Judean." The point that is being made at this juncture is that things like figurines of clothed women (employing the same iconography as, particularly, the Phoenician exemplars), model furniture, model animals, and the like *are characteristic furnishings of unquestionable shrines and sanctuaries in countries bordering Israel and Judah* and cannot, in these settings, be passed off as children's playthings, "talismans to aid in childbirth," or the like. While these last-mentioned suggestions are certainly not the only set of interpretations current, Albright's support has undoubtedly helped secure their dominant position in contemporary thought. Cf., e.g., W. F. Albright, "Astarte Plaques and Figurines from Tell Beit Mirsim," *Mélanges syriens offerts à M. René Dussaud* (Paris: Paul Geuthner, 1939) 1. 107–20, 119; idem, *From the Stone Age to Christianity* (2d ed.; Garden City, N.Y.: Doubleday Anchor Books, 1957) 311; idem, *Archaeology and the Religion of Israel* (2d ed.; Baltimore: Johns Hopkins University Press, 1946) 115; M. Tadmor, "Female Cult Figurines in Late Canaan and Early Israel: Archaeological Evidence," *Studies in the Period of David and Solomon and Other Essays* (ed. T. Ishida; Winona Lake, Ind.: Eisenbrauns, 1982) 139–73; W. G. Dever, "Material Remains and the Cult in Ancient Israel," 574. This general hypothesis no longer seems adequate to the facts as we presently know them. Since we can, at least in part, understand the functions of closely similar artifacts in Philistia and Phoenicia, we are in a better position to understand their function in Israel and Judah, particularly—as is noted below—in view of their concentrations in what must, in any serious interpretation, be viewed as "cult areas" in both Israel and Judah. The clay figurines and plastic decorations upon cult stands found at the new shrine, presumably Edomite, recently discovered by Itzhaq Beit-Arieh at Horvat Qitmit in the Eastern Negev (paper read at annual meeting of ASOR in Anaheim, 1985, cf. *AAR/SBL Abstracts 1985* [Decatur, Ga.: Scholars Press, 1985] 199), point in much the same direction and further demonstrate the fundamental difference obtaining between all "Establishment" Israelite and Judean shrines and sanctuaries found to date and those of their nearest neighbors. Further, with reference to ethnographically witnessed distinctions between magical items, cult figurines, initiation figurines, and toys, cf. M. Voight, "Functional Interpretation: Figurines," *Hajji Firuz Tepe, Iran: The Neolithic Settlement* (R. H. Dyson, Jr., gen. ed.; Hasanlu Excavation Reports, vol. 1; Philadelphia: University Museum, University of Pennsylvania, 1984) 186–95.

110. Cf. the unfinished study cited in n. 105 above. The relevant publications

are W. F. Albright, *The Excavation of Tell Beit Mirsim,* vol. 3: *The Iron Age (AASOR* 21–22; New Haven: ASOR, 1943); C. C. McCown, *Tell en-Nasbeh I: Archaeological and Historical Results* (Berkeley and New Haven: Palestine Institute of Pacific School of Religion and ASOR, 1947); J. C. Wampler, *Tell en-Nasbeh II: The Pottery* (Berkeley and New Haven: Palestine Institute of Pacific School of Religion and ASOR, 1947); Yadin et al., *Hazor I;* Yadin et al., *Hazor II;* Y. Yadin et al., *Hazor III-IV: An Account of the Third and Fourth Season of Excavations, 1957–1958* (Plates; Jerusalem: Hebrew University, 1961); Aharoni, *Beer-sheba I.*

111. A minor slackness (+ / − 2%) is introduced into the data by virtue of the fact that some house plans at Tell Beit Mirsim are incomplete or poorly preserved. A greater source of uncertainty is introduced by the fact that "a good many other fragments [of pillar-based figurines] were found but were so shapeless that no record was kept" (Albright, *The Excavation of Tell Beit Mirsim,* 3.69).

112. Aharoni, *Beer-sheba I.*

113. Given the probability that the typical Judean and Israelite house was two-storied, with the ground floor given over to storage, animal stalling areas, and work space (Holladay n.d. A), it stands to reason that we would not have recovered many (any?) typically Judean or Israelite domestic shrines *in situ.* This observation also helps to explain why items probably originally clustered together in the major upstairs room often wind up in different ground floor rooms. It is not an impossibility that the Taʿanach "Cult Structure" is an exception to this rule. Cf. also Locus 44 at Hazor, which may be the domestic shrine of a non-Israelite (probably Phoenician) resident (see n. 99, above).

114. W. G. Dever, "Iron Age Epigraphic Material from the Area of Khirbet el-Kôm," *HUCA* 40/41 (1969/70) 139–204, esp. 158–89; idem, "Asherah, Consort of Yahweh? New Evidence from Kuntillet ʿAjrud," *BASOR* 255 (1984) 21–22; A. Lemaire, "Les inscriptions de Khirbet el-Qom et l'ashérah de YHWH," *RB* 84 (1977) 597–608; J. Naveh, "Graffiti and Dedications," *BASOR* 235 (1979) 27–30, esp. 28–29; Z. Zevit, "The Khirbet el-Qom Inscription Mentioning a Goddess," *BASOR* 255 (1984) 39–47.

115. Naveh, "Graffiti and Dedications," 28–29; Meshel, *Kuntillet ʿAjrud;* Dever, "Asherah, Consort of Yahweh?"

116. F. M. Cross, *CMHE,* 34; Dever, "Asherah, Consort of Yahweh?"; Zevit, "The Khirbet el-Qom Inscription Mentioning a Goddess." For the reasonableness of the assumption that one major goddess is dominant in a particular cultus at a particular place and time, cf. J. B. Pritchard, *Palestinian Figurines in Relation to Certain Goddesses Known Through Literature* (New Haven: American Oriental Society, 1943) 85.

117. Cross, *CMHE,* 28–35; R. A. Oden, *Studies in Lucian's "De Syria Dea"* HSM 15; Missoula, Mont.: Scholars Press, 1977) 82–92, 98; Dever, "Asherah, Consort of Yahweh?" 29.

118. Note, additional to Dever, "Asherah, Consort of Yahweh?" 24–25, and more nearly in our time period, another goddess seated upon a cherub throne from Ajia Irini in Cyprus: E. Gjerstad, *The Swedish Cyprus Expedition: Finds and Results of the Excavations in Cyprus 1927–1931* (vol. 2, Plates; Stockholm: Swedish Cyprus Expedition, 1935), pl. 233: 10, 11.

119. So Cross, *CMHE,* 32–34. For an example of the "Sign of Tannit" found at 'Akko, see M. Dothan, "A Sign of Tanit from Tel 'Akko," *IEJ* 24 (1974) 43–49.

120. Cf. Y. Yadin, "Symbols of Deities at Zinjirli, Carthage, and Hazor," *Near Eastern Archaeology in the Twentieth Century: Essays in Honor of Nelson Glueck* (ed. J. A. Sanders; Garden City, N.Y.: Doubleday & Co., 1970) 218–19; Oden, *Studies,* 141. The differing placement of the arms in the typical Judean pillar-based or Israelite hollow-based figurine vis-à-vis the "Sign of Tannit" probably reflects the realities of the terra-cotta medium. Although female figurines with raised arms are common enough during this general period in Cyprus, they are either extremely rare or nonexistent in Israel and Judah. Many fewer figurines would have made it off the seller's mat in one piece if an alternative placement of the hands had not been effected. Despite their evident fragility, these figurines are designed to be as durable as possible. They seem to have been made locally and distributed either through the market economy or through pilgrim traffic at yet unknown major extramural shrines. Either explanation would suit the area-wide distribution of these regionally distinct figurine types, whose typology is more pronounced than any other class of artifact in the "distributed" repertory.

121. Assuming, against all probability, that *all* "debris" materials, streets, undefined open areas, pits, silo fills and cistern deposits were to be credited to the life of the site *prior* to the ten or twenty years preceding the posited final two (!) destructions, we would have, for these two or three centuries' accumulations, a total of only some 17 pillar-based figurines and 14 zoomorphs against 23 pillar-based figurines and 16 zoomorphs coming from the destruction debris. And, since most of the restorable street materials, debris, and general area materials probably stem from one or another of these destructions, we are left with a considerably smaller body of material reasonably antedating these destructions by more than a handful of years: 8 pillar-based figurines and 4 zoomorphs (against 32 pillar-based figurines and 26 zoomorphs coming from this broader definition of destruction debris). Using the lower date for Lachish III, fifty to seventy-five years would easily account for all the data, and would probably be too long. As with other typological arguments, placing Lachish III more than a hundred years before Lachish II makes things more difficult. This is not, however, the forum to debate this topic.

122. Holladay in Dever et al., "Further Excavations at Gezer," 114–15; Holladay, "Of Sherds and Strata," n. 82.

123. This looks nothing at all like any of the well-known Late Bronze Age bronze serpents.

124. See the "Endnote."

125. Cf. D. Ussishkin, *The Conquest of Lachish by Sennacherib* (Tel Aviv: Institute of Archaeology, Tel Aviv University, 1982) pls. 84–85, 107. R. Amiran's recent suggestion ("The Lion Statue and the Libation Tray from Tell Beit Mirsim," *BASOR* 222 [1975] 29–40) that the limestone lion and the lion-decorated basin from Tell Beit Mirsim should be associated with an Iron Age sanctuary there (Albright dated both to the Late Bronze Age) would be welcome evidence for expected cultic activity at Tell Beit Mirsim, but it flies in the face of the clear evidence for this iconography, generally exemplified as lion orthostats guarding entrances in Late Bronze Age Palestinian (and closely related) temples and its

total absence (unless the bronze weight from Arad were accorded undue significance) from presently known Israelite or Judean shrines and sanctuaries (Amiran does, however, cite a "9th century B.C. rock-cut tomb with representations of lions flanking the entrance," published by D. Ussishkin in "Tombs from the Israelite Period at Tel Eton," *Tel Aviv* 1 [1974] 109–127). See, e.g., the Late Bronze Age "Stelae Temple" and the Late Bronze Age phases of the Hazor Area H temple (Y. Yadin, *Hazor, the Head of All Those Kingdoms* [London: Oxford University Press, 1972] 72 and 83–95; cf. Yadin et al., *Hazor I*, 89–90, pls. 29:3, 30:1, 2, and *Hazor III–IV*, pls. 118:1—120:2, 328:1–3), and the Late Bronze Age temple in Alalakh Level I(b) (C. L. Woolley, *Alalakh: An Account of the Excavations at Tell Atchana in the Hatay, 1937–1949* [London: Oxford University Press, 1955] 83, fig. 34). Aharoni cites yet another head from a lion orthostat found in Late Bronze II levels "near the entryway" of the MB II–LB I Area A "Long Temple" at Hazor (Y. Aharoni, *The Archaeology of the Land of Israel* [Philadelphia: Westminster Press, 1982] 130, cf. Yadin et al., *Hazor III–IV*, pls. 13:4, 329:1–3). Note also the difficulty Amiran has in finding *crouching* Iron Age parallels to the Tell Beit Mirsim lion (Amiran, "The Lion Statue and the Libation Tray from Tell Beit Mirsim"), but note that this is exactly the posture of the orthostat from the Area H temple at Hazor, and probably that of the Area A fragment as well. The recent find of a group of horned altars at Tel Miqne, dated by the excavators to the "7th c. B.C.E.," may provide further evidence for the operation of the established cultus late in Judean history (cf. the photograph and caption on the prospectus for the fifth season of excavations of the Tel Miqne-Ekron Excavation Project).

126. A possible inference from the above might be that the primary participants in this cultus were women, but I do not presently see any way of testing this particular hypothesis, unless it were, possibly, through ethnographic analogy.

127. Such an arrangement most satisfactorily explains the contents of some of the Arad Letters, and possibly also Lachish Letter III which deals with the conduct of an unidentified prophet (*Ancient Near Eastern Texts Relating to the Old Testament* [ed. J. B. Pritchard; Princeton: Princeton University Press, 1955] 322).

128. Should further evidence develop for a belated radical centralization of the cultus in either Israel or Judah, this/these popular explosion/s could be attributed (hardly an original hypothesis) to the filling of a religious vacuum caused by removal of readily available cult symbols to remote locations. Cf. already the evidence of Beer-sheba, where the heavily supported distributed cultus appears coincident with the use of altar blocks as ordinary construction material and, possibly, the evidence of Arad. The arguments of Herzog et al., which could be taken as support of such a hypothesis, are unfortunately weakened by excessive reliance upon biblical warrants coupled with a simultaneous neglect of the reporting of the actual archaeological data unaltered by prior interpretation (Herzog et al., "The Israelite Fortress at Arad," 1–34). In my judgment, the presently available data do not unequivocally support such a hypothesis, although, on balance, it seems both attractive and possible with respect to Judah.

129. A draft version of this study was kindly read by my colleague, Paul E.

Dion, and my student, Michèle Daviau. Both offered many helpful suggestions. Any remaining errors, omissions, or distortions are mine.

ENDNOTE

According to the archaeologically witnessed materials, the officially sanctioned religious praxis of Israel and Judah seems to have been basically aniconic during both the united monarchy and the divided monarchy, especially if one exempts the floral motifs of the early chalices and tall stands with their bowls. At least two things need to be said on this point.

1. Such restraint in the use of symbols stands in sharp contrast to the emerging picture—featuring bull, lion, cherub, and anthropomorphic motifs—of cultic remains from the premonarchical and, perhaps, early monarchical period: e.g., the figurine from the "Bull Site," and the Taʿanach, Megiddo, and Jerusalem cult stands. Cf. A. Mazar, "The 'Bull Site'—An Iron Age I Open Cultic Place," *BASOR* 247 (1982) 27–42; Lapp, "The 1969 Excavations at Tell Taʿanek," 42–44; H. G. May and R. Engberg, *Material Remains of the Megiddo Cult* (Chicago: University of Chicago Press, 1935) 13–17, pls. 13–15; Shiloh, *Excavations at the City of David I*, 17, pl. 29:2. Whether these elements are antecedent to the "established" or "nonconformist" cultus (or both) is, however, a matter that cannot decisively be determined at the present time (but see below).

2. This consistently aniconic tendency in the preserved remains is astonishing, given what we know, or think we know, about the official cultus on the basis of biblical literature. (Here we must momentarily set aside our methodological exclusion of textual evidence from the Hebrew Bible). Certainly, cherub, bull, and lion iconography, to say nothing of palm trees and various floral motifs, forms a vital part of the symbolic burden of the Solomonic Temple as described in the Book of Kings. An emphasis on bull symbolism later seems to distinguish at least some factions of the northern cultus vis-à-vis the dominant cherub symbolism of the Jerusalem cultus (cf., however, the much more complex structure reconstructed by Cross, *CMHE*, 72–75, 198–215). Physical expressions of these motifs are, moreover, all very familiar from furniture ornamentation such as the Samaria Ivories (including those objects, which apparently also included bronze bowls, transported to Nimrud). Cf. J. W. Crowfoot and G. M. Crowfoot, *Samaria-Sebaste 2, Early Ivories from Samaria* (London: Palestine Exploration Fund, 1938), and Y. Yadin, "A Note on the Nimrud Bronze Bowls," in R. D. Barnett's "Layard's Nimrud Bronzes and Their Inscriptions," *EI* 8 (1967) 1*–7*. That these motifs were not peculiar to just one lot of furniture in one palace of the Northern Kingdom is witnessed by, e.g., the Hazor pyxis, handle and cosmetic spoon (Yadin et al., *Hazor I*, pls. 155, 150–51; idem, *Hazor II*, pls. 167–68). These northern exemplars are now partially paralleled by floral motifs in wood carvings from a domestic setting in early-sixth-century B.C.E. Jerusalem (Shiloh, *Excavations at the City of David I*, 19, pl. 34:1). Thus, although these motifs seem to have been Syro-Phoenician in origin, which would fit in well with the traditions of Hiram of Tyre being the prime contractor for the Jerusalem Temple (1 Kgs 5:1—6:1; 9:10–14), during most of the period of the monarchy such imagery was readily available to ancient Israelite artists and craftsmen and,

indeed, was a feature of daily life for at least the elite members of Israelite and Judean society. It could be hypothesized that such decoration, in the sphere of religion, was limited to the Jerusalem Temple (see below), but this goes against the intentionality of symbolic representation within a cultic system.

Even if most of the expected ornamentation of subsidiary cult centers (and Dan must be reckoned a major cult center) was thought to be in the form of gilded wood paneling, doors, and furnishings on the one hand and discrete gold and bronze objects and furniture on the other, and therefore subject to looting, we might expect to have found by now either some traces of gold foil (cf. the finds, by two excavation teams, in the Late Bronze Age sanctuary at Lachish [D. Ussishkin, "Excavations at Tel Lachish—1973–1977, Preliminary Report," *Tel Aviv* 5 (1978) 10, 20–21, pl. 8] and at least one scrap from the Area H temple at Hazor [Yadin et al., *Hazor III–IV*, pl. 343:39]), ivory inlays (cf. O. Tufnell, C. H. Inge, and G. L. Harding, *Lachish II: The Fosse Temple* [London: Oxford University Press, 1940] pls. 16–21), or provincial clay imitations of such furnishings. In fact, it is not impossible that the Ta'anach, Megiddo, and Jerusalem "Cult Stands" might be exactly such provincializing substitutes for the bronze wheeled stands of 1 Kgs 7:27–37 (as opposed to being "model shrines"). In favor of the attribution of these stands to a nonconforming cultus, however, might be the fact that they portray figures, e.g., naked women, "women-at-the-window," and men bearing offerings (?), not otherwise cited in connection with the Jerusalem Temple or its cultus. Note that all of these last-mentioned symbols except the naked woman are also featured on archaeologically attested four-sided bronze stands (a naked woman *is* featured on the tripod stands—playing the double oboe). Most of these stands come from Cyprus, though one was excavated at Megiddo, and their close connections, both in terms of symbolism and overall construction, with the biblical descriptions have long been apparent. E.g., May and Engberg, *Material Remains of the Megiddo Cult*, 19–20; H. W. Catling, *Cypriote Bronzework in the Mycenaean World* (Oxford Monographs on Classical Archaeology; Oxford: Clarendon Press, 1964) 203–10, pls. 33–36; O. W. Muscarella, ed., *Ladders to Heaven: Art Treasures from Lands of the Bible* (Toronto: McClelland & Stewart, 1981) 254–60. For that matter, it is fully within the realm of possibility that the rudely formed Megiddo four-sided bronze stand (not wheeled) is Solomonic in date, although, in that case, the symbolism would be completely out of line with biblical descriptions and it seems better to take it as being somewhat earlier. In any case, it is inconceivable that so perfect a description of the Solomonic wheeled carts could have been written were not actual examples present and well known to the writer of the present description. And, since all the examples of these wheeled bronze carts which we presently know seem to be concentrated either at the very end of the Late Bronze II Age or early in the Iron Age, this seems to attest not only to their actual *origins* (i.e., the exemplars in the Solomonic Temple) in the reign of Solomon but to their continued *presence* right down to the time of the writing of this description. Given the clear statement in 2 Kgs 16:17 that Ahaz "cut off the frames of the stands and removed the laver from them," such an argument, as B. Halpern reminds me, has obvious implications for the documentary history behind the Deuteronomistic historian's work (Halpern [oral communication] sees Ahaz as being—despite his bad press from the Deuteronomic historian—an important iconoclastic reformer of the cult). This astonishing fidelity of the description of the wheeled carts, moreover, tends to validate most of the other descriptions of the decoration and furnishings of the Solomonic Temple, although, here again, we cannot be certain of the date of composition of this/these document/s.

All of this seems most reasonable and, in fact, represents the present writer's operative understanding of the principal furnishings of the Solomonic Temple. But, as we have already noted, it does not easily square with the archaeological evidence we have reviewed above. If these symbols were such a vital part of the established cultus during the united monarchy and if they seem to have continued to be functioning elements of the Jerusalem Temple right down to, at the least, the second half of the eighth century B.C.E., we would expect to find the same set of symbols at least marginally present in the assemblages reviewed above.

Based upon the above line of reasoning, a number of possibilities emerge. The following four are only a selection from the more probable hypotheses.

1. We may reasonably predict a major find of precisely this sort of evidence from a provincial sanctuary. A slight variation of this hypothesis would have it that all symbolic representations either were in perishable media (paint, ungilded wood, weavings, etc.) or were so intrinsically valuable (gold or silver objects, gilded wood, ivory, bronzes, etc.) that it is highly improbable that any of them would be left unplundered. Against the former version is the fact that we already have a reasonable, self-consistent sampling of cultic materials from more than one period and more than one region of the study area, and the laws of statistical probability dictate that future finds most reasonably would be expected to follow the same trend. At a minimum we can confidently state that terra-cotta or stone artifacts employing these symbols are *not* a major feature of the typical "Establishment" sanctuary or shrine of either the united or the divided monarchy even though the symbolism seems to be characteristic of cultic artifacts generally to be ascribed to the period of the united monarchy. The decisive distinction between Israelite and Judean "Establishment" sanctuaries and shrines and those of either their neighbors or the "Nonconformist" tradition is enough to secure this line of argumentation unless or until such a "find" is made. Against the latter version is the evidence, lightly alluded to above, regarding the extant evidence for similarly nondurable or valuable cult furnishings in sanctuaries of the Late Bronze Age.

2. Another hypothesis, briefly noted above, seeking to account for this disparity between archaeological evidence and biblical data might hold that only the Jerusalem Temple itself employed such symbolism, either by virtue of Tyrian input or by virtue of its special relationship to the symbolic ornamentation of the royal palace (e.g., 1 Kgs 10:18–20). This seems contraindicated by a variety of factors, including: *(a)* the lack, to date, of evidence pointing in a similar direction from either Samaria or Tel Dan; *(b)* the violence such disjunctiveness in the set of operative cult symbols would do to any concept of a hierarchical cultic establishment, the evidence for which seems, on the basis of the present study, to be well established; and *(c)* the ubiquity of lion, bull, and cherub symbolism in various levels of biblical literature.

3. A hypothesis similar to the above would be one suggesting that the cultus developed—whether progressively or through convulsive changes such as the

Ahazic (??), Hezekianic (?), and Josianic reforms—a more aniconic/iconoclastic tradition through time (e.g., the transition from predominantly iconographic to predominantly aniconic glyptic on private seals), with only the great antiquity, unquestioned authenticity to the Yahwistic cultus, and sanctity of the Jerusalem Temple materials preventing their removal. The traditions of the bronze serpent Nehushtan (2 Kgs 18:4b), whose parallels from the Late Bronze Age become more and more numerous, and the "horses . . . [and] chariots of the sun" (2 Kgs 23:11) might be cited in defense of such a hypothesis. Against this would seem to be the fact that much of our best archaeological evidence for an aniconic tendency in cult furnishings comes precisely from the period of the united monarchy (Megiddo Loc. 2081, the apparent "Establishment" materials from the vicinity of Building 10 at Megiddo, and Building 49 in Level V at Lachish). (Note, however, the presence of floral motifs on the composite tall stands or "incense burners" from both sites.)

4. A contrary hypothesis to any of the above would argue that the "Establishment" cultus was essentially as it appears—however defectively—in subsets of the temple apparatus found in presently known sanctuaries and shrines. From the purely archaeological perspective, this must be the favored hypothesis (see the appeal to statistical probability in item 1 above). Against this are all the arguments marshaled above in defense of the essential authenticity of the physical descriptions of the decoration and fittings of the Solomonic Temple as these are related to us in a document stemming from at least the last half of the Judean monarchy.

Finally, where does this leave us? For purposes of analyzing the place in Israelite and Judean society of the various cult centers so far described in the archaeological literature, it does not matter very much whether iconography plays a major or an insignificant role in the "Established" cultus. Our hypothetical model is essentially neutral with regard to (appropriate) iconographic representation, which, however, obviously does play a major role in the "Nonconformist" tradition. On the other hand, the presently observed disparity does seem to drive a wedge between "archaeological" and "textual" reconstructions of Israelite and Judean cult settings, particularly with respect to the period of the united monarchy. For the future, much will depend upon the character of forthcoming archaeological finds. If the present tendency were to continue, and materials just now finding their first publication seem to point in this direction, we would increasingly find it difficult to maintain our earlier understandings of the decoration and furnishings of the Solomonic Temple. On the other hand, most of the richness, color, and texture of the ancient world survives only marginally—barring exceptional circumstances of preservation—in archaeologically recoverable form. If even a smattering of data supportive of a richer iconography—crafted on less durable or more precious materials—were to emerge, perhaps as a result of more careful processing of carbonized wood, fabric, and bone remains (cf. the carbonized remains of furniture, noted above, recovered by the City of David team under the direction of Y. Shiloh), we would be in a much better position to bridge the intellectual gap between "hard" archaeological evidence and "soft" literary traditions. One possible straw in the wind might be the ivory pomegranate finial to a scepter (?), inscribed *lbẙ[t yhw]h̊ qdš khnm,* "Belonging to the temp[le of YHW]H, sacred to the priests," published by A. Lemaire in *RB* 88 (1981) 236–39 (I am indebted to Paul Dion for the reminder and suggestion). As is often said in archaeological circles, "The answers lie below."

PART TWO

HISTORY AND CHARACTER

15

The Tribal League at Sinai

MOSHE WEINFELD

Sinai/Horeb[1] is named *hr h'lhym* ("the mountain of God") even before the divine call to Moses at the burning bush (Exod 3:1) and prior to the revelation to the people of Israel (Exod 4:27; 18:5). It has therefore been rightly observed[2] that this mountain was venerated long before Moses, as may be learned also from the fact that Jethro, the Midianite/Qenite priest, comes to the "mountain of God" (Exod 18:5) in order to sacrifice and partake of the holy meal "in the presence of God" (v 12). The story about this sacrificial meal has no connection with the Sinaitic theophany, which dominates Exodus 19—24,[3] and therefore scholars have made the suggestion that the sacrificial ceremony in Exod 18:12 reflects some kind of covenant between the Midianites/Qenites and the Israelites[4] (see below).

Recently Z. Weisman[5] analyzed the passages where *hr h'lhym* ("the mount of God") appears and he reached the conclusion that "the mount of God" should be seen as an extraterritorial holy site that served various tribes and ethnic groups in the area. Indeed Jethro is said to have gone *to the desert ('l hmbdr)* where Moses was encamped at "the mount of God" (Exod 18:5) and after meeting Moses and advising him about the administration of justice (vv 13–26), returned to his own land (v 27; cf. Num 10:30). Similarly, whenever the Israelites express their wish to go and worship their god, they say that they want *to go a distance of three days into the wilderness to sacrifice* (Exod 3:18; 5:3; 8:23), which points to a place far from the settled region. That the site was venerated by the nomadic tribes in the area may also be learned from the fact that the "mountain of Elohim" is associated with the divine epithet, "the god of the *'Ibrîm*" (Exod 3:18; 5:3).[6] Without committing ourselves to the identification of *'Ibrîm* with the *Ḥabiru*,[7] it is nevertheless clear that the term *'Ibrîm* refers to a population of the pre-Mosaic period with features characteristic of the *'Apiru/Ḥabiru,* people who do not have a stable

303

territorial basis and are of low social status (slaves, hired workers, or hired soldiers). Moreover, there is a significance in the fact that the verb *qrh* used for revelation in connection with the *God of the ʿIbrîm* in the mountain of *Elohim* (Exod 3:18; 5:3) is not the conventional term for revelation in Israel but is characteristic of revelation to foreigners (see Num 23:3–4, 15–16; cf. Gen 24:12).

The question may be raised: How was this extraterritorial "mount of God" turned into the mount of the worshipers of Yahweh? For this we have new evidence from Egypt. In the geographical lists of Amenhotep III (1402–1364 B.C.E.) found in the temple of Amon at Soleb in Nubia (Sudan), we find the entry *tꜣ šꜣ sw yhwꜣ*, which is to be rendered "the land of Shasu of Yhwh," meaning "the land of the nomad (tribes) of Yhwh."[8] "Yhwh" indicates here the name of the region where the deity was worshiped, or it may indicate the name of the tribes that call themselves after this deity.[9] In fact, the holy place where Jethro met Moses according to Num 10:33 is called "the mount of YHWH" and it seems that this was later changed by the Elohistic tradition into *har hāʾelōhîm* ("the mount of God") (see above). In other Egyptian topographical lists "the land of Yahweh" comes close to the other toponyms known to us from Sinai and southern Palestine associated with Midianites and Qenites, such as Seir, Laban, Šamati (or Šama), Reuel, and Punon. Thus, in the list of Ramses II from Amara-West in Nubia, which was copied from Amenhotep III's temple at Soleb,[10] we find next to *tꜣ šꜣ sw yhwꜣ* also the land of the Šasu of Seir *(sʿrr)* and of Laban *(rbn)*. Seir and Laban in the Egyptian sources should not be sought in Edom of Transjordan, as was done by some scholars,[11] because the mountain of Seir denotes also the range of mountains to the west of Arabah and to the south of the Dead Sea. Compare, for example, Deut 1:2: "Eleven days from Horeb to Kadesh-barnea by the Mount Seir route," which implies that Mt. Seir refers to the area of Sinai. Laban also belongs to the northern part of the Sinaitic peninsula close to Raphia and El Arish. It is attested in the Shishaq inscription and Sargon's annals[12] and in Deut 1:1 where it occurs together with Hazeroth in Sinai, known to us from the itinerary in Numbers 33. Seir as a region in the south of Palestine is also known to us from the El-Amarna tablets, where it is clear that the lands of Seir *(mātāti šēri)* are on the southern borders of the Jerusalemite kingdom (EA 288:26), as well as from Josh 11:17 and 12:7, where the conquest of Joshua reaches "Mt. Halaq which ascends Seir."

Next to Seir, Laban, and Yhwꜣ we find in the Shasu group of the Amara list *Šꜣmt* (also listed in the Soleb list) which has been identified with the *šamʿati* of 1 Chr 2:55.[13] This nomadic tribe is affiliated there with the Qenites, who were in close friendly relationship with the Israelites (see below).

The connection between Yhwᵌ tribes and the Qenites is reflected in another Egyptian inscription. In a geographical list from the time of Ramses III of Medinet Habu, we find the name Yahu (List XXVII 115) close to another name with great significance for our subject, and that is Reuel *(rwᵓr/l)* (XXVII 111).[14] As is well known, Reuel is associated with Jethro (Num 10:29), and in Exod 2:18 he appears as "the priest of Midian," a title given to Jethro in Exod 18:1.

Another place mentioned in the Amara list (no. 45) and connected with the Qenites is "the land of the Šasu of Punon" *(tᵌ šᵌ sw Pwnw),*[15] a place of copper industry[16] apparently associated with the Qenites, who were engaged in metallurgy. This place has to be connected (cf. the itinerary in Num 33:42) to the episode of the copper serpent in Num 21:8–9,[17] an object found in the excavation of the Midianite site in Timnah (see below).

It is quite significant that Seir opens the list of the Shasu group of the Amara list. Seir and Edom connote, in fact, the territories south of Palestine and especially the Sinaitic region. As we have seen, we find in the El-Amarna letters the lands of Seir as the extreme borders of the kingdom of Jerusalem, and similarly Mt. Seir marks the southern borderline of the Israelite territory. The descriptions of the theophany in Deut 33:2 and Judg 5:4 also open with Seir and Edom (see below).

THE NOMADS OF YAHWEH AND THEIR ALLIES

According to the crystallized Pentateuchal sources, God reveals himself to the people on a specific mountain called Sinai or Horeb. Ancient poems, however, hail several places in the Sinaitic desert as places of the theophany. In Deut 33:2 we hear about Yahweh coming, shining,[18] and appearing *(bwᵓ, zrḥ, ypᵓ)* from *Sinai, Seir,* and *Paran.* In the Deborah song we hear about Yahweh's coming forth *(yṣᵓ)*[19] and marching *(ṣᶜd)*[20] from Seir and Edom, with Sinai in the background (Judg 5:4–5). Similarly we read in Habakkuk 3 that God comes from Teman and from Mt. Paran (Hab 3:3), and in the continuation Kushan and Midian are mentioned (Hab 3:7). Teman here equals Edom and Seir (cf., e.g., Amos 1:11–12).

In Psalm 68 we find the same typology. God comes forth *(yṣᵓ)* and marches *(ṣᶜd)* before his people in the wilderness (v 8), and besides Sinai (v 9) we find there "mount of God," "mount of Bashan," and other mounts *(gabnunnîm).* As in Judg 5:4–5, the whole universe trembles before the God of Israel.

In all of these instances there is no trace of Sinaitic revelation of the type attested in Exodus 19—24. The prevailing picture is that of God setting out from his holy abode[21] (on the mountain) to save his people from their enemies on their march to the conquest,[22] not the conventional notion of God descending upon the mountain to give law. The place from which the deity sets out is not a single hallowed place (Sinai/ Horeb), as in later literature, but various places dispersed all over the Sinaitic peninsula and the Negeb: Paran in the south of Sinai, Edom in the south of Palestine, Midian, and Kushan. It seems that there were several holy mounts in this area, which served the nomads who venerated Yahweh.[23]

The outstanding Yahweh mount, however, was the one from which Moses with his ally Hobab, the Qenite, started the route for the conquest of the land. This is reflected in the ancient song of the Ark in Num 10:35–36 and in the tradition connected with it (Num 10:29–34). Here we read that upon the departure from the mount of Yahweh, Moses negotiates with Hobab, the Midianite, his father-in-law, about his joining Israel's journey to the new land and mentions his help as guide in the desert. The story then breaks off and shifts to the description about the guiding Ark (Num 10:33–36). The cooperation of the tribes of Israel with the Qenites in the settlement in the new land is attested in Judg 1:16, where it says that the sons of Qeni,[24] Moses' father-in-law, went up with Judah from the City of Palms to the wilderness of Judah in the Negeb of Arad.[25] It seems that the reference to the mundane action of Hobab as guide in the desert had been suppressed in favor of the divine guide, the Ark of the Covenant (Num 10:33–34), and therefore the disruption in the story of Num 10:28–32.

The same tendency may be revealed in Exodus 18. Here we find a detailed description of Jethro's recognition of the God of Israel and his participation in the covenantal meal accompanied by sacrifices, together with Aaron and the elders of Israel (cf. Exod 24:1, 9). After this, Jethro advises Moses concerning the administration of justice and the teaching of laws (Exod 18:20). This account with its description of the covenantal meal and the legislative actions actually parallels the traditions of giving law at Sinai attested in Exodus 19—24. However, the author who presented the glorious account of the theophany in the chapters that follow could not consider the account about Jethro as equivalent to the *Heilsgeschichte* in Exodus 19—24. He therefore dissociates Exodus 18 from the following by means of the concluding note of Exodus 18, which says that Moses sent away Jethro to his own land (Exod 18:27), exactly like Num 10:30, where Hobab says: "I will return to my own land." In such a manner, Jethro's initiative in both traditions (Exodus 18 and Num

10:29–32) was superseded by God's initiative. In Exodus the covenantal meal of Jethro and his judicial organization were overshadowed by God's covenant and his giving of the law, while, in Numbers, Hobab's guidance in the desert was replaced by the guidance of the Ark of the Covenant (Num 10:33–34). Historically the Ark of the Covenant could have marched with the Israelites while the Qenites were with them (see below concerning Deut 33:2), but theologically there was a tendency to separate the Qenites from the Israelites.

Let us now analyze the old poetic passages about the march of Yahweh in Sinai. In connection with the story about the Ark, we encounter the song:

> Arise, Yahweh, let your enemies be scattered;
>   Let your adversaries flee before you. . . .
> Return, O Yahweh, to the myriads of thousands of Israel.[26]
> (Num 10:35–36)

A similar typology occurs in Psalm 68. This psalm opens with a phrase that overlaps the song of Num 10:35–36:

> Let God arise, his enemies shall be scattered;
> his adversaries shall flee before him.
> (Ps 68:2)

In the continuance we read about God marching before his people in the wilderness while Sinai trembles before him (see above) and about myriads of thousands of warriors of Yahweh coming with him from Sinai with the holy ones (Ps 68:18).[27] The latter contains a motif identical with that of Deut 33:2: "with him were myriads of holy ones." Each of the three poems that speak about the march of God from Sinai mentions myriads of thousands of (divine) warriors accompanying Yahweh in his appearance of salvation.[28] Most interesting in this respect is the stress on the various territories serving as a background for the glorious event: Seir, Edom, Paran, Teman, Midian, and Kushan. Not less interesting, however, is the fact that the joining of Hobab the Qenite is also reflected in these traditions. We already mentioned Hobab the Midianite, who was asked by Moses to join the Israelites in their journey to the promised land (Num 10:29ff.) and the tradition in Judg 1:16 where those who joined the Judahites in their settlement in the south are Qenites (cf. Judg 4:11). This event seems to find its echo in the description of Yahweh's march from Sinai and Seir in Deut 33:2–3. Following the appearance of Yahweh, we find the peculiar phrase 'p ḥbb 'mym, which in its present reading can hardly be original. The verb ḥbb in the sense of love is found only in Aramaic and Arabic, and even if one accepts it here, the meaning of the phrase *God loving the nations* "is entirely foreign to the poet's train of thought."[29] The best solution to this phrase, which occurs in the context of a heavenly entourage guiding the people of Israel, is to read "Hobab" instead of *ḥōbēb* and then the phrase has to be understood "Also Hobab was with them" (reading *'imām* instead of *'ammîm*).[30] As in Num 10:29ff., where the guidance of Hobab stands in juxtaposition to the divine guidance, so here the heavenly entourage, which accompanies the people to its land,[31] juxtaposes Hobab's guidance. This stress on a common expedition of Israelites and Qenites toward their new land has its roots in the alliance between Moses and Jethro in the desert as reflected in the stories of Exodus.

THE ALLIANCE BETWEEN MOSES AND JETHRO

We have already referred to the close relationship of Hobab the Qenite/Midianite with the Israelites during their wanderings in the desert. This relationship is clearly reflected in 1 Sam 15:7: "Saul said to the Qenites, 'Come, withdraw at once from among the Amalekites, that I may not destroy you along with them, for you did favor *(ḥesed)* to all the Israelites when they left Egypt.'" The word *ḥesed* as well as its synonym *ṭôbah* denotes covenantal relationship,[32] and thus 1 Sam 15:6 seems to refer to the covenantal relationships between the Qenites and the Israelites in the desert (see above, n. 4). This covenantal relationship between the Qenites and the Israelites actually has its point of departure in the personal alliances between Moses, the representative of the Hebrew tribes, and Jethro, the representative of the Midianites. The story in Exod 2:15–22 is, of course, of folkloristic nature (cf. the scene of the girls at the well in Exod 2:16–19 with Gen 24:12ff. and 29:1–13). The event underlying this story, however—an Egyptian fleeing from the Egyptian court, looking for shelter among the nomadic tribes across the border and establishing relationship with them—seems plausible and indeed has its precedents in Egyptian reality. Thus we read in the story of Sinuhe, which was defined "as the story of a life as it could have been lived,"[33] that Sinuhe after fleeing from Egypt finds refuge among Asiatic nomads, whose chief gave him water and milk[34] and whose tribe "did good" (*'ir nfr*) for him and also gave him "land to land"[35] (B 20ff.). In the continuance we read that Sinuhe reaches Byblos, where he meets the Amorite ruler Ammunenshi. Sinuhe reminds him that the Egyptian king does not fail to "do good" to a land that is loyal to him, following which Ammunenshi asks Sinuhe to stay with him and promises to "do good" for him: He also married him to his eldest daughter and let him choose from his land (B 74ff.).[36] Sinuhe was able to convince Ammunenshi by stratagem[37] that if Ammunenshi will "do good" for him, the Egyptian king will see it as a sign of loyalty to Egypt and will "do good" for Am-munenshi. "Doing good" here expresses reciprocal covenantal rela-tionship,[38] which was common among rulers and their vassals. House, food, and land, which constitute doing good, are given in lieu of loyalty, and sometimes this is coupled with intermarriage, as in the case of Ammunenshi. This kind of relationship may be exemplified by the story of Hadad the Edomite. The latter flees from his country to Egypt (1 Kgs 11:17–19), the Egyptian king gives him "house, bread, and land," and in addition marries him to his wife's sister, which undoubtedly means alliance.

A similar background may be discerned in the story about Moses' relationship with Jethro. Moses finds refuge in Jethro's house where he is *called to eat bread,* an expression found in connection with the covenant of Jacob with Laban (Gen 31:43). This rite of "eating bread" is men-tioned later, in the story about the sacrificial meal with Jethro in Exod 18:12. Here, as in Gen 31:54, offering sacrifices is combined with "eating bread."

The enigmatic expression *wyw'l . . . lšbt,*[39] which comes after "eating bread" in Exod 2:20–21, seems to express some sort of subservient relationship established by formal agreement (cf. Judg 1:35; 17:11).[40] But more significant is the fact mentioned afterward of Moses' marrying Jethro's daughter, as in the case of Sinuhe, who marries the daughter of his Amorite patron Ammunenshi.

The Moses story overlaps the Sinuhe story also in the key word, which expresses establishment of covenantal relationship, "to do good." The expression is found not only in 1 Sam 15:6 but also in Num 10:29–32, where it serves as a leitmotif in the negotiations of Moses with Hobab. Moses uses the verb *hêṭîb* ("to do good") three times (Num 10:29, 32) and thus alludes to the covenantal relationship between Jethro and the Israelite tribes. As in the story of Sinuhe, this relationship is connected with *land-giving* as reward for loyalty. Moses offers to "do good" to Hobab, alluding to the promise of land to Israel, which is to be shared with Hobab (Num 10:29, 32).

An instructive detail in the passage about the negotiations of Moses with Jethro is the phrase in Num 10:31 *wĕhayîtā lānû lĕ'ênāyim* ("and you could be our guide"). In the Sinuhe story the herdsman who gives shelter to Sinuhe in the desert after leaving Egypt is called *mtn,* which is derived from *mṯn* ("road") and actually means "road finder." This is indeed what is meant by the Hebrew phrase in Num 10:31.

Though the alliance of Moses with Jethro and the Midianites and Qenites may reflect a topos and ought not to be seen as historical reality, the events underlying this story seem to be authentic, since the crystallization of the traditions about the exodus and Sinai could be explained only by means of these events.

The existence of Yhwh worship among the Qenite/Midianite tribes, now substantiated by the Egyptian toponymic list, on the one hand, and Moses, the Egyptian, establishing relationship with Midianites/Qenites where he finds shelter, on the other, are to be seen as the kernel out of which grew the whole epic of the exodus and Sinai. It is hard to believe that the information about the relationship of Jethro and Moses is spurious or fictitious. Why would such events have been invented? Why would a faithful Israelite invent a story about a Midianite priest participating in a sacred meal before Yahweh together with Aaron and the elders? And what is more, who would ascribe to this Midianite priest the introduction of judicial administration in Israel, were this not true?[41]

Furthermore, as has already been indicated,[42] the friendship with local nomads was indispensable for a group that escaped from Egypt and wanted to survive in the desert, a thing that adds credibility to the stories about Jethro, Hobab, and the Qenites and their alliance with Israelites.

THE CULT OF THE MIDIANITES

Excavations at Timnah, some thirty kilometers north of the Gulf of Aqabah, have shown that Midianites who built a shrine on top of an Egyptian sanctuary mutilated the statue of the Egyptian goddess Hathor and reused many objects from the original structure. According to the excavator, B. Rothenberg, there is evidence for a tent sanctuary that the Midianites erected on the palace of the Egyptian shrine, which brings to mind the tabernacle of the Israelites in the desert.[43]

In this Midianite sanctuary a copper snake was found that reminds us of the copper serpent made by Moses and mounted on a standard (Num 21:4–9). This was the only votive object found in the sanctuary. The Egyptian representations of the goddess Hathor were effaced and the central niche was left empty. All this could be interpreted as a reaction of the Midianite nomads against Egyptian religion and culture, not unlike the Israelite reaction toward pagan idols. Israelite monotheism is indeed described in the Book of Exodus as emerging out of a wrestling with Egyptian religion and magic (cf. Exod 7:8ff.; 8:12–13; 12:12).

Further, the aniconic tendency of Israel's religion is characteristic not only of ancient Israel but also of other nomadic tribes in the wilderness of Sinai and southern Palestine and seems to have persisted down to the period of the Nabateans in the third to the second century B.C.E.[44] The affinities of ancient Israel's faith with the faith of their nomadic confederates come to clear expression in the episode about Jehu the king of Israel, who, by his zeal for Yahweh and the opposition to Canaanite Baal, asked Jehonadab the son of Rechab to cooperate with him (2 Kgs 10:15–16). The Rechabites, who were associated with the Qenites (1 Chron 2:55; cf 4:12 [Sept. B. Luc.]), preserved their nomadic way of life for hundreds of years (cf. Diodorus Siculus 9:9 on the first Nabateans) and were persistent in their zeal for Yahwism (see 2 Kgs. 10:16), the faith of their ancestors, the nomads who, according to the Egyptian inscriptions (see above), lived in the land of Yahweh. In this connection it is worthwhile to note that Elijah the prophet, who, like Jehu, opposed the Baal worship, made a pilgrimage to Sinai to express his zeal for Yahweh (1 Kings 19) and reestablished the cult of Carmel according to the Mosaic principles and Sinaitic traditions. The anti-Baalistic trend in those days stirred a new movement that strove for a return to the old Mosaic worship.

NOTES

1. According to L. Perlitt ("Sinai and Horeb," *Beiträge zur Alttestamentlischen Theologie* [ed. H. Donner, R. Hanhart, R. Smend; Göttingen: Vandenhoeck & Ruprecht, 1977] 302–22), the appellation "Horeb" was introduced in later times by the Elohist and the Deuteronomic school instead of "Sinai" because of the association of Sinai with Sin, the moon-god of Assyria and Babylonia. Horeb, in his opinion, is a more general term, denoting desert and arid area which indeed characterized the location of the holy site in question (cf. Exod 3:1; 4:27; 18:5; 1 Kgs 19:4ff.). Since the term "Sinai" occurs in the Priestly Code (P), which is usually dated in the exilic and post-exilic periods, Perlitt argues that P reintroduced the archaic appellation. In our opinion, the contrary is true. The usage of the term "Sinai" in P is another indication of its antiquity.
2. Cf. M. Noth, "Der Gottesberg und die Midianiter," in his *Überlieferungsgeschichte des Pentateuch* (Stuttgart: W. Kohlhammer, 1948) 150ff.
3. On the difference between the "mount of God" traditions and the later Sinaitic traditions and the breach between Exodus 18 and Exodus 19, cf. most recently Th. Booij, "Mountain and Theophany in the Sinai Narrative," *Bib* 65 (1984) 1–26.
4. Cf. C. H. W. Brekelmans, "Exodus XVIII and the Origins of Yahwism in Israel," *OTS* 10 (1954) 215–24; F. C. Fensham, "Did a Treaty Between the Israelites and the Qenites Exist?" *BASOR* 175 (1964) 51–54; A. Cody, "Exodus 18, 12: Jethro Accepts a Covenant with the Israelites," *Bib* 49 (1968) 153–66; E. W. Nicholson, *Exodus and Sinai in History and Tradition* (Oxford: Basil Blackwell, 1973) 69ff. R. de Vaux's refutation of any relationship between the Qenites and the Midianites and his denial of an alliance between the Israelites and the Midianites or Qenites in the desert is hypercritical and cannot be accepted. He dismisses too easily the evidence of 1 Sam 15:6 (see his study "Sur l'origine kénite ou midianite du yahwisme," *EI* 9 [1969] 29–32).
5. Z. Weisman, "The Mountain of God," *Tarbiz* 47 (1978) 107–19.
6. Ibid., 114–15.

7. The main difficulty in the comparison is that ʿApiru/Ḫabiru never takes a gentilic form, while ʿibrî is formed with a gentilic. Etymologically, however, ʿprw, ḥabiru, and ʿbry seem to have a common root. Cf. most recently N. Naʾaman, in *The History of Eretz Israel—Introductions, The Early Periods* (ed. I. Ephʾal; Jerusalem, 1982) 1. 233–41.

8. See R. Giveon, *Les bédouins Shosu des documents égyptiens* (Leiden: E. J. Brill, 1971) nos. 6a, 16a. Cf. recently M. Görg, "Jahwe—ein Toponym," *Biblische Notizen* 1 (1976) 7–14; S. Herrmann, "Der Name Jhw in den Inschriften von Soleb," *Fourth World Congress of Jewish Studies* (Jerusalem, 1967) 1. 213–16. The objections of M. Weippert (*ZAW* 84 [1972] 491 n. 144) and M. C. Astour ("Yahweh in Egyptian Topographic Lists," *Festschrift E. Edel* [ed. M. Görg and E. Pusch; Bamberg, 1979] 17–33) to the identification of Yhwʾ in the inscriptions with the Hebrew tetragrammaton YHWH seem hypercritical and far-fetched. The fact that "the land of Shasu Yhwʾ" appears in a group of six names preceded by the words tʾ šʾsw, "the land of Shasu (= Bedouins)," most of which could be identified with places of the regions south of Palestine (Seir, Laban, Šama, see below) speaks for itself. Astour's identification of *(tʾ šʾsw) sʿrr* with the toponym *Sehlali* of EA 62 looks arbitrary.

9. For this phenomenon, cf. E. Meyer, *Die Israeliten und ihre Nachbarstämme* (Alttestamentliche Untersuchungen; Halle, 1906) 297. He calls attention to the name Aššur, which stands for a god, a land, and a nation. For a tribe being named after its god, compare also the Laws of Plato where it is enjoined that the land should be divided into twelve portions between twelve gods, every portion to be named in accordance with the name of its god (745 b, c).

10. This was first established by H. W. Fairman, in *JEA* 26 (1940) 165–68.

11. Cf. B. Grdseloff, "Edôm, d'après les sources égyptiennes," *Revue de l'histoire juive en Egypte* 1 (1947) 78ff., and the others following him.

12. Cf. *rbn* (= *lbn*) near Raphia in Shishak's geographical list; see J. Simons, *Handbook for the Study of Egyptian Topographical Lists Relating to Western Asia* (Leiden: E. J. Brill, 1937) 186, and the inscriptions of Sargon king of Assyria, where we find a sheikh of Laban *(nasīku ša URU Laban,* VA 8424:6–7); cf. E. F. Weidner, *AfO* 14 (1951) 40–53, and H. Tadmor, "The Campaigns of Sargon II of Assur: A Chronological-Historical Study (Conclusion)," *JCS* 12 (1957) 77–78.

13. Cf. E. Edel, "Die Ortsnamenlisten in den Tempeln von Aksha, Amarah und Soleb in Sudan," *Biblische Notizen* 11 (1980) 78. The identification had been previously proposed by Grdseloff. M. Weippert ("Semitische Nomaden des zweiten Jahrtansends," *Bib* 55 [1974] 271) identified it with *Šammah* of the tribe of Reuel (Gen 36:13, 17; 1 Chron 1:37).

14. Reading with M. Görg, "Jahwe—ein Toponym," 14.

15. Cf. M. Görg, "Punon—ein weiterer Distrikt der šʾsw-Beduinen," *Biblische Notizen* 19 (1982) 15–21.

16. Cf. "Punon/Pinon," *EM* 6, cols. 445–46.

17. The episode took place between the station of Hor-hahar and Oboth (Num 21:4, 10), between which we find in the itinerary of Numbers 33 the places Zalmonah and Punon (Num 33:41–42).

18. Compare recently in the Kuntillet ʿAjrud inscriptions: *wbzrḥ . . . ʾl wymsn ḥrm*, "when God . . . shines forth (= appears), the mountains melt" (cf. M.

Weinfeld, "Kuntillet 'Ajrud Inscriptions and Their Significance," *Studi epigrafici e linguistici* 1 [1984] 126). For the semantics of "shining," "appearing," and "forthcoming" in the Semitic languages, cf. S. Morag, *Tarbiz* 41 (1971–72) 4ff.

19. See Morag in the article mentioned in the previous note.

20. The pair *yṣ'* and *ṣ'd* in connection with theopany is found also in Ps 68:6. Compare Hab 3:12–13 and 2 Sam 5:24.

21. Cf. J. Jeremias, *Theophanie. Die Geschichte einer alttestamentlichen Gattung* (Neukirchen-Vluyn: Neukirchener Verlag, 1965).

22. See I. L. Seeligmann, "A Psalm from Pre-Regal Times," *VT* 14 (1964) 75–92, esp. 91; F. M. Cross, *CMHE*, 86 n. 17, 100–102.

23. This tradition is of very old age. E. Anati (cf. *Har Karkom, Montagna Sacra nel deserto dell-esedo* [Jaca Book; Milan, 1984]) discovered a cultic site in the Negeb (Mt. Karkum) from the third millennium that has a lot in common with the Sinai tradition. Most instructive are the following elements in the Mt. Karkum excavations: an encampment close to the venerated mount, 12 erected stones, and a big well in the area (for the latter, compare the well of Miriam in Num 21:16–18).

24. Read perhaps with G. F. Moore: *Hobab hāqênî* (ICC; Judges 34).

25. Cf. B. Mazar, "The Sanctuary of Arad and the Family of Hobab the Kenite," *JNES* 24 (1965) 297–303.

26. God's attribute here reminds us of the epithets of Elijah and Elisha: "Father, Father, Israel's chariot and his horsemen" (2 Kgs 2:12; 13:14), and for the myriads cf. below, n. 28.

27. Read with Albright and Cross: *b' msny bqdš*. Cf. W. F. Albright, "A Catalogue of Early Hebrew Lyric Poems," *HUCA* 23 (1950–51) 24ff.; Cross, *CMHE*, 102.

28. On the divine council accompanying God in his battle, cf. Cross, *CMHE*, 99ff. The myriads and thousands of Israel in Num 10:36 correspond to the heavenly myriads and thousands of the holy ones in Deut 33:2–3 and Ps 68:18. Cf. Cross, *CMHE*, 70: "In the holy war ideology Yahweh led the cosmic forces of heaven alongside the armies of Israel." The idea is most clearly expressed in the Qumran literature; cf., e.g., IQM 12:1ff: "With you in heaven... are armies of angels... and you have likewise put the elect of the holy people with you... you muster an army of your elected in their thousands and myriads together with your holy ones and hosts of angels... to win the battle." For the "holy ones" in Deut 33:2–3, cf. my article on the 'Ajrud inscriptions in *Studi epigrafici e linguistici* 1 (1984) 124.

29. S. R. Driver, *Deuteronomy* (ICC), 393.

30. After I had suggested the reading Hobab, I found that E. Bezredki (*'ṭ šqr swprym*, Drohibitz, 1905) had already made this conjecture and T. Sinai (*pšwṭw šl mqr'* I; Jerusalem, 1967, 234) followed him (without bibliographical reference).

31. On the relationship of the prologue of the Song in Deuteronomy 33 to the epilogue where the settlement in land is clearly indicated, cf. Seeligmann, "A Psalm from Pre-Regal Times," 84ff.

32. Cf. recently my discussion in *Maarav* 3/1 (Jan. 1982), 46–53.

33. Cf. M. Lichtheim, *Ancient Egyptian Literature*, vol. 1: *The Old and Middle Kingdoms* (Berkeley and Los Angeles: University of California Press, 1975) 211.

34. This may have its echo in Judg 5:25: "He asked for water, she gave him milk."

35. *rdi.n wỉ ḫ³st n ḫ³st*. An identical phrase is attested in a letter from Mari (A 1121 obv. 19–21): "I shall give him throne upon throne, house upon house, land upon land"; cf. A. Lods, "Une tablette inédite de Mari," *Studies in Old Testament Prophecy* (ed. H. H. Rowley; Edinburgh: T. & T. Clark, 1950) 103–10. For such constructions, compare Isa 30:1; Jer 4:20; Ezek 7:26; Ps 61:7; Job 16:14; the Aramaic Sefire inscriptions I B 30 and the Phoenician Karatepe inscription (*KAI*, 26 A I 6–8).

36. For a translation of the text, cf. Lichtheim, *Ancient Egyptian Literature*, 1.223ff.

37. Cf. the words of Sinuhe before the opening of his speech to Ammunenshi: "But I spoke in half-truths" (on this, see Lichtheim, ibid., 234 n. 5), meaning that he did not want to discover that there was a conspiracy in the court.

38. For the covenantal meaning of the expressions in the story of Sinuhe, cf. D. J. McCarthy, "Covenant 'Good' and Egyptian Text," *BASOR* 245 (1982) 63–64. McCarthy, however, did not notice the words of Sinuhe: "He will not fail to do good to a land that will be loyal (lit.: *ḥr mw.f* = on his water) to him," which is a key phrase in our discussed topic.

39. Symmachos translates *hórkise* "he swore" and Jerome, *juravit*, which is influenced by 1 Sam 14:24 and based upon rabbinic interpretation. Cf. Mekhilta Mas. Amalek, Jethro (ed. Horowitz, 191), Sifrei sec. 27 (ed. Finkelstein, 41).

40. In all these instances, the coin *y' l* with *šbt* denotes dependence by agreement, which is usually the case of a vassal who pledges loyalty for getting protection by his patron.

41. Deuteronomy, which reveals a strong nationalistic consciousness (see my article on the "Historical Antecedents of the Deuteronomic Movement" in the Louvain Volume on Deuteronomy, 1983), ignores Jethro in this matter.

42. Cf. K. Koch, "Die Hebräer vom Auszug aus Ägypten bis zum Grossreich Davids," *VT* 19 (1969) 37–81; and recently, W. H. Schmidt, *Exodus, Sinai und Mose* (Erträge der Forschung 191; Darmstadt: Wissenschaftliche Buchgesell-schaft, 1983) 124–30.

43. B. Rothenberg, "Teman," *EAEHL*, 1184–1203.

44. Cf. recently J. Patrich, "Prohibition of a Graven-Image Among the Naba-teans—The Testimony of the Maṣṣebot Cult," *Cathedra* 26 (1982) 47–104 (Hebrew).

16

"Who Is Like Thee Among the Gods?"
The Religion of Early Israel

DAVID NOEL FREEDMAN

The subject of this chapter is the religious beliefs and ideas of early Israel, that is, the description and delineation of the deity as derived from the oldest source materials in the Hebrew Bible. Before we proceed with this rather delicate and difficult task, several preliminary and qualifying remarks are in order.

In gathering, analyzing, organizing, and presenting the relevant information, I have limited the database to the major poems now embedded in the Primary History (= Torah and Former Prophets),[1] and in fact only a selection of these:

1. The Blessing of Jacob: Genesis 49
2. The Song of the Sea: Exodus 15
3. The Oracles of Balaam: Numbers 23—24
4. The Blessing of Moses: Deuteronomy 33
5. The Song of Deborah: Judges 5

These are five of the poems that I regard as the oldest literature preserved in the Bible and hence the best available source for recovering a valid contemporary account of the religion of Israel in its earliest phases.[2]

A useful and convenient way to define and delimit the period of Israel's early faith is by the establishment of the monarchy in Israel, first with Saul and his house and then on a more permanent basis with David and his dynasty. While the discontinuity and disjuncture between the Israel of the period of the Judges and earlier and that of the monarchic age may be exaggerated in much contemporary critical literature on the subject; nevertheless, the introduction of kingship into Israel represented a dramatic, if not drastic, alteration in the structure of the state as well as in essential features of its religion. While there is no reason to doubt that the literary sources from the monarchic and even later periods contain authentic traditions and valid recollections of earlier times, there is

315

equally no doubt that the traditions and source materials were shaped and colored by the concerns of the new establishment as well as reused and rewritten to suit the interests of the inheritors and administrators of the legacies of the past. Therefore we have excluded from consideration all materials that obviously and plainly belong to or come from the monarchic period: for example, the poems in the Former Prophets such as the songs attributed to David (2 Sam 1:19–27; 2 Samuel 22; 2 Sam 23:1–7) and also the Song of Hannah (2 Sam 2:1–10) with its clear references to an anointed king.

For different but similar reasons, I have not included the Song of Moses, which is in Deuteronomy 32:1–43; controversy about the date of composition has persisted for decades, and no resolution is in sight.[3] There is also considerable difference of opinion as well as doubt and confusion as to the purpose and function of the poem, not to mention the reasons and significance of its attribution to Moses. I believe and recognize that its placement in the Book of Deuteronomy and the prose exposition in which it is embedded confirm and enhance the so-called Deuteronomic connection. But that observation raises at least as many problems as it purports to solve, and the question remains as to the position and role of the poem in the Deuteronomic literature, not to speak of the religiopolitical movement associated with the corpus of writings of that "school." While affinities between two works can be seen and shown, the direction of influence and the matters of dependence and derivation are much more difficult to demonstrate, at least to a critical audience. I think that it would be worthwhile to compare the findings from the other parts of the corpus with the data independently derived from the Song of Moses to see how faithfully the latter reflects the picture presented in the former, and to assess the differences that are to be discerned, in terms of their departure from the established older norms. But in order to develop a relatively uncontaminated picture of the faith of early Israel, I will concentrate attention on the five poems listed above.

There are other poetic materials that, in my judgment, can be assigned to the premonarchic period as well. These include some shorter pieces in the prose narrative, for example, the Song of the Well in Num 21:17–18 and the longer Song of Heshbon in Num 21:27–30, not to speak of bits and fragments of larger poems such as the denunciation of Amalek in Exod 17:16 and the stopping of the sun in Josh 10:12. Lacking the larger work in these cases, or an adequate context, I am hesitant to use these bits, although generally they support or do not conflict with the findings based upon (or derived from) the longer, more complete works. Not much is to be gained, albeit little is lost, by passing over these works or using them indirectly to support or explicate views derived from the longer set pieces.

I should add that there are other poems that may reasonably be assigned to an early date as well, chiefly among the psalms. It is widely believed that Psalm 29 is an example of an old Canaanite hymn appropriated and adapted for Israelite usage but shifting the focus from the presumed Canaanite deity Baal to the Israelite God Yahweh, literally substituting the latter for the former throughout the poem. Whether or not this is the proper explanation of the contents of the psalm, there is considerable scholarly sentiment in favor of a very early date for it (perhaps twelfth century).[4] I would also call attention to Psalms 93 and 113, which bear signs of early composition. Since, however, it is almost impossible to make a convincing demonstration on the basis of language and internal evidence alone, and since suitable historical contexts are lacking, even in the tradition, for locating these poems chronologically, it is best to leave them aside as well, retaining the option of using them for illustrative or complementary or supplementary purposes only.

As a result of the previous discussion, we have left for analysis and presentation the five poems originally mentioned at the beginning of this chapter. Further remarks or comments about this group of poems are needed to establish or clarify their chronology and also the interconnections among them. Only then can we proceed to an examination of each of the poems in turn.

For the purposes here, it is sufficient to establish (or assume) that all of the poems in our group belong to or come from the premonarchic period. Elsewhere I have argued in favor of such dating for each of these poems, and I have also endeavored to establish both a relative sequence and an approximate absolute dating for the group.[5] I argued then for the following position: Exodus 15 and Judges 5 are the earliest poems in this group and can be dated in the twelfth century; the other three poems are somewhat later, roughly contemporary with one another, and can be dated in the eleventh century. While these conclusions are not susceptible of proof in the usual scientific or historical sense, they are also hard to disprove, and the debate often proceeds along familiar lines or ruts, or in cycles of circular reasoning. Usually the problem is how to interpret literary resemblances and affinities, and the results reached by different scholars depend upon how they view the connections with other poems and prose narratives. The debate will go on, probably forever, or at least until Elijah returns to clear up such matters, among other somewhat larger duties he is to perform, but the exchanges themselves are often productive, sometimes in unexpected ways. In any case, I have seen nothing in print or in private communication to dissuade me from the propositions set forth about ten years ago.

A further distinction is to be made as well. We are concerned not only with the date of composition but also with the appropriate setting whether we speak in terms of history or story (the narrative context) in which these poems are placed in the Hebrew Bible, that is, the prose narrative running from Genesis through Kings. I believe that the poems are positioned roughly where they belong, that is, they were correctly understood to reflect or relate to, and to fit into or run parallel with, the prose narrative in which they were embedded or to which they were attached. This circumstance is plainly evident in the case of the Song of the Sea and the Song of Deborah, where in each case the poem follows immediately after the prose account of the same event (that is, Exodus 15 contains the poem, while Exodus 14 describes the same event in a prose account; Judges 5 is the poem, while the corresponding prose narrative is found in Judges 4).[6] Similarly the Oracles of Balaam are embedded in the narrative about Balaam and Balak, the king of Moab, and the notably unsuccessful effort on the part of the latter to secure an effective curse against Yahweh's favored people newly entered upon and settled in territory abutting upon Balak's own, and no doubt coveted by him as well. I believe the same interpretation of the blessings attributed to Jacob and Moses should be applied—namely, that they are placed where they are at the end of Genesis and the end of Deuteronomy on purpose, because they belong to the narrative at that point and in addition describe a historical situation contemporary and consonant with the prose narrative at those points in the story. Needless to say, we must not press these points too far, or very far at all. It is not necessary in order to do justice either to the narrative or to our hypothesis to suppose that the Song of the Sea that is preserved in the Hebrew Bible was composed on the shores of the Reed Sea as suggested by the context. Since it refers directly and explicitly to the journey to the sacred mountain in the wilderness and the sojourn there, it would be quite in order to suppose that the poem was composed somewhat later, while the Israelites were encamped at the base of the mountains. At the same time, I do not believe that it includes a prospective-retrospective history of the nation designed to have Moses forecast the settlement in Canaan and the erection of a shrine or temple in Jerusalem. The case with the blessings is more complex, and additional remarks will be provided when these poems are discussed later on. Nevertheless I think it was the intention of the author/editor to describe the circumstances of the tribal league at different times in its history and in the light of, or in association with, particular historical events. Thus the Blessing of Moses was intended to reflect the status and particulars of

318

the several tribes at the time just before the death of Moses when the settlement center or headquarters was still in Transjordan. In like manner, the Blessing of Jacob should be understood, not literally as a deathbed blessing pronounced by the patriarch on his sons, but as a description of the tribal league somewhat earlier in its checkered history than the account in Deuteronomy 33. It is our contention that the blessings here are of the same genre or kind as those in Deuteronomy 33, but they deal with a vastly different historical situation, one that is set in the period before the exodus and the age of Moses. In short, it is correctly placed in the patriarchal age, although the representation of an aged father surrounded by his sons is symbolic rather than actual. We posit therefore a pre-Mosaic patriarchal Israelite league in Genesis 49, and that the blessings individually and collectively describe the circumstances of the league sometime after its formation in the late fourteenth to the early thirteenth century and reflect the dramatic confrontation with Marneptah and the Egyptian forces toward the end of the thirteenth century B.C.E. Thus the period covered by the poems extends from the end of the fourteenth century until the latter part of the twelfth, while the composition of the poems can be assigned to the twelfth to eleventh centuries B.C.E.

Cursory classification of the poems immediately reveals two major types: Victory Odes, as seen in the Song of the Sea and the Song of Deborah; and Tribal Blessings: the Blessing of Jacob and the Blessing of Moses. A significant link between the types is found in the Song of Deborah, where a third list of the tribes occurs. In the context of the War or Victory Song, the tribal roll call is not exactly a series of blessings, although some of the tribes are commended for their bravery in the military action just concluded, while others are castigated for shirking their duty. In other words, the Song of Deborah, in which an important, if not the decisive, victory over the Canaanites is celebrated, also includes a roll call of the tribes that were summoned to the battle and a critical evaluation of their respective roles in that battle. In the light of these observations, a second look at the two blessings possibly suggests similar circumstances for these roll calls. With respect to Deuteronomy 33, it appears that the role assigned to Moses is similar to that of Deborah in Judges 5, although differing in significant details. It can be said that the utterance directly attributed to Deborah consists of the roll call of the tribes, while the opening lines are spoken or sung by others, since they are addressed to her. Similarly, Moses is mentioned in the introductory section of Deuteronomy 33, and it would appear that his direct utterance begins with the roll call of the tribes. Furthermore, while no specific battle is described or mentioned in Deuteronomy 33, as it is in Judges 5, nevertheless the framework of the blessing presents Yahweh as the vic-

319

torious war-god whose march from Sinai and mighty intervention in behalf of his people has resulted in victory for the latter. The circumstances fit well the picture of Israel settled securely in Transjordan especially after the victories over Sihon and Og, the Amorite kings described in Numbers 21, and reflected vividly in the Oracles of Balaam (which are placed in the story just after those victories). Our conclusion is that the Blessing of Moses belongs to the same general category as the Song of Deborah and that both arise out of and describe or reflect the convocation of the tribes associated with circumstances and events of singular importance. Just as the Song of Deborah celebrates the climactic victory of the Israelite army over the Canaanite kings and their forces (led by Sisera), so the Blessing of Moses observes the successful conclusion of the campaign, led by Moses himself, on the East Bank of the Jordan, in which Israel was able to avoid direct conflict with Edom and Moab. However, when challenged by the Amorite kings Sihon and Og, Israel defeated them in battle and was able to establish a firm foothold east of the Jordan, a solid base from which to launch an attack upon the West Bank and the completion of the basic task of winning the promised land.

If such an analysis makes reasonable or plausible sense, then we can examine the other poems in the light of these observations: The Song of the Sea can be seen as the initial action of the warrior-god in behalf of the people he rescued from bondage in Egypt. The first decisive victory was achieved against the Egyptians, thus setting Israel free to pursue its destiny first at Sinai and subsequently in the lands on both sides of the Jordan. Victories achieved by Yahweh's interventions made the existence and viability of Israel a reality. It is no surprise that these decisive, if violent, actions are at the heart of Israel's kerygma.

The Oracles of Balaam can be fitted into the same pattern. While they do not constitute a specific victory in battle against the enemy, they nevertheless use similar vocabulary to describe the role of Yahweh and the successful outcome for Israel, a unique nation that dwells securely apart from the nations of the world. The juxtaposition of these oracles with the victories on the East Bank of the Jordan suffices to establish the connection between victory in battle and security on one's land. A larger and special element in this group of poems is the victory over, or successful defense against, enemies not armed with the conventional weapons of warfare but with sorcery and spells, black magic, and the powers of the underworld. Just as Paul remarks that the people of God must do battle with malignant spiritual beings and powers (Eph 6:12), so here Israel is confronted by the malignant forces of the evil empire—of demons and devils—and is delivered from their power, while the forces of evil are routed on their own chosen battlefield. And Balaam, who by reputation was a master wizard and magician, a diviner and seer of awesome reputation, is turned around by superior authority and power and becomes the means and instrument by which all the baleful and malevolent powers of the netherworld are defeated, dispersed, and totally nullified. Since Israel is not directly engaged in this struggle, but is protected from unseen hostile forces by equally unseen armies of God, no mention of the tribal roles is made, because none is needed. The same in a different way can be said of Exodus 15. In the violent battle at the Reed Sea, Israel played no role other than spectator and witness for Yahweh's sole power as champion of his people. Again, there is no tribal roll call, because the people of Israel were not directly involved in the struggle. We need to remind ourselves that the primary, if not exclusive, purpose of the tribal muster was military, to provide an army capable of defending the borders and the centers of population and of winning victories over the enemies of God and their enemies. So the association in the cases mentioned so far—the Song of Deborah and the Blessing of Moses—may not seem far-fetched.

One poem remains to be dealt with and that is the Blessing of Jacob in Genesis 49. While we are laboring here largely in the dark, and the prospects are relatively unpromising, nevertheless there is some basis for regarding the poem as belonging to the same category as the Blessing of Moses and the Song of Deborah. It ought to reflect or express the proceedings of a tribal conclave subsequent to or associated with some pivotal or decisive event in Israel's history or experience. Along with the author/editor who put the blessing in the mouth of Jacob and therefore in the patriarchal age, we place the poem in the early period of the tribal league, before the career of Moses and the exodus from Egypt. The origins of Israel the people, community, and nation are somewhat murky and shrouded in mystery, but there are indications here and there in the Book of Genesis and external sources about Israel the people. By combining the data from Gen 33:18–20 (esp. v 20) and 48:22 (the capture of Shechem) along with the information from the famous Marneptah stele, mentioning a decisive defeat inflicted on Israel, we can reconstruct the beginnings of Israel as follows:

a. The formation of the league consisting of twelve tribes with a cult and covenant center at Shechem. We can date the main event late in the fourteenth century or around 1300 B.C.E.

b. The defeat of Israel and partial dismemberment of the league by Marneptah toward the end of the thirteenth century. The dispersion of the closely related tribes of Simeon and Levi may be a consequence of the battle action. Neither tribe ever recovered its territory or status. Simeon was absorbed into Judah, and Levi was reconstituted as a special group associated with the Ark and the tabernacle. The kinship connections with Moses and Aaron clearly play an important role in this development, which is reflected in the tribal blessing in Deuteronomy 33 in dramatic contrast with the description of Levi in Genesis 49, which remains the one and only representation of Levi as a regular secular member of the league. On this view, Genesis 49 would present an account of the early history of Israel as a tribal league constituted by and dedicated to the patriarchal God, El Shadday, after a military victory involving the capture of Shechem and its use as the league center. Then Deuteronomy 33 would be a depiction of the reconstitution of the league after the acquisition of sufficient territory in Transjordan to justify such an action. Most important, the God of the revived league is Yahweh, the resident of Sinai, whose representative is Moses, the mediator of the renewed covenant.

We can offer an outline of Israel's history and religion on the basis of the poems in the books from Genesis to Judges.

GENESIS 49: THE BLESSING OF JACOB

In this poem, I believe that a unique survival of the patriarchal age, or more precisely of the pre-Mosaic period, has been preserved substantially intact. While the composition in its present form seems to date in the period of the Judges, the content goes back to the fourteenth to thirteenth centuries and reflects the conditions under which the tribal league first came into existence and prominence. In defense of this view we can point to several features of the collection of blessings: (1) the archaic language and style; (2) the presentation (and preservation) of the original twelve tribe grouping, which was already obsolete by the end of the twelfth century or certainly the eleventh, not to speak of the tenth and the formation of the monarchy; (3) the description of the tribe of Levi, which differs dramatically from any and all others, beginning with the Blessing of Moses; clearly the representation of Levi as a secular tribe closely associated with Simeon reflects pre-Mosaic rather than Mosaic or post-Mosaic experiences and traditions. The plundering of Shechem has patriarchal associations, and Shechem's central role in Israel's religion (as reflected in the conquest traditions (e.g., Joshua 24) has its roots in pre-Mosaic associations especially with Jacob (Gen 33:20 and 48:22); (4) at least equally significant, in my judgment, is the absence of any mention of or reference to Yahweh the God of the exodus and the Sinai experience, the principal figure in all Mosiac and post-Mosaic traditions and literature in that the name YHWH appears only once in the whole poem and then in a liturgical comment placed in the mouth of the speaker Jacob (Gen 49:18, which is not part of the blessing on Dan but comes between it and the next one on Gad). The contrast with the other group of blessings in Deuteronomy 33 is striking. In the Blessing of Moses, the name Yahweh occurs repeatedly, both in the framework of the poem (in Deut 33:1 and 29 forming an inclusio or more properly an echo) and then in several individual blessings: Judah (v 7); Levi (v 11); Benjamin (v 12); Joseph (v 13); Gad (v 21, although I believe v 21 is a complement of vv 4–5 and refers to Moses as the subject of *'śh* in v 21b and not Gad); Naphtali (v 23). Similarly, the Song of Deborah, in which the third list of tribes occurs, is a thoroughly Yahwistic work, with numerous instances of the name scattered throughout the poem, if not directly in association with particular tribes. (Note the similar usage in the Song of Deborah as in Deuteronomy 33: *yhwh* occurs at the beginning in Judg 5:2 and again in v 31—forming an envelope construction or an echo. In all, there are fourteen instances of the name, seven in the first part of the poem (vv 2–9) and seven more in the remainder.)

It should be pointed out that the phenomenon under consideration here is not related to the well-known substitution of another divine name for YHWH—namely, Elohim—in the literary strands of the Pentateuch. The parallelism between the two names, and the occurrence of Elohim in association with Yahweh or as a substitute for it, does not occur in any of the poems in our group. The word *'ĕlōhîm* is exceedingly rare, and wherever it does occur it does not represent Yahweh or the God of Israel but is the standard numerical masculine plural for other gods. We are speaking here of Elohim as an independent noun in the absolute state, which only began to appear in the old poetry of Israel with the third phase and the emergence of the monarchy. The case with the construct form *'ĕlōhê* is quite different, since in every case the defining noun in the absolute state makes clear the identity of the God in question: e.g., *'ĕlōhî yiśrā'ēl* in Judges 5 (vv 3 and 5) in association with the name *yhwh*. Note also *'ĕlōhê 'ābî* in Exod 15:2, where the identification with *Yahweh* is clearly intended.

In Genesis 49, neither form of this divine name occurs; in fact, there are very few examples of any divine name, apart from the intrusive instance of *yhwh* in v 18. These are concentrated in the Blessing of Joseph in vv 24–26 and consist principally of names and titles associated with the patriarchs, in particular *'ēl*[7] and *šadday* (v 25) and very likely *'al* in v 26 ("the most high," a title that has been recovered elsewhere and mainly in the poetry of the Bible). It is essentially equivalent in meaning with the well-known *'elyôn* (also "the most high"), also a term associated with patriarchal stories and traditions. While in the other poems of this period (eleventh century: the Oracles of Balaam and the Blessing of Moses) the patriarchal names and titles also occur, they do so in combination or parallel construction with *yhwh,* showing that the identification of *yhwh* with *'ēl* and vice versa had been firmly established by that time. But in this poem it is only the God of the fathers who plays a role at the tribal league (as reflected in the designation or expression *'ēl 'ĕlōhê yiśrā'ēl* ("El, the God of Israel") in Gen 33:20).[8]

Since the name or description *'ēl* is somewhat ambiguous, certain qualifying expressions, the purpose of which is to identify a particular deity and to distinguish him from others, are often used, and here in Gen 49:25, *šadday* is parallel to *'ēl.* The God invoked in the Blessing of Joseph is El Shadday, which can be translated variously as El the Mountaineer [or the (divine) mountain] or the God Shadday, who, however, is not different from El the chief god of the Amorite or Canaanite pantheon. It is best to regard the deity here as El himself but specifically in his mode or character as the Mountain or Mountaineer.

What follows is a series of blessings (Gen 49:25–26) six in all *(birkōt* occurs 5 times, the sixth instance being an equivalent or complementary term in this context: *ta'awat),* which are presented in traditional pairs. The first pair, "the heavens above" *(šamayim mē'āl)* and "the great sea crouching beneath" *(tĕhôm rōbeset taḥat*—which retains the flavor of the ancient myth of the sea monster Tiamat, who was split asunder by the great king of the gods in the process of creation)—is well balanced by the third pair, "the everlasting mountains" *(hôray 'ad)* and "the eternal hills" *(gib'ōt 'ōlām*—which include qualifying terms that are also applied to the deity, so that there is an additional instance of patriarchal language in connection with this deity: *'ôlām*—"the Eternal One"). It is hardly an accident that four key terms used of the God of the fathers are concentrated in these few verses: El, Shadday, *'al* (or *'elî),* and Olam.

It is the middle pair that requires closer scrutiny and attention. Here we have the following text:

birkōt šādayim wārāḥam
Blessings of breasts and womb

As in the case of the other blessings, the mythic flavor and divine features are only thinly disguised. In the two pairs previously mentioned, the sources of the blessings are natural and visible phenomena but seen as closely associated with El Shadday the divine father and serving as means or agents of his beneficent will. What about "breasts and womb"? This must also be a designation or title for a divine being, one also associated with El the Father God. It is difficult to avoid the conclusion that this is not simply a generic reference to human fertility but rather a designation of the great Mother Goddess, the consort of El who is the archetypal divine father. This brings to mind W. F. Albright's suggestion that early popular Hebrew religion may have consisted of a triad of deities: a father, mother, and son figure not unlike other early Semitic pantheons.[9]

The parallel phrase in v 26a, is difficult and the text as written and vocalized poses problems:

birkōt 'ābîkā gābĕrû 'al
The blessings of your Father are more powerful than—

But a literal rendering makes little sense and hardly fits the context and structure of the group of blessings. I think we must redivide the words and repoint the verb to produce the following: *gibbōr wĕ 'al,* "warrior and exalted one" or, taking it as a hendiadys, "exalted warrior." That the divine father (cf. El the Father in v 25) is meant seems most likely, especially in view of the chiastic structure in the two verses:

'ēl 'ābîkā, "El, thy father"
'ābîkā gibbōr, "thy father the warrior"

The association of *'El* and *gibbōr* may be noted in the name of the marvelous child of Isa 9:5, where El and Gibbor occur together. This may support the case for emending the text in Genesis 49 (cf. also Isa 10:21). If, as seems logical and reasonable, the father in Gen 49:26 is the same as in v 25 and therefore divine, then it is hard to escape the necessary conclusion that the person characterized as "Breasts and Womb" is likewise a deity. The consort of El, while not named here, is a well-known goddess in Canaanite religion and throughout the Near East and the Mediterranean world, and as well in the polemics of the biblical writers. She is Asherah who is the consort of El and later on of Baal, known as creatress of living things, the mother goddess par excellence. It is difficult to imagine such a statement in biblical literature after the establishment of Yahwism as the official religion of Israel, but as a reflection or description of pre-Mosaic patriarchal religion it is probably accurate and realistic. Probably this reference or allusion to the female deity, consort of the great high god, was sufficiently vague or ambiguous to survive the scrutiny of later editors, and its poetic form and antiquity doubtless served to save it from the censors. Nevertheless it provides a remarkable view of what the religion of the pre-Mosaic league actually was like.

In view of this information it is easier to understand the persistence of the cult of Asherah in Israel throughout the period of the First Commonwealth and the revival from time to time of the worship of this goddess and the installation of her image in various cult centers. The inscriptional discoveries at Kuntillet 'Ajrud in which Yahweh is associated with an Asherah of some kind tend to confirm the antiquity of this worship and the continuing concern for and interest in a female deity on the part of Israel. No doubt those who restored or reintroduced this aspect of worship in Israel claimed patriarchal precedent for the practice and could quote old tradition or cite the words and practices of the fathers in support of what they themselves wished to do. It is hardly an accident either that the worship of the Queen of Heaven, the Mother Goddess, persisted in Israel (Judah) right to the end of the kingdom, as recorded and reported in the Book of Jeremiah (Jer 7:18; 44:17–19, 25).

It would appear that the establishment of a new political order in the northern part of the country by Jeroboam I also involved an attempt to restore and revive the older religion of the tribal league, going back to pre-Mosaic traditions. Thus the use of a bull image in the worship of the chief male deity no doubt reflected the cult of El in the pre-Mosaic league, and no doubt the name of Aaron, if not of the fathers, could be invoked in support of, and as authorization for, such activity. At the same time, or at least somewhere in response to the same tradition, the worship of the mother goddess, Asherah the consort of El, was also reinstituted. This was not, in the proper sense, a borrowing from the Canaanites, or the local inhabitants, but rather a restoration of the older faith of the fathers.

If we follow Albright's view of patriarchal religion further, we must ask about the third member of the divine triad.[10] Was there a third god, the son of the chief god and his consort? The figure of Baal, so prominent in the later history of Israel, is very elusive in the early sources. The word itself, whether as the name or title of any deity, does not appear in the early poetry at all and does not figure in the patriarchal traditions at all.

On the one hand, it is difficult to imagine that the divine pair, El and Asherah, were childless, like Abraham and Sarah, and the crowded scenes in and around the heavenly palace testify to the plethora of the lesser divinities or *bĕnê 'ēl* (lit. "sons of El"). So it is likely that the patriarchal pantheon was not restricted to El and his consort, although in cultic and practical terms they must have dominated the scene. The presence of others must be assumed and inferred from the surviving scraps of information preserved in the text and discovered in archaeological excavations. On the other hand, Baal himself is absent entirely from the patriarchal traditions and does not make a firm appearance in the story of Israel until well after the settlement in Canaan. The apparent exception, the Baal of Peor who figures prominently in the colorful story of rampant apostasy in the Book of Numbers, may not be Baal at all but another deity altogether, namely, the otherwise unnamed god of the Midianites. It is not unreasonable to suppose that this deity is Yahweh himself, not in his Mosaic mold but rather as the traditional god of Midian, a representation drastically altered by Moses and his followers.[11]

The conclusion must be that for the most part evidence is lacking and any suggestions or inferences are largely speculative. Still it is hard to explain the enormous attraction and tight grip that Baal exerted on the population of Israel, and not in the north only, so that Baal, along with Asherah, symbolizes the most dangerous form of dereliction and apostasy from the true faith. One suspects that the reason, or a main reason, why so much fire and damnation are directed at Baal and Asherah (consorts in the later phases of this religion, whereas in an earlier version Baal would have been son, challenger, and ultimately successor to the aging El) and their adherents is that both of these deities were once approved partners and participants with the chief deity in the faith and worship of the patriarchs as well as of the pre-Mosaic tribal league which is described and reflected in the Blessing of Jacob in Genesis 49.

EXODUS 15: THE SONG OF THE SEA

In this poem, in my opinion, we are confronted with Mosaic Yahwism, in its pristine original form, the faith by which the lawgiver led his people from slavery in Egypt to freedom in the wilderness. The decisive moment when the Egyptian chariot force is destroyed, and the departing Israelites are finally set free from bondage and the threat of recapture, is caught in this powerful hymn of victory.

Yahweh is portrayed as the only actor in the drama of deliverance. He alone is responsible for the defeat of the Egyptians, the sole champion of his people, who defeats the enemy and annihilates them all.[12] On other occasions Yahweh may appoint agents and delegate responsibility, or he may assist his people in their struggles with their foes (e.g., the Song of Deborah), but here the victory is uniquely and exclusively his; the entire responsibility for the outcome rests with him, so that no one ever again can say that he had help or that others had a hand in the triumph. It is forever forbidden for Israel to boast that this was a cooperative venture or that Israel was responsible for, or capable of, delivering or rescuing themselves. On the contrary, Yahweh alone was their redeemer from bondage. He purchased them from their former owner and now has all the rights and privileges that are transferred to the new owner. The central theme of the poem is the unmatched power and authority of Yahweh, who has demonstrated this power in destroying the Egyptian host by sheer force. It is this demonstration that gains for Yahweh possession of and authority over the former slaves, who now owe to him as their redeemer all the service and obeisance previously accorded to Egypt and its divine ruler.

The emphasis upon the irresistible power of Yahweh, demonstrated through a decisive violent action against a leading military power, and the way in which it is exercised by Yahweh as sole champion without aides or assistants, and in particular without the participation of the people, who are mere spectators at a confrontation in which their fate is decided, gives a definition and structure to the faith of Israel that carries through the remainder of its history as well as its sacred books. Recognition of Yahweh's monopoly of power and his exclusive claim on Israel as his property, gained through a violent bloody decisive victory at the Reed Sea, constitutes the main content of biblical tradition and the ongoing purpose of its religion. Israel was saved at the sea and sealed to Yahweh as its sole and exclusive Lord from that moment on. Within such a historical and existential setting or framework it is not surprising that in time an appropriate theological and philosophical superstructure was developed, translating finally into the monotheistic credo of the three great biblical religions. While the theoretical underpinnings, implications, and ramifications of that single decisive action could have developed in a variety of ways, the end result is not unreasonable or excessive, although the actual development could hardly have been predicted. In the poem itself the incomparability of Yahweh is affirmed (Exod 15:11) but paradoxically by a comparison of Yahweh with other gods. In order to establish the superiority of Yahweh, comparison is necessary but compromises his uniqueness. It is like the use of substitutes for the superlative in biblical Hebrew, whereby ultimacy is predicted of the deity by calling him the King of kings, or Lord of lords, and God of gods. Such comparisons affirm that there is a valid basis for comparison but equally insist that the basis or degree of the comparison is nullified by the character and quality of the gulf between the attributes of persons compared.

At the least, however, we must affirm the face value of the statement, "Who is like thee among the gods, Yahweh?" (Exod 15:11). The expected required answer is that no other god can bear comparison, none can measure up or even be included in the comparison. But there are other gods, that is clear. Otherwise there can be no comparison to demonstrate the incomparability of Yahweh.

As already pointed out, there are too many active and articulate beings in and around the heavenly court to make a contrary claim. We may call them angels, but that term only describes or defines their activity or function, whereas their classification is the same as that of Yahweh: they belong to the category of 'ĕlōhîm, as contrasted with earthlings, who belong to the class called 'ādām. This is hardly monotheism in any philosophical or strictly rational sense of the term. At the same time, many if not most of the features of polytheism and mythology in the ancient Near East have been deleted from the biblical picture.

As for mythology in the proper sense—stories about gods—there are none in the Bible, although some vestiges survive, and these are allusions to a time before historical time when Yahweh engaged in titanic struggles with mythical monsters to establish or maintain control of the world. Similarly, all other divine beings are totally subject and subservient to the will of the one God worthy of the name.

It should be evident from all the available data that Yahweh and Yahwism did not spring full-blown from the head of Moses. Rather, *Yhwh* was a deity from olden times, with a territorial base centered around Mt. Sinai (wherever that may have been). Presumably he was the god of the Midianites, perhaps among others, and Jethro the father-in-law of Moses was his priest. Such a god would have been equipped with a mythology of his own and associated with other deities, male and female, in an appropriate pantheon. Relics, vestiges, allusions, and echoes of these elements are to be found in the Hebrew Bible, especially in the Psalter and among the prophets, but these are not likely to have been picked up later and added to the religion of Yahweh, especially since the Mosaic version developed in a different way. Rather, we may suppose that this pre-Mosaic primitive version persisted long after the break between Israel and Midian became permanent. In fact, the inscriptions and drawings at such an out-of-the-way place as Kuntillet ʿAjrud may reflect the ancient form of Yahwism practiced by Midianites and other desert peoples, although no doubt there were changes and adaptations in the course of time. Moses for his part and his followers and successors made radical alterations and adaptations while preserving essential features of the Yahwism of his time. Yahweh, the One of Sinai, remained the same as before: the mountaineer, the warrior, the storm-god, the recently crowned king of the world of gods and human beings; all this was essentially unchanged. But Yahweh the redeemer of a new people from bondage in Egypt is clearly new. So also is a high God without a consort, offspring, or heirs. Equally astonishing is the absence, even more the absolute prohibition, of images of the deity. It is difficult to say where or when or how or why such strictures became an integral part of this religion, but the tradition is both strong and persistent and points to Moses as the originator. It is these features that made the break with mythology and priestly manipulation both possible and actual.

With the revelation of the new name of God, Yahweh the One of Sinai, biblical religion set off on a new course. It is difficult to define the relationship or the difference with patriarchal religion as compared with the new faith proclaimed by Moses. While there were no doubt connections of some kind between the patriarchal communities, some of whom were in Egypt while others remained behind, and the group led out by

Moses, I do not think there was any clear or immediate connection between El Shadday, the God of the fathers and the tribal league in pre-Mosaic times, and Yahweh, the God of Sinai who revealed himself to Moses and brought Israel out of Egypt to freedom in the wilderness. Just as El is the deity mentioned in the Blessing of Jacob, so Yahweh completely dominates the Song of the Sea. It is only later that the two deities are conjoined, in poems such as the Oracles of Balaam and the Blessing of Moses, and only after bitter confrontation. The episode of the golden calf may best be understood as a confrontation between the supporters of the older patriarchal religion—for whom the molten bull symbolized not only the presence and power of El but also the other features of patriarchal religion that would obviously be in direct conflict with the faith in Yahweh proclaimed by Moses—and the proponents of Yahwism. Ultimately, compromises and accommodations were made, beginning with the principal formula for peace and concord (after the terrible bloodletting recorded in Exodus 32): Yahweh = El. There are many reasons why this equation would be acceptable to both groups, and they lie in the meaning of the names but also in the ways in which the term 'ēl came to be used all over the ancient world. Thus while El is a proper noun, the name of the chief god of the pantheon, it is also a general term meaning any god or the class of divine beings. Thus in a given nation, the principal god would be called by his own name but also by the term 'ēl. Typically, personal names would be formed with that of the national god but also with the divine element 'ēl. It is evident that the same god is intended by both designations. Many biblical names exhibit the same features; thus a well-known king of Judah bore the name Eliakim, and when enthroned by Pharaoh Necho he was given the name Jehoiakim (2 Kgs 23:34). The two names, one formed with the name El and the other with the name Yahu (short for Yahweh), are equivalent. And there are many other such pairs. Insofar as status role, attributes, and the like were concerned, there would be little to choose between them, and by blending or merging them the basic problem of a monolatrous religion was resolved. There would be no conflict between opposing deities requiring a definite choice and often resulting in disastrous fighting, since these gods would merge into each other and be one godhead. By contrast, consider the terrible struggle between adherents of Yahweh on one side and Baal on the other and the catastrophic results over the years. The alternative is well put by Elijah to all Israel at Mt. Carmel where he insists that a choice must be made: there can be no compromise between Yahweh and Baal (1 Kgs 18:29). Only one can be god of Israel, not both. At the same time, the differences and divergences are so great that it would be impossible to merge or equate them. Curiously there is some evidence that such a possibility was contemplated and perhaps worked for a time. The word *ba'al* is basically a title (= master, lord) and not a name, so it could be applied to a number of gods. Apparently it was used for Yahweh as well as for Hadad the great storm-god of Canaan and Syria, among others. So it may have been possible to denominate Yahweh by the title Baal (master) and thus blend the deities. But it was other factors, including the long history of conflict and certain characteristics of Baal, as well as his involvement in a well-defined pantheon, that ultimately made a merger impossible.

In the case of El and Yahweh, there were other concessions or changes. If we are right about patriarchal religion, then the acceptance of El as a name for Yahweh or as his alter ego required that El surrender his consort forthwith. It might have worked the other way around, and there is evidence that in Samaria (and at Kuntillet 'Ajrud) Yahweh gained a consort, and Asherah remained in view as Queen of Heaven and the Mother (Creatress) of the gods. In the end, however, the figure of Yahweh remained dominant and clear-cut. The religion of Israel was shaped primarily by Moses and the wilderness experience, more so, in terms of theology certainly, than by the patriarchal traditions. In terms of nationhood and territory, political and social structures, and the land settlement, it was the other way around, since the tribal league antedated the exodus and wanderings and provided the basic polity for the nation in the land that it occupied.

NUMBERS 23—24: THE ORACLES OF BALAAM

In this group of poems we see the firstfruits of the equation Yahweh = El. Both names occur in the pieces in parallel and complementary fashion, showing that the blending and merging of traditions has been achieved successfully, and from this point on Yahweh = El is an appropriate dual designation of the God of Israel.

In these poems we find many of the same elements already observed in the preceding pair of poems, and therefore we need not repeat some of the things already stated. The general framework of the oracles concerns the relationship between Yahweh and Israel and the unique status of the latter among the nations because of his protection. While specific military actions are not in view (except perhaps in the brief supplemental oracles at the end of Numbers 24), Israel's privileged status—dwelling alone in security and prosperity—is clearly owing to earlier victories achieved by Yahweh and the promise of his protection and the threat of divine intervention in behalf of his people if anyone tries to threaten them. Given the context of the maneuvering by Balak to secure an effective curse against these potentially serious enemies, through a proven magician or spellbinder, the seer Balaam, we can understand both the nullification of Balak's endeavors and the affirmations of Yahweh's victorious stance along with Israel's blissful existence.

A special and perhaps overriding feature of this poem in contrast to the others is the stress on a different kind of warfare being conducted by Yahweh in behalf of his people—not against armies in the field but what Paul describes (see Eph 6:10–13) as a spiritual struggle against principalities and powers and the combined and concentrated forces of evil. The Oracles of Balaam open a window on the world of magic, especially black magic that deals in curses and malevolent wishes and schemes designed to overthrow and undo enemies—the world of evil spirits and baleful omens for Israel. But an essential element in Mosaic Yahwism was the repudiation and rejection of all magic, not because it was a foolish notion or because it is demonstrably ineffectual, but because Yahweh prohibited it.

Balak was using magic, or rather hiring a successful practitioner of different kinds of malefic magic, including especially cursing and no doubt sorcery and spells, to induce the relevant gods or evil spirits to achieve by occult means what he could not achieve in battle; he was not willing to take his chances on the field and preferred to invoke the evil forces of the universe and bribe or coerce them into serving his own ends. In an ironic twist, Balaam, the acknowledged professional and master of the black arts, is turned around—a double agent, as it were—and becomes instead Yahweh's spokesman and mouthpiece pronouncing a doom on all such devices and schemes to undo his people. Yahweh can and will protect his people not only from armies doing battle but from magical spells and unseen forces trying to wreak destruction on his people.

While the oracles are set in a particular context of the alternate war waged by Balak of Moab against these unwelcome intruders on territory that no doubt he would prefer to remain in no hands at all, that is, unless he wished to acquire them himself, there are more basic considerations involved concerning the nature of Mosaic Yahwism. The war against magic, against the underworld of demons and malevolent spirits, is here declared, and it is also declared to be over. Yahweh does not deal in magic—he is not arbitrary or capricious, he cannot be bribed or seduced by flattery or rich offerings, and he works according to principles and rules, and he does what he says. Furthermore, there is no appeal from his verdict, at least not to other forces that might prove to be more amenable. There is one court and one judge; there are no tricks or maneuvers by which to avoid confrontation and decision. Balak's alternative, his politics of conducting war by other means, is doomed to failure.

332

The war against magic was never completely won; and it still isn't. But the first major blow was struck in the name of a new faith that believed in a single omnipotent deity who ruled justly and would not permit the intrusion of extraneous and malefic elements. It should be emphasized that biblical religion nowhere dismisses the world of curses and black magic as futile nonsense or even malicious mischief. There were such forces in the world and evil spirits could be invoked and convoked, but Yahweh was more powerful than all of them put together. He would not allow these purveyors of evil to gain sway on those who sought their help. He himself would wage effective war against all of them. At the same time, however, Israel was strictly, even fiercely, prohibited from having anything to do with them and from making contact with those spirits or the mediums and wizards who were their living human contacts.

CONCLUDING REMARKS

Owing to various miscalculations, and especially the limitations of space, it has proven impossible to deal specifically and individually with all of the poems in the corpus, but perhaps enough has been said about them in one context or another to make our case. In any case we must summarize our findings and our contentions.

The five poems embedded in the Primary History not only describe and reflect the circumstances and convictions of earliest Israel but were composed in substantially their present form during the premonarchic period. They thus provide a uniquely important source for analyzing and interpreting the earliest phases of Israel's experience and especially its religion.

As always, there are three phases in the evolution of Israel's religion. These may be outlined as follows:

a. The first phase is patriarchal religion: the pre-Mosaic phase. The source for this information is the Book of Genesis but more particularly the Blessing of Jacob in Genesis 49. The essential feature is that the chief God is El (Shadday) as already noted centuries later (but millennia before modern scholars) by the Priestly Editor (Exod 6:3). He is the God of the tribal league already formed in Canaan in the fourteenth to the thirteenth centuries. So far as the evidence goes, patriarchal religion shared many features with the neighboring Canaanites, including a consort for El (probably Asherah) and other divine beings.

b. The second phase, Mosaic Yahwism, is reflected in the Song of the Sea (Exodus 15). Here we meet Yahweh the God of Sinai and the deliverer of his people at the Reed Sea. The special and distinct features of biblical religion are to be found here, especially the incomparability of this God in relation to others. The main emphasis in the poem is on the overwhelming power of this God and also his unique relationship to the people he redeemed from slavery.

c. The third phase is represented especially by poems such as the Oracles of Balaam and the Blessing of Moses. Here we find the blending of the two earlier phases and the synthesis of patriarchal and Mosaic traditions. The potential and actual conflict between El (Shadday) and his partisans and Yahweh and his is resolved in the equation Yahweh = El. In the merger, greater emphasis is placed on the Yahwistic components, while the El factors are brought into conformity with them. But the political structure and the territorial entity derive from the El tradition.

(1) In the Oracles of Balaam another very significant aspect of Yahwism is revealed and presented: the absolute warfare against the underworld of black magic, evil spirits, and the like.

(2) In the Blessing of Moses the tribal league is reconstituted as the people of Yahweh. Now that a significant territorial base has been secured, it is possible to consolidate the holdings and the people in preparation for the (re)conquest of the territories on the West Bank of the Jordan.

d. A word should be added about the Song of Deborah (Judges 5). It is the last in the series and reflects the completion of the conquest with the utter defeat of the kings of Canaan and their armed forces. While details differ, nevertheless the Song of Deborah has points in common with the Song of the Sea. Together they sum up the campaign for freedom and statehood, with Yahweh overthrowing the chariot forces and Egypt at the beginning through a violent storm and ending with the equally violent destruction of the chariot forces of the Canaanites at the Wady Kishon. Thus the threads are tied together, and the comment at the end of the Song of Deborah completes the first cycle of Israel's experience from the formation of the tribal league to its final resettlement in the land:

So may all your enemies
    perish, Yahweh
And his lovers (be) like
    the going forth of the
    sun in its vigor.

And the land had rest for forty years.
        (Judg 5:31)

NOTES

1. For a discussion of the formation, development, canonization, and significance of the Primary History (Genesis through 2 Kings), see D. N. Freedman,

"Pentateuch," *IDB* 4. 711–27; idem, "The Law and the Prophets," *Congress Volume, Bonn 1962* (VTSUP 9; Leiden: E. J. Brill, 1963) 250–65; idem, "The Earliest Bible," *The Bible and Its Traditions* (ed. M. P. O'Connor and D. N. Freedman; Ann Arbor, Mich.: University of Michigan, 1983).

2. For a general introduction and discussion of the nature of Hebrew poetry and its possibilities and problems in reconstructing Israelite history and religion, see D. N. Freedman, "Pottery, Poetry and Prophecy: An Essay on Biblical Poetry," *JBL* 96 (1977) 5–26.

3. On the basis of the selection and distribution of divine names and titles I have postulated elsewhere that Deuteronomy 32 dates from the latter part of the tenth or beginning of the ninth century. See D. N. Freedman, "Divine Names and Titles in Early Hebrew Poetry, *Magnalia Dei, The Mighty Acts of God* (ed. F. M. Cross, W. E. Lemke, and P. D. Miller; Garden City, N.Y.: Doubleday & Co., 1976) 77–80.

4. Also on the basis of the distribution of divine names I have postulated a date in the latter part of the twelfth century for Psalm 29. See Freedman, "Divine Names and Titles," 60–61.

5. For a complete discussion of the sequence and dating of these five poems on the basis of the distribution of divine names and titles, see Freedman, "Divine Names and Titles," 57–70. A study of the historical elements in these same five pieces is found in D. N. Freedman, "Early Israelite Poetry and Historical Reconstructions," *Symposia Celebrating the Seventy-fifth Anniversary of the Founding of the American Schools of Oriental Research (1900–1975)* (ed. F. M. Cross; Cambridge, Mass.: ASOR, 1979) 85–96. Exodus 15 and Judges 5 are dealt with in detail in D. N. Freedman, "Early Israelite History in the Light of Early Israelite Poetry, *Unity and Diversity: Essays in the History, Literature and Religion of the Ancient Near East* (ed. H. Goedicke and J. J. M. Roberts; Baltimore: Johns Hopkins University Press, 1975) 3–35.

6. For the relationship between Exodus 14 and 15 and Judges 4 and 5, see Freedman, "Early Israelite Poetry and Historical Reconstructions," 85–87.

7. Cross provides a detailed exposition on the term *'El* and its meaning and usage throughout the Old Testament in his article in *TWAT*. See F. M. Cross, "*'ēl,*" *TDOT* 1.242–61.

8. For the designation "God of the Fathers," see Alt's seminal work on the subject, A. Alt, "Der Gott der Väter," *BWANT* 3/12 (1929). English translation in A. Alt, *Essays in Old Testament History and Religion* (Garden City, N.Y.: Doubleday Anchor Books, 1966) 1–100.

9. For a discussion of the "divine triad" in the ancient Near East and in early Hebrew popular religion, see W. F. Albright, *From the Stone Age to Christianity* (2d ed.; Garden City, N.Y.: Doubleday Anchor Books, 1957) 173 (esp. n. 44) 246–47.

10. Albright, *From the Stone Age to Christianity*, 247.

11. Cross has also suggested this in *CMHE*, 71–72.

12. For Yahweh as a "Divine Warrior," see Cross, *CMHE*, 91–194; M. C. Lind, *Yahweh Is a Warrior* (Scottdale, Pa.: Herald Press, 1980); and P. D. Miller, *The Divine Warrior in Early Israel* (HSM5; Cambridge: Harvard University Press, 1973).

17

The Nature and Purpose of the Abraham Narratives

GEORGE E. MENDENHALL

Most of the discussion and enthusiastic argumentation concerning the Abraham narratives has attempted to solve the problem of their origin and meaning by trying to define and date formal parallels to data found in the Genesis narratives. It is not surprising that conclusions concerning the date and history of the narrative, and therefore concerning the historicity and context of the personages involved, have not obtained much scholarly consensus through this method. Though there is some validity to such a procedure, it can "prove" nothing by itself simply because of the continuity of ancient cultures. Concentration on such minutiae has successfully obscured the important historical problem—which is the nature and purpose of the Abraham narrative itself in the ancient Israelite cultural history. This is a crucial and very complex historical problem that cannot be solved merely by literary criticism and source analysis, though the latter is vitally important to the history of the narrative during the biblical period.

The very fact that the narrative is not a literary and linguistically homogeneous unit is historical witness to the mutability of the past and literary witness to the fact that the narrative changed as the cultural context and ideological system of ancient society changed. This is a simple definition of the law of functional shift. A formal aspect of any culture may well be continued through time, or borrowed from outside, but the new cultural context of that form of behavior, and therefore its meaning and function, cannot be identical to the original one.[1] It follows also that the new, contemporary context or meaning is identified as the original and authoritative one. It is the purpose here to propose some solutions to this problem of functional shift in the history of the patriarchal narratives and to integrate that complex into ancient cultural history.

The main question is not whether or not there was a "patriarchal period" in ancient Israel's history. The populations that constituted ancient Israel were not spontaneously generated out of the desert sands. There is no alternative to the thesis that there must have been an enormously complex relationship between the now well attested social, cultural, and political history of the Syro-Palestinian region during the Bronze Age and those segments of that diverse population which became biblical Israel. The very knotty problems of the patriarchal narratives are themselves witnesses to this reality, and as a matter of fact those narratives were a deliberate means by which to recapture that pre-Israelite past.

The main question is why there was suddenly an interest in and an elaboration upon traditions of the remote pre-Israelite period. Secondary and dependent problems are to determine, if possible, what was the procedure and what were the "givens" that were utilized by the ancient scribes in order to produce the patriarchal narratives as we now have them. The isolation of different sources in that narrative is sufficient indication that we are not involved with a single cultural and religious context in our attempts to deal with the main and secondary problems. Obviously the history of the patriarchal narratives is intimately bound up with the history of the society itself and its changing religious ideologies. Recent extremely simplistic dismissal of the historical problems by reducing the issues to mere questions of ancient creative writing or storytelling is merely an illustration of antipathy to and inability to cope with history and the historical process[2] that is very characteristic of present-day society. At the same time, this attitude illustrates the operational relevance in modern times of the law of functional shift in that it reduces the ancient narrative to a mere aesthetic "literature."

Given that the Yahwist federation of ancient premonarchic Israel was consciously a discontinuity from all preceding social organizations as well as their operational ideological systems, then the primary question to be asked is, Why was there suddenly created a "patriarchal period" at all? It is historically and culturally no accident that there is not a single reference to the Abraham/patriarchal complex in premonarchic sources. That is excluded by the fact that Jacob is the "common ancestor" and his very name is identified with "Israel" from the earliest times. The function of the "common ancestor" in tribal society is too well known to need elaboration here, but the original function, and therefore the reason for existence in the biblical tradition, of the remote, patriarchal ancestor Abraham is a question that has hardly been raised, largely because the very late reinterpretation of the tradition has been accepted as dogma and therefore as "historical fact" in modern popular religion.

The need for a new and more remote common ancestor arose for the first time with the unification of the land by King David. As a matter of fact, only from this time on are there references to Abraham at all, and in a very restricted group of contexts. The function of the patriarchal legends is thus inseparable from the vast changes in social organization and the inevitably concomitant changes in ideology that attended the transition from a tribal federation to a centralized bureaucratic empire with decision-making power concentrated in the hands of the head of state. This working hypothesis places into a new context quite a number of elements of the patriarchal narratives, and the result is a more adequate picture not only of those narratives but also of the ideological changes necessitated by the transition to monarchy.

Eventually, it makes quite clear why there has never been a really successful "Old Testament theology," for there was not a single theology after the establishment of the state, but rather a complex of competing and mutually incompatible ideologies in spite of what seem to be repeated attempts to harmonize them. The two major ideologies may be identified as the Sinaitic/Mosaic, on the one hand, and the Abrahamic/political on the other. Ideologies, however, never exist in a social vacuum, but continue to exist, if at all, because of their operational values that determine behavior consciously or unconsciously of a sufficient number of the population to make the entire system viable.

The sudden introduction of a massive attention to a pre-Mosaic, pre-Sinaitic tradition can only be correlated with the fact that in David's empire the social element most important to the newly established political power structure was the urban population of Palestine that had never adhered to or had any use for the Yahwist/Israelite covenant tradition. The glue that holds any urban society together seems since the dawn of history to be that of political control of coercive power through the police and military organization, plus the control of the economy through the systems of internal taxation, foreign trade, and imperial tribute externally. It should be perfectly clear, however, that this bonding function works only so long as the power structure and its associated economic system continue to operate in a way that is at least tolerable and within the range of reasonable expectations of the citizenry. The problem with ancient and many modern political systems was and is the fact that the political ideology included no intrinsic qualitative motivations or controls that would guarantee for long that sort of operational tolerability. The arrogant policy of Rehoboam illustrates both the political stance and its end result, in that no concerns for external long-range consequences could overrule his simple determination to win in the power struggle. Much less could he conceive of being a servant to the people.

The rise and fall of the Davidic empire is a paradigm of the process that ran its course in a little over two generations. The thesis argued here is that the Abraham narratives originally were superimposed upon and actually displaced (so far as the political establishment was concerned) the Mosaic/Sinaitic covenant tradition. Only centuries later with the nostalgic attempt to return to past glories beginning with the reform of Josiah was the Abraham epic tradition radically reinterpreted, if not rewritten, to make it fit a now drastically changed cultural and religious context. By that time the contrast between the political ideology and the Mosaic/Sinaitic theology and their respective operational ethical systems was not at all understood. It is not surprising that the contrast was reinterpreted as a simple matter of "proper" cult practices dedicated to the deity that has the "proper" name under the control of the political state—ironically enough, precisely the dominant feature of ancient pre-Mosaic paganism. There is an essential difference, often unrecognized or misunderstood, between the original Mosaic operating system and the politically motivated readaptation of old traditions that often enough are thought to be reforms.

Once it is granted as at least a working hypothesis that the Abraham traditions are inseparably tied up with the historical and social (as well as political and ideological) process that resulted in the disintegration of the old tribal federation and the rise of the temporary empire, then many features of the patriarchal tradition fall neatly into place. Here only some of the most important can be discussed briefly as an illustration of the fact that the historical context of biblical texts and narratives is the essence of a historical-critical method over against the exegetical and form- and text-critical methods that normally are sensitive only to the verbal and textual form and context of a given passage.[3] This historical method is neither new nor unscholarly, contrary to the opinion of many types of contemporary mentality. It is, in the first place, merely an adaptation of a very old principle of interpreting Scripture by Scripture, enhanced by an enormously enlarged knowledge of the global context of ancient biblical history, and, in the second place, by the application of a global cultural method that is much called for in many modern academic fields but little practiced.

ABRAHAM THE "COMMON ANCESTOR"

The common ancestor of early federation Israel was Jacob, who was identified with Israel in the earliest sources. Nearly all genealogies included here and there in the biblical tradition end (or begin) with the specific tribal ancestor and do not extend into the pre-Mosaic period. This is the best indication that ancient federation Israel did not regard itself as the continuity of any specific social or political organization,

340

though it is quite clear that some social subunits did in whole or in part become elements of the Israelite federation, possibly including a unit that was already "Israel."[4] This is entirely in keeping with anthropological observations that new tribal organizations very often take the name of a dominant segment. In this respect, ancient societies contrast rather sharply with modern church mergers where characteristically a new name must be adopted that is not too closely identified with any participating preexisting segment.

A patriarchal period other than that represented by the eponymous ancestor Jacob/Israel himself was therefore incompatible with the fact that the new federation represented a deliberate and even vehement break from previous large-scale social or political organization and therefore also from the ideologies that loosely bonded those organizations. The religious character of those ideologies has, on the one hand, obscured to a very large extent the fact that they are political-economic concerns or even fanaticisms useful in the constant power struggle that is the normal political process itself. This has been dealt with extremely well by M. Liverani.[5] On the other hand, the similarities between those ancient pagan religious systems and the modern power struggles have likewise been obscured by the religious language of ancient political structures and the allegedly secular nature of modern political discourse. The contrast is linguistic only—a matter of sociolinguistic conventions that are radically different in different cultural contexts. The historical problem is to get behind external forms of linguistic behavior to understand the value system that is exhibited in especially the nonlinguistic patterns of behavior and the process of decision-making when alternative choices are available.

The reason for the sudden emergence of the patriarchal period in the imperial period is to be found in the needs of the greatly expanded political control system and its population base. Conversely, the patriarchal narratives could have served this function only if they were already a part of the common knowledge of at least a considerable segment of the population concerned, a probability powerfully reinforced by the association of Abraham with a large number of population centers, including some that did not even exist in the Early Bronze to Middle Bronze transition period. The epic traditions of Daniel, Noah, and Job were certainly also known, but they never became central to the ideology, simply because of the fact that they were not of critical importance to the political ideology of the monarchy.

It is in this context that the early elements of the patriarchal narratives become crucially important, for if they can be identified, they can be integrated into our understanding of the historical process that saw the rise of the empire—and its demise. The new common ancestor was certainly a part of that political attempt at bonding a population that had been polarized socially and ideologically since the rise of the federation itself. The urban centers were never Yahwist, but they were, as always, crucial to the functioning of a political state, since they were the source of specialized skills (though even then so meager that Solomon had to import specialists for his ambitious public works programs). They were also an important addition to the population base that is always a prime requisite to power structures.

Furthermore, it is clear that many Canaanite urban centers that had long been power structures, at least since the Middle Bronze II period, were important administrative bases in the system of Solomon's districts. The striking analogy to the political evolution of the Mari period is very significant, for there also formerly independent city-states were annexed by military force to become seats of district governors. Some of their populations also, incidentally, banded together to form the tribe of Benjaminites, as we know from the foundation inscription of Yahdun-Lim. I see no evidence at all of any attempt on the part of the Mari dynasts to create a new ideological bonding, for the political/religious ideology was based merely upon superior power and the "mandate from heaven" in which the will of the populace was relevant only when it was expressed through power and large organizations such as the Benjaminite tribe. Similarly, popularly based rebellions against David stemmed from Israelite, not urban, circles, notably the episode of Shemei. Absalom's rebellion is clearly a court intrigue that succeeded in exploiting dissatisfaction with David's legal administration to obtain some degree of popular support (2 Sam 15:2).

It is most probable, also, that the cities (especially Jerusalem) were the locus of a tradition of literacy so essential to the bureaucracy of a political state, for literacy was (and to a large extent still is) irrelevant to the needs of an agricultural and pastoral population and economy. The significance of the fact that the tenth-century "Canaanite alphabet" is a homogeneous entity has escaped modern specialists, for that fact alone is sufficient to establish that the scribes of tenth-century Jerusalem had the same cultural background as those of contemporary urban Canaan. The city and the political bureaucracy always regard the village population as parochial boors. Indeed, the only reason for existence of the latter is to furnish the goods and services needed to support the bureaucracy and the political establishment. Thus, the policy of Rehoboam.

The new common ancestor then represents a deliberate political ideology by which the old polarization between village Yahwist and urban Baal worshiper was proclaimed to be a thing of the past. At the same time, the policy and its concomitant party line is clearly the result of the triumph of the urban tradition. Just as clearly, there was an adaptation of old tradition to make provision for the continuity of Yahwism in certain formal aspects—most important, the name of the tutelary deity of the dynasty but also certain aspects at least of older ritual forms. The Ritual Decalogue of Exodus 34 is the monument to this radical shift in the official religious value system, though the really important ritual structure was the Temple sacrificial system, borrowed—or much more likely continued in use—by the Jerusalemite priesthood, but on a much grander scale because of the enormously enlarged population base, and therefore economic base, that resulted from the merger of the urban and village populations through military force. It is not surprising that the vast majority of the village Yahwist community did not buy into this ideology, as illustrated in the prophetic support of, first, violent removal of kings and then, subsequently, the despairing recognition of the fact that the state was doomed by its own rejection of the means by which it might be permitted to continue.

It was the ideological need of the newly established political state that motivated the new common ancestor and the creation of the patriarchal period, for, like nearly all of the formative periods of world religions, early Yahwism had absolutely no provision for the legitimizing of a political state, and the religious ideology necessary to that state could only be borrowed and adapted from earlier—that is, Bronze Age—sources that were no doubt already present and available through the urban population of Jerusalem itself, as well as Hebron. Some complex of traditions concerning Abraham were common knowledge to elements at least of both the urban and the rural populations of Palestine at the time and therefore are a "given" that was utilized and readapted to the needs of the Davidic-Solomonic monarchy. The content of that complex of tradition is, of course, difficult to establish, but the idea held by many scholars now that some literary genius created the patriarchal period out of whole cloth in the exilic period flies in the face of everything we know about the ancient Near Eastern cultures, as A. R. Millard has cogently argued.[6]

THE GIFT OF THE LAND

The enormous elaboration upon this motif both in the biblical and the modern scholarly tradition has again obscured a number of historical facts that place the biblical narrative in a quite different context—or rather three different contexts, each of which can and should be correlated with a specific historical situation.

In the first place, it needs to be pointed out and emphasized that this motif is already a part of the religio-political inventory in the Old Akkadian period, where acquisition of territory by military force is equated with the gift of land by the dynastic deity. Thus in the Old Akkadian chronicles we read:

> Enlil gave him (the region from) the Upper Sea (to) the Lower Sea.

> Sargon, the king, prostrated (himself) in prayer before the god Dagan in Tutul (and) he gave (him) the Upper Region (i.e.) Mari, Iarmuti (and) Ibla as far as the Cedar Forest and the Silver Mountain.

> ... now the god Nergal did open up the path for the mighty Naram-Sin, and gave him Arman and Ibla, and he presented him (also) with the Amanus, the Cedar Mountain and (with) the Upper Sea.

Note the contrast in the style of Hammurabi and subsequent Mesopotamian rulers:

> With the mighty power which Anu (and) Enlil have given him, he defeated all his enemies as far as the country of Subartu.[7]

This motif in the Abraham narrative is thus an extremely archaic, Early Bronze Age, survival that again became useful with the conquests of King David, and, as many have pointed out, even the definition of the territorial divine grant corresponds exactly to the ephemeral limits of David's actual conquests. It is not generally realized, however, that from all evidence now available there was little if any population existent in the region between the Damascus oasis and the Euphrates valley at Tell eth-Thadyen = Tuttul, which was the normal terminus of the desert route between Damascus/Homs and the Euphrates via Palmyra/Tadmor. The population of central Syria, like that of central Anatolia, during the Early Iron Age must have been extremely meager, in very sharp contrast to the enormously increased population of Palestine and Transjordan at this same time. The only reasonable explanation of this phenomenon is the flight or migration of populations from north to south, which is actually attested in the Egyptian sources at the Late Bronze to Early Iron transition period. This fact is reflected in numerous ways in biblical narrative, not least of which is the insistence upon the twinship of Jacob and Esau and Jacob's flight from Aram-naharaim (after having been sent back there in order to establish the connection with the Abraham genealogy, with which he originally had absolutely nothing to do).

The promise of the land was a tradition that survived into the Middle Bronze period in north-central Syria, where it is attested in the "prophetic" oracle addressed to Zimri-Lim of Mari from a source of Aleppo:

> Now, inasmuch as I restored him to the throne of his father's house, I will

take the *niḫlatu*-property from him. If he will not give (it) over, I am the lord of the throne, the land, and the city, and that which I have given I can take away. If (he does) otherwise, however, and grants my request, throne upon throne, house upon house, land upon land and city upon city I will give to him. And the country from east to west I will give to him.[8]

It is interesting to see the transition from the Early Bronze statements in which military conquest is equated with the divine gift of land, while in the Middle Bronze (Amorite) tradition it becomes a promise to be conditionally fulfilled in the future if the king acts appropriately in response to divine command (having, of course, to do with ritual/economic patterns of behavior). This represents a shift from a dogma that interprets past events to a mythical principle that permits prediction of future events.

This motif in the Abraham narrative can safely be regarded as a part of that "given" in the pre-Mosaic Palestinian tradition complex which became useful politically to the united monarchy. It was superimposed upon the earlier Yahwist tradition that knew little or nothing of the gift of the land but was enormously concerned with the individual family inheritance or family estates that were not owned and therefore could not be bought or sold.[9] Ownership of the land was held by Yahweh himself, and only enjoyment of family allotments was conditionally granted to the Israelite tribesmen.

This motif was therefore specifically political, and almost certainly it was originally the promise to the *king* as it was everywhere else in the ancient Near East. By the time the Abraham narrative was incorporated into the religious/political tradition, the actual enjoyment of family estates had been already in existence for a century and a half at least. Therefore the promise of the land could have been relevant only to those segments of the region which had never become Yahwist, namely, the existing city-states together with their territorial holdings which were now much reduced. It is these city-states that also no doubt preserved the tradition of divine grant, and thus the Abraham tradition legitimized the royal sovereignty by conquest over the old remaining *pagan* territories. The fact that Absalom and Joab had side-by-side land allocations in the environs of Jerusalem is sufficient evidence that Jerusalem and its territory had become crown property by right of conquest. The Deuteronomic version specifically emphasizes this process, by naming in some detail the various pagan urban enclaves that had not been "driven out," and therefore in the old days the "conquest" had not been complete. Judges 1 is the Josianic version of the ancient history.

It is of considerable interest that it is only the Priestly segments of the patriarchal narrative that specifically promise kings to issue from the seed of Abraham.[10] Again, this is an illustration of the naiveté of much biblical scholarship with regard to the P materials. The fact that they are the latest segment has nothing to do with the authenticity of the data they contain; conversely, the fact that they do contain very archaic and authentic data has nothing to do with their dating—as always, in archaeological strata, alphabet traditions, or ritual forms the dating is determined by the latest elements contained, not the earliest.

The divine grant of land was originally the normal archaic political motif of the ancient pre-Mosaic paganism by which legitimacy was accorded to royal conquests, and it was the more plausible in tenth-century Canaan precisely because it corresponded to the old political ideology of its urban, pagan, inhabitants. The words of poor old Rib-Addi of Byblos are most apropos: "Do you not know the land of Canaan, that they follow after the one who has power?"[11] The common Syro-Palestinian Bronze Age pagan heritage of this specific religious motif for the legitimizing of military conquests is also illustrated by its presence in Old South Arabic inscriptions.[12] It also had close parallels in Egyptian New Empire texts, while the Iron Age Assyrian ideology of conquest was entirely different.[13] Conversely, it is no accident that there was acquisition of territory through military action. It seems certain that the political ideology was applied specifically to the territories of the pagan cities. It was only there that, as crown property, land could be allocated by the king to his family and staff and could also be bought and sold.

With the Deuteronomic reform of Josiah, the old tradition had a new meaning and political utility, for the collapse of the Assyrian empire opened the way for the reunification of the land by military conquest a second time. It is no accident that the Deuteronomic tradition makes almost no use of the Abraham tradition except the Abraham-Isaac-Jacob genealogy by which the oath to the ancestors is the basis for renewed claim to possession of the entire land. The reform, however, transferred that ownership from the king to the "seed" of Abraham, thus superimposing the old Sinaitic/federation tradition of the divine allocation of family fields upon the royal claim to ownership of the entire territory, and at least in theory furnished the necessary ideological ground for the unification of the long-polarized populations of the kingdoms of Israel and Judah. Of necessity, however, there could be only *one* Yahweh (Deut 6:4) and one place for his name and therefore his cult. Deviant ritual observances were tantamount to a declaration of political independence and therefore treason. It was a sort of compromise that steered a middle course between the position of Naboth and that of King Ahab in the famous episode of Naboth's vineyard. At the same time, it was obvious that only the true "seed of Abraham" could inherit the land, and therefore all non-Israelites were to be driven out or exterminated in this holy war. It seems that as a matter of political policy anyone who deviated from Josiah's party line was exterminated, especially those associated with the old high places.

THE DIVINE CHARTER THEOLOGY

Whether or not the Davidic covenant had a direct connection in the tenth century to the covenant with Abraham is a much-discussed problem to which there has been no solution (and probably won't be). Studies have again concentrated upon forms of language and literature, but, useful as those may be, they do not address the primary question, which is what that form did in society and why it existed at all.

The identity of structure between the covenant of Abraham in Genesis 15 and the covenant of David mediated through the prophet Nathan as reported in 2 Samuel 7 has already been discussed at length elsewhere and need not be reiterated here, except to reemphasize that Genesis 15 does not include a covenant-based obligation, nor does the Priestly revision of Genesis 17. By its very nature, circumcision is no obligation assumed by the eight-day-old baby. It is an obligatory ritual necessary to mark the child as a member of the group that has the covenant. There is in the existing texts no indication of any direct relationship between the Abrahamic and Davidic covenants, and in fact none need be expected simply because both narratives in their transmitted form have been readapted to the theological and cultural situation of the seventh to sixth centuries, when for the first time circumcision became important as a religious group marker (Ezek 44:9).

Though more careful search of the texts is necessary, it is difficult to believe that the conditionality of the divine charter, in which the obedience of the king to Torah was necessary in order to secure the divine promise, was an original part of that royal theology. It was certainly a part of the Deuteronomic complex of political theology that tried valiantly to merge mutually incompatible ideologies. Certainly there is little indication in the actions of most of the kings after David that there were any scruples involved in their policies that derived from the old religious tradition. On the other hand, the extraordinarily powerful reaction of Josiah himself to the discovery that there actually *was* another and authentic religious tradition strongly suggests that any ethical control over the royal behavior was mediated through public opinion, not through any official royal theology of conditional divine support. The conditionality was the result of the merging of the Sinaitic and Davidic covenant traditions.

As argued above concerning the divine grant of land, however, such a

347

promise involving territory necessarily implies a royal recipient, and this aspect of the tradition can safely be assumed to have been part of that "given" in the original Abraham tradition. Combined with the traditions very closely connecting Abraham with Hebron, and especially the tradition of the burial cave of Machpelah and its necessary connection with the cult of the dead that we now know to have been very characteristic of Middle Bronze West Semitic royal houses, it is virtually certain that the Abraham narrative or even epic tradition had to do specifically with the establishment of the Hebronite kingship that was by tradition also linked with the Middle Bronze Hyksos regime of Egypt, being founded "seven years before Zoan."

That the burial tradition and the cave were also "given" in the epic tradition of Abraham is demonstrated beyond reasonable question by its mere existence and by the fact that there is not the slightest hint of any *other* significance of its existence in the entire Bible other than the very important narrative of Genesis 50 that was required in order to support the genealogical linkage between Abraham and Jacob. Isaac also had, of course, to be buried there as a sort of afterthought, but poor Rachel already had two tombs of her own by the time the narrative was created and only the unfavored wife Leah shared the sepulcher of honor with the patriarchs.

The entire Abraham tradition does not make sense other than as one that was transmitted through a variety of sources from the Middle Bronze "Heroic Age" on, like the epics of Daniel, Noah, and Job. Even the two forms of that name which, like all other such archaic names, was connected with a popular etymology ("father of a multitude") can now be correlated with the fact that the Early Bronze coastal dialect of Palestine and the East Mediterranean littoral had very often a medial *h* that had been lost in Amorite and presumably other inland dialects. In the Byblos Syllabic inscriptions of the Early Bronze Age, even the root *ra'* ("evil") is spelled *ra-ha-'a* in the perfect tense form. The two forms Abram and Abraham are thus witnesses to the linguistic process of fusion (sometimes called now creolization) of two distinct West Semitic dialects that actually took place in the Early Bronze to Middle Bronze transition period and resulted in a new language that has been long termed "Canaanite" and whose most significant witness is the corpus of texts from Ugarit.[14]

No doubt with the "Amorite" migration that resulted in their dynastic control over most of the cities of the coastal region, including Palestine, came also the political ideology of the divine charter, so well attested in the literature of the similarly Amorite dynasties of Mesopotamia.[15] In that ideology the ruling king whose status resulted from military superiority was formally declared to be the "chosen" of the deity or committee of deities, and the presumption at least was that his dynasty should remain on the throne until the gods changed their minds because of the successful feats of some later military genius.

It is quite clear, or should be, that what is expressed as the will of a deity or the pronouncement of a deity is an expression of a *value judgment* on the part of the adherents to this old pagan ideology as well as a way of describing what they believed to be the normal process of history. This is the mythical idealism of ancient paganism known in Old Testament thought as Baal worship, for historical events are considered to be only the pale "reflection upon the wall of the cave" of those mythic conflicts which already had been decided on the cosmic plane. It is for this reason that ancient political mythmaking and modern fundamentalisms alike have little or no concern for mere history and even less concern for historical fact. Unfortunately, for the same reason this sort of ideology likewise has no understanding for long-range historical processes and little concern for the future. Politicians cannot afford to be concerned about anything beyond the next election, over against the old Yahwist formula that Yahweh brings home the consequences of rejection to the third and fourth generation of those who have no use for him.

Whatever the specific connections may have been, it is clear that the whole complex of Bronze Age political ideology was called upon to furnish what the authentic Mosaic Yahwism vehemently rejected, namely, the elevation of the political state as the "Ultimate Concern," as P. Tillich's theology (for once rightly) puts it. It is thus a matter of no particular significance whether there was a direct linkage between the Davidic covenant and that of Abraham tradition. They stemmed from the same source, no doubt through the political traditions of Jerusalem itself whose structure as well as whose bureaucracy was necessarily taken over in the course of David's coup d'état. The prophet Nathan as well as the priest Zadok were both part of that bureaucracy, for only in this way can there be an accounting for the identity of the Temple ritual with that of the Canaanites.[16] Furthermore, the oldest Zadokite genealogy is exactly five generations too long, because their own Jebusite genealogy had been inserted into that of the Shiloh priesthood.[17]

The legitimizing theology of the Davidic dynasty was thus a simple substitution of names in the ongoing divine charter political ideology, and this was a process that was no doubt familiar to urban prestige centers for many centuries, if not millennia. As usual, the whole complex was of no particular significance to the village population to whom the family, the kin group, and the village remained the primary social relationship.

GEORGE E. MENDENHALL

THE TRIUMPH OVER PAROCHIALISM

Within the framework of the historical reconstruction presented here, one passage of the Abraham narrative takes on a remarkably lucid meaning that had an equally remarkable continuity in spite of the enormous transformations that the narrative suffered in subsequent reinterpretations. It is the passage at Gen 12:3 that evidently captured the minds of the political establishment, for it underwent so many repetitions and modifications. The oldest and simplest formula may well have been a long-standing part of the royal theology: *wnbrkw bk kl mšpḥt h'dmh* ("by means of you shall all the families of the land be blessed").

The use of the *nif'al* form of the verb in this passage is the crux. It was usually translated as a passive until E. A. Speiser's commentary in the Anchor Bible, where he treated it as a reflexive, and most commentators and translations since then seem to have followed his lead. It is certainly wrong, however, the best evidence for which is the later (especially P) substitution of the *hithpa''el*, the specific purpose of which could only have been to forestall the idea that the common ancestor now of the Jews could be anything but an object of envy to the *goyim* who use him as a model for invoking divine blessings upon themselves.

J. Hoftijzer[18] has already commented upon the fact that in this complex of promises to the patriarchs, kings are mentioned in connection with the *goyim*, but never when there is reference to *'ammim* or as here *mišpaḥōt*. The phrase represents precisely that which was the actual political propaganda of King David's empire, namely, that this fulfillment of ancient prophecies had come to fruition. There were no more "kings" beside him in the land, and his regime was a blessing to all the "families" of the land who previously had been *goyim* under a king.

The *nif'al* form of the verb has fortunately been subjected to a thorough study by B. Bicknell, who points out that, as usual, grammatical categories based upon traditional Indo-European grammars simply do not work in biblical Hebrew (or other Semitic languages, for that matter). The so-called passive especially in this context is better described as a resultative.[19] It does not designate primarily an action undergone by a subject, but a result that happens to that subject through the agency designated by the prepositional phrase *bk*.

The correlation of ancient tradition with imperial political practice is the essence of such passages as this in the time of the Davidic empire, and no doubt it enjoyed considerable public esteem during this period of growth enhanced by the economic income from the imperial conquests stretching all the way to the Euphrates, according to the preserved traditions. From the point of view of the original Israelite population of

350

the countryside there developed rapidly one important fly in the imperial ointment: The dominant politicoreligious tradition (officially they *could not* be two separate traditions, though the social differentiation required two different priests) by the reign of Solomon had little or nothing to do with the religious traditions or the social and economic needs of that Yahwist population. The old urban paganism had again won out, but the collapse of the empire in the waning days of Solomon's reign meant that his successors had far too little military and economic power to maintain the unity of the state, and it divided.

It was no doubt intended to be a noble enterprise of healing the rift between the grass-roots religiously based community of Yahwism and the politically based urban power centers, but as always the political power structure won out temporarily—and that is why we usually have to go dig them up to find out much about them. The patriarchal narrative deliberately served the purpose that is much too rarely conceived of in political circles—of attempting to find some higher ground within which existing social polarizations can be resolved for the maintenance of both the peace and the economic well-being of both sides.

The function of the Abraham tradition as an ideological ground for the transcending of social polarizations continues even into the New Testament period, for not only does John the Baptist indignantly reject descent from Abraham as a ground for claiming special status with God (Matt 3:9 = Luke 3:8) but also for Paul, the Abraham tradition continues to be the basis for the claim of Gentiles to the promises of God (Galatians 3). This introduces the next motif of this remarkable patriarchal tradition.

THE GENEALOGIES OF ABRAHAM

The Abrahamic genealogies exhibit an almost archaeological stratification that has a significance so far largely overlooked. It is a basic principle of symbolic genealogies that the authoritative one functioning in the power centers of a given society is of course the most recent.[20] The older the genealogical remnant, the more meager is the information it provides. Thus we have pretty good evidence for a long continuity of the Abraham tradition, probably extending centuries back into the past, well into the Bronze Age, and representing repeated reuses of that epic tradition long before it was taken up for political purposes in the time of the united monarchy.

The most archaic and thus the most intractable is that of the heir *ben mešeq* (Gen 15:2), for whom we have only the curious and unintelligible gloss *hw' dmśq 'ly'zr*. Since this is embedded in the archaic narrative of Genesis 15, it can be safely regarded as part of that "given" in the epic tradition at the time it was adopted by the Davidic dynasty.

The next most archaic are the two genealogical traditions associated with the wife Keturah, and the concubine Hagar. It is extremely difficult to explain those traditions upon any historical basis other than that they were already present in the substance of the Abraham narrative at the time it was taken over by the Davidic dynasty. There had to be a Hagar before she and her son could be put away in favor of the *most* recent son Isaac and his mother Sarah. The virtual absence of any independent tradition about Isaac clearly points to his function as the necessary link between the Amorite Abraham complex and that of the authentic Israelite Aramean "ancestor" Jacob. In very similar fashion, the Joseph narratives furnish the necessary link between the Mosaic exodus band of ʿApiru escapees and the Palestinian tribes of the federation period—the more necessary, since according to the traditions themselves only Caleb and Joshua of Moses' contemporaries survived into the federation of Palestine proper.

The priority of the older genealogical traditions is guaranteed not only by the impossibility of accounting otherwise for their presence in the Genesis narrative but also by a number of details that could only have been "given" in the tradition as it existed in Palestine before the united monarchy. First is the statement that "Abraham gave all his possessions to Isaac. To the sons of his concubine (sic!) Abraham gave presents, and during his lifetime he sent them away from his son Isaac eastward, to the east country" (Gen 25:6). Whoever wrote this knew of the Palestinian origins of those tribes listed as descendants from the "concubines" of earlier times.

Until more information was available about the history of occupation of Northwest Arabia, and until a better perspective was available concerning the linguistic history of the Semitic languages, this statement simply had no connection with what was known about ancient history and was considered as mere learned speculation of the ancients. Now it seems clear that it is a reminiscence, of course radically interpreted, of actual cultural and linguistic history reaching well back into the Bronze Age. There is now no reasonable alternative for the primary origin of the enormously varied complex of pre-Islamic dialects than the Early Bronze Age dense population of Palestine, Lebanon, and Transjordan, no matter how much the eastern provinces of the Arabian Peninsula may have contributed to the cultural heritage of those Iron Age cultures of the south.[21]

It was in this region of high population density that the complex of dialects with an essentially Arabic grammatical structure developed already in the Early Bronze Age and was radically modified by the Amorite migrations of the Early Bronze to Middle Bronze transition period. The resulting language is what has usually been termed Canaanite, or North-west Semitic. So far as can now be determined, the language of the Palestinian, Transjordanian, and East Mediterranean littoral still remained structurally Arabic until the entire disintegration of the Bronze Age linguistic structure at the transition to the Iron Age. By the time the destruction of the Late Bronze empires took place, population elements had already been settled for some time in the northwest of Arabia, and there they preserved largely intact the language that had previously been predominant in the Palestinian and Transjordanian countryside.

THE IDENTIFICATION OF YAHWEH
WITH EL SHADDAI

The clearest and most definitive proof of the thesis that with the united monarchy there was a deliberate fusion of the old Yahwist and the Canaanite (and probably specifically the Jebusite) religious ideologies for political purposes is the specific identification of the pre-Mosaic god or gods with Yahweh. This is not only deliberately stated in Exod 6:3 but is also taken for granted in the most archaic strata of the Abraham narrative as we now have it. For there it is asserted without hesitation that it was Yahweh who appeared to Abraham and gave him the various promises. The statement of Exod 6:3 therefore in all probability presupposes the archaic form of the Abraham narrative that likely stems from the time of Solomon at least if not David, for it "explains" the anomaly and attributes it to the initial mission of Moses himself. It thus represents the same sort of modification of the Moses tradition as is shown also in the Ritual Decalogue where the provisions of the Sinai covenant are reduced to the various cultic traits of the monarchic period. For with the monarchy, the whole substance of socially enforced law had to come under the direct jurisdiction of the king and his courts, not remaining in the hands of village procedures or tribal leaders.

The linguistic phenomena associated with Yahweh and El Shaddai have been well dealt with by F. M. Cross and need not be reiterated here. The evidence is massive enough to prove what should no longer be necessary, namely, that the language of earliest Israel was for all practical purposes just what Isaiah said it was: "the lip of Canaan." Anything that could be said of Yahweh had to be couched within the framework of linguistic possibilities furnished by that language and its religious terminology. It is the functioning social and ideological systems represented by the two deities that is the important historical datum of prime significance. The merger of the two deities is a function of the merger of the two contrasting and hostile social and religious population groups that took place by military conquest under David, and therefore they had to be represented by two priests until Solomon's accession, when the old Yahwist priesthood was done away with.

To be sure, there are still enormous mysteries connected with El Shaddai. I suggested diffidently in *The Tenth Generation* that the name is actually a toponym,[22] but of course there is no way in which this can be proven. That it designates the chief deity of Tuttul (= *tell et-tadyēn*) remains a most attractive hypothesis that would explain a number of curious features. In the first place, as H. Levy has pointed out,[23] the names are semantic equivalents, but it is strange to find an important city in the mid-Euphrates Valley with a Sumerian name (another Tuttul, of course, lies farther north). I would diffidently suggest that the royal scribes from Old Akkadian times on deliberately used the Sumerian name as less crass and more refined than the earthy local name (the meaning of which to the present day seems not to be known to the local population of the village, since they pronounce it *es-sadyēn*).

El Shaddai, then, would be one of the deities brought to Palestine with the Amorite migrations or invasions such as the Dagon attested at Ashdod. The name in the Balaam oracles is striking, and the significance is difficult to assess until we have more reliable information concerning the date, provenance, and historical context of those poems. The very bizarreness of the entire narrative, including the oracles, strongly suggests an authentic foundation in historical fact as well as folklore, which would be further supported if the Balaam texts of Tell Deir ʿAllā also include references to Shaddai (I am quite dubious about that interpretation, however).[24]

It is inherently quite probable that it was precisely the obscurity of this deity that made the name useful as a mediator between the authentic Yahweh of the federation and the El cult of Jerusalem and elsewhere. It thus facilitated the syncretistic "Yahweh" as the tutelary deity of the political establishment of Jerusalem (as well as Dan and Bethel). It was evidently known in the popular religion and tradition, but there is no evidence that it was particularly closely tied to any existing organized political entity—and in fact may have been resurrected specifically because it was so old that it posed no threat to conservative village Yahwist society. In fact, as its occurrence in archaic personal names proves, El Shaddai must have been an element in the pre-Mosaic popular religion and therefore quite familiar.

CONCLUSION

All of the important elements of the Abraham narrative thus point to their function in the legitimizing of the monarchy, particularly from the standpoint of the old pagan urban traditions. All that had to be done was to take over those traditions and proclaim their fulfillment in the dynasty of David. This process probably was and remained irrelevant to the original Yahwist village population, until the political policies brought about the predicted destruction of both Samaria and Jerusalem. After those events the old polarizations themselves became irrelevant and largely forgotten. But by the time of the exile, the old Abraham narratives had become firmly entrenched as a part of the total tradition. They were reinterpreted within the framework of the exilic and post-exilic situation, and Abraham supplanted Jacob permanently as the "common ancestor."

Evidently, the function of the Abraham epic as the means by which the divine blessings were extended to the non-Yahwist population was not forgotten, for this was the basis for Paul's presentation of the extension of the divine promise to the Gentiles—but this time without the political apparatus of military conquest and therefore the more easily recognizable by those walking in darkness.

NOTES

1. Cf. the discussion at p. 6 in G. E. Mendenhall, *The Tenth Generation: The Origins of the Biblical Tradition* (Baltimore: Johns Hopkins University Press, 1973), and especially the quotation from B. N. Cardozo: "We may think the law is the same if we refuse to change the formulas. The identity is verbal only."

2. The present fads for storytelling and substituting of genre labels for serious attempts to understand the course of ancient cultural history can easily degenerate into Orwellian rewriting of history to make it fit some modern political obsession.

3. Cf. T. L. Thompson: "The recovery of the earliest traditions is not a task proper to the historian, but is rather a literary task involving analysis of the traditions and their intention(s)," *Israelite and Judaean History* (ed. J. H. Hayes and J. M. Miller; Philadelphia: Westminster Press, 1977) 178. The recovery of "intention(s)" is the primary *historical* problem, inseparable from the total historical context of the literary corpus and equally inseparable from the understanding of the actual past.

4. The acceptance of the mention of "Israel" in the Merneptah stele as a reference to some social organization of pre-Mosaic times simply reinforces powerfully my contention that the twelve tribe federation was a religiously based unification of the *existing* population of Palestine.

5. M. Liverani, "The Ideology of the Assyrian Empire": "The divine approval is not the cause of the legitimacy of the action, it is clearly its expressed form. . . . Assur is precisely the hypostasis of the Assyrian kingship" (*Power and Propaganda: A Symposium on Ancient Empires* [ed. M. T. Larsen; Mesopotamia 7; (Copenhagen: Akademisk Forlag, 1979)] 301).

6. A. R. Millard, "Methods of Studying the Patriarchal Narratives as Ancient Texts," *Essays on the Patriarchal Narratives* (ed. D. J. Wiseman and A. R. Millard; Winona Lake, Ind.: Eisenbrauns, 1983) 35–51.

7. *ANET,* 267, 268, 270.

8. H. B. Huffmon, "Prophecy in the Mari Letters," *BAR,* 3.199–224.

9. H. Bess, "Systems of Land Tenure in Ancient Israel" (unpublished diss., University of Michigan, 1963).

10. For example, Gen 17:6 and elsewhere.

11. El Amarna 73:14–16.

12. J. Biella, *Dictionary of Old South Arabic* (Chico, Calif.: Scholars Press, 1982) 298: *hwfyhmw ḥ whnfhmw ḥ wF tny ḥllyn:* "(the god) granted them (the territory?) *h.* and enriched (?) them (with the territories?) *ḥ.* and F., the two pieces of (land taken as) plunder (?)." Cf. the discussion of Byblos Syllabic Spatula f, in G. E. Mendenhall, *The Syllabic Inscriptions of Byblos* (1985) 133.

13. For example, Tiglath-pileser I: "At the command of my lord Ashur I was a conqueror ... from beyond the Lower Zab River to the Upper Sea." *ANET,* 275. Cf. also Liverani, "The Ideology of the Assyrian Empire."

14. See Mendenhall, *The Syllabic Inscriptions of Byblos,* chap. 10, "Prologomena to a Linguistic History of the Semitic Languages."

15. The similarity of the Davidic "Divine Charter" with that so well illustrated in the Mesopotamian Amorite dynasties seems consistently to have been passed over lightly. Note the motive of the divine "chosenness" of the king, e.g., the Code of Hammurabi, line 22 and elsewhere (*ANET,* 164).

16. R. Dussaud, *Les origines cananéennes du sacrifice israélite* (Paris, 1921). Cf. W. F. Albright, *From the Stone Age to Christianity* (2d. ed.; Garden City, N.Y.: Doubleday Anchor Books, 1957) 294, on the "Canaanizing" sacrificial practice that certainly goes back to the "patriarchal age." He failed to recognize the fact that most of the prophets condemned those practices, that could only have been brought back in by a priestly cadre to whom that tradition was native.

17. Other genealogies that end with the tribal designation, e.g., that of David, exhibit roughly half the number of generations that are included in the Zadokite genealogy. The insertion of the Zadokite genealogy into an older one was a well-known ancient "historical" method.

18. J. Hoftijzer, *Die Verheissungen an die drei Erzväter* (Leiden: E. J. Brill, 1956) 10.

19. B. Bicknell, "Passives in Biblical Hebrew" (unpublished diss., University of Michigan, 1984). The function of Niphal and the inner passive stems should "be viewed in terms of the aspect of action which they signify.... It includes only the end result of the action or signifies the resulting state of the patient" (p. 128).

20. Curiously, R. Wilson entirely ignores the Keturah and Hagar genealogies except for some passing references to literary motifs (*Genealogy and History in the Biblical World* [New Haven: Yale University Press, 1977] 191). The motif of the "barren wife" is necessary to the replacement of an older tradition by a later one and presupposes that older tradition.

21. Mendenhall, *The Syllabic Inscriptions of Byblos,* esp. chap. 10.

22. Cf. the toponym *El-bethel.* Cf. also Mendenhall, *The Tenth Generation,* 44.

23. H. Levy seems first to have identified Tuttul with *tell et-ṭadyēn* on etymological grounds. See A. Goetze, "The Syrian Town of Emar," *BASOR* 147 (1957) 24 n. 24, where he rejects the identification that is now certain. The chief god of Tuttul already in Sargonic times was Dagan.

24. But see also chap. 9 (Hackett) in this volume.—Ed.

18

David as Temple Builder

CAROL MEYERS

I

The rich collection of insights and analyses and of important scholarly advances in the understanding of Israelite religion that comprise F. M. Cross's *Canaanite Myth and Hebrew Epic* also contains the following cautious statement about the putative role of David in the construction of a permanent temple for Yahweh in Jerusalem:

> We cannot be sure, despite later traditions, that David considered the tent provisional and that he himself persisted in planning to build a temple of cedar, that is, a dynastic shrine in the Canaanite pattern. Certainly the temple and its cult were largely, if not exclusively, the creation and innovation of Solomon.[1]

This reluctance to attribute much, if any, of the initiative for the Jerusalem Temple to the reign of David is predicated, for Cross, upon an awareness that other programs and events, which later became associated with David, were in fact the result of Solomonic activity that was at odds with the regnal policies of David. The most flagrant instance of such a reversal[2] is probably the attribution to David, on his deathbed, of instructions for the murders of Joab and Shimei (1 Kgs 2:5–9). Other factors, however, contribute to the hesitancy to ascribe the Temple project to Davidic policy. Recognition of the tradition of a God who wanders, for example, as well as the political hypothesis that a shrine fixed in one geographical locale would be discriminatory against all the tribes not favored by having that site in or near their territories, has led others to suggest that the notion of a permanent sanctuary could not have materialized until Solomon's reign.[3]

The difficulty in ascertaining David's actual part in the decision to build a temple and in the steps taken to carry out that plan clearly arose from the problematic nature of the biblical sources that provide information about David's activities in the cultic sphere. Prominent among those sources are 2 Samuel 7, which contains Nathan's oracular statements about the permanence of the Davidic dynasty as well as about the assignment to Solomon of the task of constructing a house for Yahweh's name; Psalm 132, which is a liturgical hymn marking the transfer of the Ark from Ephrathah/Jaar to Jerusalem; and 1 Chronicles 22, which describes David's preparation of the site and materials to be used by Solomon in building the Temple.[4] In addition to these major texts, certain other references bear directly upon the issue of David's involvement in the Temple project: the narratives about the threshing floor of Araunah, which was apparently the location of the future temple (2 Samuel 24; cf. 1 Chronicles 21 [and 22:1]; the tradition present already in 1 Kgs 8:16–21 that "it was in your [David's] heart" to build Yahweh's house; and 2 Chron 6:41–42, which cites Psalm 132 (vv 8–10) in the context of the Temple's dedication under Solomon and in so doing reflects an understanding, at least on the part of the Chronicler, that Psalm 132 implies a temple building and not a tent or tabernacle as the intended abode for the Ark. The Ark narratives, in particular 2 Sam 6:1–19 (= 1 Chron 13:1–14; 15:1—16:3), are also relevant because they concern the sacred object that was to be housed in the holiest chamber of the Temple in Jerusalem.

Arguments about David's role as initiator of the Temple project that depend directly upon any of these texts inevitably become bogged down in the notorious uncertainty about the integrity, context, and dating of these passages, particularly the three major sources mentioned above. The extent to which the Deuteronomist may have shaped pre-Solomonic materials in Nathan's oracle is a matter of extensive scholarly debate.[5] Similarly, no clear consensus has emerged concerning the origin, date, or function of Psalm 132.[6] Although most would agree that the psalm concerns the movement of the Ark to Jerusalem, even that viewpoint is open to question.[7] More serious, from the perspective of this investigation, is the problem of establishing whether or not the psalm refers to a permanent building in Jerusalem as the ultimate destination for the Ark that David brought to his dynastic capital. As for 1 Chronicles 22, the most widely divergent of opinions have been expressed concerning the antiquity and reliability of the attribution to David of activities expressly directed toward the construction of a monumental religious edifice.[8]

It is clear from the problematic nature of the biblical evidence that a fresh perspective on David's participation in the Temple project cannot rest entirely on any reexamination of the literary sources but rather must draw upon methodologies that diverge from traditional literary and historical analysis of relevant biblical texts. The construction of a major edifice, such as a temple, is surely a religious act but is also one that cannot be understood on that level alone. Activities that we deem religious because of our modern Western tendency to divide the world into the secular on the one hand and the sacred on the other were, in the biblical world, integrally and systematically part of the social, political, and economic fabric of any community. Therefore, "religious" or cultic institutions can fruitfully be studied by using approaches that take into account the intimate relationship of religious beliefs and activities with the dynamics of human organization, the latter including economic, political, and social factors. The recent outpouring of works employing sociological analysis is evidence of the recognition of this methodological potential and to some extent is a development of the older trend toward the use of political analysis. In both cases, the shift is away from the traditional judgment of Israelite history from an exclusively theological viewpoint.[9]

Considerable progress has been made in exploring the beginnings of the Israelite monarchy as political history. Less attention has been granted to the sociological and economic dynamics involved in the transition from tribal league to monarchy. This chapter will consider both of those aspects of David's rise to power. More specifically, the appearance of monumental architecture, of which temples are the prime example, as a feature in the emergence of centralized political configurations will be investigated as a way of bringing information derived outside the biblical sources to bear upon the problem of the Davidic role in temple-building. In another context I have attempted to show that Solomon's accomplishment in constructing a temple-palace complex of enormous proportions and elaborate decoration was not simply a matter of his materialistic personal inclinations or of his decadent distortion of the ideals promulgated or achieved in the Davidic synthesis of tribal traditions.[10] Rather, Solomon's architectural program can be seen as the logical and essential continuation of the national unification and imperial expansion achieved by David. Perhaps this perspective on Solomon's projects should be pushed further in its observation of the inextricable link between David's conquests and Solomon's various enterprises. Can any of Solomon's activities be appraised as having more than functional origin in David's deeds? Would it be more accurate to attribute to David himself as the architect of the monarchy and the empire the full range of organizational characteristics normally associated with the centralizing forces of David's monarchic system?

At the outset one must acknowledge the perspective of most, if not all, of the biblical passages dealing with David and the Temple. Whether or not any of those passages can be taken as a reliable indication that David in fact had set out to provide a house for Yahweh is a moot point. Yet it is clear that these texts are operating from a mind-set that expects David to have been determined to do just that. Many of the texts are blatantly apologetic; they take pains to explain just why it is that Solomon, rather than David, carries out the project. Surely this characteristic reveals an attitude expecting David to have been the one to have built the Temple. The attitude certainly was present not long after David's death, and hence it is not impossible to suppose that it existed during his lifetime.

II

The formation of the monarchy must be understood in terms considerably more complex than the assertion that the rise to power of Saul and David was a response to the pressures exerted upon the Israelite tribes by the Philistine hegemony.[11] It is beyond the scope of this work to evaluate or even summarize the existing scholarly investigations of the dynamics involved in state formation in Israel, particularly because the focus here is on the control mechanisms and developmental features inevitably arising from the needs of a centralized government, no matter how the origins of such a system are explained or described. Instead, the political complexity of the monarchic state, once it had been established by David, must first be examined. For that task, the application of concepts from modern political science is appropriate.[12]

Not the least of the features of the Israelite monarchy that have been considered unique is the unparalleled preeminence of a Palestinian-based superpower in the Near East. The kingdom ruled by David and then Solomon was hardly a "gigantic homogeneous bloc" but rather was a remarkably varied structure, composed of at least five discrete levels of political interrelationships.[13] The political organization achieved by roughly the midpoint of David's forty-year reign was that of a true empire, which can be conceived schematically as consisting of five concentric circles, each of which represents both a different stage in the formation of the empire and a different category of domination by the central government in Jerusalem. The heart of the empire was the tribal kingdom of Judah (governed at first from Hebron), which soon became a national kingdom that included the northern tribes.[14] With the united tribes providing military and material support, David proceeded to establish no fewer than five types of dominance over adjacent territories.[15] Closest to home, David conquered enclaves of Canaanite settlement in conjunction with his subjugation, not without considerable difficulty, of the expansionist Philistine threat on the western edge of the Israelite holdings. The lands thus occupied were consolidated with existing tribal lands to form a territorial state. The Israelite armies next subjugated Moab, which was one of several areas made into vassal states (2 Sam

8:2), and Edom. The latter, like Damascus later, was more severely subjected to Israelite domination: David put garrisons in these regions (2 Sam 8:6, 14), making them provinces. Ammon was apparently annexed (2 Sam 12:30). In a final expansionist move, David confronted the Aram-Zobah bloc, defeated Hadadezer, and ultimately established sovereignty over the complex of Aramean states. This accomplishment apparently also provided the Israelite kingdom with ascendancy over some areas beyond Damascus (2 Sam 8:10).[16] In short, David within twenty years had established a variegated supranational state with its peripheral territories controlled in various ways by the centralized power structure in Jerusalem.

Not only does the structure of the empire show evidence of careful and strategic application of divergent mechanisms for relating the subjugated regions to the center of the realm but also the success of David's military venture bespeaks foresight and astute advance planning.[17] One can detect, in the early years of Israelite expansion, signs that David's goals were both long range and well defined. Since David's marriages signify political alliances, the list of wives in 2 Sam 3:2–5 indicates his consolidation of a Judean power base as well as his anticipation, by means of his marital union with the daughter of the king of Geshur, of the future advance of his forces toward the northeast across the Jordan and north of Ammon.

David's remarkable success in achieving national unity and international ascendancy was clearly dependent upon his military and political strategy. Interwoven with the strategic dimension was David's ability to muster support by convincing his three-tiered constituency—his immediate followers, his Israelite tribal coalition, and his imperial subjects—of the legitimacy of his rule. He had to persuade them that their tribute, service, and loyalty—their material, personal, and psychological surrender to royal domination—would be amply rewarded by internal peace and stability, by agricultural fecundity, and by military security (cf. the language of Ps 132:12, 15, 18). The mechanisms for securing the support of the different components of the population would not necessarily be the same, although some overlap might be expected. The most powerful mechanisms could well be the ones that would have reached equally all three segments of David's realm. This three-tiered model admittedly does not reflect the variation that existed within each segment: different ranks and categories of leadership, alignments among the tribal components on the national level, and variegated forms of subjugation imposed upon the conquered states. Nonetheless, these three segments represent a legitimate arrangement with respect to the question of how David was able to achieve control of a vast realm.

David's initial force of arms went a long way toward establishing his authority at all levels, but his military prowess alone cannot account for his ongoing maintenance of political domination. David would have had to use other means of persuasion or influence to assert in a convincing manner the legitimacy of his position.[18] He would have to have used various forms of propaganda to achieve such a goal. Despite its negative connotations, the term "propaganda" is appropriate and has often been applied to various sections of the biblical canon. Cross, for example, would label the Deuteronomistic history as Josianic propaganda, an ideological platform establishing a case for Josiah's reform and his hopes for restoring northern allegiance to Jerusalem.[19]

Written documents such as the Hebrew Bible or the various sources that ultimately formed the canon would have been effective as propaganda only insofar as they reached a literate audience. For the period of the early monarchy, one can speculate that the population to which a written brief for the monarchic power of David might be presented would be limited to the royal bureaucracy, that is, the uppermost level in the three-tiered population of the empire. It is possible to view 1 Samuel 9 to 1 Kings 2 as a "defense of David," a written apologia originating in David's court and directed to the elite, in much the way that other royal courts in the ancient Near East produced literature aimed at exalting and so legitimizing the occupant of the throne.[20]

The extent of the ideological impact of the written or even the spoken word would have been necessarily limited in the ancient world. Consequently, other forms of propaganda, notably those employing visual symbols, were extremely important.[21] Both verbal and visual modes of communication stressed that dynastic power derived its legitimacy from its close connection with divine sovereignty. With the religious sphere existing as an integral and critical aspect of political authority, divine sanction of a regime provided the ultimate and incontrovertible justification for its coercive power.[22] A religious text could convey that sanction to a privileged, literate audience; a religious symbol or edifice could provide that message to a wider public.

The Ark of the Covenant surely served as a prime symbol of Yahweh's presence among the tribes and of divine support for the king who had possession of it. Scholars widely recognize that the coming of the Ark to Jerusalem signified the granting of Yahweh's favor for the new era, the bestowal of divine blessings upon and through the regime that was inaugurating the shift from tribal organization to statehood, and God's approval of the new status of Jerusalem as the center of a far-reaching polity.[23] Bringing the Ark to the new capital helped immeasurably in transferring the ancient religionational traditions of premonarchic Israel to the new dynastic order and hence in securing the support of the tribal components of the national kingdom. If the Ark itself signified God's legitimating presence, the procession and the festivities connected with it constituted a media event that reached "all the people, the whole multitude of Israel, both men and women" (2 Sam 6:19). It should not go unnoticed that this festal occasion included the distribution of provisions to all the people, another royal action associated with cultic sacrifice and hence not without its value in eliciting the favor and support of the people, much as the distribution of parcels of land to the royal elite (see 1 Sam 22:7 and 2 Sam 9:9–11; cf. Ezek 46:16) was a mechanism, along with a written defense, for securing the loyalty of the bureaucracy.[24]

The presence of the Ark in Jerusalem was apparently a powerful and effective instrument for securing both monarchic and dynastic legitimacy in the eyes of the people who were heirs to Israel's ancient order. That it was not the only mechanism for achieving national solidarity will be discussed below; but it was the major symbol in the religious sphere for sanctioning the reordering of Israelite national life. The question remains, which returns us to our consideration of David's relationship to the construction of a permanent structure to house the Ark, as to whether the Ark alone, without a "house of cedar" (i.e., a permanent monumental building, according to ancient Near Eastern idiom; 2 Sam 7:7), was an adequate form of propaganda for communicating with the nonliterate population of the empire. Was the archaic Ark tradition sufficient to meet the needs of a dynastic order in a world in which the building of a temple was a requisite component of the establishment of monarchic rule, in which the construction of a shrine simultaneously actualized and symbolized the divine sanction of human rule?

Had Israel's boundaries in the Davidic era been limited to the national kingdom or even to the territorial state that included Canaanite enclaves wrested from the Philistines, the Ark traditions might have been powerful enough to have taken on successfully the added burdens of royal iconography and to have helped form the image of rightful human kingship under Yahweh's sovereignty. Yet the dissension among the tribal components of David's kingdom, as evidenced by the conflicts portrayed in the succession story which comprises a major portion of 2 Samuel, perhaps belies the shaky unity of a diverse population that might have been brought closer together in support of David had an imposing temple building superseded the more modest tent enclosure for the Ark.

The question about the need for a temple as a propaganda measure beyond that provided by the Ark with respect to the internal Israelite population is perhaps rendered inconsequential in the light of the fact that David's constituency contained a third segment, the subject populations of the adjoining states conquered by the Israelite armies. For them the Ark symbolism would have been far less meaningful on a political level (as opposed to the military aspect, the Ark having served effectively as Israel's palladium in the Philistine wars). David's task of communicating to a non-Israelite population the legitimacy of his dominion would have been made immeasurably easier by the existence in Jerusalem of a shrine of grand dimensions and rich design, a building commensurate with the international preeminence of the Davidic throne.

It has long been recognized that the relationship between God, king, and temple in the ancient Near East was an intimate and essential one.[25] One of the tasks of the king, as representative of a centralized community that depended upon the official administration for its welfare, was to erect an earthly home for the deity who was the source of the bounty and stability that the populace hoped would prevail. Without the deity's presence in a temple building, where he or she was accessible to the public (or at least the priestly leadership) and available to receive the offerings that were meant to help secure divine favor, the authority of the king to rule his people was not clearly established. Conversely, the decay or disrepair of a temple was seen as evidence of divine anger; and kings were as anxious to set about the restoration of existing temple buildings as they were to initiate the construction of new ones.[26]

On these grounds alone, one could assert that it would have been David's next logical step, after bringing the Ark to Jerusalem, to set about building a temple for it in conformity with ancient Near Eastern attitudes,[27] even though the presence of the Ark alone might have served David's purposes vis-à-vis the top and middle tiers of his constituency. However, the imperial populace also needed to be presented with a convincing image of royal dominance. Temples were the structures par excellence for communicating to a wide audience the authoritative rule of the regime responsible for erecting them. It is important to note that in the case of the Jerusalem Temple, when it finally was completed by Solomon, the architectural style as well as the nature of the embellishments were in the Syro-Canaanite mode. The use of a ground plan and of decorative motifs similar to those used in the states surrounding Israel and subjugated by Israel was not simply a matter of slavish borrowing; rather, it can be seen as a deliberate use of a visual idiom that would be clearly understood by the population to which the Temple's existence and hence its political significance had to be conveyed.[28] The efficacy of temple buildings in convincing subjugated or allied peoples of the supremacy of a particular god and of the regime associated with that god can be further seen in the way in which the gods of a polity were invoked in the procedures for making international treaties.[29]

III

The arguments from a political perspective that David as an imperial Near Eastern ruler intended to construct a temple for the Ark and for Yahweh in Jerusalem can be augmented by a consideration of the socioeconomic factors that were features of temple-building in archaic states. The rapid emergence of Israel as an imperial power in the lifetime of David marked a radical change not only in political orientation but also in socioeconomic structure. The leadership of Saul and of David in his early years set Israel on a course marked by the increasingly centralized organization of local communities and a growing body of individuals whose statuses in the community were hierarchically ranked. These two principles of social organization can be identified with a chiefdom stage in the evolution of a complex state.[30]

The features of a centralized, hierarchical government as they can first be perceived in the chiefdom stage have long been recognized by anthropologists engaged in ethnographic studies of contemporary social groups. Anthropological theorists have also sought to isolate aspects of archaeological data that might be used to identify centralizing social units in ancient populations. The lists of relevant data vary, but certain items pertinent to temple-building recur and are worth noting insofar as they constitute evidence of societies moving toward or having already achieved the institutional transformation that accompanies state formation.

Perhaps the most comprehensive list (twenty items) is that compiled by C. Renfrew.[31] Three of the items can be cited: increase of rituals and ceremonies for various social purposes; growth of the priesthood; and use of public labor for public works, agricultural (e.g., irrigation) and/or religious (temples, pyramids, tombs). For C. S. Peebles and S. M. Kus,[32] five major distinctive attributes can be recognized in the emergence of ranked societies. One of these concerns the existence of organized productive labor that transcends the household group, with the construction of monumental architecture as a major object of such activity. A third theorist, T. Earle, proposes a simple, or less nuanced, collection of three essential features.[33] The existence of central places, the importance of which can be ascertained by the labor expended in their construction is one; and the utilization of cooperative labor for capital improvements (e.g., irrigation and dams) or other supradomestic construction activities is a second (with the presence of mortuary practices exhibiting the differentiation of wealth being the third).

All of these models include as a prominent feature the existence of construction activities that serve the state. Some of these activities can be seen as public works of overtly pragmatic value, such as the hydraulic projects.[34] Yet the most notable projects, monumental temples and/or tombs, are those whose pragmatic value is more subtle yet equally important in integrating the various components of a complex society and in establishing the authority of the ancient theocratic state. Not only can monumental architecture be identified as a diagnostic feature of the shift to nonegalitarian societies[35] but it also can be perceived as signifying institutional and societal transitions involved in state formation. Public monuments such as temples, even if they could be approached or entered only by an elite clergy, nonetheless were institutions that pertained to the whole of society. This would have been particularly true for the time period in which such projects were undertaken, when the human and material resources of the state were called upon to an extent beyond that required to support bureaucratic structure. The requirements of manpower and materials that are part of the effort to produce monumental architecture contribute to the solidarity of a political unit insofar as the feeling of commonality is a consequence rather than an antecedent of a state composed of discrete segments.[36] The appearance of a temple on the human landscape meant that a wide spectrum of the population had participated in some way in the construction process and hence shared in the communal welfare that the temple inaugurated.

Furthermore, the temple as a state institution had many specialized functions that were directed toward self-maintenance but also provided services to the realm, to the palace and populace alike. The manifold ritual activities of a temple meant the existence of workshops and storerooms, the latter being the repository of at least part of the state's revenues. Its complex administration would have been supported by temple revenues; but the surpluses were available, it seems, for redistributive purposes, at least at festivals and probably at other times as well.[37] The temple clearly represented the intersection of the social and material aspects of a nation with its ideological values. Temples were every bit as utilitarian, though perhaps in a more abstract way, as were other public works such as irrigation systems.

IV

These remarks about the integrative role of monumental (temple) architecture in state formation and social stability can now be grounded in an examination of the evidence that ancient Israel at the inception of its monarchic period exhibited characteristics similar to those identified in the models proposed by anthropologists. Although our focus is on temple construction, other religiopolitical aspects of centralizing states—the growth of the priesthood and attention to ritual—can be identified in the policies associated with Davidic rule and will first be examined.

The rise of the priesthood does not have to be tied to the construction of the Temple. The two lists of high officials attributed to the Davidic era (2 Sam 8:15–18 and 2 Sam 20:23–26; cf. the Solomonic list, 1 Kgs 4:1–6) indicate the proliferation of priestly involvement at the highest levels under David. In the first list, the king's own family is included ("David's sons, priests"), although this may simply mean, since the sons lack the specific designation by name that all of the other officials mentioned in the lists enjoy, that David himself is particularly attuned to priestly affairs. Both lists involve additions to the established incumbency of Abiathar, who was a descendant of Eli and a close associate of David especially in the beginning of the latter's career. Zadok is appointed a priest along with Abiathar in the first list; and Ira the Jairite appears as "David's priest" in the second list. Factional juggling or tribal politics may indeed be responsible for the specific individuals selected,[38] but attempts to discern the political aspect of the appointments of Zadok and Ira should not obscure the fact that they represent additions to the priestly hierarchy. At the end of David's reign there are two military officers (Joab over the army and Benaiah over the mercenaries) and three priests. Just as the army has increased at all levels and required two high-level administrators, so too an expansion of the priesthood at lower echelons would have accompanied the added high-level posts. The Chronicler's record of the Davidic organization of the Temple servitors may indeed reflect a proliferation of priestly personnel implied by the cabinet lists of 2 Samuel. In addition, David's direct involvement in cultic matters and his association with psalmody (and hence liturgy) are not simply matters of personal patronage or preference but rather reflect his utilization of public cultural forms that have propaganda value and socially integrative potential.

David's expansion of the priestly bureaucracy and his attention to ritual need not be viewed as anticipatory of the needs of a temple institution, although it would be reasonable to consider them in that way. Other features of David's rule, however, may point more decisively to his intention to embark upon the sort of monumental architecture, a temple, typically associated with the transition to complex sociopolitical structures. It is worth pointing out that there was little opportunity, given the ecological circumstances of ancient Israel, for Israelite state formation to have undertaken hydraulic works, which are typically the diagnostic sign of a centralizing government. Among the possibilities that existed for the channeling of productive resources into a national enterprise, only a temple project would have been appropriate for Israel during the second half of David's reign. Construction of his own residence and the rebuilding of Jerusalem after it was taken from the Jebusites evidently occurred very early in David's career (2 Sam 5:9–12).

Temple-building required both materials and manpower. There is evidence that David had taken steps to secure both. Although it is difficult to say conclusively that a temple project was directly involved in his amassing of materials, such a supposition can be made on the basis of texts (e.g., 2 Sam 8:10–12) that describe the valuable materials that David collected from the subjugated nations and "dedicated to Yahweh." The relationship between periphery and center in an imperial structure inevitably produced a primary accumulation of wealth, derived at first from booty and tribute and eventually secured in the form of taxation as well. David does not seem to have levied taxes; the inpouring of goods from provinces and vassal states along with the income from crown property apparently was sufficient for the expenses of his court, army, and bureaucracy, with surplus for Yahweh—and for the projected temple. Parallel motifs in Near Eastern literature of subject peoples bringing precious commodities to the capital typically depict the gifts as offerings to the sovereign god of the capital, either to be put in the temple's treasuries or to be used in building the dynastic sanctuary.[39]

Manpower was a different matter. David created, according to the second listing of his chief officers, a new position in his administration, a superintendent over the labor force (*'al hammas,* 2 Sam 20:24). This levy, or corvée, apparently refers to persons conscripted for labor, probably on a temporary basis in contrast with the permanent labor force *(mas 'ōbēd),* which may have been comprised exclusively of non-Israelites.[40] That is, Israelites could be conscripted on an interim basis for the levy but not for the permanent institution of forced labor. That David instituted a cabinet post to oversee a levy meant that he intended to secure a labor force, probably for the public work of temple construction, just as Solomon later did (1 Kgs 5:27–31) expressly for temple work. David's conscriptive labor policies must be related to his census, which was taken by Joab and the army against their will (2 Sam 24:2–3) and so could not have been for augmentation of the military. What else could David have intended by this census than to secure native Israelite labor for a project that demanded more workmen than were readily available to him? A project such as the construction of a national shrine would be effective in its integrative function to the degree that it involved the population whose solidarity was to be advanced by the effort. We shall return below to the tragic consequences of David's census.

V

Examination of the political and socioeconomic conditions attendant upon the formation of imperial states corroborates the scanty biblical evidence that David had embarked upon the normal course of action for someone in his position, namely, a program of monumental architecture embodied in the construction of a temple in Jerusalem. Literary factors also contribute to this understanding of David's role in temple-building. Just as the Temple in Jerusalem, once erected, adheres in nearly every way to the array of motifs that form a common temple typology in ancient western Asia,[41] so too the description of the steps involved in its construction adheres to a common thematic structure found in a selection of Mesopotamian and Northwest Semitic building accounts. Although there are differences among the various building texts, each one exhibiting certain unique features of style or content, nonetheless a consistent five-part structure can be found in all such texts.[42] As might be expected, the narrative of Solomon's construction of the Temple follows the same five-part thematic arrangement and, at least structurally, is a typical Near Eastern building document. The biblical information about David's relationship to the Temple project obviously would not adhere to the full pattern of such building accounts. The last three items of those accounts—a description of the edifice itself, a portrayal of the ceremonies of dedication, and a blessing for the king or prayer by him—would be found only in the Solomonic materials. However, the first two parts of the typical building narrative are indeed present in the David story.

The first is the decision to erect a building, a decision inevitably linked to an expression of divine sanction. The essential approval of the deity could be made in a variety of ways, such as through dreams, divination, natural portents, or prophetic revelation. However divine authorization may have been secured, it is clear that a monarch hoping to build a temple experienced great anxiety about receiving approval for a project so essential to securing his own regnal authority,[43] for the god evidently could withhold consent and deny the king the sanction to carry out his task. In the David stories, Nathan is the prophetic conveyor of both the granting of Yahweh's permission (2 Sam 7:1–3) and then, in a striking reversal, the denial of permission (2 Sam 7:4–13). The promise of a dynastic house becomes substituted for the promise of a house for Yahweh. The originality of the sanction, preceding the denial, is hard to dispute, considering the effort that the denial makes to lessen what must have been a substantial setback to a king intent upon instituting a project with crucial political, economic, and social significance.

The second item of a temple-building account is the description of the preparations for the task of construction. This part was often elaborate; it dealt with the acquisition of materials, the drafting of an adequate labor force, preparation of the building site, and sometimes even the laying of the foundations as a separate ceremony.[44] The first two of these components, materials and manpower, have already been considered; and David's probable involvement in them has been established. The preparation of the location on which the Temple was to be built is directly attributed to David. Furthermore, this is the only element of the five-part typology that is vague in the Solomon narrative. David's purchase of the threshing floor of Ornan the Jebusite in the Chronicler's account (1 Chron 21:18—22:1) marks the acquisition of the site on which the Temple is to be built.[45] The Samuel account has the story curiously displaced to the end of 2 Samuel (24:15–25). In both accounts, however, divine sanction for the purchase comes through the prophet Gad.

Both accounts also describe a sacrificial ceremony carried out at an altar, built by David, which may have been the holocaust altar of the Solomonic Temple since the 1 Kings description of that edifice strangely omits mention of the main sacrificial altar. This ceremony adumbrates the elaborate dedicatory celebration held by Solomon. In the Davidic ceremony, the sacrifice elicits a response from Yahweh (2 Sam 24:25; 1 Chron 21:26). Such a response, which in itself can represent the consecration of a sanctuary,[46] is absent from the description of Solomon's dedicatory sacrifices (1 Kgs 8:62–64; 2 Chron 7:4–7; cf. 2 Chron 7:1–3, an insertion recording divine response to the sacrifices even before they were made!). Although it may not be justified to suggest that David's sacrifices fulfill in advance the dedicatory aspect of temple-building, it seems reasonable to interpret that action as part of the foundation ceremonies that were included in the second unit of the temple-building sequence (cf. Ezra 3:10–11, which describes the foundation ceremonies for the postexilic Temple and in so doing involve the "directions of David king of Israel").

To summarize: the common Near Eastern literary structure of temple-building accounts finds its place, albeit an incomplete one, in the Davidic materials. This observation lends further support to the supposition that David fully intended to build a temple in Jerusalem.

VI

Given the compelling evidence for David's temple-building intentions, it remains to consider what deterred David from carrying out his task. The biblical authors and the modern critics share both an interest in that question and a propensity to suggest imaginative explanations rather than probable causes. The biblical authors suppose either that David was too busy because of his enemies (1 Kgs 5:17), a possibility that does not take into account his relative freedom from military engagement in the latter half of his long reign; or that his hands were too bloody from his wars (1 Chron 22:8–9; 28:3), a proposal that apparently emerges from the desire to draw a contrast with Solomon as man of peace and to create a pun on his name; or that a tent had sufficed for Yahweh since the wilderness period and would continue to be an appropriate dwelling, an appeal to traditions in Nathan's oracle (2 Sam 7:6–7). The modern critics offer a variety of equally plausible suggestions, all based on the biblical explanations or on theoretical notions rather than on the dynamics of social processes.[47]

An alternative solution derives from the possibility that the census/plague episode of 2 Samuel 24 was placed in its present position at the end of 2 Samuel very late in the literary history of the book and that originally it had been attached to the materials contained in 2 Samuel 5—7.[48] The census, we have posited, was ordered by David in order to raise a levy of Israelite workers to build the Temple. What would have been the response? Despite the larger social value of cooperative Israelite labor on a national project for the sovereign god, the very concept of forced labor implies reluctance. This would be particularly true in Palestine, where the nature of an agricultural system adapted to the semiarid environment meant that chronic seasonal labor shortages were inevitable, especially in periods of agricultural intensification such as seems to have characterized the early stages of the monarchy. With David having established a standing army in addition to the traditional militia that had constituted the military during the premonarchic era, labor shortages were even more likely to have been a serious problem. In addition, the growth of the empire entailed the dispatching of diplomatic envoys and garrisons, probably composed of civilian employees as well as of soldiers, to the various parts of the conquered territories.

Because labor shortages can be posited for this particular point in Israelite history, the response to a census aimed at removing additional workers from their agricultural tasks could not have been viewed favorably. Samuel's warning (1 Sam 8:11b–13) about the liabilities of a monarchy with respect to conscription and corvée speaks to this question, in language that shows Samuel's awareness at the outset of Saul's reign of the negative aspects of a monarchic system.[49]

The census account is inextricably linked with the report of a devastating outbreak of disease. There is no reason to object to the historicity of that epidemic. On the contrary, the occurrence of such dramatic outbreaks in close association with some other, unrelated but potentially traumatic events inevitably creates the kinds of cause-and-effect theological explanations that are typical of human responses everywhere until the modern era, when medical science can demonstrate otherwise. The biblical corpus is replete with examples of outbreaks of pestilence or plague interpreted as the work of the angel of the Lord in furthering or bringing a halt to the event to which it is coincidentally linked.[50] Since census-taking is typically a dreaded event, it is not difficult to imagine that a population would grasp at any circumstance that would make the census invalid. The association of census and plague in the Bible suggests that a causal connection between the census and a not infrequent outbreak of disease was often made. The terror with which pestilence was viewed by a medically helpless population created the emotional willingness to seek cause and understanding, and we must strive not to allow our present scientific knowledge to keep us from acknowledging that fact.

To return to David and the Temple: the census/plague narrative, originally part of the section of 2 Samuel in which David's temple-building program would have been initiated, contains the information that can explain David's failure to carry out his strategy of having his newly formed state produce a monumental building in the capital. The plague was seen as a dramatic message from Yahweh that David should desist from the project that required the levy that a census would help secure. It is no wonder that, overnight, Nathan's oracular message of approval was reversed. It remained for Solomon to complete the project. Insofar as the initial approval, site selection, and amassing of materials, if not manpower, can be attributed to David, his role as temple builder transcends his inability to bring the project to fruition. Although he was not to receive the glory associated with the completion and dedication of a major edifice in the ancient world and in the history of Israel, he was also thereby to escape the opprobrium attached to the monarch responsible for completing a building that seemed unnecessarily opulent and dangerously open to paganism.

NOTES

1. F. M. Cross, *CMHE*, 231.

2. Ibid., 231 n. 50.

3. See M. Weinfeld, "Zion and Jerusalem as Religious and Political Capital: Ideology and Utopia," *The Poet and the Historian: Essays in Literary and Historical Biblical Criticism* (ed. R. E. Friedman; Harvard Semitic Studies 26; Chico, Calif.: Scholars Press, 1983) 89.

4. The succeeding chapters (22—26) of Chronicles proceed to attribute to David the organization of the priests and Levites as Temple servitors.

5. See the literature cited by P. K. McCarter, *II Samuel* (AB 9; Garden City, N.Y.: Doubleday & Co., 1984) 209–24, in his excellent discussion of the major approaches to the issues of date and unity.

6. The liturgical role of Psalm 132 seems assured by virtue of its position in the Psalter (cf. Cross, *CMHE*, 94–97), and the antiquity of the material has been established with some surety (see M. Dahood, *Psalms III: 101–150* [AB 17A; Garden City, N.Y.: Doubleday & Co., 1970] 241). However, the very archaic nature of the language has created considerable latitude in the interpretation of many of the terms of the poem and even in the syntactical relationship of the elements; compare, e.g., the readings and interpretations in F. M. Cross, "The Divine Warrior in Israel's Early Cult," *Biblical Motifs: Origins and Transformations* (ed. A. Altman; Cambridge: Harvard University Press, 1969) 22 and n. 36; in Dahood, *Psalms III,* 245; and in T. E. Fretheim, "Psalm 132: A Form-Critical Study," *JBL* 86 (1967) 289–300.

7. So D. R. Hillers, "Ritual Procession of the Ark and Ps 132," *CBQ* 30 (1968) 48–55.

8. The general tendency is to see in this chapter, which has no parallel in the Kings account, an example of the Chronicler promulgating his own viewpoint, which favors cultic matters and tends to idealize David. David's preeminent role in deciding to build the Temple and in laying out all the plans and materials for his inexperienced son would be just the convergence of interests that would characterize the Chronicler. A serious counter-tendency can be found in the observation by J. Bright, among others, that the tradition in Chronicles "ought not lightly to be dismissed" in the light of the strong traditions of David's concern with the cult; see J. Bright, *A History of Israel* (3d ed.; Philadelphia: Westminster Press, 1981) 206. Recently, B. Halpern has emphasized the existence of an extensive older literature, largely unknown but surely underlying at least some of the original sections in Chronicles, in his essay "Sacred History and Ideology: Chronicles' Thematic Structure—Indications of an Earlier Source," *The Creation of Sacred Literature* (ed. R. E. Friedman; Near Eastern Studies 22; Berkeley and Los Angeles: University of California Press, 1981) 35–54.

9. See Halpern's sharp critique of the use of theological history as the basis for historical theology, particularly with respect to the treatment of the foundation of the monarchy: "The Uneasy Compromise: Israel Between League and Monarchy," *Traditions in Transformation* (ed. B. Halpern and J. D. Levenson; Winona Lake, Ind.: Eisenbrauns, 1981) 59–63.

10. See my "The Israelite Empire: In Defense of King Solomon," *Michigan Quarterly Review* 22 (1983) 412–13.

11. The seminar papers presented to the SBL/ASOR seminar on the monarchy since 1980 have been instrumental in working toward a nuanced understanding of state formation in Israel.

12. A. Malamat has written extensively about the monarchy from such a perspective. One of his earlier treatments of this subject is "Organs of Statecraft in the Israelite Monarchy," *JNES* 28 (1965) 34–65. Recently his work has drawn more directly upon the work of political scientists dealing with imperial systems, such as S. N. Eisenstadt, M. T. Larsen, and M. Liverani, all of whom have made

valuable contributions to *Power and Propaganda: A Symposium on Ancient Empires* (ed. M. T. Larsen; Copenhagen: Akademisk Forlag, 1979).

13. A. Malamat, "A Political Look at the Kingdom of David and Solomon and Its Relations with Egypt," *Studies in the Period of David and Solomon and Other Essays* (ed. T. Ishida; Winona Lake, Ind.: Eisenbrauns, 1982) 189–204; see also Malamat's similar study, "The Monarchy of David and Solomon," *Recent Archaeology of the Land of Israel* (ed. H. Shanks; Washington, D.C.: Biblical Archaeology Society, 1984) 161–72.

14. G. Buccellati (*Cities and Nations of Ancient Syria* [Rome: Istituto di Studi del Vicino Oriente, 1967] 137–93) follows A. Alt ("The Formation of the Israelite State in Palestine," in Alt, *Essays in Old Testament History and Religion* [Garden City, N. Y.: Doubleday Anchor Books, 1966]) in characterizing this stage of Israelite monarchy as a regime of "Personal union," i.e., a situation in which two units are ruled by one person but without concomitant integration of those units. But see the discussion by J. A. Soggin, "The Davidic-Solomonic Kingdom," *Israelite and Judaean History* (ed. J. H. Hayes and J. M. Miller; Philadelphia: Westminster Press, 1977) 352–56.

15. Cf. n. 13.

16. Malamat ("The Monarchy of David and Solomon," 168) calls this alliance one of "satellite nations."

17. Ibid., 164–65.

18. K. Whitelam ("The Defence of David," *JSOT* 29 [1984] 61) points out that the rise to power of figures such as Augustus, Caesar, Napoleon, Hitler, Stalin, and Mao was closely associated with their utilization of various forms of media so as to be able to influence the attitudes of the people they had come to dominate at least partly by force.

19. Cross, *CMHE*, 284.

20. Whitelam, "The Defence of David," 61–87; cf. the discussion by S. N. Eisenstadt, "Observations and Queries About Sociological Aspects of Power in the Ancient World," *Power and Propaganda*, 14–16, of the need for an ascendant ruler to secure, in the preliminary stages of his rise to power, the services of loyal personnel who would be as independent as possible from traditional groups.

21. See M. Liverani, "The Ideology of the Assyrian Empire," *Power and Propaganda*, 301–2.

22. Eisenstadt, "Observations and Queries," 21–33.

23. Cross, *CMHE*, 230–31; A. F. Campbell, *The Ark Narrative* (SBLDS 16; Missoula: Scholars Press, 1975) 244–49; T. Ishida, *The Royal Dynasties in Ancient Israel* (BZAW 142; Berlin: de Gruyter, 1977) 146; Weinfeld, "Zion and Jerusalem," 101.

24. T. N. D. Mettinger, *Solomonic State Officials: A Study of the Civil Government Officials of the Israelite Monarchy* (Lund: Gleerup, 1971) 80–110.

25. H. Frankfort, *Kingship and the Gods* (Chicago: University of Chicago Press, 1978 [orig. ed., 1948] 267–74; more recently, G. W. Ahlström, *Royal Administration and National Religion in Ancient Palestine* (Leiden: E. J. Brill, 1982), and B. Halpern, *The Constitution of the Monarchy in Israel* (HSM 25; Chico, Calif.: Scholars Press, 1981) 21–31. J. M. Lundquist ("The Legitimizing Role of the Temple in the Origin of the State" [SBLASP 1982] 271–97) would go

so far as to say that the state in archaic societies, the Davidic empire included, could not have been considered as having come into being until the national temple was constructed and dedicated. Contrast the view of Bright (*A History of Israel*, 217–18), who, failing to grasp the integral relationship of state formation and temple-building, relegates the temple to the status of one of the various building projects by which "Solomon's wealth was put to work."

26. Some examples of the evidence of this state of affairs in Ugaritic and Mesopotamian literature are cited in M. Ota, "A Note on 2 Sam 7," *A Light Unto My Path* (ed. H. N. Bream et al.; Gettysburg Theological Studies 4; Philadelphia: Temple University Press, 1974) 404–5; in Halpern, *The Constitution of the Monarchy*, 21–23; and in Frankfort, *Kingship and the Gods*, 267–68.

27. So Soggin, "The Davidic-Solomonic Kingdom," 363.

28. See my "The Israelite Empire," 420–22. The specific role of the external appearance of the Temple, with the pillars of Jachin and Boaz as the dominant features, in communicating that Yahweh indeed had taken up residence in his earthly abode is explained in my "Jachin and Boaz in Religious and Political Perspective," *CBQ* 45 (1983) 167–78. See also Whitelam, "The Defence of David," 61–65.

29. Buccellati, *Cities and Nations*, 63 and n. 171.

30. J. W. Flanagan ("Chiefs in Israel," *JSOT* 20 [1981] 47–73) suggests that describing the Saul-David transition to monarchy in terms of the dynamics of chiefdom can help account for the "forces and counter-forces" that accompanied the rise of the monarchy. He draws heavily upon social anthropological discussion as exemplified by the essays in *Origins of the State* (ed. R. Cohen and E. R. Service; Philadelphia: Institute for the Study of Human Issues, 1978).

31. C. Renfrew, "Beyond a Subsistence Economy: The Evolution of Social Organization in Prehistoric Europe," *Reconstructing Complex Societies* (ed. C. B. Moore; *BASOR* Sup 20; Cambridge, Mass.: ASOR, 1974) 73.

32. C. S. Peebles and S. M. Kus, "Some Archaeological Correlates of Ranked Societies," *American Antiquity* 42 (1977) 431–33.

33. T. Earle, *Economic and Social Organization of a Complex Chiefdom* (Anthropology Papers, Museum of Anthropology, University of Michigan, no 63; Ann Arbor, Mich.: University of Michigan, 1978). Earle and Peebles and Kus both use a cybernetic model; the usefulness of such a model is a debatable issue only in the consideration of the dynamics of state formation and does not affect the descriptive elements relating to the chiefdom or state once it exists.

34. E. R. Service ("Classical and Modern Theories of the Origins of Government," *Origins of the State*) asserts that nearly all of the classic archaic civilizations had complex systems of state-controlled water systems.

35. B. Price, "Secondary State Formation: An Explanatory Model," *Origins of the State*, 165; Renfrew, "Beyond a Subsistence Economy," 78.

36. See Buccellati, *Cities and Nations*, 63.

37. J. J. Janssen ("The Role of the Temple in the Egyptian Economy During the New Kingdom," *State and Temple Economy in the Ancient Near East* [ed. E. Lipiński; Louvain, Department Oriëntalistiek, 1979] 2.514–15) offers the intriguing suggestion that the periodic provision of foodstuffs, collected by the temples as offerings, to villagers on the West Bank at Thebes meant that the

"temples played a part not unlike the parish-relief boards of the Christian Churches." Cf. 1 Sam 21:1–6, where David, lacking provisions, receives supplies from Ahimelech the priest at Nob; Ahimelech, short of a supply of "common bread," nonetheless agrees to supply David with "holy bread."

38. E.g., see the proposal of S. Olyan concerning "Zadok's Origins and the Tribal Politics of David," *JBL* 101 (1982) 177–93.

39. Weinfeld, "Zion and Jerusalem," 108–15.

40. See Mettinger's analysis, *Solomonic State Officials,* 128–37.

41. As described by J. M. Lundquist, "What Is a Temple? A Preliminary Typology," *The Quest for the Kingdom of God: Essays in Honor of George E. Mendenhall* (ed. H. B. Huffmon et al.; Winona Lake, Ind.: Eisenbrauns, 1983) 205–19, and "The Common Temple Ideology of the Ancient Near East," *The Temple in Antiquity* (ed. T. G. Madsen; Religious Monograph Series; Provo, Utah: Religious Studies Center, Brigham Young Univ., 1984) 53–76.

42. An investigation of over twenty building stories, analyzed as to both content and structure, can be found in A. Hurowitz, *Temple Building in the Bible in Light of Mesopotamian and North-West Semitic Writings* (doctoral diss., Hebrew University; Jerusalem: 1983; Hebrew).

43. Ota, "A Note on 2 Sam 7," 404–5; Ishida, *The Royal Dynasties,* 85; and R. S. Ellis, *Foundation Deposits in Ancient Mesopotamia* (New Haven: Yale University Press, 1968) 6–8.

44. Ellis's work as a whole *(Foundation Deposits)* deals with the ceremonial and ideological dimensions of this stage of a temple project. See pp. 8–17 for a discussion of the extraordinary measures taken to secure and prepare building sites and pp. 17–31 for an account of the collection and manufacture of suitable materials with the direct involvement of the king.

45. The question of prior sanctity of the site is difficult to answer. It is unlikely that a Jebusite shrine had been situated on Ornan's property, but the threshing floor in itself may have had some special significance. See S. Smith, "The Threshing Floor at the City Gate," *PEQ* (1946) 5–14.

46. J. Milgrom ("Altar," *EncJud* 1. 764) observes that it is "an assumption common to biblical tradition that a sanctuary is not fully consecrated—or is not divinely sanctioned—unless it has a tradition of theophany upon its altar."

47. For explanations not based directly on the biblical ones, see Weinfeld, "Zion and Jerusalem," 88: "It was almost too difficult for a single generation to assimilate two innovations [fixed dynasty and fixed sanctuary] at once"; Ishida, *The Royal Dynasties,* 95: David was too preoccupied with a struggle between priestly factions; and V. W. Rabe, "Israelite Opposition to the Temple," *CBQ* 29 (1967) 8, 229: conservative elements influenced David to keep the tent.

48. So McCarter, *II Samuel,* 516–17. Its relocation probably was the result of the manipulation of the altar story in anticipation of the Solomonic material that dominates the beginning of 1 Kings.

49. See I. Mendelsohn, "Samuel's Denunciation of Kingship in the Light of the Akkadian Documents from Ugarit," *BASOR* 143 (1956) 17–22.

50. E.g., Exod 32:35; Num 16:11–15; 2 Kgs 19:35–36. For examples of pestilence, understood as divine action, altering the course of human affairs, see W. H. McNeill, *Plagues and Peoples* (Garden City, N.Y.: Doubleday, 1976).

19

In Defense of the Monarchy:
The Contribution of Israelite Kingship
to Biblical Theology

J. J. M. ROBERTS

It is very difficult to write a dispassionate evaluation of the contribution that the Israelite monarchy made to biblical theology. The monarchy arose and developed in controversy, and that ancient debate continues to provoke sharp controversy in modern attempts to evaluate the theological significance of the Israelite kingdom. In the ancient debate some voices claimed that the mere request for a human king was tantamount to a rejection of God, to a rebellion against divine rule (Judg 8:22–23; 1 Sam 8:7; 12:12, 17–20). Others, arguing less theologically but equally opposed to the monarchy, saw kingship as a totally unnecessary and unproductive drain on the resources of a healthy society (Judg 9:7–15; 1 Sam 10:27). Still others, the ancient promonarchists, viewed kingship as God's gift that finally brought order to an irresponsibly chaotic society in which formerly "every man did what was right in his own eyes" (Judg 17:6; 21:25; cf. 18:1; 19:1). Which of these ancient opinions is the voice of authentic Yahwism? Or, more to the point, which of these ancient opinions, if any, represent the authentic word of God?

Given these several discordant opinions, all of which are preserved and positively presented in Scripture, one might have expected contemporary scholars to be cautious about adopting any of them uncritically. Nonetheless it is fairly common today for biblical scholars to characterize the monarchy as an essentially alien development in Israelite history.[1] Its development, and especially the creation of an imperialistic ideology to undergird it, is typically seen as the progressive paganization of Israel,[2] and some scholars who hold this view are quite extreme in rejecting any theological construct that is dependent on the monarchy for its creation or development.[3]

The implications of such a stance are profound, because many of what have been taken to be central biblical themes owe their existence or their peculiar biblical shape to the imperial theology first developed in the

Davidic-Solomonic court and then transmitted and elaborated in the royal cult of the subsequent Judean court. I have discussed the formation and the shape of that imperial theology extensively elsewhere,[4] so here I will simply list some of the central biblical themes that are dependent on this royal theology.

While the conception of Yahweh as king is premonarchical in origin[5] and at one stage in Israelite history even functioned polemically to retard the development of human kingship,[6] the imperial conquests of David played an essential role in the development of the theological claim that Yahweh's rule was universal, that he was the great king over all the earth.[7] The royal theology's claim that God had chosen David and his dynasty as God's permanent agent for the exercise of the divine rule on earth was the fundamental starting point for the later development of the messianic hope, and the particular contours that this hope took reflect to a large extent the portraits of the ideal king projected in the royal cult.[8] Those portraits include mythological elements, some borrowed from other cultures, but Christians have claimed that even these mythological elements find a surprisingly literal fulfillment in Jesus Christ.[9] Finally, the imperial theology's claim that Yahweh chose Jerusalem for his dwelling place, a claim that resulted in the creation of a mythological mystique for this royal city, is the ultimate source for the later prophetic vision of universal peace and for the hope of eternal life in the new Jerusalem.[10]

If one dismisses the imperialistic theology of the Davidic-Solomonic court as sheer apostasy, as nothing but the progressive paganization of the Yahwistic faith, what does that do to the content of biblical theology? Must all of those biblical themes dependent on this theology for their development or elaboration also be condemned as pagan aberrations? If so, biblical theology as it has been traditionally understood will be gutted. The knife will have to remove far more than just the messianism that J. L. McKenzie is willing to sacrifice to his antimonarchical principle.

Before undergoing radical surgery, a patient is always wise to get a second opinion, and before sacrificing so much of the traditional content of biblical theology, one should question whether the Israelite monarchy has been correctly diagnosed as an alien, malignant growth in the body of genuine Yahwism. This negative diagnosis is based on several arguments: (1) The establishment of the monarchy involves significant borrowing from the surrounding, non-Israelite cultures; (2) the setting up of a human king stands in fundamental opposition to the recognition of God as king; and (3) the motivations behind the royal theology are transparently human and reflect all too clearly the inevitable coercive abuse of any human monopoly on power. Each of these arguments must be reappraised to see whether it justifies such a negative appraisal of the royal theology.

FOREIGN ELEMENTS

The monarchy is generally regarded as alien to genuine Yahwism, because the development of the monarchy in Israel involved the adaptation of elements taken over from the surrounding cultures. This is indicated by the Deuteronomic and Deuteronomistic motif that Israel asked for a king "like all the nations" (Deut 17:14; 1 Sam 8:5) or "to be like all the nations" (1 Sam 8:20). Moreover, a comparison of the Israelite monarchy with the monarchies in the surrounding states shows that Israel obviously adapted many features from these older models. Egypt, in particular, appears to have exercised a strong influence over the development of the Israelite monarchy. This is not surprising, given the fact that Egypt had been the nominal overlord of Palestine down to the time of the formation of the Israelite monarchy and that Egypt experienced a resurgence of its imperial power while the Israelite monarchy was still quite young, during the reign of Solomon and especially of Rehoboam, his successor. David and Solomon both appear to have followed Egyptian models in setting up their imperial administrations,[11] the Israelite coronation service seems to have adapted the Egyptian practice of giving five royal names,[12] and the conception of the new king as the offspring of the deity has certain connections to the Egyptian material.[13] The practice of anointing the new king may also go back to Egyptian antecedents, but this is debated.[14] Other elements associated with the monarchy seem to have connections with Mesopotamia,[15] though these may have been mediated through the smaller kingdoms that lay between Israel and the major empires of Assyria and Babylon.

Nevertheless, despite these borrowings, it is not at all clear whether one is justified in characterizing the monarchy as alien to the essence of Yahwism. As far as one is able to judge, given the nature of the sources, Yahwism has always been characterized by the adaptation of elements from its surroundings. If one can characterize the Mosaic period as the period when Yahwism was born, following the biblical tradition about the revelation of the name Yahweh, one finds a religious faith quite open to external religious influences. The revelation of the divine name takes place at a mountain site that had apparently long been sacred to tribes in the area (Exod 3:1), and in organizing the new religious community, particularly with regard to its cultus, Moses seems to have been heavily influenced by his Mideonite family connection (Exod 18:1–27).[16] Moreover, Israel's earliest religious poetry seems to have been heavily dependent on the poetic canons and the religious motifs of contemporary Canaanite culture.[17] It is difficult to speak of the essence of Yahwism without speaking of its ability to take up elements of its environment, even hostile elements, and transform them into supporting structures for the Yahwistic faith. In view of this well-attested power of absorption, the mere presence of foreign elements in the development of the Israelite monarchy is hardly sufficient grounds for rejecting it as pagan aberration.

THE CONFLICT BETWEEN HUMAN
AND DIVINE KINGSHIP

But is not the conception that Yahweh is king fundamentally at odds with any attempt to set up a human king? Is not the desire for a human king tantamount to the rejection of Yahweh as king? Such a view was current in ancient Israel. Both Gideon (Judg 8:22–23) and Samuel (1 Sam 8:7; 10:19; 12:12, 17–20) give expression to it, but the modern theologian would do well to consider the issue carefully before simply adopting this view as the authentic word of God on the matter.

In the first place, this is only one of the points of view preserved and positively presented in the biblical text. Even the Deuteronomistic historian (Dtr), who is normally considered rather critical of kingship, preserves both the promonarchical and the antimonarchical sources in his account of the transition from tribal confederacy to monarchy, and he, along with many other biblical writers, invests the monarchy with the sanction of Yahweh's promissory covenant to the Davidic dynasty.[18] If one takes canon seriously as an important factor in theological debate, then it must be significant that the voices of the promonarchists were not erased from the biblical record in the editing process. If the critique of kingship preserved in the biblical record relativizes kingship and destroys any claim which that form of human government may make to being *the* divinely authorized form of government,[19] the positive appreciation for kingship relativizes the claims of any competing form of human government. In fact, one can hardly find any clear portrayal of a rival form of government. The tribal alliance remains a nebulous scholarly reconstruction even for the period when it functioned politically, and after the establishment of the monarchy there seem to have been no efforts to return to this earlier form of organization. Both the prophetic visions of the future government and the actual forms the government took when Israel gained a measure of independence, as in the Maccabean era, were in some sense monarchical.[20] Contrary to S. Herrmann,[21] there was even an attempt to restore the monarchy in the early postexilic period.[22] Its failure was due to Israel's status as an insignificant but potentially troublesome part of the Persian empire. Israel simply did not have the freedom to choose its own form of government.

The apparent assumption of later Israel that a free Israel would be constituted as a kingdom and Dtr's clear incorporation and preservation of both promonarchical and antimonarchical sentiments in his history suggest that one be very careful in evaluating Dtr's attitude toward the monarchy. It is doubtful whether one can simply identify the anti-monarchical sentiments of either Gideon or Samuel with the opinion of Dtr. The law of the king (Deut 17:14–20) found in the Deuteronomic law code, the theological base for Dtr's treatment of history, contains no trace of the notion that the appointment of a human king implies the rejection of Yahweh as Israel's king.[23] While Dtr incorporates traditions in his history that attribute that notion to Gideon and Samuel, two of his heroes, his treatment of both contains certain undercurrents which, taken seriously, tend to distance the narrator from his leading character. As has long been noted, while Gideon rejected the popular attempt to make him and his son after him "ruler" over Israel since only Yahweh should be Israel's "ruler," this rejection appears to have been more the rejection of a title than of the substance behind that title.[24] Immediately after rejecting this title, Gideon asks for tribute from his followers (Judg 8:24), establishes a cult center in his city of Ophrah (Judg 8:27), and creates a large harem for himself (Judg 8:30). Abimelech, his son through the concubine, clearly understood that despite Gideon's disclaimer, his father did in fact "rule," and he assumed that that rule would pass to Gideon's sons (Judg 9:2). Some ancient sources have probably been conflated in Judges 8—9,[25] but Dtr has allowed these texts to stand together, thereby relativizing Gideon's rejection of the "rule" and at the same time distancing himself from this rigid position.

Dtr similarly distances himself from the opinion of Samuel voiced in 1 Samuel 8 and 12. In addition to preserving the more promonarchical narratives in 1 Samuel 9—11, including the notice in 10:27 that identifies those who opposed Saul's rule as "worthless fellows," Dtr gives some justification to the people's demand for a king even in 1 Sam 8:1–5, when he preserves the tradition that the sons of Samuel perverted justice and ruled unjustly.[26] Moreover, in 1 Sam 8:7 Yahweh has to remind Samuel that the people are rejecting Yahweh, not Samuel, as their ruler, and it is curious how easily Yahweh, in contrast to the irate Samuel, gives in to the people and grants their request. R. Klein comments that the rationale for this paradoxical behavior of Yahweh is not satisfactorily explained.[27] I would suggest that Yahweh's paradoxical behavior is a better reflection of Dtr's views than the antimonarchical formulations that God, no less than

Samuel, utters. Dtr found this antimonarchical polemic in his sources, preserved it, but by interspersing it within and thereby juxtaposing it to other traditions he softened it, thereby bringing it more into line with his own qualified acceptance of kingship.

In the light of Yahweh's reminder to Samuel that it was not Samuel that the people were rejecting, it may be profitable to examine Samuel's attitude toward kingship more closely, paying attention both to the narrative and the possible historical realities behind the narrative. Yahweh's comment suggests that Samuel's unhappiness over the people's request (1 Sam 8:1–6) had a large personal element in it. In fact, whatever else the people may have been doing, they *were* rejecting the rule of Samuel and his sons. The transition to royal rule would certainly weaken the authority of Samuel, and it would seriously undercut any attempt to hand down any of his authority to his children.

It is difficult to evaluate Samuel's opposition to Saul in the following stories in 1 Samuel 13–15. On the narrative level, Saul is portrayed as too weak, fearful, rash, or self-willed to wait for and follow God's direction, but it is easy for the reader, at least the modern reader, to regard the king sympathetically as a tragic character. In contrast, Samuel appears brutally harsh, particularly in 1 Sam 13:5–14, since the prophet was late (v 8) and the situation was desperate.[28] P. K. McCarter apparently does not respond to the text in the same way, or he assumes that the ancient Israelite readers would not have responded in that way. He attributes this material to a pre-Deuteronomistic prophetic author who took over an older, pro-Saulide complex of traditions, and revised it in order to "introduce paradigmatically the relationship between king and prophet" and "to establish the ongoing role of the prophet."[29] I have difficulty with this analysis. McCarter sees no sign of prophetic reworking of the Davidic material in 1 Samuel 16—31, except for the introduction in 16:1–13, a late addition in 19:18–24, the brief notice in 25:1, and the séance at En-dor (28:3–25).[30] But it is clear that the older Davidic material consciously portrays David as having precisely those virtues which Saul was lacking. Saul was too impatient to wait for the divine oracle (1 Sam 13:8–14; 14:18–19, 36), but David scrupulously consulted it (1 Sam 23:2–4, 6–12; 30:7–9; 2 Sam 2:1–2; 5:19, 22–25). Saul was antagonistic toward the priestly bearers of the old religious traditions and eventually slaughtered most of them (1 Sam 22:12–19),[31] but David respected the traditions (1 Sam 21:6; 22:14–15) and saved the survivor of that slaughter (1 Sam 22:20–23). Saul apparently showed no concern for the ancient religious symbol of Yahweh's presence, the Ark,[32] but David returned it to a place of honor in Israel's religious life (2 Samuel 6). Finally, while Saul disobeyed the divine oracle in his campaign against the Amalekites (1 Samuel 15), David followed the oracle in his campaign against the same people (1 Sam 30:7–8).[33]

These contrasts were apparently a part of the History of David's Rise, David's apologetic justifying his irregular succession to the throne.[34] If that is so, the religious critique of Saul antedates any use of it that a later prophetic writer may have made, and it suggests that the tensions reflected in the narrative between the older religious authorities, including Samuel, and the new king Saul are actually rooted in early historical realities.

On the historical level, the text seems to reflect a conflict between representatives of the old order trying to maintain their former prerogatives and a representative of the new order, forced to move forward cautiously because of the jealous reluctance of the older religious authorities to give up their former control over political life in Israel. The religious opposition to Saul all seems to have come from professional religious types whose status was threatened by any growth in Saul's royal power. Samuel attacks Saul for usurping his old prerogative of presiding over the sacrifices at state functions (1 Sam 13:8–14; cf. 1 Sam 7:5–10; 9:12–13), even though Saul acts out of concern for the well-being of his army. Samuel also attacks him for failing to adhere rigidly to Samuel's prophetic call for the ban (1 Samuel 15). Finally, the narrative faults him for not directing his campaigns according to the oracular responses of the priests (1 Sam 14:18–19, 36–38). One wonders whether Saul's hostile attitude toward the priests of Nob (1 Sam 22:12–19), the successors of the influential Shiloh priesthood, may not have had deeper roots than the incident that provoked Saul's massacre of this priestly clan. The restrictions on Saul's freedom already noted suggest that the representatives of the old order did their best to limit Saul's kingship. The *mishpaṭ* of the kingdom that Samuel wrote in a document at Mizpah (1 Sam 10:25) was probably a treaty specifying the rights and limitations of the king,[35] and the comment in 1 Sam 14:47 that Saul "seized the kingship over Israel" may suggest that Saul had extended his authority beyond the limits that the older authorities had envisioned for an Israelite king.[36]

If many ancient biblical writers, including Dtr, did not share the view of Gideon and Samuel that the choice of a human king implies the rejection of Yahweh, that notion can hardly be regarded as self-evident. In fact, seen in the broader perspective of general Near Eastern thought, the notion is anything but self-evident. In Mesopotamia the human king was easily accepted as the agent or regent of the real king, the deity. Thus in the Assyrian enthronement ritual one stresses that the real king is Asshur, but the human king is allowed his place in the scheme of things nevertheless.[37] Likewise in Babylon, the real king is Marduk, but his human agent is still permitted the title king of Babylon.[38] The accommodation of human kingship to divine kingship appears to have taken place without any serious theological friction. Moreover, once Israel developed the monarchy, it related the human king and the divine monarch to each other in precisely the same way as had been done in Mesopotamia.[39] The texts that come out of the royal cult betray no indication that the presence of a human king compromises the position of the divine king.

HUMAN MOTIVATIONS BEHIND KINGSHIP
AND THE ROYAL IDEOLOGY

No one will deny that quite human and sometimes sinful motivations played a role in the formation of the kingship and of the imperialistic royal ideology that was developed to undergird it, but theologically one must ask, So what? The God portrayed in the Bible has never seemed averse to working through human agents who were less than perfect. Moreover, anyone with a basic theological understanding of human nature knows that there was never a time in Israel's history when quite human motivations were out of play, and that includes the creative Mosaic period.

In his canonization of this period as the ideal period that should serve as a touchstone for judging what is authentically Yahwistic, G. E. Mendenhall seems to imply that Israel's leaders at this time were completely open to God's leading, that the selfish human desires and motivations that later perverted this ideal situation were dormant or ineffective in this period.[40] Such a claim is heavily dependent on sheer hypothetical reconstruction. There is almost no direct historical evidence for this period and relatively little for the subsequent period of the Judges, so any reconstruction of the Israelite political and religious order during these formative periods is quite hypothetical at best. To canonize one such fragile reconstruction as the touchstone for deciding what is "authentically Yahwistic," as Mendenhall and others do, hardly seems compelling.

Even if one agrees in many respects with Mendenhall's reconstruction of early Israel's organization, it does not follow that the human motivations that led to that structure were as pure and devoid of the desire for power as Mendenhall suggests. In my opinion, Mendenhall is correct in seeing the Mosaic covenant as very early and as intimately tied to the idea of Yahweh's kingship over Israel.[41] Moreover, Israel's covenantal recognition of Yahweh as king and its acceptance of the covenantal law in the tribal assembly probably reflected a rejection of Pharaonic rule and of Canaanite kingship, both of which had been experienced by different elements in the assembly as oppressive.[42] Assuming that this is correct, however, the creation of this rival theological ideology for self-government was not without its selfish human motivations. By uniting under a divine overlord, the tribes gained a supratribal strength that aided them in their struggle to wrest living space from the established city-states in Canaan. Moreover, by vesting that unifying power in a divine king rather than in a human king they preserved the maximum freedom for the pursuit of their own tribal interests as well as scoring a propaganda victory against their opponents in the struggle for Canaan. The burden of taxation that was needed to support Israel's divine king was far less than that required to support the human kings of the Canaanite city-states. Thus, for large elements of the population of Canaan capitulation to the Israelites offered the advantage of lower taxes as well as relief from the economic disruption that hostile Israelite tribes could cause to the cities that opposed this confederacy. As N. K. Gottwald has correctly noted, the Israelite confederacy in no way represented the renouncement of the human exercise of coercive power; it simply redistributed the power in a less centralized fashion than the contemporary monarchies.[43] While Yahweh was the acknowledged suzerain, the actual governmental power lay in the hands of the tribal leaders and the religious authorities. Moreover, while that power was diffuse and apparently ill-defined, it was clearly enough recognized that any shift in its distribution could provoke intertribal warfare.[44] Tribal leaders during the period of the league could be just as defensive of the status quo as any court theologian of the later monarchy, and I have already indicated the political stake that religious leaders like Samuel had in maintaining the old system.

Finally, while more diffuse, the exercise of coercive power during the league could be just as brutal as anything seen during the later monarchy, and because the power was so diffuse, its coercive exercise tended to be far more ad hoc and arbitrary. If one gives any credence to the texts, both the early wars of conquest and the intertribal conflicts were brutal, bloody affairs with no lack of what people today would consider atrocities. Thus when Mendenhall blasts Saul for the illicit conduct of war, David for his glorification of the professional soldier's "superior ability to commit murder," and the monarchy in general for the horrendous atrocities that marked the royal wars of the united monarchy and the divided monarchy of ancient Israel and Judah,[45] that critique appears anachronistic, self-contradictory, and hardly worthy of rebuttal. Unless one is prepared to accept G. von Rad's claim that the early wars of Israel were purely defensive wars,[46] a claim that contradicts the biblical tradition and represents perhaps the weakest point in his classic study,[47] one cannot sanitize the early wars of the "divine warrior." The *herem,* that religious obligation which called for, among other things, the sacral execution of prisoners of war, is quite clearly a heritage from these early wars of conquest, and the great promoters of the *ḥerem* or ban were not the kings of Israel and Judah but the religious leaders of the league and their later successors among the prophets. Samuel condemned Saul for not carrying out the ban. If one wants to speak of atrocities, it was Samuel, not Saul, who hacked the living Agag into pieces before Yahweh (1 Sam 15:32–33), and it was the prophets who wanted to preserve this ancient practice against the tendency of the later kings to treat their captives with politically motivated clemency (1 Kgs 20:30–43). It was the Deuteronomistic heirs of the Mosaic tradition, not the court theologians of the Zion tradition, who preserved and codified in Deuteronomy 20 the rules of war so offensive to modern sensibilities.

The transition to royal rule took place in Israel because the old system was no longer working. Under the combined pressure of Philistine and Ammonite expansion, the loosely organized Israelite confederacy could not muster and maintain sufficient military forces to deal with the continuing threat. The advantages the league offered during the earlier period of the struggle with the Canaanite city-states no longer worked against the new enemies. An Israelite king might require taxes, but the alternative was to pay an even more onerous tribute to the Philistines, the Ammonites, or some other invading enemy. Some Israelites opposed the development, but apart from important officials in the old regime, it is difficult to identify these opponents. The opposition probably came from those who had the most to lose and the least to gain from such a change, that is, from tribal leaders whose own territories were least threatened by the growing Philistine and Ammonite power.[48]

With the establishment of the monarchy, a new religious ideology was developed to legitimate the human monarch as the chosen agent of the divine king, and under David this royal ideology was elaborated to provide justification for his imperial conquests. On the one hand, one can see how this ideology served to stabilize the power structure, but while it certainly served royal interests, that ideology can hardly be dismissed as all bad. The ideology of kingship emphasized the king's duty to promote justice, and the royal administration of justice probably offered the powerless the first effective check against the oppression of powerful local leaders that they had experienced in a long time. Judicial corruption did not begin with the monarchy; on the contrary, the monarchy was understood as offering a corrective to such corruption. While Israelite kings did not live up to the ideal promulgated in the royal ideology, the ideology promoted the understanding of justice that the prophets were later to exploit in their critique of particular kings and their royal officials.

Curiously enough, the same point may be made in regard to the imperialistic aspects of the royal ideology. The Zion tradition's conception that Yahweh would subject all the surrounding nations to the Davidic hegemony in Jerusalem, thus bringing about peace and well-being in the Davidic empire, is nationalistic, imperialistic, and even chauvinistic, but it also lies at the base of the great prophetic visions of universal peace. Again, the ideal reflected in the ideology could provide a weapon for criticizing any contemporary ruler. Though originally formulated to justify the Davidic imperial expansion, it could be employed by an Isaiah to attack the militaristic activities of an Ahaz or a Hezekiah.[49] It will not do to dismiss this theology as a purely pagan development. Theologically the doctrine of the election of the Davidic dynasty is no more problematic than the doctrine of the election of the Israelite people. Both doctrines can and have been perverted by sinful human beings who want to claim privilege without responsibility, but even without that perversion the doctrines may seem offensive in their particularity. There is an undeniable human and self-serving element in the formulation of both these doctrines, yet despite this human element, both these doctrines are authentically Yahwistic and characteristically biblical. To reject either is simply to rebel against the particularity of biblical faith, to reject the God who chose to work his work through a particular nation and through particular individuals despite their sins and shortcomings.

NOTES

1. One may cite S. Herrmann (*A History of Israel in Old Testament Times* [2d ed.; Philadelphia: Fortress Press, 1981] 132) as fairly representative of this view: "All this confirms the common view that the monarchy was a late phenomenon in Israel, forced on it by historical circumstances and essentially alien to its original nature." Herrmann goes on to argue that Israel was by nature a tribal alliance and ideally remained so throughout its history, and this in turn is the major reason why the monarchy was not renewed in the postexilic period once it had collapsed (ibid.).

2. This view is expressed in its strongest form in a number of studies by G. E. Mendenhall. In his article "The Monarchy" (*Interpretation* 29/2 [April 1975] 155–70), he argues that "a systematic reversion to Bronze Age paganism took place in less than two generations" with the development of the monarchy (p. 157). Since Israel's formative period was the time of Moses and the covenant legal tradition, this "reversion to the old Bronze Age paganism of the United Monarchy" was "a process of rapid erosion of the basic principles of the new religious ethic" that Moses introduced (p. 158). The process began under Saul's rule, and the erosion took place so fast that by David's time little was left of the basic convictions of the Old Yahwist federation outside isolated segments of the society (p. 161). David and Solomon finished the job. Mendenhall assumes that David simply took over the Jebusite bureaucracy of Jerusalem, and he identifies Zadok, Nathan, and Bathsheba as Jebusites (pp. 162–64). He admits that he

cannot prove that Zadok and Nathan were Jebusites, but he asserts, "What we can prove is the fact that the cultic/political system of Jerusalem during the Monarchy had nothing to do with the Yahwist revolution and was actually completely incompatible with that religious movement" (p. 166). Similar blasts against the monarchy may be found in his book *The Tenth Generation: The Origins of the Biblical Tradition* (Baltimore: Johns Hopkins University Press, 1973), where he blames the state with breaking down both the old tribal structure of early Israelite society and the religiously centered value system, thus making possible the corruption of the law courts so bitterly denounced by the prophets (p. 209), and in his contribution to the Wright Festschrift, "Social Organization in Early Israel," *Magnalia Dei, The Mighty Acts of God* (ed. F. M. Cross, W. E. Lemke, and P. D. Miller; Garden City, N.Y.: Doubleday & Co., 1976) 132–51—note esp. 140.

Other scholars who in some way share Mendenhall's negative view of the monarchical development are far more restrained and careful. Cross is not especially critical of the "limited monarchy" of Saul and David, but while he spares Saul and David, he has hardly anything good to say about Solomon, who, according to Cross, began a pattern of innovations that "Canaanized" the royal ideology and cult (*CMHE*, 233–34, 239–41). J. Bright's reconstruction of the historical development of the monarchy has much in common with that of both Mendenhall and Cross, but in sharp contrast to Mendenhall and far more explicitly than Cross, Bright points to the ambiguity in the institution: "From our modern point of view at least, the new order brought to Israel so much that was good and so much that was bad that no simple evaluation is possible. It is, therefore, scarcely surprising that Israel was herself never of one mind on the subject. The monarchy was a problematical institution that some believed divinely given and that others found intolerable. In speaking of Israel's notion of kingship and state we are warned never to generalize" (*A History of Israel* [3d ed.; Philadelphia: Westminster Press, 1981] 224; see also 225–28).

In recent years a third group of scholars has attacked the basic underlying notion according to which the monarchy was an alien development in Israel. As long ago as 1967, G. Buccellati vigorously and brilliantly debunked this idea (*Cities and Nations of Ancient Syria* [Rome: Istituto di Studi del Vicino Oriente, 1967] 240–41), and his conclusion is well worth quoting: "And, to my mind, the conclusion is that the monarchy, far from being an 'alien institution,' was the natural development of forces present among the Israelites and stimulated by circumstances such as the conquest of Palestine and the fight against the Philistines. In other words, the monarchy was the institution which best met the political exigencies of the Israelites at a given time: since institutions could originate and develop freely, there is no reason to deny the monarchy validity and authenticity as a real Israelite institution" (p. 241). J. A. Soggin also raises questions about the standard treatment of the monarchical development in his new history, though he approaches the question quite differently from Buccellati. Basically he rejects the reconstruction of the premonarchical period as the formative period of Israelite identity when Yahwism was pure and orthodox. The monarchy could not represent the progressive paganization of an originally pure Yahwism, because that golden age of noble and pure origins never existed (J. A.

Soggin, *A History of Ancient Israel* [Philadelphia: Westminster Press, 1985] 167–8).

3. J. L. McKenzie, who basically follows Mendenhall's historical reconstruction, is even more radical, or at least more explicit, than Mendenhall in drawing such radical theological conclusions from this historical reconstruction. Since he believes "that the monarchy makes sense only as the imposition of a foreign aristocracy upon Israel," in his *A Theology of the Old Testament* (Garden City, N.Y.: Doubleday & Co., 1974) 267–317, he "refused to include the theme of messianism as proper to the theology of the Old Testament" ("The Sack of Israel," *The Quest for the Kingdom of God: Essays in Honor of George E. Mendenhall* [ed. H. B. Huffmon, F. A. Spina, and A. R. W. Green, Winona Lake, Ind.: Eisenbrauns, 1983] 34). Moreover, the section on messianism in his article "Aspects of Old Testament Thought," *The Jerome Biblical Commentary* (ed. R. E. Brown, J. A. Fitzmyer, and R. E. Murphy; Englewood Cliffs, N.J.: Prentice-Hall, 1968) art. 77, secs. 152–63, was, according to McKenzie, added by the editors without his knowledge or consent, and he publically disavowed it ("The Sack of Israel," 34).

4. See especially my article, "Zion in the Theology of the Davidic-Solomonic Empire," *Studies in the Period of David and Solomon and Other Essays* (ed. T. Ishida; Winona Lake, Ind.: Eisenbrauns, 1982) 93–108. Cf. also my earlier studies: "The Davidic Origin of the Zion Tradition," *JBL* 92 (1973) 329-44; "The Religio-Political Setting of Psalm 47," *BASOR* 221 (1976) 129–32; and "Zion Tradition," IDBSup, 985–87.

5. For further discussion of this point, see T. N. D. Mettinger, "YHWH Sabaoth—The Heavenly King on the Cherubim Throne," *Studies in the Period of David,* 130 n. 87.

6. Despite F. Crüsemann's recent attempt to date this religious rejection of kingship to the post-Solomonic period (*Der Widerstand gegen das Königtum. Die antiköniglichen Texte des Alten Testamentes und der Kampf um den frühen israelitischen Staat* [WMANT 49; Neukirchen-Vluyn: Neukirchener Verlag, 1978] 74–81, 124), K. H. Bernhardt's earlier discussion that situated this outlook to the transitional period between tribal league and monarchy is far more convincing (*Das Problem der altorientalischen Königsideologie im Alten Testament* [VTSup 8; Leiden: E. J. Brill, 1961] 154–55). As Bernhardt says, the total rejection of kingship presupposes a situation in which the decision whether to remain with the patriarchal rule of the tribal leaders or to adopt monarchical rule was still in doubt, and this transitional period prior to the monarchy is the only period in which the alternative, patriarchate or kingdom actually existed for Israel: "Wenn es gilt, einen Ursprungsort für die gründsätzliche Ablehnung des Königtums zu finden, dann dürfte keine Epoche israelitischer Geschichte so geeignet sein wie diese Übergangszeit von der patriarchalischen Herrschaft der Stammeshäupter zur Monarchie. Es ist die einzige Situation, in der die Alternative Patriarchat oder Königtum überhaupt für Israel bestanden hat. Die grundsätzliche Verneinung des Königtums setz eine Situation voraus, in der das gewohnte Nomadendasein mit der neuen Notwendigkeit des Königtums noch im Streite lag; nicht anders, als die spätere polemische Kritik an einzelnen Regenten ein durch lange Erfahrung mit der Monarchie zur festen Norm gewordenes

Königsideal zur unbedingten Voraussetzung hat. Kein Anzeichen aber deutet darauf hin, dass die antimonarchischen Äusserungen im Alten Testament allmählich aus dieser Kritik an unbeliebten Fürsten zur grundsätzlichen Ablehnung der Königsherrschaft herangewachsen sind" (pp. 154-5). For further discussion of the historical and theological background of this ancient Israelite debate, see below.

7. Roberts, "Zion in the Theology of the Davidic-Solomonic Empire," 98–99; idem, "The Religio-Political Setting of Psalm 47," 221, 132.

8. Cross, *CMHE*, 263–65. For my own views on this development, see J. J. M. Roberts, "The Divine King and the Human Community," *The Quest For the Kingdom of God*, 127–39, esp. 132–33; idem, "Isaiah in Old Testament Theology," *Interpretation* 36/2 (1982) 130–43, esp. 138–39.

9. The Christian claims that Jesus is the Son of God and that he shares the divine nature with the Father have their scriptural roots in the royal theology's mythologumenon of the divine birth of the Davidic king which raises him to the position of Yahweh's firstborn (Pss 2:7, 89:27–28; perhaps 110:3; and possibly Isa 9:5) and secondarily in the hyperbolic deification of the king which took place in the extravagant language of the royal cult so that the king on occasion was addressed with divine titles, e.g., "Mighty God" (Isa 9:5), "Elyon" (Ps 89:28), and "God" (Ps 45:7–8).

10. Roberts, "Isaiah in Old Testament Theology," 136–37; idem, "Isaiah 33: An Isaianic Elaboration of the Zion Tradition," *The Word of the Lord Shall Go Forth: Essays in Honor of David Noel Freedman in Celebration of His Sixtieth Birthday* (ed. C. L. Meyers and M. O'Connor; Winona Lake, Ind.: Eisenbrauns, 1983) 15–25; idem, "Isaiah 2 and the Prophet's Message to the North," *JQR* 75 (1985) 209–308; idem, "Yahweh's Foundation in Zion (Isa 28:16)," forthcoming in *JBL;* and the excellent study by B. C. Ollenburger, *Zion, The City of the Great King: A Theological Investigation of Zion Symbolism in the Tradition of the Jerusalem Cult* (1982 Princeton Theological Seminary diss. soon to appear in the *JSOT* Supplement Series, no. 41).

11. See especially T. N. D. Mettinger, *Solomonic State Officials: A Study of the Civil Government Officials of the Israelite Monarchy* (Lund: Gleerup, 1971), and the earlier literature cited there.

12. S. Morenz, "Ägyptische und davidische Königstitular," *Zeitschrift für ägyptische Sprache* 79 (1954) 73–74 = *Religion und Geschichte des alten Ägypten* (Cologne and Vienna: Bölan Verlag, 1975) 401–3. For the Egyptian enthronement ritual, see H. Bonnet, "Krönung," *Reallexikon der ägyptischen Religionsgeschichte* (Berlin: Walter de Gruyter, 1952) 395–400; H. Brunner, *Die Geburt des Gottkönigs. Studien zur Überlieferung eines altägyptischen Mythos* (Ägyptologische Abhandlungen 10; Wiesbaden: Otto Harrassowitz, 1964); and note especially the accounts of the coronation of Horemhab (G. Roeder, *Der Ausklang der ägyptischen Religion mit Reformation, Zauberei und Jenseitsglauben* [Die ägyptische Religion in Text und Bild 4; Zurich and Stuttgart: Artemis Verlag, 1961] 72–89) and Thutmosis III (G. Roeder, *Kulte, Orakel und Naturverehrung im alten Ägypten* [Die Ägyptische Religion in Text und Bild 3; Zurich and Stuttgart: Artemis Verlag, 1960] 195–215). For the Israelite evidence, see A. Alt's seminal study, "Jesaja 8, 23–9, 6. Befreiungsnacht und

Krönungstag," *Kleine Schriften zur Geschichte des Volkes Israel* (Munich: C. H. Beck'sche Verlagsbuchhandlung, 1964) 2. 206–25, and the careful treatment by H. Wildberger, *Jesaja* (BKAT X/1; Neukirchen-Vluyn: Neukirchener Verlag, 1972) 362–89.

13. Cross thinks any Egyptian influence on Israelite royal ideology must have been indirect, mediated through the Canaanites, both because "the Egyptian royal theology with its conception of the king as a physical son of the god and the Israelite conception of the adoptive sonship of the king were not identical" and because of "the rapidly increasing evidence of the specifically Canaanite origin of Israelite ideas of the king as son of god" (*CMHE*, 247). Unfortunately Cross does not give any specifics as to what makes up this "rapidly increasing evidence." The Keret Epic does suggest that the Canaanites, at least those circles from which this text came, considered their kings as in some sense the offspring of the deity. Keret is referred to as the "lad of El" (*ǧlm il*, CCA 14.40–41, 61–62, 306; 15.2.16, 20), El is called his father (14.40, 49, 169), and as the son and progeny of El, immortality was expected of Keret—he should not die like a mere mortal (16.3–23, 98–111). Since Keret is king and the text is about kingship, one may conclude that this text reflects a conception of the divine sonship of the king, but nothing suggests that it is adoptive rather than physical. If anything, the emphasis on the expected immortality of the king points in the other direction. Moreover, I see nothing in the Ugaritic or El Amarna texts that suggests that Canaanite conceptions, in contrast to Egyptian conceptions, were more influential in the Israelite development. There are quite striking parallels between the Egyptian and the Israelite coronation ritual. Besides the giving of the royal names, note the similar divine acknowledgment of the human king as his offspring using the language of birth. Amon's words to Horemhab, "You are my son and my heir who has come out of my members" (G. Roeder, *Zauberei und Jenseitsglauben*, 88 [my translation of the German], and Yahweh's words to the Davidic king, "You are my son, today I have given birth to you" (Ps 2:7), are similar, if not identical, and both were apparently spoken on the day of the king's enthronement.

It may be that the Israelite conception is adoptionistic, Yahweh's word being a performative utterance, as Mettinger has very skillfully argued (*King and Messiah: The Civil and Sacral Legitimation of the Israelite Kings* [Coniectanea Biblica, OTS 8; Lund: Gleerup, 1976] 265–66), but, contrary to Cross, that does not rule out direct Egyptian influence on the Israelite conception. Mettinger believes that there is a genetic connection between the two conceptions, and he suggests that this may reflect a deliberate Israelite "adaptation and reinterpretation of the Egyptian mythological conception" (ibid.). While I think Mettinger has demonstrated that there is a subtle difference between the Israelite and the Egyptian conception of the king's sonship, I am dubious whether the Israelite conception was as free of mythological color as Mettinger would have us believe. In that regard I share the skepticism that H. Donner ("Adoption oder Legitimation? Erwägungen zur Adoption im Alten Testament auf dem Hintergrund der altorientalischen Rechte," *OrAnt* 8 [1969] 87–119, esp. 114), G. W. Ahlström (*Psalm 89. Eine Liturgie aus dem Ritual des leidenden Königs* [Lund: Gleerup, 1959] 112), M. Görg ("Die 'Wiedergeburt' des Königs [Ps. 2, 7b]," *Theologie und Glaube* 60 [1970] 413–26, and P. A. H. de Boer ("The Son of God in the Old

Testament," *OTS* 18 [1973] 204) have expressed toward the adoptionist interpretation of the Israelite conception. In short, I think Egypt, with all its differences, still provides the best background for understanding this aspect of Israelite royal theology, and it is probably the dominant influence on Canaanite royal theology as well.

14. R. de Vaux argued for an Egyptian influence behind the Israelite practice ("Le roi d'Israël, vassal de Yahvé" *Mélanges Eugène Tisserant* I [Studia e Testi 231; Città del Vaticano: Biblioteca Apostolica Vaticana, 1964] 119–33), E. Kutsch suggested a Hittite background mediated through Canaan (*Salbung als Rechtsakt im Alten Testament und im alten Orient* [BZAW 87; Berlin: Walter de Gruyter, 1963] 56), and Mettinger argues for an autochthonous development in Israel (*King and Messiah*, 185–232). Mettinger's argument against de Vaux's view is dependent on Mettinger's historical reconstruction of the development of the rite in Israel (ibid., pp. 210, 232), however, and I cannot accept his reconstruction, according to which the rite was originally secular and only became sacralized in the time of Solomon (ibid., pp. 207, 229–30). His dating of the texts seems arbitrary, if not circular—e.g., he makes the tradition of Saul's anointing dependent on the "late" tradition of Samuel's anointing of David, thus enabling him to reject the anointing of Saul as unhistorical! (ibid., pp. 194–97)—and he assigns far more significance to the use of the plural form of the verb *māšaḥ* ("anoint") than seems justified (ibid., p. 208).

15. The characterization of the king's rule as "from sea to sea" (Ps 72:8) picks up Mesopotamian geographical terminology ("from the upper sea [Mediterranean] to the lower sea [Persian Gulf]"), though the borrowing of such imperialistic language actually grows out of the imperialistic expansion of David's rule (see H.-J. Kraus, *Psalmen* [BKAT 15/1; 2d ed.; Neukirchen-Vluyn: Neukirchener Verlag, 1961] 14, 498). Note that the similar motif in Ps 89:26 is colored by the Canaanite cosmogonic myth. Other motifs that Israel's royal ideology shared with Mesopotamia include the divine election of the king and his royal city (Pss 78:72; 132; see the prologue to the Code of Hammurabi [E. Bergmann, *Codex Hammurabi, Textus Primigenius* {Rome: Pontificium Institutum Biblicum, 1953}, i 1–50]) as well as the conception that the real king was the imperial deity (Code of Hammurabi, ibid., and the Assyrian enthronement ritual—K. Fr. Müller, *Das assyrische Ritual, Part 1: Texte zum assyrischen Königsritual* [*MVAG* 41/3; Leipzig: J. C. Hinrichs Verlag, 1937], esp. i 29; and compare the similar text edited by E. F. Weidner in *AfO* 13, 210ff., esp. line 15). The king's responsibility for maintaining justice is common to Egypt, Mesopotamia, and Canaan, so one cannot attribute that element of Israelite royal theology to any one specific background.

16. Cross, *CMHE*, 200–1; D. N. Freedman, "Early Israelite History in the Light of Early Israelite Poetry," *Unity and Diversity: Essays in the History, Literature, and Religion of the Ancient Near East* (ed. H. Goedicke and J. J. M. Roberts [Baltimore and London: Johns Hopkins University Press, 1975]) 6–7, 25 n 16; Herrman, *A History of Israel in Old Testament Times*, 75–77.

17. Cross, *CMHE*, 121–34, 141–44.

18. According to Cross, God's promise to David and his dynasty is one of the

two major themes in the first edition of the Deuteronomistic History (*CMHE*, 278–85).

19. J. D. Levenson, *Sinai and Zion: An Entry Into the Jewish Bible* (Minneapolis: Winston Press) 74–75.

20. One may argue about the authenticity of the passages concerned, but at least in the form in which the oracles of Amos (9:11), Hosea (3:5), Micah (5:1–5), Isaiah (8:23—9:6; 11:1–9, 10; 32:1–8), Jeremiah (23:5–6; 33:14–22), and Ezekiel (34:23–31; 37:24–28) have come down to us, they envision a future Davidic monarchy. Isaiah of Jerusalem's vision of the future government hardly differed in structure from the government of his own day (Roberts, "The Divine King and the Human Community," 132–33), and while the Davidic king plays no significant role in Second or Third Isaiah or in the Isaianic Apocalypse, none of these collections really address the issue of the structure of the future government of Yahweh's community; they are content to concentrate on the divine king (Roberts, "Isaiah in Old Testament Theology," 140–42). The question has been raised, however, whether the monarchs in Ezekiel 40—48 and in First Zechariah are actually envisioned as functioning politically in a manner that would justify the term "monarchy" for their government. Levenson characterizes the Davidic prince of Ezekiel 40—48 as no more than a liturgical figurehead (J. D. Levenson, *Theology of the Program of Restoration of Ezekiel 40—48* [HSM 10; Missoula, Mont.: Scholars Press, 1976] 143), and D. L. Petersen sees the governmental ideal portrayed in the oracles of Zechariah as a diarchy rather than a monarchy (*Haggai and Zechariah 1—8* [OTL; Philadelphia: Westminster Press, 1984] 118). Given the higher status assigned to the royal figure in Zech 6:9–15 (ibid., p. 277), however, I am dubious whether diarchy is really a more appropriate designation than monarchy.

21. Herrmann, *A History of Israel in Old Testament Times*, 132.

22. The oracles concerning Zerubbabel in Haggai and Zechariah (Hag 2:20–23; Zech 3:8; 4:6–10, 11–14; 6:9–15) clearly express the expectation that God will elevate Zerubbabel to royal honor, even if Petersen is right in suggesting that Haggai, at least, was very careful in his formulation of this expectation so as not to stir up political problems with the Persians (*Haggai and Zechariah 1—8*, 104–6). The textual problems in Zech 6:9–15 still suggest to me, contrary to Petersen (ibid., pp. 273-81), that Zechariah was not so cautious, that the expectations attached to Zerubbabel were rudely dashed, probably by the Persian authorities, and that the text was secondarily corrected away from the emphasis on the crowning of Zerubbabel.

23. Bernhardt, *Das Problem der altorientalischen Königsideologie*, 136–39.

24. J. Gray, *Joshua, Judges and Ruth* (NCB; London: Oliphants, 1977) 175–76.

25. G. F. Moore indicates the tensions in the narrative quite clearly (*Judges* [ICC; Edinburgh: T. & T. Clark, 1895] 229), even if one is not convinced by his analysis of the sources.

26. A. Weiser: *Samuel. Seine geschichtliche Aufgabe und religiöse Bedeutung* (FRLANT 81; Göttingen: Vandenhoeck & Ruprecht, 1962) 30; H. J. Stoebe, *Das erste Buch Samuelis* (KAT 8/1; Gütersloh: Gerd Mohn, 1973) 183; J. Mauchline, *1 and 2 Samuel* (NCB; London: Oliphants, 1971) 88–89.

27. R. Klein, *1 Samuel* (Word Biblical Commentary 10; Waco, Tex.: Word Books, 1983) 75.

28. Ibid., 126–27.

29. P. K. McCarter, *1 Samuel* (AB 8; Garden City, N.Y.: Doubleday & Co., 1980) 20.

30. Ibid., 20–21.

31. Note how Ahimelek's initial fear on seeing David coming alone (1 Sam 21:2) parallels Samuel's fear when told to go anoint David (1 Sam 16:2).

32. The reference to the Ark in the MT of 1 Sam 14:18 is generally considered a textual corruption for "ephod" which most critics adopt as the correct reading (McCarter, *1 Samuel*, 237).

33. One should note, however, that the same harsh sacral demands were never imposed on David; no one complained when he returned from his campaigns loaded with booty.

34. For the identification of the date, genre, and purpose of this History, see McCarter, *1 Samuel*, 27–30.

35. Ibid., 194.

36. The use of the term *lākad* for assuming kingship is unusual; it is nowhere else attested either for assuming kingship or any other office, and this leads McCarter to adopt the reading *ml'kh* ("territory") for MT's *hmlwkh* ("the kingdom") (*1 Samuel*, 253). But McCarter can show no real parallel for translating *ml'kh* as "territory" (p. 255), and to translate it and the following prepositional phrase as "territory outside of Israel" is simply an unjustified tour de force. H. J. Stoebe points out that the use of the verb *lākad* here picks up on its use in 1 Sam 10:20–21, where Saul was "taken" by lot to be Israel's king (*Das erste Buch Samuelis*, 276). The use of the active voice here suggests that Saul was now grasping after royal authority rather than simply allowing himself to be grasped by God's call, and the placement of this fragment of tradition (14:47–52) between Saul's clash with sacral tradition in the account of his botched success in chap. 14 and his final rejection in chap. 15 heightens the impression that it functions editorially to prepare for Saul's approaching downfall.

37. K. Fr. Müller, *Das assyrische Ritual,* esp. i 29, where the priests proclaim, "Asshur is king! Asshur is king!", ii 30–31, where Asshur and Ninlil are referred to as the lords of the royal crown that has just been placed on the head of the new king, and iii 5–7, where the first present brought to the newly enthroned king is taken away to the temple of Asshur and presented to the god. Note also the ritual for King Asshur-ban-apal edited by E. F. Weidner (*AfO* 13, 210ff.; = E. Ebeling, *Literarische Keilschrifttexte aus Assur* [Berlin, 1953] no. 31). Lines 15–16 say: "Asshur is king! Asshur alone is king! Asshur-ban-apal is [the beloved] of Asshur, the creation of his hand. May the great gods establish his reign, may they protect [the life of Asshur-ba]n-apal, the king of Assyria."

38. See, e.g., the prologue to the Code of Hammurabi (Bergmann, *Codex Hammurabi,* cols. i–v).

39. Levenson, *Sinai and Zion,* 70–71.

40. Mendenhall's grudging admission that the old pagan tendency toward local aggrandizement at the expense of groups beyond the tribal border continued even

under the *pax Yahweh* hardly affects his unrealistic idealization of this formative period (*Magnalia Dei,* 145).

41. Despite the recent tendency of some scholars to return to a Wellhausian late dating of the covenant concept following L. Perlitt (*Bundestheologie im Alten Testament* [WMANT 36; Neukirchen-Vluyn: Neukirchener Verlag, 1969]), and despite D. J. McCarthy's more restrained judgment that the earliest covenant form in Israel was a ritual covenant, that the treaty form was first called upon to express some profound ideas about the people's relation to God after the fall of Samaria by the circles that produced Ur-Deuteronomy (*Treaty and Covenant* [AnBib 21A; Rome: Biblical Institute Press, 1978] 290), Mendenhall has maintained the position he spelled out in his classic *Law and Covenant in Israel and the Ancient Near East* (Pittsburgh: Biblical Colloquium, 1955), and many Old Testament scholars, particularly in North America, would still agree with his claim that the religious foundations of the premonarchic tribal federation "stemmed from Moses and the Sinai covenant" (Mendenhall, "The Monarchy," 158).

P. D. Miller has shown, following Wright, that Deut 33:4–5 links Israel's recognition of Yahweh as king, Israel's acceptance of covenantal law, and the constitution of the people of Israel in a tribal assembly (*The Divine Warrior in Early Israel* [HSM 5; Cambridge: Harvard University Press, 1973] 82). As translated by Miller, the text reads as follows:

Moses commanded for us torah,
A possession of the assembly of Jacob.
Then (Yahweh) became king in Yeshurun
When the leaders of the people gathered together.
The assembly of the tribes of Israel

It is difficult to assign a specific date to this text, but even if one agrees with Miller in regarding it as a secondary insertion in the very ancient introductory frame to the Blessing of Moses, the text is quite old (ibid.) and may reflect an authentic tradition· about the formation of the Yahwistic federation. Given our limited knowledge of the premonarchic period, it is hard to take seriously Crüsemann's confident rejection of this possibility: "Es ist nach all unserer Kenntnis historisch-unmöglich, dass eine Versammlung des vorstaatlichen Israel Jahweh zum König über sich proklamiert hätte" (*Der Widerstand gegen das Königtum,* 81).

42. J. D. Levenson has shown quite convincingly that Israel's religious rejection of kingship stems from Israel's covenant conception in which God is seen as suzerain of the people: "If all Israelites are vassals of the great king, then it follows that one Israelite may not be set up over his fellows as king. There is no such thing as a 'vice-suzerain' to whom vassals in covenant may do homage without harming their relationship with the great king. In short, the directness of the two-party relationship of YHWH and Israel, including even the individual Israelite, precludes human kingship. YHWH is her suzerain, YHWH alone (*Sinai and Zion,* 72–73).

43. N. K. Gottwald, *The Tribes of Yahweh: A Sociology of the Religion of Liberated Israel 1250–1050 B.C.E.* (Maryknoll, N.Y.: Orbis Books, 1979) 226, 599–602.

44. Note especially the recurring motif of Ephraim's claim to hegemony in Israel (Judg 8:1–3; 12:1–6).

45. Mendenhall, "The Monarchy," 159.

46. G. von Rad, *Der heilige Krieg im alten Israel* (3d ed.; Göttingen: Vandenhoeck & Ruprecht, 1958) 26.

47. Miller, *The Divine Warrior*, 2.

48. Thus, in contrast to McKenzie's claim that the elders pushed for a king in order to enrich an oligarchy (in *The Quest for the Kingdom of God*, 29), I would argue that much of the opposition to kingship came from an oligarchy that feared that its privileges and freedom would be curtailed by this new authority.

49. See especially my forthcoming study, "Yahweh's Foundation in Zion (Isa 28:16)," *JBL*.

20

The Place of Women in the Israelite Cultus

PHYLLIS BIRD

Despite the timeliness of the question posed in the title of this essay, it is not a new one in the history of Old Testament scholarship.[1] It occasioned lively debate at the turn of the century, in terms remarkably similar to arguments heard today. A key figure in that early debate was J. Wellhausen, whose analysis of Israelite religion emphasized its masculine, martial, and aristocratic nature, positing an original coincidence of military, politicolegal, and religious assemblies, in which males alone had full rights and duties of membership.[2] Others argued that women were disqualified from cultic service by reference to an original ancestral cult of the dead which could be maintained only by a male heir.[3] A further argument associated women's disability or disinterest in the Yahweh cult with a special attraction to foreign cults or pre-Yahwistic beliefs and practices involving local numina.[4]

Underlying these arguments and assumptions concerning the marginal or subordinate status of women in the Israelite cultus was a common understanding of early Israel as a kinship-structured society of nomadic origin, whose basic social and religious unit was the patrilineal and patriarchal family.[5] Though it was the agricultural village with its assembly of free landowners that Wellhausen had in mind when he correlated political and religious status, the principle he articulated had broader applicability: "Wer politisch nicht vollberechtigt war, war es auch religiös nicht."[6] Women, who were disenfranchised in the political realm, were disenfranchised in the religious realm as well.

Stated in such terms of disability—or disinterest and disaffection—the widely held view of women's inferior status in the Israelite cultus, exhibited in the critical historiography of the period, elicited vigorous rebuttal in a series of studies aimed at clarifying, and defending, women's position in ancient Israelite religion and society.[7] While the arguments and conclusions of these studies differed, the general outcome was to demonstrate that women's participation in the religious life of ancient Israel was in fact broader and more significant than commonly depicted.[8]

Today many of the same arguments and much of the same evidence put forward in the earlier discussion are being employed once more in a renewed debate over the androcentric and patriarchal character of Israelite religion.[9] This time, however, the discussion appearing in scholarly publications, or in works by biblical scholars, is fueled by a debate arising outside the academy and borne by a literature that is primarily lay-oriented and largely lay-authored, a literature marked by the anger and urgency of profound existential and institutional conflict.[10] Modern feminist critique of the Bible as male-centered and male-dominated has elicited widely differing historiographical and hermeneutical responses, ranging from denial of the fact or intent of female subordination to rejection of the authority of the Scriptures as fundamentally and irredeemably sexist.

In the current debate, with its heavy charge of personal and theological interest, the biblical historian has a limited but essential contribution to make by isolating and clarifying the historical question. The task of Old Testament historiography must be to determine as accurately as possible the actual roles and activities of women in Israelite religion throughout the Old Testament period and the meaning of those roles and activities in their ancient socioreligious contexts. The question for the historian today is the same as that addressed to earlier scholars, but it must be answered in a new way—because of new data, new methods of analysis, and a new understanding of history. The following is an attempt to set forth a rationale and a plan for that new answer.

The question about the place of women in the Israelite cultus exposes a defect in traditional historiography—beginning already in Israelite times. It is a question about a forgotten or neglected element in traditional conceptions and presentations of Israelite religion, which typically focus on the activities and offices of males. Where women appear at all in the standard works, it is in incidental references, as exceptional figures, or in limited discussions of practices or customs relating especially to women. This skewed presentation may be explained by the limits of the available sources and may even be understood as an accurate representation of the Israelite cultus as a male-constituted or male-dominated institution. But it can no longer be viewed as an adequate portrait of Israelite religion. The religion of Israel was the religion of men and women, whose distinctive roles and experience require critical attention, as well as their common activities and obligations. To comprehend Israelite religion as the religion of a people, rather than the religion of males, women's roles, activities, and experience must be fully represented and fully integrated into the discussion. What is needed is a new reconstruction of the history of Israelite religion, not a new chapter on women. Until that is done, the place of women in the Israelite cultus will remain incomprehensible and inconsequential in its isolation, and our understanding of Israelite religion will remain partial, distorted, and finally unintelligible.

A first step toward this integrated reconstruction must be an attempt to recover the hidden history of women and to view the religion through their eyes, so that women's viewpoint as well as their presence is represented in the final account.[11] The obstacles to that effort are immense, but, I shall argue, not insurmountable. They do, however, require that critical attention be given to methodology before any reconstruction can proceed. That being the case, this chapter can offer no more than a highly provisional sketch of the assigned subject, prefaced by a summary of the methodological study that forms the essential introduction.

PRELIMINARY METHODOLOGICAL CONSIDERATIONS

1. Two fundamental shifts in focus or perspective are necessary to the reconstruction I have proposed: *(a)* The cultus must be understood in relation to the total religious life in all of its various forms and expressions, "private" as well as public; heterodox, sectarian, and "foreign" as well as officially sanctioned;[12] and *(b)* religious institutions and activities must be viewed in relation to other social institutions, such as the family, and in the context of the total social, economic, and political life. While both of these shifts are essential to an understanding of Israelite religion as a total complex, they have particular consequence for the understanding of women's place and roles.

2. The information needed to give a fully adequate account of the place of women in Israelite religion, including the cultus, is in large measure unavailable—and unrecoverable—from either biblical or extra-biblical sources. We have at best isolated fragments of evidence, often without clues to context. As a consequence, any reconstruction must be tentative and qualified. The same, however, is true, though in less extreme degree, of our knowledge of men's roles, and demands similar caution and qualification. Our fullest and best information is partial and skewed.

3. A comprehensive and coherent account of Israelite religion and of women's place in it requires the use of an interpretive model, not only to comprehend the available evidence but also to locate, identify, and interpret missing information—which is often the most important.[13] The blanks in the construct are as essential to the final portrait as the areas described by known data. They must be held open (as the boxes in an organizational chart)—or imaginatively filled—if the structure is not to

collapse or the picture is not to be rendered inaccurate or unintelligible. The primary means of filling the blanks is imaginative reconstruction informed by analogy.

4. The closest analogies may be found in other ancient Near Eastern societies. They are limited, however, by dependence on written documents, most of which come from the spheres of men's activities and reflect male perspectives.

5. Modern ethnographic studies of individual societies and institutions and cross-cultural studies of women's roles in contemporary non-Western societies can aid the Old Testament historian in formulating questions and constructing models.[14] Such studies are especially valuable for their attempts to view societies as total systems as well as for their attention to features that native historians and lay members of the society may overlook or deem unimportant. Because they do not depend on written records but are based on observation and interview of participants, they give us access to women's roles and experience that is otherwise unavailable.

6. Androcentric bias is a pervasive feature of the ancient sources, their subjects, and their interpreters. It has also characterized most anthropological research and writing until recently.[15]

SUMMARY OF FINDINGS OF CROSS-CULTURAL STUDIES

The most important finding of cross-cultural studies for a reconstruction of women's religious roles in ancient Israel is the universal phenomenon of sexual division of labor, which is particularly pronounced in pre-industrial agricultural societies.[16] Basic to this division of labor is an understanding of women's primary work as reproductive work, including care of children and associated household tasks, with a consequent identification of the domestic sphere as the female sphere, to which women's activities may be restricted in varying degrees.[17] This fundamental sexual division of labor has far-reaching consequences for the status and roles of women in the society as a whole as well as their patterns of activity and participation in the major social institutions. In all of the primary institutions of the public sphere, which is the male sphere, women have limited or marginal roles, if any. Thus leadership roles in the official cultus are rarely women's roles or occupied by women.[18]

Conversely, however, women's religious activities—and needs—tend to center in the domestic realm and relate to women's sexually determined work. As a consequence, those institutions and activities which appear from public records or male perspective as central may be viewed quite differently by women, who may see them as inaccessible, restricting, irrelevant, or censuring. Local shrines, saints and spirits, home rituals in the company of other women (often with women ritual leaders), the making and paying of vows (often by holding feasts), life-cycle rites, especially those related to birth and death—these widely attested elements of women's religious practice appear better suited to women's spiritual and emotional needs and the patterns of their lives than the rituals of the central sanctuary, the great pilgrimages and assemblies, and the liturgical calendar of the agricultural year.[19] But the public sphere with its male-oriented and male-controlled institutions dominates and governs the domestic sphere, with the result that women's activities and beliefs are often viewed by "official" opinion as frivolous, superstitious, subversive, or foreign.[20]

WOMEN IN ISRAELITE
RELIGION AND CULTUS:
OBSERVATIONS AND HYPOTHESES

We have argued that an adequate understanding of the place of women in the Israelite cultus requires attention both to the place of the cultus in the total religious and social life of the society and to the place of women in the society—including consideration of the society's understanding of male and female nature, capacities, and inclinations and its organization and assignment of male and female roles, activities, rights, and duties. Despite the efforts of the Israelite cultus to exert a controlling influence over the total life of the society and despite its significant stamp on the culture, the cultus must still be seen as one institution among others, influenced by general social and cultural norms, especially as they define appropriate male and female roles and activities. Consequently, we should expect significant correspondence between women's roles and status in the cultus and in the society as a whole. Three prominent elements of that general understanding of women's nature and duty have direct bearing on women's place in the cultus: (1) the periodic impurity of women during their reproductive years;[21] (2) the legal subordination of women within the family, which places a woman under the male authority of father, husband, or brother, together with a corresponding subordination in the public sphere in which the community is represented by its male members; and (3) an understanding of women's primary work and social duty as family-centered reproductive work in the role of wife-mother.

The effect of each of these determinants is to restrict the sphere of women's activities—spatially, temporally, and functionally. Only roles that were compatible with women's primary domestic-reproductive role and could be exercised in periods or situations free from ritual taboo, or from the requirement of ritual purity, were open to women. While restrictions also existed on men's ability to participate in particular cultic roles and activities (e.g., economic constraints on offering vows and sacrifices and restriction of priestly office to members of priestly families), these did not affect all males as a class. A significant distinction between male and female relationships to the cultus may be seen in the fact that for women, but not for men, conflict between social and cultic obligation is a recurring phenomenon—which is resolved by giving priority to social demands. Examples may be seen in the annulment of a woman's vows by her father or husband (Num 30:1–15)[22] and in the "exemption" of women from the requirement of the annual pilgrim feasts (Exod 23:17; 34:23; Deut 16:16). In both of these cases one may argue that responsibility to the family is the underlying principle and that it is understood as a religious, not merely a social, obligation; but a contrast remains between the understanding of a male and a female religious obligation.[23]

This explanation assumes a conflict of duty or interest (defined socially, not individually) as grounds for women's limited role in the Israelite cultus, but the limitation might also be explained by an understanding of the cultus as an originally, or essentially, male institution or association. The evidence suggests that there is truth in both views.

Wellhausen was surely right in recognizing behind the generic language of many texts and translations a cultus conceived and operated as a male association to which women were related, if at all, in a marginal and mediated way. Evidence for an understanding of the cultic community as fundamentally a body of males is substantial. While the best examples relate to the early period, they are not confined to it: for example, the prescription for the pilgrim feasts ("Three times in the year shall all your males appear before the Lord God," Exod 23:17; cf. Deut 16:16); the instructions to the "people" at the mountain of God ("Be ready by the third day; do not go near a woman," Exod 19:15); the tenth commandment ("You shall not covet your neighbor's wife," Exod 20:17); and other injunctions, exhortations, blessings, and so forth, that address the cultic community as male ("Blessed is everyone who fears the Lord. . . . Your wife will be like a fruitful vine," Ps 128:1–3; "Jeremiah said to all the people and all the women," Jer 44:24).

Further evidence may be seen in the Hebrew onomasticon, where theophoric names describing the individual as a worshiper or votary of the deity (names compounded with 'ebed/'ōbēd, i.e., "servant of") are reserved to males and have no female counterpart—in contrast to Akkadian and Phoenician practice.[24]

Objections to Wellhausen's view that seek to show broad participation of women in religious and cultic activities fail to challenge his basic argument, which is not that women were prohibited from participation, but rather that their participation was not essential and that it played a less central or less important role in women's lives than in men's. Well-hausen's insight was also sound in positing an "original" coincidence or congruence of military, legal, and cultic assemblies; the three represent the primary institutions of the public sphere, which is everywhere the sphere of male activity. His understanding of the correspondence of rights and duties in these overlapping realms can also be substantially affirmed, though areas of divergence require greater attention together with cases of status incongruity. A further modification is required by the extension of both the cultic and the legal spheres beyond the circle of males to encompass the broader community.[25] As a consequence, women, who were excluded from the governing or representative institutions of both (namely, the priesthood and the cultic assembly, and the council of elders and the assembly of landholders), were nevertheless brought within their spheres of interest and authority.[26] Thus women possessed dual status in the legal and cultic realm, being members of the outer circle governed by the community's norms but restricted in varying degree from the inner circle where the norms were formulated, inculcated, and rationalized.

In the cultic realm, differentiation of roles is associated with a hierarchy of offices and prerogatives ordered according to a concept of graduated degrees of holiness (represented spatially, e.g., in the plan of the Temple and its courts). At the center, which is also the apex of authority, stands the priest or high priest, surrounded by other members of the priesthood and/or other orders of cultic personnel (the local shrine represents the simplest form of cultic leadership, invested in a resident priest—and his family—while the Temple cultus occupies the other end of the spectrum, with its elaborate, graded system of special orders and offices). Beyond the priesthood stand members of the community (more specifically, the free citizens), bound by duty of pilgrimage, addressed directly by the cultic proclamation and having limited rights of sacrifice (varying according to period). The outer circle is represented by women, dependents, and resident aliens. They are also addressed by the cultic proclamation, but usually indirectly; both their hearing and their response is commonly mediated by a male guardian.

While this scheme gives a general picture of the relationship of women to the Israelite cultus, it must be qualified in a number of ways, especially with regard to changes or variations in internal and external relationships over the Old Testament period, some of which appear to have significant consequence for the nature and extent of women's participation. Factors requiring consideration include the number of cultic centers, the types of activities associated with them, and the relationships among them; the status and affiliation of the cultic personnel, the degree of centralization, and the extent of professionalization or specialization of cultic maintenance roles; and the relationship of the central cultus to other institutions and spheres of life.

While this chapter does not permit detailed study of the complex assortment of data embedded in the Old Testament text, a summary review of the more prominent features of the major periods may help to provide a context for a series of concluding hypotheses concerning patterns of participation and changes in women's relationship to the cultus.

The fullest and richest evidence for women's religious activity is found in literature pertaining to the premonarchic period, which also provides the richest portrait of women in leadership roles. We see Miriam leading the Israelites in a song of victory at the sea (Exod 15:20–21), punished for claiming equality with Moses as one through whom the Lord had also spoken (Num 12:2), and ranked with Aaron and Moses as leaders of the people (Num 12:2–8; Mic 6:4);[27] women "ministering" at the tent of meeting (Exod 38:8; 1 Sam 2:22); Deborah honored as a "mother in Israel" (Judg 5:7), as a judge and a prophet summoning the forces of Israel to holy war at Yahweh's command and accompanying them into battle (Judg 4:4–10; 5:7, 12–15), and as a singer of Israel's victory through Yahweh (Judg 5:1); Jephthah's virgin daughter "initiating" an annual ritual of mourning by the daughters of Israel (Judg 11:34–40);[28] Micah's mother commissioning an image for the family shrine established by her son (Judg 17:1–13, esp. v 4); women dancing at the yearly feast at Shiloh (Judg 21:19–21); Hannah and Peninnah accompanying their husband on his annual pilgrimage to Shiloh and sharing the portions of the sacrifice (1 Sam 1:1–4); and Hannah, weeping, praying, vowing at the sanctuary, and finally paying her vow with the dedication of the child (1 Sam 1:9–28). In these images we see most of the roles attested in the later period.

Sources pertaining to the period of the monarchy and to the postexilic period expand the references to heterodox practices and sharpen the distinction between legitimate and illegitimate roles and activities. Two female prophets, Huldah (2 Kgs 22:14–20) and the unnamed něbî'â of Isa 8:3, are the only women portrayed in approved cultic roles.[29] The rest are viewed as illegitimate. These include references to qědēšôt (Hos 4:14; Deut 23:18);[30] to queens and queen mothers who introduced foreign cults and cult objects (Maacah—1 Kgs 15:13; Jezebel—1 Kgs 18:19 [cf. 16:31–32]; Athaliah—2 Kgs 11:18; cf. Solomon—1 Kgs 11:1–8); to women weaving vestments for Asherah (2 Kgs 23:7); and to women baking cakes/burning incense for the Queen of Heaven (Jer 7:17–18; 44:15–25), weeping for Tammuz (Ezek 8:14), and engaging in sorcery ("prophesying"—Ezek 13:17–23). Postexilic literature yields only a prophet opponent of Nehemiah (Noadiah—Neh 6:14), showing a continuation of women in the class of prophets.[31] The number and nature of references to women's religious roles and activities during the monarchy appear to reflect the consequences of the centralization of the cultus under royal control and a tendency, culminating in the Deuteronomic reform, to brand all worship at the local sanctuaries idolatrous/promiscuous.[32]

Evidence from the patriarchal traditions depicts a family-centered or clan type of cultus in which the patriarchs perform all of the roles of sacrifice and blessing and are portrayed as founders of various local shrines or cults (Gen 22:9–14; 26:23–25; 28:18–19; 35:6–7, 14–15).[33] Rachel's stealing of the teraphim (as cultic objects belonging to her father) is further witness to clan-based religious practice, but it tells us nothing about women's religious roles. Her audacious and amusing act of theft and coverup in which she "protects" the sacred objects by professing defilement does not describe the institutionalization of an action. Rachel remains a dependent as she cleverly assists her husband in robbing her father.

SUMMARY GENERALIZATIONS

The following is an attempt to summarize the evidence in a series of preliminary generalizations.

Women in Cultic Service

1. Leadership of the cultus appears at all times to have been in the hands of males (though with differing patterns and sources of recruitment into the leadership group). Women, however, were not excluded absolutely from cultic service or sacred space, though increasing restriction is suggested, correlated with increasing centralization, specialization, and power (at least in Judah) under a royally sanctioned Zadokite priesthood. Persistence of women in cultic roles in the later period is identified in the canonical texts with heterodox practice.

2. The attested roles of men and women in the service of the cultus appear to exhibit a sexual division of labor corresponding closely to that discernible in the society as a whole.

   a. Males occupy the positions of greatest authority, sanctity, and honor and perform tasks requiring technical skill and training. They preside over the presentation of sacrifices and offerings,[34] have charge of the sacred lots, interpret the sacred law and instruct the congregation, pronounce blessing and curse, declare absolution and pardon, and guard the purity of the sanctuary and the worshipers; that is, they perform the priestly service in both sacrificial and oracular functions. Priestly office in Israel, as in the rest of the ancient Near East, was reserved to males. Contrary to popular opinion, Israelite Yahwism was not distinguished from the surrounding religions by its rejection of women in priestly office, but conformed to common practice.[35] The Israelite cultus in its basic institutional forms appears to have shared the essential features of the cultus known in surrounding cultures.

b. Women's cultic service seems to have been confined largely to maintenance and support roles, essential to the operation of the cultus but not requiring clergy status—or prescription in texts concerned with the proper performance of the required rituals. Since these roles are poorly documented in the biblical sources, we can only speculate based on chance clues, parallels in domestic life, and the suggestions afforded by comparative studies of cultic organization and maintenance elsewhere in the ancient Near East. The following tasks appear likely (further suggestions must await a fuller study of comparative materials): the weaving and sewing of vestments, hangings, and other textiles for cultic use;[36] the preparation of cultic meals or foods used in the ritual;[37] and the cleaning of cultic vessels, furniture, and quarters.[38]

c. Some references to women associated with the cultus point to more public and representative or symbolic roles, suggesting a need to include within the cultus activities or attributes specifically identified with women, for example, as singers and dancers[39] or as attendants in the sanctuary. Both the *ṣōbĕʾôt* (Exod 38:8; 1 Sam 2:22)[40] and the *qĕdēsôt* (Gen 38:21–22; Deut 23:17; Hos 4:14)[41] are associated with the service of the sanctuary, though the exact nature and form of their respective service remains unclear. Both represent classes rejected or superseded by the normative cultus that preserved the record of their existence, suggesting that they played a larger role (for a longer period of time) than the meager references would at first intimate. The identifying symbol or implement of the former group (a mirror) and the innuendo in references to the latter suggest that in both cases female sexuality was a significant aspect of the role.

d. If we posit any specialized service of women within the cultus, we must also consider the social organization that would enable permanent or continuous (short-term or long-term) cultic activity. Since women's place in society is determined by their place within the family, women are not normally free to operate for extended periods outside this sphere. The well-known exceptions are the widow, the prostitute, and the hierodule. Two possible arrangements may be suggested to account for women's service in the Israelite cultus. One would see the women as members of priestly families, hence resident at or near the sanctuary and sharing in some degree the special sanctity of the priest, which would give them access to the sacred space. The other would assume that they are women without families (whether widows, virgins, or women separated from their families by a vow). In the latter case we may expect, as in the case of the various classes of Babylonian hierodules, that the cultus will assume the authority and control of father or husband and that restrictions, comparable to those applying within the family, will be placed on the woman's sexual activity for the duration of her service (whether as a prohibition of sexual activity or of having or keeping children).

e. Women might also on occasion play a role in the royal cultus through their roles in the ruling house. A queen, in the absence of a male ruler (or in the presence of a weak one), might assume the role of titular head and patron of the state cult. Since our best Old Testament example is provided by a foreign queen (Jezebel), presiding over a foreign cult, the cultic role of the king's wife or mother may not have been as fully developed in Israel as elsewhere—or it may have been rejected. This specialized cultic role is in any case dependent upon a secular role and the particular politicoreligious relationship of the royal cultus.

3. The most important and best-documented religious office occupied by women in ancient Israel, that of prophet, stands in an ambiguous relationship to the cultus. Whatever the role of the prophet within the cultus, it was clearly not a priestly office. Since recruitment was by divine designation (charismatic gift) and not dependent upon family or status, it was the one religious office with broad power that was not mediated or directly controlled by the cultic or civil hierarchy and the one religious office open to women. Because recruitment to and exercise of the role did not depend on socially or sexually defined status but on personal attributes, it was also the one role shared by men and women, a pattern attested in Mesopotamia and in cross-cultural studies.

The lack of formal restrictions to women's assumption of the office does not mean, however, that women were equally free to exercise it. Here, as in the case of other extrafamilial roles, women were confronted with a dual vocation, which was normally—and perhaps always—resolved in favor of the domestic obligation. Women prophets probably exercised their charismatic vocation alongside their family responsibilities or after their child-rearing duties were past. As a consequence of this complementary or sequential pattern of women's prophetic activity—and as a consequence of the normal patterns of social organization, which placed women as dependents in family-centered units—one would not expect to find women organized in prophetic guilds (the professional guild is a male form of organization). Nor would one expect to find women prophets as heads of schools or having the freedom of action and access to political and cultic power that is apparent in the case of their most prominent male counterparts. It is therefore not unexpected that no prophetic books carry the names of women, and it requires no explanation of prejudice or conspiratorial silence—but rather conflict of duty, which made every woman a mother before she would exercise another vocation.

4. Some forms of cultic service by women associated with the central Yahwistic cultus were judged heterodox or foreign by the canonical sources. In addition to these references the Old Testament contains frequent references to local cults of alien gods and to foreign cults brought into the central cultus. These references, which are always polemical and usually formulated in very general terms, do not supply us with adequate information about the related cultic personnel, but presumably some of these were women (e.g., *qědēsîm* in 1 Kgs 15:12; 2 Kgs 23:7 may be understood as an inclusive use of the generic plural). It is impossible on the basis of our sources, however, to determine whether women played a larger role in the service of non-Yahwistic cults. Evidence for a female deity or female aspect of deity as a persistent and at times, perhaps, legitimate element of the Yahwistic cultus requires reassessment of the terms "foreign" and "syncretistic" as descriptions of discredited worship as well as a reassessment of the ritual and personnel of such cults. The sources suggest that disavowal, rather than discontinuance, of the practices and beliefs is what is indicated in the increasing and increasingly polemical attention to "foreign" cults and cultic practices in late sources.

Women as Worshipers

1. Since women rarely emerge in the text from behind the facade of generic male terminology, it is impossible to determine with certainty the extent of their participation in prescribed or reported activities. Isolated clues suggest, however, that women attended the major communal feasts and rituals, insofar as personal and domestic circumstances permitted, and presumably contributed to the preparation of meals and of food (especially grain) offerings. Animal slaughter and sacrifice, as an action of the worshiper, was reserved to males—as elsewhere generally—but this appears to have been the sole specific exclusion or reservation. In the major pilgrim feasts and other festivals at local shrines, as well as in family-based ritual meals, the woman participates as a member of a family unit. But she may also exercise her role in "the great congregation" and as "a daughter of Israel" bound by covenant law in individual acts of

devotion and duty: in songs of praise (1 Sam 2:1–10) and prayers of petition (1 Sam 1:10–16), in the making and performing of vows (1 Sam 1:11, 24–28; Num 30:3–15), in seeking oracles (2 Kgs 4:22–23; cf. 1 Kgs 14:2–5), in bringing offerings, and in performing the rituals prescribed for ritual cleansing, absolution, and so forth (Lev 12:1–8; 13:29–39; 15:19–29). The locus of these activities might be the central shrine (on occasions of pilgrimage) but was surely most commonly a local shrine or holy place or simply the place of daily activity. That women's communion with the deity was common and that women were recipients of divine communications is indicated by a number of the-ophany traditions—though where the response to the appearing deity takes cultic form, as in the case of Manoah's wife, the action shifts to the male (Manoah presents the offering and questions the angel, cf. Judg 13:2–7 and 8–20).

2. Of family-centered ritual we know even less, except in the case of the Passover. We may expect in this and in other cases that the normal male and female roles in the family will be reflected in the ritual, with food preparation belonging to the women and the presiding role, reading and recitation, assumed by males. The alternative practice of segregated dining and ritual, common in Islamic custom, was more likely the rule in cultic meals of larger groups or societies formed for such purposes.

3. Peculiarly or predominantly female forms of ritual and worship are suggested in the canonical sources only in reference to heterodox cults, the clearest examples of which are the women weeping for Tammuz (Ezek 8:14) and making offerings to the Queen of Heaven (Jer 7:17–18; 44:19). Though the whole population is explicitly implicated in the latter case, the women seem to have a special role. Prophetic use of the metaphor of the promiscuous bride to describe Israel's apostasy may reflect a special proclivity of Israelite women for "foreign" cults, but the sin that is condemned is the sin of the people, and this usage alone is insufficient to demonstrate a pattern. Of possible greater significance for an understanding of women's religious participation and the total re-ligious life of the community is the hidden realm of women's rituals and devotions that take place entirely within the domestic sphere and/or in the company of other women. Cross-cultural studies show that these often constitute the emotional center of women's religious life as well as the bulk of their religious activity, especially where their participation in the central cultus is limited. For such practices, however, we have little or no direct testimony, as this order of religious practice is generally seen as unworthy of note unless it challenges or undermines the central cultus. (Women's rites may even be unknown to men, who have no part in them.) Ceremonies and practices that belong to this category might include birth

and mourning rites and other rituals of the life cycle performed in the home or the village, especially with a woman as ritual specialist; prayers; vows and their performance in such actions as holding a feast, endowing a shrine, or dedicating some prized possession; making pilgrimages; consulting mediums and seers; and participation in spirit-possession cults or rituals. The line between religion and magic or orthodox and heterodox is more difficult to draw in this realm of practice and belief since the controls of the central cultus, its priesthood and theology, are largely absent. Like folk religion everywhere, it is typically seen as debased or corrupted and often as syncretistic.

The freedom to engage in such actions may vary considerably, relating in part to the degree to which they may be seen as convergent with or contrary to cultically prescribed duties. For example, ritual prescriptions governing the state of impurity associated with childbirth draw the otherwise private birth event into the sphere of the central cultus in its attempt to maintain the purity of the people as a cultically defined community. But the satisfaction of the cultic requirement does not exhaust the ritual need associated with the birth, which may be supplied by a naming ceremony, circumcision feast, and/or special rituals to assist the mother in the birth—rituals in which a female specialist such as a midwife may play a role closely analogous to the role of a priest in other situations of crisis. Women's private rituals or actions favored by women may also be opposed by male authorities as frivolous, superstitious, costly, and unnecessary. But opposition does not always mean compliance. Women may take vows that are costly and undertake forbidden pilgrimages as actions of rebellion or flight from oppressive household responsibilities and restrictions. As religiously sanctioned actions they may offer limited relief to women whose options for action were often severely circumscribed.

4. On the boundary of the sacred sphere that is organized by the central cultus or claimed by rival cults, a sphere extended in the name of the principal deity, or deities, to the rituals of daily life, there exists a quasi-religious sphere of spirits, demons, and various malevolent or amoral forces that trouble people and over which they attempt to gain control by special knowledge and defensive action. Those skilled in discerning and controlling these forces, by sorcery, witchcraft, necromancy, medicine, or other means, may be acknowledged by the cultus as practitioners of valuable practical arts or proscribed as challenging the fundamental claims of the deity to embody or control all forms of superhuman power. While some religions might incorporate such beliefs and practices into their belief systems, Israelite Yahwism, from the time of Saul, proscribed the practices and banned the practitioners (1 Sam

23:3, 8). It has often been suggested that women had a special attraction to these quasi-religious practices, both as clients and as practitioners, and it makes sense that women should prefer to seek help for their problems from a local specialist than from a general practitioner or ritual specialist serving a remote God. That women should also constitute a significant proportion of the mediums and other specialists in spirit manipulation is also understandable. However, the Old Testament evidence is insufficient to confirm such a pattern of preference and contains more references to male than to female classes of occult practitioners.

CONCLUSION

During the period reflected in the Old Testament sources there appear to have been a number of changes within the cultus and in its relationship to the population as a whole that had significance for women's participation. The progressive movement from multiple cultic centers to a central site that finally claimed sole legitimacy and control over certain ritual events necessarily restricted the participation of women in pilgrim feasts and limited opportunities for women to seek guidance, release, and consolation at local shrines, which were declared illegitimate or demolished. At the same time, increased specialization and hierarchal ordering of priestly/levitical ranks within the royal/national cultus deprived males in general (as well as Levites) of earlier priestly prerogatives, increasing the distance or sharpening the boundary between the professional guardians of the cultus and the larger circle of male Israelites who comprised the religious assembly. Reorganization of the cultus under the monarchy and again in the postexilic period appears to have limited or eliminated roles earlier assigned to women. On the other hand, there appears to have been a move (most clearly evident in the Deuteronomic legislation) to bring women more fully and directly into the religious assembly, so that the congregation is redefined as a body of lay men and women. As the priesthood becomes more powerful and specialized, the primary cultic distinction or boundary within the community becomes that between priest and laity rather than between male and female.

NOTES

1. This chapter is a preliminary and highly abbreviated form of the introduction to a book-length work (in preparation) on women in Israelite religion.
2. J. Wellhausen, *Israelitische und jüdische Geschichte* (3d ed.; Berlin: Georg Reimer, 1897) 89–90.
3. I. Benzinger, *Hebräische Archäologie* (Freiburg im Breisgau and Leipzig:

J. C. B. Mohr, 1894) 140, and W. Nowack, *Lehrbuch der hebräischen Archäologie* (Frieburg im Breisgau and Leipzig: J. C. B. Mohr, 1894) 154, 348.

4. See, e.g., B. Stade, *Biblische Theologie des Alten Testaments* (Tübingen: J. C. B. Mohr, 1905) 1. 40. Cf. E. König, *Geschichte der alttestamentlichen Religion* (Gütersloh: Bertelsmann, 1912) 216 n. 1.

5. See, e.g., Benzinger, *Archäologie* (1907), 102; Nowack, *Lehrbuch,* 153–54.

6. Wellhausen, *Geschichte,* 94.

7. The earliest (1898) and most positive in its assessment was that of I. Peritz, "Women in the Ancient Hebrew Cult," *JBL* 17 (1898) 111–48. Other major studies include the following: M. Lohr, *Die Stellung des Weibes zur Jahwe-Religion und-Kult* (Leipzig: Hinrichs, 1908); G. Beer, *Die soziale und religiöse Stellung der Frau im israelitischen Altertum* (Tübingen: J. C. B. Mohr [Paul Siebeck], 1919); and E. M. McDonald, *The Position of Women as Reflected in Semitic Codes of Law* (Toronto: University of Toronto Press, 1931).

8. For an excellent review and assessment of the history of scholarship on women in Israelite religion, see chap. 1 of U. Winter's *Frau und Göttin. Exegetische und ikonographische Studien zum weiblichen Gottesbild im alten Israel und in dessen Umwelt* (Freiburg and Göttingen: Universitäts/Vandenhoeck & Ruprecht, 1983). Winter's work, which became available to me only after the completion of my initial draft, exhibits substantial parallels to my own approach and significant accord with my analysis.

9. See, e.g., C. J. Vos, *Woman in Old Testament Worship* (Delft: Judels & Brinkman, 1968); J. Otwell, *And Sarah Laughed: The Status of Women in the Old Testament* (Philadelphia: Westminster Press, 1977); and Winter, *Frau und Göttin.*

10. By "lay" I mean nonbiblical specialist. This literature, which is a product of, or response to, the modern women's movement, is largely, though by no means exclusively, written by women and is characterized by a high degree of existential involvement and political intention (protest and advocacy). In the three decades since the appearance of S. de Beauvoir's *The Second Sex* (New York: Alfred A. Knopf, 1953; French orig., 1949), it has swelled to a flood, establishing itself as a major new category in both religious and secular publishing—and affecting the entire field of publishing in its attention to gendered language and images. While this literature treats a broad range of social, psychological, and historical issues, a recurring theme, in secular as well as religious writings, is the legacy of biblical tradition in Western understanding of the nature and status of women. Recent scholarly attention to women in the biblical world has arisen, in part at least, as an effort to correct and inform the "popular" discussion (cf. Winter, *Frau und Göttin,* 17).

11. Cf. E. Schüssler Fiorenza's groundbreaking work for the New Testament, *In Memory of Her: A Feminist Theological Reconstruction of Christian Origins* (New York: Crossroad Publishing Co., 1983).

12. By cultus I understand the organized, usually public, aspects of religious life centered in a temple, shrine, or other sacred site, maintained by a priesthood and/or other specialized offices and roles, and finding expression in sacrifices, offerings, teaching and oracular pronouncement, feasts, fasts, and other ceremonies and ritual actions. Since our knowledge of Israelite religion is limited

almost entirely to the "national" cultus and its several schools of theology or streams of tradition, it is easy to slip from analysis of the cultus to generalizations about the religion. This tendency has been qualified to some extent by the recognition that we have no direct evidence for North Israelite theology and practice and by attempts to recover and reconstruct it from elements surviving within Judean compositions. It is also being qualified by new attention to local or folk traditions of Israelite Yahwism evidenced in extrabiblical texts. The question about women in the cultus, I shall argue, raises the question about the role of the cultus in the total religious life of Israel in an even broader and more radical way.

13. The need for consciously articulated interpretive models has been convincingly argued in recent decades and needs no further defense. It does need reiteration, however, as paucity of evidence intensifies the need. For example, if we assume that the Israelite congregation was composed of all adults, we will picture women as a silent constituent even where no reference is made to their presence. But if we construe the congregation as a body of males, we must give a different account of the missing women—and of the role of the cultus in the society.

14. This is an exceedingly rich and suggestive literature combining descriptive and theoretical interests. It is also expanding so rapidly that it is impossible to list even the most important works. The following is a sample of works I have found useful: M. K. Whyte, *The Status of Women in Preindustrial Societies* (Princeton: Princeton University Press, 1978); M. K. Martin and B. Voorhies, *Female of the Species* (New York: Columbia University Press, 1975); M. Rosaldo and L. Lamphere, eds., *Woman, Culture, and Society* (Stanford: Stanford University Press, 1974); N. A. Falk and R. M. Gross, eds., *Unspoken Worlds: Women's Religious Lives in Non-Western Cultures* (San Francisco: Harper & Row, 1980); E. W. Fernea, *Guests of the Sheik: An Ethnography of an Iraqi Village* (Garden City, N.Y.: Doubleday & Co., 1969); E. Bourguignon et al., *A World of Women: Anthropological Studies of Women in the Societies of the World* (New York: Praeger Publishers, 1980); and S. W. Tiffany, ed., *Women and Society: An Anthropological Reader* (Montreal: Eden Press Women's Publications, 1979).

15. For efforts to identify and counter this bias and an introduction to the study of gender as a major new field of anthropological theory, see especially J. Shapiro, "Anthropology and the Study of Gender," *A Feminist Perspective in the Academy: The Difference It Makes* (ed. E. Langland and W. Gove; Chicago: University of Chicago Press, 1981) 110–29; N. Quinn, "Anthropological Studies on Women's Status" (*Annual Review of Anthropology* 6 [1977] 182–222); and S. Ortner and H. Whitehead, eds., *Sexual Meanings* (Cambridge: Cambridge University Press, 1981).

16. M. Rosaldo, "Woman, Culture, and Society: A Theoretical Overview," Rosaldo and Lamphere, *Women,* 18, and J. K. Brown, "A Note on the Division of Labor by Sex," *American Anthropologist* 72 (1970) 1074–78. Cf. Martin and Voorhies, *Female of the Species,* 276–332, and Whyte, *Status of Women,* esp. 156–73.

17. Rosaldo, "Woman, Culture, and Society," 26–27. See further H. Papanek and G. Minault, eds., *Separate Worlds: Studies of Purdah in South Asia* (Delhi: Chanakya Publications, 1982) esp. 3–53 and 54–78; Fernea, *Guests;* and Martin

and Voorhies, *Female of the Species,* 290–95. Women's activities are never completely confined to the home, but sexual division is the rule in both work and play wherever mixed groups are found. See Brown, "A Note"; P. R. Sanday, "Female Status in the Public Domain," Rosaldo and Lamphere, *Woman,* 189–206; and E. Friedl, *Women and Men: An Anthropologist's View* (New York: Holt, Rinehart & Winston, 1975) 8. For Old Testament examples, cf. the young women *(ně'ārôt)* as distinct from the young men *(ně'ārîm)* working in Boaz's field (Ruth 2:8, 9; cf. 2:22, 23). Note the sexual division of labor described in 1 Sam 8:11–13. Cf. also Old Testament references to women drawing water (Gen 24:11; 1 Sam 9:11), grinding grain (Job 31:10; cf. Matt 24:41), cooking and baking (1 Sam 8:13; Lev 26:26), and dancing and singing (Exod 15:20; 1 Sam 18:6–7).

18. Rosaldo, "Woman, Culture, and Society," 17, 19–21. Cf. Ortner and Whitehead, *Sexual Meanings,* 4 and passim; P. R. Sanday, *Female Power and Male Dominance* (Cambridge: Cambridge University Press, 1981); and Shapiro, "Anthropology," 118–22.

19. These generalizations summarize an extensive review of descriptive literature and case studies, which cannot be documented here. For a fuller analysis with examples and references, see my forthcoming work.

20. Cf. I. M. Lewis, *Ecstatic Religion* (New York: Penguin Books, 1971) 86–88, 96–97, 101.

21. While the menstrual taboo is cultically defined and regulated, it is so universal a factor of human culture that it may be viewed as a general social concept apart from its specific interpretation and institutionalization in the Israelite cultus.

22. The divorced woman and the widow alone are free of overriding male authority.

23. The consequences and implications of this conflict in ordering, or contrast in defining, the religious priorities for women are far-reaching. In a society in which cultic service is accorded highest value, women are disadvantaged when they are excepted from that obligation. The various attempts within the Old Testament to extend to women obligations and options that were originally formulated with males in mind leave unaddressed the tension between the requirement and the ability to fulfill it.

24. Old Babylonian *amat*-DN names, i.e., "handmaid of [divine name]," exceed *warad-* ("servant-") names proportionally, even when the names of *nadītu* women are excluded as cloister names. The data for these comparisons together with a full analysis of sexual distinction in naming are found in my unpublished study, "Sexual Distinction in Israelite Personal Names: A Socio-Religious Investigation."

25. The cultic assembly is not, I believe, to be understood as a male sect or society (though the early cultus has many of the features of a men's religious organization) but rather as a male-constituted and directed institution at the center of Israelite society, representing the community as a whole and directing and controlling its life. The way in which it related to the larger community and the understanding of its own constitution seem to have changed over time in the direction of greater openness and inclusiveness, in respect not only to women but

also to slaves, dependents, and resident aliens (cf. Deut 16:10–11, 13–14). See Conclusion.

26. Thus women shared many of the same rights and duties as men, made use of the same aid provided or mediated by the institutions, and, as men, were held accountable by them. Women, in common with men, prayed, consulted oracles, attended festivals and sought justice in the courts, received theophanies and divine commissions, sought oracular judgments and legal redress for wrongs suffered and received punishment for wrongs committed. It appears that they were not as a rule prohibited from general religious practices but rather were hindered from fuller participation by competing interest or duty (see below) or attracted by their own particular circumstances to make use of some means of religious expression more than others.

27. Miriam's historical role is impossible to reconstruct, but her ranking alongside Moses and Aaron suggests a position of considerable importance—and a cultic role. She is not identified by a husband but by her "brothers," the priest and the prophet. The roles of cultic singer and prophet are suggested.

28. The mythic and aetiological character of the narrative does not limit its value as evidence for a women's ritual.

29. The meaning of *nĕbî'â* in the latter case is disputed. It is clear, however, that the term in Isa 8:3 is used as a role designation ("*the* prophetess," not "my wife") whether or not it designates Isaiah's wife, and that it designates one who is to assist in the symbolic act that will complete Isaiah's sign.

30. The term used in Gen 38:21–22 is intended to describe a Canaanite practitioner in a Canaanite (and pre-Israelite) setting. Cf. n. 41, below.

31. Here opponents of Nehemiah. The Greek and Syriac apparently understood the name as masculine.

32. The narrowing of acceptable roles for women is correlated with a general narrowing of options in religious practice. The greater variety of roles and the fuller or more candid descriptions of practice in the premonarchic period in comparison with the later period raises the question whether the earlier practices disappeared or were simply reinterpreted (as heterodox) and/or suppressed. What is allowed to stand in the tradition of the earlier period was interpreted, in part at least, as evidence of the low moral state of the time—a judgment made explicit in the final editing of the Book of Judges (19:1, 30; etc.).

33. Use of the patriarchal traditions as sources for social reconstruction requires particular caution; they depict individuals or families with little attention to social context and treat them as representative or symbolic figures.

34. The one religious activity from which women appear to have been excluded by principle rather than circumstances was the offering of sacrifices, which eventually became the sole prerogative of the priest. The exclusion may ultimately be connected with the menstrual taboo, but it is not confined to periods of menstrual impurity. It appears, rather, to have been common practice elevated to a principle (cf. Winter, *Frau und Göttin*, 38–40) or to have been understood more in symbolic than in practical terms. Efforts to show that women offered sacrifices fail, I believe, in the case of biblical evidence. Presenting a sacrificial offering to the priest is not itself a sacrificial action (contra Peritz, "Women," 126–27) but an act of offering to which all are bound. In the case of

the offering required for a woman's purification (Lev 12:6–7), a clear distinction is made between the woman's presentation of the animal to the priest ("she shall bring a lamb . . . to the priest," v 6) and the offering made *by* the priest *for* the woman ("and he shall offer it . . . and make atonement for her," v 7) (cf. Lev. 15:19–33). Nor is the sharing of a sacrificial meal an act of sacrifice, though it is an important form of cultic participation, as Peritz insists ("Women in the Ancient Hebrew Cult," 123–25). Manoah prepares and offers the sacrifice on behalf of his nameless wife to whom the angel has appeared (Judg 13:19), and Elkanah sacrifices *(wayyizbaḥ)* at the shrine of Shiloh, distributing portions to his wives and children (1 Sam 1:4).

35. J. Renger's study of the Old Babylonian "priesthood" based on the *lú = amēlu* list shows only one among the nineteen classes identified as *Kultpriester* in which men and women are identified by a common term, namely, the *en,* the highest ranked and earliest attested office in the list ("Untersuchungen zum Priestertum in der altbabylonischen Zeit" [*ZA* NF 24 (1967) 110–88] 113). The sex of the *en* appears to have been complementary to that of the deity, suggesting that the *en* was understood to represent the divine spouse. The rest of the classes are distinguished by gender and nomenclature and grouped (with the exception of the *entum,* the later Akkadian designation of the female *en*) in the typical hierarchical order of male-female, strongly suggesting sexual division of labor within the cultus rather than shared roles. Despite Renger's use of the term *Priesterinnen* to describe the female classes, they do not appear to have performed activities that would properly be described as "priestly." Use of the term "priestess" to describe such women is misleading, since it suggests comparable, if not identical, roles and equal status with priests.

The third group in the *lú = amēlu* list, exorcists, consists of five classes, all male—as we might expect, since these represent offices requiring technical skills and mastery of a body of esoteric knowledge, like the *baru* diviners in the second group. It is only in the second group, comprising the oracular speakers, that we find professional classes with both male and female members, namely, the *šā'iltum/(šā'ilum), maḫḫum/maḫḫūtum,* and *āpilum/āpiltum.* The pattern presented in the Old Babylonian sources corresponds exactly to that which the more meager, and less specialized, Old Testament data suggest: priestly roles involving technical expertise and leadership in the sacrificial cult or other cultic ritual were male, as well as other roles demanding specialized knowledge, while the more charismatic forms of divination open to lay as well as professional practitioners involved women as well as men, just as their Old Testament prophetic counterpart. Cf. R. Harris: "Except for the religious functions of royal women and dream interpretation and divination, women played a minor role in cultic life. Only in the lower echelons of the 'clergy' did female singers, dancers, and musicians participate in the cult" ("Woman in the Ancient Near East," *IDBSup,* 960–63 62).

Syrian and Canaanite sources are too meager to confirm a pattern. The Ugaritic texts contain no reference to any class of female cultic personnel as a recognizable group. Phoenician and Punic sources contain the only known ancient feminine form of *khn* ("priest"). In the Eshmunazar sarcophagus inscription (*KAI,* 14:15) it is applied to the queen of Sidon as royal patron, and hence chief official, of the city god Ashtart. I would interpret this as evidence of a royal cultus in which the king/queen, qua ruler, assumed the title and role of priest/presider in the official cultus, not as evidence for a class of female priests. The status and function of the women bearing this title in several Punic inscriptions (*KAI,* 70:1; 93:1; 145:45[?]; 140:2) cannot be determined. See now J. A. Hackett, *The Balaam Text from Deir 'Allā* (Chico: Scholars Press, 1984) 25.

36. While the women weavers expelled from the Temple by Josiah were associated with the service of a "foreign" deity or cult object, the Yahweh cultus also had need of such service. According to Exod 34:25–26, the material for the tabernacle hangings was spun by women. The weaving of the hangings, however, was supervised by the master craftsman Bezalel or his male assistant (Exod 34:35), an example of the male professionalization of female crafts observed in cross-cultural studies of gender roles. It is not certain who actually did the work; the *kol ḥăkam-leb bĕʿōśeh hammĕlāʾkāh* ("everyone able to do the work") with its masculine plural verb could be a generic use of the masculine to describe a group of workers of mixed gender.

37. This is suggested on the analogy of work in the domestic sphere, though cultic specialization might well make cooking and baking male activities. Nevertheless it is worth speculating who prepared the sacrificial victims for the communion meals eaten at the sanctuary and who baked the shewbread. In the report of the "priests' custom with the people" in 1 Sam 2:13–17, it is clear that neither the priest nor the priest's servant is involved in boiling the meat, since the priest's servant takes or demands the portion desired by the priest. The man sacrificing is addressed in 1 Sam 2:15, but did he cook as well as slaughter the animal? Might not his accompanying wife have performed her usual work for the family feast? Or when the sacrifice later became a priestly prerogative, might not women of priestly families have performed this service?

Ezekiel's provisions for the restored Temple include designation of areas for cooking and baking within the Temple complex, carefully separating the place where the priests were to boil the *'āšām* and the *ḥaṭṭā't* offerings and bake the *minḥâ*—which was to be within the inner court (Ezek 46:20)—and the "kitchens" *(bē hammĕbaššĕlîm)* where "those who minister at the Temple" *(mĕšārĕtê habbayit)* were to boil the "sacrifices of the people" *(zebaḥ hā 'am)*—which were located in the outer court (Ezek 46:21–24). This late scheme clearly assigns all actions related to the sanctuary to priests, guarding this sphere from that in which the preparation of meals for the people took place. Hearths are provided for the latter purpose and the activity was supervised by a lower class of Temple personnel (not priests). This stage of prescription for the cultus has professionalized actions earlier performed by the worshiper, including the slaughter of the sacrificial victims, which is now assigned to the Levites (Ezek 44:12; cf. Lev 2:4–7 and 3:1–17).

The mention of women as cooks and bakers in the palace service (1 Sam 8:13) may also provide a clue, at least for the earlier period, since the administration of the Temple was similar in many ways to the administration of the palace. A third type of female work mentioned in 1 Sam 8:13, that of "perfumers," has a counterpart in the cultus in the preparation of the holy anointing oil, a special skill described by the use of the same verb *(raqqāḥôt; rōqēaḥ,* Exod 30:25).

However, the distinction in the use of the aromatic oils produced for the cultus may make this a male specialty in the cultic setting.

38. The suggestion is again by analogy to the almost universal assignment of housecleaning to women—or slaves. In large public buildings, palaces, etc., such work is usually done by slaves or low-caste groups, with tasks divided by sex, and that may have been the case in the Temple too. But at local shrines presided over by a single priest, the housekeeping chores of the deity's house might well have fallen to the female members of the priest's family.

39. Women are widely identified with singing and dancing as well as instrumental musicmaking in both biblical and extrabiblical texts and in pictorial representations (see, e.g., *ANEP*, 63–66, 111, 346; I. Seibert, *Woman in Ancient Near East* [Leipzig: Fortschritt Erfuhrt, 1974], pls. 10, 34, 99; O. Keel, *The Symbolism of the Biblical World* [New York: Seabury/Crossroad, 1978] 336–39). None of these activities was restricted to women (cf. *ANEP*, 63–66, David's reputation as a singer, and his dance before the Ark, 2 Sam 6:14, 16), though some types of instruments and performance may have been regarded as peculiarly or typically female. The "timbrel," *(top)*, e.g., appears to have been a preferred instrument of women (cf. Winter, *Frau und Göttin,* 33 n. 164; E. Werner, "Musical Instruments" [*IDB* 3. 469–76] 474); women musicians and dancers are widely attested as professional entertainers of men (cf. the Arabic *shayka,* the Japanese geisha, and the Old Testament image of the prostitute as a troubadour, singing to the tune of her harp [Isa 23:14–15]); and women typically formed a welcoming chorus line to greet warriors returning from battle (Exod 15:20; 1 Sam 18:6). The disputed question is whether women participated as musicians or dancers in cultic celebrations and whether they belonged to the personnel of the sanctuary.

The question is too complex for adequate treatment here. It may be that references to cultic dancing should be eliminated altogether, or at least those described by *māḥôl/mĕḥōlâ* and verbal forms of *ḥwl,* which appear always to designate actions of the congregation or groups of lay women, not a professional activity, and may refer to antiphonal singing rather than dance (see J. M. Sasson, "The Worship of the Golden Calf," *Orient and Occident: Essays Presented to Cyrus H. Gordon,* AOAT 22 [1973] 151–59 157; cf. Winter, *Frau und Göttin,* 32–33). The function of the three daughters of Heman, mentioned in a parenthetical note in 1 Chron 25:5, is unclear, though the sons constituted a major Levitical guild of musicians in the Second Temple. The *mĕšōrĕrîm ûmĕšōrĕrôt* of Ezra 2:65 clearly represent a different class from the Temple singers described by the same term (masculine plural) in Ezra 2:41; Neh 7:44. Their place in the list following male and female servants and preceding the horses suggests a menial class of entertainers.

It seems likely that the public, professional roles of musicians in the Temple service were assigned to males, at least in the later period of the monarchy and the Second Temple period, while women's specialized musical activity was limited to secular entertainment and funeral dirges (a "home" ritual). The earlier period, however, suggests a different picture in the attribution of two important songs of praise to women, both called prophets (Exod 15:20–21; Judg 4:4; 5:1; cf. 1 Chron 25:1, which describes the function of the Temple musicians as "prophesying" with lyres, harps, and cymbals). While the narrative contexts point to a traditional secular role of women in greeting returning warriors (cf. Winter, *Frau und Göttin*, 33), both texts may also be understood to describe cultic actions, whose setting is the celebration of Yahweh's victories, not simply as one-time historical acts, but as repeated cultic actions recalling the great victories (or does the shift in attribution of the Song at the Sea from Miriam to Moses reflect a cultic institutionalization of the victory song in which the secular/lay role of the woman leader is transformed into a cultic/professional male role?). Psalm 68:26 suggests that in the Temple period at least women formed a recognized group among the Temple musicians (*'ălāmôt tôpēpôt*, mentioned between *šārîm* and *nōgĕnîm* in the procession to the sanctuary; cf. Winter, *Frau und Göttin*, 34–35).

40. The many questions about these women cannot be explored adequately here, much less resolved. For the most recent discussion and review of literature, see Winter, *Frau und Göttin*, 58–65. Both the Samuel and the Exodus passages suggest the persistence of the office or institution after the initiation of the Yahwistic cultus and its tent shrine in the desert. Winter has seen rightly, I believe, that the significant information in the archaic Exodus tradition is the reference to the mirrors (*Frau und Göttin*, 60). For a critique of his interpretation, which views the mirror as the symbol of a female deity associated with fertility and the women as *Hofdamen* visiting the sanctuary, rather than cultic personnel, see my forthcoming work. Cf. J. Morgenstern, "The Ark, the Ephod, and the Tent," *HUCA* 17 (1942–43) 153–265, *HUCA* 18 (1943–44) 1–52, for an interpretation of the women as shrine attendants based on pre-Islamic Arabic parallels.

41. This is not the place to review the evidence and arguments concerning the *qĕdēšâ*. The literature is far larger than that on the women at the entrance to the tent of meeting and the presence of cognates and of presumed parallel institutions in other ancient Near Eastern cultures requires a more thorough investigation and report than the chapter in this present volume permits. Of the three Old Testament references, two suggest a foreign origin or, at least, a non-Yahwistic institution (Deut 23:17 and Gen 38:21–22), while all three parallel the term with *zônâ* ("prostitute"). The cultic nature of the office or role is clear from the etymology and from the one text that describes an activity (Hos 4:14): "[The men] sacrifice with *qĕdēšôt*." Since the term is paired in Deut 23:17 with the masculine *qādēš*—in the reverse of the normal male-female order—any judgment about the *qĕdēšâ* must involve consideration of the whole class of cognate terms. In overview, it appears that the Old Testament usage is so generalized and polemical that it may serve more as a cover term for proscribed cultic roles rather than as the precise designation of a particular office or function. Since all of the masculine references (all apparently collective, except Deut 23:17, and therefore conceivably inclusive) are in Deuteronomic contexts, the possibility must be considered that the term was used in Deuteronomistic circles to describe roles or offices, such as that of the *ṣōbĕ'ôt* of the Tent of Meeting, that were at one time considered a legitimate part of the Israelite cultus.

21

The Marriage Motif in Israelite Religion[1]

HELMER RINGGREN

Isaiah's song of the vineyard (Isa 5:1–7) begins with the following words:

> I will sing for my beloved,
> a love song concerning his vineyard.
> (Isa 5:1)

In the prophet's audience, the terms "beloved" *(yādîd)* and "love song" *(šîrat dôdî)* would immediately bring to mind a certain genre of poetry, namely, the one most fully represented in the Song of Songs.[2] Since "vineyard" in those love songs is sometimes a symbol of the beloved lady (e.g., Cant 8:12), the audience is led to expect a song about the friend and his wife. And in the sequel, when the prophet speaks of his friend's care and attention for his vineyard, one easily gets the impression that he is actually referring to what his friend did for his wife. The failure of the vineyard to bear good fruit could very well be interpreted as an allusion to the unfaithfulness of the wife. As the prophet asks his audience to "judge" between the owner and his vineyard, their reaction has to be: The unfaithful wife should be punished. Only then does the prophet reveal what he is talking about: His friend is God and the vineyard is the people of Israel.

It is true that "vineyard" is used as a symbol for the people elsewhere, too, without associations with love and marriage, as in Isa 27:2–3.[3] But the allusions to love poetry in the song of the vineyard are too strong to be neglected.

This song is obviously one of the numerous examples of the prophets' free use of various literary forms to convey their message. Nevertheless, one question remains: What is the reason for the applicability of love poetry to the relationship between Yahweh and his people? We have to turn first to the genre of the love song as such, especially as represented by the Song of Songs.

421

Obviously, the Song of Songs is a composite work. The speaker is alternately a woman and a man, several literary genres are represented, and there is no obvious progress of action or thought. Scholars who have tried to interpret the song as a kind of drama have been able to do so only by rearranging the poems. It thus seems that we have before us a collection of love lyrics without any logical arrangement. But should these love songs be taken literally, or are they meant as allegory? There is little, if anything, in the texts themselves to suggest the latter alternative. But if they refer to human love in general, why are they included in the collection of sacred Scriptures?

A closer study of literary parallels is somewhat inconclusive. Such a characteristic genre as the description song (Arabic *waṣf*),[4] in which the beauty of the beloved is described according to the various parts of the body (Cant 4:1–7; 5:10–16; 7:2–10), has parallels in Egyptian love songs, in an Akkadian Tammuz hymn,[5] in the Keret epic from Ugarit (*UT* Krt VI.24–30), in the *Genesis Apocryphon* from Qumran (1QapGen XX 2–8, a description of Sarah's beauty), and in great number in modern Arabic wedding songs from Syria-Palestine.[6] The genre is thus spread from the second millennium B.C.E. down to our own age and from cult lyrics and mythology to secular love songs in folklore. A similar observation can be made when metaphors and comparisons are concerned. The wealth of images taken from plant life is striking (flowers—Cant 2:1–2; apples—2:3; 7:9; pomegranates—4:3, 13; 6:7, 11; 7:13; 8:2; palms—7:8–9; cedars and cypresses—1:17; garden—4:12–13; 5:1; vineyard—8:12). All of these are found as love symbols in ancient cult lyrics as well as in modern folklore.[7] The same is true of the dove (1:15; 2:14; 5:12; 6:9); it is the bird of the love goddess and well known also in modern folklore.[8] Honey is another symbol (2:14; 4:11) found in Sumerian cult lyrics and modern songs.[9]

Chronologically the Song of Songs stands between the ancient cult songs and the wedding songs of Palestinian folklore. Geographically it stands between the Egyptian love songs—which *may* be secular but certainly contain religious elements—and the Sumerian and Akkadian songs from the Ishtar-Tammuz religion. The only conclusion that can be drawn from these observations is that the Song of Songs belongs to a stream of tradition that is very old and reaches down to our modern age and is spread at least from Mesopotamia to Egypt. It is not very meaningful to ask whether this poetic tradition has its roots in the cult or in secular life. Obviously, nobody would have used the language of love in cult lyrics unless there had been such a thing as human love, but on the other hand the use of symbolic language in secular songs seems to show that these have been influenced by cultic songs. Secular and religious love songs represent one single stream of tradition and can hardly be separated on stylistic grounds.

One indication that the Song of Songs might have cultic roots is that the bride is described as "seeking" her bridegroom (Cant 3:1–5; 5:6–8). For it is well known that the theme of seeking and finding is characteristic both of the Ishtar-Tammuz religion and of the Egyptian Osiris-Isis mysteries. In the Old Testament the motif is found in similar contexts in Hos 2:7 (Israel seeks her lovers, that is, the idols) and Prov 7:15 (the "foreign woman" seeks the young man). But the seeking motif is rather vague and general and can hardly bear the burden of proof.[10]

A strong argument could be found in the fact that it is always the bride who takes the initiative in the Song of Songs. This hardly makes sense in a secular wedding but is easily explained if the bride was originally a goddess.

A closer look at the Song of Songs reveals a number of details which, if taken literally, might very well point to cultic celebrations (at least originally). There is a procession from the "wilderness" that is expressly said to be a wedding procession (Cant 3:6–11). Several allusions point to events taking place in a garden or vineyard (Cant 1:7; 2:10–13, 15; 6:1, 10); the time is spring (Cant 2:10, 13). The bridegroom approaches the bride and calls on her: "Rise, and come out!" (Cant 2:10, 13). The bride rises to open the door, but the bridegroom has disappeared and she has to seek him (Cant 3:1–5; 5:6–8). The scene takes place in the night (Cant 2:17; 4:6; cf. 7:11). The references to raisins, apples, milk, and honey may allude to a ceremonial meal, but might of course be mere metaphors.[11]

The persons of the play are "the king" (Cant 1:4, 12) or "Solomon" (Cant 3:7–11; 8:11) and "Shulammith." The first epithet can be understood literally. Between Solomon and Shulammith there must be some kind of connection, but there is no consensus as to its nature (is Shulammith a goddess?).

In the time of the synagogue, the Song of Songs was read at the Passover festival. One might ask, therefore, if there is any trace of an original connection with this festival. The evidence is weak. Hypothetically we might point to the procession from the wilderness with its pillar of smoke (Cant 3:6–8) and the *beter* mountains in Cant 2:17, *if* there is any connection between these and the *beter* sacrifice which in Gen 15:7ff. and Jer 34:18–19 accompanies the conclusion of a covenant—the covenant was concluded at Sinai shortly after the exodus. Otherwise it is spring and the renewal of vegetation that is in the focus; some allusions to the fertility of the herds and flocks complete the picture.[12]

From the point of view of literary form, language, and motifs it is thus possible that the Song of Songs has a cultic origin. But in its present form it is hardly a cultic text. It is not believable that a text belonging to a *hieros gamos* ceremony should have been included in the Israelite canon. We do not even know that such a ceremony was ever practiced in Israel, though prophetic polemics against syncretism, the occurrence of the goddess Anath together with Yahweh in the Elephantine texts, and the recently discovered references to Yahweh and his Asherah at Kuntillet ʿAjrud give a certain amount of probability to such a hypothesis. It is more likely, however, that the original function of the songs had been forgotten and that they had received a new interpretation before they were included in the canon.

A clue to this interpretation is probably found in the following passage in the Song of Songs:

> For love is strong as death,
> its zeal as hard as Sheol. . . .
> Many waters cannot quench love,
> neither can floods drown it.
> (Cant 8:6–7)

Death and Sheol, on the one hand, and *mayim rabbîm* and floods *(nĕhārôt),* on the other, are well known as representatives of the forces of chaos, which threaten life and the order of the world. But love is stronger than them all. In other words, the divine force that pervades the cosmos and sustains life and order can be called "love."[13] This love is present in the relationship between man and woman as well as in the order of nature in general. Human love is an expression of the principle that sustains life in general.

Whether or not such ideas were present in the ancient fertility religion of Canaan cannot be proved by textual evidence, but it is a fact that the Sumerians considered fertility, prosperity, victory, and success in general as the result of the king's functioning in the *hieros gamos* ceremony.[14] Behind this is some kind of analogy thinking: Everything that furthers life in all its forms belongs together and pervades the cosmos as a divine force.[15] The "pagans" identified this force with deities of love and fertility; in Israel the conviction grew that it was Yahweh who stood for all of this. An illustration of this process is provided by the prophet Hosea.

The marriage of Hosea became a sort of symbolic action. Just as his wife turned out to be unfaithful, so Israel had been unfaithful to Yahweh. By analogy, then, Israel is the wife of Yahweh. The covenant is understood as a marriage relationship. It emerges from the context that there is a hidden polemic against the Canaanite practice of *hieros gamos* behind

Hosea's preaching. The people of Israel was Yahweh's wife, but she thought that it was her lovers, that is, the fertility gods, who gave her bread and water, wool, flax, oil, and drink (Hos 2:5; cf. 2:12—vines and fig trees "are the hire which my lovers give me"). So Yahweh will show his people who is really the giver of fertility. "She will pursue her lovers but not overtake; she shall seek them but shall not find them" (Hos 2:7). There we have again the seeking motif of the Song of Songs and clearly connected with fertility gods. Israel did not realize that it is Yahweh who gives fertility (Hos 2:8), but they will realize the truth when he withholds it (Hos 2:9).

In other words, the real sacred marriage which produces fertility is that between Yahweh and his people, not the one celebrated in the fertility cult. We have before us a transformation of the fertility religion. The love that pervades nature is Yahweh's love, and it should be met by the people's love for their God.

Yahweh's love is steadfast, however, and he will renew his relationship with Israel. This is again expressed in terms of betrothal and marriage:

> Therefore, I will allure her
> and bring her into the wilderness
> and speak tenderly to her. . . .
> And there she shall respond as in the days of her youth,
> as at the time when she came out of the land of Egypt.
> And in that day, says Yahweh,
> you will call me "My husband,"
> and no longer will you call me "My *ba'al.*"
>
> (Hos 2:14–16)

The last verse contains a wordplay. *Ba'al* is the normal word for "husband," but it is also the name of the god that should be rejected. At the same time, the expression seems to imply that in this particular form of syncretism Yahweh was also called *ba'al.* On the other hand, *'îš* is a more rare word for "husband" and "apparently an endearing expression" correspondent to *'iššâ* as term for "wife."[16]

In any case, the result will be that "the sky will answer [cf. the same verb in Hos 2:15b above] the earth," and the earth will bring forth grain, wine, and oil (vv 21–22). In the wilderness Yahweh will make a covenant (v 18) with his people just as he did at Mt. Sinai.[17] Marriage and covenant are the same thing, but the main point here is fertility as in the Baal religion. Yahweh replaces Baal as the partner, and he gives exactly that which the people expected from Baal. In other words, Hosea uses the concepts of the fertility religion in order to convey the idea that it is Yahweh who is the true God. It should not be forgotten that in the promise of a happy fortune as set forth in Hosea 14 it is again the concept of fertility that is in focus:

> I will be as the dew to Israel,
> he shall blossom as the lily,
> he shall strike root as the poplar,
> his shoots shall spread out,
> his beauty shall be like the olive.
>   (Hos 14:5–6)

Yahweh—not Baal—is the answer to the quest of the people. This, at the same time, adds a new dimension to the covenant relationship. If in Deuteronomy, for example, loving God has the connotation of vassal loyalty, the word has here more emotional overtones. It may even be that when Hosea asks for *da'at 'elōhîm*, he does not only mean "knowing about God"[18] but the kind of intimate relationship that is characteristic of marriage.

The fertility overtones are absent in other prophetic passages where marital symbolism occurs. Jeremiah refers to the happy time in the wilderness when the people loved him as a bride in true devotion (Jer 2:2) and accuses the people of having broken the relationship.

Ezekiel 23 is a marriage allegory, in which the two sisters Oholah and Oholibah represent Samaria and Jerusalem. But the emphasis is rather on the harlotry of the two sisters than on the marriage aspect (only v 4, "They became mine, and they bore sons and daughters"). Another interesting example is Ezek 16:8: "When I passed by you again and looked upon you, you were at the age of love. I plighted my troth to you and entered into a covenant with you, and you became mine." Here again, the emphasis is on the unfaithfulness of the wife. But we notice that covenant and marriage are identical concepts.

Another example is found in Isaiah:

> You shall no more be termed Forsaken,
> and your land shall no more be termed Desolate,
> but you shall be called "My delight is in her"
> and your land "Married,"
> for Yahweh delights in you,
> and your land shall be married. . . .
> For as the bridegroom rejoices over the bride,
> so shall your God rejoice over you.
>   (Isa 62:4–5)

There may be a faint trace of the fertility symbolism here in that the land of the forsaken wife (people) is "desolate," while the land of the beloved is "married" *(bĕ'ûlâ),* which obviously is meant to denote the opposite of a desolate and barren country (cf. the Mishnaic expression *šĕdê habba'al* and Arabic *'ard ba'l* for land which is watered by rain).[19] The emphasis here is on the restitution of normal (happy) conditions.

A second transformation of the marrage motif is found in the wisdom literature. The relationship between the disciple and (sometimes personified) Wisdom is often described in terms of love and marriage:

> Say to wisdom, "You are my sister,"
> and call insight your intimate friend,
> to preserve you from the "foreign woman."
> (Prov 7:4–5)

> Do not forsake her [wisdom], and she will keep you,
> love her, and she will guard you . . .
> she will honor you if you embrace her,
> she will place on your head a fair garland.
> (Prov 4:6, 8)

> [Blessed is the man] who peers through her windows
> and listens at her doors. . . .[20]
> She will come to meet him like a mother,
> and like the wife of his youth she will welcome him.
> (Sir 14:23; 15:2)

> I directed my soul to her,
> my hand opened her gates.
> I entered to her and saw her
> and found her in her purity.
> (Sir 51:19–20, Hebrew text)

Of course, this is all metaphorical language, but it seems probable that it has developed in competition with and in polemic against a form of religion in which there was a goddess who was the object of *hieros gamos* ceremonies. The "foreign woman" from whom Wisdom is to protect her disciple is also described in terms that remind us of a sexual cult.[21] Thus, just as Hosea presented Yahweh as the alternative of Baal, the wisdom writers present Wisdom as the alternative of the foreign woman/the goddess. At the same time, Wisdom represents the principle of creation, the order that pervades the cosmos, as is shown by Prov 8:22–31, where Wisdom is presented as the assistant creator, that is, the one who set up the principles according to which the world was arranged in its wise order.[22] And when Wisdom in Sirach 24 is equated with the law, we are reminded of the Jewish saying that God looked up in the Torah and then created the world. In the Song of Songs the all-pervading force or principle is *'ahăbâ* ("love"); here it is wisdom, later identified with the Torah.

NOTES

1. A preliminary essay *"Hieros gamos* in Egypt, Sumer and Israel" was published in Swedish in *Religion och Bibel* 18 (1959) 23–51. Parts of that essay have been utilized for this study.

2. This idea was first developed by A. Bentzen, *AfO* 4 (1927) 209–10; cf. H. Junker, "Die literarsiche Art von Is. 5, 1–7," *Bib* 40 (1959) 269ff.

3. This vineyard metaphor may go back to Canaanite usage. According to one possible translation of *UT* 77, 22–23, Nikkal promises his bride to "make her fields into vineyards, the fields of her love into orchards"; the reference seems to be to the sexual act. Cf. H. P. Müller, *"kerem" (THAT* 4. 329).

4. Cf. G. Gerleman, *Das hohe Lied* (BKAT 18; Neukirchen-Vluyn: Neukirchener Verlag, 1965) 65ff.

5. E. Ebeling, *Tod und Leben nach den Vorstellungen der Babylonier* (Berlin, 1931) no. 10.

6. For further details, see S. Linder, *Palästinische Volksgesänge*, ed. H. Ringgren, I (UUÅ 1952:5) 82–86.

7. Ibid., 86–94.

8. Ibid., 96–97.

9. For example, the poem quoted in H. Ringgren, "Hohes Lied und hieros gamos," *ZAW* 65 (1953) 300–301; cf. Linder and Ringgren, *Palästinische Volksgesänge*, 97–98.

10. Cf. A. Haldar, *Associations of Cult Prophets Among the Ancient Semites* (Uppsala: Almqvist & Wiksell, 1945) 129, where "the Lord whom you are seeking" in Mal 3:1 is interpreted as "the dead god being sought."

11. Cf. Ringgren, *"Hieros gamos* in Egypt," 49.

12. Ibid., 50.

13. See my commentary in *Das Alte Testament Deutsch* 16 (3d ed.; Göttingen: Vandenhoeck & Ruprecht, 1981) 287.

14. A. Falkenstein and W. von Soden, *Sumerische und akkadische Hymnen und Gebete* (Zurich and Stuttgart: Artemis, 1953) 101; cf. Ringgren, *"Hieros gamos* in Egypt," 41–42.

15. Comparable is H. Frankfort's interpretation of Osiris, *Ancient Egyptian Religion* (New York: Columbia University Press, 1948) 108–9.

16. H. W. Wolff, *Hosea* (Hermeneia; Philadelphia: Fortress Press, 1974) 49.

17. Cf. G. Östborn, *Yahweh and Baal* (Lunds universitets årsskrift 51:7; 1956) 79–80.

18. As argued by H. W. Wolff, "'Wissen um Gott' bei Hosea als Urform der Theologie," *EvTh* 12 (1952–53) 533–44.

19. *HALAT* 136b.

20. Cf. Cant 5:1ff.

21. See H. Ringgren, *Word and Wisdom* (Lund: Håkan Ohlsson, 1947) 105, 133ff.

22. Ibid., 95ff.

22

The Place of Covenant in the Religion of Israel

ROBERT A. ODEN, JR.

This chapter is an investigation into some of the changing and recurring perspectives in Old Testament scholarship during the course of the past century. Specifically, my purpose is to examine in broad outline major shifts during this period in critical assessments of the role that the covenant relationship between Yahweh and Israel played in the history of Israelite religion. The congruence between the assessments of the date and significance of the covenant relationship that obtained at the beginning of this period and again at the end of this period is my particular focus. Why was the covenant concept characterized as relatively late in the date of its appearance and of peripheral importance by scholars a century ago? Why has this same characterization appeared again recently? Why did many scholars in the period between, and especially in the period from about 1930 until about 1960, reach a conclusion so nearly the opposite of this?

THE ROLE OF THE COVENANT IN
BIBLICAL SCHOLARSHIP:
1880–1980

As in so many instances of tracing a line of inquiry within biblical scholarship, it is appropriate to begin this investigation with J. Wellhausen. Even though Wellhausen's general assessment of the covenant relationship—that it appeared late and was not of central importance for Israelite religion for several centuries—is well known, so thoroughly was this assessment rejected by most scholars in the middle of the twentieth century that looking again at either the *Prolegomena* or the articles assembled in *Die Composition des Hexateuchs*[1] still occasions some surprise at how little space Wellhausen devotes to any account of the covenant relationship. In the *Prolegomena,* for example, fewer than three pages are devoted directly to a discussion of the meaning and development of the term *běrît* in the Hebrew Bible.[2] In this brief section,

Wellhausen argues that the use of *bĕrît* to characterize the relationship between Yahweh and Israel is something unknown to the preexilic prophets, including Hosea,[3] and is "an entirely new thing" when it appears later.[4] Such use appears, Wellhausen continues, only after Josiah's introduction of the Deuteronomic law; and "it prevails" only in Deuteronomy, Jeremiah, Ezekiel, Second Isaiah, Leviticus 17—26, and, of course, "in the Book of the Four Covenants," one of Wellhausen's designations for Q or P.[5] Nor does this minimalizing assessment of the role of the covenant change in any significant or widely influential way for the next quarter of a century. Thus the studies of R. Kraetzschmar[6] or J. J. P. Valeton[7] are those from the end of the nineteenth century to which most frequent reference is made on the subject of covenant; and neither scholar appears to depart from the position of Wellhausen.

In several areas of biblical study, the turn of the century is marked most centrally by the work of A. Eichhorn, H. Gunkel, H. Gressmann, and others of the history of religion school.[8] However, it is not as true for a thorough reassessment of the place of covenant as it is for areas such as tradition history or the inaugural steps in the rise of form criticism. For the covenant issue, it is rather the conclusions of W. R. Smith and M. Weber that mark a dramatic turn. Since the concluding section of the present study will concentrate upon Smith's work, it might be appropriate here to accent the role of Weber.[9] The two chief emphases of much of Weber's work, those which have been aptly characterized as "the structural institutional" on the one hand and the "religious-ideological" on the other,[10] come together in his writings on the place of the covenant in the religion of Israel. Weber entitles the first part of his study of ancient Judaism "The Israelite Confederacy and Yahweh"[11] and discovers "periodic amphictyonic ritualistic acts" at the basis of the Israelite religious community,[12] an idea that would soon play a key role in Old Testament study. Of even more importance, if less frequently remembered, are Weber's statements on the role of the covenant. After specifically rejecting the conclusions of Kraetzschmar, Weber argues that the singularity of ancient Israel is best seen in Israel's use of the concept of *bĕrît* as the foundation of Israel's legal and ethical life.[13] Though many nations' gods protect the social order, Weber argues (and to this argument we will return), only in Israel did "the 'covenant' idea" become "the specific dynamics informing the ethical conception of priestly teaching and prophecy."[14] How might one, then, best describe Yahweh for ancient Israel? As, Weber concludes, "a god of social organization" or, even more plainly influential for the later discussion, as "the contractual partner [*Vertragspartner*] of its law established by *berith*."[15]

Though Weber's conclusions about the social nature of the religion of

Israel and especially about Yahweh as a "treaty partner" foreshadow much of the twentieth-century emphasis upon the centrality of the covenant relationship, some years passed before Weber's analysis of the religion of Israel was appropriated by biblical scholars. Thus, A. S. Peake's Society for Old Testament Study Presidential Address in 1924 surveys the developments in the area of the religion of Israel since the time of Kraetzschmar and Valeton and concludes, "The net result of the recent critical movement, it seems to me, is that we are left in the main very much where we were a quarter of a century ago" and "I am disinclined to anticipate that we shall see any great movement in the direction of reclaiming Deuteronomy for the pre-prophetic period."[16] Of course, "great movement" is just what did obtain within a very few years after Peake's statements, and precisely in the area of redating covenant traditions, such as those in Deuteronomy, to a much earlier era.

This change of direction is usually, and fairly, located above all in W. Eichrodt's *Theology of the Old Testament,* which first began to appear in 1933.[17] As G. Hasel correctly notes, Eichrodt here "broke once and for all with traditional God-Man-Salvation arrangement" for Old Testament theology and found instead "the covenant concept" to be the Old Testament's "overriding and unifying category."[18] Eichrodt's chapter titles already make this clear: "The Covenant Relationship"; "The Covenant Statutes"; "The Name of the Covenant God"; "The Nature of the Covenant God;" and others.[19] For Eichrodt, from the Mosaic period on, the foundation of Israel's relationship with Yahweh was seen as a covenant.[20] Of course, this notion comes to the fore, as Wellhausen had noted, in materials influenced by Deuteronomic law; but Eichrodt argues that the covenant concept was also a key to understanding the older prophets, even if these later avoided explicit use of the term *běrît*.[21] However, for the tradition we are tracing here, it is important to remember that Eichrodt was not alone in asserting the centrality of covenant—that we have to do here with an entire tendency and not just the work of a single scholar. Thus, half a dozen years before Eichrodt's *Theology* was published, N. Glueck's dissertation on the term *ḥesed* appeared.[22] Here, anticipating much future work on further technical terms viewed as comprehensible only in terms of the covenant relationship, Glueck stresses throughout the mutuality implied in the various uses of the term *ḥesed* in the Hebrew Bible. *Ḥesed,* for Glueck, is the very content of *běrît*[23] and can be translated "covenant loyalty."[24] In the same era, E. G. Kraeling was to affirm that for the religion of Israel, "the *berīth* or covenant is the fundamental thing upon which the cult rests; it is the basic relation between the divinity and the group and the chief concern of the cult is its 'renewal' from time to time."[25] Hence, the reconstruction of

Eichrodt was hardly one without a willing audience. Rather, an entire tradition of scholarship had begun a shift toward asserting the antiquity and centrality of the covenant relationship.

Not everyone was immediately enveloped in the developing drift away from Wellhausen's position. This is hardly surprising, since such shifts in any academic discipline only appear unanimous retrospectively and temporarily.[26] As late as 1950, for example, R. H. Pfeiffer could still assert, "I have been unable to discover any reference to the divine covenant with Israel in passages which are earlier than 621."[27] Pfeiffer's opposition, however, was, even in 1950, lingering opposition which was soon to find fewer and fewer adherents. What put an end, for a time, to the older view, which found covenant late and peripheral, was, of course, the alleged discovery of ancient and exact parallels between the Israelite covenant and ancient Near Eastern treaties.[28] The most widely cited and clearly argued of the initial claims for these treaty-covenant parallels was a pair of articles by G. E. Mendenhall.[29] Mendenhall began his discussion of the importance of the Hittite vassal treaties for understanding the Israelite covenant by summarizing several of the basic assumptions lying behind his reconstruction of the religion of Israel—assumptions that were at once very different from the bases of Wellhausen's position and that were to become fundamental for the "covenant centrality" views of the following decade or two. Thus, for Mendenhall, the existence of a covenant-bound community of tribes as a religious federation can hardly be doubted on rational grounds so far as the period of the Judges is concerned;[30] "the messages of the prophets are essentially indictments of Israel for breach of covenant";[31] and Deuteronomy is not a "pious forgery" but rather represents "a continuity of old traditions."[32] After this summary, Mendenhall turned to a search for "some objective criteria for reconstructing the course of Israelite history and religion." These he found in the Hittite treaties.[33] Both before and after he listed V. Korošec's now familiar six-part structure to these treaties, Mendenhall emphasized the importance of the second millennium B.C.E. date—and no other—of this structure.[34] Adding this new information to the amphictyonic thesis of Weber, Mendenhall then concluded that Israel came into existence as a religious community through the covenant with Yahweh, that a text like Joshua 24 reflects just such an event, and that "the history of Israel before the monarchy can be understood and reconstructed only on the assumption that a covenant did exist."[35]

Given the empirical support that these conclusions seemed to give to those, like Eichrodt, who had previously defended the centrality of the covenant notion for the religion of Israel, it is not surprising that the decade or so after the publication of Mendenhall's articles witnessed the high point of this position. Two publications from this period will serve to document this. The first is J. Muilenburg's "The Form and Structure of the Covenantal Formulations."[36] Like many in this period, Muilenburg begins with the assumption that "behind the promulgation of the Deuteronomic Code of 621 B.C. lies a long history of literary and cultic activity."[37] Proof of this Muilenburg finds, as were others to do, in Exod 19:3–6, in which he denies the presence of any Deuteronomic or Deuteronomistic editing and which is thus "the *fons et origo* of the many covenantal pericopes which appear throughout the Old Testament."[38] Muilenburg can then conclude that both Joshua 24 and 1 Samuel 12 rest upon old traditions as well and that these covenant traditions "formed the background against which the prophets (especially from the north) launched their invectives and threats."[39] A second example is K. Baltzer's *The Covenant Formulary.*[40] The thesis of this volume, in perhaps conscious refutation of Wellhausen and agreement with Weber, is that the notion of the *běrît* "designates the basis of the relationship between the God of Israel and his people."[41] Baltzer's study of Joshua 24, Exodus 19—34, and Deuteronomy then demonstrates for him that the genre of the covenant formula was known in Israel, so that from an early date the pattern represented in the ancient Near Eastern treaties was applied in the religion of Israel.[42]

So widely known are the many related areas of inquiries generated by this basic set of conclusions that detailed summary is doubtless unnecessary here. It may be useful simply to note some of these areas, in order to indicate how much explanatory power was accorded to the covenant relationship. First, and in a manner begun quite early in Glueck's study of *ḥesed,* the understanding of a whole series of technical terms began to be revised against the background of the treaty-covenant structure. These terms include *'āhēb,*[43] *yāda',*[44] *ṭôb,*[45] and *rîb.*[46] Second, the thesis of a cultic background for many Old Testament texts was seen to receive support in the supposition of a ritual of covenant renewal.[47] Third, the perennial problem of the preexilic prophets' reticence in using the term *běrît* was explained on the basis of such arguments as that which saw the covenant relationship as so basic and ancient in Israel that no explicit mention of *běrît* was expected or required from the earlier prophets.[48] Fourth, the demonstrable ideological differences between the Southern and the Northern Kingdom were schematized by the appeal to two different understandings of covenant: a promissory relationship, modeled upon the royal grant, and a conditional relationship, modeled upon the suzerain-vassal treaty.[49] And finally, in this greatly abbreviated list, what may well be the most lasting contribution of the inquiries prompted by the covenant-treaty discussion was the observation that the Book of

Deuteronomy, or an earlier form of the book, is structured according to the standard schema of the suzerain-vassal treaty, especially the treaties of the Assyrian period.[50]

However, the same years that witnessed these expansions upon the thesis of the centrality and antiquity of the covenant relationship in the religion of Israel also saw the beginnings of what would become a complete return, on the behalf of many scholars, to the position of Wellhausen. Since our purpose here is to follow the course of an entire tradition within biblical scholarship, it is best not to attempt to designate any individual scholar or study as the first in this return but rather to indicate a series of studies in this direction.[51] Among the initial studies that presage the full return is A. Jepsen's 1961 reevaluation of the terms *rhm* and *hsd*.[52] His conclusions about the meaning of the latter of these terms are particularly relevant, since we noted above that Glueck's earlier monograph on *hesed* was among the first works to signal the rise of the "covenant centrality" tradition. After summarizing Glueck's argument for the intimacy of the link between *hesed* and *běrît,* Jepsen states plainly that his conclusion is rather that there is "no clear relationship between *hsd* and *bryt.*"[53] *Hesed,* for Jepsen, contains little or no suggestion of any mutual relationship, and rather indicates an act of free will, a conclusion to which more recent studies of the same term have also come.[54] This same general tendency to remove any sense of mutuality from a host of terms previously associated with covenant and translated as relational terms is one that characterizes the entire return to the position of Wellhausen.

Within a short period after Jepsen's 1961 study of *hesed,* there appeared an article by C. F. Whitley that denied the fundamental correctness of the proposed analogy between the Israelite covenant and the Hittite treaty form and also found the covenant concept irrelevant to the question of Israel's origins.[55] Like Wellhausen, Whitley accented the prophetic ignorance of the covenant and found those prophetic passages (e.g., Hos 6:7 and 8:1) which others had used to establish a pre-Deuteronomic awareness of the covenant relationship to be no proof of any true awareness of the covenant.[56] Again foreshadowing subsequent tendencies, Whitley also saw heavy Deuteronomistic editing or composition in passages such as Exod 19:3b–8 and Exod 24:1–11, thus concluding, "We may doubt if there was any notion of such a covenant before Deuteronomic times."[57]

With regard to influence upon a wide group of scholars, neither Jepsen's nor Whitley's study was as important as was the first edition of D. J. McCarthy's *Treaty and Covenant,* which appeared in 1963, "at exactly the right time," McCarthy was later to say, when "debate about covenant and especially treaty covenant in the Old Testament was at its height."[58] Central arguments in this volume were the denial that the Sinai narrative resembles the structure of Near Eastern treaties and the demonstration that a single treaty form was used throughout the Near East over a very long period, and hardly alone for a few centuries contemporary with the origins of Israel. Though McCarthy remained convinced that the basic covenant notion was quite old, he stated first here that which would soon become something like a consensus, that the treaty parallels are found best in the Book of Deuteronomy.[59]

Much more pessimistic about the centrality and antiquity of the covenant relationship, and hence closer still to the position of Wellhausen, is G. Fohrer's 1966 article on amphictyony and covenant.[60] Though this article is often cited for its attempted refutation of the amphictyonic hypothesis, more significant for our purposes is the allied argument seeking to refute the equally prevalent view "that the relationship between Yahweh and Israel fundamentally and always" was a covenantal relationship.[61] After summarizing the recent work of Jepsen, Whitley, and others, Fohrer presents his own case. This is that the social setting of early Israel is completely inappropriate for the national state setting of the treaties;[62] that those biblical texts which speak of Yahweh's relationship to Israel as a běrît (e.g., Exod 19:3b–8, Genesis 15, or Joshua 24) are all late and the results of a theologumenon created by the Deuteronomists;[63] and that it is the Priestly school which then takes up this covenant concept and fashions it into a total historical system.[64]

Though the works of many others might be cited here,[65] the most extended presentations of this revisionist position are doubtless the volumes of L. Perlitt and E. Kutsch. Given that both volumes develop arguments summarized above, neither requires elaborate description here. Perlitt's *Bundestheologie im Alten Testament*[66] is, as McCarthy correctly noted, "a direct attack on much of the received wisdom concerning covenant."[67] *Běrît*, Perlitt affirms as had others before him, referred early not to a relationship but rather to an obligation; hence, *běrît* in Israel was not originally modeled after anything like the structure of international treaties. The witnesses to the covenant as a divine-human relationship in the Sinai narrative, for example, are not, for Perlitt, a result of any early traditions but rather are confined to a chronologically limited period in the development of this narrative—that is, to the period of the Deuteronomists.[68] Building upon the preliminary conclusions in a series of articles,[69] Kutsch's *Verheissung und Gesetz* concentrates upon the meaning of the term *běrît*.[70] His conclusion too is that *běrît* before Deuteronomy refers to "self-obligation" (*Selbstverpflichtung*) or the obligation of another, and not primarily to a mutual relationship between

God and human beings, which sense it acquires only in the late monarchic period.[71] With regard to the existence of a covenant festival, Kutsch affirms that since "Israel did not understand its relationship to Yahweh as a covenant, . . . there was therefore in Israel no 'covenant' festival."[72]

With Perlitt and Kutsch, we are very clearly back behind the position of Weber to that of Wellhausen.[73] Many of Perlitt's affirmations are strikingly similar to those of Wellhausen. And just as Weber had concluded "that *berith* is rightly rendered through 'confederation,'"[74] so Kutsch concludes the opposite, that in discussions of covenant "we ought to remove 'confederation' from our vocabulary."[75] Though some of the apparent testimony on behalf of the antiquity of the covenant concept has not been refuted or even directly addressed in the recent turn,[76] it remains clear that many voices from various quarters now call for a relatively late date and a relatively peripheral role for this concept, and that the boundaries of the chronological disputes that remain are greatly diminished.[77]

Let me conclude this one-hundred-year summary with some final examples. E. W. Nicholson has recently published three studies of Exod 24:9–11,[78] a pericope that McCarthy earlier found to be "a particularly clear case" of the covenant meal in Israel of the nomadic era;[79] Nicholson concludes that the tradition here is indeed ancient but witnesses to a theophany tradition and not at all to the sealing of a covenant. J. D. Levenson's important article on "the theologies of commandment" has as its chief agendum the aim of speaking about law theologically without speaking about the covenant; and here Levenson observes "that most of the laws of the Hebrew Bible are nothing like the stipulations in the extra-biblical covenants."[80] W. M. Clark's summary of the treatment of law in recent form-critical studies concludes that "covenant must not be looked to for an explanation of the origin of most Old Testament law genres."[81] J. A. Soggin's recently translated Old Testament introduction is, with regard to the issue of the role of the covenant, in basic agreement with Perlitt and Kutsch: "The use of the term [*bĕrît*] is rare in the time before Deuteronomy;" "it is only with Deuteronomy that it came to represent a central concept."[82] And J. Barr's semantic analysis of *bĕrît* begins with the observation that "several decades of animated research and discussion seem in the end to have left us rather uncertain about the theological direction in which this term might lead us."[83] The range of opinions about many key issues in the study of the religion of Israel is widely represented in these studies; yet the author of each is more restrained about the role of the covenant than have been many biblical scholars for much of this century.

THE INTELLECTUAL TRADITION OF
"COVENANT CENTRALITY"

The tradition within biblical scholarship receiving wide assent in the period from about 1930 to about 1965 is a tradition that might fairly be labeled that of "covenant centrality."[84] Since the more recent turn to a position like the one obtaining a century ago is both too near to the present and too incompletely assessed to merit full treatment here, it is to an account of the origins of the covenant centrality tradition that I wish to move now. Just as the summary above began with Wellhausen, so here the origins of this tradition can usefully be thought of as a reaction against Wellhausen and the entire literary-critical and idealist position he and others represent. Of course, the aims of the history of religion circle are a part of this reaction (and also a part of the tradition itself); but the concentration here will be upon the works of others, works that have received less attention than that devoted to Gunkel and others and are of greater relevance to the particular issue of the role of the covenant.

Initially, and quite obviously, the reaction against Wellhausen was a reaction against a kind of social evolutionism that obtained in many historical reconstructions from the latter half of the nineteenth century. Wellhausen had argued that in the period when Israel was first threatened by Assyria, "the natural bond" between Yahweh and Israel was severed and replaced in the course of Israel's evolution by "conditions of a moral character."[85] Already Weber observed that this reconstruction could be described as an "immanent evolutionary" position.[86] The present century's emphases upon oral tradition, upon the sophistication of what was before called "the primitive mind," or upon the various examples of monotheistic religions at an early date are all efforts to combat these evolutionary schemes. But so too is the tradition of covenant centrality. The view that the covenant relationship was foundational to the religion of Israel carries with it several advantages in this battle. It finds very early in the history of this religion the significant use of a metaphor drawn from the combined political and legal sphere, thus denying any gradual development from a natural, kinship bond to a legally conditioned relationship. Of equal importance, it finds in the covenant relationship an area where the uniqueness of Israel can be accented. That is, the evolutionary historiographic tradition appeared to have denied much, or any, specificity to Israel: Israel grew quite naturally, as have many or all other nations. The emphasis upon covenant finds here something by which to differentiate Israel from every other nation. Though this reminds one of the more general concentration of Gunkel and others upon Israel's "specificity" or "individuality" *(Eigentümlichkeit)*,[87] the covenant tradition in biblical scholarship plays a particular role here. It is thus no accident that Weber, as we noted above, discovers in the covenant a ground for Israel's uniqueness and that, quite recently, M. Weinfeld can affirm that "the idea of a covenant between a deity and a people is unknown to us from other religions and cultures" and that "the covenantal idea was a special feature of the religion of Israel."[88]

Second, the covenant symbol has played a most useful role in schematizing the religion of Israel, especially for theological purposes, as already those responsible for Deuteronomy and for the Deuteronomistic History discovered. This too accords with developments after the time of Wellhausen. Clearly, Wellhausen himself was not writing a theology of the Old Testament; and the years of his initial publications witnessed a more general hiatus in such activity. When W. R. Smith summarized for a British audience the fruits of biblical scholarship in 1876, he observed: "In the hands of the latest writers on the subject, Old Testament theology is passing almost entirely into researches into the history of the religion of Israel."[89] With, of course, some exceptions, this hiatus lasted into the twentieth century, until the period of K. Barth's initial publications and the increased attention to biblical theology that this work signaled.[90] Eichrodt was, of course, a colleague of Barth in Basel at the time of the publication of his *Theology*;[91] but it would be an error to point solely to this setting, since, as we have seen, the covenant centrality tradition went beyond Eichrodt and beyond Basel. The powerful if subtle effect of the larger theological movement was such that even histories of the religion of Israel began to take on a notable theological (even a Deuteronomy-like) cast, most especially in their descriptions of the covenant relationship. Thus, Pfeiffer, whom we have seen to be one of the last holdouts in the covenant centrality tradition, lamented in 1951 what he called "this trend backwards to Deuteronomistic historiography."[92]

Important as are the movements away from evolutionary schemes and toward biblical theology, neither is as significant as is the third and final impetus to the covenant centrality tradition to which I wish to point: the perceived discovery at about the time of the turn of the century of the place of the social in the meaning and function of religion. This discovery begins, as both E. Durkheim and Weber were later to admit, with W. Robertson Smith.[93] It is of great interest to observe Smith's discovery of the relationship between religion and its social setting in the course of his own career. His earliest work betrays none of this and is still indistinguishable from much of the kind of evolutionary thinking typical of this period. For example, in 1870 he could still affirm that "the prophetic writings are the true key to the marvelous religious development, which is, in fact, the kernel of all Israel's history."[94] This begins to change with the publication in 1880 of his "Animal Worship and Animal Tribes Among the Arabs and in the Old Testament,"[95] an article that forms the basis of many of the positions taken in his *The Religion of the Semites*. In the latter work, Smith argued that for the religion of Israel and other ancient religions one must note that religion was "a part of the citizen's public life," so that the scholar must ask "what place the gods held in the social system of antiquity" and "what the working religious institutions were."[96] Smith can then conclude that "religion did not exist for the saving of souls but for the preservation and welfare of society."[97] Though his work on the role of the covenant remains quite undeveloped, these presuppositions led Smith directly on to a new appreciation of this institution. The God of Israel, Smith asserts, is "the god of a confederation," and this notion presents us with "the idea of a covenant religion."[98]

It is this set of explanations for the origin and meaning of religion upon which Durkheim and Weber expand and which then becomes a major impetus to the covenant centrality tradition. For Durkheim, "an essential postulate of sociology" is that religion deals with matters that are not individual but, rather, social.[99] Durkheim therefore rejects both animism and naturism as explanations for religion, since both assume that religion is a matter of "hallucinatory representations" or "imaginary conceptions" and neither offers "an objective value," which is rather to be found in society itself.[100] Durkheim's central thesis is then "that religion is something eminently social."[101] Weber's point of departure, as we have already seen, is much the same. He too, as R. Bendix correctly notes, "approached the study of religious ideas in terms of their relevance for collective actions, and specifically in terms of the social processes whereby the inspirations of a few became the convictions of the many."[102] That it was Weber who introduced the thesis of early Israel as an amphictyony and who seized upon the role of *bĕrît* as the generative center of the religion of Israel becomes far less surprising given this background. Equally unsurprising is the observation that Mendenhall's initial article on covenant and treaty cites near its opening Weber's *Ancient Judaism*, which had just (in 1952) been translated into English.[103] So too, when Eichrodt returns in 1965 to a defense of the role of covenant, it is a defense that accents the covenant's place in creating Israel as a sacred community and that in general attempts to convict the opposition of ignoring the actual, day-to-day social setting of the religion of Israel.[104]

The origin and *floruit* of the covenant centrality tradition thus is both chronologically and methodologically coincident with the birth and maturity of that tradition within the study of religion more broadly that began with Robertson Smith and received its clearest expression from Durkheim and Weber. That this latter tradition began to receive sharp criticism and then recede in the 1950s and beyond may well be a part of the reason for the similar fate of the covenant centrality tradition. Support for a causal link between these two traditions may be found in the fact that the recent opponents of the antiquity and central importance of the covenant relationship have both removed any sense of mutuality, any sense of social bond, from their reading of *bĕrît* and also have taken up a sort of literary criticism at wide remove from the contextual, tradition-historical research prompted by the methods of Smith, Durkheim, and Weber. The literary criticism currently in fashion is quite different in many ways from what Wellhausen intended. But like Wellhausen, many recent scholars have read Old Testament texts divorced from any inquiry into these texts' possible social contexts. It is this, more than any other factor, that explains the convergence between Wellhausen and many biblical scholars today on the issue of the role of the covenant.

NOTES

1. J. Wellhausen, *Prolegomena zur Geschichte Israels* (2d ed. of *Geschichte Israels*, vol. 1; Berlin: Georg Reimer, 1883); but for the addition of a seven-page foreword that responds to some of the receptions accorded the first edition, this edition is little changed from the first edition of 1878. Idem, *Die Composition des Hexateuchs und der historischen Bücher des Alten Testaments* (Berlin: Georg Reimer, 1899); the articles assembled in this volume originally appeared in the *Jahrbücher für Deutsche Theologie* in 1876–77, and in the fourth edition of Bleeks's *Einleitung*, 1878. For the sake of convenience, the present study will cite the English translation of the *Prolegomena* (*Prolegomena to the History of Ancient Israel* [Gloucester, Mass.: Peter Smith, 1973]) and of other German works available in English translation, though occasional reference to the original editions of these works will be necessary.

2. Wellhausen, *Prolegomena*, 417–19.

3. Whether or not Hosea was familiar with anything like the developed covenant concept is an issue that returns periodically and is treated in many of the studies that have appeared in the period of the renewal of the covenant debate during the past twenty years. These studies will be noted below. For Wellhausen, Hos 6:7 is no problem, since Wellhausen finds here no real awareness of the use of *bĕrît* to characterize Yahweh's relationship with Israel, and Hos 8:1 is a secondary interpolation (*Prolegomena*, 418).

4. Wellhausen, *Prolegomena*, 418.

5. Ibid., 419.

6. R. Kraetzschmar, *Die Bundesvorstellung im Alten Testament in ihrer geschichtlichen Entwicklung* (2d ed.; Marburg: Elwert, 1896).

7. E.g., J. J. P. Valeton, "Bedeutung und Stellung des Wortes *bryt* im Priester-

codex," *ZAW* 12 (1892) 1–22, or "Das Wort *bryt* in den jehovistischen und deuteronomischen Stücken des Hexateuch," *ZAW* 12 (1892) 224–60.

8. On the goals and achievements of this circle, see my "Hermeneutics and Historiography: Germany and America," *SBL 1980 Seminar Papers,* 135–57, with the many sources cited there.

9. Since scholarly studies of M. Weber have long been an industry (as Weber himself might dolefully have predicted), no attempt will be made here to summarize anything like Weber's total achievement. For a readable and accurate introduction to Weber, see R. Bendix, *Max Weber: An Intellectual Portrait* (Garden City, N.Y.: Doubleday & Co., 1960), and for an acute analysis of Weber's reconstruction of the religion of Israel, see S. N. Eisenstadt, "The Format of Jewish History—Some Reflections on Weber's Ancient Judaism," *Modern Judaism* 1 (1981) 54–73, 217–34.

10. Eisenstadt, "The Format of Jewish History," 61.

11. M. Weber, *Gesammelte Aufsätze zur Religionssoziologie,* vol. 3: *Das antike Judentum* (Tübingen: J. C. B. Mohr [Paul Siebeck], 1921; originally published in *Archiv für Sozialwissenschaft und Sozialforschung* (1917–19) vii. The chapter heading I translate above is absent from the English translation of Weber's volume (*Ancient Judaism* [New York: Free Press, 1952]), from which all further citations from Weber will be taken.

12. Weber, *Ancient Judaism,* 90.

13. Ibid., 75.

14. Ibid., 120.

15. Ibid., 130–31 (German ed., pp. 140–41).

16. A. S. Peake, "Recent Developments in Old Testament Criticism," *BJRL* 12 (1928) 73. This article represents extracts from Peake's Society for Old Testament Study Presidential Address delivered on 1 January, 1924.

17. W. Eichrodt, *Theology of the Old Testament* (Philadelphia: Westminster Press, 1961; a trans. of the 5th ed. of *Theologie des Alten Testaments* [Stuttgart: Klotz Verlag, 1957]).

18. G. F. Hasel, *Old Testament Theology: Basic Issues in the Current Debate* (Grand Rapids: Wm. B. Eerdmans Publishing Co., 1972) 20. Hasel does note that Eichrodt was hardly the first to mention the role of covenant as an organizing principle for Israelite religion; but Eichrodt's schematization was the first to find a wide response—i.e., the first to alter for a time the tradition of Old Testament scholarship.

19. Eichrodt, *Theology,* 1.7–8.

20. Ibid., 1.36–37.

21. Ibid., 1.51–52.

22. N. Glueck, *Hesed in the Bible* (Cincinnati: Hebrew Union, 1967; a trans. of *Das Wort ḥesed im alttestamentlichen Sprachgebrauche als menschliche und göttliche gemeinschaftgemässe Verhaltungsweise* [BZAW 47; Giessen: Alfred Töpelmann, 1927]). For a recent and comprehensive return to many of the issues raised by Glueck, see K. D. Sakenfeld, *The Meaning of Hesed in the Hebrew Bible: A New Inquiry* (HSM 17; Missoula, Mont.: Scholars Press, 1978). Both Sakenfeld (*The Meaning of Hesed,* 3–13) and G. R. Larue ("Recent Studies in Ḥesed," 1–32 in the English translation of Glueck's monograph) offer summaries

of other studies of *ḥesed* in the years following the appearance of Glueck's volume.

23. Glueck, *Ḥesed in the Bible*, 74 n. 32.

24. Ibid., 77.

25. E. G. Kraeling, "The Real Religion of Ancient Israel," *JBL* 47 (1928) 136.

26. The classic inquiry into this phenomenon remains T. S. Kuhn, *The Structure of Scientific Revolutions* (Chicago: University of Chicago Press, 1962), on which see, e.g., I. Lakatos and A. Musgrave, eds., *Criticism and the Growth of Knowledge* (Proceedings of the International Colloquium in the Philosophy of Science 4; Cambridge: Cambridge University Press, 1970).

27. R. H. Pfeiffer, "Facts and Faith in Biblical History," *JBL* 70 (1951) 4. This entire article (pp. 1–14) is the text of Pfeiffer's 1950 SBL Presidential Address. See also R. H. Pfeiffer, *Introduction to the Old Testament* (New York: Harper & Bros., 1941) 285 and 551.

28. For recent summaries of the great range of issues that have come to be treated under the heading of treaty and covenant, see D. J. McCarthy, *Treaty and Covenant: A Study in Form in the Ancient Oriental Documents and in the Old Testament* (2d ed.; AnBib 21A; Rome: Biblical Institute Press, 1978) 1–24; M. Weinfeld, "*bĕrîth*," *TDOT* (1977), 2.266–69; W. M. Clark, "Law," *Old Testament Form Criticism* (ed. J. H. Hayes; Trinity University Monograph Series in Religion 2; San Antonio: Trinity University Press, 1974) 99–139; and R. Clifford, *Deuteronomy, with an Excursus on Covenant and Law* (Old Testament Message 4; Wilmington, Del.: Michael Glazier, 1982) 186–91.

29. G. E. Mendenhall, "Ancient Oriental and Biblical Law," *BA* 17 (1954) 26–46, and "Covenant Forms in Israelite Tradition," *BA* 17 (1954) 50–76. Much of the basis for the treaty analysis portion of these studies was the work of V. Korošec, *Hethitische Staatsverträge. Ein Beitrag zu ihrer juristischen Wertung* (Leipziger rechtswissenshaftliche Studien 60; Leipzig: Weicher, 1931); and some of Mendenhall's analysis was apparently anticipated in E. Bickermann's "Couper une alliance," *Archives d'histoire du droit oriental* 5 (1950–51) 133–56 (I have not had access to this article). The role of Mendenhall's work in seeming to make certain the conclusions of Eichrodt has been noted by many; see, e.g., E. Gerstenberger, "Psalms," *Old Testament Form Criticism*, 194; Clark, "Law," 109; and Weinfeld, "*bĕrîth*," 275.

30. Mendenhall, "Ancient Oriental and Biblical Law," 28.

31. Ibid., 42.

32. Ibid., 44.

33. Ibid., 52.

34. Ibid., 53, 61.

35. Ibid., 62–68 (quotation from 68).

36. J. Muilenburg, "The Form and Structure of the Covenantal Formulations," *VT* 9 (1959) 347–65.

37. Ibid., 347.

38. Ibid., 352.

39. Ibid., 365

40. K. Baltzer, *The Covenant Formulary* (Philadelphia: Fortress Press, 1971);

a trans. of *Das Bundesformular* (WMANT 4; 2d ed.; Neukirchen-Vluyn: Neukirchener Verlag, 1964).

41. Ibid., 2 (a statement documented by reference to Eichrodt).

42. Ibid., 19–38.

43. See W. L. Moran, "The Ancient Near Eastern Background of the Love of God in Deuteronomy," *CBQ* 25 (1963) 77–87. Note that Moran carefully argues here that Deuteronomy's use of *'āhēb* may "represent an innovation in Israel's covenant tradition" (p. 83). Again, throughout this section, I make no claims to comprehensiveness and rather list a major study or two for each of these terms.

44. H. B. Huffmon, "The Treaty Background of Hebrew *Yāda'*," *BASOR* 181 (1966) 31–37, and H. B. Huffmon and S. B. Parker, "A Further Note on the Treaty Background of Hebrew *Yāda'*," *BASOR* 184 (1966) 36–38.

45. M. Fox, "*Ṭôb* as Covenant Terminology," *BASOR* 209 (1973) 41–42.

46. H. B. Huffmon, "The Covenant Lawsuit in the Prophets," *JBL* 78 (1959) 285–95; J. Harvey, "Le 'Rîb-Pattern,' réquisitoire prophétique sur la rupture de l'alliance," *Bib* 43 (1962) 172–96; and G. E. Wright, "The Lawsuit of God: A Form-Critical Study of Deuteronomy 32," *Israel's Prophetic Heritage: Essays in Honor of James Muilenburg* (ed. B. W. Anderson and W. Harrelson; New York: Harper & Row, 1962) 26–67.

47. See the summaries of this position offered by Weinfeld ("*bĕrith*," 262–65), by Gerstenberger ("Psalms," 179–223), and by J. A. Soggin (*Introduction to the Old Testament* [OTL; Philadelphia: Westminster Press, 1976] 120–22). Very influential extensions of the position appeared in the many works of G. von Rad.

48. This prophetic reticence and the problems it appears to create for any view of the covenant relationship as central throughout Israelite history have been noted for generations. See, e.g., R. E. Clements, *Prophecy and Covenant* (SBT 43; Naperville, Ill.: Alec R. Allenson, 1965) 54–55; D. J. McCarthy, "Covenant in the Old Testament: The Present State of Inquiry," *CBQ* 27 (1965) 240; or Weinfeld, "*bĕrith*," 275–78. Eichrodt used here a line of defense often imitated: though it appears, Eichrodt argued, that the "covenant concept" has receded into the background of prophetic thought, this is to be explained as a part of the larger battle by the prophets against all *opus operatum* thinking for which the covenant idea might seem to provide some basis (*Theology*, 1.51–52). Eichrodt returned to this line of reasoning, e.g., in "Prophet and Covenant: Observations on the Exegesis of Isaiah," *Proclamation and Presence: Old Testament Essays in Honour of Gwynne Henton Davies* (ed. J. I. Durham and J. R. Porter; Richmond: John Knox Press, 1970) 167–88, esp. 187 (Isaiah "avoids the temptation of getting lost in the intricacies of a dispute about a concept so rich, but also so variegated, as that of the covenant").

49. The work of Weinfeld has been especially valuable in this regard. See M. Weinfeld, "The Covenant of Grant in the Old Testament and in the Ancient Near East," *JAOS* 90 (1970) 184–203; idem, "*bĕrîth*," 270–72; and idem, *Deuteronomy and the Deuteronomic School* (Oxford: Clarendon Press, 1972) 74–81.

50. See, again, Weinfeld, *Deuteronomy*, 66 ("It is only in Deuteronomy that we encounter all the elements which characterize the Hittite and Assyrian treaties") and 67–126, or Clifford, *Deuteronomy*, 3–5. For the most useful summaries of much of this century's research on the Book of Deuteronomy, see E. W.

Nicholson, *Deuteronomy and Tradition* (Philadelphia: Fortress Press, 1967) and, very recently and with massive bibliography, H. D. Preuss, *Deuteronomium* (Erträge der Forschung 164; Darmstadt: Wissenschaftliche Buchgesellschaft, 1982).

51. McCarthy cites F. Nötscher's 1965 article ("Bundesformular und 'Amtsschimmel': Ein kritischer Überblick," *BZ* NF 9 [1965] 181–214) as "the first heavy shot in the anti-covenant campaign" (*Treaty and Covenant* [2d ed.], 15 n. 25). Several of the works cited below antedate Nötscher's article; but no purpose would be served here by the effort to refine the definition of a "heavy shot."

52. A. Jepsen, "Gnade und Barmherzigkeit im Alten Testament," *KD* 7 (1961) 261–71. Most of this article (264–71) is devoted to the term *ḥesed*.

53. Ibid., 265 (my translation).

54. Ibid., 266–70. The other studies I am thinking of include J. Barr, "Some Semantic Notes on the Covenant," *Beiträge zur Alttestamentlichen Theologie. Festschrift für Walther Zimmerli zum 70. Geburtstag* (ed. H. Donner, R. Hanhart, and R. Smend; Göttingen: Vandenhoeck & Ruprecht, 1977) 23–38; and E. Kellenberger, *häsäd wä'ämät als Ausdruck einer Glaubenserfahrung* (Zurich: Theologischer Verlag, 1982), on which see the review of D. Pardee, *CBQ* 46 (1984) 547–48 (I have not had access to Kellenberger's monograph). Sakenfeld also reports that "by 1970 [Sidney] Hills believed there was no connection at all between *ḥesed* and *bᵉrît*" (*The Meaning of Hesed*, 13 n. 31), a view that Sakenfeld herself does not endorse.

55. C. F. Whitley, "Covenant and Commandment in Israel," *JNES* 22 (1963) 37–48.

56. Ibid., 38–39.

57. Ibid., 41–42. The issues of the presence or absence of any Deuteronomistic editing in the Tetrateuch, and of the literary sources of Exod 19:3b–8; Exod 24:1–2, 9–11; and Exod 24:3–8 are issues for which there is nothing like consensus. For the question of Dtr composition/editing in the Tetrateuch, see conveniently Soggin, *Introduction*, 132–34. On Exod 19:3b–8, see B. S. Childs, *The Book of Exodus: A Critical, Theological Commentary* (OTL; Philadelphia: Westminster Press, 1974) 360–61; A. W. Jenks, *The Elohist and North Israelite Traditions* (SBLMS 22; Missoula, Mont.: Scholars Press, 1977) 48; and R. McC. Good, *The Sheep of His Pasture: A Study of the Hebrew Noun 'Am(m) and Its Semitic Cognates* (HSM 29; Chico, Calif.: Scholars Press, 1983) 72–73. On Exod 24:1–11, see Wellhausen, *Die Composition*, 88; Cross, *CMHE*, 312; Childs, *Exodus*, 497–509; Jenks, *The Elohist*, 49; and E. W. Nicholson, "The Interpretation of Exodus XXIV 9–11," *VT* 24 (1974) 78–80.

58. D. J. McCarthy, *Treaty and Covenant* (2d ed.), ix. See also McCarthy's "Covenant in the Old Testament."

59. A position stated with equal strength in the second edition of *Treaty and Covenant*, 186. Unlike others whose works are noted in this section, McCarthy continued to believe that Exod 19:3b–8 and Joshua 24 are pre-Deuteronomic (*Treaty and Covenant* [2d ed.], 15–16, 221–42, and 265–79).

60. G. Fohrer, "Altes Testament—'Amphiktyonie' und 'Bund'?" *TLZ* 91 (1966) 801–16 and 893–904.

61. Ibid., 893 (my translation).

62. Ibid., 898.

63. Ibid., 897–900.

64. Ibid., 900–901.

65. E.g., E. Gerstenberger, "Covenant and Commandment," *JBL* 84 (1965) 38–51.

66. L. Perlitt, *Bundestheologie im Alten Testament* (WMANT 36; Neukirchen-Vluyn: Neukirchener Verlag, 1969).

67. D. J. McCarthy, "*bᵉrît* in Old Testament History and Theology," *Bib* 53 (1972) 110.

68. Perlitt, *Bundestheologie,* 232.

69. E.g., E. Kutsch, "Gesetz und Gnade. Probleme des alttestamentlichen Bundesbegriffs," *ZAW* 79 (1967) 18–35; or "Von *bryt* zu 'Bund,'" *KD* 14 (1968) 159–82.

70. E. Kutsch, *Verheissung und Gesetz. Untersuchungen zum sogenannten "Bund" im Alten Testament* (BZAW 131; Berlin and New York: Walter de Gruyter, 1973). For other semantic and/or etymological studies of *bᵉrît,* see J. Begrich, "*berit.* Ein Beitrag zur Erfassung einer alttestamentlichen Denkform," *ZAW* 60 (1944) 1–11; Cross, *CMHE,* 265–73; Weinfeld, "*bᵉrith,*" 253–56; and Barr, "Some Semantic Notes," 23–38.

71. Kutsch, *Verheissung,* 149–50.

72. Ibid., 173 (my translation).

73. This, of course, has been noted with some frequency. See, e.g., Eichrodt, "Prophet and Covenant," 167, or McCarthy, "*bᵉrît* in Old Testament History," 111.

74. Weber, *Ancient Judaism,* 441 n. 22.

75. Kutsch, *Verheissung,* 206.

76. This is hardly the appropriate setting in which to marshal or assess this evidence. I am thinking of material such as the following. First, some of the Old Testament poems (e.g., Judges 5; parts of Psalm 132; of 2 Sam 23:1–7) that many continue to place at an early stage in Israel's history do appear to contain terminology that is difficult to divorce completely from the covenant and treaty context. This is true, e.g., of the conclusion to the Song of Deborah (see Moran, "The Ancient Near Eastern Background," 85) and of some of the language in the Last Words of David (see Cross, *CMHE,* 234–36, and P. K. McCarter, *II Samuel: A New Translation with Introduction, Notes, and Commentary* [AB 9; Garden City, N.Y.: Doubleday & Co., 1984] 485–86). Second, the traditional arguments for a connection between the northern, E stream of tradition in the Tetrateuch and the origins of Deuteronomy (see S. R. Driver, *A Critical and Exegetical Commentary of Deuteronomy* [ICC; 3d ed.; Edinburgh: T. & T. Clark, 1902] lvii–lxi, and Nicholson, *Deuteronomy and Tradition,* 58–82) have hardly been demolished in more recent works; and these traditional arguments too support the thesis of a developing awareness of the covenant relationship in *some* quarters within ancient Israel, though hardly for any unanimity in this regard (J, e.g., is as reticent in its use of *bᵉrît* as are the preexilic prophets).

77. With regard to this latter issue (that of chronology), it is most revealing to note that today where there is disagreement on the issue of the date of the

introduction of the covenant concept, such disagreement most often focuses upon the boundaries of a quite limited period—upon whether this concept should be dated to the mid-eighth century or rather to the late seventh century. This is in great contrast to what obtained only a generation ago, when many were prepared to support a Mosaic or tribal league date for the covenant's origin.

78. E. W. Nicholson, "The Interpretation of Exodus XXIV 9–11," *VT* 24 (1974) 77–97; idem, "The Antiquity of the Tradition in Exodus XXIV 9–11," *VT* 25 (1975) 69–79; and idem, "The Origins of the Tradition in Exodus XXIV 9–11," *VT* 26 (1976) 148–59.

79. McCarthy, "*bᵉrît* in Old Testament History," 113.

80. J. D. Levenson, "The Theologies of Commandment in Biblical Israel," *HTR* 73 (1980) 17–33 (citation from 23).

81. Clark, "Law," 115–16.

82. Soggin, *Introduction,* 131.

83. Barr, "Some Semantic Notes," 23.

84. Though many other descriptions might be suggested, I consider this phrase to be both accurate and less offensive than some of the labels others have applied to this tradition.

85. Wellhausen, *Prolegomena,* 442–43.

86. Weber, *Ancient Judaism,* 426. Weber's terminology here has been repeated with some frequency; see, e.g., McCarthy, "Covenant in the Old Testament," 217, or Levenson, "Theologies of Commandment," 17–18.

87. For the importance accorded the identification of and stress upon each nation's and each religion's particularity by Gunkel and others of his era, see my "Hermeneutics and Historiography," 146.

88. Weinfeld, "*bĕrit,*" 278.

89. W. R. Smith, "The Study of the Old Testament in 1876," *Lectures and Essays of William Robertson Smith* (ed. J. S. Black and G. Crystal; London: Black, 1912) 391.

90. As noted by both Gerstenberger ("Psalms," 186–87) and Levenson ("Theologies of Commandment," 18).

91. Gerstenberger, "Psalms," 193.

92. Pfeiffer, "Facts and Faith," 12.

93. For recent summaries of the important step taken by W. R. Smith in "discovering" the social genesis of many religious ideas and institutions, see T. O. Beidelman, *W. Robertson Smith and the Sociological Study of Religion* (Chicago: University of Chicago Press, 1974), and, more briefly, J. W. Rogerson, "Biblical Classics: IX. W. Robertson Smith: Religion of the Semites," *ExTim* 90 (1979) 228–33. For Durkheim's statement of his debt to W. R. Smith, see Emile Durkheim, *The Elementary Forms of the Religious Life* (Glencoe, Ill.: Free Press, 1965) 61 n. 62. Many others in the first third of the twentieth century also noted the significant role played by W. R. Smith's key thesis; e.g., Driver, *Deuteronomy,* xv–xvi; M. Jastrow, Jr., "Constructive Elements in the Critical Study of the Old Testament," *JBL* 36 (1917) 19; S. A. Cook, Preface and Introduction to W. R. Smith, *Lectures on the Religion of the Semites* (3d ed.; London: Black, 1927) x and lxiv; and Glueck, *Ḥesed in the Bible,* 38, 43, 46, 49. The second edition of W. R. Smith's *Lectures* (1894) was reprinted four times between 1901 and 1923;

the third edition was completed in 1927 and has been reprinted several times (Rogerson, "Biblical Classics," 231).

94. W. R. Smith, "On the Question of Prophecy in the Critical School of the Continent," *Lectures and Essays,* 166.

95. Originally published in 1880 and reprinted in *Lectures and Essays,* 455–81.

96. W. R. Smith, *The Religion of the Semites: The Fundamental Institutions* (New York: Schocken Books, 1972) 21–22.

97. Ibid., 29.

98. Ibid., 319 n. 2.

99. Durkheim, *Elementary Forms,* 14.

100. Ibid., 86, 106–7, and 173.

101. Ibid., 22, cf. 388–89.

102. Bendix, *Max Weber,* 259.

103. Mendenhall, "Ancient Oriental and Biblical Law," 28 n. 8.

104. W. Eichrodt, "Bund und Gesetz. Erwägungen zur neueren Diskussion," *Gottes Wort und Gottes Land. Hans-Wilhelm Hertzberg zum 70. Geburtstag am 16. Januar 1965* (ed. H. G. Reventlow; Göttingen: Vandenhoeck & Ruprecht, 1965) 30–49, esp. 34 and 40.

23

Religious Dimensions of Israelite Wisdom

ROLAND E. MURPHY

In several ways Hebrew wisdom presents itself as a mine field to those who trek across it. It is exceedingly difficult to find a *Sitz im Leben* for wisdom. The existence of school(s) in the preexilic period has been denied almost as vigorously as it has been affirmed.[1] The class of "sages" or wise men has been replaced in some quarters by an "intellectual tradition."[2] The concept of wisdom has been extended so as to include the Joseph story, the Succession Narrative, some prophets, Esther, and other books of the Bible.[3] (For the purposes of this essay, the discussion of wisdom is restricted to Proverbs, Job, Ecclesiastes, and, among the apocrypha, Sirach and the Wisdom of Solomon.) Comparisons with Egyptian literature have spawned interpretations of Israelite wisdom out of Egyptian mentality; one might call it the "ma'atizing" of wisdom.[4] The dating of the literature presents problems. Proverbs is a mixed bag: Are Proverbs 1—9 from the postexilic period? The dating of Job is still a moot point.[5] At least, the three remaining books are clearly postexilic, with the Wisdom of Solomon difficult to pinpoint. The dating is further complicated by an alleged evolutionary pattern of development from secular to religious wisdom.[6] Finally, Hebrew wisdom is not widely regarded as a serious source of Hebrew religion; it is the "Yahwistic" tradition (defined mainly in terms of the patriarchal promises, exodus, covenant) that yields the "real" biblical faith.[7] This position is argued *à outrance* by H. D. Preuss, who has warned Christians against preaching from wisdom texts.[8]

In the light of the above it seems hazardous to write about the religious dimensions of *Israelite* wisdom. The prevailing view recognizes perhaps the religious character but at the expense of its being a real expression of Israelite faith.[9] Or only at the end of a certain evolution does an alleged "Yahwistic" influence make itself felt. This view claims that the "older" wisdom (e.g., most of the sayings in Proverbs 10ff.) is a kind of surrogate

449

of Egyptian wisdom. It seeks to find out and even to create a world order, an order of life in the area of everyday events. True, this order is supervised by the deity, but the whole idea is alien to Yahwism. Indeed it is a mentality shared by the entire Fertile Crescent, and especially matched by the Egyptian conception of *ma'at*.[10] As regards "retribution" specifically, God is not directly at work in the reward/punishment events of life.[11] Rather, the deity is a kind of midwife who watches over the mechanical correspondence that is perceived to exist between an action and its consequence. The good act automatically begets a good effect, and the evil act an evil effect (Prov 10:2, 6 and passim). The awareness of the limitations of wisdom (e.g., Prov 16:9; 19:21; 21:30–31) is not due to the influence of Yahwism; they are commonplaces in ancient Near Eastern wisdom, which also recognizes the mysteriousness of the deity. This brand of wisdom falls into a crisis with the books of Job and Ecclesiastes. The authors of these books saw that the traditional wisdom scheme was not adequate and did not fit the facts of life for the believing Israelite. It is the influence of Yahwism, finally, that is responsible for the breakthrough. Yahweh appears in a theophany to Job; he is affirmed as the *gō'ēl* (Job 19:25; cf. the use of *g'l* in Exod 6:6; 15:13 and especially in Isa 43:1; 44:22–23; etc.).

What is wrong with this scenario? (1) The issue of retribution. One need not deny that the understanding of the mechanical correspondence between act and consequence formed part of the Hebrew mentality. But in fact the direct intervention of the Lord in the life of the Israelite is affirmed throughout the Hebrew Bible even more frequently and emphatically. There seem to be two ways of understanding retribution. No exclusive choice is made, nor is there evidence of an evolution from one to the other. (2) It assumes that Yahwistic theology of covenantal salvation is incompatible with wisdom's emphasis on creation and personal well-being. Yahwism is understood as a belief system derived solely from the historical experience of the people in its initial founding events (promises, exodus, etc.) and continued in the representation in the cult and in the preaching of the prophets. As against this, wisdom is interpreted as secular and human, an exercise on the plane of creation in which one deals with an *Urhebergott*, and not the saving God of Israel. It is hard to see how the average Israelite, to whatever extent he or she recognized the Lord as God (Deut 6:4), would have made the academic distinction that is implied by this view. Wisdom and salvation are not incompatible in human experience; prosperity and adversity are personal as well as communal. The teaching of Deuteronomy and Proverbs suggests that the Yahweh of both books is the same Yahweh who is at work on every level of experience. (3) This view rests partially on the questionable assumption that Israelite wisdom (Proverbs) is the creation of court school(s) where sages were preoccupied with royal and secular interests. Hence, they cultivated the model of the "cool" person on the make. (4) One may not argue against this view that the sayings make use of the sacred name of YHWH or that the Lord's direct intervention is more prominent in the Bible than the act-consequence mentality. Rather, one can claim that there is absent from wisdom thinking any intimation that a buffer zone of order comes between the sage and the Lord (Prov 16:9, 20; 19:21; etc.). (5) The scenario does not represent the message of the wisdom books as they stand among the Writings. Whether it describes a prehistory of biblical wisdom is problematic.

This preliminary discussion of current interpretation of Israelite wisdom is necessary if we are to discuss religious dimensions of Israelite wisdom. If this interpretation is correct, one might as well begin the discussion by reading from Ptahhotep or Amenemope.[12] If it is not correct, then one can turn to the consideration of the religious dimensions of *Israelite* wisdom. No attempt will be made to point out what is "Yahwistic" or due to the influence of Yahwism. Even if such elements could be identified (such as the identification of Torah with wisdom in Sirach), this is the wrong way of putting the question. It presupposes a Yahwism as opposed to wisdom, as though one had to make a supposedly secular wisdom "religious" in the tradition of patriarchal promises and exodus experience. This is to forget that the extant wisdom literature was formed by Yahwists. They found salvation to be an issue in everyday life, where a (religious) wisdom perspective was at work. Whether salvation is termed *yeša'* or *šālôm* or simply *ṭôb*, the issue is the same.

It is a fact that wisdom has many faces, and hence there are many aspects that might qualify as "religious dimensions." Several of these will be merely mentioned here, but only one can be singled out for development.

1. Fear of the Lord. This phrase, or the idea, is found in wisdom books, from Proverbs to Sirach, and cuts across the rest of the Bible as well. Hence it will be the selected topic of this chapter.

2. Wisdom theology as creation theology. Although this was succinctly affirmed by W. Zimmerli, it is G. von Rad who has shown the direction in which it is best developed: "The most characteristic feature of her [Israel's] understanding of reality lay, in the first instance, in the fact that she believed man to stand in a quite specific, highly dynamic, existential relationship with his environment."[13]

3. The mystery of God. It is a striking fact that the mystery, otherness, or, better, *Unverfügbarkeit*, of God appears in the wisdom literature with greater starkness than in the rest of the Hebrew Bible. Mystery is culti-

451

vated by wisdom, as much as if not more than by history, and wisdom encountered the Lord at his most puzzling.[14]

4. The relationship between wisdom and the praise of God (hymns). This has been mentioned by von Rad but deserves fuller treatment.[15]

5. The personification of wisdom. The religious implications of this development, which spans the wisdom books (Proverbs 1; 8; 9; Job 28; Sirach 24; Wisdom 7—9), deserve a monograph rather than an article.[16]

6. In Sirach and the Wisdom of Solomon there is an unabashed, and, for wisdom, an unparalleled incorporation of traits of salvation history: the identification of wisdom and Torah (Sirach 24; cf. Bar 3:9—4:3) and the praises of the fathers (Sirach 44—50). Wisdom appears as a savior figure to a cast of characters ranging from Adam to Moses (Wisdom 10), and there is a lengthy development of the exodus plagues (Wisdom 12—19). The union of wisdom and Torah is clear from Eccl 12:14 and from the Book of Sirach. Unfortunately the details of this shift cannot be documented: Did the sage become the scribe? When did experience yield pride of place to the law? This development is an important factor within the religious dimensions of biblical wisdom (cf. *Pirqê 'Abôt*). In any case this correlation of Torah and wisdom is so late that it cannot illuminate the religious dimensions common to all of wisdom.

For our purposes, "fear of the Lord" and "fear of God" are not to be distinguished. The use of the name YHWH does not imply "Yahwehizing," nor does the use of Elohim imply a reference to another deity. There is one God in Israel's wisdom literature. Previous studies of "fear of God/Lord" in the Old Testament have noted the origin of the idea in the human reaction to the numinous.[17] It is at least arguable whether the phrase has ever lost the direction given by its origins. But it is quite clear that it has taken on other nuances in various parts of the Bible. In the Deuteronomic literature, fear of God/Lord reflects loyal response to the covenant God (e.g., Deut 6:2, 13, 24). Those who fear the Lord in the psalms are the worshiping community (e.g., Pss 33:18; 34:10). Fear of God also acquires a nomistic meaning whereby it designates observance of the Torah (e.g., Ps 119:63; Eccl 12:13). On all sides it is acknowledged that fear of the Lord is a central concept in the wisdom literature. What is not obvious is why fear of the Lord became so closely identified with wisdom and was so emphatically nourished in this literature, even in the Book of Ecclesiastes. Our particular purpose is to portray the manner in which the concept "fear of the Lord" functioned in wisdom.

Proverbs is made up of several collections, presumably written over an extended period of time, and hence various nuances of "fear" can be expected in the light of the contrast between Proverbs 1—9 and 10—31. An important cue appears in Prov 1:7, a saying apparently intended to determine the role of "fear of God" in this book: "The fear of the Lord is the beginning of knowledge," or, as in Prov 9:10, "The beginning of wisdom is the fear of the Lord." The idea appears elsewhere in variant forms (Prov 15:33; Ps 111:10; Job 28:28). Here it sets the tone for Israel's understanding of wisdom. Von Rad has made the formidable claim that this thesis "contains in a nutshell the whole Israelite theory of knowledge."[18] Epistemology may be overtaxed here, if it is taken in its Greek sense. Israel had no real theory of knowledge apart from praxis. A statement such as Prov 1:7 is fundamental to a wisdom approach to reality. It is rooted in a basic attitude toward God, which determines progress in wisdom. Whatever the sages judged worthy of teaching, and this touched on manifold levels of creation, flowed from fear of God. Moreover, the wisdom associated with fear of the Lord was itself a gift of God (Prov 2:6). But it was a tenuous gift, for if ever one really considered oneself to be wise, the gift was automatically lost (Prov 26:12; cf. Jer 9:22).

The saying in Prov 1:7 not only provides an orientation to the collections in the book, it is also a major statement concerning a function of fear of the Lord. The latter is seen as leading to knowledge, preparing one to become wise. In Prov 1:7, *rēʾšît* does not mean the "best part," as if the two ideas were being evaluated. It means "beginning," as *těhillat* in Prov 9:10 indicates. Similarly in Prov 15:33, fear of the Lord is seen as a discipline *(mûsār)* that leads to wisdom. The whole wisdom enterprise is inconceivable without discipline (e.g., Prov 1:7b; 10:17; etc.); now it is fear of the Lord that is the primary factor in this discipline. Although Prov 8:13 appears to be glossed, there is a strong moral connotation attached to fear of the Lord (v 13b, c). Probably the same meaning is contained in Prov 3:7, where fear is associated with turning away from (moral, rather than physical) evil; compare Job 1:1, 8. In the collected sayings of Proverbs 10—22 fear of the Lord is most often associated with the optimistic doctrine of retribution. It guarantees life (Prov 10:27; 14:27; 19:23, 22:4). In Prov 23:17–18 and 24:13–14 there is a striking equation of fear of the Lord with wisdom (understood as moral conduct), since both are given the same motivation: the certainty of having a future (Prov 23:18; 24:14).

The LXX of Prov 31:30 reads: "A wise woman will be praised; let her praise the name of the Lord." MT is usually translated: "The woman who fears the Lord will be praised." But it is possible to regard *yirʾat YHWH* as in apposition to *ʾiššâ*. If so, the intention of the author is to take up the personification of wisdom as a woman—now incarnate in the *ʾēšet ḥayil*—as well as the theme of fear of the Lord from 1:7. However, the text remains uncertain (did the original read *ʾēšet bînâ*?).

"Fear of the Lord" is not frequent in Job, but it plays an important role in the prologue. Here "God-fearing" (Job 1:1, 8–9; 2:3) clearly has a moral connotation; Job is a just man who "avoids [moral] evil" (Job 1:1). Eliphaz, as might be expected, understands "fear" as traditional piety or right conduct (Job 4:16; 15:4; 22:4), which guarantees prosperity. Whatever may be the origins of the great poem on wisdom and the concluding verse in Job 28, there seems to be a deliberate tie-in with the prologue: "The fear of the lord [*yir'at 'ădōnāy*; cf. also Job 6:14] is wisdom; and avoiding evil is understanding" (Job 28:28; cf. 1:1, 8). This moral understanding is, of course, not in harmony with Job's claims in the dialogue.

As in so many other ways, Ecclesiastes is unique among the wisdom books in its understanding of the fear of God.[19] The phrase itself never appears. Twice (Eccl 3:14; 5:6) "fear" carries the nuance of awe before the numinous. The only time Qohelet attributes a purpose to God's action in the world is in Eccl 3:14: "Thus has God done that they [human beings] may fear him." This is far from the consoling "fear of God" in Proverbs, because it is rooted in the inscrutable mysterious action that human beings cannot understand (Eccl 3:11). In Eccl 5:6 he issues a simple command, "Fear God!" This is set in a context of admonitions against a casual or chatty attitude toward divinity: "God is in the heavens and you are on earth; therefore let your words be few" (Eccl 5:1). The divine mystery is clearly up front, and Qohelet offers little consolation to the worshiper except for the possibility of rejoicing in the gifts of God, *if* they come one's way (e.g., Eccl 3:12–13).

The meaning of Eccl 7:18 is difficult to establish: "The one who fears God will go forth" (?). If it means that such a person will succeed, then Qohelet is recommending fear of God, probably in the numinous sense, as the bottom line for those who are given conflicting prescriptions about wisdom and moral conduct (Eccl 7:16–18). The entire passage has been interpreted in various ways.[20]

"Those who fear God" in Eccl 8:12 is to be understood in the traditional sense of the just, as opposed to the wicked. Although many commentators argue that Eccl 8:12b–13 is an insertion, it seems better to recognize this as a reference to, but not an adoption of, the traditional view of retribution. In other words, Qohelet is saying that he is aware of this point of view, which rewards fear of God.

In the epilogue, fear of God is joined with the keeping of the commandments (Eccl 12:14). Such a union is foreign to Qohelet, who never mentions *miṣwôt* in the book. Rather, this is a cautious thematizing of the work by the epilogist who is editing it for the community.[21] The fear of God here has a nomistic sense: Observe the Torah. We can conclude that

Qohelet's understanding of the fear of God is colored by his appreciation of the mystery of the divine ways. Within the wisdom literature this serves as a salutary and necessary correction of the more frequent traditional understanding. But his work is far from being "The Song of Fear of God," as F. Delitzsch suggested.[22] In short, one has to understand Qohelet's statements against the background of the mystery of God and his actions and against Qohelet's ongoing dialogue with traditional wisdom, which is stripped of the consoling aspects of fear of God.

The nomistic understanding of fear of the Lord has been widely accepted as the view of Ben Sira (see Sir 9:15–16). But the study of J. Haspecker has shown that he is much more versatile than that.[23] One need not adopt Haspecker's view that fear of God is *the* theme of the book and determinative of its literary structure. But he shows clearly the attitudes that crystallize around the notion. At several points Ben Sira describes fear of the Lord in some detail:

> You who fear the Lord, wait for his mercy;
> and turn not aside, lest you fall.
> You who fear the Lord, trust in him,
> and your reward will not fail;
> you who fear the Lord, hope for good things,
> for everlasting joy and mercy.
>
> (Sir 2:7–9)

> He who fears the Lord will accept his discipline,
> and those who rise early to seek him will find favor.
> He who seeks the law will be filled with it,
> but the hypocrite will stumble at it.
> Those who fear the Lord will form true judgments,
> and like a light they will kindle righteous deeds.
>
> (Sir 32:14–16)

The emphasis on trust and hope is aimed at the inner being. In Sir 2:6–14, the consoling aspect of reward is not absent, but trust in the Lord is the key to the passage. It is not based on "works." As Haspecker remarks, the tenor of the passage is not that the God-fearing can trust in God because they are God-fearing; rather, they must trust in God in order that they become more God-fearing.[24]

In no fewer than three passages there is a clear parallelism between fearing God and loving him: Sir 2:15–16; 7:29–30; and 34:15–16. In 7:29 the verb for fear is *pāḥad*:

> With all your soul fear the Lord,
> and honor his priests.

> With all your might love your Maker,
>> and do not forsake his ministers.[25]
>> (Sir 7:29)

Another attitude that is associated by Sirach with fear of the Lord is humility (*'nwh; prautēs, tapeinotēs*). The term occurs in Hebrew or Greek six times (Sir 1:27; 3:17; 4:8; 10:28; 13:20; 45:4). The following is an example:

> If you desire wisdom, keep the commandments,
>> and the Lord will supply it for you.
> For the fear of the Lord is wisdom and instruction.
>> and he delights in fidelity and humility.
>> (Sir 1:26–27)

Humility is coupled with fidelity as constitutive of fear of the Lord. Humility is referred also to neighbor as Sirach warns against pride (Sir 7:16–17).

These and other attitudes of Sirach deserve to be considered along with his emphasis on observance of the law. He does insist on the latter as well, but it springs out of deeper roots than a mere nomistic standpoint. He is open to the sovereign disposition of the Lord who has spoken to Israel in the Torah. In short, trust and humility are the essential elements of fear of the Lord/wisdom for this second-century sage.

We have seen how fear of God has functioned within Israelite wisdom. The result is almost as varied as wisdom itself, for the concept fluctuates across the centuries, between a sense of the numinous and a serenity in the worship of God. This is not a linear development; it merely underscores how wisdom is unthinkable without fear of God. Although wisdom seems to be taken up with the ordinary, everyday events, it retains its basic relationship to God, and the fear of the Lord is an essential ingredient in this achievement.

NOTES

1. Cf. A. Lemaire, *Les écoles et la formation de la Bible dans l'ancien Israël* (OBO 39; Fribourg: Editions universitaires, 1981); F. W. Golka, "Die israelitische Weisheitsschule oder 'des Kaisers neue Kleider,' " *VT* 33 (1983) 257–70. In turn, Lemaire has disputed Golka in "Sagesse et écoles," *VT* 34 (1984) 270–81.

2. So R. N. Whybray, *The Intellectual Tradition in the Old Testament* (BZAW 135; Berlin: Walter de Gruyter, 1974).

3. For convenience, see the discussion by J. L. Crenshaw, "Method in Determining Wisdom Influence Upon 'Historical' Literature," *JBL* 88 (1969) 129–42,

reproduced in J. L. Crenshaw, *Studies in Ancient Israelite Wisdom* (New York: KTAV Publishing House, 1976) 481–94.

4. The clearest manifestation of this is in H. H. Schmid, *Wesen und Geschichte der Weisheit* (BZAW 101; Berlin: Alfred Töpelmann, 1966); cf. also H. Gese, *Lehre und Wirklichkeit in der alten Weisheit* (Tübingen: J. C. B. Mohr [Paul Siebeck], 1958).

5. Cf. M. H. Pope, *Job* (AB 15; 3d ed.; New York: Doubleday & Co., 1973) xxxii–xl: "still an open question" (xl).

6. This grid is applied by W. McKane in *Proverbs* (OTL; Philadelphia: Westminster Press, 1970). The distinctively religious trend of Proverbs 1—9 is obviously intended as an orientation for comprehending the collections that follow. This interpretation makes more sense than a hypothetical reconstruction of God-talk.

7. This is the old problem of aligning wisdom with the rest of the Old Testament theology. For a recent discussion, see H. G. Reventlow, *Problems of Old Testament Theology in the Twentieth Century* (Philadelphia: Fortress Press, 1985) 168–86.

8. H. D. Preuss, "Erwägungen zum theologischen Ort alttestamentlicher Weisheitsliteratur," *EvTh* 30 (1970) 393–417. See also idem, "Das Gottesbild der älteren Weisheit Israels," *Studies in the Religion of Ancient Israel* (VTSup 23; Leiden: E. J. Brill, 1972) 117–45, and idem, "Alttestamentliche Weisheit in christlicher Theologie?" *Questions disputées d'Ancien Testament* (BETL 33; Louvain: University Press, 1974) 165–81.

9. See the references in n. 4. Another standard presentation is E. Würthwein, *Die Weisheit Ägyptens und das Alte Testament* (Marburg: Elwert Verlag, 1960), reproduced in English translation in Crenshaw, *Studies*, 113–33.

10. On the concept of *ma'at*, see S. Morenz, *Egyptian Religion* (London: Methuen & Co., 1973) 133ff. He makes three observations about the *Pilatusfrage* (What is *ma'at*/truth?): (1) *ma'at* is the correct situation or harmony established in creation between nature and society, out of which flows justice, truth, etc. (2) It is important to preserve or restore this harmonious order; hence *ma'at* is the goal or task of human activity. (3) At the same time, *ma'at* is the reward of human activity. See also the discussion of H. Frankfort, *Ancient Egyptian Religion* (New York: Harper & Row, 1961) 59–87.

11. Cf. K. Koch, "Gibt es ein Vergeltungsdogma im Alten Testament?" *ZTK* 52 (1955) 1–42. For a different point of view, cf. P. D. Miller, *Sin and Judgment in the Prophets* (SBLMS 27; Chico, Calif.: Scholars Press, 1982) 5–6, 134–39.

12. Two observations are in order here. First, there is no intent to deny the clear influence of Egyptian wisdom on that of Israel (e.g., Amenemope and Prov 22:17—23:11). The "Instructions" of Egypt are important for understanding both form and content of Israelite wisdom. Second, whatever may be the similarities with the wisdom of the ancient Near East, Israel did not judge her wisdom to be in conflict with her own self-understanding, and eventually canonized her views in the Writings. The religious dimension of Israelite wisdom is to be found here, not in a hypothetical reconstruction of the prehistory of wisdom.

13. The statement of Zimmerli is: "Wisdom thinks resolutely within the

framework of a theology of creation"; cf. "The Place and Limit of the Wisdom in the Framework of the Old Testament Theology," *SJT* 17 (1964) 146–58, reproduced in Crenshaw, *Studies,* 148/316. See G. von Rad, *Wisdom in Israel* (Nashville: Abingdon Press, 1972) 301. Also pertinent are von Rad's further remarks in *Wisdom,* 307: "The wisdom practiced in Israel was a response made by a Yahwism confronted with specific experiences of the world. In her wisdom Israel created an intellectual sphere in which it was possible to discuss both the multiplicity of trivial, daily occurrences as well as basic theological principles. This wisdom is, therefore, at all events to be regarded as a form of Yahwism, although—as a result of the unusual nature of the tasks involved—an unusual form and, in the theological structure of its statement, very different from the other ways in which Yahwism reveals itself."

14. It appears as though the God problem was taken up in a "safe" area, daily life, and so the patriarchal and exodus promises were not threatened. One can point to challenges to the salvation promises, as in Psalm 89, or Habakkuk, or the challenge that Amos puts to salvation history (Amos 9:7), but these are hardly comparable to the probing of Job and Qohelet, or the complaints of the psalmists.

15. Cf. von Rad, *Wisdom,* 162, 199.

16. Although Lady Wisdom's secrets are far from being revealed, some insights can be gained from B. Lang, *Frau Weisheit* (Düsseldorf: Patmos Verlag, 1979).

17. See the works of S. Plath, *Furcht Gottes* (Stuttgart: Calwer Verlag, 1962); J. Becker, *Gottesfurcht im Alten Testament* (AnBib 25; Rome: Biblical Institute Press, 1963); L. Derousseaux, *La crainte de Dieu dans l'ancien testament* (Paris: Editions du Cerf, 1970). M. L. Barré has pointed out that fear of God or gods is "a concept common to all areas of the ancient Near East, a concept moreover which is regularly encountered in the wisdom literature of this region." Cf. M. L. Barré, " 'Fear of God' and the World of Wisdom," *BTB* 11 (1981) 41–3; the quotation is from p. 43. However, it can be said that only in Israel do we find an explicit and intimate association of wisdom with "fear of God."

18. Von Rad, *Wisdom,* 67.

19. Cf. E. Pfeiffer, "Die Gottesfurcht im Buche Kohelet," *Gottes Wort und Gottes Land* (ed. H. G. Reventlow; Göttingen: Vandenhoeck & Ruprecht, 1965) 133–58.

20. It is commonly interpreted in the sense of Qohelet advocating a just mean, but this can hardly be correct. In any case, the ambiguity of the phrase we are discussing remains: *yēṣēʾ ʾet kullām.*

21. Cf. G. T. Sheppard, *Wisdom as a Hermeneutical Construct* (BZAW 151; Berlin: Walter de Gruyter,1980) 121–29.

22. Cf. F. Delitzsch, *Commentary on the Song of Songs and Ecclesiastes* (Grand Rapids: Wm. B. Eerdmans Publishing Co., 1982 reprint) VI, 183.

23. J. Haspecker, *Gottesfurcht bei Jesus Sirach* (AnBib 30; Rome: Biblical Institute Press, 1967).

24. Ibid., 254.

25. Cf. ibid., 281–312, for a detailed exegesis.

24

The Cult Reform of Josiah of Judah: 2 Kings 22—23 as a Source for the History of Israelite Religion*

NORBERT LOHFINK

Within the Bible there is a "Deuteronomic phenomenon." At its center stands the Book of Deuteronomy. Around this is grouped the "Deuteronomistic" literature. There also appears to be evidence, especially in the Tetrateuch, of early- and proto-Deuteronomic work. Even earlier than de Wette the Deuteronomic phenomenon was linked to the cult reform of Josiah of Judah, in 621 B.C.E. Actually, the sēper hattôrâ ("book of the law") discovered in the Temple at that period was thought to be an early form of the present Deuteronomic law. But in other respects it would be rash in presenting the history of Israelite religion to identify the Deuteronomic phenomenon simply with the period of Josiah.

The Deuteronomic phenomenon has a diachronic dimension, beginning probably in the premonarchic period and extending into the postexilic period. From a synchronic perspective it is therefore unlikely that the lively period of the late seventh century alone came under Deuteronomistic influence. Unfortunately there is almost no consensus within scholarship over the beginnings and precise history of the Deuteronomic literature. The internal stratification of Deuteronomy itself has not been convincingly explained. It remains an open question what kind of historical and sociological reality stands behind the Deuteronomic phenomenon. Was there actually a "movement"? Or are we concerned with "literature," behind which stand only a few individuals, be they writers, theologians, or government officials? Is there a determinable geographical or sociological point of origin (Northern Kingdom or Jerusalem at the beginning; Judah or Babylon during the exilic period; Levites or prophets, wisdom teachers or court figures as tradants)?[1] Archaeology and epigraphy are not of much further help. It appeared for a brief while as though Y. Aharoni had succeeded in establishing that cult centralization had taken place in two phases, during the reigns of

---

*Translated from the German by Christopher R. Seitz.

459

Hezekiah and Josiah,[2] a fact that would have proven valuable for other questions facing Deuteronomic research. But there is now again doubt concerning this. F. M. Cross had already harbored this doubt years ago.[3] So at the present time we cannot, unfortunately, make full use of one of the most important literary complexes of the Bible for the history of Israelite religion—assuming "history of religion" to be an actual historical science, which links what is reported with a point in time, a place, and names.

What we can do is more modest. We can use historical information contained within the Deuteronomic literature to illuminate individual events of significance for the history of Israelite religion. In the following, what I should like to do is examine that event which, despite all uncertainties, is our firmest point of orientation: the cult reform of Josiah. What can we say about it historically? I proceed with the notion that the Chronicler's presentation (2 Chronicles 34—35) contains no new or independent information beyond that in 2 Kgs 22:1—23:20.[4] This then is our only source worth considering. It is found in a biblical book which, in its final form, dates from no earlier than the middle of the sixth century.[5] Thus it reports about Josiah and events that proved truly cataclysmic for Judah from a distance of several generations. Consequently, (1) 2 Kings 22—23 must first be examined as to its prehistory, and thus its value as a source, before (2) it can be put to full use for the history of Israelite cult and religion.

I

The limited scope of this essay will not allow the presentation of individual literary-critical analyses. Therefore I present straightaway the results of my analysis, starting with the final text and working back to the earliest recoverable levels.[6]

The definitive text of 2 Kgs 22:1—23:30 appears without major modification to be the text of the exilic edition of the Deuteronomistic historical work. One can characterize it as tightly structured throughout, though its form betrays a peculiar tension. The usual concluding formulas of the Books of Kings comprise its frame. At the end of the actual body of the text, the evaluation of the king is repeated (elsewhere only for Asa at 1 Kgs 15:11, 14; Hezekiah at 2 Kgs 18:3, 5–6 and Manasseh at 21:2, 9), and as such it still belongs with the frame. Even within the body of the text itself one finds further framing motifs.[7] The full text is divided into five action units, each of which begins with a royal initiative.

This organizational structure transforms the entire report concerning Josiah into a cult report. Josiah's covenant-making stands at the center of the presentation. According to it, Josiah is a cult reformer, nothing more.

CHART I

1. Introductory formula (22:1)
  2. Evaluation (22:2)
    3. *CORPUS (22:3—23:24)* (Framework elements: 22:3, 8 and 23:23–24)
      I. 22:3 "King Josiah sent"   *Temple, book, repentance*
      II. 22:12 "The king commanded"   *Prophetic inquiry*
      III. 23:1 "The king sent"   *Covenant-making*
      IV. 23:4 "The king commanded"   *Cult reform*
      V. 23:21 "The king commanded"   *Passover in Jerusalem*
  4. Evaluation (23:25–27)
5. Concluding formula (23:28–30)

Political and military elements are found only in connection with the death of the king (23:29–30). Prophetic speech appears in connection with the cult-reform (22:15–20) or with the evaluation of the king (23:26–27—if this is even prophetic speech at all and not God's own monologue). These elements are thus subordinated by the cultic orientation of the text.

In terms of content, however, there is yet another orientation which lies below the cultic disposition of the text. The question exists as to whether a Judah threatened by the curse of Yahweh can still be rescued, or must go under. Within the framework of the cultically oriented structure, this question appears in a concealed way. The first evaluation of Josiah is positive (22:2), leading one to expect Yahweh's blessing. Then, however, the discovery of the *sēper hattôrâ* sets off a feeling of panic. Josiah rends his clothes (22:11), Josiah's mission to Huldah anticipates the worst (22:13), and, while Huldah's oracle (22:15–20) does grant a postponement during Josiah's lifetime, it keeps the threat of destruction alive. This fact remains in the reader's consciousness when, during the covenant making, the subsequent cult reform, and the reintroduction of the Passover festival, Josiah's repentance and faithfulness to the Torah shine forth. In his reforms he cancels on behalf of Judah the sins of all the kings since Solomon (23:4–14) and nullifies the cultic transgression, so fatal in the unfolding of history, of Jeroboam at Bethel (23:15–20). Thus, the Passover festival forms a bridge back to the early period of the Judges (23:21–23). There then follows a final, still generalized notice of cult-reform (23:24), which recalls especially the sins of Manasseh (cf. 2 Kgs 21:6, 11). Will these also be blotted out? The second evaluation which follows now (23:25–27) indicates no. Even the premature, violent, and obviously far from honorable death of Josiah indicates that Huldah's oracle itself, as it postponed the destruction for Josiah's lifetime, had thus prevented the utter darkness of Yahweh's wrath to come to full prominence: Josiah would die before this time (23:28–30).

CHART II

Framework (beginning part)	positive
Corpus I and II	*negative*
Corpus III (center)	positive
Corpus IV and V	positive
Framework (concluding part)	*negative*

In contrast to what the beginning promised, at the end what dominates the picture is the coming catastrophe. God holds fast to it, despite Josiah's repentance and faithfulness to the Torah (23:25).

At a point in time when practically all of biblical scholarship was fascinated with M. Noth's concept of a single, exilic "Deuteronomist," it is to the credit of Cross that he renewed the theory, already advanced by A. Kuenen and J. Wellhausen, of a double Deuteronomistic redaction of the Books of Kings: one Josianic and one exilic.[8] This distinction also explains most easily the internal tension evidenced in the structure of the Josiah presentation.[9] The basic structure, oriented entirely around the cult reform of Josiah, is the work of the Josianic Deuteronomist (Dtr I). By contrast, the orientation around the question of whether or not the catastrophe will be halted originates with the exilic editor of the larger historical work (Dtr II).[10] Dtr II introduced his new theme into the text by placing the motif of Yahweh's wrath, already burning for many generations, into Josiah's request for an oracle (22:13),[11] by greatly reworking Huldah's oracle (22:15–20),[12] by calling to mind the sins of Manasseh with the insertion of a yet more extensive reform notice (23:24),[13] by reversing with 23:26–27 the positive verdict of Dtr I over Josiah (found at 23:25),[14] and by extending the narrative beyond 23:28 to report events that had taken place in the meantime. The text of Dtr I thus consists of 22:1–12, 13*, 14, 15–20*; 23:1–23, 25*.

This text forms the conclusion of the work of Dtr I. His final chapter presents the last king of Judah to be chronicled as the consummate cult reformer, the one whose repentance (23:25) again calls forth the great age of "his father" David (22:2). That structure of the text which resisted to a certain extent Dtr II's interpretation of Josiah was the work of Dtr I, and it can be identified throughout by content as his text.

At the center stands the pledge of king and people to the Torah

CHART III

1. Introduction and Evaluation of Josiah (22:1–2)
    2. *CORPUS (22:3–12, 13*, 14, 15–20*; 23:1–23)* (Framework: 22:3; 23:23)

I. 22:3	"King Josiah sent"	*Temple, book, repentance*
II. 22:12	"The king commanded"	*Prophetic inquiry*
III. 23:1	"The king sent"	*Covenant-making*
IV. 23:4	"The king commanded"	*Cult reform*
V. 23:21	"The king commanded"	*Passover in Jerusalem*

3. Concluding Evaluation of Josiah (23:25)

document found in the Temple (III). The discovery occurs as the king seeks to renovate the Temple. This forms the beginning of the text unit (I). The great Passover festival in the Temple forms a mirror image at the end (V). In between, the central scene is preceded by the prophetic authorization to undertake the covenant (II); it is followed by the carrying through of the demands of the discovered Torah (IV). Part II breaks open the future, while the mirror-image Part IV draws the line on the past.

It is hardly conceivable that the text would have been composed in this form after the sudden death of Josiah at Megiddo. In all probability what we have before us is a text from Josiah's last years, just a few years removed from the events it reports. This could suffice for the question of the text's historicity. However, the text itself forces us to examine once again its sources.

One can detect a style of reporting that does not otherwise appear in those sections of the work composed by Dtr I. This indicates that in these places Dtr I utilized one or more earlier documents. In fact, between the frames (22:1–2; 23:25) and the accounts of reform (23:4–20) on the one hand, and the remaining text on the other, tensions in narrative presentation and language are to be noted.[15] The following assumptions can be made. The basis for the work of Dtr I consisted of a narrative about the discovery of the Torah, a prophetic inquiry, the sealing of the covenant, and the Passover festival. Into this, Dtr I skillfully inserted notices concerning Josiah's reform measures, between the scenes of covenant-making and Passover festival.[16] At least in the graveyard episode (23:16–18), he made use of a preexistent prophetic narrative.[17] Around the whole he has placed his frame.

Most characteristic and easy to recognize is the short story

(Kurzgeschichte) concerning the discovery of the Torah and the sealing of the covenant: 22:3–12, 13*, 14, 15–20*; 23:1–3, 21–23. It begins "in the eighteenth year of King Josiah" and ends with a reference to "the eighteenth year of King Josiah." Within the narrative, it is always "the king" who is spoken of. The story unfolds in four separate action units, each of which regularly begins with an initiative of the king. Working with this presentation, Dtr I formed his own picture of Josiah, with the modification that the covenant-making ceremony was given a central position. In the original short story, the covenant-making was just one episode among others in a connected course of action.

CHART IV

I.	22:3	"King Josiah sent"	*Temple, book, repentance*
II.	22:12	"The king commanded"	*Prophetic inquiry*
III.	23:1	"The king sent"	*Covenant-making*
IV.	23:21	"The king commanded"	*Passover in Jerusalem*

The short story revolves entirely around the king and the Torah. It appears to have been composed shortly after the events that it relates, perhaps as a memorandum, perhaps as propaganda. Conceivably, it was clear to Dtr I, who no doubt worked under a higher authority, that this text would serve well as the crowning chapter for his history of Israel.[18]

While the short story was taken over by Dtr I in an apparently unaltered form, the same is not true of the reform report (23:4–20). Here there is evidence of linguistic accommodation to the framework already provided by the short story. Moreover, the presentation of Josiah's reforms has clearly been composed with care and attention to the whole product.[19] There are ten reform notices for Judah and two for the Northern Kingdom.[20] In both cases, at the center a narrative fragment can be spotted. For Judah it is quite brief (23:9),[21] while for the Northern Kingdom it is more extensive (23:16–18).

In the Judah section, the elimination of the foreign cults frames the elimination of the Yahweh high places.[22] As such, two completely different concerns, the exclusive worship of Yahweh and the centralization of the cult, are dealt with.[23] The schematic presentation of the destruction of cult objects gives indication of relationship to Deut 9:21. In the background of the report, methods of presentation and action common to the wider orient can be spotted.[24] As such, one must be cautious about historical arguments (and even more, those with literary-critical conclusions), which stress the impossibility of many of the actions depicted. Many, though not all, cultic matters that are mentioned hearken back to

CHART V

JUDAH (23:4–14)

1. Vessels (4)
2. Idolatrous priests (5)
3. Asherah (6)
4. Houses of the cult prostitutes (7)
    5. High places in the country (8a)
    6. High places at the gates (8b)   Narrative: Priests (9)
7. Topheth (10)
8. Horses and chariots of the sun (11)
9. Altars on the roofs and in the courts (12)
10. High places for Ashtoreth, Chemosh, and Milcom (13–14)

THE NORTHERN KINGDOM (23:15–20)

1. High places in Bethel (15)   Narrative: Prophet (16–18)
2. The other high places of the Northern Kingdom (19–20)

details already provided in the Books of Kings.[25] When all of this is taken into account, it appears highly unlikely that Dtr I here simply worked in a text which already existed, in other words, a (frequently proposed) "Reform Report." On the other hand, it is possible that Dtr I may have used a preexistent document which he freely adapted. It is rather unlikely that he worked from his own memory or from what was reported to him. Consequently, we are not able to get behind the text of Dtr I for an exact report of the Cult reform. This is, however, not all that unfortunate, since his text seems to have been composed shortly after the events, based upon underlying sources.

II

With this the situation of the sources appears clarified. We can attempt a *historical evaluation.* Just as the Chronicler falls away as a historical source, so evidently does everything in 2 Kings 23—24 which is to be ascribed to Dtr II. In the text elements from Dtr II there are no statements that contain purely historical information. The light these statements throw on information in the earlier levels of the text originates in the exilic period, with all its problems. This light should be dimmed when one raises historical questions concerning the cult reform of Josiah.

A. Can one ascribe informational value to the *sequence of events* presented by Dtr I? Here one must distinguish two aspects: first, the sequence of reform measures that presently exists in 2 Kgs 23:4–20; and second, the placement of all these reform measures between the act of obedience narrated at 23:1–3 and the report of the great Passover festival at 23:21–24. Both of these are of course closely related. For Dtr I had clearly wanted to depict the oath of obedience to the newly discovered Torah as the internal motivation for, and the Passover festival as the crowning act of, the reform measures proper. Therefore he spliced them in and represented them as a kind of great, single action initiated by the king (23:4), at whose conclusion stood a return to Jerusalem (23:20). But is there something more here than an internal logical connection as expressed in narrative sequence? This possibility at least cannot be excluded. Indeed, the highly stylized arrangement of the reform measures, with cult centralization occupying the central position in the section concerning other Judahite reforms, argues against an actual sequence of events being reported. This holds true as well for the sequence Judah to Northern Kingdom. Here too the text is clearly schematized. It is not to be ruled out that perhaps the expedition to Bethel did not take place earlier than the completion of all the cultic activity mentioned in Judah. Then the notice at 23:4, that ashes had "already" been brought to Bethel with the "first" reform measure, would perhaps not seem so strange as is the case when one assumes historicity in the sequence. Yet if we are in the dark concerning the actual sequence of individual reform measures and their original relationship, we remain all the more ignorant of their precise time frame and their causal connection with the discovery of the Torah and the making of the covenant.[26] If the turn of the year is calculated in autumn, then, if pressed, one could locate all the cult reforms mentioned between a covenant-making in the fall and a Passover celebration in the spring.[27] But is it likely on historical grounds that all this occurred in such a compressed fashion? For which reform measures is it necessary to assume a closer connection with the early stage of the Deuteronomic law, as it can be presupposed for the period of Josiah, and for which is it sufficient merely to assume the general desire to resist Assyrian cultural influence, as far as possible, and at the same time eliminate Assyrian control? Cult centralization remains the surest reform measure to link with the Deuteronomic legislation of that period.[28] The dismantling of foreign cults could already have long been under way when the discovery of "Deuteronomy" occurred. After all, the discovery took place during renovation of the Temple.[29]

We have now identified as at least conceivable the positions that Th. Oestreicher had brought into the discussion.[30] However, Oestreicher granted historical value to the Chronicler as a source and therefore spoke not of the conceivable or the possible, but of the actual course of events. If one evaluates the Chronicler's presentation differently, this will not work. From 2 Chronicles 34—35 one can only assume that the Chronicler also did not understand the reported sequence in 2 Kings 22—23 as making claims for historicity. And because the Chronicler also had free reign with his sources, nothing much more can be added to the discussion.

So a good deal of darkness hangs over the sequence of individual events, when viewed historically. Josiah carried out a whole series of cult reforms. There are fairly good grounds for connecting the elimination of Yahweh worship on the "high places," reported at 23:8, with the chance discovery of the Torah made during work on the Temple, and with the subsequent prophetic inquiry, covenant-making, and Passover festival in Josiah's eighteenth year. The purification of the cult from non-Yahwistic elements is not necessarily related to this. Working from the data, those cult reforms unrelated to the discovery of the Torah are naturally to be seen as having taken place before, rather than after, these events. If one wants to consider them in historical terms, they may be best understood as expressions of the growing distance from Assyrian sovereignty.

B. The next historical question concerns *which foreign cults* were eliminated by Josiah—regardless of when or in what actual sequence. Dtr I is undoubtably concerned to establish the comprehensive nature of Josiah's cult purification. Thus he makes explicit reference to the entire history of the monarchic period which is depicted earlier in his work: at the beginning he speaks of the (idolatrous) activity of the "kings of Judah" (23:5; also vv 11, 12), and at the end, of the activity of the "kings of Israel" (23:19). At points in between, he also refers by name to Manasseh (23:12), Solomon the "king of Israel" (23:13), and Jeroboam the son of Nebat, "who made Israel to sin" (23:15). Originally, therefore, not all of the non-Yahwistic cults destroyed by Josiah could have been Assyrian imports. Josiah's actions were aimed at a more fundamental level. As such, they were not just "anti-Assyrian" moves.

On the other hand, cults imported, if not in fact imposed, by Assyria surely played a role in the series of reforms. The question of Assyrian imposition is not without controversy. In the more recent period, J. W. McKay has in particular promoted a picture of religious tolerance on the part of the Assyrians toward their subjugated peoples.[31] Shortly thereafter, M. Cogan painted a substantially darker picture of Assyria's stance in matters religiopolitical.[32] But he also made a sharp distinction between provinces that had been annexed and more loosely allied vassal states— Judah would have been in the latter group. In the meantime, H. Spieckermann has brought forth convincing evidence calling into question this distinction in several respects.[33] We have to assume that the Assyrian cult did not just spread into Jerusalem and Judah through cultural influence but rather through official imposition, especially in Jerusalem itself. Based on Assyrian practices, it appears clear that Josiah's cult reform consisted in great measure of the destruction of Assyrian cults. The notices at 2 Kgs 23:4–14 give the deities Canaanite names in part, and that may have also been true in actual practice—certainly there were more or less clearly syncretistic elements everywhere. But especially at the time when the Assyrian empire was collapsing, Assyrian religiosity began to make itself felt with greater and greater intensity in the daily life of the cult in Jerusalem and Judah. We are not in a position to discuss all of the ramifications and the concrete reality that might stand behind the individual notices of cult reform; we recommend that one simply refer to the excellent new monograph by Spieckermann.[34]

C. If all the actions directed against non-Yahwistic elements in the cult can well be explained historically as direct reflexes of a putative, slowly growing, national independence move away from Assyria, this does not yet explain the *concentration of the cult in Jerusalem.* We still do not have a plausible explanation for this development. Neither purely fiscal[35] nor purely theological hypotheses are convincing. The latter is often characterized by the catch phrase: *"One* God, *one* people, *one* cult." But apart from its ring, this triad lacks convincing logic. Deuteronomy itself speaks against it. Never does Deuteronomy ground the exclusive claim for one cult site in the exclusive worship of Yahweh or the uniqueness of Israel. The sole explanation it offers is to be found in the so-called centralization formula. According to it, all is simply Yahweh's will: his "election" of one single cult site within all the many tribes. In this way, cult centralization (in the veiled form found in Deuteronomy) is linked to the promise to David.[36] Of course the former does not proceed all that logically from the latter. But at a minimum, centralization appears to have been viewed in this connection.

The full structure of the work of Dtr I also speaks in favor of this connection. In the view of Dtr I, the ups and downs of the monarchic period are primarily related to two factors: first, the promise of a *nîr* for David (which preserves Judah from the fate of the Northern Kingdom); and second, the charge to destroy the "high places" (if not carried out, assuring yet further disaster). The two factors could have appeared, when Josiah made his unique act of royal "repentance" (23:25), as simply two sides of one and the same coin.

In concrete terms, cult centralization was not simply a concentration of the cult in Jerusalem but also in the Temple proper. For, according to 23:8, Josiah razed not only the rural sanctuaries but also the "high places of the gates" at the walls of Jerusalem. A problem growing out of these actions concerned the future of the priesthood in these many cult places. What then occurred is briefly described in 23:9.[37]

That the entire undertaking deeply engaged the sentiments of the populace or called for a major effort at convincing the people is far from obvious in 2 Kgs 23:8–9. In view of the full presentation of the monarchic period by Dtr I, the destruction of the high places, finally accomplished but long overdue by centuries, would seem a rather obvious matter of concern for the Yahweh cult in Israel. But it is precisely on these terms that the presentation *is* a piece of royal propaganda for cult centralization.[38] The stylized nature of almost all of Deuteronomy's laws of centralization as joy-filled festivals indicates that the people had to be talked out of feeling they had lost something.[39] The young Jeremiah also appears to have been active as a propagandist for a pilgrimage to Jerusalem, springing from joy over new salvation to be wrought by Yahweh.[40]

D. Therefore, while the accounts of cult reform must on literary-critical grounds be separated from the "short story" relating *Torah discovery, covenant-making, and Passover celebration,* we must at the same time assume a closer factual connection between the events it reports and at least the cult centralization. Only in the sort of climate brought on by the making of the covenant, that of a new religious start and a return to Israel's origins, was it possible to view such radical restructurings of religious conduct as acceptable for a whole population.

The "short story" may report the events from the discovery of the Torah to the Passover festival in a highly selective way and may stylize them in a one-sided fashion—nevertheless they are a testimony to the consciousness of the hour. Of course it is just the kind of consciousness the royal propaganda wanted to create. But we must assume that the wider populace accepted these odds. Otherwise Josiah could not have carried out the changes he did.

Admiration for the energetic, God-pleasing king was certainly a decisive element in the consciousness of this brief historical moment. It permeates the entire short story.[41] Along with this is the feeling of return to the beginnings of premonarchial Israel. This is particularly clear in the closing paragraph concerning the Passover celebration (23:22–23). We know as well from the Book of Jeremiah that Josiah could be characterized precisely as the one who stood for justice and equality.[42] This too was certainly born of the desire to revitalize a nation, now already in the process of decay, as from the early time. However, the Torah which was discovered at that moment seems to have recognized this aspect, insofar as it contained it at all, only as related to a proposal for the cultic life of

Israel.[43] It depicts Israel as a cultically assembled people of God; this was the center of its restorative impulse.

The main catalyst took the form of what we usually call "covenant." Was that something new, or was it likewise a return to Israel's origins? It was clearly understood as a return. And contrary to the many recent claims,[44] already in the premonarchic period a kind of relation which later on in Roman law was called *privilegium* existed between Israel and Yahweh,[45] already Hosea could speak of *berît* as a matter of course,[46] and among the many other rites there was also something in the royal ceremony in Jerusalem that resembled the making of a covenant between Yahweh, king, and people.[47] Nevertheless, the covenant pledge that Josiah made and to which the people gave assent, while it may have looked like a return to beginnings was also something completely different: the transference of a major principle from the consciousness of the ruling Assyrians, together with their own linguistic and ritual forms of expression.[48] Here the competing world view had its core extracted, while Israel's own faded national memory received a shot of new life. The whole unfolding of Deuteronomic theology, which is essentially covenant theology, originated with Josiah's covenant-making. However, at the same time this was possible only because, as a result of the confluence of rivulets of Israelite tradition with the waters of the Assyrian world view, it conformed exactly with the larger expectations, in the eighteenth year of King Josiah, of the people of Judah and Jerusalem[49]—and likewise with the newly discovered "Deuteronomy," whose prehistory is not to be examined here.[50]

NOTES

1. For my view, see N. Lohfink, s.v. "Deuteronomy," *IDBSup,* and more recently "Kerygmata des deuteronomistischen Geschichtswerks," *Die Botschaft und die Boten* (ed. J. Jeremias and L. Perlitt; Festschrift H. W. Wolff; Neukirchen-Vluyn: Neukirchener Verlag, 1981) 87–100. For the most recent survey of scholarship and bibliography, H. D. Preuss, *Deuteronomium* (Erträge der Forschung 164; Darmstadt: Wissenschaftliche Buchgesellschaft, 1982).

2. Y. Aharoni, "Arad," *BA* 31 (1968) 2–32.

3. F. M. Cross, "Two Offering Dishes with Phoenician Inscriptions from the Sanctuary of Arad," *BASOR* 235 (1979) 75–78.

4. On this, lastly, H. Spieckermann, *Juda unter Assur in der Sargonidenzeit* (FRLANT 129; Göttingen: Vandenhoeck & Ruprecht, 1982) 30–41.

5. The last recorded event is the pardoning of Jehoiachin by Amel-Marduk (2 Kgs 25:27–30).

6. My work is based upon the following preliminary studies: "Die Bundesurkunde des Königs Josias (Eine Frage an die Deuteronomiumsforschung),"

Bib 44 (1963) 261–88, 461–98; "Die Gattung der 'Historischen Kurz-geschichte' in den letzten Jahren von Juda und in der Zeit des babylonischen Exils," *ZAW* 90 (1978) 319–78; "Zur neueren Diskussion über 2 Kön 22—23," *Das Deuteronomium. Entstehung, Gestalt und Botschaft* (ed. N. Lohfink; BETL 68; Louvain: Peeters/University Press, 1985) 24–48. A bibliography on 2 Kings 22–23 is supplied there (fn. 60) for the years 1960—1982.

7. On this, see H.-D. Hoffmann, *Reform und Reformen. Untersuchungen zu einem Grundthema der deuteronomistischen Geschichtsschreibung* (Abhandlungen zur Theologie des Alten und Neuen Testaments 66; Zurich: Theologischer Verlag, 1980) 35–38, 169, 204. By contrast, he reverts to literary-critical logic for his arrangement of the text corpus.

8. See especially F. M. Cross, "The Themes of the Book of Kings and the Structure of the Deuteronomistic History," *CMHE,* 274–89. For further publications on this subject from Cross's students, see Lohfink, "Zur neueren Diskussion," n. 50.

9. In the tension described above, one can see a further argument in support of the two-editions theory. This goes beyond the well-known arguments regarding extensive tensions in statements from Kings and detailed text and language observations—in what follows, these are presupposed without further explanation.

10. There are small details in the text that could only have emerged in connection with the text's subsequent transmission. However, I see no compelling reason to posit a further level of redactional activity at random points within 2 Kgs 22:1—23:30—which does not mean that I doubt the existence of editorial work subsequent to Dtr II at other points in the Deuteronomistic History.

11. At a minimum, the text of Dtr I contained the charge: "Go, inquire of Yahweh for me concerning this document that has been found." A reference to Yahweh's wrath is not to be excluded: it would fit well between the rending of the garments and the prophetic authorization to adopt a new relationship with Yahweh—without having to assume thereby that Judah and Jerusalem's destruction had already occurred, in historical terms. On the other hand, at least the reference back to the sin of previous generations (Manasseh comes naturally to mind) certainly came first from Dtr II.

12. I do not have the courage to reconstruct Huldah's oracle as composed by Dtr I (which, moreover, would still not be its actual historical wording). Dtr II appears in general never to have altered texts but rather only to have expanded them. But here convincing grounds for a precise delimiting of the text are missing. It seems possible, but not certain, to me that the oracle was already in two parts for Dtr I: interpretation of the situation (wrath of Yahweh) and opportunity for a new chance (and therewith authorization for the covenant-making of 23:1–3). Certainly a pre-form of 22:20 stood in the oracle, for, if it were a new creative work of Dtr II, the verse would have to read differently. See on this Lohfink, "Historische Kurzgeschichte," 340 n. 53. For more recent theories concerning the Huldah oracle, see Lohfink, "Zur neueren Diskussion," n. 87.

13. I see no particular reason to assume further elaborations by Dtr II in the area of the reform report.

14. Concerning Dtr II from 23:26 on, see especially G. Vanoni, "Beobachtungen zur deuteronomistischen Terminologie in 2 Kön 23:25—25:30," *Das Deuteronomium,* 357–62. Presumably, the end of 23:25 ("nor did any like him arise after him") is also to be ascribed to Dtr II, who thereby created a transition to 23:26. But the statement could also belong with the full concluding word of a Dtr I, who is certain of his cause on into the future.

15. Since here I cannot, as previously, refer to observations made by many scholars, the most important factors will be mentioned. (1) The distinctive style of the reform presentations. This fact has been frequently discussed. Much remains obscure, especially the frequent but not completely consistent use of the narrative *waw* perfect. The solution, provided once again by Spieckermann, that here the style is determined by the circumstances, is far from satisfactory. (2) The discovered document is spoken of differently in 23:2–3, 21 (no naming of Moses or the statutes of Yahweh) than in 23:25 (Torah of Moses). (3) The wording "*this* document" at 23:21 speaks in favor of the verse having once been located not too far away from the last mention of the document, namely, at 23:3. (4) While at 23:3 an expression not attested in the language of Deut/Dtr ("with whole heart and whole soul"—no suffixes!) occurs, the usual form of the expression appears at 23:25 (with suffixes!), in fact with the full form attested otherwise only at Deut 6:5: "with all his heart and with all his soul and with all his might." (5) The terms used for Josiah are different and are distributed as follows: *(a)* Josiah: 22:1; 23:16, 19; *(b)* King Josiah: 22:3; 23:23; *(c)* the king: 22:9, 10, 11, 12, 20; 23:1, 3, 4, 13, 21; *(d)* the king of Judah: 22:18. This series of observations urges again a differentiation between the actual reform notices and the graveyard scene at 23:16–18. (6) The individual action units begin alternatively with "the king sent" and "the king commanded." Only between 23:4 and 23:21 does this pattern drop out.

16. It begins with "the king sent." Except for the graveyard scene, it says "the king."

17. In this section "Josiah," not "the king," is spoken about.

18. I have spoken further about this short story in previous works: Lohfink, "Bundesurkunde"; idem, "Historische Kurzgeschichte."

19. Hoffmann has the most fruitful analysis here: *Reform und Reformen,* 212–52. For further critical comment on Hoffmann, see Lohfink, "Zur neueren Diskussion," 36–42.

20. For a refutation of the usual claim, that in 23:9 we have a supplement to 23:8a separated by the intervening 8b, see Hoffmann, *Reform und Reformen,* 213ff.

21. The text is even longer than can be recognized in the MT. At 23:16 a portion of the text, which can be reconstructed from G*, has fallen out because of homoioteleuton. See D. Barthélemy, *Critique textuelle de l'Ancien Testament, 1* (OBO 50/1; Fribourg: Editions universitaires; Göttingen: Vandenhoeck & Ruprecht, 1982) 421.

22. The customary, widespread emendation of *haššĕʿārîm* at 23:8 to *haśśĕʿîrîm,* first attested with Houbigant, cannot be justified either on text-critical or tradition-historical grounds. See N. H. Snaith, "The Meaning of *śʿyrym,*" *VT*

25 (1975) 115–18; Hoffmann, *Reform und Reformen,* 234ff.; Barthélemy, *Critique textuelle,* 419.

23. For the Deuteronomist, the cults of the high places during the period of the monarchy as well as foreign cults are considered a violation of the First Commandment. At the same time, this does not foreclose our seeing the differences which are made clear in our text, e.g., in the distinction between *hakkᵉmārîm* and *kohᵃnê habbāmôt.*

24. On this, see C. T. Begg, "The Destruction of the Calf (Exod. 32:20//Deut. 9:21)," in *Das Deuteronomium,* 208–51.

25. See the table in Hoffmann, *Reform und Reformen,* 253.

26. Here we have a clear contrast especially with Spieckermann's position. It is an all too obvious matter for him that the "oath to the covenant" is the "prerequisite for the following reforms." Discovery, covenant, and reform are "the three acts of the Josianic drama"—so in *Juda unter Assur,* 79. And this is apparently so obvious prior to literary-critical analysis that the reasons which support a literary-critical break after 23:3 are played out. Here everything depends on the order in which questions are asked. Is one to begin with a basic intuition that discovery, covenant, and reform proceed from one another, or is one in the first instance to operate with exclusively literary-critical criteria?

27. On the problem of determining the year's end, see my exchange with E. Würthwein in "Zur neueren Diskussion," n. 91.

28. Without my going into detail on the difficult topic of literary-criticism of the Book of Deuteronomy, let it be remarked that: (1) Yahweh's demand for exclusive worship in Israel was not purely a Deuteronomic theologumenon, and therefore it did not first come into effect with the discovery of the Torah. (2) The express commands to eliminate foreign cults extend on the one hand well into the past (see Exod 34:13; 23:24), and they may also have already found their place in the Josianic Deuteronomy (if an earlier form of Deuteronomy 7 belonged with it—see Deut 7:5), but their formulation inside Deuteronomy 12 (12:2–3; see 12:29–31) is deuteronomistic (see Lohfink, "Kerygmata," 96ff.) and, due chiefly to the actual connection of cult centralization and foreign-cult elimination under Josiah, it also is worked into the law concerning one cult place (as a framing motif, exactly as at 2 Kgs 23:4–14). (3) The requirement of a single cult place, by contrast, must be regarded as Deuteronomic proper. In Deuteronomy 12 it is certainly to be found in layers which were in Josiah's Torah. For within Deut. 12:4–28, the oldest Deuteronomistic level (at least 12:8–12, see G. Braulik, "Zur deuteronomistischen Konzeption von Freiheit und Frieden," *Congress Volume, Salamanca* [VTSup 36; Leiden: E. J. Brill, 1984] 29–39) presupposes still older versions of the single cult place regulation (generally sought in the context of 12:13–19).

29. Regarding the much-discussed question as to how 2 Kgs 12:10–17 and 22:4–7 are related to each other, Spieckermann (*Juda unter Assur,* 179–82) might have the most enlightening proposal: chap. 12 is dependent upon chap. 22, and not the reverse. Therefore one can fully regard 22:4–7 (with perhaps a small question mark at 22:6) as the oldest, historically reliable level.

30. The best overview of the discussion of the 1920s, sparked especially by

Oestreicher, is found in W. Baumgartner, "Der Kampf um das Deuteronomium," *TR,* NF 1 (1929) 7–25.

31. J. W. McKay, *Religion in Judah Under the Assyrians* (SBT, 2d series, no. 26; London: SCM Press, 1973).

32. M. D. Cogan, *Imperialism and Religion: Assyria, Judah and Israel in the Eighth and Seventh Centuries B.C.E.* (SBLMS 19; Missoula, Mont.: Scholars Press, 1974).

33. Spieckermann, *Juda unter Assur,* 200–25 and 307–72.

34. Ibid., esp. 307–70 ("Religionspolitische Massnahmen der Assyrer gegenüber Juda und anderen besiegten Völkern") and 30–160 ("Der Reformator Josia"). Despite all of the literary-critical distance I would maintain from the last-named section of the book, it is still highly recommended for its information concerning the history of the cult.

35. See W. E. Claburn, "The Fiscal Basis of Josiah's Reform," *JBL* 92 (1973) 11–22.

36. See N. Lohfink, "Zur deuteronomistischen Zentralisationsformel," *Bib* 65 (1984) 297–329.

37. On the much-discussed "contradiction" between 2 Kgs 23:9 and Deut 18:6–8: (1) It is by no means certain that both of the texts are concerned with the same groups of people or the same subjects (so Hölscher [1923], Gunneweg [1965], Lindblom [1971], and Abba [1974]); (2) presumably Josiah's Torah does not yet include the Deut 18:6–8 passage at all, since the legislation concerning offices was first worked out by Dtr II (on this, see provisionally N. Lohfink, "Die Sicherung der Wirksamkeit des Gotteswortes durch das Prinzip der Gewalten-teilung nach den Ämtergesetzen des Buches Deuteronomium," *Testimonium Veritati* [ed. H. Wolter; Festschrift W. Kempf; Frankfurt: Knecht, 1971], 143–55).

38. I leave undiscussed the question of whether there was an earlier Hezekiah edition of the Books of Kings with the same basic approach. On this, see especially: H. Weippert, "Die 'deuteronomistischen' Beurteilungen der Könige von Israel und Juda und das Problem der Redaktion der Königsbücher," *Bib* 53 (1972) 301–39.

39. Deut 12:7, 12, 18; 14:26; 15:20; 16:11, 14, 15; 26:11. Cf. G. Braulik, "Die Freude des Festes," *Leiturgia-Koinonia-Diakonia* ed. R. Schulte; Festschrift F. König; (Wien: Herder, 1980) 127–79.

40. See N. Lohfink, "Der junge Jeremia als Propagandist und Poet. Zum Grundstock von Jer 30—31," *Le livre de Jérémie* (ed. P.M. Bogaert; BETL 54; Louvain: Peeters/University Press, 1981), pp. 351-68.

41. More details in Lohfink, "Bundesurkunde," 275–77.

42. Jer 22:15–16.

43. The "Deuteronomy" of Josiah would hardly have yet contained anything from Deuteronomy 19—25. See provisionally G. Braulik, "Die Abfolge der Gesetze in Deuteronomium 12—26 und der Dekalog," *Das Deuteronomium,* 252–72. However, concepts of social leveling and equality, at least with the Passover festival, were closely tied to the laws of centralization now found at Deut 12:14–16.

44. Especially as a consequence of the work of E. Kutsch and L. Perlitt.

45. See J. Halbe, *Das Privilegrecht Jahwes Ex 34:10–26* (FRLANT 114; Göttingen: Vandenhoeck & Ruprecht, 1975).

46. See R. Kümpel, "Die Berufung Israels. Ein Beitrag zur Theologie des Hosea" (diss.; Bonn, 1973) 93–104.

47. I maintain my position (N. Lohfink, "Dt 26:17–19 und die 'Bundesformel,'" *ZTK* 91 [1969] 517–53, esp. 526) that the formulation of 2 Kgs 11:17 is neither Deuteronomic nor Deuteronomistic. I regard as completely quixotic the tour de force of C. Levin (*Der Sturz der Königen Atalja* [Stuttgarter Bibelstudien 105; Stuttgart: Katholisches Bibelwerk, 1982] 72), who not only sees here no distinction with other *b^erît* statements but then also explains over twenty *b^erît* attestations in Joshua through 2 Kings as later additions in order to arrive ultimately at a date around the year 500. For a conceivable origin of the rite, see N. Lohfink, "Beobachtungen zur Geschichte des Ausdrucks '*m jhwh*," *Probleme biblischer Theologie* (ed. H. W. Wolff; Festschrift G. von Rad; Munich: Chr. Kaiser Verlag, 1971) 275–305, esp. 299f.

48. For more detail, see N. Lohfink, "Gott im Buch Deuteronomium," *La notion biblique de Dieu* (ed. J. Coppens; BETL 41; Gembloux: Duculot/Louvain: University Press, 1976) 101–26, esp. 111–15; idem, *Great Themes from the Old Testament* (Chicago: Franciscan Herald/Edinburgh: T. & T. Clark, 1982) 17–37.

49. L. Perlitt (*Bundestheologie im Alten Testament* [WMANT 36; Neukirchen-Vluyn: Neukirchener Verlag, 1969] 8–12), who is primarily concerned with refuting my assertion that the "short story" presupposes that its readers already have a "world" marked by covenantal thinking, may be right with respect to the assumption, circulating widely at the beginning of the 1960s, of a "covenant cult" or even a "covenant festival." However, with respect to the view presented above, his arguments have little force. The reference to 2 Kgs 23:22–23 is off target, for here it is specifically stated of the Passover festival that it had not existed previously; of the "covenant" there is no mention.

50. Concerning that which I proposed as conceivable in "Bundesurkunde" from the nature of the discussion at that time, I still maintain that at a minimum the covenant text of Exodus 34 and the "book of the covenant" belong to the prehistory of Deuteronomy.

25

Liberation from Debt Slavery After the Exile in Second Isaiah and Nehemiah

KLAUS BALTZER

The writings of Second Isaiah begin with the charge, "Comfort ye, comfort ye my people" (Isa 40:1–2). The motto epitomizes the author's message. In every generation this divine decree of consolation has been construed afresh. Its language has infused sermons and great music, such as Handel's *Messiah*.

One must ask, however, whether, beyond proclaiming generally the consolation of God, the motto does not also address a concrete situation. At first glance, this would seem to be the return from the exile in Babylon. While correct, such a reconstruction of the context is not complete. It entails reductionism in our interpretation of the author's meaning.

Reconstructing the historical context of poetry is always difficult; it is even more so when the text is anonymous and not clearly dated. In this realm, conclusions attain at best a greater or lesser degree of probability. Nevertheless, what follows is an attempt to explore the possibilities and the limits of tradition history for the understanding of the text.

In Second Isaiah, "consolation" originates primarily with Yahweh (Isa 49:13; 51:3, 12; 52:9). The command in Isa 40:1 originates with God as well, but it remains an open question who is to carry it out. According to B. Duhm, "everyone who can console" is meant.[1] In most cases, the consolation is directed toward Zion/Jerusalem, that is, to the city (see Isa 40:1; 51:3, 12, 19; cf. 54:11). The object of consolation is the "people" in Isa 40:1; but the context here and in 52:9 makes it clear that Jerusalem is again in view.

Recently, H. J. Stoebe has stressed "the concreteness of the consolation": "That consolation implies real help whenever necessary and possible."[2] But what could "concreteness" consist of in reference to the city of Jerusalem? In order to answer this question, one must examine the semantic field of the term "consolation." What interrelationships charac-

477

terize its components? What implications and associations do they have at the literal and conceptual levels? Trunk, branch, leaf: these are elements of the semantic field "tree." One cannot meaningfully invoke such concrete elements without bringing the overarching but more abstract field into consciousness. Conversely, one cannot speak of the abstract field without evoking thoughts of its concrete constituents. Only the dynamic between the abstract and the concrete lends meaning to either.

For "consolation" in Second Isaiah, the vocables of the context in each instance provide an adequate point of departure. Isaiah 40:2 speaks of the completion of "service" (ṣbʾ), the discharge (rṣh) of "guilt"; 49:13 presents the parallel, "he takes pity on those in misery" ('ny; cf. 54:11); in 52:9, the subject is "redemption" (gʾl). These words pertain in common to the larger semantic field with which the term "consolation" (nḥm) has its primary associations.

The lexeme ʿebed has a considerable breadth in Hebrew.[3] Its meaning ranges from "slave," "hired hand," and "servant" to "subordinate," "official," and "minister"—from the lowest stratum of society to the highest. "Servant" inevitably calls the antonym "master" (ʾădōnāy) to mind. But the standing of the "servant"—both position and role—can be determined only if the "master's" social status is known. At every level, the master-servant relationship evinces identical characteristics: regulation under law and custom, with mutual rights and responsibilities. Service and unconditional allegiance are demanded of the servant. The master provides sustenance and protection. He replaces the bayit (the clan, the family) as the source and focus of the servant's life. Depending on how each fulfills his role in the relationship, one is a better or worse master or a better or worse servant.

The relationship between master and servant is a basic element of Second Isaiah's theological language. It can be described as a "sociomorpheme." As the anthropomorphism employs human traits to describe the deity, the sociomorphism draws on societal models to express the nature of the relationship between God and human beings. The master-servant sociomorpheme can be applied at different levels of abstraction. The "servant of Yahweh" in the Servant texts is, for the purposes of the literary presentation, an individual.[4] His position is comparable to that of a vizier in relation to his king. But the author develops a collective connotation when he designates Israel as "my servant." This represents a concretization: The fate of the people of Yahweh is personified in the figure Jacob/Israel. At the same time, it is an abstraction: The fate of the individual melts into that of the collective. Perhaps one should speak of "concrete abstractions." These are comparable to our pyramidal categoric abstractions, but their use makes possible

478

a simultaneous exploitation of the differentiated registers of a conceptual scale. The author integrates diverse conceptual levels into a network, maintaining all the while an overall consistency of thought.

The idea that Israel "serves" Yahweh, its God, draws on an age-old mode of conceiving relation to the deity. It can have a concrete cultic meaning. For Israel, the "service" had long since implied fulfillment of Yahweh's commandments with the consequence that Israel could not "serve" other gods. Out of this prohibition and the master-servant so-ciomorpheme comes Second Isaiah's parody of the idols on trial. The idols are useless, powerless to succor, in the sense that a master may succor his servant. Yet the nature of the sociomorpheme, as a means of communication, a linguistic convention, becomes clear when Second Isaiah plays on it to the point of absurdity, having Yahweh say, for example, "You have made me 'serve' (*'bd-hiphil*) by your sins" (Isa 43:24).

It is characteristic of a sociomorpheme that it must be internally coherent, in any case with regard to its core elements, which can be expanded and recombined.[5] When the core elements are widely known, as within a single cultural tradition, minor changes can convey important signals. It can be shown that Second Isaiah is extremely precise in his language: Yahweh as master has property rights[6] over his servant, whom he made[7] and chose.[8] To the servant's "service," the aid and protection of the master correspond.[9] Should the servant fail to serve, he can be admonished and punished; in extreme cases, this means the slave's sale,[10] abrogating his legal relationship to the master. If the master buys the slave back, at his request—redeems him[11]—he far exceeds the limits of his obligation. In this instance, it is the master who pays the price for the servant's redemption.[12] Jacob/Israel does not bear the cost.[13] His formal renaming[14] restores the status quo.

Second Isaiah's cultural inheritance furnished him with a discrete semantic field in which the language he employed had its bearings and in which the lexemes he used were intermeshed in an integrated conceptual unity. This is characteristic of tradition. Units of conception—reflected, for example, in the construction of a semantic field—are juxtaposed in a mutually illuminating way. The element of "sale to the foe" provides an example. This expression is prominent in the Book of Judges (Judg 4:1; cf. 2:14; 3:8, 12; 6:2; 10:6) and, in the context of the Deuteronomistic History, in 1 Sam 12:8ff. Psalm 44:13 reads, "You sold your people for a pittance, without profit from their price." Isaiah 52:3 takes up the inherited topos: "For nought were you sold; without money shall you be redeemed (*g'l*)." Deutero-Isaiah bases himself on the exodus tradition. In this, the sojourn in Egypt is regarded as "slavery."[15] By means of this tradition, an archetypal "sale" and "release," Second Isaiah apprehends and communicates the experience of exile in Babylon. The ending of the exile, seen as an act of his God's salvation, constitutes one of Second Isaiah's basic themes concerning his people. As obvious as all this is, I should nevertheless like to ask, whether the exodus from Egypt in its narrow sense is the only element of this theme that Second Isaiah means to apply to the return from exile, whether he does not also apply the associated complexes of slavery and the whole Moses tradition with its wider implications.

It has often been observed how vague the details regarding the situation of the exiles are in Second Isaiah. About this subject we learn a great deal more from a line of literature running from Jeremiah 29 through the Book of Ezekiel to Daniel 1—6. There are texts describing captivity in Second Isaiah. The difficulty is that the portrait they paint does not fit with what we know otherwise about the circumstances of the deportees in Babylon. It is more likely that these could move relatively freely in their assigned settlements than that they sat imprisoned. The nature of the problem emerges from an examination of three typical texts: Isa 42:22ff.; 49:8ff.; and 51:11ff.

Regarding Isa 42:22, A. Schoors summarizes, "The vast majority of interpreters think that the condition of the exile is meant. They invoke the figurative and hyperbolic language of the prophet."[16] He recognizes the historical problem: Does this verse reflect the conditions of exile that exegetes assume? He registers the minority opinion of Duhm: "The statement that all the Israelites were confined in holes, if taken as a stark hyperbole, is also proof that Second Isaiah did not live in Babylon."[17] But what if v 22 is intimately interwoven with the whole fabric of Second Isaiah's writing? And what if it is not figurative here but double-edged, with sharp relevance for the present? Verse 23 demands from the hearer "attentive listening." K. Elliger summarizes the verse's content: "It is not enough that the people have lost everything that they had; above all, they have lost their freedom."[18]

In Isa 49:8–12, Yahweh orders the reallocation of the ancestral lands *(naḥălâ)* and the liberation of captives. The return from exile is described in pastoral terms. But it is not completely clear in this text either what exactly is figurative. "Fetters," "darkness," "hunger," and "thirst" pertain to prison. The "return" takes place not just from Babylon but from every point of the compass.

In Isaiah 51, in connection with the restoration of Zion/Jerusalem, v 14 addresses the conditions of captivity: "He who is fettered hastens to be free; he will not die in the pit, nor will he lack bread." But the straitened existence before the liberation is viewed here as "sorrow and sighing" (v 11), fear before others (v 12), and persistent, daily coercion (v 13).

Comparison of these and other texts[19] produces a relatively consistent picture of desperation. What circumstances could be the subject of this portrait? A key is to be found in Isa 51:11: "Those whom Yahweh has redeemed will return; and they will enter Zion with jubilation." For "redeeming," the expression *pādâ* is used here. It is a *terminus technicus* for freeing in the context of the institution of debt slavery. Instead of this term, Second Isaiah normally employs the verb *ga'al*,[20] which has a broader meaning, in the sense of the restoration of a previous status. The word *ga'al* is primarily oriented toward legal relations in the clan; *pādâ* belongs to the realm of commercial relations. Both are used to describe release from debt slavery.[21] The legal procedure and its associated terminology can be extracted from the Holiness Code in Leviticus 25.[22] There, *ga'al* is used; there, as in Second Isaiah, the exodus from Egypt provides the legal and logical premise. Debt slavery, one of the many forms of slavery,[23] has various facets. Debts or crop failure or other factors leading to naked hunger can drive the free man, stripped of his possessions, to indenture himself as a last resort, simply to survive. The creditor can try, by distraining the debtor, to extract the debt from his clan as "ransom." This is the most probable background for the appearance of "imprisonment" in the texts cited above. The creditor can exploit the debtor's manpower but also has the option of selling him to another as a slave. Various texts in the Old Testament reflect the specifically legal and institutional measures taken in Israel against such potentially destructive economic practices.[24] Despite the ethos these texts reflect, the practices persisted particularly in times of general impoverishment, as Jer 34:8–22 attests for the preexilic period.

It is against this background that the writing of Second Isaiah must be situated. This permits a much sharper focus both on its conceptual and on its economic content. The poetic form of his work does not imply vagueness on his part. It is only the medium for the conveying of his meaning.

The best illustration comes from Neh 5:1–13, a text that can be located in specific historical circumstances.[25] In genre, Nehemiah's prose could hardly differ more from Second Isaiah. But the economic background and the conceptual approach are similar. In Neh 5:1–13, Nehemiah carries through a general release of debts. According to vv 1–5, the history of each social group is different, but the result in each case is the same: On the loss of property follows enslavement, whether simply to survive, or in order to pay duties and taxes. Nehemiah lectures the members of the upper class (v 8): "We have to the best of our ability purchased the freedom of our Jewish brethren, who had to sell themselves to the nations, yet you are still selling your brothers, so that we must purchase them back." The word *pādâ* here denotes ransom. The connection between impoverishment, debt slavery, and slave trade in foreign lands is clear. The debt release is a premise of the rebuilding of Jerusalem.[26]

The texts in Second Isaiah and Nehemiah are probably closer to one another than has previously been noted. The issue in both cases is the refoundation and restoration of Jerusalem's integrity as a city *(metropolis)*. They share the structure and concept of the *'ebed,* of service, as an integrated entity on different levels of thought (cf. esp. Nehemiah 1). They agree in their acceptance of Persian overlordship as a *translatio imperii.* The relationship between Second Isaiah and Nehemiah demands a more exact explanation; its historical consequences need to be explored.[27] A later dating of Deutero-Isaiah seems under the present circumstances a possibility that deserves more serious consideration.

It can be seen that Second Isaiah makes no distinction between "redemption" and "liberation." The transformation of the exile is and remains a divine wonder. It demands a human response. They must proclaim the release of debt; they must make possible the return of those who have been sold into slavery abroad; they must return from the *gôlâ* in Babylon.[28] Only these acts together permit a new beginning.[29] It is the "consolation of God" that makes human consolation meaningful and necessary. "Consolation," helping others to "breath easy," "providing relief from burdens," is, according to Isa 40:1, the obligation of all who hear, so that human beings need no longer suffer.

An epitome of this aspect of Second Isaiah's theology is found in the parable of "the generous king and the unforgiving servant" in Matt 18:21–35.[30] The point of the tale is this: If you have enjoyed release from debt, how much more should you, too, make like allowance for others. The rule applies to every "servant" of the one Lord and King.

NOTES

1. B. Duhm, *Das Buch Jesaja* (HKAT III 1; 3d ed.; Göttingen: Vandenhoeck & Ruprecht, 1914) ad loc.

2. H. J. Stoebe, *"nḥm,"* THAT 2, col. 62.

3. See the lexica; literature in C. Lindhagen, *The Servant Motif in the Old Testament* (Uppsala: Almqvist, 1950); C. Westermann, *"'ebed,"* THAT 2, 182–200.

4. See my *Die Biographie der Propheten* (Neukirchen-Vluyn: Neukirchener Verlag, 1975) 171–77. For recent discussion, cf. H. J. Hermisson, "Israel und der

Gottesknecht bei Deuterojesaja," *ZThK* 79 (1982) 1–24; T. N. D. Mettinger, *A Farewell to the Servant Songs* (Lund: Gleerup, 1983).

5. Particularly noteworthy in Second Isaiah is the coupling of the sociomorpheme, master-servant, in reference to Jacob/Israel, with the sociomorpheme, husband-wife, referring to Zion/Jerusalem. In both realms, the term "redeem" *(g'l)* had originally a very specific meaning. The two can be integrated into a single network by deployment of the term and the concepts it entails. The verb retains its two distinct connotations, yet serves simultaneously in the context of the conceptual combination to produce a higher level of abstraction (for *g'l* and the "servant," see below; for Zion/Jerusalem, cf. Isa 49:26; 52:9; 54:5, 8).

6. Isa 41:8, 9; 42:1; 43:1, 10; 44:1, 2; 45:4; 49:3.

7. Isa 44:2, 21; 49:5.

8. Isa 41:8, 9; 42:1; 43:10; 44:2; 45:4.

9. Isa 41:10; 44:2; 50:7.

10. Cf. Isa 50:1; 52:3.

11. Isa 48:20; cf. 41:14; 43:1; 44:23.

12. Isa 43:34; cf. 45:13; 50:2.

13. Isa 52:3, 5; cf. 55:7.

14. Isa 44:5. This text corresponds even in its particulars to a *manumissio* of slaves.

15. Cf. Deut 5:15; 15:15; 16:12; 24:18, 22. In the Decalogue the formula is "who has brought you out of Egypt, out from the house of bondage *(bêt ʿabādîm),"* Exod 20:1; Deut 5:6. See N. Lohfink, *Das Hauptgebot* (AnBib 20; Rome: Pontifical Biblical Institute, 1963) 98–101.

16. A. Schoors, *I Am God Your Saviour* (VTSup 24; Leiden: E. J. Brill, 1973) 205.

17. B. Duhm, *Das Buch Jesaja,* ad loc.

18. K. Elliger, *Deuterojesaja* (BKAT XI 1; Neukirchen-Vluyn; Neukirchener Verlag, 1978) ad loc.

19. Isa 41:11–12; 43:5; 48:16–17; 49:22–26; 51:7; 54:14–15; 55:6 are the texts that should be taken into account.

20. See J. J. Stamm, "gʾl," *THAT* 1, 383–94; H. Ringgren, "gʾl," *TWAT* 1. 884–90, esp. III, 4.

21. See J. J. Stamm, *Erlösen und Vergeben im Alten Testament* (Bern: Franke, 1940); idem, *THAT* 2. 389–406.

22. Cf. Exod 21:2–11 *(pdh* in v 8); Deut 15:12–18 (v 15 relates to status of "servant" [ʿebed], during the sojourn in Egypt, with *pdh* for the liberation).

23. Cf. I. Mendelsohn, *Slavery in the Ancient Near East* (Westport, Conn.: Greenwood Press, 1978 reprint); M. I. Finley, ed., *Slavery in Classical Antiquity: Views and Controversies* (Cambridge, England: W. Heffer & Sons, 1961). Further: M. I. Finley, *Studies in Land and Credit in Ancient Athens 500–200 B.C.* (New Brunswick, N.J.: Rutgers University Press, 1952); idem, "The Servile Statuses of Ancient Greece," RIDA III 7 (1960) 166–89; idem, "Die Schuldknechtschaft," H. G. Kippenberg, *Seminar Die Entstehung der antiken Klassengesellschaft* (Frankfurt am Main: Suhrkamp, 1977) 173–204 (revised by the author; first appeared in *Revue historique de droit français et étranger* 43

(1965) 159–84; E. Neufeld, "Inalienability of Mobile and Immobile Pledges in the Laws of the Bible," RIDA III 9 (1962) 33–44; R. Yaron, "Redemption of Persons in the Ancient Near East," RIDA III 6 (1959); E. Neufeld, "Ius redemptionis in Ancient Hebrew Law," RIDA III 8 (1961) 30–40.

24. See, among others, E. Neufeld, "Socio-Economic Background of Yōbēl and Šemiṭṭā," *Rivista degli studi orientali* 33 (1958); N. P. Lemche, "The 'Hebrew Slave,' " *VT* 25 (1975) 129–44; idem, "The Manumission of Slaves—The Fallow Year—The Sabbatical Year—the Jobel Year," *VT* 26 (1976) 38–59; cf. E. Lipiński, "L' 'Esclave Hébreu,' " *VT* 26 (1976) 120–24.

25. See the commentary of W. Rudolph, *Esra und Nehemia* (HAT I 20; Tübingen: J.C.B. Mohr [Paul Siebeck], 1949); U. Kellermann, *Nehemia. Quellen, Überlieferung und Geschichte* (BZAW 102; Berlin: Walter de Gruyter, 1967); H. G. Kippenberg, *Religion und Klassenbildung im antiken Judäa* (2d ed.; Göttingen: Vandenhoeck & Ruprecht, 1982) esp. 54–77.

26. Apposite is the comparison to Solon's reform in Athens with its "cancellation of debts *(he apokope tōn chreōn)*" and "shaking-off burdens *(he seisachtheia)*." See Aristotle, *The Athenian Constitution XI–XII*; cf. Plutarch, *Lives, Solon XV–XVI.*

27. Coincidence cannot be ruled out, but *nḥm* forms the basis of the name, Nehemiah *(nĕḥemyâ)*. Three times, at salient points, the sentence *kî niham yhwh* (49:13; 51:3; 52:9) occurs. Is the name a reflection of the program represented in Second Isaiah, or does Second Isaiah play on the name for programmatic reasons? A decision in this question has to take into account the genre of the book.

28. Comparison with the measures taken by Solon to repatriate different groups in Athens is instructive. See Aristotle, *The Athenian Constitution* XII 4:

> And many sold away I did bring home
> To god-built Athens, this one sold unjustly,
> That other justly; others that had fled
> From dire constraint of need, uttering no more
> Their Attic tongue, so widely they had wandered,
> And others suffering base slavery
> Even here, trembling before their masters' humours,
> I did set free.

(Translation by H. Rackham in Loeb Classical Library) Cf. also Plutarch, *Lives, Solon* XV 5:

> And of the citizens whose persons had been seized for debt, some he brought back from foreign lands.... And some who here at home in shameful servitude were held."

(Translation by B. Perrin in Loeb Classical Library)

29. For the problem of depopulation, see Isa 44:25. For the economic evaluation of the program implied in Second Isaiah, the indication of redistribution of the land is important *(naḥălâ,* see 49:8); so, possibly, is the distribution of seed-grain and bread, according to 55:10–11.

30. This text was called to my attention by Jo Baltzer. I would like to thank Baruch Halpern for his help in translating this article, as well as Thomas Krüger for his assistance in preparing the final draft.

26

Israelite Religion in the Early Postexilic Period

PAUL D. HANSON

THE VITAL ROLE OF ANTECEDENT
TRADITIONS

The religious life of the Jews in the early postexilic period is incomprehensible if the effects of the devastating events of the first decades of the sixth century B.C.E. are not taken fully into account. Within a community characterized by a considerable diversity, no group emerged from this period without experiencing considerable change, due in no small part to a spiritual trauma that called into question some of the most fundamental principles of the Yahwistic faith.

To be sure, the Judahite nation had not been spared adversity in the past. Its position between Egypt and the empires of Mesopotamia virtually guaranteed constant threats of aggressive encroachment upon both its northern and southern borders. The demise of its sister nation in the north at the hands of the Assyrians in 722 B.C.E. stood as a grim reminder of the fragile nature of its own political existence. That reminder, reinforced by the harsh lessons of its own history such as Sennacherib's devastating invasion of the land in 701 B.C.E., had already nurtured within the nation several distinct ways of coping with the ominous threats posed by foreign aggressors. Within circles closely associated with Zion and the Davidic house a theologumenon had developed that based the security of Jerusalem and the stability of the Davidic dynasty upon divine election. Likely fostered by the royal house since the latter days of the united monarchy, this tradition clearly influenced the thought of the great eighth-century prophet Isaiah (see esp. Isaiah 7—11), and it received powerful historical corroboration by the near-escape of the capital city during the massive assault on the land by the Assyrians at the very end of the eighth century. The majestic Ariel prophecy in Isa 29:1–8 gives testimony to the miraculous divine intervention that the adherents of this view awaited from God against any enemy that plotted to destroy the holy

City of David (see Psalm 2). The persistence of this view into the period of Babylonian ascendancy is indicated by the confident attitude of Jeremiah's opponents (see Jer 7:1–15, and even more emphatically, the version of the Temple incident in Jeremiah 26).

Jeremiah speaks from a vastly different perspective and is a prime witness to a second tradition that was developing in the period leading up to the exile. Rather than taking comfort in the allegedly eternal promises of God to protect the royal city and its king, those who subscribed to this tradition took their clues from the religious and moral conditions prevailing in the land, which conditions they measured against the standards of classical Yahwistic faith. They concluded that the situation of Judah was essentially the same as the one that Amos and Hosea had described on the eve of the decline and destruction of the Northern Kingdom, a situation characterized by apostasy and the repudiation of the divine standards of righteousness and compassion. Jeremiah, for his part, concluded that the king and the people were locked by the perversity of their hearts into a path leading to destruction, which was to be Yahweh's judgment on the disobedience of the land (Jer 17:9–10). What hope he saw was a hope lying beyond this judgment.

A third tradition flourished in the years between the destructions of Samaria and Jerusalem, namely, that of the Zadokite priestly family. After years of gradual ascendancy at the cost of the wider circle of levitical priests,[1] and perhaps following the example of an earlier reform program sponsored by Hezekiah, the high point was reached when Josiah, as a part of his thoroughgoing reform, closed outlying sanctuaries and centralized all cultic activities in Jerusalem, under the leadership of the Zadokites. It was during this period that many of the legal and narrative traditions found in the so-called Priestly stratum of the Pentateuch developed toward their final form. The influence of this tradition is also manifested by the Book of Ezekiel, for example, in the application of theological themes such as the "glory of Yahweh," in the emphasis placed on the centrality of the Temple and its Zadokite priesthood, in the downgrading of the royal figure (named *nāśî'* ["prince"] rather than *mélek* ["king"]), and in the elaborate program of restoration found in Ezekiel 40—48, a program resting solidly upon a Zadokite Temple theology. Especially when one bears in mind the central role exercised by the Zadokite priests both during the exile and in the years of rebuilding that followed Cyrus's edict, it comes as no surprise that this third tradition was in a favorable position to continue guiding the thought of many as they sought to work out the riddles of the postdestruction era.

Finally, we mention a fourth preexilic tradition, one broadly cosmopolitan in perspective and related to similar phenomena in the great cultures of ancient Mesopotamia and Egypt, the so-called wisdom tradition. With a distinctly empirical orientation, its practitioners sought to grasp the harmony underlying all phenomena by tracing them to their grounding in an order both unchanging and eternal. Equipped with wisdom, kings were enabled to reign wisely over a citizenry living in prosperity within a society in which virtue was rewarded and wickedness punished. To this universal tradition the Jews added their own confession, whereby they specified wisdom's ultimate Source: "The fear of Yahweh is the beginning of knowledge" (Prov 1:7a).

Given the rich legacy of the four well-developed traditions that we have briefly surveyed, it is quite natural that when tragedy struck in the form of a crushing foreign invasion and consequent destruction of Temple and nation, many people turned to those same traditions in search of explanations. In identifying four traditions that were to continue to play a key role in the religious thought of the Jews, we must avoid the danger of oversimplifying either the preexilic or the postexilic situation. As indicated by the prophet Isaiah, these traditions could be melded with a high level of effectiveness and without consequent evisceration. And though the writings of the postexilic period give evidence that group identity was in part fostered by the particular stream of tradition to which a specific group adhered, such adherence must not be construed in a rigid sense. Zadokites naturally continued to cultivate the theological and cultic notions with which their ancestors had identified; those whose interests were tied to the Davidic house looked to royal traditions with special favor; those who felt called to extend the concerns of the prophets into the new period displayed a predisposition toward the writings of figures such as Amos, Hosea, Isaiah, and Jeremiah; those dedicated to wisdom continued to search for the harmony uniting all reality. Still the common legacy shared by all of these groups far outweighed the differences in emphasis. For example, central in the thinking of all groups was the role of righteousness (especially as it was expressed in *tôrâ*). So long as the abiding significance of this common legacy is kept clearly in mind, distinguishing between the specific traditions drawn upon by different groups in the early postexilic period can add a measure of clarity to our knowledge of the religious groups active during that time and to our understanding of the specific ways in which they responded to the recent tragedy experienced by the nation.

There is much truth in the claim that Yahwism survived the loss of nationhood, the destruction of Temple, and the incalculable human shame and suffering of this period in no small part due to earlier prophetic tradition. Second Isaiah could argue that this calamity did not disprove Yahweh's might or mercy precisely because he could assume knowledge of the judgment prophecies of the preexilic prophets (see Isa 42:24–25). And in the wake of Second Isaiah there arose devoted disciples who relied primarily on the classical prophetic writings, and especially on the oracles of judgment against Israel, as a key to their own experiences. The stream of tradition they constituted will provide one of the foci of our ensuing discussion.

But the judgment prophecies were not the only words recalled as people struggled to make sense out of the humiliating situation to which they had fallen and to lay the foundations for a new life as God's people. The royal tradition recalling God's promises to David and Zion was also remembered and applied to the new situation. Haggai applied this tradition to the Davidide Zerubbabel and emerged with a daring messianic prophecy (Hag 2:20–23). Zechariah entertained similar notions (Zechariah 4). This tradition also played an important role in the earliest edition of the Chronicler's History, as shall be discussed below.

The Book of Zechariah also gives ample evidence that the third preexilic tradition that we mentioned above also continued to exert its influence on the thoughts of the survivors of the Babylonian destruction. For many, the most reliable path into the future had already been charted within the traditions handed down by the Zadokite priests (e.g., Ezekiel 40—48 and the Priestly recension of the Pentateuch). There can be little doubt that the Zadokite priests themselves were actively engaged in cultivating such traditions further and in defending them against the attacks of rival groups (see Zechariah 3 and Ezekiel 44).

Finally, there is abundant evidence in Psalms and Proverbs, as well as in later collections of sapiential sayings, that the wisdom tradition enjoyed a popular following in the exilic and postexilic periods and provided a medium through which thoughtful individuals puzzled over the anomalies of their new situation.

We shall now attempt to describe the general social situation within which these four traditions were drawn upon in attempts to understand harsh new realities. This will be followed by an examination of representative writings of the early postexilic period to discern more specifically how the older traditions of royal cult, priesthood, prophecy, and wisdom functioned as a guide to understanding the tragedy of the Babylonian destruction.

THE SOCIAL CLIMATE IN THE WAKE OF
THE BABYLONIAN DESTRUCTION

Over the span of some seven centuries Jewish court officials, priests, prophets, and sages had developed their systems of religious thought, which had ordered the lives of their people and provided them with the symbols and images necessary for interpreting new experiences and choosing between the options forced upon them by world events. Specifically in the case of the Southern Kingdom of Judah, the capacity of the Jerusalem Temple theology to provide direction and undergird social and political stability was quite remarkable. The fact that a single dynasty was able to remain in power for over four centuries bears clear witness to that capacity. And the often harsh criticism directed at the political and religious leaders of Judah by certain prophets does not gainsay this observation, for internal criticism was to some degree tolerated by the system (albeit often begrudgingly) and represented one of its most progressive qualities.

As even some of the religious symbolism found in the prophetic writings indicates, the faith of Judah had developed in intimate association with the Jerusalem Temple. Individual groups could dispute over the division of religious leadership in the land, but their conceptualization of divine providence was ever tied to the Temple that Solomon had built on Zion. The attacks of certain prophets on the misuse of sacrificial practices and on the false sense of security derived by some people from a high form of royal ideology do not obscure the fact that the celebration of Yahweh as king that occurred amid sacrifice and praise in the Temple united the hearts and nurtured the aspirations of most of the inhabitants of Judah. This is to say that the Temple, both as home of the cult and symbol of Yahweh's presence in the land, was a master symbol in the religious faith of the Jewish inhabitants of Judah on the eve of the Babylonian invasion. This is a fact corroborated equally by prophetic and hymnic literature of the preexilic period and by laments arising out of the exile.

Recognition of the pivotal role of the Yahwistic religious symbol system in the life of the nation, and specifically of the central religious significance of the Temple, provides background for considering the effects of the destruction of Zion on the survivors. Here we can be aided by the insights of modern social scientists into such situations of calamity.

The destruction of the Temple, and all of the repercussions attending that destruction, represent a classical case of social anomie. C. Geertz has written:

> The thing we seem least able to tolerate is a threat to our powers of conception, a suggestion that our ability to create, grasp and use symbols may fail us. Man depends upon symbols and symbol systems with a dependence so great as to be decisive for his creatural viability and, as a result, his sensitivity to even the remotest indication that they may prove unable to cope with one or another aspect of experience raises within him the gravest sort of anxiety.[2]

To this Geertz adds this vivid description of the "uncanny" by S. Langer:

> [Man] can adapt himself somehow to anything his imagination can cope with; but he cannot deal with Chaos. Because his characteristic function and highest asset is conception, his greatest fright is to meet what he cannot construe—the "uncanny," as it is popularly called. It need not be a new object; we do meet new things, and "understand" them promptly, if tentatively, by the nearest analogy, when our minds are functioning freely; but under mental stress even perfectly familiar things may become suddenly disorganized and give us the horrors. Therefore our most important assets are always the symbols of our general *orientation* in nature, on the earth, in society, and in what we are doing: the symbols of our *Weltanschauung* and *Lebensanschauung.*[3]

It is no accident that the literature of the exilic and early postexilic periods frequently deals with the themes of chaos and creation. As the great civilizations of the ancient Near East had struggled with these themes in their myths and rituals as a means of dealing with the threats and changes of nature and history, so too the Jews found themselves forced to address the fundamental problem of life's viability afresh (cf. Isaiah 24—27; 65:17–25; Zechariah 14). To be sure, the physical and economic hardships they faced were severe. But far worse was the threat posed by the new situation to the fundamental system of thought and belief that had sustained the people in their own land, that is, the threat to the Yahwistic symbol system or *Weltanschauung.* What was to be said in defense of a god whose temple had been destroyed by the followers of other gods? Who was now determining the destiny of the Jewish people, now that they found themselves in a land in which Marduk rather than Yahweh was worshiped as the supreme ruler of the universe? Such questions threatened to undo the fabric of the religious system that had enabled the Jews to cope with life in a viable way. They describe the state of mind to which L. Festinger has attached the now fashionable term "cognitive dissonance."[4] Left to fester without satisfactory resolution, they can destroy the identity of a people, replacing social, political, and religious order with chaos, and making it vulnerable to complete assimilation to the captors.

Geertz has gone on to specify three points at which chaos "threatens to break in upon man: at the limits of his analytic capacities [= bafflement], at the limits of his powers of endurance [= suffering], and at the limits of his moral insight [= intractable ethical paradox]."[5] All three of these manifestations of chaos are amply documented in the literature of the time of the Babylonian destruction. Bafflement is readily apparent in the terse note made within the Deuteronomistic History by one of its final editors. It focuses on the Davidide whose early successes in battle and

490

religious fervor had raised nationalistic and even messianic expectations to a high pitch in the closing decades of the sixth century. Without comment or explanation the stinging contradiction of all that pious Yahwists held dear is recorded: "Pharaoh Neco king of Egypt went up to the king of Assyria to the river Euphrates. King Josiah went to meet him; and Pharaoh Neco slew him at Megiddo." (2 Kgs 23:29).[6] The terrible suffering of the population of Judah is recorded in another note in the Deuteronomistic History:

Nebuchadnezzar king of Babylon came with all his army against Jerusalem, and laid siege to it; and they built siegeworks against it round about. . . . On the ninth day of the fourth month the famine was so severe in the city that there was no food for the people of the land. . . . And he burned the house of the Lord, and the king's house and all the houses of Jerusalem; every great house he burned down. (2 Kgs 25:1, 3, 9)

Finally, expressions abound of the intractable ethical paradox pressed upon the Jewish consciousness by the devastation of their land, their Temple, and their possessions, as these examples from the Book of Lamentations illustrate:

The precious sons of Zion,
    worth their weight in fine gold,
how they are reckoned as earthen pots,
    the work of a potter's hands!
(Lam 4:2)

The tongue of the nursling cleaves
    to the roof of its mouth for thirst;
the children beg for food,
    but no one gives to them.
(Lam 4:4)

Happier were the victims of the sword
    than the victims of hunger,
who pined away, stricken
    by want of the fruits of the field.
(Lam 4:9)

The numbing paradox of the situation is summarized by this comparison with Sodom: "For the chastisement of the daughter of my people has been greater than the punishment of Sodom" (Lam 4:6a).

Given this frontal attack on cherished traditions of the past such as the divine election of Israel and the special status of Zion, its Temple, and its Davidic king, it was inevitable that tremendous strains would arise within the various groups seeking to preserve the religious beliefs and values of the past. And such strains would necessitate changes varying all the way from minor adjustments, to major changes, to outright abandonment of Yahwistic tradition in favor of other options (e.g., Jer 44:16–18). We turn now to specific texts to examine some of the changes that arose in response to Judah's brush with chaos in its various forms of bafflement, suffering, and intractable ethical paradox.

RESPONSES TO CALAMITY

The social and political conditions we have been describing are of the type that commonly abet otherworldly tendencies among those who have experienced the shaking of the fundamental conceptual foundations that have upheld their beliefs, customs, and institutions in the past.[7] In medieval Europe, groups experiencing chaos in the form of unstable political conditions and religious persecution became the breeding ground of millenarian movements.[8] During the Hellenistic and Roman periods, the experience of oppression at the hands of both foreigners and rivals within the Jewish community gave rise to apocalyptic movements.[9] Recent study has traced the roots of apocalypticism back to the period that is the focus of our present study, especially among circles seeking to apply certain prophetic traditions to the new postexilic conditions in the face of stiff opposition from the dominant Zadokite priestly leadership.[10]

One of the peculiarities of the early postexilic situation that has not been explained satisfactorily, however, is the fact that visionary literary conventions and images that would be adopted and further developed in later centuries by apocalyptic circles can be found not only among the distinctly dissident circles of the late sixth century B.C.E. but also within circles comprised of or allied to the Zadokite leadership. This poses a problem, however, only if the element of deprivation commonly associated with apocalyptic and millenarian movements is narrowly construed along socioeconomic lines. This is not to deny the general truth of this statement by Y. Talmon: "Radical millenarism found support in all levels of society at one time or another but essentially it is a religion of the deprived groups—oppressed peasants, the poorest of the poor in cities and towns, populations of colonial countries."[11] Any apparent contradiction disappears when one recognizes that social groups and individuals possessing roles of leadership and authority can also experience deprivation, if not specifically in socioeconomic terms, then in terms of a perceived diminution of power vis-à-vis the world powers of the time.[12] As we turn to examine the varied responses to the Babylonian conquest arising within the Jewish community, we must avoid the oversimplification of associating apocalyptic themes solely with explicitly dissident groups. We must take careful note of expressions of bafflement, suffering, ethical paradox, cognitive dissonance, and deprivation in its various forms, and analyze the impact that such experiences had upon the reapplication of earlier tradition by each of the groups in the early postexilic period.

The Reapplication of Royal Tradition

Deeply ingrained in the thinking of many Jews was a very ancient belief, a belief perhaps more widely held throughout the ancient Near East than any other, namely, that the well-being of a nation depended on the maintenance of the central cult, a responsibility primarily residing in the hands of the king. From a transcendent point of view, the smooth operation of the sacrificial system located in the temple assured that the demands of the patron deity of the land were being fulfilled, a condition upon which the prosperity of any nation depended.[13] From a more mundane point of view, an efficiently operating cult assured that the resources of the land were being properly distributed in such a way as to assure the highest level of economic prosperity and political stability possible.[14]

Among those viewing the world from the perspective of royal tradition, it was quite natural that the hardships being experienced in the land in the years immediately following the exile would be traced to the fallen state of temple and cult. The prophet Haggai gives explicit expression to this world view as he delivers his divine oracles:

> Thus says the Lord of hosts: This people say the time has not yet come to rebuild the house of the Lord. . . . Is it a time for you yourselves to dwell in your paneled houses, while this house lies in ruins? Now therefore thus says the Lord of hosts: Consider how you have fared. You have sown much, and harvested little; you eat, but you never have enough; you drink, but you never have your fill; you clothe yourselves, but no one is warm; and he who earns wages earns wages to put them into a bag with holes. (Hag 1:2–6)

The solution Haggai presents, again in the form of the divine oracle, is fully in harmony with the basic royal ideology we described above:

> Thus says the Lord of hosts: Consider how you have fared. Go up to the hills and bring wood and build the house, that I may take pleasure in it and that I may appear in my glory, says the Lord. You have looked for much, and, lo, it came to little; and when you brought it home, I blew it away. Why? says the Lord of hosts. Because of my house that lies in ruins, while you busy yourselves each with his own house. Therefore the heavens above you have withheld the dew, and the earth has withheld its produce. And I have called for a drought upon the land and the hills, upon the grain, the new wine, the oil, upon what the ground brings forth, upon men and cattle, and upon all their labors. (Hag 1:7–11)

The deplorable economic and social conditions of the land could be changed only if the root of the problem was addressed. For what the land was experiencing was more than a poor harvest or a dry season; it was experiencing divine curse! The nerve center of the nation, indeed of the cosmos, had to be restored to its proper order, and this could occur only if the Temple, which was the earthly center of the cult and the mundane counterpart to the heavenly temple, were rebuilt and its sacrificial system brought back into full operation.

That Haggai's message is continuous with the central themes of the royal theology of the preexilic Jerusalem cult is obvious. Beyond this, is there any indication that the Babylonian destruction contributed an impact of its own to the manner in which royal themes were applied to the changed circumstances of the postexilic period? Though we believe there is, the nature of that impact is sufficiently subtle to require careful delineation.

Haggai's line of reasoning can be summarized as follows:

1. Era of Curse
    a. Indictment for laxity in rebuilding the Temple (Hag 1:2–4)
    b. Query: "Consider how you have fared" (Hag 1:5, 7; 2:16)
    c. Description of the land under divine curse (Hag 1:6; 2:16–17)
2. Era of Blessing
    a. Admonition: "Build the house, that I may take pleasure in it and that I may appear in my glory, says the Lord" (Hag 1:8)
    b. Query: "Consider from this day onward" (Hag 2:18)
    c. Description of divine blessing (Hag 2:6–9, 18–19)

The logic behind this formulation of the problem and its solution is derived from the heart of the royal ideology that had been developed into a specifically Yahwistic form within the Temple cult of Jerusalem. For example, Psalm 68 celebrates the God of Israel with the words:

> Ascribe power to God,
>> whose majesty is over Israel,
>> and his power is in the skies.
> Terrible is God in his sanctuary,
>> the God of Israel,
>> he gives power and strength to his people.
>> (Ps. 68: 35–36 [Eng. vv 34–35])

Israel's God is sovereign over all creation, yet his sanctuary is in Jerusalem. From that sanctuary flow the power and the blessing that are the basis of the prosperity of the nation. The importance of honoring God through careful maintenance of the Temple cult is implicit throughout the royal hymns.

The key to Haggai's message relates directly to this theologumenon. The admonition, "Build the house!" carries a twin mandate: (1) Give proper glory to God and (2) Restore the economic system of the land. These are ultimately two sides of the same phenomenon. If we are to look for evidence of the impact of the Babylonian destruction in this message, it must be found in terms of *specific* nuances rather than in terms of fundamental changes, for continuity here is much more conspicuous than change. Our attention, therefore, must be directed toward Haggai's words of promise as they describe the results of the restoration of Temple and cult:

> For thus says the Lord of hosts: Once again, in a little while, I will shake the heavens and the earth and the sea and the dry land; and I will shake all nations, so that the treasures of all nations shall come in, and I will fill this house with splendor, says the Lord of hosts. The silver is mine, and the gold is mine, says the Lord of hosts. The latter splendor of this house shall be greater than the former, says the Lord of hosts; and in this place I will give prosperity, says the Lord of hosts. (Hag 2:6–9)

The imagery in this passage is familiar. The hymnody of the Temple had celebrated Yahweh's rule over all creation, and his victories on Israel's behalf over all enemies (e.g., Psalms 46; 47; 48). What is notable here, however, is the application of the most lofty of royal/mythic imagery to *one moment in history* and to *one particular historical figure.* The moment is a specific day in 520 B.C.E.: "the twenty-fourth day of the ninth month" (2:18), that is, the day on which the foundation stone of the new temple was laid. The historical figure is Zerubbabel, who was a Davidide, to be sure, but not a king, for Israel was kingless under the dominion of a foreign lord, Darius the Persian. At this specific moment and to this particular figure was given a dazzling promise:

> The word of the Lord came a second time to Haggai on the twenty-fourth day of the month, "Speak to Zerubbabel, governor of Judah, saying, I am about to shake the heavens and the earth, and to overthrow the throne of kingdoms; I am about to destroy the strength of the kingdoms of the nations, and overthrow the chariots and their riders; and the horses and their riders shall go down, every one by the sword of his fellow. On that day, says the Lord of hosts, I will take you, O Zerubbabel my servant, and son of Shealtiel, says the Lord, and make you like a signet ring; for I have chosen you, says the Lord of hosts." (Hag. 2:20–23)

What in the royal psalms were quasi-mythic formulations of God's creative power and universal sovereignty have here been transformed into a lofty eschatological promise, one that had direct bearing on the historical realities of the time. Specifically, this promise implied the overthrow of Persian hegemony, the glorification of Judah, and the ascendancy of the Davidide Zerubbabel as Yahweh's "servant," "signet ring," and "chosen."[15] This eschatologization of mythic themes is one of the hallmarks of biblical apocalypticism,[16] and the influence exercised on the later development of Jewish apocalyptic by Haggai's application of royal/mythic themes to the early postexilic situation cannot be denied. For a related phenomenon, we now turn to a second example of the reapplication of royal tradition, namely, in the prophecy of Zechariah.

Though later redactors treated Haggai and Zechariah as "identical twins,"[17] a close reading of the two books gives no evidence that they took each other's mission or message into account. What is more, their messages appear to have been quite distinct from one another. Zechariah seemed to be more reticent than Haggai in making a public announcement that a messianic turn of events was about to be inaugurated specifically by Zerubbabel. Zerubbabel is mentioned by name only in Zech 4:6aβ–10a (four times!), a passage that is clearly intrusive (the angel's answer, introduced in Zech 4:4–6aα, is answered in 4:10b). Elsewhere, reference is made more obliquely to the "Branch" ($ṣemaḥ$ in Zech 3:8 and 6:12). This term, designating "royal heir" in Hebrew as well as in Phoenician, perhaps provided Zechariah with a more guarded means of proclaiming his eschatological message than would have been possible had he named Zerubbabel explicitly.

The major tradition upon which Zechariah drew stemmed from the program of the prophet Ezekiel, in which a restoration was envisioned led by a diarchy consisting of a Zadokite priest and a Davidic prince (Ezek 37:24–28; 43:18–27) and in which the former enjoyed the preeminent position, with the latter occupying a position within the second order of sanctity (Ezek 43:6–9; 46:18; 45:1–8). Zechariah, a prophet given to elaborate images and symbols, delineated his notion of a diarchy most clearly in the oracle in Zechariah 4, where a vision is described in which two olive branches flank the Temple lampstand as symbols of the two anointed ones, priest and prince, who were to preside over the nation as Yahweh's representatives. Though Zechariah seems to have exercised greater political restraint in his prophecies than Haggai—perhaps out of a more realistic view of the probable harsh response of the Persians to prophecies describing the meteoric rise of an explicitly named Davidic prince—it is clear that he was active within the same nationalistically charged environment as Haggai, to which he too responded in an eschatological mode by reformulating the priestly/royal tradition upon which he drew. The seven visions forming the core of his prophecy (the vision in Zechariah 3 was independent of this cycle of visions) picture a reconstituted Jewish community with Temple located veritably at the *omphalos mundi* and with the indwelling of Yahweh's glory assuring security and blessing.[18] As in the case of Haggai, the faith crisis precipitated by the failure of lofty hopes of restoration to materialize after the return of the exiles occasioned a prophetic response. To the question, "O Lord of hosts, how long wilt thou have no mercy on Jerusalem and the cities of Judah, against which thou hast had indignation these seventy years?" (Zech 1:12), the prophet brings Yahweh's impassioned reply:

I am exceedingly jealous for Jerusalem and for Zion. And I am very angry with the nations that are at ease; for while I was angry but a little they furthered the disaster. Therefore, thus says the Lord, I have returned to Jerusalem with compassion; my house shall be built in it. (Zech 1:14b–16a)

The "theology of glory *(kābôd)*" of the first Temple that had been cultivated by the Zadokite priests in the exile and that gave structure to Ezekiel's theology is here renewed:

Jerusalem shall be inhabited as villages without walls, because of the multitude of men and cattle in it. For I will be to her a wall of fire round about, says the Lord, and I will be the glory *(kābôd)* within her. (Zech 2:8b–9 [Eng. 2:4aβ–5])

The basic pattern of the Jerusalem royal theology is again clearly visible: rebuilding of the Temple, indwelling of Yahweh's glory, renewal of the blessing, and security of the land. Here, however, a development earlier discernible in Ezekiel[19] is abetted: The leadership position of the Zadokite priesthood, with its high priest at the head, waxes at the expense of the incumbent of the Davidic house.

This tendency is to be detected also in Zechariah 3, a chapter that seems to have been added as an introduction to the central vision of Zechariah's cycle of seven in Zechariah 4 in order to enhance the position of the priestly member of the diarchy, even as the interpolation in Zech 4:6aβ–10a seems to have been added to heighten the visibility of the Davidide within that same central vision. Without going into the question of the authorship of Zechariah 3, its function seems to have been that of defending the legitimacy and purity of the Zadokite high priest Joshua against charges perhaps relating to his having spent years in exile on pagan soil. None other than Satan is the accuser, and none other than Yahweh defends the priest! Vindicated and sanctified, the priest then receives from an angel this solemn charge: "If you will walk in my ways and keep my charge, then you shall rule my house and have charge of my courts, and I will give you the right of access among those who are standing here" (Zech 3:7). The loftiness of this promise is realized when it is understood that "those who are standing here" are Yahweh's heavenly attendants! The high priest's authority rests upon no less a basis than his being privy to Yahweh's council, a claim that was earlier the unique prerogative of the prophets (e.g., Isaiah 6 and Jer 23:21–22). For a brief moment, attention turns to the Davidide ("the Branch"), only to return to

Joshua, with whose office is tied the cleansing of the land and the return of paradisaical conditions to Judah (Zech 3:9–10), the latter being a concern that traditionally had fallen under the aegis of the king.

Zechariah thus bears witness to a stream of tradition in the early postexilic period that synthesized royal and priestly elements in a well-defined program of restoration and, for reasons no longer transparent to us, expanded the authority of the Zadokite priests so as to encompass areas earlier controlled by prophets and kings. The history of the growth and transmission of the Book of Zechariah thus gives us a glimpse of the development of the Jewish community from a diarchy under a Davidic prince and a Zadokite priest to a hierocracy under a Zadokite functioning as high priest.

This development is documented even more dramatically by another major biblical source, the Chronicler's History. Through the research of D. N. Freedman[20] and F. M. Cross[21], a new reconstruction of the history of that source has emerged, throwing valuable light on the question of the reapplication of antecedent tradition during the early postexilic period. In this case one can trace stages of development from a program supporting the reestablishment of monarchy under the Davidic house to one heralding the hierocracy under the high priest of the Zadokite house as the culmination of God's history with the Jewish people.

The promonarchical stage (Chr_1) consists of an early version of the genealogies in 1 Chr 1—9, 1 Chr 10—2 Chr 34, plus the *Vorlage* of 1 Esdras 1:1—3:13. Given its ideological predilection, it is not surprising to find Chr_1 drawing heavily upon the "Josianic" edition of the Deuteronomistic History (Dtr_1), a work that functioned in similar fashion in support of the Davidic house during its earlier renaissance in the latter half of the seventh century.[22] The reapplication of royal tradition (in this case in the form of the history of the house of David) and of the priestly tradition inextricably tied to the Solomonic Temple is thus comparable to the process of reapplying royal and priestly tradition which we have found in the late-sixth-century books of Haggai and Zechariah. It seems that we are dealing with several manifestations of the same restoration effort in which the career of Zerubbabel was viewed as the fulfillment of God's covenant with the Davidic house and as the occasion for the renewal of the institutions and practices established by God during the reigns of David and Solomon and valid by divine promise for all time. Freedman describes this "legitimate pattern of institutions and their personnel" as follows: "They are the monarchy represented by David and his house, the priesthood by Zadok and his descendents, the city and the temple in the promised land."[23]

The later editions of the Chronicler's work, which originated in the middle to late fifth century (Chr$_2$ consisting of Chr$_1$ plus the Aramaic source in Ezra 5:1—6:19 and the Ezra narrative beginning at Ezra 7:1, and Chr$_3$, in which the genealogies in 1 Chronicles 1—9 were brought up to date and the Nehemiah memoirs were added), give clear evidence of the eclipse of the Davidic leader and the exaltation of the Zadokite high priest to the position of preeminence within the Jewish community. Naturally, David and Solomon are established figures in the history that the final editors of the Chronicler's History continue to hand down, which makes all the more noteworthy the fact that their earlier function of legitimizing the reestablishment of the David house is deflected and redirected toward the priestly house of Zadok. In the added material, Zerubbabel's royal titles are dropped (Ezra 2:2; 3:2, 8; 4:2, 3; 5:2; Neh 7:7; 12:1, 47), even as the heroic tale exalting his wisdom and piety is suppressed (cf. 1 Esdr 3:1—5:2), as the focus moves squarely upon the Zadokite priesthood presiding over a people living under Persian rule. There is no hint any longer of hope for the restoration of an indigenous Davidic kingdom. To the contrary, the Persians are hailed as God's chosen rulers, for whom prayers are to be offered in the Temple and to whom obedience is to be paid in all civil matters in return for freedom to live a life of fidelity to the Torah of Moses (Ezra 1:1; 6:4, 22; 7:27–28; 9:9; Neh 2:8, 9, 18). Eschatological expectations have disappeared. As with the latest redactional stages of Ezekiel and Zechariah, we thus find reflected in these later stages of the Chronicler's History a fifth-century community that has moved—in part because of changed international circumstances—away from a royal Davidic model of community, and even beyond a model of a balanced royal-priestly diarchy, toward an exclusively priestly form of rule most accurately described as a hierocracy. We have entered the era in which the patrons of the Zadokite leaders were no longer the kings and princes of the house of David but the members of the imperial house of Persia.

Having examined writings within which royal traditions were reapplied to the changing circumstances of the early postexilic period, and having noted that in these writings one sees evidence for the enhancement of the Zadokite priesthood at the expense of the royal house of David, we turn next to ask whether there is evidence in the literature of this period for an appropriation of earlier tradition that was priestly in its orientation from the start.

The Reapplication of Priestly Tradition

The results of a major literary effort to reapply earlier priestly traditions associated with the Jerusalem Temple are found in the so-called Priestly Writing (the name used by scholars to designate the final stratum of the Pentateuch). Both in the way earlier materials were arranged and in the new theological framework into which such materials were placed, we witness a highly creative process of adapting beliefs and practices of the past to a radically changed situation.[24] In Genesis 1, the chaos originally at home in ancient cosmogonic myth was transformed into a vivid metaphor for the threatening new situation faced by the exiles, even as the efficacy of God's magisterial command in bringing forth out of chaos a harmonious created order offered them a firm basis upon which to build hope for their own future. The great heroes of the past, like Noah, Abraham, and Moses, became mediators of the signs and practices that formed the heart of Jewish identity in exile: covenant, circumcision, Sabbath, and the commandments. The wilderness wandering of the ancient ancestors of Israel became a poignant model for their own sojourn in a foreign land. Antecedent temple rituals of expiation and atonement were subjected to profound reinterpretation against the background of the recent tragic events and within the new exilic setting (e.g., Leviticus 16 and 17). Theological concepts such as God's *kābôd* ("glory") and God's "tenting" *(škn)* in the midst of Israel were reapplied as powerful conceptual resources for contemporizing God's abiding presence in a pagan land.[25] It is striking, moreover, how this comprehensive picture of the people of Israel is dominated through and through by the priesthood, with no hint of an envisioned role for a Davidic "prince" or "king."[26]

The hands of the priestly circles engaged in directing developments during the restoration period on the basis of antecedent priestly material are also to be detected in Zech 6:9–14. In what was originally an oracle celebrating the diarchy of priest and prince in the balanced manner characteristic of Zechariah, the present text betrays a rather crude textual surgery in which a place of equal honor has been denied Zerubbabel, resulting in the enhancement of the position of Joshua the high priest. Much speculation has poured into the attempt to explain this textual puzzle, out of which has emerged the likelihood that it reflects the efforts of the Zadokite priests to capitalize on the reversal suffered by the Davidides, perhaps due to Persian intervention brought about in response to what was perceived as a potentially dangerous resurgence of nationalism around the figure of Zerubbabel. Though the genealogy of the house of David continued to be compiled (cf. 1 Chronicles 3), the available evidence indicates that in the period between Zerubbabel and Nehemiah, Jewish governors of non-Davidic descent presided over the civil affairs of Judah.[27]

Ezekiel 44 gives us a further glimpse into the efforts of the Zadokites to consolidate power. Here the rivalry is not with the house of David but with the Levites. The end result, however, is the same, namely, the enhancement of Zadokite power though the diminution of the power of another group. On the basis of charges of apostasy (which seem to be without historical basis), the right of the Levites to offer sacrifices in the Temple is denied, with the result that they are consigned to duties of a lesser order.[28]

In Zechariah 6 and Ezekiel 44 we thus see a second distinct pattern of response to the harsh new realities of the early postexilic period gaining momentum. Both in response to power vacuums and in response to rival claims, the Zadokites moved to consolidate their own power until it became preeminent and in a position to fashion the future of the Jewish community in keeping with the contours of their priestly program.

As we search the literature of this period, we find traces of another group that was outmaneuvered by the Zadokites in the course of the latter's rise to preeminence. It consisted of those who drew upon the third complex of antecedent tradition cited in the introductory section of this chapter, namely, the writings of Israel's major prophetic figures.

The Reapplication of Prophetic Tradition

There is evidence that the energetic Zadokite reform movement encountered considerable opposition. In response to Haggai's oracles urging the rebuilding of the Temple under Davidic/Zadokite leadership came the protest that this effort was not divinely sponsored at all but rather was the result of human perversity and rebelliousness (Isaiah 57; 65; 66).[29] An alternative program was accordingly advanced, one repudiating the exclusive claims of the Zadokites and focusing on an incisive intervention by God that would miraculously transform both the Jewish community and its natural habitation, resulting in the acknowledgment of God's reign throughout the world and in the establishment of unblemished righteousness within a nation of priests (Isaiah 60—62). While circles close to the Davidic house were favoring royal traditions and the Zadokites were drawing on materials deriving from their own past, what we may call a visionary group found its closest affinities with early prophetic writings, especially those gathered under the name of the prophet Isaiah. In some cases, they were specific in reapplying the words of Second Isaiah to the crises of the early postexilic period.[30] They also found relevance in the genre favored above all others by the preexilic prophets, the judgment oracle, for as they surveyed the conditions prevailing in their community, it seemed apparent to them that theirs was a nation standing not under divine favor but continuing judgment. In their reapplication of that classical prophetic genre, the new situation left its mark, leading to the transformation of the judgment oracle into the

501

hybrid "salvation-judgment oracle," in which was announced simultaneously doom for the wicked and eschatological salvation for the righteous (e.g., Isaiah 59 and 65). On a deeper level, the prophetic message underwent significant transformation, for the restoration beyond judgment, which the classical prophets had conceived of mainly in historical terms, was envisioned increasingly with the aid of otherworldly categories, especially ones ultimately tracing back to ancient cosmogonic myth (e.g., Isa 59:15–20; 65:17; 66:15–16). This otherworldly tendency seemed to grow in direct relation to the disintegration of the life situation and social status of the dissident group.

We noted earlier that the eschatologization of ancient mythic themes pointing in the direction of later Jewish apocalypticism was evident in the oracles of Haggai and Zechariah, at the base of which development could be detected the experiences of bafflement, suffering, and ethical paradox resulting from the tragic events of the early sixth century B.C.E. This "proto-apocalyptic" tendency did not develop further within Zadokite circles in the remaining Persian period, but was arrested in large part because of a normalization of society and cult under their leadership with a concomitant alteration in their perception of the world. Such was not the experience of the visionaries. To the general hardships suffered by all Jews during this period was added the stinging experience of progressive marginalization within their own community. They sensed that they were losing a grip not only on the world situation but on the situation within their own community as well, as they were removed from positions of power and forced into the kind of disenfranchisement that historically has been the breeding ground of apocalyptic speculation. While the initial experimentation of the Zadokite group with apocalyptic forms and images gave way to a more pragmatic posture generally inhospitable to otherworldly speculation, the apocalyptic predilection of the visionaries was only strengthened by their experience of unmitigated hardship. This gave rise to a rather persistent stream of eschatological speculation that later resurfaced in the mature apocalyptic writings of the Seleucid period.

It is characteristic of the writings of the early postexilic period that the programmatic statements of various groups were not circulated independently under the name of their author but were embedded in writings that had already achieved a position of honor within the Jewish community. As the Zadokites advanced their cause by inserting into the Book of Ezekiel a polemical statement against the Levites (Ezekiel 44), so too the visionaries laid claim to the authority of Ezekiel by inserting Ezekiel 38—39. In so doing, they disputed the claim of the Zadokites that their implementation of the program formulated in Ezekiel 40—48 represented the fulfillment of God's promises to the Jewish community. By adding a vision of judgment outstripping the Babylonian invasion in horror, they proclaimed that Israel still stood within the era of divine wrath and that nothing less than direct divine intervention could remove obstacles of mythic dimensions and inaugurate the era of blessing envisioned by the prophet Ezekiel in chaps. 40—48.

A similar statement was made in the small anonymous collections of oracles entitled *maśśā' děbar yhwh* which in the course of transmission became attached to the collection of Zechariah's writings (Zechariah 9—11 and 12—14). Only after passing through awful trials and terrible judgments would a remnant of Israel be delivered by the divine warrior Yahweh and established in a realm portrayed in rather fully developed apocalyptic terms (cf. esp. Zechariah 14). Though the so-called Isaiah Apocalypse of Isaiah 24—27 offers little concrete evidence for its original setting, it seems to have originated in the early postexilic period within a similar climate of prophetic protest and apocalyptic speculation.[31]

The caution inserted at the beginning of this chapter regarding oversimplification of data in the attempt to detect streams of tradition in the early postexilic period must here be reiterated and amplified by way of an example. Zechariah 14 could serve as a clear illustration of a visionary formulation of the future, combining rather lofty apocalyptic themes with notions reflecting the concerns of priests (Zech 14:10–21). Even more dramatically, however, the Book of Malachi, which is another anonymous collection originally bearing the title *maśśā' děbar yhwh,* bears witness to a dissident group combining priestly and prophetic themes and concerns. The present writer earlier has argued that the interests of Levites combined with those of prophetic disciples in the oracles of Isaiah 56—66.[32] This is clearly the case also in the Book of Malachi. Though the concerns reflected are thoroughly priestly in nature, the attack on the presiding priesthood, that is, the Zadokite Temple priests, is scathing. And the denouement is envisioned in lofty eschatological terms. This combination of themes and concerns can be accounted for most felicitously by assuming that the Book of Malachi originated among dissident Levites who formulated their own position with the aid of an old tradition concerning God's covenant with Levi, a tradition that by antedating the one depicting a similar covenant with the Zadokites was useful as an argument in favor of the authoritative status of the Levites. Moreover, in their conflict with their Zadokite opponents, these Levites welcomed the support of visionaries who combined condemnation of existing institutions and leaders with visions of divine judgment and reversal. This solution seems preferable to the suggestion that the Book of Malachi results from the combination of two sources, one priestly and the other apocalyptic.

The Reapplication of Wisdom Tradition

As indicated by certain passages in Jeremiah (e.g., Jer 17:5–10, and quite generally the "confessions" of Jeremiah) and in Ezekiel (especially Ezekiel 18), the late seventh and early sixth century was a time of increased concern with the plight of the individual within a community beset with problems and existing in a threatening world. Though certain traditional concepts were stretched through such questioning, the basic retributive structure of thought remained intact, preserved by Ezekiel within the full apparatus of the Temple theology and by Jeremiah within a more critical prophetic structure of thought.

The perspective of the individual and the mood of questioning were pressed much farther in the Book of Job. Here the transformation of earlier tradition was accomplished by way of an appeal to both wisdom and prophetic themes, combined with a harsh critique of the traditional Temple theology and aspects of the royal theologumenon that continued to adhere to it. The end result was a unique readaptation of antecedent tradition that involved such a thoroughgoing transformation as to lead F. M. Cross to conclude: "Job brought the ancient religion of Israel to an end."[33] While this assessment has recently been challenged,[34] it is clear that traditional beliefs and assumptions were subjected to such a severe reexamination in Job as to leave a deep and lasting mark on the history of Israelite religion.

The effort to place the Book of Job within its historical setting must appeal to a rather broad typology of biblical religion in the absence of unambiguous linguistic or historical data. Specifically regarding its place within the wisdom tradition, it is important to note that the mood of preexilic Jewish sapiential writings is generally optimistic and life-affirming. This is as true of the earlier sections of the Book of Proverbs as it is of early narrative materials that scholars have assigned to wisdom circles, such as the Joseph story in the Book of Genesis. According to the world view pervading these writings, there underlies all of life's experiences a cosmic order that is dependable, assuring success to the righteous and judgment to the wicked (e.g., Proverbs 16). The task of the sage is to probe behind the variegated phenomena constituting human experience to the divine order that explains everything according to one all-encompassing and integrated system of justice. The basic retributive theologumenon underlying this world view is essentially the same as that upheld by the Priestly Writing and the Deuteronomistic History.

Against this background, the probing and questioning of traditional beliefs found in Job seems to be best explained on the assumption that, as in the case of similar self-examination within the other traditions we have examined, the experience of the catastrophe of 587 B.C.E. has raised for Israel's sages a hard, new set of questions. A difference in perspective is also to be noted: Whereas the other writings we have examined arose as a communal response to the experiences of deprivation, bafflement, and paradox, the Book of Job reveals the tortured soul of the individual seeking to make sense out of a world in which the righteous suffer and the wicked prosper. In the face of bitter contradictions and inexplicable paradoxes, the theme of the righteous sufferer found already in ancient Sumerian, Egyptian, Babylonian, and Canaanite sources becomes the suitable vehicle for arguing with God.

The heart of the crisis revolves around Job's refusal to allow his experiences to be forced into the interpretive framework of an orthodoxy that raised too many contradictions and left unanswered too many questions to remain viable for the honest believer (Job 8:3–7; 22:29–30). For Job, faith could be preserved only if inadequate human constructs were banished in favor of an experience of the transcendent God of ineffable mystery who evokes awe and worship, not in return for blessings bestowed, answers given, or puzzles solved, but out of the sheer fact of incomparable majesty and holiness. The conceptual idiom that proved to be appropriate for expressing this confession was one ultimately rooted in ancient mythology but long since integrated into Yahwistic faith, especially within Israel's hymns of worship and within the creation traditions. And the correspondence style that proved appropriate was one more interrogative than indicative in nature, and depending on a lavish use of irony and indirect statement.[35]

The danger accompanying the delineation of the retributive doctrine found in the Priestly Writing, the Deuteronomistic History, the Chronicler's History, and wisdom tradition that Yahwistic faith would become the privileged right of life's winners was incisively checked by Job's outcry and the transformation of tradition it set in motion. Religious faith was for the God-fearing, regardless of their earthly fortunes, for it relied not upon human proofs but upon encounter with holy transcendence (Job 38:1—42:6). This lofty view of religion did not, however, create a wider gulf between the believer and other human beings. For it fostered an awareness of God's majesty conducive of genuine humaneness, the kind of openness that reaches out to others out of a true sense of solidarity with all mortals (cf. Job 19:21–22).

After Job, wisdom writing would never return to its earlier optimism. It would remain dedicated to the search for the order underlying human existence and giving it meaning, but in that search it would be much more open to the ambiguity and contradiction that faces every human being, and especially the one facing crisis. Though the Book of Ecclesiastes is a clear example of this transformation, the transforming effect of the Book of Job was felt by wider circles as well in a period of considerable hardship in which the sagacious heirs to Israel's sapiential traditions came to play an increasingly influential role in the Jewish community.

CONCLUSION

The various streams of tradition that constituted the religious community of the Jews underwent considerable transformation in the wake of the Babylonian destruction of Jerusalem. As a result, there arose patterns of leadership, belief, and practice that, while maintaining distinct connections with traditions of the past, nevertheless in part inaugurated and in part pointed the way toward a new era. The early postexilic period is thus important not only in itself, and not only as a witness to the direction in which biblical tradition had moved, but also as indispensable background to understanding the religious movements and parties that would develop during the Hellenistic and Roman periods. For the shape of these parties, within both Judaism and Christianity, was in part adumbrated by princes, priests, visionaries, and sages of the Persian period as they sought both to be faithful to traditions received from the past and to adapt to new conditions within a rapidly changing world.

NOTES

1. See, e.g., 1 Sam 2:12–17, 22–25, 27–36.

2. C. Geertz, *The Interpretation of Cultures: Selected Essays* (New York: Basic Books, 1973) 99.

3. S. Langer, *Philosophy in a New Key* (4th ed.; Cambridge: Harvard University Press, 1960) 287.

4. L. Festinger, *A Theory of Cognitive Dissonance* (Stanford: Stanford University Press, 1953).

5. Geertz, *Interpretation of Cultures,* 100.

6. See S. B. Frost, "The Death of Josiah: A Conspiracy of Silence," *JBL* 87 (1968) 369–82.

7. Y. Talmon, "Pursuit of the Millennium: The Relation Between Religious and Social Change," *Archives européennes de sociologie* 3 (1962) 125–48.

8. N. Cohn, *The Pursuit of the Millennium* (New York: Oxford University Press, 1957).

9. Most recently, see J. Collins, *The Apocalyptic Imagination: An Introduction to the Jewish Matrix of Christianity* (New York: Crossroad Publishing Co., 1984).

10. P. D. Hanson, *The Dawn of Apocalyptic: The Historical and Sociological Roots of Jewish Apocalyptic Eschatology* (2d ed.; Philadelphia: Fortress Press, 1979.

11. Talmon, "Pursuit," 136.

12. This point has been made clearly by A. Y. Collins in an unpublished manuscript entitled "Apocalypse and Politics."

13. This mythologumenen lies at the heart of the monumental Babylonian text, the *Enūma eliš* (E. Speiser, *ANET*[3], 60–72).

14. See G. Anderson, "Sacrifices and Offerings in Ancient Israel: Studies in their Social and Political Importance" (unpublished diss., Department of Near Eastern Languages and Civilizations, Harvard University, 1985).

15. The contrast between Haggai's royal perspective and Jeremiah's earlier pronouncements on the Davidic house is sharp (cf. Jer 22:24 with Hag 2:23; see further S. Japhet, "Sheshbazzar and Zerubbabel—Against the Background of the Historical and Religious Tendencies of Ezra-Nehemiah," *ZAW* 77 [1965] and fn. 25).

16. See S. B. Frost, *Old Testament Apocalyptic: Its Origins and Growth* (London: Epworth Press, 1952); and idem, "Eschatology and Myth," *VT* 2 (1952) 70–80.

17. The final redactor who added the chronological framework to Haggai and Zechariah 1—7 has been identified by P. Ackroyd as the Chronicler ("Studies in the Book of Haggai," *JJS* 2 [1951] 163–76 and *JJS* 3 [1952] 1–13, and "The Book of Haggai and Zechariah I—VIII," *JJS* 3 [1952] 151–56). In Ezra 5:1, the two prophets are treated as one phenomenon.

18. P. D. Hanson, "In Defiance of Death: Zechariah's Symbolic Universe," *Love and Death* (ed. J. Marks; New Haven: Four Quarters Publishing, forthcoming).

19. Ezekiel's preference of the term *nāśî'* ("prince") rather than *melek* ("king") to designate the future Davidide has been understood correctly by critics as a reflection of Ezekiel's pro-priestly posture.

20. D. N. Freedman, "The Chronicler's Purpose," *CBQ* 23 (1961) 436–42.

21. F. M. Cross, "A Reconstruction of the Judean Restoration," *JBL* 94 (1975) 4–18, reprinted, with revisions, in *Interpretation* 29 (1975) 187–203.

22. Cross, *CMHE*, 274–89. Recent study has strengthened the conclusion that the Chronicler used the Dtr_1 edition of the Deuteronomistic History. Cf. S. L. McKenzie, *The Chronicler's Use of the Deuteronomistic History* (HSM 33; Atlanta: Scholars Press, 1984). Chr_1 exudes a deep interest in the Davidic monarchy, the Temple, and a unified Israel throughout. McKenzie has suggested to me in private communication that 2 Chronicles 23—24 even presents a diarchy of sorts, with Jehoiada directing Joash in obedience to the *tôrâ*, and with Joash straying from obedience after the death of Jehoiada.

23. Freedman, "Chronicler's Purpose," 196.

24. Cf. P. D. Hanson, *The People Called: The Growth of Community in the Bible* (New York and San Francisco: Harper & Row, 1986), chap. 7.

25. See Cross, *CMHE*, 293–325.

26. See W. Zimmerli, *Ezekiel* 2. 539–40.

27. The position advanced in 1934 by A. Alt ("Die Rolle Samarias bei der Entstehung des Judentums," reprinted in *Kleine Schriften zur Geschichte des Volkes Israel* II [Munich: C. H. Beck, 1953] 316–37), and subsequently widely held by scholars, has been convincingly refuted by N. Avigad, who on the basis of a thorough study of seals, bullae, and stamped jar handles of the early Second

Temple period as well as the evidence of the Books of Ezra and Nehemiah, has offered a plausible reconstruction of the non-Davidic Jewish governors beginning with Sheshbazzar and ending with Nehemiah. Avigad goes on to suggest that the jar handles stamped with *yhd* plus the names of the governors and their officers are from jars used in gathering wine from the populace as part of the system of heavy taxation referred to in Neh 5:15 (N. Avigad, *Bullae and Seals from a Post-exilic Judean Archive [Qedem* 4; Monographs of the Institute of Archaeology, Hebrew University; Jerusalem: Hebrew University, 1976] 1–36).

28. See·Hanson, *Dawn,* 263–69.

29. For a more complete discussion of the dissident group behind the oracles of Isaiah 56—66, see Hanson, *Dawn,* 32–208.

30. W. Zimmerli, "Zur Sprache Tritojesajas," in *Gottes Offenbarung* (Munich: Chr. Kaiser Verlag, 1963) 217–33.

31. W. R. Millar, *Isaiah 24—27 and the Origin of Apocalyptic* (HSM 11; Missoula, Mont.: Scholars Press, 1976). Whether the visionaries behind Isaiah 56—66, Ezekiel 38—39, Isaiah 24—27, Zechariah 9—11 and 12—14, and Joel were all members of one dissident movement is a difficult problem, and will not be discussed here. Much work remains in seeking to untangle the social-historical matrix of these and related writings of the postexilic period.

32. Hanson, *Dawn,* 94–96.

33. Cross, *CMHE,* 344.

34. J. G. Janzen, *Job* (Interpretation; Atlanta: John Knox Press, 1985).

35. J. G. Janzen, "The Place of the Book of Job in the History of Israel's Religion," chap. 28 in this volume.

27

The Persian Period and the Judean Restoration: From Zerubbabel to Nehemiah

ERIC M. MEYERS

The intention of this chapter is to sketch the broad outlines of the Judean restoration from the reign of Darius I (522–486 B.C.E.), to Artaxerxes I (465–424 B.C.E.). This period embraces several epochal events in the history of Israel.[1] The first of those is the response of the Babylonian exiles to the Edict of Cyrus (538 B.C.E.) that enabled many Judahites to return to their native Palestine, presumably some of them under the governor Sheshbazzar (cf. Ezra 5:14 with Ezra 1:8) but mostly under the governor Zerubbabel (Hag 1:1, 14), in 520 B.C.E. in what is usually called the Second Return to Yehud. This historic move coincided with the reign of Darius I, who upon consolidating his claim to the throne after the death of Cambyses (530–522 B.C.E.) devoted considerable effort to reorganizing the entire empire into satrapies. Such an understanding presupposed a common vision of the empire, and its success depended to a large extent upon the king's ability to implement those views.[2]

The second major event in Yehud that fundamentally affected the course of the Second Temple Judaism was the response of the Jewish leadership to the completely changed social circumstances that governed life in the early postexilic restoration period.[3] The dominant response that influenced at least the first generation after the Second Return in the reign of Darius I was a pragmatic and tolerant attitude toward Persian rule in the satrapy of Beyond the River.[4] This response is reflected best in the composite prophetic work intended for presentation at the dedication of the Second Temple in 516 or 515 B.C.E., Haggai and Zechariah 1—8. The first generation of civil leadership in Yehud culminated with the governorship of Elnathan (510–ca. 490 B.C.E.), who is associated with or married to Shelomith his *'āmāh* ("maidservant"), Davidic descendant and daughter of Zerubbabel (1 Chron 3:19).[5] In all, it is a period of approximately thirty years in which a high measure of stability is achieved and maintained in the empire by Darius I. It seems reasonable to suppose, despite a popularly held view to the contrary,[6] that a similar degree of internal stability was to be found in Yehud as well.

There must have been an enormous common effort to bring about such a stabilization within Yehud, on the part of both the Persian authorities and the Yehudite leadership. The postexilic economy was not strong, and bad crops and a lazy populace had impeded progress on the rebuilding of the Temple.[7] But the success of Haggai's and First Zechariah's ministries was such that this terrible situation was turned around and success achieved in time for the rededication of the Temple. The success of the rebuilding effort was not merely a response to these two prophets, it was also a testimony to the efficiency of the dyarchic rule of Joshua, the high priest, and Zerubbabel, the civil governor and descendant of the house of David.[8] It is quite probable, therefore, that the momentum of those successful years carried over into the next century, and to strengthen and consolidate the governor's claim to civil leadership, Elnathan married into the Davidic family and even assigned Shelomith substantial administrative responsibilities. The fate of the Davidic line after Shelomith is difficult to recover, but the presence of the Davidic genealogy in 1 Chron 3:17–24 indicates that it continues through the fifth century. Whether Zech 12:7–9 refers to a period following Elnathan and Shelomith in which the Davidic line is challenged by elements within Yehud is still a matter too difficult to ascertain with any degree of certainty.

What is clear to all students of the early Persian period, however, is that a high degree of uncertainty is imposed upon the territory of Yehud and the satrapy of Beyond the River immediately following the governorship of Elnathan. Indeed, events in the empire and in the eastern Mediterranean were such that instability and insecurity were very much the order of the day until the strong governorship of Nehemiah (445–433 B.C.E.). The first of these events occurred in the year of Darius's death, 486 B.C.E., when Egypt attempted to break away from the control of the empire. Xerxes I, Darius's successor, in order to suppress the burgeoning revolt had to pass through the coastal territories of Beyond the River. A report in Ezra 4:6 notes that Xerxes received a written accusation directed against the population of Judea and Jerusalem. Although the late J. Morgenstern laid great emphasis on this as a pivotal moment in Jewish history, nothing more is known about this affair.[9] What is most significant is that the notice in Ezra coincides with this first sign of Egyptian rebellion. It is possible that Xerxes dealt with the matter en route to Egypt. In any case, Persian control over Egypt was resecured by 483 B.C.E.

In 482 B.C.E. the Babylonians rebelled and murdered their satrap Zopyrus. The king's brother-in-law, Megabyzus, was sent to crush the rebellion and to inflict severe punishment.[10] The Persians removed the estates from the nobles and took them over for their own use. As a result, Beyond the River was separated from Mesopotamia and became an independent administrative unit in that same year. Megabyzus was ultimately appointed satrap sometime prior to 456 B.C.E., and was later involved in another rebellion on the eve of Nehemiah's mission in 445 B.C.E.

The most serious uprising to affect the relative quiet of Yehud, however, was the Egyptian revolt of 460 B.C.E.[11] On this occasion Egypt enjoyed the support of the Athenian fleet. The new alliance sent shock waves throughout the western provinces and undoubtedly set in motion a series of countermoves in Persia that were designed to prevent the secession of Egypt from the empire and to check the expansion of Athens into the eastern Mediterranean. Persia had had its difficulties with the Greeks when the Greek cities of Asia Minor had broken away from Persian control from 500 to 494 B.C.E. In 490 B.C.E. the Athenians bested the Persians at the Battle of Marathon; Xerxes I (486–465 B.C.E.) unsuccessfully attempted to bring the Greek states under Persian control in the years following.[12]

It is no wonder that Persia by the mid-fifth century was embarked upon an administrative policy vis-à-vis the coastal territories that tended to reverse the more liberal policies implemented by Darius I or even Cyrus the Great earlier. Moreover, Palestine underwent a fairly extensive period of fortification to shore up Persian control of the important lines of communication.[13] It is hard to imagine that events and circumstances of such magnitude did not impact greatly on the community in Yehud. Indeed, Ezra's words in the prologue to the reaffirmation of the covenant in the Book of Nehemiah testify to just how greatly conditions had changed since the days when Zerubbabel was governor: "Behold, we are slaves this day; in the land that you gave to our fathers to enjoy its fruit and its good gifts, behold, we are slaves! And its rich yield goes to the kings whom you have set over us because of our sins; they have power over our bodies and over the cattle at their pleasure, and we are in great distress" (Neh 9:36–37). The rebuilding of the walls of Jerusalem by Nehemiah must also be viewed within the larger context of the tightening of Persian controls in the area and of the building of a series of fortifications along the major arteries linking the coast with the inland territories.[14]

A strong case thus can be made that the political fortunes of Yehud in the restoration era had changed dramatically merely seventy years after the rededication of the Second Temple (515–445 B.C.E.). We have suggested that whatever accommodation with Persian rule was achieved by the high priest Joshua and Zerubbabel the governor, it already began to become unraveled by 485 B.C.E. when the first serious threat of rebellion in Egypt seems to have impinged on Palestinian consciousness.

It is quite clear that Palestinian feelings had to be placated to a considerable degree during the early restoration period just prior to the successful Temple rebuilding effort that culminated in 515 B.C.E. More than any other factor, the absence of any realistic opportunity to reinstate the office of kingship necessitated a basic readjustment of attitudes. Both the prophets Haggai and First Zechariah presuppose the hegemony of Persian authorities in all local affairs and never question the appropriateness of the office of governor or high priest.[15] The same is true in Ezra. In other words, there seems to be a complete readiness to accept the apparent largesse of a Persian government that had earlier authorized the return of the exiles to their homeland and the rebuilding of their religious sanctuary. Not only did Second Isaiah welcome the period of return about to begin but he assigned to Cyrus, sponsor of the Edict of Return in 538 B.C.E., the ultimate sign of approval, referring to him as "shepherd" and "messiah," Yahweh's special instrument of deliverance.[16]

The internal adjustments that had to be made by the Judahite community in exile and consequently in Yehud were few but very significant. The Persian authority, perhaps recognizing the seriousness of the loss of kingship in Israel, appointed a governor of the royal house of David. Moreover, the Yehudites, recognizing the unique opportunity, reinstituted the title of high priest to designate the chief officer of the Temple hierarchy who was to rule alongside the governor. The prophetic vision of Zechariah 3 best expresses symbolic support of the expanded powers that the high priest came to enjoy in the restoration when Joshua is granted access to the heavenly council (Zech 3:7). A concomitant of a strong high priest was the diminution, at least by First Zechariah, of the role of the Davidic scion, who is relegated to an eschatological status (Zech 3:3; 4:6b–10a; 6:12). The attitude of the prophet is that the Davidic line will be reestablished at a future time of God's choosing, but for the meantime a Davidic governor—possibly groomed for the job in the court of Darius I[17]—was thought to be sufficient evidence of Persian goodwill and Yehudite aspirations.

It is not surprising, then, that the high priest and not the Davidic governor becomes the principal actor in the drama of Temple refoundation presented in Zechariah 3 and 6:9–15. Yehudite hopes for the restablishment of the monarchy are thrust into an undefined and uncertain future, though a dyarchic pattern of local leadership within the Persian administrative system is reaffirmed in Zech 6:9–15. A certain difference in emphasis on this point may be noted in the books of Haggai and Zechariah 1–8. Haggai, whose career falls more closely in time to the period of the beginning of Darius's rule, when rebellion and problems of succession plagued him in 522 B.C.E.,[18] reflects a more heightened eschatology, especially in his final oracle, Hag 2:20–23. He repeatedly uses Zerubbabel's name and refers to his office as governor. Zechariah, however, utilizes Zerubbabel's name without mention of office and only in the Oracular Insertion (Zech 4:6b–10a).[19]

In neither book, however, is there any sense that the present order is about to break down. Although Haggai's final oracle is often thought to reflect a renewed sense of Davidic messianism, I believe that it refers to a future time, one not able to be realized in the present or in the immediate future. Indeed, Haggai not only is caught up in the present by encouraging and exhorting his fellow Yehudites to go about their work on the Temple but he utilizes a priestly ruling (Hag 2:10–14) to do so and to elaborate on the moral dimensions of sanctity and defilement. By making reference to an active priesthood in his day and through utilization of a prophetic question and answer Haggai presages a new role for the postexilic prophet, one that is drawn more and more closely to the priesthood.[20]

For First Zechariah, society has already begun to be transformed and revitalized. Progress on the rebuilding of the Temple is so far along that he provides symbolic, prophetic legitimization to the ceremony of refoundation that marked the beginning of the new era (Zech 3:9 and 4:10). He also further elaborates upon the new and expanded powers of the high priest (Zech 3:7). Although the construction of a temple without dynastic sponsorship ran counter to centuries of Israelite practice when Davidic leadership was associated with it and counter to the general integration of temple and palace in the political states of the ancient world, Zechariah's visions and oracles provide the necessary religious and symbolic justification for a Yehud with a temple and without a king.

It is possible that Darius's attempts to have the laws of conquered Persian territories codified manifested itself in First Zechariah in several ways.[21] Zechariah's vision of the flying scroll (Zech 5:1–4) no doubt refers to the authoritative Law of the Covenant. His repeated reference to the authority of the words of earlier prophets (e.g., Zech 7:7, 12) and his utilization and assumption of the existence of the Primary History (Genesis—2 Kings) both reaffirm what is commonly held to be axiomatic in biblical scholarship, namely, that the sixth century is a critical period in the development of the Old Testament canon. Indeed, it is possible that Persian encouragement to codify laws in the provinces could well have been the impetus to combine Zechariah 1—8 with Haggai into a single composite piece that was probably intended for presentation at the rededication ceremony of the Second Temple. Both prophets of the early restoration era then undertook to guide the Yehudite community through one of the most difficult transitions in their history, and the redactor or editor of the composite work Haggai and Zechariah 1—8 organized the two prophetic works as if they were a single literary piece that would serve as a showpiece of the Temple rededication ceremony.[22] The new Persian administrative machinery had assured that Yehud's world was to be one fundamentally different from the one in which classical prophecy had emerged, one in which monarchy had played so central a role. Haggai and First Zechariah accept, present, and justify that situation to their fellow Jews.

The consensus forged in the early years of the restoration assured not only the survival but the vitality of Judaism in the Second Temple period. Indeed, it is the prophets Haggai and First Zechariah who are credited in rabbinic literature with transmitting biblical religion into the hands of the men of the Great Assembly.[23] That claim is surely not justified on historical grounds but does give credibility to the significant role they played in history. I am not convinced that the so-called followers of Second Isaiah who articulated an alternative visionary view of the future can be securely dated to this narrowly restricted time frame or that anything in either Haggai or First Zechariah clearly can be related to social contention.[24]

In my opinion, it is still too soon to date all books in the prophetic corpus with precision. I am convinced that Trito-Isaiah (Isaiah 56—66) should be dated to the early Persian period along with Deutero-Zechariah, Malachi, and Joel. I am also convinced that the social circumstances they reflect are vastly changed from the ones presupposed by Haggai and Zechariah 1—8. Whether or not any of them or all of them reflect the repercussions of the first serious hints of rebellion in the Persian empire and the changed social circumstances that might have resulted from those developments is simply too difficult to say at this time. It seems useful, however, to examine in some further detail the conditions that led to Nehemiah's mission in 445 B.C.E. with a view toward understanding features common to some of these biblical works. Those elements would include the problem of mixed marriages and the corruption of the priesthood (Mal 2:1–4, 10–16; 1:7–10; 3:8), the future of the Davidic line (Zech 11:15–16; 12:7–8), a deterioration in the economy of Yehud (Joel 1—2; Isa 58:3–4; 59:6, 9–15), and an increasing lack of confidence in prophecy itself (Mal 3:22–24 = RSV 4:4–6; Zech 10:2; 13:2–6) together with a focusing upon a final eschatological day [25] or divine warrior language.[26] Though this by no means constitutes an exhaustive list of themes and motifs in the last books of the prophetic corpus, it does suggest the range of social and religious problems that could have surfaced by the second quarter of the fifth century B.C.E.

Shortly after Artaxerxes I (465–424 B.C.E.) became king of Persia, the satrapy of Beyond the River was administered by the king's brother-in-law Megabyzus, who was sent by the king to quell the Egyptian rebellion. In this endeavor he enjoyed the full support of the Phoenician fleet. The situation in nearby Cyprus is not quite clear, and despite a struggle between the Greek and the Phoenician cities on the island, Cyprus appears to stay within the Persian empire.[27] Upon return to Persia from Egypt, Megabyzus was greatly angered at the harsh policies of the king toward the Egyptian prisoners and returned to his own satrapy of Beyond the River, where he declared a new revolt against the Persian monarch.[28] After at least two known major battles the revolt ended and Megabyzus was reconciled to the king.[29] He undoubtedly was forced to give up the administration of his satrapy, however.

These tumultuous events coincide with events reported in Ezra 4:7–23. Although the material in Ezra 3—5 has been incorporated into the canon in a very awkward arrangement—the letter from Shimshei and Rehum to Artaxerxes comes before the report of the recommencement of work on the Temple in the second year of Darius I (Ezra 4:24)—it nonetheless appears to preserve reliable information from this period. The officials of the satrapy of Beyond the River make the following accusation: The Jews who had come up from Persia to Jerusalem are rebuilding that "wicked" and "rebellious" city (Ezra 4:12), a city that had a long history of revolt against the monarchy (Ezra 4:19). Furthermore, the text goes on to say, rebellion and strife had long been rife in the city in which powerful kings had ruled, exercising authority over the whole province of Beyond the River in at least fiscal affairs (Ezra 4:20).

The question is whether or not this letter of the officials of Beyond the River in Ezra refers to a truly indigenous revolt in the province of Yehud or simply to the aftermath of Megabyzus's brief engagement with Artaxerxes, suggesting perhaps that he had used Jerusalem to support his cause. The consequences of either the Egyptian revolt or the rebellion of Megabyzus in any event are certainly reflected in the vividness of the report in Nehemiah regarding the broken walls of Jerusalem and its burnt gates (Neh 1:3). At the conclusion of the reading of the reply of King Artaxerxes' letter to Rehum and Shimshei a delegation is sent to Jerusalem to halt work on the Jerusalem fortification (Ezra 4:23). What business the Yehudites had in mid-fifth century undertaking such a venture remains a puzzle yet to be answered. Were the Yehudites declaring their intention to follow suit and declare their independence from Persian authority? Was there a kind of messianic uprising in Yehud that evoked a counterresponse from other Jews in the province (Zech 12:7ff.)?

We have suggested above that the mission of Nehemiah to rebuild the walls of Jerusalem in 445 B.C.E., coming armed with title of governor of the province of Yehud and in the face of opposition from the neighboring governors, may be interpreted as part of a larger Persian effort to fortify the routes to the coastal lands and Egypt.[30] The inclusion of Jerusalem and other Judean highland sites in a list of possible Persian military outposts most probably has to do with providing a secondary route south through Palestine in the event that the Greeks might cut off the coastal route. This could well have been a live concern if the Athenians had established a foothold by this time at Dor. If a renewed and vigorous effort at Persian militarization can be documented for the mid-fifth century, then it is not difficult to imagine how many foreigners and mercenaries were required to hold these stations. It is also possible to imagine that the presence of so many foreigners led to a good deal of intermarriage, as it had in times past.

Most scholars[31] have explained Nehemiah's actions on the basis of having to establish a loyal following in Palestine at a critical juncture in time, a motivation that had always inspired neighbors of Palestine to woo their support. But Nehemiah's activities in Jerusalem are a bit too elaborate for such a theory to suffice. Nehemiah requested a royal subvention not only to rebuild the walls of the city but also to construct the "fortress" (Neh 2:8; cf. 7:2, where Hanani is called "governor of the fortress"). The Hebrew term for "fortress" (*bîrâ*) is derived from Akkadian *bîrtu* and always has a military context; and Nehemiah is accompanied by military personnel (Neh 2:9) who are involved in the rebuilding process.[32] In short, it seems more reasonable to assume that Nehemiah's mission is part and parcel of a much larger Persian effort to militarize and fortify the major lanes to the west, with Jerusalem representing a critical point in controlling a secondary route south through the Judean highlands.

If we have endeavored to use Ezra and Nehemiah to fill in some of the gaps prior to the mission of Nehemiah, what has emerged from this presentation is that Yehud, at least from 460 B.C.E. and possibly as early as 485 B.C.E., was in constant turmoil because of major disturbances in the satrapies of Egypt and Beyond the River. Ezra's mission in 458 B.C.E. was most probably motivated by the Egyptian revolt in 460 B.C.E. By the time Nehemiah is authorized to go to Jerusalem, the Persian empire had apparently been forced to strengthen its direct presence in some of the territories, reversing a policy of self-rule that had marked the beginning of the Second Temple period for Yehud. Although this view seems to contradict that of E. Stern and others who want to place the beginning of limited Yehudite autonomy in the era of Nehemiah, I believe both the biblical sources and the archaeological data suggest an earlier date in the time of Zerubbabel.[33]

It is unfortunate that our prophetic sources for this era are so difficult to date and so obscure in content. The use of chronological headings, which is so characteristic of Haggai and Zechariah 1—8, is entirely lacking in Trito-Isaiah, Deutero-Zechariah, Malachi, and Joel. The disappointment, reflected in these works, in the management of the Temple cult no doubt comes about as a result of Persia's increasing dependency on Yehud as an ally or friendly province in times when the western provinces were either in danger of leaving the empire or falling under Greek control. It is not difficult to imagine how the office of high priest, so greatly strengthened in the days of Joshua and Zerubbabel, especially in fiscal affairs, became ever more closely involved in state affairs. By the time Nehemiah comes, however, the office of governor has apparently been strengthened once again. Throughout the entire Persian period one may observe a shifting pattern in the relationship between ecclesiastical and secular control of Yehud. A high point in ecclesiastical rule was certainly the high priesthood of Joshua. The fact that both Ezra and Nehemiah have so much to do with religious affairs suggests that ecclesiastical rule in the first half of the fifth century had not been successful.

The last of the prophetic writings thus provide indirect testimony to the changing fortunes of the high priesthood and to the profound social upheaval that resulted from tensions in the Persian empire. The difficulties which the Persian empire had to face at this time could well have spawned a renewed, awakening sense of the need for independence in Yehud—as well as an enlivened commitment to the house of David. Despite these forces and despite a strong assimilationist trend which was effected through intermarriage, there were always voices around to caution their fellowmen. It may well be that we will never be able to make complete sense of the seventy years from Zerubbabel to Nehemiah, but in many ways they were as much a crucible as the seventy years from the beginning of exile to the rebuilding of the Temple (Zech 1:12; 7:5).

NOTES

1. For the most recent general review of Jewish history in the Persian period one must consult W. D. Davies and L. Finkelstein's *The Cambridge History of Judaism*, vol. 1: *Introduction: The Persian Period* (Cambridge: Cambridge University Press, 1984). Of special interest in this volume are the two essays of E. Stern, "The Persian Empire and the Political and Social History of Palestine in the Persian Period," 70–87, and "The Archaeology of Palestine," 88–114. For a

fuller treatment of the archaeology of this period, see E. Stern's *Material Culture of the Land of the Bible in the Persian Period, 538–332 B.C.* (Warminster, England: Aris & Phillips, 1982).

2. A fresh and exciting treatment of Darius I may be found in the excellent volume of J. M. Cook, *The Persian Empire* (London: J. M. Dent and Sons, 1983) 67–90.

3. Many of the views presupposed in this chapter are based on my forthcoming work with C. L. Meyers in the Anchor Bible, *Haggai and Zechariah 1—8: A New Translation with Introduction and Commentary* (Garden City, N.Y.: Doubleday & Co., 1987).

4. A. Rainey's article ("The Satrapy 'Beyond the River,'" *AJBA* 1 [1969] 51–78) is still the best English-language essay on the subject. A more recent version of it has just appeared in Hebrew, "The Province of Eber Nahara," 105–16, *The World History of the Jewish People: The Restoration—The Persian Period* (ed. H. Tadmor et al.; Jerusalem: Am Oved Publishers, 1984). Rainey also has let me read the English version of that article which is scheduled for the translation of that volume.

5. E. M. Meyers, "The Shelomith Seal and the Judean Restoration: Some Additional Considerations," *Eretz Israel* 18 (1985).

6. I refer to P. D. Hanson's influential work, *The Dawn of Apocalyptic: The Historical and Sociological Roots of Jewish Apocalyptic Eschatology* (Philadelphia: Fortress Press, 1975). His reconstruction of postexilic history has more to do, in my opinion, with the fifth century than with the sixth century. I am much indebted to him for stimulating much of my thinking despite the fact that we have come to different conclusions.

7. See esp. Hag 1:6–11.

8. It is clear that we may now reconstruct the list of governors from Cyrus to Artaxerxes I with a high degree of probability. Based on N. Avigad's reconstruction, which is published in *Qedem* 4 of the Hebrew University Institute of Archaeology Monograph Series, *Bullae and Seals from a Post-exilic Judean Archive* (Jerusalem: Hebrew University, 1976), we may propose the following: Sheshbazzar, 538–520 B.C.E. (*phh*, Ezra 5:14; "prince," Ezra 1:8); Zerubbabel, 520–510? B.C.E. (*pht yhwdh*, Hag 1:1, 14); Elnathan, 510–490? B.C.E. (*phw',* bulla and seal; Shelomith, *'āmāh* of Elnathan, b. ca. 545 B.C.E.); Yehoʿezer 490–470? B.C.E. (*phw',* jar impression); Ahzai, 470–? B.C.E. (*phw',* jar impression); Nehemiah, 445–433 B.C.E. (*hphh*, Neh 5:14; 12:26). Although we can reconstruct the high priesthood with some degree of probability, without the kind of archaeological support we have for the governor list we must regard it as only tentative: Joshua, b. ca. 570; Joiakim, b. ca. 545; Eliashib I, b. ca. 545; Johanan I, b. ca. 520; Eliashib II, b. ca. 495; Joiada I, b. ca. 470. Cf. F. M. Cross, "A Reconstruction of the Judean Restoration," *JBL* 94 (1975) 17.

9. J. Morgenstern, "Jerusalem—485 B.C.," *HUCA* 27 (1956) 101–79; *HUCA* 28 (1957) 15–47; *HUCA* 31 (1960) 1–29; and idem, "Further Light from the Book of Isaiah Upon the Catastrophe of 485 B.C.," *HUCA* 37 (1966) 1–28.

10. A. T. Olmstead, *History of the Persian Empire* (Chicago: University of Chicago Press, 1948) 237 n. 23. Olmstead's reconstruction is based on Ctesias, *Pers.* Epit. 52–53.

11. A. R. Burn, *Persia and the Greeks: The Defense of the West 546–478 B.C.* (New York: Minerva Press, 1962) 5–16. See also Olmstead, *History,* 289–90, and Cook, *The Persian Empire,* 127.

12. E. Bresciani, "Egypt and the Persian Empire," *The Greeks and the Persians from the Sixth to the Fourth Centuries* (ed. H. Bengtson; New York: Delacorte Press, 1968) 339–40. The Greeks apparently also had intentions on Cyprus in 460 B.C.E. (Burn, *Persia and the Greeks,* 560).

13. For example, the residency at Lachish is to be dated to 450 B.C.E., a date proposed by O. Tufnell, *Lachish III: The Iron Age* (London: Oxford University Press, 1953) 279 and reconfirmed by D. Ussishkin, "The Destruction of Lachish by Sennacherib and the Dating of the Royal Judean Storage Jars," *Tel Aviv* 4 (1977) 38–39. We suggest below that Nehemiah's repair of the walls and "fortress" or citadel of Jerusalem is also to be understood in this context. Other mid-fifth-century sites would include stratum IV at Beth Yerah, Megiddo Area C Stratum I, Meṣad Ha-Yarkon, Ashdod, Tel el-Ḥesi, Tell Jemmeh, Tell el-Farah, South (Sharuhen), Tel el-Ful, Ramat Rahel, Phase I of the citadel of Beth-Zur, and Khirbet Abu Twain. This is only a partial listing of sites that seem to be fortified in the fifth century and that conceivably date after the 460 Egyptian revolt. A systematic survey of this evidence is being undertaken by K. Hoglund of Duke University as part of a dissertation on the Persian period directed by the author.

14. One should not underestimate the fear of Greece on the part of the Persians in the fifth century. The Athenian tribute lists of 454/53 B.C.E. list a "Dor" which may have been part of the Delian League which might well have served as an outpost for Athenian ships involved in the Egyptian and Cypriote revolts. On this point, see B. D. Merritt et al., *The Athenian Tribute Lists* (Princeton: American School of Classical Studies at Athens, 1939–53) 1:483, 3:10–11. M. Smith, *Palestinian Parties and Politics That Shaped the Old Testament* (New York: Columbia University Press, 1971) 391–92 has argued that the fear of a potential alliance between Jerusalem and Athens is what motivated the Persians to support Ezra's return to Jerusalem. Whether or not Dor was a Greek outpost at this time may well be answered by the new excavations undertaken there by E. Stern of the Hebrew University.

15. I am in basic agreement with Rainey ("The Satrapy 'Beyond the River' ") that Yehud constituted a subprovince of the larger satrapy of Beyond the River and was administered by a *peḥâ* ("governor"). See an extended discussion of this in C. L. Meyers and E. M. Meyers, *Haggai and Zechariah 1—8,* Note to "governor" in Hag 1:1. The term "high priest" is also extensively discussed here in the Note to *hakkohēn haggādôl.*

16. A cautionary note of the benign quality of Persian rule has been sounded by A. Kuhrt, "The Cyrus Cylinder and Achaemenid Imperial Policy," *JSOT* 25 (1983) 83–97. Zechariah's vision, The Four Horns and the Four Smiths (Zech 2:1–4; RSV 1:18–21), also suggests that the Persians could instill a great deal of fear also.

17. So Cook, *The Persian Empire,* 48–49, 71.

18. Much discussion has traditionally been focused upon the accession problems of Darius I and the degree to which they influenced the Book of Haggai and First Zechariah. Although Darius had quelled all opposition by 522 B.C.E. (Cook,

The Persian Empire, 50–55), the revolt in Babylon continued until 521. The earliest chronological marker in the Haggai–Zechariah 1—8 corpus is 29 August, 520 (Hag 1:1), and to my mind that is late enough to argue that not only was Darius I fully in control but also the reorganization of the provinces was well along, an activity that can be understood of a monarch who is fully in charge of his territories. Cf. the view of J. Blenkinsopp, *A History of Prophecy in Israel* (Philadelphia, Westminster Press, 1983) 231 and 244.

19. It is curious that Zerubbabel's name occurs with patronymic in Zech 4:6, 7, 9, 10. Of its seven occurrences in Haggai only two of them lack the patronymic, ben-Shealtiel. There is a good deal of confusion in the sources about Zerubbabel's lineage because of the mention in 1 Chron 3:19 that he is descended from Pedaiah. It would seem, however, that he is the nephew or brother of Sheshbazzar governor of Yehud in 538 B.C.E. For a fuller discussion of this question, see Meyers and Meyers, *Haggai and Zechariah 1—8,* Note to "Zerubbabel ben-Shealtiel" in Hag 1:1.

20. So E. M. Meyers, "The Use of Torâ in Haggai 2:11 and the Role of the Prophet in the Restoration Community," *The Word of the Lord Shall Go Forth: Essays in Honor of David Noel Freedman in Celebration of His Sixtieth Birthday* (ed. C. L. Meyers and M. O'Connor; Winona Lake, Ind.: Eisenbrauns, 1983) 69–76.

21. So Cook, *The Persian Empire,* 71. Plato refers to Darius I as the great lawgiver, and Olmstead (*History,* 119–34) credits him with the establishment of a penal law code. In Egypt, Darius ordered Aryandes to set up a commission to collect and codify laws, and within sixteen years they were codified on papyrus and published in Egyptian demotic and Aramaic. It is likely that Darius's efforts in the provinces in this area also touched Yehud, where we can imagine that the Primary History underwent further refinement and that other sacred writings, notably the prophets, were collected and organized.

22. This view is a novel one not previously published to the best of my knowledge. A detailed justification for this assumption is presented in the introduction to Meyers and Meyers, *Haggai and Zechariah 1—8.* D. L. Petersen's recent commentary treats Haggai as a "brief apologetical historical novel" and Zechariah as a theological statement of the renewal of life in postexilic Yehud with the Temple at its center. See D. L. Petersen, *Haggai and Zechariah 1—8,* (Philadelphia: Westminster Press, 1984) passim.

23. *Soṭah* 486; *Yoma* 9b; *Sanhedrin* 11a; *'Abot de Rabbi Nathan* 1. On the end of prophecy, see Y. Kaufmann, *History of the Religion of Israel* (New York: KTAV Publishing House, 1977) 4. 450–51.

24. Cf. Blenkinsopp, *A History of Prophecy,* 225–67, and Hanson, *Dawn,* passim.

25. Blenkinsopp, *A History of Prophecy,* 261ff.

26. Hanson, *Dawn,* 292ff.

27. Cook, *The Persian Empire,* 127–28. The Greek's major victory was won at Salamis against Phoenician and Cilician forces, but the Athenians did not have the will to fight further.

28. Cook, *The Persian Empire,* 169. There is no independent confirmation of this secondary revolt outside of Ctesias, *Pers.* Epit., 68–70. Since Megabyzus is

credited in Diodorus as commanding the forces opposing the Greek assault on Cyprus in 450 B.C.E., one should be skeptical about the reliability of this account. Stern ("The Persian Empire," 73) maintains that Megabyzus together with Arsames, satrap of Egypt, destroyed the Athenian fleet in Cyprus that had unsuccessfully besieged Kition and Salamas.

29. Ctesias mentions that Megabyzus was supported by his two sons Zopyrus and Artyphius. One force directed against him was led by an Egyptian named Usiris and the other was commanded by the Persian, Menostanes, the king's brother and satrap of Babylon.

30. See in this regard the helpful article of M. Dunand, "La défense du front méditerranéen de l'empire achemenide," *The Role of the Phoenicians in the Interaction of Mediterranean Civilizations* (ed. A. Ward; Beirut: American University of Beirut, 1967) 43–51.

31, For example, P. R. Ackroyd, *Israel Under Babylon and Persia* (London: Oxford University Press, 1970) 175–78, and G. Widengren, "The Persian Period," *Israelite and Judean History* (ed. J. H. Hayes and J. M. Miller; Philadelphia: Westminster Press, 1977) 528–29.

32. Our discussion has presupposed the traditional ordering of the canonical books. We believe it to be proper and defensible despite the debate on the subject. On this point, see Ackroyd, *Israel,* 191–96; M. Smith, *Palestinian Parties,* 120–23; and H. H. Rowley, *The Servant of the Lord* (3d ed.; Oxford: Basil Blackwell, 1965) 135–68. Our view that Ezra's mission comes as a direct response to the Egyptian uprising is supported by Blenkinsopp (*A History of Prophecy,* 244) and inter alia by Rainey (see above n. 4).

33. Stern's views (*Material Culture,* 237 and inter alia) support the traditional view of A. Alt, who maintained that Yehud was annexed to Samaria after the Babylonian conquest and that it enjoyed very limited autonomy until the visitation of its first true governor, Nehemiah. Cf., however, Avigad, *Bullae and Seals,* 33, and nn. 125–26; M. Smith, *Palestinian Parties,* 193–201; and Widengren, 509–11. See also a recent supporter of Stern, S. McEvenue, "The Political Structure in Judah from Cyprus to Nehemiah," *CBQ* 43 (1981) 353–64. I support Avigad's position of relative autonomy for Yehud in the early restoration but reserve judgment on the precise character of the province in relation to Beyond the River. For the time being I am content to use Rainey's term "subprovince" to describe the status of Yehud in the time of Zerubbabel.

28

The Place of the Book of Job in the History of Israel's Religion

J. GERALD JANZEN

I.

By and large, studies of the Book of Job have situated this book primarily with reference to the sort of theology represented in the Book of Deuteronomy and, in a wider context, the sort of questioning of theology represented in Mesopotamia in *Ludlul bêl nêmeqi* and in the Babylonian Theodicy. But the contrast between Deuteronomy and Job provides much too narrow and static a basis for analysis within the Israelite context; and reference simply to the two above-mentioned Mesopotamian works, without consideration of the respective history of religion contexts, likewise is too narrowly focused. Recently T. Jacobsen and F. M. Cross have indicated much more comprehensively the proper context for our assessment both of how Job is to be interpreted and of the place of Job in the history of ancient Near Eastern religions.[1]

Jacobsen's comment on Job comes in the context of his characterization of three millennia of religious understanding in terms of three fundamental metaphors for the gods: (1) the gods as powers immanent in the phenomena of nature, powers willing to come to specific form as the phenomena (fourth millennium); (2) the gods as royal divine figures transcending nature and society, creating nature as a complex artifact and humankind as slaves of the gods, and ruling nature and society by the display of "absolute power . . . selfish, ruthless, and unsubtle"[2] (third millennium); and (3) the gods as "personal" deities related "parentally" to the individual family or clan head, responsible for birth, nurture, protection, and guidance, present to the devotees as the power within the individual for success, and sensitively responsive to the devotee's familiar, trusting petition for every felt need (second millennium).

According to Jacobsen, this personal religion with its parental metaphor gave way in the first millennium in Mesopotamia before the resurgence of older modes of perception of divine nature and activity. But first it entered into the religious experience of Israel's ancestors and formed the basis of Israelite Yahwism. Jacobsen writes:

> As far as we can see, it is only Israel that decisively extended the attitude of personal religion from the personal to the national realm. The relationship of Yahweh to Israel—his anger, his compassion, his forgiveness, and his re-newed anger and punishment of the sinful people—is in all essentials the same as that of the relation between god and individual in the attitude of personal religion. With this understanding of national life and fortunes as lived under ultimate moral responsibility, Israel created a concept of history as purposive.[3]

Nevertheless, Jacobsen draws attention to what he considers "the paradoxical character of personal religion, with its conspicuous humility curiously based on an almost limitless presumption of self-importance, its drawing the greatest cosmic powers into the little personal world of the individual, and its approach to the highest, the most awesome, and the terrifying in such an easy and familiar manner."[4] This paradox issues in a crisis, in the tension between belief in the gods as encountered in the way things really are (cosmic lords) and belief in the gods as human beings would like them to be (personal parents). The crisis comes to a focus in the problem of the righteous sufferer (*Ludlul bêl nêmeqi* and the Babylonian Theodicy) and is resolved by acknowledging the ways of the gods to be incomprehensible. It is in such a context that Jacobsen then comments on the Book of Job:

> The personal, egocentric view of the sufferer—however righteous—is re-jected. The self-importance which demands that the universe adjust to his needs, his righteousness, is cast aside, and the full stature of God as the majestic creator and ruler of the universe is reinstated. The distance between the cosmic and the personal, between God in his infinite greatness and mere individual man, is so great and so decisive that an individual has no rights, not even to justice.[5]

Cross picks up the analysis of the origins of Israelite religion where Jacobsen leaves it, connecting the religion of Israel's ancestors with the personal religion of second-millennium Mesopotamia.[6] Throughout *Canaanite Myth and Hebrew Epic* he reiterates the essentially covenantal and law-centered character of Israel's religion, developed from ancestral bases; and he identifies as extraneous, peripheral, and suspect the thematics of gratuitousness (negative or positive) wherever they are discernible in Israelite thought and practice.

However, Cross concludes, the great exilic reformulations of tradition, in the Priestly form of the Epic and the revised Deuteronomistic History, were inadequate to the shocks of Israel's experience, insofar as they suppressed the ambiguities of history and found the hand of God "plainly visible in the course of historical events."[7] It is in the late exilic and early postexilic literature—especially in the utterances of Second Isaiah and company, and partly in Ezekiel— that Cross identifies the continuing evolution of Israelite religion. There, he finds, "the Epic themes of old Israel become transfigured in a new, complex view of history, given dark dimensions with dualistic elements of myth, yet affirming the sovereignty of Yahweh in history and confirming the vocation of Israel as the people of God."[8] As for the Book of Job, Cross places it between the revised Epic and Deuteronomistic. History, and the proto-apocalyptic developments arising at the end of the exile. In such a context, the role of Job is largely negative, exposing the inadequacies of the unambiguous reading of history in the Epic and the Deuteronomistic History:

> The argument of Job attacked the central theme of Israel's religion. It repudiated the God of history whose realm is politics, law, and justice, whose delight is to lift up the poor and to free the slave. The God who called Israel out of Egypt, who spoke by prophet, the covenant God of Deuteronomy, did not reveal himself to Job. It is true that God spoke, but note that he spoke from the storm cloud. It is true that he revealed transcendent wisdom and power, but they were revealed in thunder and lightning, in the language of Ba'l. He was revealed in the defeat of the dragon of chaos, in the myths of creation. There is a sense in which Job was opaque. Job viewed the flux of history in despair; he detected no pattern of meaning there. History was a riddle beyond man's fathoming. The Lord of History failed to act. 'El or Ba'l, the transcendent creator spoke. Only he lived. Job saw him and bowed his knee.[9]

If Job indeed belongs "in the main line of the evolution of Israel's religion," its function in that line is deconstructive, clearing the way for others to attempt creative reconstructions.

The history of religion analyses of Jacobsen and Cross provide us with a more ample context for the study of Job than was available hitherto; and the issues that they identify as exercising Job are largely correct. Yet, in my judgment, their assessment of the Joban resolution of those issues is wide of the mark. A few unelaborated remarks will indicate my chief problems with their conclusions.

To begin with Jacobsen, his reading of Job focuses entirely on the questions that Job addresses to God and ignores completely the question raised in heaven concerning Job. Methodologically, to drive such a wedge between the prologue and the dialogues is a misstep that cannot but skew one's conclusions. Second, and inexplicably, Jacobsen moves from a historically contextual discussion of *Ludlul bêl nêmeqi* and the Babylonian Theodicy directly to Job, as though the latter text arose at the same point in the same cultural context—a curiously ahistorical piece of analysis. For, of course, Job arose after a thousand years of cultural and religious formation not shared by the Mesopotamian communities.

In second-millennium Mesopotamia, of the two coexisting religious metaphors the personal metaphor was the newcomer, whereas the lordly metaphor enjoyed the weightier sanction of more ancient tradition. This more weighty sanction received the reinforcement of historical shocks that extinguished the relatively tender religious and existential consciousness nascent in personal religion. By contrast, in Israel the personal metaphor was no latecomer but was remembered as foundational (e.g., Deut 32:6 and Exod 4:22–23; and the common early divine kinship names, beginning with Abra[ha]m), whereas loyal Yahwists identified the gods of the other nations as newcomers and interlopers (e.g., Deut 32:16–18). This means that the dialectic between rival religious metaphors operated differently within Israel and Mesopotamia. Whereas in Mesopotamia two metaphors native to the culture vied for survival, in Israel the struggle was between the personal metaphor experienced as foundational for the community and alien metaphors viewed as temptations (cf. Jer 6:17).[10] Finally, Israel's religious history did not end, as did Mesopotamia's, in a dark age. The descendants of Abraham and Sarah emerged from the exile with views that, however transformed, continued to ground themselves firmly in the traditions concerning those ancestors and concerning the exodus and the Sinai covenant. It is possible, of course, that Job is an alien voice amid Israel's religious traditions. But when we read Job against the background of the leading themes of Israel's preexilic traditions, in my view we may discern the outlines—limned in agony and tentativeness, adumbrated under a cloak of rhetorical ambiguity, yet soliciting the consent of the bold—of a positive resolution of those issues which in *Ludlul bêl nêmeqi* and the Babylonian Theodicy were resolved so pessimistically. It is this resolution (and not merely a deconstructive function) which gives Job its place in the history of Israel's religion.

For, where Cross reads disjunction ("Job brought the ancient religion of Israel to an end"), I read critique, deepening, and the seeds of transformation—in any case a fundamental continuity in which, under historical shocks, the radical and (*pace* Jacobsen) realistic implications of the personal metaphor were unflinchingly faced and accepted. The following items will indicate in part my identifications of continuity where Cross identifies discontinuity.

1. Is it the case that " 'El or Ba'l, the transcendent creator spoke"? It is precisely in the dialogues that we encouter the generic and common Semitic names for God (El and eloah) alongside the ancestral Šadday, as

though the ancestral god may be identifiable with an alien, inscrutable deity. In the narrative introductions to the divine speeches, why is this usage discontinued in favor of the exodus and covenant name Yahweh? Surely it is misleading to equate the voice of a transcendent creator ipso facto with the voice of El or Baal. By the exile, such creation themes were long at home in Yahwism.

2. Similarly, after Exodus 19—20; Psalm 18; and Ezek 1:4 it is not self-evident that storm and cloud, thunder and lightning betoken Baal's voice rather than Yahweh's.

3. The god revealed in the defeat of dragon is not thereby disclosed as divorced from the concerns of history, as is clear from Job's near-contemporary Second Isaiah (Isa 51:9–11). These three features of the divine speeches are present in later apocalyptic in a much more robust mythic fashion, where Cross, however, takes them as enabling a more complex, dark, somewhat dualistic reading of a history that nevertheless "affirm[s] the sovereignty of Yahweh in history and confirm[s] the vocation of Israel as the people of God."[11] That positive enablement, I suggest, begins in Job.

4. The God who called Israel out of Egypt did so from a habitation in the wilderness, sometimes called *tōhû*. This God who acted in justice to lift up the poor and the slave as "children of God" (Exod 4:22–23; Hos 11:1; Deut 32:6, 10–12) and to feed them (Deut 32:13; Psalm 81) also acted in the wilderness to try them and know their heart, whether they serve God for bread alone (Deut 8:2–3). Job, with its heavenly question concerning the basis for human piety (Job 1:9–10), falls well within such a tradition.

5. Similarly, the God who spoke by prophet apparently sometimes spoke through conflicting prophetic voices to test the hearts of kings (1 Kings 22). Job may be a critique of prophetic religion, but it is a critique internal to that tradition.

6. The God of covenant is identified as such in the tradition not solely by the presence of covenant terminology or formularies but by the presence of certain fundamental conceptions of the nature of the divine-human relation. Cross elsewhere asserts that "the covenant relation is properly described as a substitute kinship relation."[12] If that is so (and I think it is), covenant conceptions and forms (including law) and concerns (including justice) have their ground in deeper human sensibilities and concerns native to kinship relations. In my view, Job does not so much break with covenant and law as circumscribe their adequacy when they are in danger of losing effective contact with that organic ground and becoming a logically mechanical moral calculus. In Job, covenant and law are rerooted in their personal ground.

7. The assertion that "the Lord of history failed to act" assumes that the epilogue formed no original part of Job—an assumption that, for all its scholarly currency, may be questioned by a close reading of the epilogue. The assertion also assumes a one-level reading of the divine speeches as an unambiguous put-down of Job. But the divine speeches are to be read, not as a rebuff—or not unambiguously as such—but rather or also as a call to a worldly and historical task supposedly impossible (as Moses in Exod 3:11—4:13 felt his to be) yet crucial to the divine purpose in and for creation. (The cosmic scope of this worldly and historical call is significant for Job's propaedeutic to apocalyptic.) Indeed, given the "place" in which Job finally situates himself existentially, as a form of wilderness (Job 30:28–31), one may go so far as to take the divine speeches, in their numinosity, as a renewed call analogous to the speech from the burning bush, where this time it is Job who burns and is not consumed. As I shall hope to show, that numinosity is not only terrifying but also attracting; and the terrifying and attracting dimensions of the numinosity are conveyed by means of a climactic employment of rhetorical means for which the way has been prepared since the prologue.

II

By way of introducing my reading of Job, I should like to draw attention to those aspects of the Israelite tradition upon which chiefly, in my view, the text of Job works its transformations and to two prominent rhetorical means by which that transformation is effected. The most relevant traditions are the following:

1. *Genesis 1.* It is commonly recognized, of course, that creation themes abound in Job. But Genesis 1 in particular is reflected in Job 3.[13] Leading elements played upon in Job are the themes of God as cosmic creator and humankind as *imago dei*, *'ādām* from the *'ădāmâ* yet given royal dominion over the earth and over the denizens of sea, air, and land.

2. *Psalm 8.* The parody of Psalm 8 in Job 7:17–18 is well known, but another play on the psalm occurs also in Job 25. Moreover, in the divine speeches the catalogue of creatures climaxes in the figures of *běhēmôt* and *liwyātān*; and this catalogue is best taken as an elaboration of that in Psalm 8, which itself comes to a double climax in the *běhēmôt* (Ps 8:8 [Eng. 8:7], summing up the nonhuman creatures made on the sixth day) and "whatever passes along the paths of the sea" (Ps 8:9 [Eng. 8:8], summing up the creatures of the fifth day; cf. esp. Job 41:24 [Eng. 41:32]). Over all of these creatures, humankind in Psalm 8 is to exercise royal dominion—*tamšîlēhû*—with which we may compare the taunting "upon earth there is not his *mōšēl*," best read as "his ruler" (Job 41:25

[Eng. 41:33]). Again, then, in this psalm we note the twin emphases on God as creator of all and on mortal, earthly, human being *('ĕnôš/ben 'ādām)* called to royal function.

3. *Genesis 2—3.* The Joban prologue and dialogues variously resonate with the thematics of the Garden story. The thematics of a human vocation to live loyally before God on earth, in the face of a temptation to interpret that vocation otherwise through a "wisdom" indicated by the agency of a divinely given tempter, are integrally related to the thematics of a vocation to rule the animal realm through naming, a vocation which however becomes problematical.

4. *The traditions of the exodus and of Sinai* (and therefore, to be sure, of Deuteronomy), including the call of Moses at the bush, the covenant, and the testing in the wilderness. To be sure, the absence in Job of explicit reference to these traditions stands in loud contrast to the prominence of creation thematics. (Though Job 24:1–12 may challenge Exod 2:23–25 the way Job 7:17–18 challenges Psalm 8.) Job's anguished query concerning *justice* in Job 9 and then concerning *creative purpose* in Job 10 exemplifies a movement toward the radical form of the issue: If God's creative purpose is in doubt, a fortiori questions concerning redemption and covenant are likewise in jeopardy. For by this time in Israel, creator and redeemer/covenanter are one God.

5. *Second Isaiah.* The thematic, rhetorical, and lexical connections between these two books are virtually innumerable. At the center of the connection lies the issue of the status and vocation of Israel as mortally human (Isa 40:6–8; 41:14a) yet called to a democratized royalty (Isa 55:1–5) in the face of inexplicable suffering (Isa 52:13—53:12). In Second Isaiah this status and vocation are affirmed not merely in the face of such suffering but somehow in and through it. In my view, Job does not merely clear the way for such a vision by negating a mechanical moral-retributional calculus for history but also implies a similar vision by the rhetorical means to which I shall shortly turn.

One aspect of the general historical setting of Job remains to be indicated, and that has to do with what we may call the evolution of human consciousness. Whether or not one finds suggestive the eccentric thesis of J. Jaynes, in more general terms one may argue the appearance of personal religion in the ancient Near East as marking the rise and intensification in that region of individuated consciousness vis-à-vis both the social group and the divine realm.[14] Job then may be viewed as one exploration of the vocational implications of the gift and the burden of consciousness. What does it mean to be a sentient, suffering, solitary consciousness in problematic relation to God and to the created world both human and nonhuman? What is the nature of the claims laid upon such an individual by others, by tradition, by God, in the face of experiences that isolate oneself within a self-awareness that itself is being called into question? What becomes of the nature of covenant and community when consciousness takes on such a solitary dimension? (One of the problems of the customary rejection of the epilogue is that the resultant picture of Job leaves him in the posture and circumstance of a modern existentialist hero. As I believe I have shown, the epilogue reintroduces individuated Job into a solidly communal context in such a way that both individuality and community are intensified.)[15] In this respect Job carries to a further point the issues of individual and community articulated in Jeremiah and Ezekiel.

The two chief rhetorical means by which the Israelite religious traditions are transformed are *irony* and a *questioning* mode of address. These two means often, though not always, occur in tandem. It should be noted that these two means are displayed in the prologue and that by these means Job is presented already in chap. 2 (*not* only first in chap. 3) as harboring a divided consciousness.

Irony, as W. Booth puts it, admirably serves the purposes of deconstruction and reconstruction. But irony serves such purposes indirectly, by appearing to inhabit the very structure that it in fact subverts and by offering its own positive alternative only implicitly, in the mode of invitation to entertain that alternative. The "soft" logical or assertorial force of irony (invitatory rather than logically indicative or coercive) allows those who miss the irony to "dwell in happy ignorance in the shaky edifice, thus adding to its absurdity."[16] At the same time, Booth says, "a kind of morally active engagement is invited by the irony."[17] For, "having decided for myself that the ostensible judgment (based on the apparent meaning of the text) must somehow be combatted, I make the new position mine with all the force that is conferred by my sense of having judged independently."[18] This last feature of irony, its invitation to morally active engagement, is one of the keys to the reading of the divine speeches. These speeches offer a parade example of how content, or meaning, is conveyed in and through form, in this instance through the use of rhetorical questions posed ironically. By such means Job is not rebuffed but challenged and invited (much in the spirit of Jer 12:5) to move beyond the merely creatural expostulatory position that he inhabits to a stance of morally active engagement and participation with the Creator in the making of meaningful form in the face of what is formless.

The last two sentences lead us to the other prominent rhetorical means, the questioning mode of address. For from Job 1:7 onward, all that is narrated or spoken either moves toward or proceeds from questions posed by one or another character, including God. But questions come in various kinds. The kinds most relevant to a reading of Job are rhetorical, impossible, and existential questions.

The *rhetorical* question concerns that which is known by the questioner but is posed as a question for the purpose of enlisting the addressee's own energies of affirmation or "morally active engagement," to draw the addressee onto ground already occupied by the questioner. (Thus the language modes of irony and the rhetorical question display an intrinsic affinity, and their efficacy is intensified in their joint use.) The rhetorical action here is unilateral, and the moral relation that it opens up is asymmetrical: The addressee is moved to move toward a stationary questioner (like Aristotle's God). A special form of the rhetorical question is the *impossible* question, which has the effect of heightening the disparity and the asymmetry between two parties, inasmuch as it discloses the limits of the addressee's intellectual and physical powers and ventures.[19] The "common ground" onto which the addressee thereby is drawn turns out to be the common recognition of what the questioner already knew—the asymmetrical relation of disparity between addressee and questioner. Rhetorically, the impossible question is an ideal form for the portrayal of lordly power which may ask all questions and need answer none.

Existential questions stand in manifold contrast to impossible questions. For an existential question, as here understood, comes to its addressee as a possibility for existence, for becoming, to which the answer comes, if at all, in the form of the self that the addressee becomes as the result of the venture of life enacted in the power and direction offered by such a question. The risk integral to an existential question— the sense of a "void" residing alongside the question's power, or perhaps constituting that power—is the fact that what is posed questioningly as a possibility may prove to have been impossible. Likewise, however, the openness and the invitatory character of such a question lies in the fact that its possibility or impossibility is properly decidable only in and through the venture.

As a source and form of power, an existential question may be entertained and channeled through unilateral ventures of solitary becoming. To disclose one's existential question to another party is to offer to share one's power of becoming, such that the other is in a position partially to determine one's future. Relations founded on the sharing of existential questions are one form of covenant relation, just as the posing of existential questions (whether ironically or unironically) to another is a form of offer of such a covenant relation. Such a relation may be asymmetrical, where only one party discloses an existential question. In contrast to the impossible question, however, in this asymmetrical relation it is the addressee who becomes the unmoved mover. Where the disclosure of existential questions is reciprocal, the covenant relation becomes symmetrical and parity exists. Both parties are moved by each other's questions. Such a covenant relation is the fullest form of historical existence, in which (to use Jacobsen's language) history is purposive and lived under ultimate moral responsibility. But the personal metaphor for the divine implies that both human and divine parties are morally responsible. The crisis that Jacobsen effectively identifies can, then, be formulated this way: What sort of question is most appropriate to the divine-human relation? Reciprocally existential? Asymmetrically existential? Or unilaterally rhetorical and, finally, impossible?

Elsewhere I have attempted to initiate a line of reflection upon Israel's religious traditions, according to which those traditions imply a view of God, not as some sort of mythic or epic precursor of Aristotle's metaphysical unmoved mover (in Cross's terms, some sort of divine source and exemplification of "static structures of meaning behind or beyond the historical flux")[20] but as the living God, as dynamic and self-creative process of becoming through that self-naming—"I will be who I will be"—which is self-enacting and, therein radically historical, is the free and freeing (Exod 3:14 in context!) ground of the temporal process in the created and finite world.[21] In such an implicit vision, the divine-human covenant may be said to be initiated already in the divine creation of the world, though the covenant therein implicitly initiated awaits more overt presentation. The significance of the creation, viewed as a covenanting act, lies in the possibility that the aboriginal life of God, purely self-determining, by an act of decision brings into being derivative and dependent, yet finitely originative centers of life, with whom then God seeks freely to share what M. Buber calls the "power of fate-deciding"[22] and what I would call the power of the divine existential question. This shared question eventually in Israel takes on the contours of eschatological symbolism.[23]

It is within the framework of such an understanding of existential questions that I approach the questions that loom so prominently in the Book of Job in both its narrative and its dialogical sections. Two questions are primary: From the human side arises the question as to the meaning of innocent suffering for one's understanding of one's own life and of human existence in general and for one's understanding of the divine purposes and character. But this human question is correlative to—and in Job is presented as arising out of—the question as to the motivation and character, and therefore the meaning to God, of human piety and rectitude. Indeed, the human question is generated by the divine question. It is perhaps only some sort of theological veto or inhibition that prevents us from detecting in the divine question concerning Job's piety a prior reflexive question—an existential question—concerning God's intrinsic capacity to evoke freely covenanting worship. Behind the question as to whether Job is pious only in grateful response to God's "parental" goodness lies the question as to whether God can elicit Job's loyalty only through such unilateral and asymmetrical benevolence. Insofar as this existential question is not answered unilaterally within the solitariness of the divine realm, but is given into the hands of Job to answer, the full implications of the personal metaphor of divine-human relations (and of the covenant metaphor, which, in Cross's words, is a substitute for the personal/kinship relation) are now realistically drawn.

The resolution of the Joban drama is here understood to come in the divine speeches and in Job's response in 42:1–6. The divine speeches, of course, come almost entirely in the mode of questions. Commonly they are taken to be rhetorical, or impossible to answer.[24] No doubt they apparently have that character. But it is here proposed that they have that character ironically. By this time the reader has encountered so many instances of irony, including questions that appear to be offered rhetorically but which the context clarifies (at the time or in retrospect) as in fact operating nonrhetorically, that the way is prepared to read the divine questions ironically. Appearing to rebuff Job, as utterance of the *mysterium tremendum,* they thereby offer Job the option of understanding himself as one rebuffed and abased. But as utterance of the *mysterium fascinans* they in fact convey an invitation to understand himself in the light of such questions posed existentially. These two voices correspond climactically to the two voices initially heard in the prologue, that of questioning Yahweh and that of questioning Satan. These two voices correspond to the two sets of voices that are heard in the dialogues, those of the friends and that of Job. These two voices within the divine speeches, moreover, may be said to internalize within those speeches the tension between Elihu's (supposedly and perhaps in fact) divinely inspired utterances and the divine speeches themselves. For it is likely that we should recognize in the juxtaposition of Elihu's (inspired?) utterances and the utterances of Yahweh an analogue of the voices of the many prophets and the juxtaposed voice of Micaiah ben Imlah in 1 Kings 22 as also an analogue of the voices of Yahweh God and of the snake in Genesis 2—3. By this rhetorical means, both the voices that in the prologue were heard only within the secret chambers of heaven now address Job. By the combined means of irony and rhetorical questions, then, Job is drawn (like a classical prophet) into the divine council, there to participate as a morally responsible agent.

There is not space here to treat the divine questions one by one, so as to demonstrate the ironic undertow that subverts the apparent rebuff and to disclose the real character of the questions as existential. Such a demonstration is attempted in detail in my commentary. A few examples will indicate the nature of my analysis. Yahweh asks whether Job has journeyed in the realms of sea, deep, deep darkness, and the underworld (Job 38:16–18). That the apparent answer "No, I have not" is *not* the answer being solicited is suggested by the fact that repeatedly this very language of the realm of darkness and death and Sheol has occurred on Job's own lips as a way of describing his current experience and existential state. Like Jonah of both the whale narrative and the poem, Job has descended into those regions. In the light of all this, the only way Job can continue to hold fast his integrity is to say, "Yes, I have." In Job 38:39—39:30, Yahweh parades before Job a realm of nonhuman creatures wild as at the day of their creation, or perhaps we should say wild as at the day of their original presentation to human view for domination. Against the background of Genesis 1 and 2, and of Psalm 8, Job is invited (like the reader) to take this parade as a re-presentation of the human vocation to royal function, in the face of Job's experience of the "wildness" present in creation in the form of inexplicable suffering. (Compare again *mōšēl* in Job 41:25 [Eng. 41:33] with *tamšîlēhû* in Ps. 8:9 [Eng. 8:8]. It is, of course, unnecessary to decide between mythological and zoological connotations of these two figures, for they function both ways. Finally, the absence of any mention of the human creature from the catalogue of the denizens of creation may be taken in either of two ways. Either human existence is so insignificant cosmically that it can be left out of the picture with no loss or the omission may signify that the status of the human creature is open for revision. This creature is not merely a creature along with the rest but is that creature who is addressed by God concerning creation and who therein is being invited to enter with deepened, or newly awakened, awareness into the vocation implicit in the anthropological metaphor of dust and ground (*'āpār* and *'ādām*/*'ădāmâ*) as *imago dei*.

As for Job's response, of which a close reading is likewise offered in the commentary, we may note only this: The customary translation of the preposition "I repent *in* dust and ashes" in Job 42:6 is indefensible. There is no Hebrew analogy for the construal of *niḥḥam 'al* as "repent in"; every other instance, without exception, requires the translation "repent or change the mind *concerning*." As for the phrase "dust and ashes," this combination occurs only three times in the Hebrew Bible, here and in Gen. 18:27 and Job 30:19. In the one instance, Abraham uses the phrase to characterize his own creaturely finitude, yet precisely in that situation where dust and ashes argues with deity concerning divine justice and righteous humanity. In the other instance, in Job 30:19, Job utters a tightly constructed couplet that trades on multiple meanings of both verbs: "God has cast me into the mire, //and I have become like dust and ashes," and "God has directed me to consider mire, //and I liken myself therefore to dust and ashes." The student supposedly is instructed by the wise teacher, through suffering, to learn from nature of his own nature, to think of himself as merely dust and death in the light of his experience at God's hands. God has subverted Job's formerly royal self-understanding (19:9—"He has stripped from me my glory, //and taken the crown from my head"; also, for example, 29:25) and directed him to dust and ashes and mire. Now, as a result of the divine speeches, Job comes to a new understanding of what it means to be a human being, of what it means to be dust and ashes. What that understanding is is left veiled from the reader. Perhaps this veil exists in order to draw the reader to participate in Job's response, by the way in which the reader attempts to hear the import of the divine questions. This much, in any case, is clear: Job now rejects the former interpretation, in Job 30:19, according to which his experience meant God's abasement of him. In such a reading, Job 42:6b portrays Job as hearing in the divine speeches something other than a lordly put-down. That translators and interpreters have persistently construed Job 42:6b against the clear import of a common and unambiguous idiom *(niḥḥam ʿal)* is hard to explain except by reference to a theological preunderstanding of the very sort that the Book of Job was designed to overturn.

Purely in the context of a history of religion investigation, it is intriguing to note that the ironic use of a seemingly impossible question, in respect to precisely the same complex of issues and themes, appears in Mark 10:35–45. There, two disciples request to be given positions of rule "in your glory," that is, in Jesus' kingdom. The request is met with the apparent rebuff, "You do not know what you are asking. Are you able to drink the cup that I drink, or to be baptized with the baptism with which I am baptized?" To the reader's acute embarrassment on their behalf, the disciples obtusely and brashly answer, "We are able." Thereupon Jesus' response discloses that their answer, however unwitting, is correct—they shall drink that cup. Yet, he says, kingly rule is not to be seized, for it is conferred. Nor is it enacted in the fashion suggested by conventional wisdom, for it is displayed in precisely those modes of worldly existence in which it would seem to have been relinquished or to have been taken away. Such a vision of human vocation, of course, is present already in Second Isaiah, as Cross has succinctly intimated in the last two pages of *Canaanite Myth and Hebrew Epic.* If my demurral from his reading of Job is persuasive, such a reading may, on the other hand, take us a step farther in appreciating his placement of Job between the earlier Epic and Deuteronomistic works and the proto-apocalyptic works of the late exile and the early postexilic period. In that situation we may now appreciate that, if Second Isaiah was able to affirm a Servant of Yahweh who walks in darkness and has no light, yet trusts in the name of Yahweh and relies upon his God (Isa 50:10), that affirmation rested upon a basis already laid in Job, where that walk is traced in its excruciating detail of solitary yet faithfully covenanting consciousness.

NOTES

1. T. Jacobsen, *The Treasures of Darkness: A History of Mesopotamian Religion* (New Haven: Yale University Press, 1976); and F. M. Cross, *CMHE*, 343–44.

2. Jacobsen, *The Treasures of Darkness*, 121.

3. Ibid., 164.

4. Ibid., 161.

5. Ibid., 163.

6. Cross, *CMHE*, 75 and note.

7. Ibid., 343.

8. Ibid., 346.

9. Ibid., 344.

10. The point that I am trying to make is treated in E. W. Said, *The World, the Text and the Critic* (Cambridge: Harvard University Press, 1983). In chap. 10, "Traveling Theory," Said analyzes and exemplifies the ways in which "by virtue of having moved from one place and time to another an idea or theory gains or loses in strength" and the ways in which "a theory in one historical period and national culture becomes altogether different for another period or situation" (p. 226). The point is treated also by L. Hartz in *The Liberal Tradition in America* (New York: Harcourt, Brace & Co., 1955) and in *The Founding of New Societies* (New York: Harcourt, Brace and World, 1964). According to the summary of Hartz in G. Horowitz, "Conservatism, Liberalism, and Socialism in Canada: An Interpretation" (*The Canadian Journal of Economics and Political Science* 32 [May 1966]), when new societies are founded as "fragments" thrown off from a parent society, "[t]he key to the understanding of ideological development in a new society is its 'point of departure' from [in the instances being studied] Europe: the ideologies born by the founders of the new societies are not representative of the historic ideological spectrum of the mother country. The settlers represent only a fragment of that spectrum" (p. 143). According to Horowitz, Hartz goes on to argue that "the significance of the fragmentation process is that the new society, having been thrown off from Europe, 'loses the stimulus to change that the whole provides' [quoting Hartz]. . . . The ideology of the founders is thus frozen, congealed at the point of origin" (p. 144). I adapt the latter part of Hartz's hypothesis as follows: Israelite religious culture represents only a fragment of Mesopotamian religious culture. The religious metaphor of the founders is not so

much frozen, but enabled to grow and develop, uninhibited by the changes internal to Mesopotamia whereby the older lordly metaphor eventually overpowered the younger personal metaphor.

11. Cross, *CMHE,* 346.

12. Ibid., 257–358.

13. The allusions to Genesis 1 are by no means confined to this chapter, but they are present in a programmatic way here.

14. J. Jaynes, *The Origin of Consciousness in the Breakdown of the Bicameral Mind* (Boston: Houghton Mifflin Co., 1976). See my brief comments in "Jeremiah 20:7–18," *Interpretation* 37 (1983) 178–83.

15. J. G. Janzen, *Job* (Interpretation; Atlanta: John Knox Press, 1985).

16. W. C. Booth, *A Rhetoric of Irony* (Chicago: University of Chicago Press, 1974) 36.

17. Ibid., 66.

18. Ibid., 41.

19. J. L. Crenshaw, "Impossible Questions, Sayings, and Tasks," *Semeia* 17 (1980) 19.

20. Cross, *CMHE,* viii.

21. See the essays listed in the bibliography to my commentary *Job,* where a fuller presentation of the overall interpretation given here may be found.

22. M. Buber, *The Prophetic Faith* (New York: Harper & Brothers, 1949) 104.

23. See, preliminarily, J. G. Janzen, "Metaphor and Reality in Hosea 11," *Semeia* 24 (1982) 36–38, and idem, "Eschatological Symbol and Existence in Hosea," *CBQ* 44/3 (1982) 394–414.

24. So, e.g., Crenshaw, "Impossible Questions."

29

The Place of Apocalypticism in
the Religion of Israel

JOHN J. COLLINS

In a seminal essay, published in 1969, F. M. Cross claimed that "in many respects the most serious lacuna in the study of apocalyptic has been in the early era, in its relations to older biblical religion."[1] Much study has been devoted to this issue in the intervening years, but the lacuna has not been definitively filled. Instead, expanding research on the apocalyptic literature has shown that the issue is even more complex than had been thought and that any theory of "the origins of apocalyptic" necessarily involves some over-simplification and confusion.

It is now widely recognized that the word "apocalyptic" used as a noun obscures some quite basic distinctions. In 1970, K. Koch distinguished between "apocalyptic as a literary type" and "apocalyptic as a historical movement."[2] This distinction was refined by P. D. Hanson in 1975 in his definitions of "apocalypse" as a literary genre, "apocalypticism" as the ideology of a particular kind of socioreligious movement, and "apocalyptic eschatology" as a religious perspective that is not confined to either apocalypses or apocalyptic movements.[3] While these distinctions are quite fundamental, it is also important to appreciate the relationship between the three terms. As Koch already argued, the starting point for any discussion of "apocalyptic" matters must lie in those texts which are recognized as apocalypses.[4] Apocalyptic eschatology is most appropriately defined as the kind of eschatology that is typical of apocalypses, although it may also be found elsewhere. The movements most appropriately called apocalyptic are those which either produced apocalypses or were characterized by the beliefs and attitudes typical of the genre.[5] Whether some postexilic prophecy should be called apocalyptic or taken to attest an apocalyptic movement depends on our assessment of the similarities between this material and the literary genre apocalypse.

One of the problems that has beset the quest for "the origin of apocalyptic" is that the apocalypses are not simply uniform but contain diverse subgenres and motifs that may be traced to different sources.[6] If we wish to arrive at an understanding of the historical development of apocalypticism, it is necessary to differentiate the various apocalyptic texts and the movements that may be inferred from them. The two major types of apocalypse—the "historical apocalypse," characterized by an extended review of history in the guise of prophecy, and the otherworldly journey[7]—are both first exemplified in developed form in the Hellenistic period, in the books of Daniel and *1 Enoch*. It is on the development of this material that we wish to focus here.

The dominant trend in recent scholarship on apocalyptic origins has sought to establish an unbroken connection with postexilic prophecy.[8] O. Plöger believed that a selection of postexilic eschatological passages such as Isaiah 24—27; Zechariah 12—14; and Joel could produce "a line, when joined together, that leads from the older restoration eschatology, which is certainly within the sphere of influence of the pre-exilic prophetic promises, to the rather different, dualistic and apocalyptic form of eschatology, such as we find in a fairly complete form in the Book of Daniel."[9] Plöger admitted that the line was a broken one but affirmed continuity nonetheless and related the whole development to the rise of the Hasidim, who are known from the Maccabean books. Hanson also "views Daniel as one station along a continuum reaching from pre-exilic prophecy to full-grown apocalyptic, very much at home on Jewish soil and manifesting foreign borrowing only as peripheral embellishments."[10] Hanson, however, has denied that the development of apocalypticism can be attributed to a single movement or party. Since he dates compositions such as Isaiah 24—27 earlier than Plöger, he posits a gap in the continuum in the fourth century B.C.E. The later apocalypses are analogous to the postexilic prophecies in their revival of ancient myth and their sociological matrix but are not the products of a continuous movement.[11]

It is fair to say that Plöger and Hanson have concentrated on the development of cosmic eschatology, which they regard as the heart of apocalypticism, and trace the connections primarily with Daniel rather than Enoch.[12] Even in the case of Daniel, many scholars have questioned whether cosmic eschatology is an adequate rubric for understanding the book. On the one hand, there has been renewed interest in the visionary form of the material, which also has biblical precedents, to be sure.[13] On the other hand, some features of Daniel's eschatology, which are not attested in late prophecy, especially the belief in resurrection, can hardly be regarded as peripheral embellishments.[14] Continuity with the biblical tradition is less obvious in the journeys of Enoch than in the symbolic visions of Daniel. Plöger's thesis, which sought to tie the development of apocalypticism to a particular party, is especially vulnerable. Both Daniel and *1 Enoch* provide internal evidence of developing movements in the pre-Maccabean period. These movements are not related to Plöger's eschatological conventicles but in each case have strong links with the eastern Diaspora.

THE ENOCH MOVEMENT

The publication of the Aramaic fragments of *1 Enoch* from Qumran by J. T. Milik in 1976 has been a turning point in the recent study of apocalypticism. Milik claimed, on the basis of paleography, that a copy of the Astronomical Book (*1 Enoch* 72—82) dates "from the end of the third or the beginning of the second century," while a manuscript of the Book of the Watchers (*1 Enoch* 1—36), including fragments of chaps. 1—12, dates from the first half of the second century B.C.E.[15] If we assume that these manuscripts were not autographs, both compositions may well date from the third century, appreciably earlier than had previously been thought. Consequently new attention has been focused on the Enochic writings as evidence for apocalypticism prior to Daniel and the Maccabean revolt.[16]

The early date of several Enochic writings seems assured even apart from the paleography of the Qumran fragments. The Animal Apocalypse (*1 Enoch* 85—90), which is part of the Book of Dreams (*1 Enoch* 83—90), clearly alludes to the Maccabean revolt and is roughly contemporary with the Book of Daniel. Yet it seems to presuppose the Book of the Watchers at *1 Enoch* 86—87 (the story of the fallen angels). The Apocalypse of Weeks (*1 Enoch* 93:1–10; 91:11–17) does not refer to the desecration of the Temple by Antiochus Epiphanes and was probably written before it. This apocalypse is now embedded in the Epistle of Enoch (*1 Enoch* 91—105) and may have always been an integral part of it. The Epistle fits as well in the pre-Maccabean era as in the Hasmonean period to which it was dated by R. H. Charles, and its polemic against idolatry can be more plausibly assigned to the earlier date. Moreover, the *Book of Jubilees,* itself of Maccabean origin, seems to refer not only to the Astronomical Book, the Book of the Watchers, and the Book of Dreams but also to the Epistle of Enoch (although this allusion is disputed).[17]

It appears, then, that we have a corpus of writings in the name of Enoch, composed over roughly the half century before the Maccabean revolt.[18] It is reasonable to suppose that the literary continuity is due to the ongoing activity of a group, and there are indications within the books themselves of an emerging group identity. *1 Enoch* is introduced as "the words of the blessing of Enoch according to which he blessed the chosen and righteous who must be present on the day of distress." The chosen and righteous appear to be technical terms throughout the book for a particular group, which is not simply identical with the Jewish people. (Contrasts between the righteous and the sinners are especially sharp in the Epistle.) The Book of the Watchers and the Astronomical Book, which seem to be the oldest sections of *1 Enoch,* give least indication of a distinct group identity. In *1 Enoch* 10:16 "the plant of righteousness and truth" is apparently Israel, and there is no reference to a further off-shoot—on the contrary, "all the sons of men shall be righteous" (*1 Enoch* 10:21). By contrast, the Apocalypse of Weeks assigns the origin of the plant of righteousness to the third week, in the time of Abraham, but has another development at the end of the seventh week. Then "the chosen righteous from the eternal plant of righteousness" will be chosen.[19] This special group is evidently an offshoot from Israel. The Animal Apocalypse also recounts the rise of a special group in *1 Enoch* 90:6: "and small lambs were born from those white sheep, and they began to open their eyes and see." Modern scholarship has often associated this development with the rise of Hasidim, who, like the lambs, take up arms and make common cause with Judas Maccabee.[20] The Apocalypse of Weeks also endorses the use of the sword against the wicked and is compatible with what we know of the Hasidim.

The apocalyptic movement underlying the early Enoch literature appears to have become more sharply defined in the crisis under Antiochus Epiphanes, but it must have originated some considerable time before that. The "symbolic universe"[21] of the movement, also, may have undergone some adjustments at that point, but the main outlines of the Enochic system may be found already in the Book of the Watchers and the Astronomical Book, which may be as old as the third century.

Our knowledge of the history of this early Enoch movement is very sketchy, but some points have been clarified by recent study.[22]

A MESOPOTAMIAN CONTEXT

The figure of Enoch is fashioned after Mesopotamian prototypes, especially Enmeduranki, who appears as seventh king in several antediluvian lists.[23] This association is already evident in the P source in Gen 5:21–24, where Enoch is placed seventh from creation.[24] The age of Enoch, 365 years, suggests an association with the solar year. Enmeduranki was associated with the sun-god Shamash. It is less certain whether the biblical phrase *wayyithallek 'et-ha'ĕlōhîm,* usually translated "he walked with God," reflects the tradition that Enmeduranki was admitted to the divine assembly and implies the later tradition that Enoch sojourned with the angels.[25] Even if the use of the article with *'ĕlōhîm* reflects a polytheistic source, it is possible that his walking was still on earth.[26] The motif of Enoch's final translation is derived from the Babylonian flood hero Utnapishtim.[27] The general context of these associations is clear enough. The Jewish writer constructs Enoch as a counterpart to legendary Mesopotamian heroes, no less than they in fame and distinction. This kind of competition between traditions is quite old and is reflected, for example, in the biblical appropriation of the flood story. It becomes much more blatant in the Hellenistic period, when Ps. Eupolemus attributes the discovery of astrology to Enoch and Artapanus credits Moses with inventing the Egyptian animal cults.[28]

The Priestly portrait of Enoch in Genesis stops far short of the legend developed in *1 Enoch*. Enoch is not said to transmit revelations or to write books, and he is not contemporaneous with the fallen angels. Whatever association with the heavenly world is implied, it does not yet have the revelatory function that is crucial to *1 Enoch*.

Enoch's role as revealer is, however, illuminated by the parallel with Enmeduranki. The Sumerian king was admitted into the divine assembly and shown mysteries that included the tablets of heaven and the techniques of divination. Enoch reveals "that which appeared to me in the heavenly vision and which I know from the words of the holy angels and understand from the tablets of heaven" (*1 Enoch* 93:2). Enmeduranki was regarded as the founder of the *bārû* guild of diviners and the mediating revealer of its methods. Enoch, the "scribe of righteousness" (*1 Enoch* 12:4), is the prototype of the "righteous and chosen" and is cast as their mediator of revelation. The analogy with Enmeduranki suggests that the Enoch movement was in some sense a Jewish counterpart to the Mesopotamian diviners.

On the evidence of the literature, however, the influence of divination was strictly limited.[29] Enoch does not employ the techniques of the *bārû*—consulting entrails, observing oil on water, or manipulating the cedar rod. The only Babylonian medium of revelation that he endorses is the dream, which had some precedent in biblical tradition (cf. Jacob and Joseph), although it had also been subject to criticism.[30] Interestingly, dream interpretation was not especially characteristic of the *bārû* guild.[31] The Enochic interest in the astral world may have been stimulated by the science of the astrologers, but Enoch does not use the stars for divination.

The relation of the Enoch movement to the Babylonian diviners may be clarified by consideration of two biblical parallels. Second Isaiah vehemently ridicules the diviners and wise men of Babylon and contrasts them with the servant of the Lord (Isa 44:25–26; 47:13). Yet his demonstrations of Yahweh's superiority are colored by this polemic. He places exceptional emphasis on the claim that his God has foretold things from of old. The ability to predict is accepted as a criterion of divine power. The prophet is not a diviner, but he claims to outdo them at their primary task.[32] The court legends in Daniel 1—6 also have a Babylonian setting. Here Daniel is trained as a Babylonian wise man and, at least in Daniel 2, appears to be a member of a guild.[33] He too outdoes the Chaldeans at their own task of interpreting dreams and mysterious writing, but he does so by the power of the God of Israel. Daniel, like Enoch, endorses the dream as a medium of revelation but does not resort to the divinatory techniques of the *bārû*. In each of these cases, the Jewish prophet or wise man is in competition with his Babylonian counterparts and accepts some of their presuppositions but also maintains a distinctive identity. The competitive aspect is not so explicit in the case of Enoch but is implied by the comparison with Enmeduranki.

The analogy with Daniel is especially interesting for the present discussion. It is well known that the tales in Daniel 1—6 represent a pre-apocalyptic stage of the Daniel tradition, which is primarily concerned with problems of Jewish identity in the eastern Diaspora.[34] It seems that the Enoch tradition had its roots in a similar context. What is especially important is that the interest in the revelation of mysteries that is fundamental to apocalypticism[35] is introduced in both traditions in this context—in Daniel's role as dream interpreter and Enoch's ascent to heaven. Both go well beyond Second Isaiah and come closer to Babylonian models in the manner in which revelation is received. To be sure, both traditions undergo some development, both in the manner of revelation and in the area of eschatology, before we can speak of apocalypses, and the development involves some reappropriation of Israelite traditions. Yet the understanding of revelation as the interpretation of mysteries, especially through dreams, which was developed in the Babylonian setting, remained an important constituent of the apocalyptic world view.[36]

The differences between the Daniel and Enoch traditions should also be noted. Daniel is a practitioner of courtly wisdom, concerned with the rise and fall of kingdoms. The earliest Enoch tradition is characterized by pseudoscientific speculation on cosmology and astronomy. These interests derive from the ascent of Enoch and his connection with the solar calendar.[37] The distinctive interests suggest that each tradition originally had a different *Sitz im Leben* and explain some of the differences between the apocalyptic movements that developed.[38]

The Daniel tradition first takes on a clearly apocalyptic character during the crisis of the Maccabean era. It is now apparent that Enochic apocalypticism had taken shape before then. The "symbolic universe" of this movement is most fully described in the Book of the Watchers, which contains the oldest extant account of Enoch's ascent, as distinct from his final translation.[39]

THE SYMBOLIC UNIVERSE OF ENOCH

The report of Enoch's ascent is embedded in the Book of the Watchers, *1 Enoch* 12—16. This passage occupies a pivotal place in the book. The myth of the Watchers in *1 Enoch* 6—11 makes no mention of Enoch and is widely thought to be woven from two older traditions.[40] Chapters 12—16, where Enoch is introduced for the first time, has aptly been called "a kind of commentary" on that myth.[41] It pronounces a verdict on the Watchers of the preceding chapters and highlights some aspects of their sin: they abandoned heaven and became unclean with human women, and they spread a worthless mystery on earth. On the other hand, this passage prepares us for the "true" revelation, which will be furnished in the journeys of Enoch in *1 Enoch* 17—36. This revelation is also directly related to the story of the Watchers. While the various segments of the Book of the Watchers may have had diverse origins, they are now related to each other in a coherent apocalypse.[42]

In view of Enoch's other associations with Enmeduranki, we must assume that the idea of his ascent for revelatory purposes was suggested, at least in part, by that king's admission to the divine assembly. The actual account in *1 Enoch* 14, however, does not even mention the heavenly tablets that are noted in *1 Enoch* 81:1 and 93:2. Instead, it is shaped in large part by the tradition of prophetic throne visions, reaching back to Micaiah ben Imlah (1 Kings 22) and Isaiah 6.[43] Prophetic influence is conspicuous in the climax of the vision, where Enoch is given a mission to rebuke the Watchers. There are also several noteworthy departures from the prophetic tradition. The whole experience is set in a dream, a "mantic" medium but one that had ancient Israelite precedents. It should be noted, however, that dreams of journeys to heaven or the netherworld are not recorded in the Hebrew Bible but are attested in Mesopotamia.[44] The actual upward travel of the visionary is recorded. The vision of the heavenly mansion is far more complex than what we find in the prophets and has affinities with later, mystical, literature.[45] It would seem to presuppose already some tradition of mystical speculation. Most significantly, Enoch is implicitly cast as a revealer of mysteries. The Watchers are angels who descend to reveal a worthless mystery. Enoch is a human being who ascends to get the true revelation.[46]

The sin of the Watchers is specified in *1 Enoch* 12–16 as improper marriage and improper revelation. Both of these factors are prominent in *1 Enoch* 6—11, where they lead to the spread of violence on earth. By analogy with other apocalyptic writings, it is very probable that the myth is used paradigmatically to describe the author's own time, although we cannot demand an exact correlation of all details. There is a growing consensus that the editorial section in *1 Enoch* 12—16 implies a critique of the Jerusalem priesthood (see esp. *1 Enoch* 15:2: "You ought to petition on behalf of men, not men on behalf of you").[47] The description of Enoch as a "scribe of righteousness" suggests that the author and his circle may have been scribes too. The application of the myth can hardly be restricted to the priesthood, however. It surely entails a more general description of a world gone awry. In view of the analogies with Greek myths, especially that of Prometheus,[48] the general situation is most probably the spread of Hellenistic culture in the third century. The myth would seem to imply that superhuman forces are at work, but human responsibility is not necessarily excluded thereby. Rather, the paradigm of the Watchers underlines the responsibility of sinners and their liability to punishment.[49]

Enoch's own revelation is derived from his tour, which begins in *1 Enoch* 17 and takes him to the ends of the earth, accompanied by angelic guides.[50] It is evident that the author draws on a learned tradition of cosmology and mythical geography. It is inappropriate, however, to ask whether "scientific" or eschatological interests predominate in this composition. The pseudoscientific lore is placed at the service of eschatology. Enoch's first tour in chaps. 17—19 culminates with the prison for the stars of heaven. The second tour begins in chap. 20 again with the place of punishment of the stars and proceeds to the abodes of the dead in chap. 22. Subsequently, Enoch sees the fire of all the lights of heaven, the place where God will set his throne in the end time and the place of judgment for sinners (chaps. 23—27).[51] The remainder of the tour, to the ends of the earth, serves to fill in the cosmological context of the places of judgment and reaffirm the order of the universe, which had been eclipsed by the revolt of the Watchers.[52]

Enoch's tour cannot be adequately explained either as a midrash on "walking with the angels" or by the precedent of Enmeduranki. While there are many partial parallels, it does not seem that this tour was based on a clear model.[53] Rather, it expresses the new symbolic universe of one Jewish movement in the Hellenistic age. The orderly world traversed by Enoch stands in sharp contrast to the anomie of the story of the Watchers and presumably reflects the disparity between the author's faith in a divinely controlled universe and the actual historical experience of the time.

The symbolic universe of Enoch is expressed in mythological terms although it embraces pseudoscientific cosmology. Two aspects are especially important. First, there is a transcendent world, which is not accessible to humanity without special revelation.[54] It includes the heavenly council of God and his angelic hosts. It also includes an elaborate cosmology that is undisturbed by the disruptions of the Watchers. Second, there is the assurance of a definitive judgment. This is not only foretold. It is built into the cosmology in the places of judgment. This judgment will deal not only with the fate of the earth but also with the fate of individuals beyond death. Both these aspects serve to restore the sense of order and justice disrupted by the Watchers.

The Astronomical Book has a similar mythological framework. It is presented as an angelic revelation mediated by Uriel, the guide of all the heavenly bodies. Several angelic leaders of the stars are named, especially in *1 Enoch* 82.[55] The eschatological horizon is shown in the allusion to "the new creation which will last forever" in *1 Enoch* 72:1 and the upheavals "in the days of the sinners when many heads of the stars will go astray" (*1 Enoch* 80).[56] Reward after death is implied at *1 Enoch* 81:4. The predominant interest of the Astronomical Book is in calendrical and cosmological matters, but they are presented in the context of an apocalyptic view of the world.

The cosmological interest recedes in the "historical" Enoch apocalypses, the Animal Apocalypse and the Apocalypse of Weeks. These works represent a new stage in the Enoch movement, marked by a more sharply defined group identity and the appropriation of new literary forms. Their novelty over against the Book of the Watchers should not be underestimated. Here we can only note some points of continuity. The periodization of history is already adumbrated, though certainly not developed, in *1 Enoch* 10:12, where the Watchers are bound for seventy generations. Both "historical" apocalypses provide for a final judgment that involves the destruction of the Watchers. The Animal Apocalypse is allegorical throughout and attaches great importance to angelic activity, notably the seventy angelic "shepherds" of the nations. Yet it evidently endorses the human initiative of Judas Maccabee (the horned ram in *1 Enoch* 90:9). The Epistle (*1 Enoch* 91—105) speaks more directly in terms of human causality, but angels figure prominently in the judgment and the life beyond death (*1 Enoch* 102—104).

It appears then that the Enoch movement has its own distinctive history, which has little relation to the eschatological conventicles posited by Plöger. Rather, it originated in the confrontation with Mesopotamian culture in the eastern Diaspora[57] and its "scientific" interests developed in that setting. The subsequent development of an eschatologically oriented apocalyptic movement seems to have been prompted by the culture crisis of the Hellenistic age, well in advance of the Antiochan persecution. The "symbolic universe" constructed in the Book of the Watchers draws on many traditions, including biblical prophecy, but also retains the imprint of a tradition of pseudoscientific learning.

RELATION TO BIBLICAL TRADITION

The question of continuity with the biblical tradition does not admit of a simple answer, not only because of the diversity of Enoch's sources but also because of the diversity within the older Israelite religion. The biblical canon is shaped to a great degree by Deuteronomic influence. In Deut 30:12 we are assured that God's commandment "is not in heaven, that you should say, 'Who will go up for us to heaven, and bring it to us, that we may hear it and do it?' " The whole premise of Enochic revelation is thereby undermined. A similar perspective is found in the wisdom literature in the rhetorical question of Agur: "Who has ascended to heaven and come down?" (Prov 30:1–4). There is no reason to suppose that the Enoch group rejected the Mosaic law, but it was not sufficient for them; hence the need for the higher angelic revelation. The heavenly revelations cannot be understood as an explanatory midrash on the Torah. They give new information, things that Enoch alone is supposed to have seen (*1 Enoch* 19:3). It is significant that these revelations are ascribed to a figure far older than Moses, older even than the Israelite people.

1 Enoch is very sharply in contrast with Deuteronomic religion.[58] There were other strands of Israelite religion, however, that allowed more room for mythological speculation.[59] The angelic world which enjoys such prominence in *1 Enoch* is a direct development of the heavenly council and host that are widely attested in the Hebrew Bible.[60] The throne vision in *1 Enoch* 14, with its entourage of holy ones, stands in the tradition of the prophetic visions of Micaiah ben Imlah and Isaiah.

Cosmic eschatology also has strong Israelite roots, as Hanson and others have argued. An intriguing passage in Isa 24:21–23 says that "on that day the Lord will punish the host of heaven, in heaven, and the kings of the earth, on the earth. . . . They will be shut up in a prison, and after many days they will be punished." In its context, this passage is related to the reign of the Lord of hosts on Zion. It evidently presupposes a mythical story that is not explicit in the text and raises the possibility that Enoch's concept of the prison for the host of heaven is derived from a tradition that was at home in the Jerusalem cult. Other allusions to the punishment of heavenly beings are found in Psalms 82 and 58. The idea that Yahweh will judge the nations and the world is widely attested in the psalms and the prophets (e.g., Psalms 96; 98; Isa 2:4).

Even in the light of the mythical traditions associated especially with the Jerusalem cult, there is much that is new in Enoch, much of which may be attributed to the distinctive character of the Enoch tradition. No biblical prophet enjoys the same degree of access to the heavenly world. Enoch's revelation is the disclosure of a mystery, which contains extensive information about the heavenly world or about history. It is not simply the proclamation of God's plan. The range of cosmological speculation is greatly enlarged. The angels are now given names and are the focus of much greater attention than was the case in the Hebrew Bible. We may note here the rabbinic tradition that the names of the angels were brought back from Babylon.[61]

Two other points are of more far-reaching importance. First, the hope for judgment after death radically alters the biblical view of salvation. The language of resurrection is used a number of times in the Hebrew Bible for the restoration of the Jewish people—for example, Ezekiel 37 and Isa 26:19.[62] The discussion in *1 Enoch* 22, however, is presented in the context of mythical geography and is indebted both to Babylonian and to Greek traditions.[63] The motif of awakening from sleep used in *1 Enoch* 91:10 echoes Isa 26:19, but the extended discussion in *1 Enoch* 102—104 speaks in terms of the elevation of the righteous to the stars and to the host of heaven.[64] We cannot now be sure of the circumstances in which the belief in the afterlife began to play a role in the Enoch tradition. In view of the cosmological context in the Book of the Watchers, and the association with the angels in the Epistle, we must suspect that reflection on the translation of Enoch himself played a part in this development.

Personal afterlife is not, of course, the only aspect of apocalyptic eschatology. *1 Enoch* also looks for the end of this world and a new creation in which the earth will be transformed, ideas more in accordance with prophetic eschatology. Yet the hope for a blessed afterlife, especially in the angelic form that is explicit in *1 Enoch* 104 has great implications for apocalyptic piety and goes hand in hand with the tendency to mysticism evident in Enoch's association with the angels and in his throne vision.[65]

Second, the claim of a special exclusive revelation often entails a tendency to sectarianism.[66] *1 Enoch* presents an elaborate view of the world based on Enoch's alleged experience. The movement that accepts Enoch as its authority is likely to be at variance with those who do not. It is difficult to assess how far the Enoch movement was estranged from the rest of Jewish society at the various stages of its history. If we can assume that the lunar calendar of rabbinic Judaism was already in force in the third century, the 364-day calendar of the Astronomical Book would have been an obstacle to participation in the cult.[67] However, we are poorly informed about the history of the calendar, and the Enoch group may not have been located in proximity to the Temple in any case. A few passages reflect a negative attitude to the Second Temple or to the priesthood.[68] Yet the Animal Apocalypse seems to mourn the death of Onias III (*1 Enoch* 90:8) and make common cause with Judas Maccabee. The message of the Epistle is intended broadly for the "sons of earth" (*1 Enoch* 105:1–2). If the Animal Apocalypse and the Apocalypse of Weeks are correctly associated with the Hasidim, this would imply active participation in the events of the Maccabean era. It is noteworthy, however, that the books of Enoch were treasured in the Qumran community, which eventually made a cleaner break with Jewish society.[69]

DANIEL AND ENOCH

The apocalyptic visions of Daniel seem prima facie to stand in clearer continuity with biblical prophecy. Two recent studies have independently traced the development of the symbolic vision form from Amos to the apocalypses.[70] Yet the development is also significantly modified by the form of the dream report, as we might expect in the light of Daniel 1— 6.[71] Dream reports throughout the ancient Near East are characteristically presented within a conventionalized frame that tells about the dreamer, the locality, and the circumstances and often reports his reaction at the end.[72] This frame is an important formal element in the visions of Daniel.

Daniel lacks the cosmological interests of Enoch (which recede even in the "historical" Enochic apocalypses of the Maccabean era). Yet the symbolic universe of Daniel is closer to that of Enoch than to its biblical precedents.[73] The heavenly host is more active here than in any other biblical book.[74] The patron angels of the nations are the forces behind history in Daniel 10, as in the Animal Apocalypse, and the victory of Michael in Dan 12:1 is evidently of crucial importance for the Jews on earth.[75] The vision of the divine throne in Daniel 7 is remarkably similar to that of *1 Enoch* 14, and the analogy strongly supports the view that the "holy ones" in Daniel are heavenly beings.[76] The resurrection in Daniel 12, where the wise teachers will shine like stars, directly parallels the formulation of *1 Enoch* 104:2. Further parallels can be drawn between the periodization of history as seventy weeks of years in Daniel 9, the seventy shepherds in the Animal Apocalypse, and the schema of weeks in the Apocalypse of Weeks.

Daniel also attests the rise of a distinct group, the *maśkîlîm*, who act in the time of persecution by instructing the masses. The instruction they give is presumably the view of the world disclosed in Daniel's visions. Here again, the claim to a higher revelation involves a sectarian tendency, although the *maśkîlîm* are actively engaged with the rest of Jewish society. The stance of the Danielic group is rather different from the militant posture of the righteous in *1 Enoch* and does not correspond to what we are told of the Hasidim in the books of Maccabees.[77] The various apocalyptic groups of the Maccabean era can be classified together only if Hasidim is used as a very broad umbrella term. It is noteworthy, however, that both the Danielic and the Enochic writings were preserved at Qumran.

In Daniel as in *Enoch*, we find a movement that has its own historical roots, quite distinct from earlier prophetic groups. In the stress of the Antiochan persecution, it formulated an apocalyptic symbolic universe that owed much to ancient myth.[78] The fact that the canonical Daniel draws so heavily on myth has scandalized some pious commentators, but this was in fact a point of continuity with Israelite tradition, especially with the cult traditions of Jerusalem.[79] Again, the innovations are significant. Daniel does not explicitly expect a new creation, and the hope for a "kingdom" (presumably on earth) has strong biblical precedents, but the hope for salvation is changed radically by the belief in the resurrection of the dead. We must emphasize that the increased use of myth does not detract from the seriousness of human actions in history. It does, however, place those actions in a new perspective, where their value cannot be measured by their success in this world.[80]

CONCLUSION

Jewish apocalypticism, as we find it in *1 Enoch* and Daniel, cannot be adequately described as a child of prophecy any more than it can be adequately attributed to Babylonian influence or any other single source. It was essentially a new creation, designed for the needs of a new age, and one that embraced different movements and traditions. Novelty, of course, is not an obstacle to authenticity. Every stage of Israelite religion is marked by changes, often stimulated by contact with neighboring, pagan religions. Jewish apocalypticism was one of several ways in which Jews of the Hellenistic age attempted to adapt their traditions. Despite their sectarian tendencies, these groups continued to interact with other areas of Jewish society. Even the Essenes, who were extreme in their withdrawal, were still recognized as a Jewish "philosophy" by Josephus. It is increasingly evident that apocalypticism continued to play a part in Judaism long after the rise of Christianity,[81] although it is true that it had a far more central place in the new religion.[82]

NOTES

1. F. M. Cross, "New Directions in the Study of Apocalyptic," *Apocalypticism, JTC* 6 (1969) 161.

2. K. Koch, *Ratlos vor der Apokalyptik* (Gütersloh: Gerd Mohn, 1970; English trans. M. Kohl, *The Rediscovery of Apocalyptic* [SBT 2/22; Naperville: Alec R. Allenson, 1972]).

3. P. D. Hanson, "Apocalypticism," *IDBSup*, 28–34. M. E. Stone ("Lists of Revealed Things in Apocalyptic Literature," *Magnalia Dei, The Mighty Acts of God* [ed. F. M. Cross, W. E. Lemke, and P. D. Miller; Garden City, N.Y.: Doubleday & Co., 1976] 414–52) distinguishes between apocalypse and apocalypticism or apocalyptic, in a manner closer to Koch.

4. Koch, *The Rediscovery*, 23. Koch's list (Daniel, *1 Enoch*, 2 Baruch, 4 Ezra, *Apocalypse of Abraham*, Revelation) is too brief. For the full corpus, see J. J. Collins, ed., *Apocalypse: The Morphology of a Genre, Semeia* 14 (1979). The list of Jewish apocalypses should at least include *2 Enoch*, *3 Baruch*, and *Apocalypse of Zephaniah*, and arguably also *Jubilees* and *Testament of Abraham*. Most of these texts can be found in J. H. Charlesworth, ed., *The Old Testament Pseudepigrapha*, vol. 1: *Apocalyptic Literature and Testaments* (Garden City, N.Y.: Doubleday & Co., 1983).

5. See further my discussion in *The Apocalyptic Imagination: An Introduction to the Jewish Matrix of Christianity* (New York: Crossroad Publishing Co., 1984), chap. 1.

6. See my discussion of the forms of apocalyptic literature in *Daniel, with an Introduction to Apocalyptic Literature* (FOTL 10; Grand Rapids: Wm. B. Eerdmans Publishing Co., 1984).

7. For the typology, see J. J. Collins, "The Jewish Apocalypses," *Semeia* 14 (1979) 12–15, and *The Apocalyptic Imagination*, chap. 1.

8. The rival thesis of G. von Rad (*Die Theologie des Alten Testaments* [5th ed., Munich: Chr. Kaiser Verlag, 1968] 2.316–38) that apocalypticism is derived from wisdom has stimulated much discussion but won little following. For a recent review of scholarship, see M. Knibb, "Prophecy and the Emergence of the Jewish Apocalypses," *Israel's Prophetic Tradition: Essays in Honour of Peter Ackroyd*; (ed. R. Coggins, A. Phillips, and M. Knibb; Cambridge: Cambridge University Press, 1982) 155–80. An important by-product of the discussion has been the observation of affinities between apocalypticism and "mantic wisdom" (H. P. Müller, "Mantische Weisheit und Apokalyptik," VTSup 22 [1972] 269–93).

9. O. Plöger, *Theocracy and Eschatology* (Richmond: John Knox Press, 1968) 108.

10. P. D. Hanson, "Old Testament Apocalyptic Reexamined," *Visionaries and Their Apocalypses* (ed. P. D. Hanson; Philadelphia: Fortress Press, 1983) 53 (originally published in *Interpretation* 25 [1971] 454–79).

11. Hanson, in his article "Apocalypticism" in *IDBSup*, speaks repeatedly of apocalyptic movements.

12. Note, however, Hanson's later essay, "Rebellion in Heaven, Azazel and Euhemeristic Heroes in 1 Enoch 6—11," *JBL* 96 (1977) 195–233.

13. For example, C. Rowland, *The Open Heaven: A Study of Apocalyptic in Judaism and Early Christianity* (New York: Crossroad Publishing Co., 1982) 13–14.

14. J. J. Collins, "Apocalyptic Eschatology as the Transcendence of Death,"

Visionaries and Their Apocalypses, 61–84 (originally published in *CBQ* 37 [1974] 21–43).

15. J. T. Milik, *The Books of Enoch* (Oxford: Clarendon Press, 1976) 5–7.

16. See especially M. E. Stone, *Scriptures, Sects and Visions* (Philadelphia: Fortress Press, 1980) 27–47; reprinted in *Visionaries and Their Apocalypses*, 85–100), and J. C. VanderKam, *Enoch and the Growth of an Apocalyptic Tradition* (CBQMS 16; Washington: Catholic Biblical Association of America, 1984).

17. *Jub* 4:16–25. VanderKam, *Enoch*, 142–49; G. W. E. Nickelsburg, *Jewish Literature Between the Bible and the Mishnah* (Philadelphia: Fortress Press, 1981) 149–50. For the date of *Jubilees*, J. C. VanderKam, *Textual and Historical Studies in the Book of Jubilees* (HSM 14; Missoula, Mont.: Scholars Press, 1977) 214–85.

18. The Similitudes of Enoch (*1 Enoch* 37—71) are a later development, although they are Jewish and no later than the first century C.E. See D. W. Suter, "Weighed in the Balance: The Similitudes of Enoch in Recent Discussion," *RelSRev* 7 (1981) 217–21.

19. On the terminology, see F. Dexinger, *Henochs Zehnwochenapokalypse und offene Probleme der Apokalyptikforschung* (Leiden: E. J. Brill, 1977) 164–77.

20. 1 Macc 2:42; 1 Macc 7:12–13; 2 Macc 14:6. See especially M. Hengel, *Judaism and Hellenism* (Philadelphia: Fortress Press, 1974) 1.179. See the comments of G. W. E. Nickelsburg, "Social Aspects of Palestinian Jewish Apocalypticism," *Apocalypticism in the Mediterranean World and the Near East* (ed. D. Hellholm; Tübingen: J. C. B. Mohr [Paul Siebeck], 1983) 641–54. Related developments are attested in *Jubilees* 23 and CD 1.

21. Hanson ("Apocalypticism," 30) defines apocalypticism as "the symbolic universe in which an apocalyptic movement codifies its identity and interpretation of reality."

22. VanderKam *(Enoch)* has provided the most complete discussion to date.

23. Ibid., chaps. 1 and 2. The association with Enmeduranki was proposed by H. Zimmern in 1903 and has been widely accepted.

24. In the J source (Gen 4:17), Enoch is son of Cain, grandson of Adam.

25. So VanderKam, *Enoch*, 44. For the texts about Enmeduranki, see W. G. Lambert, "Enmeduranki and Related Matters," *JCS* 21 (1967) 126–38.

26. The same phrase is used in connection with Noah in Gen 6:9. Cf. similar expressions for a relationship with God in Mal 2:6 and Mic 6:8.

27. *ANET*, 95. Note also the suggestion of R. Borger ("Die Beschwörungsserie BĪT MĒSERI und die Himmelfahrt Henochs," *JNES* 33 [1974] 183–96), who relates Enoch to Utuabzu, seventh sage and counselor of Enmeduranki, who ascended to heaven.

28. See J. J. Collins, *Between Athens and Jerusalem: Jewish Identity in the Hellenistic Diaspora* (New York: Crossroad Publishing Co., 1983) 32–39, and, more broadly, M. Braun, *History and Romance in Graeco-Oriental Literature* (Oxford: Basil Blackwell, 1938).

29. VanderKam, who has argued at length for the relevance of divination as a background for apocalypticism, notes that the two "certainly have not produced comparable literature" *(Enoch, 62)*.

30. On dreams in the biblical tradition, see E. L. Ehrlich, *Der Traum in Alten Testament* (Berlin: Alfred Töpelmann, 1953). Note the negative evaluations of dreams in Deut 13:1–3; Jer 23:25–28; 29:8; Sir 34:1–8.

31. VanderKam, *Enoch*, 61.

32. See P. von der Osten-Sacken, *Die Apokalyptik in ihrem Verhältnis zu Prophetie und Weisheit* (Theologische Existenz heute 157; Munich: Chr. Kaiser Verlag, 1969) 18–23.

33. J. J. Collins, *The Apocalyptic Vision of the Book of Daniel* (HSM 16; Missoula, Mont.: Scholars Press, 1977) 27–36.

34. W. L. Humphreys, "A Life-Style for the Diaspora: A Study of the Tales of Esther and Daniel," *JBL* 92 (1973) 211–23; J. J. Collins, "The Court-Tales in Daniel and the Development of Apocalyptic," *JBL* 94 (1975) 218–34.

35. This has been repeatedly emphasized in recent years. See the definition of apocalypse in *Semeia* 14 (1979) 9; Rowland, *The Open Heaven,* 13–14; J. Carmignac, "Qu'est-ce que l'apocalyptique? Son emploi à Qumrân," *RQ* 10 (1979) 3–33; H. Stegemann, "Die Bedeutung der Qumranfunde für die Erforschung der Apokalyptik," *Apocalypticism* (ed. Hellholm) 495–530.

36. See the formulation of VanderKam (*Enoch*, 62), who argues that a common structure of revelation through enigmatic signs distinguishes both Mesopotamian divination and Jewish apocalypticism from biblical prophecy. Compare J. J. Collins, "Jewish Apocalyptic Against Its Hellenistic Near Eastern Environment," *BASOR* 220 [1975] 27–36), where I emphasize revelation by interpretation as a widespread characteristic of the Hellenistic age (cf. also *The Apocalyptic Vision,* 67–93). J. Carmignac ("Description du phénomène de l'apocalyptique dans l'Ancien Testament," in *Apocalypticism* [ed. Hellholm] 163–70) argues that dreams are at the origin of apocalypticism, without regard to extrabiblical material.

37. The antiquity of this material is supported by the fact that the Astronomical Book does not reflect a dispute between solar and lunar calendars, as does *Jubilees* in the Maccabean era. Instead, it polemicizes against a 360-day calendar which was never official in Judaism and has its closest parallels in Babylonia. See VanderKam, *Enoch,* 91–104. The primitive character of Enoch's astronomy is emphasized by O. Neugebauer, *The "Astronomical" Chapters of the Ethiopic Book of Enoch (72—82)* (Copenhagen: Munksgaard, 1981).

38. Compare the argument of R. R. Wilson ("From Prophecy to Apocalyptic: Reflections on the Shape of Israelite Religion," *Semeia* 21 [1981] 93) that "the shape of a particular group's religion and literature will depend on the group's social and religious background."

39. The oldest fragments ascribed to the Astronomical Book by Milik have not actually been published and do not overlap at all with the Ethiopic text, although they do overlap with another Qumran fragment of the Astronomical Book. The pre-Maccabean Astronomical Book seems to have been quite different from the text that survived. The original form cannot be reconstructed simply by excising supposed additions from the Ethiopic text. The book as we have it does not describe Enoch's ascent, but clearly presupposes a heavenly tour (cf. 76:1). The clearest reference is in 81:5, where three angels set Enoch down in front of his house. Since these have not been mentioned before, they are thought to be

derived from the Animal Apocalypse (cf. 87:3). The tour framework then may be part of a secondary recension of the Astronomical Book.

40. Hanson, "Rebellion in Heaven," 197, and, in more detail, G. W. E. Nickelsburg, "Apocalyptic and Myth in 1 Enoch 6—11," *JBL* 96 (1977) 384–86, and D. Dimant, "1 Enoch 6—11: A Methodological Perspective," SBLASP (1978) 1:323–39.

41. G. W. E. Nickelsburg, "Enoch, Levi and Peter: Recipients of Revelation in Upper Galilee," *JBL* 100 (1981) 575.

42. J. J. Collins, "The Apocalyptic Technique: Setting and Function in the Book of the Watchers," *CBQ* 44 (1982) 91–111; J. C. Thom, "Aspects of the Form, Meaning and Function of the Book of the Watchers," *Neotestamentica* 17 (1983) 40–48.

43. I. Gruenwald, *Apocalyptic and Merkavah Mysticism* (Leiden: E. J. Brill, 1980) 21–42; Rowland, *The Open Heaven*, 78–80.

44. A. L. Oppenheim, *The Interpretation of Dreams in the Ancient Near East* (Philadelphia: American Philosophical Society, 1956) 214. Note especially the "Vision of the Nether World" attributed to an Assyrian prince in a tablet from the seventh century (*ANET*, 109–10).

45. So esp. Gruenwald, *Apocalyptic and Merkavah Mysticism.*

46. While Enoch is given the privilege of entering to the divine presence that is denied to some angels, VanderKam's statement that he "attains at least the status of an angel" (*Enoch,* 131) does not seem to be justified in the Book of the Watchers. Such a definitive exaltation is attested, however, in the later tradition: *1 Enoch* 71; *2 Enoch* 22, and the so-called *3 Enoch* 4.

47. D. W. Suter, "Fallen Angel, Fallen Priest: The Problem of Family Purity in 1 Enoch 6—16, *HUCA* 50 (1979) 115–35; Nickelsburg, "Enoch, Levi and Peter," 586.

48. Nickelsburg, "Apocalyptic and Myth," 383–405. Nickelsburg sees an allusion to the wars of the Diadochi in *1 Enoch* 6—11.

49. *1 Enoch* 98:4 counters the deterministic implications of the story of the Watchers by insisting that "sin was not sent on the earth but man of himself created it."

50. M. Himmelfarb (*Tours of Hell: An Apocalyptic Form in Jewish and Christian Literature* [Philadelphia: University of Pennsylvania Press, 1983] 50–60) comments on the form of the tour and points to analogies in Ezekiel 40–48 and in ancient dream interpretation. These analogies do not account for the range of the content.

51. Stone (*Scriptures, Sects and Visions,* 34–35) acknowledges "some eschatological interest, particularly in chapters 1—6 and 10:14–16" but passes over the eschatological significance of Enoch's tour.

52. VanderKam's statement that the order of the universe is presupposed and unchanging in the Book of the Watchers (*Enoch,* 7 n. 24) does not appear to take the descent of the Watchers into account.

53. See VanderKam, *Enoch,* 137–38. The parallels that have been adduced include the travels of Gilgamesh and the Odyssey, esp. bk 11.

54. It is often observed that many of the places observed by Enoch are actually located on earth (e.g., Rowland, *The Open Heaven*, 124–26). His experience is

transcendent, however, in the sense that it goes beyond the normal range of human experience.

55. VanderKam's statement that the Astronomical Book "does not disclose a transcendent reality beyond the perceivable universe" (*Enoch,* 109) is odd, since he recognizes the pervasive role of the angels (103 n. 84).

56. VanderKam (*Enoch,* 106–7) argues that chaps. 80 and 81 are secondary additions. The allusion to Enoch's return to earth at 81:5 seems to presuppose the Animal Apocalypse (87:3), but this may be part of a broader revision rather than simply an addition. The objection to chap. 80 is that the disruption of the stars allegedly contradicts 72:1, which says that their regulations will last until the new creation. Whether there is a real contradiction here is questionable. The regulations may still be in force if some stars digress, or the events described in chap. 80 may be part of the transition to the new creation.

57. This is not to say that any of the extant *Enoch* books were necessarily written in Babylonia. It is generally agreed that at least the Book of Dreams and Epistle were written in Palestine. The provenance of the Book of the Watchers is quite uncertain. The book draws on various traditions besides Babylonian ones. Milik thinks the author "was perhaps himself a Jerusalemite, for he has an excellent knowledge of the environs of the Holy City (26:2—27:1)" (*The Books of Enoch,* 26). Nickelsburg has a stronger case for Galilean origin because of the peculiar prominence of the region around Dan and Mt. Hermon in the story of the Watchers ("Enoch, Levi and Peter," 586–87) but even here the geographical location may have been attached to one of the sources of the Book of the Watchers.

58. The covenantal allusions noted by L. Hartman in *1 Enoch 1—5* (*Asking for a Meaning: A Study of 1 Enoch 1—5* [Lund: Gleerup, 1979]) are placed in a new context of cosmic rather than Deuteronomic law. Consequently it seems misleading to describe Enoch's "pattern of religion" as "covenantal nomism" (as does E. P. Sanders, *Paul and Palestinian Judaism* [Philadelphia: Fortress Press, 1977]). See the discussion of law in *1 Enoch* in C. Münchow, *Ethik und Eschatologie. Ein Beitrag zum Verständnis der frühjüdischen Apokalyptik* (Göttingen: Vandenhoeck & Ruprecht, 1981) 16–42.

59. See the suggestive article of M. Barker, "Some Reflections Upon the Enoch Myth," *JSOT* 15 (1980) 7–29, although she greatly exaggerates the importance of the fallen angels in the Enochic corpus. See also Stone, *Scriptures, Sects and Visions,* 30.

60. F. M. Cross, "The Council of Yahweh in Second Isaiah," *JNES* 12 (1953) 274–77; P. D. Miller, *The Divine Warrior in Early Israel* (HSM 5; Cambridge: Harvard University Press, 1973) 66–74; E. T. Mullen, Jr., *The Assembly of the Gods: The Divine Council in Canaanite and Early Hebrew Literature* (HSM 24; Chico, Calif.: Scholars Press, 1980).

61. *Bereshit Rabba,* at Gen 18:1. H. Bietenhard, *Die himmlische Welt im Urchristentum und Spätjudentum* (Tübingen: J. C. B. Mohr [Paul Siebeck], 1951) 12.

62. Isa 26:19 is sometimes taken as a reference to the resurrection of individuals (e.g., L. J. Greenspoon, "The Origin of the Idea of Resurrection," *Traditions in Transformation* [ed. B. Halpern and J. D. Levenson; Winona Lake, Ind.:

Eisenbrauns, 1981] 284–86), but the context is clearly concerned with the well-being of the nation rather than of individuals.

63. See the thorough study by M.-T. Wacker, *Weltordnung und Gericht. Studien zu 1 Henoch 22* (Würzburg: Echter, 1982). Babylonian influence is apparent in the location of the underworld inside a mountain, Greek influence in the differentiation of groups after death.

64. See especially G. W. E. Nickelsburg, *Resurrection, Immortality and Eternal Life in Intertestamental Judaism* (Harvard Theological Studies 26; Cambridge: Harvard University Press, 1972) 112–29.

65. On apocalyptic piety, see J. C. H. Lebram, "The Piety of the Jewish Apocalyptists," *Apocalypticism* (ed. Hellholm), 171–210.

66. This is not necessarily always the case. *2 Baruch* uses the claim of special revelation to buttress the authority of the Mosaic law.

67. The history of the calendar is in dispute. See J. C. VanderKam, "The Origin, Character and Early History of the 364-Day Calendar: A Reassessment of Jaubert's Hypotheses," *CBQ* 41 (1979) 390–411; P. R. Davies, "Calendrical Change and Qumran Origins: An Assessment of VanderKam's Theory," *CBQ* 45 (1983) 80–89; and VanderKam, "The 364-Day Calendar in the Enochic Literature," SBLASP (1983) 157–65.

68. We have noted that a critique of the priesthood may be implied in the Book of the Watchers. The Apocalypse of Weeks dismisses the entire postexilic period as "an apostate generation" and ignores the restoration of the Persian era. The Animal Apocalypse says that the offerings of the Second Temple were impure.

69. On the affinities of the Enoch literature with the Qumran sect, see especially G. W. E. Nickelsburg, "The Epistle of Enoch and the Qumran Literature," *JJS* 33 (1982) 333–48.

70. S. Niditch, *The Symbolic Vision in Biblical Tradition* (HSM 30: Chico, Calif.: Scholars Press, 1983); K. Koch, "Vom profetischen zum apokalyptischen Visionsbericht," *Apocalypticism* (ed. Hellholm) 413–46.

71. Collins, *Daniel.*

72. Oppenheim, *The Interpretation of Dreams,* 187.

73. See my remarks in "Apocalyptic Genre and Mythic Allusions in Daniel," *JSOT* 21 (1981) 83–100.

74. The extraordinary claim of W. S. Towner (*Daniel* [Interpretation; Atlanta: John Knox Press, 1984] 173) that "a de-mythologizing of angels and the heavenly forces has already taken place in the Danielic corpus" cannot be defended historically.

75. His importance is all the greater if he is identified with the "one like a son of man" in chap. 7. See my arguments in *The Apocalyptic Vision,* 144–46. See also Rowland, *The Open Heaven,* 178–83.

76. Ibid., 123–44. See also A. Lacocque, *The Book of Daniel* (Atlanta: John Knox Press, 1979) 130–32.

77. Collins, *The Apocalyptic Vision,* 201–5. Compare Nickelsburg, "Social Aspects of Palestinian Jewish Apocalypticism," 647–48.

78. Especially in the adaptation of the Canaanite Baal/Yamm myth in chap. 7. See Collins, *The Apocalyptic Vision,* 96–104. A. J. Ferch (*The Son of Man in Daniel 7* [Berrien Springs, Mich.: Andrews University Press, 1979]) mis-

construes the nature of mythic allusions, which inevitably involve a transformation of the mythic source. See my comments in "Apocalyptic Genre and Mythic Allusions," 91–95.

79. This has been shown especially by Hanson, "Old Testament Apocalyptic Reexamined" and idem, "Jewish Apocalyptic Against Its Ancient Near Eastern Environment," *RB* 78 (1971) 31–58.

80. Collins, "Apocalyptic Eschatology as the Transcendence of Death."

81. A. J. Saldarini, "Apocalypses and 'Apocalyptic' in Rabbinic Literature and Mysticism," *Semeia* 14 (1979) 187–205; Gruenwald, *Apocalyptic and Merkavah Mysticism;* Rowland, *The Open Heaven,* 271–348.

82. See my essay, "The Apocalyptic Context of Christian Origins," *The Bible and Its Traditions, Michigan Quarterly Review* 22 (1983) 250–64.

30

The Sources of Torah: Psalm 119 and the Modes of Revelation in Second Temple Judaism

JON D. LEVENSON

I

An essential aspect of the traditional Jewish understanding of Scripture is the priority of the Pentateuch. The rabbis of the Talmudic era assumed that the first five books of the Hebrew Bible, with the possible exception of only a few verses,[1] were revealed to Moses on Mt. Sinai, a claim that neither those books nor others in the Hebrew Bible actually make. Following the ascription of unique prophetic gifts to Moses, which *is* in the biblical text,[2] the rabbis recognized only a subordinate and corroborative role for non-Pentateuchal, which for them meant post-Pentateuchal, revelation. In fact, they tended to assume that occurrences of the term *tôrâ* elsewhere in biblical literature refer to the deposit of Mosaic revelation. Thus, when the psalmist beatifies the man "whose delight is in the teaching *(tôrâ)* of YHWH, and who meditates on his teaching *(tôrâ)* day and night" (Ps 1:2), a rabbinic midrash explains that "if one occupies himself with the Torah and puts it into practice, it is as if he had received it from Mount Sinai."[3] For the rabbis, the psalmist's *tôrâ* can only be Moses'. The faithful Jew studies the Torah continually, explores its treasures, and absorbs its beauty, but even a prophet may not change the ancient and eternal revelation. "Forty-eight male and seven female prophets prophesied to Israel," reports an anonymous source in the Talmud, "and they neither took away from nor added to that which is written in the Torah, with the exception of the reading of the Scroll [of Esther on Purim]."[4] Even this apparent innovation is then legitimated by reference to the exodus and thus shown to be no innovation at all but only the implementation in a new situation of a Mosaic principle. In fact, in the light of the prestige of origins that surrounded the Pentateuch in the Pharisaic-rabbinic mind, any innovation, no matter how minor or how radical, required a Pentateuchal argument. Similarly, the ex-Pharisee Paul, in arguing that observance of the Mosaic law was not incumbent

559

upon gentile Christians, cited Deuteronomy (of all books!) as a proof text, and he supported his claim that Sinaitic revelation is actually a form of slavery with an allegorical reading of the rivalry of Sarah and Hagar in Genesis, a book revealed on Sinai.[5]

In both the rabbinic and the apostolic cases, the doctrine of the priority of the Pentateuch serves to thwart consciousness of change and thus to uphold the insistence of the Pentateuch itself upon the finality of Mosaic revelation (Deut 4:2; 13:1). The tradition is unitary; its ostensible innovations came from within, not from without, and they have been part of the tradition all along. The derivation of change from an immutable archetype serves to defeat time, for both the ancient and the contemporary traditionalist. The modern, critical study of the Hebrew Bible (and of the New Testament), on the other hand, moves in the opposite direction. It aims to promote a consciousness of time by focusing on innovations and change and challenging the putative immutability, unity, and self-referentiality of the tradition. One of the programmatic discoveries of biblical criticism was the idea that large parts of the Pentateuch date from *after* the prophets, not before.[6] It is for this reason that almost none of the "latter" prophets mention Moses, Sinai, the tablets of the covenant, or the like, or quote from the Pentateuch. This, in turn, raises the possibility that biblical references to *tôrâ* need not refer to the Pentateuch at all. The reference may be simply to any oracle or other piece of sacred lore. Indeed, critical scholarship has established that the term *tôrâ* has many meanings in the Hebrew Bible. Those meanings can contradict each other.[7]

In a very limited way, rabbinic tradition anticipates this non-identification of Torah and Pentateuch. Numerous rabbinic sources assume that the Pentateuch is only part of Moses' Torah. In addition to this "Torah in writing," there is, they assert, also a "Torah on the mouth," an Oral Torah, which is identical with rabbinic teaching. Thus, another midrash on Ps 1:2 affirms that God made a covenant with Israel "that the Oral Torah would never be forgotten," and sees an allusion to this in Isa 59:21: "The words which I put in your mouth will not leave your mouth and the mouths of your descendants... ever."[8] The rabbis did not originate the idea that ostensibly new norms had already been revealed to Moses on Sinai. Instead, they inherited it from their antecedents in the Second Temple period. In *Jubilees,* for example, one sees the fruit of such an interaction. This pseudepigraphal book claims to be the secret revelation by the Angel of the Presence to Moses on Mt. Sinai.[9] In fact, it is a recomposition of Genesis 1—Exodus 12. To call it a supplementation or interpretation of that bloc of Pentateuchal material is not quite accurate, for the author or authors of *Jubilees* did not view the Pentateuch as so

560

fixed that new material could be only appended to it or derived exegetically from it. Instead, for them, the Pentateuch is authoritative, but not definitive; it is *tôrâ,* but not yet a fixed text. The traditionary process that produced the Pentateuch remains alive; Genesis 1—Exodus 12 has not yet reached its final form.[10] What made this fluidity possible was the fact that, despite many traditional and critical statements to the contrary, divine inspiration *(rûaḥ haqqôdeš)* was not universally thought to have departed from Israel with the death of the last of the canonical prophets.[11] Prophecy survived, even though the growing influence of the book religion required it to deal increasingly with Scripture, a new phenomenon.[12] We cannot say for sure that the Pharisees saw inspiration as a source of the non-Pentateuchal ingredient of their twofold Torah. We do know, however, that books like *Jubilees* can document the first occurrence of an institution presupposed by the rabbis but unattested in the Pentateuch or elsewhere in the Hebrew Bible. The Mishnah, for example, assumes that wine is drunk during the Passover banquet *(sēder).*[13] But there is no mention of wine in the Passover regulations in the Pentateuch. Instead, we find the first reference to the custom in *Jub* 49:6. In short, although the rabbis did not recognize *Jubilees* and although it contradicts their *hǎlākâ* on numerous points (most important, the calendar), the inspired revelation of *Jubilees* is a witness to at least one important item of rabbinic non-Pentateuchal Torah.

II

In all biblical literature, no text is more preoccupied with *tôrâ* than Psalm 119. M. Dahood, perhaps influenced by the title given this poem in the Vulgate *(Divinae legis encomium),* termed it the "Psalm of the Law." Yet, as he too recognized, *tôrâ* can refer to many different forms of divine instruction.[14] The chief object of the following pages is to probe the meaning of the term in Psalm 119. In so doing, we should be able to uncover the psalmist's own theology and his place in the history of Israelite religion.

Unfortunately it is not the theology of Psalm 119, but its sheer formal complexity, that has preoccupied exegetes for generations. The psalm is an acrostic in which each of the twenty-two letters of the Hebrew alphabet is given one stanza of eight bicola, for a total of 176 verses. In 1898, D. M. Müller published a study in which he asserted an even more elaborate organizing principle.[15] Each stanza, he maintained, has exactly eight synonyms for "law," and every verse has one and only one of these terms. The eight synonyms—*tôrâ* ("teaching," "revelation"), *ʿēdâ* or *ʿēdût* ("decree"), *piqqûd* ("order"), *miṣwâ* ("commandment"), *'imrâ* ("utterance"), *mišpāṭ* ("law"), *ḥōq* ("ordinance"),[16] and *dābār* ("word," "prophecy")—were derived from the Torah doxology of Ps 19:8–11, of which our psalm is an expanded version. Nine years later, C. A. and E. G. Briggs, charting the placement of the eight synonyms, thought that they had come upon an even more intricate system, one so complex that only an examination of their diagram can do it justice.[17] The essence of it is an elaborate, although imperfect order of occurrence for the eight synonyms, one marked by frequent chiasmus cutting across stanzas. As if this were not enough, B. Bonkamp found significance in the number of appearances of the various synonyms. *Miṣwâ, ḥōq,* and *dābār* appear twenty-two times, *mišpāṭ* and *ʿēdût* twenty-three times, *piqqûd,* twenty-one times, *tôrâ* twenty-five times, and *ʾimrâ* nineteen times. If this seems to destroy Müller's original observation and to suggest randomness where he saw consummate regularity, note that the sum of these figures is 177, or—if we omit *miṣwâ* in v 48 as a dittography from the prior verse—176, exactly the number of verses in the poem![18]

The eightfold acrostic format, by far the most elaborate in the Hebrew Bible, is alone persuasive evidence for the high value the author placed on discipline and formal constraints, a value that is no less prized in his theology. On the other hand, the elaborate patterns discovered by modern scholars can be sustained only through massive textual emendation— in other words, through a circular process by which a pattern is intuited from the text and the text "corrected" so as to conform to the pattern. A. Deissler, in his fine doctoral dissertation on this psalm, pointed out that in the Masoretic Text only four stanzas correspond to Müller's pattern.[19] The numerous emendations proposed by Müller and others are indefensible on text-critical grounds. In truth, Deissler lists not eight synonyms but ten.[20] *ʾŌraḥ* ("path") in v 15 and *derek* ("way") in vv 3 and 37 are certainly synonyms of the octad; the emendation to *dābār* in the last verse, suggested by a small minority of Hebrew manuscripts and by a Targum, is unwarranted and does not solve the problem of the textually unimpeachable attestation of *derek* in v 3. Only five of the eight synonyms appear in Ps 19:8–11. Even if one emends the "fear" *(yirʾat)* of YHWH in v 10 to the "utterance" *(ʾimrat)* of YHWH (without versional support), one still has to invent *ḥōq* and *dābār.* Furthermore, not every verse in Psalm 119 shows one of the eight synonymous terms. Verses 90 and 122 lack a term for "law,"[21] whereas, by contrast, vv 15, 16, 43, 160, 168, and 172 have two each.[22] If this is correct, and circular reasoning is not implemented, we come to 182 terms, not the 176 that Bonkamp counted. In sum, the evidence suggests that the author of Psalm 119 was committed to using one of the ten synonyms in each verse of his poem, but not so rigidly as to preclude deviation. The rarity of two of the synonyms relative to the other eight suggests that the equation of the number of frequently used terms with the number of bicola in each stanza is not coincidence. On the other hand, it does not seem to have been the author's intention to employ each of the eight terms only once in each stanza, and the presence of five of those eight in Ps 19:8–11 is best explained by reason of the identity of the subject matter and not by appeal to literary influence.

III

In spite of the lack of necessary connection with Psalm 19, the observation that the style of Psalm 119 is anthological[23] is correct. That is, the psalm tends to paraphrase other biblical texts. One notes, for example, a very high degree of affinity with Jeremiah. "Though princes sit in session and speak against me," avers the author to his God, "your servant meditates upon your ordinances" (v 23). The wording recalls Baruch's reading of Jeremiah's scroll to a session of the princes (Jer 36:1–2), an episode that forces Jeremiah into hiding (v 26). The psalmist's cry, "When will you execute justice upon those who persecute me?" (Ps 119:84) recalls Jeremiah's demand that YHWH "avenge me of those who persecute me" (Jer 15:15). In fact, of the nine attestations of *rōdĕpay* ("those who persecute me"), three are in Jeremiah and two in Psalm 119. When the psalmist complains, that "arrogant men have dug pits for me" (Ps 119:85), he echoes Jeremiah's complaint in Jer 18:20, 22. These verses account for three out of only seven attestations of *šûḥâ/šîḥâ* ("pit").[24] And when the psalmist begs God to "champion my case and redeem me" (Ps 119:154), he is most likely influenced by Jer 50:34, in which it is asserted that "their powerful redeemer will champion their case." Although references to Jeremiah, such as these, are the most frequent, Deissler has demonstrated that the psalmist makes ample use of several biblical books,[25] especially Isaiah, Proverbs, and Job.

In his theology, the psalmist is, with certain important qualifications that I shall make, closest to Deuteronomy. The affinity is also lexical. Of the forty-nine attestations of the form *lišmôr/lišmōr* ("to observe"), for example, fifteen appear in Deuteronomy, thirteen in the Deuteronomistic History, and six in Psalm 119. These three corpora thus account for over two-thirds of the appearances of this familiar expression. *Bĕkol lēb(āb)* ("with all the heart"), when applied to praise of God or inner commitment to him and his will, appears a total of thirty-two times, of which Deuteronomy accounts for seven and the Deuteronomistic History and Psalm 119 for six each. Of the remaining thirteen attestations, three are the Chronicler's duplications of the Deuteronomistic History. In the light of the psalm's striking affinity with Jeremiah, which is theologically and lexically close to Deuteronomy and was redacted by Deuteronomistic sources, this strong overlap with Deuteronomy itself is predictable.

The concern with commandments, under various names, is also common to Psalm 119 and Deuteronomy. Indeed, in some Deuteronomistic paraenetic texts (e.g., Deut 4:1–6), one can hear as many as five of the eight synonyms of Psalm 119 in only a few verses. In contrast, distinctive Priestly terminology is largely absent in the psalm. For example, in spite of the penitential tone of the psalm, the expressions *wěnislaḥ (lô)* ("and he shall be forgiven") and *kippēr* ("to make atonement") are missing, although they are mainstays of the P idiom and denote central items of Priestly theology. The poet stands in the Deuteronomic tradition of repentance,[26] not in the Priestly tradition of atonement and expiation. He stresses recommitment to the commandments (e.g., v 59) but never mentions the cult or the priesthood.

This familiarity with so much of the Hebrew Bible has suggested to many scholars the period of Ezra and Nehemiah as the date or at least the *terminus a quo* of Psalm 119. (The clear influence of Deuteronomy fits Nehemiah's circles better than Ezra's.)[27] On the other hand, certain salient Deuteronomic concepts are absent from the psalm. For example, the word and the idea *běrît* ("covenant") are nowhere to be found in this poem. Their absence suggests that it is an error to derive all concern for law and commandments in the Hebrew Bible from covenant theology, as many scholars of "biblical theology" are inclined to do.[28] Similarly, the exodus and the promised land and even the people Israel—all central to the Deuteronomic (and Priestly) covenant theology—are unmentioned in this longest of psalms. Even more surprising in a composition so influenced by Deuteronomy and other Scripture is the absence of any mention of Moses. In fact, whereas Moses is the great teacher of Torah in Deuteronomy,[29] in Psalm 119 God himself is the teacher. It is he who discloses commandments, teaches, enlightens, and imparts discernment to the psalmist.[30] This seems usually to occur without an intermediary, in spite of some slight reference to teachers and elders (vv 99–100). The unmediated character of the revelation of commandments is in pointed contradiction to Deuteronomic tradition[31] and to the whole exaltation of Moses' prophetic gifts upon which the doctrine of the priority and preeminence of the Pentateuch is founded. "Teach me!" "Reveal to me!" "Make me understand!" "Grace me with your Torah!" "Give me wisdom!" Although a rigid application of form-critical method would confirm H. Gunkel's view that Psalm 119 is a *Mischgedicht*,[32] a poem of mixed form, the composition does have a thematic center: it is a prayer for illumination and revelation. The author insists that however much he has strayed (vv 67, 71), never having forgotton the laws of God, he is still worthy to come into a charismatic experience of them or others like them:

Give me discernment, and I will keep your Torah,
I will observe it with all my heart.
Lead me in the path of your commandments,
For in it have I found delight.
(Ps 119:34–35)

On the one hand, he knows the Torah and has spent his life learning it. On the other, he prays to have it disclosed to him as if it is new. The likelihood is that the psalmist's Torah lacks a constant identity. It is like the *tôrâ* of a prophet, which comes sporadically. Between oracles, the prophet can only cherish the old ones and prepare himself spiritually for a new one:[33]

Do not utterly strip away *(taṣṣēl)* from my
mouth your word of truth,
For I have put my hope in your laws.
(Ps 119:43)

The only other appearance of *'āṣal*[34] in this sense occurs when God "strips away" some of Moses' spirit in order to impart it to the seventy elders, who validate their office by prophesying (Num 11:17, 25). Nothing in the psalm hints that the author considers his own pneumatic experience inferior to Moses' and only corroborative of it. In fact, in contradiction to all Deuteronomic tradition (including Jeremiah), Psalm 119 lacks any trace of book consciousness. In contrast, the Deuteronomistic History, in language reminiscent of our psalm, commends conformity to the Torah of Moses (by which is meant Deuteronomy), for example:

You shall observe the charge of YHWH your God to walk in his ways *(derek)*, to keep his ordinances *(ḥōq)*, his commandments *(miṣwâ)*, his laws *(mišpāṭ)* and his decrees *('ēdût)*, as is written in the Torah of Moses, that you may succeed in all that you do, wherever you may turn. (1 Kgs 2:3)

If our psalmist's Torah had been written, if, in other words, his prayer were only for the gift of pneumatic exegesis, then the exigencies of the acrostic format should have made some reference to a book and to writing all the more likely. Instead of beginning the first two *kaf* verses (Ps 119:81–82) with different forms of the same verb *(kālâ)*, he could have begun, in good Deuteronomic idiom, with a clause like this:

kātûb bělibbî sēper tôrātěkā . . .
Inscribed on my heart is the Book of your Torah . . .

Instead of using *mâ* and *mikkol* each twice in the *mēm* stanza (vv 97, 103; 99, 101), he could have employed the name of Moses at least once. And in place of the exceedingly rare word *sāmar* ("creeps") in v 120, he might have begun the verse with *sēper* ("book") or *Sīnay* ("Sinai"). But he did not, and there is no reason to assume that his Torah is limited to the Pentateuch or even dominated by it or any other book.[35]

The absence of awareness of Moses and his Torah Book casts into doubt the association of Psalm 119 with the agenda of Ezra and Nehemiah, for in both of their careers, the Moses Book was a central feature.[36] In contrast, the psalmist receives his laws from teachers and elders (Ps 119:99–100), but especially from unmediated spiritual experience, including the charismatic gift of wisdom. His anthological style does indeed suggest a date well into the period of the Second Temple. But his openness to private illumination argues that he is closer typologically, although not necessarily chronologically, to the position of *Jubilees*, in which Scripture, still fluid, and prophecy, still active, interact to produce more Scripture and perhaps, in those who read it, more spiritual experience. It seems likely that the psalm was written to serve as an inducement for the kind of revelation and illumination for which it petitions. Its high degree of regularity and repetition can have a mesmerizing effect upon those who recite it, with the octad of synonyms functioning like a mantra and providing a relaxing predictability while banishing thoughts that distract from the object of contemplation. If the goal of the author was to create the psychic conditions conducive to the spiritual experience he seeks, then those commentators who wish the psalm were shorter have missed the point of it.[37] Its idea can be communicated in a verse or two, indeed in any verse or two of the 176. But merely knowing the theology is not equivalent to being in the state of mind that comes from reading it in a deliberate and reflective fashion, such as that which the medieval Catholics called *lectio divina*. There are liturgies that are best short, and others, like Psalm 119, that work only if they are long.

IV

What are the commandments that the author of Psalm 119 insists that he has always observed? To those who see the author as devoted to the Pentateuch, the answer is obvious: he is speaking of the Pentateuchal laws, for example, the Sabbath, love of one's neighbor, the dietary laws, the pursuit of justice. But, if so, then why does he never mention any specifics? Why does he not insist, with Moses and Samuel, that he has never misappropriated property, or, with Ezekiel, that he has never eaten forbidden food?[38] The utter lack of concreteness and specificity in his discussion of commandments is further evidence against the assumption that the Pentateuch is uppermost in his mind. Instead, the usage in Psalm 119 is close to that of Proverbs, where *miṣwâ* (and its synonyms) indicates the counsel of a sage rather than juridical or cultic norms:

[13]He who disdains a "word" (*dābār*) will thereby suffer injury,
And he who reveres a commandment (*miṣwâ*) will be rewarded.
[14]The teaching (*tôrâ*) of a sage is a fountain of life,
Enabling one to avoid deadly snares.
[15]Good sense brings favor,
But the way (*derek*) of the treacherous is harsh.
(Prov 13:13–15)

Here, as always in the Hebrew Bible, the Torah of the sage refers to prudent advice which enables his disciples to succeed in the world. Wisdom literature sees this advice, not as one person's opinion, but as a revelation of the will of God. It is for that reason that the proverbs can be certain that those who spurn a "word" will suffer calamity. In fact, the wisdom the sage imparts is itself often seen as divine knowledge:

[4]Those who forsake instruction *(tôrâ)* praise the wicked,
But those who heed instruction *(tôrâ)* fight them.
[5]Evil men do not understand justice *(mišpāṭ)*,
But those who seek YHWH understand everything.
(Prov 28:4–5)

Wisdom *(ḥokmâ)* is a gift of God, as we see, for example, for the cases of Bezalel, Solomon, and the coming Davidide in Isaiah 11.[39] Like Solomon, the author of Psalm 119 prays that God endow him with discernment, which, in turn, will enable him to understand the commandments. Here too, these are most likely the general maxims whose observance ensures prosperity and victory (v 98) rather than the covenant stipulations of the Pentateuchal codes, which were thought to produce the same effect. The strictly sapiential concept of commandments, which pays no attention to covenant, is a significant deviation from Deuteronomy, which blends the two theologies.[40] In this, Psalm 119 is closer to Proverbs.

How shall we put together the evident influence of Deuteronomic tradition (including Jeremiah) and this sapiential morality? On the one hand, the idiom of the psalm and even, as we shall see, its content show too much of the influence of Pentateuchal literature for the author to have been a classic wisdom teacher *(ḥākām).* On the other hand, I have argued that the inclusion in his understanding of Torah of immediate revelations and sapiential motifs, but not of book awareness, indicates considerable distance from the emerging Pentateuchal focus of much postexilic Judaism. In short, the author knows the Pentateuch (or at least parts of it), but does not limit Torah to it.[41] In this, he resembles Joshua ben Sira, the savant of the early second century B.C.E. who left us the book that the Catholic Church calls Ecclesiasticus. Ben Sira regularly imitates the Hebrew Bible, shows a special predilection for Deuteronomy, and even identifies Wisdom with Moses' covenant book (Sir 24:1–29).[42] Apparently the oldest witness we have to what became the central Jewish institutions of the *bêt midrāš* and the *yĕšîbâ* (Sir 51:23, 29), both meaning an academy,[43] he was a teacher whose curriculum included Pentateuch, wisdom collections, and prophecy (Sir 39:1–11). Great though the scriptural influence on him was, his book is hardly a collection of scholia on the Hebrew Bible. In fact, it is remarkable how rarely Ben Sira refers to Scripture. Most of his book is a collection of maxims and poetic essays on proper behavior, in the style of the Hebrew Bible, but without the citation of it, and presented through the prism of Ben Sira's own theology. His translator and grandson identifies the themes of the book as "discipline (or, education) and wisdom" (*paideian kai sophian*, Prologue, v 12). The highly pedagogical idiom (e.g., Sir 31:22) indicates that this sapiential material, too, formed part of the curriculum of his *bêt midrāš*, evidently the larger part. His theology was one that saw the Pentateuch as the Jewish particularization and the supreme exemplification of something larger, Wisdom, but did not seek to limit Wisdom to the Pentateuch (or the other sections of the Hebrew Bible) or to require a scriptural base for all valid teaching. Ben Sira's use of pneumatic language to describe wisdom teaching (Sir 39:6) recalls Psalm 119 and suggests that he regarded his own book as inspired. But unlike Psalm 119, he manifests an acute consciousness of the book, a deep commitment to the cultus (Sir 50:1–21), and no reticence about naming the heroes of Israel's sacred history (Sir 44—50).

The psalmist so focuses upon *ethos* that he barely notices *mythos*, in this case, the history of redemption. The latter is reflected only in the form of ostensibly autobiographical statements that show the influence of the old stories. When, for example, the psalmist cries out, "I am an alien in the land!" (Ps 119:19), he recalls both Abraham's self-introduction to the Hittites ("I am alien resident among you") and Moses' naming his son Gershom, "because he said 'I was an alien *(gēr)* in a foreign land.' "[44] The use of "house of my sojourning" (*bêt mĕgûrāy*, Ps 119:54) to express the same idea is similarly reminiscent of the great Pentateuchal story. Of the other nine attestations of *mĕgûrê*, six appear in Genesis and Exodus, and one of the others (Ezek 20:38) in the context of the new Exodus. His final self-characterization—"I have wandered like a lost *('ōbēd)* sheep" (Ps 119:176)—recalls the confession of the farmer presenting his firstfruits: "My father [Jacob] was a lost *('ōbēd)* Aramean" (Deut 26:5). In short, the resonance of the diction implies an identification of the *persona* of the psalmist with a homeless Israel, trusting in an unfulfilled promise. The focus narrows, however, in Ps 119:46, when the psalmist declares that he speaks of YHWH's decrees "in the presence of kings, and I am not embarrassed." This is not Israel, but an ideal Israelite modeled on any or all of a number of figures who spoke fearlessly before kings, even chastizing them—Abraham, Isaac, Moses, Aaron, Daniel, Esther, Nehemiah, and many of the prophets, especially Jeremiah (e.g., Jer 38:14–28). In good prophetic fashion, the author identifies fidelity with a subgroup of the Jewish nation. His cry in Ps 119:126, "It is time to act, YHWH; they have nullified your teaching *(tôrâ),*" is reminiscent of Elijah's protest that "I have acted zealously for YHWH, God of hosts, because the Israelites have abandoned your covenant. . . . I alone have survived, and they are trying to take my life" (1 Kgs 19:14). In fact, the persecutions of Elijah and Jeremiah have had an important influence upon the self-image of the psalmist, that is, upon the self-image he wishes Jewry to have. That he has suffered for the sake of the commandments is one of his constant protestations;[45] he is a near-martyr. Only his faithfulness to the commandments has kept him alive. His identification with a faithful minority of a generally nonobservant people suggests a situation of sectarian conflict. But the language is too formulaic and stereotypical for us to be confident of the precise identities of the parties.

Just as the highly variegated national history has been telescoped into one person's biography, so have all the messages of the tradition been reduced to one great dichotomy—to keep the commandments or to forsake them. This choice, the psalmist seems to say, is the constant in every situation the Jew faces. Its invariability makes the particulars of the situations irrelevant—hence, no overt reference to the heroes of *Heilsgeschichte,* in striking contradiction to Ben Sira's "Praise of the Famous Men" (Sir 44—50).[46] For the psalmist, everything is a consequence of the *dābār,* a term that denotes not only a commandment or a promise but also the energetic transformative "word" through which God effects his will.[47] The *dābār* of God is "posted in the heavens" and governs the astral bodies (Ps 119:89–91),[aj1038] yet it is also available to the speaker, who has striven to observe it (v 101). bin other words, the commandments that the psalmist practices, even those which may be Pentateuchal, constitute a kind of revealed natural law. They enable him to bring his own life into harmony with the rhythm of the cosmos and to have access to the creative and life-giving energy that drives the world. The commandments, of whatever origin, are not simply positive law or testimonies to specific events in the history of redemption. The reverse is the case: the history of redemption is a consequence of the laws of God. *Mythos* is an expression of *ethos.* The person who conforms to that *ethos* replicates the national story within that person's own life. The commanded deed continues, focuses, and actualizes the meaningful past.

V

We have seen that the author of Psalm 119 recognizes three sources of *tôrâ:* (1) received tradition, passed on most explicitly by teachers (vv 99–100) but including perhaps some sacred books now in the Hebrew Bible, (2) cosmic or natural law (vv 89–91), and (3) unmediated divine teaching (e.g., vv 26–29). The importance for him of books we consider "biblical" must not be minimized. They hold a kind of normative status for him; they provide the language with which to formulate a significant statement. Nonetheless, he never identifies *tôrâ* with the Pentateuch. His own perspective is too close to that of the older wisdom tradition for him to do so.[49] Deissler's opinion that the author of Psalm 119 was a proto-Sadducee whose law was the Scriptures[50] is the reverse of the truth. In fact, he is more like a Pharisee in that his spiritual life is informed both by Scripture and by the teachings of sages and elders. But a simple identification of his theology with that of the Pharisees is also not possible, principally because of his emphasis upon divine illumination and his lack of interest in so much Pentateuchal material, especially the cult. Indeed, the central theme of the poem is the author's hunger for illumination and his flawed yet impressive worthiness of it—the worthiness of a penitent.

Until very recently, modern scholarly literature has tended to see the idea of non-Pentateuchal *tôrâ* as having derived from the need to supplement the Pentateuch. J. Bright's remark about the Pharisees in his valuable *History of Israel* puts it well: "The oral law [had been] developed to interpret the written."[51] He is, of course, largely correct. But his statement implies that earlier in the history or prehistory of the Pharisaic movement lay a theology that recognized *only* the written Torah, the Pentateuch, as normative and that only as this theology became unworkable did the notion of another Torah, an oral Torah, emerge to supplement the written. In this implication, one cannot avoid hearing overtones of an old Reformation polemic: Revelation comes through Scripture alone *(sola scriptura)*, and tradition is valid only to the extent that it is an accurate transmission of scriptural truth, and not an independent source of revelation.[52] Thus, Scripture is prior to tradition, both chronologically and axiologically. In recent years, however, this rather Protestant view has weakened, as scholars of all backgrounds ha2ve become icreasingly aware of the fluidity of tradition in the Second Temple period and of the relative lateness of the idea of a fixed text. In J. A. Sanders's view, from the first century B.C.E. on, "earlier fluid rather shamanistic views of inspiration of patriarchs, prophets and psalmists gave way to the more formal view of the inspiration of each word of those scriptural traditions which were considered old and which were recognized as widespread among the various scattered Jewish communities in the Mediterranean world."[53] In other words, just as Scripture generates tradition, so does tradition generate Scripture. Neither can be said to have absolute chronological priority. The Sadducaic limitation of Toraitic authority to the Pentateuch is no less an innovation than the Pharisaic doctrine of non-Pentateuchal Torah. There is no evidence whatsoever for a period in which the Pentateuch (or any other parts of the Hebrew Bible) alone held the allegiance of *all* Jewish groups, to the exclusion of contemporary prophecy, inspired wisdom, the enactments of legal authorities, and the like, including ultimately the Oral Torah of the rabbis and the gospel of the Church.[54] In the light of this new awareness of the fluidity of the idea of inspiration in late Second Temple times, the essential question is no longer why the idea of nonscriptural authority developed, but, instead, why some groups came to think of a book as the exclusive repository of truth.

NOTES

1. *b. B. Bat.* 15a.
2. Num 12:6–8; Deut 34:10.
3. *Tanḥuma' Rĕ'ēh* 1.
4. *b. Meg.* 14a.
5. Gal 3:13, citing a strange Greek rendering of Deut 21:23; Gal 4:21–31.
6. See J. Wellhausen, *Prolegomena to the History of Ancient Israel* (Gloucester, Mass.: Peter Smith, 1973) 3–4 (The *Prolegomena* was first published in 1878 as *Geschichte Israels,* vol. 1). Wellhausen traces his own momentous reception of the idea back to K. H. Graf, who got it from E. Reuss. L. George and W. Vatke developed it independently of Reuss and of each other.
7. E.g., see B. Lindars, "Torah in Deuteronomy," *Words and Meanings* (ed. P. R. Ackroyd and B. Lindars; Cambridge: Cambridge University Press, 1968) 117–36; and J. Jensen, *The Use of Tôrâ by Isaiah* (CBQMS 3; Washington: Catholic Biblical Association of America, 1973).
8. *Tanḥuma' Nōaḥ* 3.
9. E.g., *Jub* 1:27, 29.
10. Comparisons with the theology of the sect that produced most of the writings found at Qumran immediately suggest themselves. See S. Talmon, "The Textual Study of the Bible—A New Outlook," *Qumran and the History of the Biblical Text* (ed. F. M. Cross and S. Talmon; Cambridge: Harvard University Press, 1975) esp. 378–81; and J. C. VanderKam, *Textual and Historical Studies in the Book of Jubilees* (HSM 14; Missoula, Mont.: Scholars Press, 1977) esp. 255–83.
11. See D. E. Aune, *Prophecy in Early Christianity* (Grand Rapids: Wm. B. Eerdmans Publishing Co., 1983) 103–6. It is important to note that the claim that prophecy died, whether made by ancient sources or contemporary scholars, is a norm masquerading as a description. Its purpose is to discredit all prophecy outside the professed canon, especially the oracles of contemporary prophets.

12. See J. Blenkinsopp, *Prophecy and Canon* (University of Notre Dame Center for the Study of Judaism and Christianity in Antiquity 3; Notre Dame and London: University of Notre Dame Press, 1977).

13. *m. Pesaḥ.* 10:1ff.

14. M. Dahood, *Psalms III: 101–150* (AB 17A; Garden City, N.Y.: Doubleday & Co., 1970) 172–73. In the Vulgate, the poem is Psalm 118.

15. D. M. Müller's study, "Strophenbau und Responsion," has not been available to me, although summaries of his analysis have been. B. Bonkamp (*Die Psalmen* [Freiburg: Wilhelm Visarius, 1949] 534) lists the bibliographic information as *Biblische Studien* II (1898), 54ff. A. Deissler (*Psalm 119* [*118*] *und seine Theologie* [Münchener Theologische Studien 1/11; Munich: Karl Zink, 1955] xvii and 55 n. 173) lists the place of publication as Vienna, the date as 1904, and the pages as 54–61.

16. According to Deissler (*Psalm 119*, 69), Müller emended *huqqôt* in v 16 to *tôrâ*.

17. C. A. Briggs and E. G. Briggs, *A Critical and Exegetical Commentary on the Book of Psalms* (ICC; New York: Charles Scribner's Sons, 1907) 2.418.

18. Bonkamp, *Die Psalmen,* 523–24 n. 8.

19. On the problems with Müller's theory, see Deissler, *Psalm 119,* 68–70, and A. Robert, "Le sens du mot loi dans le Ps. CXIX (Vulg., cxviii)," *RB* 46 (1937) 185–86.

20. Deissler, *Psalm 119,* 75–86.

21. Or is *'ĕmûnâ* ("faithfulness") in v 90 a synonym of the ten?

22. *Miṣwôtêkā 'ăšer 'āhābtî* in v 48 is a dittography from v 47. In its place, read *'ēlêkā*, as suggested in *Biblia Hebraica* (Stuttgartensia).

23. On this, see Deissler, *Psalm 119,* 19–31.

24. One of the others occurs in Jer 2:6.

25. Deissler, *Psalm 119,* 270–77.

26. See H. W. Wolff, "Das Kerygma des deuteronomistischen Geschichtswerk," *ZAW* 73 (1961) 171–86; J. D. Levenson, "Who Inserted the Book of the Torah?" *HTR* 68 (1975) 203–33, esp. 231–33; and J. D. Levenson, "From Temple to Synagogue: 1 Kings 8," *Traditions in Transformation* (ed. B. Halpern and J. D. Levenson; Winona Lake, Ind.: Eisenbrauns, 1981) 143–66, esp. 162–64.

27. See, e.g., A. F. Kirkpatrick, *The Book of Psalms* (Cambridge: Cambridge University Press, 1951) 700; A. Robert, "Le Psaume CXIX et les sapientaux," *RB* 48 (1939) 20; and Deissler, *Psalm 119,* 47.

28. See J. D. Levenson, "The Theologies of Commandment in Biblical Israel," *HTR* 77 (1980) 17–33.

29. E.g., Deut 4:5, 10, 14; 5:31; 6:1.

30. Ps 119:12, 18, 26, 27, 29, 33, 36, 64, 66, 68, 102, 108, 124–125, 135, 169. See J. P. M. van der Ploeg, "Le Psaume 119 et la sagesse," *La Sagesse de l'Ancien Testament* (ed. M. Gilbert; BETL 51; Gembloux: Duculot/Louvain: University of Louvain, 1979) 87.

31. E.g., Deut 5:20–24.

32. See Deissler, *Psalm 119,* 59–60.

33. E.g., see Hab 2:1–4.

34. On the problematic root of *taṣṣēl*, see Deissler, *Psalm 119*, 143. A derivation from *nṣl* is semantically difficult.

35. There is no reason to assume that the objects of the author's sight in vv 6, 15, and 18 are literary rather than visionary. Whereas *hibbîṭ* ("to look at") can denote prophetic vision (e.g., Num 12:8, of Moses), it is never used in connection with reading a document. *Gal-'ênay* (lit. "uncover my eyes," Ps 119:18) is also characteristic of visionary experience. See its use in connection with the Mesopotamian mantic Balaam ben Beor in Num 22:31; 24:4, 16.

36. E.g., Ezra 7:14; Neh 8:1; 1:7. The precise identity of the Moses Book(s) in question is unknown.

37. E.g., A. Weiser, *The Psalms* (OTL; Philadelphia: Westminster Press, 1962) 739: "The psalm is a many-coloured mosaic of thoughts which are often repeated in a wearisome fashion; in the hymn 'Wohl denen, die da wandeln vor Gott in Heiligkeit' they are condensed with welcome brevity."

38. Num 16:15; 1 Sam 12:3–5; Ezek 4:14.

39. Exod 31:3; 1 Kgs 3:12; Isa 11:2. It would thus be dangerous to interpret the natural theology of Wisdom literature as precluding announcement through an experience of revelation. Note, in addition, Eliphaz's description of how he came to know that no person can ever be in the right against God. The idea came to him as a "word" *(dābār)* in his sleep, during which he beheld a vision and heard a voice (Job 4:12–21). The resemblance of vv 14–15 to Ps 119:120, the only verbal attestations of the root *smr* in the Bible, suggests that the psalmist's attitude toward the commandments has been colored by this account of sapiential revelation. See S. Holm-Nielson, "The Importance of Late Jewish Psalmody for the Understanding of Old Testament Tradition," *ST* 14 (1960) 31.

40. See M. Weinfeld, *Deuteronomy and the Deuteronomic School* (Oxford: Clarendon Press, 1972) 244–319.

41. See Robert, "Le Psaume CXIX," 14; and Kirkpatrick, *The Book of Psalms*, 700.

42. See G. T. Sheppard, *Wisdom as a Hermeneutical Construct* (BZAW 151; Berlin and New York: Walter de Gruyter, 1980) 19–83.

43. F. Vattioni, *Ecclesiastico: Testo ebraico con apparato critico e versioni greca, latina, e siriaca* (Publicazioni del Seminario di Semitistica 1; Naples: Istituto Orientale di Napoli, 1968) 282–83. The meaning of *yšybty* in v 29 is not certain. On the importance of the academic setting for understanding this sort of literature, see P. A. Munch, "Die jüdischen 'Weissheitpsalmen' und ihr Platz im Leben," *AcOr* 15 (1936) 112–40, esp. 128–31.

44. Gen 23:4; Exod 2:22; 18:3.

45. E.g., Ps. 119:25, 28, 61, 71, 82, 86, 87, 95.

46. But there is a close parallel in the Wisdom of Solomon, which epitomizes the stories of Adam, Cain, Noah, Abraham, Jacob, Joseph, Israel in bondage, and Moses without providing a single name (Wisd 10:1—11:14). These men are not the great protagonists of *Heilsgeschichte* here; rather, it is *sophia*, Wisdom, which is the energizing force and the unique constant in each incident of the great national story. *Sophia* functions in the Wisdom of Solomon as the entity designated by the ten synonyms does in Psalm 119.

47. See Deissler, *Psalm 119*, 19.

48. See Robert, "Le Psaume CXIX," 5–11.

49. The same would seem to be true also of Psalms 1 and 19. The division of the Psalter into five books and the placement of Psalm 1 at its head may indeed show the influence of the Pentateuch. On this, see C. Westermann, "Zur Sammlung des Psalters," *Forschung am Alten Testament* (Munich: Chr. Kaiser Verlag, 1964) 336–43. But, if so, the absence of any mention of Moses or his Book suggests that the process is a midrashic specification of the psalmists' *tôrâ*. For the opposite view, see inter alia Holm-Nielson, "The Importance of Late Jewish Psalmody," 26.

50. Deissler, *Psalm 119,* 286. One of the problems here and with scholarly treatment of Psalm 119 in general is the tendency to accept as factual traditional Christian defamations of the Pharisees and the rabbis. See Deissler's statement (p. 286) that the halakhic tradition of the rabbis lacks mystical inwardness or Robert's remark that the Torah here is not a matter of formal observance, as it was for the Pharisees, but one of love and devotion ("Le sens du mot loi," 206). These positions are unbecoming in critical scholars. A particularly deleterious approach to this material is one that dichotomizes and polarizes spiritual experience into "law" (bad) and "grace" (good). On this, see H.-J. Kraus, "Zum Gesetzverständnis der nachprophetischen Zeit," *Kairos* 11 (1969) 122–33. On the other hand, Kraus's tendency to identify Torah and Pentateuch (e.g., p. 126) is an unfounded anachronism.

51. J. Bright, *A History of Israel* (3d ed.; Philadelphia: Westminster Press, 1981) 461. See also 437.

52. See R. E. McNally, "Tradition at the Beginning of the Reformation," *Perspectives on Scripture and Tradition* (ed. J. F. Kelley; Notre Dame: Fides, 1976) 69–77.

53. J. A. Sanders, "Text and Canon: Old Testament and New," *Mélanges Dominique Barthélemy* (ed. P. Casetti et al.; OBO 38; Fribourg: Editions Universitaires/Göttingen: Vandenhoeck & Ruprecht, 1981) 381.

54. On the oversimplification involved in the dichotomy of Written Torah/Oral Torah and in the characterization of Mishnah-Tosefta as Oral Torah, see M. I. Gruber, "The Mishnah as Oral Torah: A Reconsideration," *JSJ* 15 (1984) 112–22. It must be stressed that there is no secure basis for the assumption that the Pharisaic traditions were, like the Tannaitic, orally formulated and transmitted. See J. Neusner, "The Rabbinic Traditions About the Pharisees Before 70," *Early Rabbinic Judaism* (SJLA 13; Leiden: E. J. Brill, 1975) 73–89 (reprinted from *JSS* 22 [1971] 1–18). Here Neusner develops M. Smith's point ("A Comparison of Early Christian and Early Rabbinic Traditions," *JBL* 82 [1963] 169–76). The term "non-Pentateuchal Torah" is preferable to the term "Oral Torah" for use in discussions of pre-rabbinic and non-rabbinic literature.

31

Ideal Figures and Social Context: Priest and Sage in the Early Second Temple Age

MICHAEL E. STONE

The present study should be regarded as part of a broader investigation of the history of Judaism in the Persian and early Ptolemaic periods. Here our primary aim is to investigate how certain social structures are reflected in ethical ideals set forth in the literature of the age. In particular, those ideals evidenced in the presentation of certainly socially fixed figures have proven to be important in the attempt to isolate these social structures.

The student of Judaism of the age of the Second Temple is beset by a dearth of documents from the earlier part of this period that is balanced by a plenitude in its later centuries.[1] Furthermore, the literature written after the Seleucid conquest of the land of Israel is almost all religious and to a large extent hortatory in character. Relatively little of it is halachic, while all the narrative works have moral or explicitly religious intent.

Throughout this literature are found numerous passages of outright exhortation to a life of righteousness. These are diverse in content and tone as well as in genre and literary type.[2] Often they aim to present patterns of righteous conduct applicable in principle to all human beings without any consideration of social status or function,[3] so that the ideals they propagate and the aspirations they seek to encourage are not determined by a specific social group or class toward which they are directed.

One such passage is Tobit's address to his son Tobias before the latter set out for distant parts (Tob 4:21–25).[4] In addition to a general summons to follow the way of the Lord, Tobit calls on Tobias to give charity, to beware of mixed marriages, not to withhold wages, and to conduct himself properly with God and man. His sentiments are not directed toward any particular social group or role. His injunctions, terminology, and message are rather general; they stress a fairly practical view of the world, and although based on a clearly Jewish (in opposition, say, to a pagan) viewpoint, do not reflect any very developed metaphysical outlook.[5]

In this respect they contrast with numerous hortatory passages and sentiments in the literature of the Qumran sect. The sectaries conducted their life according to a very distinct view of human beings, of God, and of the world.[6] This view governed their religious writing and thinking and permeated their outlook on morals and ethics. A passage such as the *Manual of Discipline* 3:20—4:10 illustrates this well. In it a dualistic view is urged, dividing all human beings into two camps led by two angels called "the Prince of Light" and "the Angel of Darkness." The pattern of conduct for these two camps is set forth in structured, semi-poetic, contrastive discourse. The sectarian world view led to the development of a distinctive terminology to express their deterministic dualism. Moreover, this dualism informs the contrastive literary style of this passage and many others in the writings of the sect.[7]

The deterministic ideology of the sect implies that there is an overall, perhaps even a complete, identity between the sons of light and the members of the sectarian community. Nonetheless, the sectarian system as such is based on cosmological principles and therefore poses its demands to those human beings whose position in the lot of God is predetermined. This group of individuals, as far as we can tell, was not drawn from any given social class, group, or role bearers, nor does it reflect the interests of such.

Such exhortations to the life of righteousness are common in documents stemming from after the early century B.C.E. The situation during the preceding two centuries remains largely enshrouded in darkness. However, it is the purpose of the following paragraphs to penetrate that darkness and to clarify, in some measure, moral and ethical structures of that age. To do this we shall examine certain texts that treat of ideal patterns of conduct and exemplary figures whose primary characteristics flow from their social and religious function.[8] The fact that the roles of these figures are socially and religiously fixed has the advantage of providing a norm, an important instrument for our analysis. This can aid us to isolate and assess the value systems and world views expressed in the presentation of these ideal figures or paradigms of conduct. Such figures are the Sage and the Priest.[9]

In the Wisdom of Ben Sira, chaps. 38—39, there is a discussion of various callings and walks of life that reflects the attitudes of the author/ wisdom teacher and scribe in Jerusalem at the very start of the second century B.C.E.[10] He opens:

> The wisdom [i.e., proficiency] of the scribe will increase wisdom,
> And he who is with[out] any business may become wise.[11]
>
> (Sir 38:24)

Farther on in the chapter, Ben Sira enumerates the various callings in life—the farmer, the smith, the silversmith, the potter. He praises the special virtues of each of these occupations, paying particular attention to the skill required by each of them and the devotion of mind and hand that each demands.

> All of these rely upon their hands,
>   and each man is skilled at his craft.
>   (Sir 38:31)

Moreover, he emphasizes their essential contribution to the proper functioning of society, which cannot survive without them, as well as the comfortable income and living that they provide to their practitioners. But, he goes on:

> Yet they are not sought out in the council of the people,
>   nor do they attain eminence in the public assembly.

They will not be judges, they will not teach "wise counsel" but instead will understand mundane matters.

After this exposition Ben Sira turns to the description of the sage. He distinguishes the following characteristics. First, in contrast to the craftsmen who "keep stable the fabric of the world," the sage "devotes himself to the study of the Torah of the Most High" (Sir 39:1). He knows the profound meaning of the Torah, of the prophecies, of riddles and mysteries. Second, as a result of this knowledge and devotion, the sage will come to serve in high places of society, in elite positions, and "will judge men" even in foreign countries.[12] Ben Sira, however, speaks extensively, not about these features and functions of the sage, but about religious characteristics of his conduct. Third, the sage will pray to the Most High, he will confess his sins. By the will of the Most High he will be filled with the spirit of understanding and will confess to the Lord with wisdom.[13] It is important to observe, in this passage, the lack of any distinction between the "wisdom" characteristics of this figure and the "religious" ones. Moreover, wisdom is granted to the sage by God Most High. As a result of these characteristics and the conduct they entail, according to Ben Sira, the sage will gain eternal renown (Sir 39:11).

This description of the sage, which is one of the most detailed in ancient Jewish literature, can be analyzed from a variety of points of view. In the light of the aims of the present study, three points are particularly noteworthy: (1) To be a wise scribe in Ben Sira's view demands complete devotion. It is neither a task nor a profession that can be pursued together with another calling in life, such as the various sorts of crafts.[14] (2) The rewards offered to the sage for his devotion to his vocation are twofold. The first is social position and status—recognition; he will be a famous judge or a minister of state or an ambassador; he will be prominent in society. The second reward is equally socially rooted—eternal fame and renown. (3) The sage is by no means a purely secular functionary. His wisdom is accompanied by and expressed in prayer and is granted to him by God. It is to that extent inspired wisdom.[15]

Consequently, Ben Sira's conception of the sage is rather elevated. He has a fixed, prominent role in society and not merely intellectual and technical qualifications but also religious and ethical ones. This distinct social role is permeated with Jewish religious values, and wisdom is even compared with prophecy.[16] A clear outcome of the religious dimension of the sage is the notion that repentance and confession of sins, prayer, and petition will lead to the sage's receiving divine inspiration, which is his teaching.[17] Ben Sira seems to have combined an ancient social role with newer conceptions and then to have set the resulting figure before his students as an exemplary type. Yet, obviously, not all men could aspire to this ideal, let alone achieve it. "Sages in training" could only come from certain strata and groups in society. This is clear, *inter alia,* from the statements that Ben Sira makes about the various professions.

It is interesting to compare the sage with another central figure in the life of Judaism in the era of the Second Temple, that of the priest.[18] The priest, even more than the sage, is tied to a specific role and function in the society of the time, and since the office is hereditary, the measure of determination is magnified.

The Testaments of the Twelve Patriarchs is one of the more problematic works in the pseudepigraphical literature, and indeed the prevalent view is that the Greek *Testaments of the Twelve Patriarchs* is basically a Christian composition incorporating earlier Jewish sources and writings.[19] This view is nicely confirmed in the case of the *Testament of Levi,* for Aramaic fragments and parts of a Greek translation of what seems to have been one of its sources have survived. That source stemmed in our view from the third pre-Christian century at least. Aramaic fragments were discovered both in the Cairo Genizah and among the Dead Sea Scrolls, while the Greek fragments occur in one single manuscript.[20]

Since *Aramaic Testament of Levi* (hereafter *Aramaic Levi*) serves as a source for the *Testament of Levi* which is part of the *Testaments of the Twelve Patriarchs* (hereafter *Greek Levi*), it is permissible cautiously to use the evidence of the latter to supplement information gained from the fragmentary *Aramaic Levi. Aramaic Levi* v 88 reads: "Now, my children, teach your children reading and writing and wise instruction."[21] Here the instruction to teach writing and reading (*spr 'lypw*) is combined with two clear wisdom terms, "wise instruction." Similar language also occurs at the end of this verse, namely, "and wisdom shall be with you as eternal honour" (cf. *Greek Levi* 13:3). Further it should be recalled that on the last column of the Bodleian Genizah fragment is a poem of praise to wisdom, apparently set in Levi's mouth, phrases from which were also introduced into *Greek Levi*.[22] In *Greek Levi* 13:1–5, which is based on *Aramaic Levi* 83—95, we read the following:

1. And now my children, I command you:
   Fear our Lord with all your heart,
   and walk in simplicity according to all his Law.[23]

2. You too, teach your children to read and write,
   so that they may have knowledge all their life,
   and read continually in the Law of God.

3. For everyone who knows the Law of God will be honoured,
   and he will not be a stranger wherever he goes;

4. And he will gain more companions than his parents,
   and many men will desire to serve him,
   and to hear Law from his mouth.

5. Do righteousness, my children, upon the earth,
   so that you will find [scil. righteousness] in the heavens.[24]

It is interesting to observe that, although elsewhere in *Greek Levi* the patriarch addressed his children about cultic matters as such (see, e.g., vv 17–18), here the teaching of the Torah of God is foremost in his instructions. Naturally a number of aspects of those instructions are drawn from the Bible, and in the passage cited the author is dependent on the blessing that Moses pronounced on the tribe of Levi according to Deut 33:10: "They shall teach Jacob your ordinances, and Israel your laws." Yet it is striking that he does not avail himself of the latter part of the verse of Deuteronomy: "They shall put incense before you, and whole burnt offering upon your altar."[25] In *Greek Levi* 13, then, the stress is almost exclusively on the priest's role in teaching the Torah. Noteworthy is the instruction to teach children reading and writing, which is made explicitly. As Levi had taught them to write, they should teach their children (v 2). This is clearly related to *Aramaic Levi* 88. Certain aspects of the themes detected in *Aramaic Levi* are further developed in *Greek Levi*. It is possible, moreover, that *Greek Levi* may preserve ancient material lost from the fragmentary Aramaic text. In this passage, in any case, its additional material is fully consonant with what is found in *Aramaic Levi* and illuminates it.

These texts indicate a very interesting development: the circles responsible for *Aramaic Levi* laid a very strong emphasis on the instructional function of the priesthood and this aspect of the priesthood attracted sapiential motifs. This process was fully developed by the third century B.C.E. at the latest. As a result of it the figure of the ideal priest became imbued with features of the sage. Incidentally, *Aramaic Levi* cannot be accused of ignoring or downplaying the cultic aspect of the priestly office. To the contrary, it includes detailed instructions about sacrificial cult, most of which were omitted by *Greek Levi* (see vv 18–60). Furthermore, the centrality of the Levitical line was so stressed in *Aramaic Levi* that biblical verses referring to Judah, which came to be interpreted messianically, were transferred to Levi.[26]

The wisdom of Ben Sira also supplies us with information about the priesthood. In the "Praise of the Fathers of Old," as has been remarked often in the past, the priesthood plays a special role. Thus, Ben Sira devotes only a few verses to Moses (Sir 45:1–5), [27] while his treatment of Aaron and his sons is very extensive (Sir 45:6–26). Ben Sira, however, pays no special attention to the instructional function of the priests, and it is mentioned only in one verse (Sir 45:17). This verse is based on Deut 33:10a but departs from it in its wording. Yet in the course of rewriting and expanding the biblical text Ben Sira uses no sapiential terminology. This is well contrasted with *Greek Levi*'s treatment of the same biblical verse (see above). Throughout the whole section, Ben Sira emphasizes primarily the cultic function of the Aaronids, the high priest's vestments, the offering of sacrifices, and the Temple cult. The same attitude is evident in chap. 50, which is devoted to the description of Simon the high priest as he leaves the sanctuary.[28]

All the sources about the priest and the sage that have been discussed here stem from or draw on material that originated before the Maccabean revolt. In them certain aspects of ideals aspired to may be discerned. Ben Sira, a sage and teacher of wisdom, repeatedly emphasizes the religious dimension of the ideal sage, and it is reasonable to assume that this was the ideal that permeated his own life. Likewise he emphasizes the affinity between the sage and the prophet and the fact that only members of certain social classes, who conduct a particular way of life, can hope to achieve this ideal. On the other hand, for Ben Sira the priest is predominantly a cultic figure with certain administrative responsibilities (Sir 50:1–2).

In *Aramaic Levi*, however, it is precisely the priestly office that attracts sapiential language and function; cultic instructions given to the priest by his fathers contain a strong element of ethical exhortation. Ben Sira's sage and *Aramaic Levi*'s priest share an affinity with wisdom. Ben Sira's wise sage is endowed with prophetic characteristics, while *Aramaic Levi*'s wise priest has messianic overtones. A certain structural symmetry appears here.

In evaluating these two perceptions, which clearly differ from each other, we can speculate that Ben Sira's views result from his being a sage himself. Ben Sira "clearly considers the wise man to be the most necessary and effective person in the Jewish society of his own day. Do not forget," D. Harrington urges, "that Ben Sira was in the business of training just such wise men."[29] Consequently, his ideal sage holds center stage and has drawn to himself a prophetic dimension, and the whole of the learned and sapiential tradition centers on him to the virtually complete exclusion of the priest, who is limited, in Ben Sira's presentation, to his official, cultic function.

In contrast, then, *Aramaic Levi* stems from circles in which the priesthood held a far more prominent role and in it the figure of the priest attracted strong wisdom motifs as well as messianic themes originally at home in relationship to Judah.[30] Yet it is open to question whether *Aramaic Levi* came from Temple circles. It certainly seems to base its calculations on a calendar like that of *Jubilees,* the Enochic *Book of the Heavenly Luminaries,* and the Dead Sea sect.[31] Moreover, some aspects of its sacrificial theory, and particularly that attributing a complex sacrificial cult to the patriarchs, are known only from apocryphal literature, admittedly later, but of distinctly peculiar characteristics.[32] Even though *Aramaic Levi* is rather older than Ben Sira, its interpretation of the priesthood is ignored by Ben Sira, or unknown to him.

These permutations and combinations of themes and ideals, the interchange of many of the functions of ideal figures, can be assessed in view of the norms of these figures. The background of priests and sages is known, and consequently the particular dimensions of the presentation of Ben Sira and *Aramaic Levi* are the more striking. The information gained from them about attitudes (and implicitly about the social groups that cultivated these attitudes) must be added to the meager store of knowledge we have and, if possible, integrated with it.[33]

We may particularly remark on the role played by sapiential ideals in these developments. Elsewhere, attention has been drawn to the development of complex wisdom/apocalyptic figures in this period.[34] Enoch and Daniel are prime examples. Above, some features were noted that bring Ben Sira's conception of the sage close to the apocalyptic seer, particularly in actions and attitudes relating to inspiration. These are complemented by other traits common to wisdom sages and apocalyptic seers.[35] Levi is to teach his children writing (*Aramaic Levi* 88), but it was Enoch who invented it (*Jub* 4:27). Indeed, some aspects of knowledge and "science" cultivated by the earliest apocalypses are not, apparently, rooted in the known Israelite and Jewish wisdom traditions[36] and may derive from traditions of mantic wisdom or other sources.[37] However, these do not detract from the role played by wisdom terminology, which, in the texts we have examined, wanders from figure to figure. Not the less remarkable are the inspirational aspects that are stressed for the wisdom teachers and for the apocalyptic seers.

From all these interrelationships certain patterns emerge and these are determined, so it appears, largely by the interests of the writers (see n. 30). But the writers do not seem to have been just isolated individuals. It is not a daring assumption to say that Ben Sira stands within a wisdom tradition rooted in a particular context. *Aramaic Levi*, at least as far as is revealed by the affinities of its calendar (see above), also probably stems from a group or tendency within Judaism of the third century, or even earlier. That group clearly had priestly concerns, but its relation to the priestly establishment is unclear.

It would be ill-considered and premature to tie these circles of particular interests to such actual groups as happen to be known to us from the historical sources. The agendum must be first to examine other aspects of the literature of the age for its contribution to the map of Jewish society. What will remain true is that the social role of the two ideal figures discussed, the priest and the sage, is deeply influenced by social context, and this provides an important instrument for evaluating the actual historical existence of specific groups or circles.

PROSPECT

In the course of the investigation of two such figures, the priest and the sage, however, a number of other issues have arisen that cannot be resolved in the scope of this chapter but will be addressed in a continuing study. The first is the apparent chronological contrast, arising from the first part of this chapter, between the socially determined ideal figures in the texts of the fourth and third centuries and the socially more generalized paradigmatic types of the later texts. This contrast may be in part a *trompe l'oeil* resulting from the fragmentary literary evidence, on the one hand, and the necessarily partial selection of texts dealt with here, on the other. The absence of socially non-role determined ideals in the earlier texts is the much more important phenomenon, since the presence of such ideals in the later texts is to be assumed. Second, the investigation of the uses of these ideals may be of potential importance as a way of analyzing texts of later periods as well. Third, the significance of the phenomenon of "magnetism," the tendency of certain ideal figures to attract broad and significant characteristics, as a way of discovering which ideals were considered central to people's world views seems likely to be of use in continuing study (see n. 30, above). This may prove to be an important diagnostic tool for the reconstruction of religious history. Finally, questions have been raised, but not yet fully answered, about the relationship between the sort of information that is yielded by this analysis and certain other pieces of knowledge that have been garnered about the shape of Judaism in the fourth and third centuries.

NOTES

1. For a recent survey of the literature, see M. E. Stone, ed., *Jewish Writings of the Second Temple Period* (CRINT 2/II; Philadelphia: Fortress Press, 1984); G. W. E. Nickelsburg, *Jewish Literature Between the Bible and the Mishnah* (Philadelphia: Fortress Press, 1981). Both these works contain bibliographies for further reference. Concerning the distribution of sources and its implications for the historian of Judaism, see M. E. Stone, *Scriptures, Sects and Visions* (Philadelphia: Fortress Press, 1980) 20–25.

2. A selection of such texts is presented by G. W. E. Nickelsburg and M. E. Stone, *Faith and Piety in Early Judaism* (Philadelphia: Fortress Press, 1982) 91–115.

3. Further examples of such preaching permeate the *Aramaic Testament of Levi*, the *Epistle of Enoch* and the *Testaments of the Twelve Patriarchs*, among other works.

4. See Nickelsburg and Stone, *Faith and Piety*, 91–93.

5. Ibid.

6. On the relationship between cosmology, anthropology, and ethics at Qumran, see the still apposite remarks by D. Flusser, "The Dead Sea Sect and Pre-Pauline Christianity," *Scripta Hierosolymitana* 4 (1958) 215–66.

7. Basic outlines of sectarian thinking are given, in addition to Flusser's paper (n. 6), in H. Ringgren, *The Faith of Qumran* (Philadelphia: Fortress Press, 1963). Perhaps the most sensitive analysis of the sectarian ideology is to be found embodied in the introductions to and commentaries on the *Manual of Discipline* and the *Thanksgiving Psalms* by J. Licht: see *The Rule Scroll* (Jerusalem: Bialik Institute, 1965) and *The Thanksgiving Scroll* (Jerusalem: Bialik Institute, 1957) (both in Hebrew).

8. There have been few studies that have attempted to use the types of ideals set up in ancient Jewish texts as a key to the hopes and aspirations of the authors. A number of essays along these lines may be found in J. J. Collins and G. W. E. Nickelsburg, *Ideal Figures in Ancient Judaism* (SBLSCS 12; Chico, Calif.: Scholars Press, 1980). A penetrating analysis important, from the point of view of the subject of this chapter, chiefly for its approach, is G. Scholem, "Three Types of Jewish Piety," *Eranos Jahrbuch* 38 (1969) 331–48.

9. The present exercise, it should be stressed, is not an essay in exegesis; it is an attempt to infer from the texts something about the ideals prevailing in Jewish society in the early part of the period of the Second Temple.

10. We have had much benefit from the edition by M. H. Segal, *Sefer ben Sira HaShalem* (Jerusalem: Bialik Institute, 1958). Illuminating remarks on the social

role and function of Ben Sira, as well as on his attitude toward Hellenism were made by M. Hengel, *Judaism and Hellenism* (Philadelphia: Fortress Press, 1974) 1.131–38 and notes in vol. 2. Most of the terms with which we deal here from our particular perspective were carefully annotated by Hengel. The figure of the sage in Ben Sira is clearly analyzed by D. Harrington, "The Wisdom of the Scribe According to Ben Sira," *Ideal Figures*, 181–88. Further bibliography may be found there.

11. The text of this colon is problematic. We translate Geniza Ms B. RSV gives, according to the Greek, "The wisdom of the scribe depends on the opportunity of leisure." The citations in this chapter follow RSV except where noted.

12. Hengel would discern an autobiographical element in this characterization of the positions to be held by the sage; see *Judaism and Hellenism*, 1.32–33 and notes to there. This is very likely the case, but these types of functions were ancient and traditional for the sage, such as Daniel and Ahikar. See also *IDB*, s. v. "Wisdom," and *IDBSup*, s. v. "Wisdom in the Ancient Near East" and "Wisdom in the OT," and further bibliography there. Harrington analyzes the role and function of the sage very nicely, and we accept most of his categories and analysis, in spite of some minor differences of emphasis; see "Wisdom of the Scribe," 184–86.

13. Sir 39:6. See Segal, *Ben Sira,* on this verse. For Ben Sira, of course, at another level of discourse, wisdom is domesticated as the Torah of Moses, cf. 24:8–12, 23. Harrington discusses this development clearly and succinctly ("Wisdom of the Scribe," 181–83). We now add that it is related to the interpenetration of the sapiential and "religious" features of the scribe. Yet it is impossible to know which development was prior.

14. See n. 16, below.

15. It is intriguing to ponder whether there is any special meaning to the fact that the scribe-sage is set in opposition to the various craftsmen and the farmer but not to functionaries of religious character such as the priest.

16. Compare further the language used of his wisdom by Ben Sira in chap. 24:30–34, where it is compared to prophecy, or, according to the Syriac version, said to be prophecy. Such an attitude to wisdom is also explicit in Wis 7:7; 8:21; 9:17–18; and elsewhere. The point is stressed by Hengel, *Judaism and Hellenism*, 1.134–35. Furthermore, on a literary level, wisdom and prophecy can be seen coming together in the "prophetic" wisdom poem in Bar 3:9—4:4. Yet Ben Sira recoils from attributing too mythological a dimension to wisdom. See the comparisons made by Harrington, "Wisdom of the Scribe," 183. This may reflect Ben Sira's "conservative" character, which indeed makes the penetration of the sapiential tradition by "religious" elements the more striking.

17. On this collocation of activities in various modes, see D. Satran, "Daniel: Seer, Philosopher, Holy Man," *Ideal Figures,* 33–48. They are commonplace activities of the apocalyptic seer prior to his receiving a vision. In the apocalypses, however, fasting also plays a prominent role in this context.

18. On the central role of the priesthood, see the comments in M. E. Stone, "Reactions to Destructions of the Second Temple: Theology, Perception and Conversion," *JSJ* 12 (1982) 198 and n. 14 and further references there.

19. For a collection of recent studies and some fine overall assessments of the research, see M. de Jonge, ed., *Studies in the Testaments of the Twelve Patriarchs* (VTSup 3; Leiden: E. J. Brill, 1975). A history of scholarship is given by H. D. Slingerland, *The Testaments of the Twelve Patriarchs: A Critical History of Research* (SBLMS, 21; Missoula, Mont.: Scholars Press, 1977).

20. On these fragments, with bibliography, see J. C. Greenfield and M. E. Stone, "Remarks on the Aramaic Testament of Levi from the Geniza," *RB* 86 (1979) 214–30. We assume a third-century date, because this document or something very like it must have served as a source for *Jubilees*, which is dated most recently to the first third of the second century B.C.E.; see J. C. VanderKam, *Textual and Historical Studies in the Book of Jubilees* (HSM 14; Missoula, Mont.: Scholars Press, 1977) 214–85. Nickelsburg (*Jewish Literature*, 78) seems to favor a somewhat earlier date about 168 B.C.E. *Jubilees* is also apparently referred to in the Damascus Document, which dates from the second century (see CD 16:3–4); on the date of the latter, see F. M. Cross, *The Ancient Library of Qumran and Modern Biblical Studies* (rev. ed.; Garden City, N.Y.: Doubleday Anchor Books, 1961) 82. Concerning the Qumran manuscripts of *Jubilees*, see J. A. Fitzmyer, *The Dead Sea Scrolls: Major Publications and Tools for Study* (SBLSBS 8; Missoula, Mont.: Scholars Press, 1977) 16, 19, 30, 37. Their numbers include 1Q 17, 1Q 18, 2Q 19, 2Q 20, 3Q 5, 4Q 221, 4Q Jub a–e, and 11Q Jub. Information about these manuscripts is not yet complete.

21. *wk'n bny spr <w>mwsr ḥwkmh 'lypw lbnykwn*. For the emendation of *mwsr* to *<w>mwsr*, cf. *Aramaic Levi* 90. Compare Greenfield and Stone, "Remarks on the Aramaic Testament of Levi," 226–27.

22. In remarks made on the use of sapiential terminology in certain apocalypses and other Second Temple period literature, we noted the spread of this terminology, and in the later part of the age it became a chameleon, serving to denote whatever teaching or doctrine the writer using it considered to be highest "wisdom" or "understanding." "Meaningful contacts should be posited where there is common ground in conceptual or at least formal structure" (M. E. Stone, "Apocalyptic Literature," *Jewish Writings of the Second Temple Period* [CRINT 2/II; Philadelphia: Fortress Press, 1984] 384). We stand by this statement, but maintain that here, both because of the antiquity of *Aramaic Levi* and because of the qualitative similarities between the conceptual contacts involved, shared "meaningful structures" between it and the wisdom tradition can be said to exist. One point of entry for these traditions might have been Deut 33:10 and the function implied by it.

23. Greek *nomos*, and so throughout the passage.

24. Translated from the text edited by M. de Jonge, *The Testaments of the Twelve Patriarchs* (PVTG 1.2; Leiden: E. J. Brill, 1978).

25. Here and elsewhere the Bible is cited according to RSV, except that the second person singular pronoun is always "you" and the possessive adjective "your."

26. Greenfield and Stone, "Remarks on the Aramaic Testament of Levi," 219 (on v 9) and 223–24 (on vv 66–67). Some indications are also noted there of the secondary character of certain of the "Judah" references in *Greek Levi*. These "Judah" references would then be a modification of the originally very marked

centrality of Levi in *Aramaic Levi*. That central role is expressed in the endowing of the priest with characteristics of the sage of wisdom and of the eschatological Anointed.

27. Note the similarity between Sir 45:5 and the reference to Levi's instruction in Deut 33:10—"to teach Jacob the covenant and Israel his judgments" (Sir 45:5) and "They shall teach Jacob your ordinances, and Israel your law" (Deut 33:10). Yet the sentiment as expressed in the context of Moses by Ben Sira is commonplace. So it is difficult to say, though we might be tempted to do so, that Ben Sira tends to present the Levite Moses as fulfilling Deut 33:10a and the Levite priest Aaron as fulfilling Deut 33:10b. Indeed, Ben Sira adduces Deut 33:10a of Aaron in 45:17 (see below, in this paragraph).

28. See Nickelsburg and Stone, *Faith and Piety*, 58–60, on this chapter.

29. Harrington, "Wisdom of the Scribe," 185. Note his just assertion (contra Rivkin) of the central position of the scribal ideal in Ben Sira's thought.

30. Ben Sira attributes great importance to the priest, as has been pointed out above. Yet, for him, it is the figure of the sage that has the "magnetic" quality of attracting features of other social functions. The same "magnetic" quality is to be observed in *Aramaic Levi*'s treatment of the priest. It seems to be a correlative of the systematically central role of the figure in a given writer's outlook.

31. See Greenfield and Stone, "Remarks on the Aramaic Testament of Levi," 224–25.

32. Such is *Jubilees* (of course largely dependent on *Aramaic Levi*) and as a further example *2 Enoch*. On the sacrificial cult in the latter book, see S. Pines, "Eschatology and the Concept of Time in the Slavonic Book of Enoch," *Types of Redemption* (ed. R. J. Z. Werblowsky and C. J. Bleeker; SHR 18; Leiden: E. J. Brill, 1970) 72–87. Yet too much should not be made of this point, since our knowledge of the third pre-Christian century is so thin.

33. An analogous attempt with certain other sorts of material is made in M. E. Stone, "The Book of Enoch and Judaism in the Third Century B.C.E.," *CBQ* 40 (1978) 479–92; idem, *Scriptures, Sects and Visions*, 24–27.

34. Stone, *Scriptures, Sects and Visions*, 39–47; idem, "Apocalyptic Literature," 383–441; idem, "Lists of Revealed Things in Apocalyptic Literature," *Magnalia Dei, The Mighty Acts of God* (ed. F. M. Cross, W. E. Lemke, and P. D. Miller; Garden City, N.Y.: Doubleday & Co., 1976) 414–54. From another perspective, see J. Z. Smith, "Wisdom and Apocalyptic," *Religious Syncretism in Antiquity* (ed. B. A. Pearson; Missoula, Mont.: Scholars Press, 1975) 131–70. Much of interest is also to be found in J. J. Collins, "Cosmos and Salvation: Jewish Wisdom and Apocalyptic in the Hellenistic Age," *HR* 17 (1977) 121–29.

35. G. von Rad (*Theologie des Alten Testament* [Munich: Chr. Kaiser Verlag, 1965] 2.319ff.; idem, *Wisdom in Israel* [Nashville: Abingdon Press, 1972] 272–83) probably laid too much stress on the relationship between wisdom and apocalyptic writers. See in response P. von der Osten-Sacken, *Die Apokalyptik in ihrem Verhältnis zu Prophetie und Weisheit* (Theologische Existenz heute 157; Munich: Chr. Kaiser Verlag, 1969). Here we shall not tread again the well-worn track of this debate. See in detail, Stone, "Apocalyptic Literature," 388–89.

36. See Stone, "Lists"; idem, "Third Century B.C.E."

37. Stone, "Apocalyptic Literature," 388–89; Collins, "Cosmos and Salvation"; and H. P. Müller, *Ursprünge und Strukturen alttestamentlicher Eschatologie* (Beiheft ZAW 109; Berlin, 1969) 268–73.

32

The Emergence of Jewish Sectarianism in the Early Second Temple Period

SHEMARYAHU TALMON

I

This chapter focuses on the beginnings of Jewish sectarianism between the fourth and the second century B.C.E. Concomitantly it attempts to reevaluate some central aspects of M. Weber's work concerning postexilic Israel, bringing under scrutiny new materials discovered since his days and the results of post-Weberian scholarly research. Thus it may be seen as an addendum to Weber's *Ancient Judaism.*[1]

The student of the Bible who purports to review Weber's seminal sociological analysis of ancient Judaism perforce vacillates between praise and criticism in his appreciation of that work.

One cannot escape being impressed by the audacious attempt to portray the societal life and the world of ideas of ancient Israel on an immensely wide and colorful canvas that reveals a powerful faculty for integrating the diverse components into a highly suggestive and meaningful picture; to trace the reverberations of the mores and modalities of that ancient civilization in later stages of the development of Judaism; and, beyond these limits, to relate them to phenomena that come to the fore in other religions and civilizations, predominantly, but not exclusively, in Protestant ethics.

Weber was not concerned with particularized historical investigations but rather with the exposure of overall processes that he believed he could discern in often quite disparate historical societies and situations. Therefore, says T. Parsons: "The total result of Weber's comparative study becomes much more reliable than the judgement of one particular case can be from its own data, taken alone."[2] It is precisely this comprehensiveness of the endeavor that constitutes the most conspicuous innovation in Weber's presentation of ancient Judaism, as was pointed out by J. Guttmann in a review of *Das antike Judentum* a few years after its publication.[3]

True, the praise that Weber drew from specialists in diverse branches of Jewish studies, not only from Bible scholars, was always accompanied by more than a grain of criticism. A caveat was sounded against Weber's "typological"[4] approach which, in the eyes of his critics, sometimes played havoc with or at least clouded historical realities, as far as they could be extracted from the transmitted sources.

The strictures raised against Weber's methodology meant that *Ancient Judaism* had only a marginal impact on the "professional" study of Israel's history, the biblical cult, and even biblical prophecy which is at the very center of his interest. He did, however, influence some Old Testament scholars who, like him, inclined toward conceptual generalizations[5] and could readily subscribe to his dictum: Concepts are not reflections of reality but intellectual constructs for the purpose of its control.[6] It would appear that the lack of attention given to Weber's work may be related to the waning of the "Pattern of Culture" school and the concomitant increase of an anti-type orientation in Old Testament studies which tends to stress the particular and the atypical in biblical society and its conceptual universe.

It follows that while, to quote H. Liebeschütz, "the work of the Heidelberg sociologist can still serve us as starting point for further inquiries,"[7] at the present day, Weber's study must be subjected anew to scrutiny.

We have to go beyond Weber and integrate into the picture new evidence that had not been available when *Ancient Judaism* was written.[8] In this respect, issues and problems pertaining to "Jewish sectarianism" constitute a most promising field of inquiry. A host of recent discoveries such as the Gnostic materials from Nag Hammadi[9] and foremost the Scrolls from Qumran[10] throw welcome light on dissenting religious groups and trends in the Second Temple period. They help in illuminating, even though only partially, the otherwise undocumented age in the spiritual history of the late biblical and the early postbiblical era. The decisively richer information on the socioreligious profile of Judaism in the Second Temple period that the new documents provide calls for a reassessment of Weber's typology and his presentation of some phenomena pertaining to postexilic Israel and its socioreligious structure. A case in point is his treatment of the Samaritans, to whom he refers only in passing.[11] The opposition Jews versus Samaritans (as a prefiguration of the dichotomy Pharisaism versus heterodoxies) now must be viewed in the light of the Qumran finds, which add a new dimension to the phenomenon of Jewish sectarianism.[12]

An investigation of the new materials, and especially of the Qumran writings, may throw light on processes that Weber traced in *Ancient*

Judaism and on concepts that constitute the warp and woof of his typology. Let me mention just a few to which reference will be made in the ensuing discussion:

1. Weber's crucial assumption that postexilic Israel experienced a decisive transition from peoplehood and nationhood to a (mere) "confessional community" *(Glaubensgemeinschaft)* must be put to the test by its application to the self-understanding of the Samaritans and the Qumranians.

2. In this connection, also his contention that it was then that Israel developed to an increasing measure traits of a pariah community will come up for review. An analysis of the Qumran (and Samaritan) world of ideas provides tools for a reconsideration of the "in-group—out-group morality," which in Weber's view is rooted in the early biblical ethos, grew stronger in the setting of the Babylonian exile, and since Pharisaic times has shaped the attitude of Jews toward the non-Jewish world. Concurrently, some attention must be given to the question whether at all, and if so to what degree, the presumed dual morality was indeed conducive to or precipitated the crystallization of a stringent behavior pattern that consolidated Judaism from within and at the same time cut it off from the surrounding society.

3. The constitution of the Qumran community may serve as a touchstone for Weber's proposition that in the last centuries before the rise of Christianity a rigid cultic code, the rabbinic *halakhah,* prevented Jews from engaging in agricultural occupations that by their very nature engender infringements of ritual prescriptions and that accordingly Judaism became urbanized and developed an intrinsically urban ethic.[13]

4. As already mentioned, the study of the dissenters' Commune of Qumran may bear on the more general question of how the socioreligious phenomenon "sect" should be defined in distinction from other socioreligious structures.[14] The results of this inquiry may prompt a reevaluation of Weber's description of the Pharisees' religious stance as a sect religiosity.

5. The presentation of the Righteous Teacher, the dominant figure of leadership in the Qumran writings, invites a reconsideration of Weber's typology of religious leaders.

6. These writings also reflect the progressive denouement of the process of growing rationalization that plays such an important role in Weber's thinking, as well as the increasing democratizing of one-time esoteric religious learning. Because of its many ramifications, however, this process requires a rather involved exposition, which cannot be attempted here.

II

At this stage of our inquiry, a characteristic of the sources on which all observations concerning ancient (biblical) Judaism are founded must be brought under consideration: Any attempt to retrace the social and religious development of Israel in the preexilic period is perforce based almost entirely on inferences drawn from the interpretation of literary materials that already in the biblical age itself had been handed down over centuries and are now before us in the forms and formulations given to them by the latest tradents or redactors. While the extent of the time lag between the occurrence of a particular event and its recording remains a matter of scholarly debate, that fundamental characteristic of the biblical traditions is generally recognized in modern biblical scholarship. Weber was cognizant of these facts. He knew full well, for example, that the patriarchal stories reflect, to a degree, concepts and conditions of the early monarchy and that they "were influenced by the social problems produced by kingship."[15] It follows that in the endeavor to recover the mainstays of the Israelites' socioreligious organization and world of ideas in the preexilic age, scholars by necessity have recourse to the extrapolation of sources that are a melange of historical facts and historiographic fantasy. This is an irremediable predicament that Weber shares with all students of early biblical society and, for that matter, of the ancient civilizations also.

At times one suspects that Weber, although aware of the inherent dangers, did not sufficiently take into account that crucial gulf between the historical actualities and their recordings that are colored by the recorder's existential situation. Notwithstanding his critical acumen, he tends to take the biblical traditions at face value whenever it suits his purpose, as has been pointed out by critical reviewers of his work.[16] This, at times unqualified, reliance on the biblical sources attenuates especially the reliability of the presentation of "The Establishment of the Jewish Pariah People," for which the analysis of the historicosocial and religious phenomena pertaining to the Israelite confederacy and prophecy serves as a launching pad.[17]

No such chronological gap between the historical circumstances and their reporting manifests itself in the biblical account of the early postexilic times. The books that relate the details of the return from the exile— foremost Ezra, Nehemiah, Haggai, and Zechariah—are contemporaneous with or were composed shortly after the actual occurrence of the events they record. While the contemporaneity does not yet allay the scholar's concern over the "objectivity" of these presumed eyewitness reports, for once the biblical records are practically synchronous with the historical situation and reflect, *grosso modo*, the ideonic stance of that age.

Viewed from the same angle, the Qumran Scrolls have quite a special significance. They are the only extensive contemporary documentation that relates to a Jewish group from the last centuries before the turn of the era. Being firsthand records, penned by scribes of the New Covenant–Commune for the benefit of its members, and having come to us in their pristine form,[18] these documents are of unsurpassed value for a sociological case study of an ancient religious group or sect.

The task obviously cannot be adequately carried out in the framework of this chapter. But the Bible scholar can at least try to whet the sociologist's appetite by presenting some basic information on the Covenanters. In doing so, I shall restrict my remarks to aspects of their communal life, societal structure, and theology that bear directly on issues treated by Weber in the essays "The Establishment of the Jewish Pariah People" and "The Pharisees."[19]

III

Let me stress once again that I am concerned here with the beginnings of Jewish sectarianism between the late fourth and the early second century B.C.E. My thesis will be that the emergence of sectarianism at that time must be viewed in conjunction with the Judaism of the sixth and fifth centuries B.C.E. that presents itself to the scholar in the postexilic biblical literature. The internal diversification that then arose in Judaism and ultimately found its salient structural expression in the formation of *sects* can be fully and adequately appreciated only against the backdrop of the experience of the Babylonian exile and the return from the exile. Viewed from this angle, the very phenomenon of Jewish sectarianism links up directly with the history and the spiritual history of early postexilic Israel.

I shall direct my comments to two pivotal aspects of the socioreligious transformation to which the biblical body politic was exposed in the wake of the cataclysmic events of 586 B.C.E., that is, the destruction of the Temple, the capture of Jerusalem, and the concomitant loss of political sovereignty: (1) changes in the internal structure of Israelite society and in the interaction of the main societal agents of leadership: king, priest, and prophet; and (2) the transformation from the preexilic monocentric nation, defined by the geopolitical borders of the Land of Israel, to the postexilic people characterized by a multicentricity resulting from deportations and voluntary or semivoluntary emigration.[20]

1. The social structure of Israel in the monarchical period hinged upon the interaction of three pivotal socioreligious institutions—kingship, priesthood, and prophecy—that gave expression to a basic cohesiveness

and unity, notwithstanding social and economic differentiation and the political division into two realms.

The priests embodied the guardianship over established norms that found their tangible expression in the temple—whether in Jerusalem or in Bethel—and the sacrificial service. By their very call and nature, the priesthood and the cult signified permanence and stability in the public and personal domain. The kings, motivated by the realism that the mundane affairs of the realm dictated, on the whole shared with the priests the overriding interest in permanence and continuity. Against this, the prophets would not acquiesce in the pragmatism that guided kings and to a degree also priests in their decisions. Never doubting the legitimacy of these institutions,[21] they aimed at elevating their status by impressing upon them the demand to emulate in historical reality the ideal standards of personal and public conduct that informed their own utopian visions.[22]

The societal integrity of Israel in the monarchic period rested upon the equilibrium maintained between the forces of "constancy"—kings and priests—and the generators of "creative movement"—the prophets. An undue gravitation toward institutional realism could impair Israel's uniqueness shaped by the precepts of biblical monotheism. An over-emphasis on utopian idealism could intensify eschatological speculations and messianic dreams to a degree that would undermine the will to live in actual history. Neither of these extremes appears to have materialized before the end of the First Temple period.

2. In the days of the monarchy, and essentially also in the preceding stages of the Hebrew tribes' implantation in the Land of Canaan, the life of the people of Israel was marked by a fundamental geographical circumscription which furthered social, religious, and political cohesion. Shared traditions of a common ethnic extraction and a common historical past meant that the division into two rival kingdoms—since approximately 900 B.C.E.—was generally considered a temporary breach that would be healed at some future time in history. In the last analysis, it did not sap the Ephraimites' and Judeans' consciousness of being one nation. Although constituted in historical actuality, of two political entities, (all-) Israel thus retained a basic unity, safeguarded by the geographical compactness that encompassed all those who considered themselves of Abraham's stock. The external pressure of the surrounding "foreign nations," and ongoing contacts between Judah and Ephraim—of war and intermittent alliances, commerce, and the two-way migration of groups and individuals among whom prophets such as Amos stand out—helped in preserving the pathos of an intrinsic oneness, symbolized in the tradition of the Twelve Tribes. Even when no one place was recognized by all Israel

as the nation's religious and political pivot, the very boundaries of the land sufficed to circumscribe Israel's monocentricity. No constituted group or groups of Israelites existed outside the space of the divinely promised and sanctified land. Also the recurrent deportation of Ephraimites in the wake of the conquest of Samaria by the Assyrians in 722 B.C.E. did not materially affect this monocentricity. There is no tangible evidence to suggest that the relocations effected the emergence of Ephraimite centers in Mesopotamia or elsewhere. Even if this should have been the case, as is sometimes surmised, those presumed Ephraimite exilic communities disappeared within a comparatively short span of time. In any event, there is nothing to show that a new lasting understanding of Judaism differing significantly from that of predestruction Samaria ever was conceived by Ephraimites in exile.

One readily acknowledges the existence of differences in the social structure of the Southern Kingdom on the one hand and the Northern on the other. In both, one observes a diversity of interpretations of Israelite monotheism, entertained by various strata of society. It appears, however, that the latitude of deviation remained sufficiently restricted to prevent the complete estrangement of any segment of Israelite society from the fundamental tenets and patterns of life that distinguished Israel as a whole from neighboring societies and cultures. The cohesion indeed was at times strained because of socioeconomic, politicoreligious, and even ethnic differences prevailing in the citizenry of the two realms. But it would appear that at no stage in the history of the monarchies did the stratification into poor and rich, oppressors and oppressed, pure monotheists and syncretists effect a fundamentally different development in the existing societal structures, either in Judah or in Ephraim.

In sum, throughout the First Temple period, thanks to internal cohesion and geographical compactness, homogeneity prevailed in Israel over heterogeneity, uniformity over multiformity.

IV

All this changed abruptly after the debacle of 586 B.C.E. when Judah and its capital city fell prey to the Babylonians. With the political framework in shambles, the monarchy in actual history lost its raison d'être. However, the idea and the ideal of "royalty," in the configuration of the "anointed shoot of the house of David" (cf. Isa 42:1–3 with 11:1–5),[23] gained strength and became the embodiment of a restoration—hope and ideology. With the Temple sacked, the cultic paraphernalia looted and carried away by the conqueror, the priests were in effect deprived of their sphere of function and influence. This did not result in a religious reorientation leading to a search for new means and forms of worship; rather, it resulted in the emergence of an intensified dream of a future restitution of the age-honored holy place and the sacrificial cult.[24] In short, the institutionalized political and religious agencies, and their representatives who had been imbued with office charisma, survived the historical setback by a temporary transfer from the plane of facticity to that of conceptuality. Their reactivation in historical reality was considered a certainty, depending on Israel's conduct that would lead to a reconciliation with God and the restitution of its fortunes.

Most severely affected was the prophetic leadership and the very phenomenon of prophecy. The prophet's personal charisma lacked the staying power that the institutional character of the monarchy and the priesthood conferred upon them. Thus, the fall of Judah and Jerusalem signaled the wane of prophecy. Although there would be a short-lived reemergence of prophecy in the period of the return (Haggai, Zechariah, and Malachi), the need for a replacement of personal inspiration as a principle of public guidance, by more rational and controllable forms of instruction, had become acute. Ultimately, the transformation would crystallize in new classes of spiritual leaders—the scribes and then the sages. Their authority rested on expert exposition of the hallowed traditions by techniques whose reliability can be objectively ascertained rather than on personal inspiration which cannot be subjected to any generally acknowledged checks and controls.

Concomitant with the developments that affected the leadership, the original geographical compactness of Israel was shattered. An era of multicentricity set in. Multiformity replaced uniformity; heterogeneity supplanted the former homogeneity. It is to these features that we must now turn our attention.

After the fall of Jerusalem, the Babylonians, emulating a strategy introduced by the Assyrians, deported segments of the Judean population to other parts of their empire and settled them in various places in Mesopotamia. The biblical records imply that the exile (deportation) affected mainly the upper strata of the society. The figures of deportees adduced in the biblical sources may not be altogether accurate or may not give the correct total of all Judeans removed. Allowing for some latitude, a total of thirty thousand to forty thousand may be considered a conservative estimate. But more important for the subsequent historical development than the sheer numbers is the circumstance that the expatriates either were forcibly settled by the conquerors on specific sites or elected out of their free will to cluster in compact localities. Some of these are mentioned by name in biblical sources, for example, Tel-abib (Ezek 1:3; 3:15) and Casiphiah (Ezra 8:15–20). Also the Ephraimites deported after the fall of Samaria in 722 B.C.E. had been settled by the Assyrians in specific locales (2 Kgs 17:6; 18:11; 1 Chr 5:26). But in contrast to them, the deported Judeans seem to have turned their ghettolike settlements to advantage. The concentration enabled them to maintain their identity and, in effect, to further their tradition in ways and manners that were not shared by the remnant left by the conquerors in the Babylonian province of Judah (Yehud). Thus, there emerged in Babylonia a new center of Judaism in which a particular understanding of biblical mono-theism was cultivated. The Babylonian community entertained a fervent messianic hope for an imminent return to the homeland which restrained them from sinking roots in the foreign soil (Jer 29:4–7). Therefore it could provide echelons of returnees when the liberating edict of Cyrus the Great in 538 B.C.E. made a return possible. However, not all exiles returned. It well may be that those who remained even constituted the majority. In any case, they were to become the matrix of a flourishing community which in later days would compete with, and at times sur-pass, Palestinian Judaism in literary achievements and social weight.

Another center emerged in Egypt. Information on the presence of Jewish communities comes from two disparate sources that are some 150 years apart. The more detailed evidence can be gleaned from the archives of a Jewish garrison stationed in Elephantine and Syene (Assuan) in Upper Egypt.[25] The documents pertain to a period of approximately forty years, between 420 and 380 B.C.E. References, however, to earlier histor-ical events indicate that the settlement preceded the conquest of Egypt by the Persian king Cambyses in 525 B.C.E. Of special importance for our purpose is the knowledge gained from the Elephantine papyri on the internal structure of the garrison and its religious outlook[26] as well as its relations to their homeland. We learn that already before 525 B.C.E., that is, merely some decades after the destruction of the Jerusalem Temple, the Jewish garrison had built a temple in Elephantine. The construction of a permanent sanctuary outside Jerusalem, in a foreign land, constitutes a significant departure from biblical precepts. The very existence of that sanctuary in Elephantine flaunted the uniqueness of the Jerusalem Tem-ple and its exclusive legitimacy. We must conclude that Egyptian Jewry had adjusted to their Diaspora conditions. They had accepted life "away from the land" as final and did not entertain any hope of a restoration, or at least did not believe in the possible realization of such hope in histor-ical times.

The other set of evidence derives from the Book of Jeremiah, chaps. 43—44. There it is reported that an unspecified number of Judeans fled to lower Egypt a short while after the fall of Jerusalem, fearing Babylo-nian reprisals for the murder of Gedaliah, the governor whom the con-queror had appointed over the province (Jeremiah 41). They interpreted the calamity that had befallen them as proving the inefficacy of YHWH rather than as a punishment for their sins and disregard of his commands. It may be presumed that this attitude ultimately led to a complete separation between them and their former compatriots and coreligionists in the Land of Israel and in the Babylonian Diaspora. In consequence, Egyptian Jewry would have no share in the founding of the new community in the land by the returnees from the exile in the wake of Cyrus's declaration.

The estrangement of Egyptian from Babylonian and Palestinian Jewry was deepened by one other historicopolitical factor. Egypt was conquered by the Persians only in 525 B.C.E. in the reign of Cambyses. Thus the Jews in Egypt were not included in the decree of 538 B.C.E. which had been addressed foremost to the exiles in Babylonia-Persia (Ezra 1:2–4; 4:3) but probably also to other Jews living in territories within the reaches of the Persian empire (see Ezra 7:11–25).

A synoptic view of the constitution of the Jewish people after the fall of the Kingdom of Judah in 586 B.C.E. reveals a situation that is fundamentally different from the one that obtained in the First Temple period. Not only has multicentricity replaced the former monocentricity but, what is more, the different Jewish communities present to the viewer diverse sociological and spiritual, in short, existential profiles: Those who had been permitted by the Babylonians to remain in the land in essence did not change their life style, economic structure, and religious-cultic customs, notwithstanding the loss of political sovereignty and cultic institutions and the incurrence of economic hardship. They were the conservatives who clung to their established system of values, despite the changed circumstances. In Egypt there emerged an émigré community of Jews who had elected to leave their homeland, even though under pressure. The severance of ties with the land and with biblical monotheism severely undermined their staying power and their will to resist the inroads of the surrounding society and its conceptual universe. Hated and persecuted by their Egyptian neighbors, as some Elephantine papyri evidence, they nevertheless could not preserve their identity and social cohesion. They embraced an accommodating syncretistic stance, which ultimately caused their community to dry up.

In contrast, the community of exiles in Babylonia-Persia, at least in part,[27] persisted in its particularity. The exiles indeed re-formed and reinterpreted traditional values so as to be able to cope with the situation of a stubborn minority into which they had been precipitated. Their unmitigated sense of being in exile reinforced their insistence on strict adherence to their spiritual heritage and furthered the formation of societal structures adjusted to exilic conditions, for example, by concentrating in specific locales. More than that, the consciousness of being expatriates intensified the hope of repatriation in an appreciable historical future and reconstitution of their political sovereignty under an anointed king of the Davidic line. It stimulated an intrinsically activist stance.

V

Before proceeding to the next stage of our inquiry, we need to highlight some salient characteristics of Israel in exilic times, characteristics that seem to have a special bearing on Weber's conceptual framework.

1. Postdestruction Palestinian Jewry did not come to be divorced from agriculture, nor did it become urbanized. Quite the opposite appears to have been the case, as the biblical sources intimate and archaeological research bears out.[28] The cities became the pivots and mainstays of the imperial civic and military administration, with the concomitant influx of foreign bureaucrats, army personnel, and population groups that first the Assyrian and then the Babylonian suzerain transplanted into the conquered territories of Samaria (see 2 Kgs 17:24–41) and most probably also of Judah (see Ezra 4:7—6:5; Neh 3:33—4:2; 6:1–7; 13:16). It may be postulated, in fact, that then and there the Jewish population of the land became increasingly deurbanized, being forced out of the cities and pushed into the rural periphery.

The continued attachment of considerable parts of the Jewish populace to agricultural pursuits persisted into or was renewed in the period of the return from exile and beyond it into rabbinic times.[29] This fact clearly emerges from the accounts preserved in the postexilic biblical literature, which prove that the people of the land played an important role in the reconstituted body politic of the returnees. Recurrent references to cattle, vineyards, fields and crops, and the failure of crops (Hag 1:6, 10, 11; 2:15–19; Zech 8:10–12; Ezra 3:7; Neh 5:1–15, 18; et al.) point to the existence of a substantial rural class with agricultural interests and not to a landless urbanized citizenry as Weber surmised. Biblical reports have it that Nehemiah was forced to have recourse to the conscription of every tenth member of the returnees' families for settlement in Jerusalem, so as to ensure that former exiles would predominate in the citizenry of the capital (Neh 7:4–5; 11:1–2). Equally revealing is the "roster of returning exiles" that has been preserved in two slightly diverging versions (Ezra 2:1–70 and Neh 7:6–72).[30] It served Nehemiah as a basis for the repopulation of Jerusalem with trustworthy men. In part this list is arranged according to localities in the Land of Israel (Ezra 2:21–35), mostly villages and rural townships. The arrangement reflects the returnees' intention to take root in domiciles in which their forebears had been settled before their expulsion. The concluding line of that roster, "The (returning) priests . . . Levites . . . and all Israel [settled] in their villages" (Ezra 2:70 = Neh 7:72), is echoed in the "conscription notation," which directs that nine out of ten members of each family should remain in their "locations," whereas one should transfer to Jerusalem (Neh 11:1).

2. The enforced status of a confessional community had been regarded by the Babylonian exiles as a mere temporary adjustment to prevailing adverse circumstances. However, as will be explicated, once this new form of communal life had come into existence, it would not be discarded even when the conditions that brought it about were seemingly reversed or attenuated by the return to the land, which did not, however, put an end to the existence of an exilic community. The structure of the credal community will be absorbed into the future societal framework of Jewry, in transformations that are concordant with its changing religiosocietal configuration.

When the returning exiles reconstituted the political framework of Judah in the early Persian period, there evolved a symbiosis of credal community with nation. After that time, Jewish peoplehood would embrace communities that accentuate their national-religious heritage differently. Rather than one replacing the other, *pace* Weber, mutually exclusive types of sociopolitical and religious organization—confessional community and nation—would coalesce.

3. The continuing adherence to preexilic socioreligious structures finds its expression also in the circumstance that immediately upon their return to the land, the former exiles began to rebuild the Temple (Ezra 3:2; 4:1–3; cf. Haggai passim; Zech 3:1–10; 6:9–15) and reinstituted the sacrificial service (Ezra 3:2–6; 6:16–22; 7:17; Neh 10:35–39; 12:43–47; 13:30–31; cf. Mal 1:6–14; 2:12). As in the past, the Temple was considered not only an institution exclusively dedicated to religious concerns but also a symbol of nationhood and political sovereignty, as was well understood by the local Persian officials (see Ezra 5:6–8 and 4:12–22, 24). In this respect, the Temple differs from the synagogue, which replaced it at a later stage in the Second Temple period, as Weber correctly recognized, but which has no discernible roots either in the exilic setting[31] or in the days of the return.

4. Weber's contention that, since access to the religious confessional community was regulated primarily by ritual law, proselytism became a constitutive phenomenon of postexilic Judaism[32] certainly does not apply to the returnees' community. The above-mentioned roster of returning paternal houses is obviously intended to help preserve the ethnic-national circumscription of its membership and to block altogether, or at least brake, the infiltration of outsiders. The restrictive effect of the self-identification thus achieved becomes clearly visible in the ensuing cam-

paign of Ezra, Nehemiah, and their followers against the intrusion of "foreign women" into the Judeans' society. The traditional endogamy principle, which precludes intermarriage with ethnic foreigners, is now expanded to apply also to non-Judean Israelites whose version of the biblical faith was at variance with the returnees' understanding of biblical monotheism. Again one encounters the concentric structure of confessional community within nation: The confessional religious-credal factor causes *connubium* to become operative exclusively within the society of the former exiles. Only returnees can be counted among the "righteous remnant," the "holy seed" whose preordained restoration the preexilic prophet Isaiah had announced, so that it should become the stock out of which the people (nation) of Israel would rise again (cf. Ezra 9:2 and Neh 9:2 with Isa 6:13). There emerged a triad of relationships that was not recognized by Weber or, for that matter, by other students of the period:

(credal-national)	inner-group
(national)	in-group
(credal-ethnic-foreign)	out-group

This pattern prevailed in later Second Temple Judaism. It determined, to a large degree, the very character of Jewish sectarianism and the interrelation of the diverse factions that are but structured-societal manifestations of diverging interpretations of the common tradition shared by all. The above analysis and the suggested three-tier model lend additional force to J. Taubes's observation that in contrasting people and religion in reference to Judaism, Weber created a false polarity.[33]

VI

The multicentricity and heterogeneity of Judaism effected by the dispersion that followed upon the dissolution of the Kingdom of Judah, and the socioreligious characteristics outlined above, constitute the backdrop against which the overall population in the land after the return of contingents of exiles from Babylonia-Persia must be viewed and its internal diversification and the conflicts and clashes that resulted from it appreciated. Against this background one can identify the most prominent factors that separated the returnees from "the people(s) of the land" and caused some factions of these "Palestinians" to become prototypical dissenters. I submit that the issue should be regarded initially as a confrontation of two factions in the people (or nation) of Israel pitted against each other, with the controversy being triggered by motives of a historicopolitical, economic, and religious-cultic nature. This multifariousness of aspects puts the ensuing Samaritan schism in a category by itself, within the wider compass of "Conformity and Dissent" or "Mainstream versus Sectarian Judaism" in the Second Temple period. This schism appears to offer the earliest tangible evidence of a shift in the substance of the problems that confronted Judaism and foremost the returnees' "Torah Community."

The "in-group—out-group" ethos that had characterized Israel's relations with its pagan neighbors in the land in the predestruction period, and in the Diaspora during the exile, now manifested itself in new configurations. The need for a close circumscription of Jewish identity that had been especially pressing in the setting of a surrounding pagan-foreign majority in Babylonia-Persia was turned inward, so to speak. The insistence on the observance of religious-ritual norms—foremost Sabbath, festivals, and circumcision—in the Diaspora had acted as a defense mechanism in the quest for self-preservation vis-à-vis the ethnically "other." After the return, the question at issue progressively became internalized. Compliance with the specific-particular execution of these rites now became a criterion that set apart constituents of one Jewish "inner group" from others. Weber seemingly did not take note of this transmutation, nor did he take it into account in his analysis of "in-group—out-group" behavior patterns.[34]

The biblical sources indicate that the Israelites (and the Judeans) in the land at first expressed a readiness to join with the returnees in their efforts to rebuild the Temple and their community and probably to subscribe to their religious norms and values. The Book of Ezra reports that in distinction from "the people(s) of the land" who sought to prevent the restoration of the Temple (Ezra 3:3), some inhabitants proposed to participate actively in the building operations. These petitioners are designated "adversaries of Judah and Benjamin" (Ezra 4:1). This designation implies that they were considered opponents of the returnees whose community was predominantly, if not exclusively, constituted of exiled Judeans and Benjaminites (Ezra 1:5; 2:1—Neh 7:6; Ezra 10:9; 2 Chr 34:9), citizens of the former Kingdom of Judah. The precise specification of the petitioners' identity suggests that the report revolves on an internal Israelite matter, namely, the question of whether the returnees should completely separate themselves from the "Palestinian" Ephraimites (and Judeans) who had not undergone the exile experience or whether they should agree to integrate them into their midst. At that time, that is, around 520 B.C.E., Zerubbabel and his followers rejected them (Ezra 4:1–3), obviously acting under prophetic pressure.[35] The refusal caused bad blood between the two factions. But this apparently did not prevent the locals from trying again in the days of Ezra and Nehemiah to win acceptance into the Judean *res publica*,[36] once more to no avail. The finality of the rift between the two strata of Israelites in the land comes to the fore in the pronouncements of the last biblical prophet Malachi, who assumedly was active then. At the end of his book, which signals the closure of the collection of prophetic writings and indeed the termination of biblical prophecy (as a whole), the author records a controversy between two (certainly "Jewish") factions: "those who fear God and serve him" and "those who do not fear God nor serve him" (Mal 3:13–21). The first are promised good fortunes and salvation,[37] the other misery and damnation on the "[appointed] day,"[38] when God will sit in judgment over his people. It goes without saying that the author sides with those whom he considers to be obedient to God. They may be regarded as akin to those "who revere [or abide by] the word of God" (Isa 66:5; contrast Isa 65:11) and to the *'anawim* (= "humble") or *ṣadiqim* (= "righteous") of the psalms, and as forerunners of the later *hasidim* (= "pious") of early Maccabean times.[39]

Having been repeatedly spurned by the returned Judeans, the *Samarians*[40] or Ephraimites—subsequently also known as Shechemites—abstained from further overtures. Approximately a century later, they struck out on their own. Renouncing any adherence to the Jerusalem Temple, they reportedly built a rival sanctuary on Mt. Gerizim near the city of Shechem. Josephus relates that Menachem, a member of the high priestly family whom Nehemiah had ousted from Jerusalem (Neh 13:28), then married the daughter of Sanballat, whom the Samaritans considered to have been the leader of their community at that time. The priest had taken with him from the temple of Jerusalem a Torah scroll which he placed in the sanctuary on Mt. Gerizim.[41] Josephus's story is not without difficulties. He appears to have telescoped historical events. He linked the priest whom Nehemiah drove out of Jerusalem in approximately 430–425 B.C.E., and who may have been the son-in-law of the Sanballat of Nehemiah's days, with another Sanballat, probably the third,[42] who flourished a hundred years later, in the time of Alexander.

But these inaccuracies and inconsistencies do not invalidate Josephus's statement on two points:

1. By the end of the fourth century, the erstwhile *Samarians*, who now will become known as the *Samaritans*, had entirely severed their links with the Jerusalem community. The foundation of a holy place on Mt. Gerizim, whatever form it took, gave finality to the break.

2. The secessionists adopted the Torah as the fundament on which they built their communal life.[43] Thus, both major derivates of preexilic Israel—the returnees from Babylon and the Palestinian Israelites—proclaimed the Torah the mainstay of their beliefs and practices.[44] Each conceived of itself as "the Torah Community" and strove to outdo the other in professing and exhibiting faithfulness to Torah laws. Paganism had been totally overcome.[45] On this common platform of basic consent,

each faction emphasized particular aspects in the execution of the shared tradition. Dissent expressed itself in differences of interpretation resulting in deviating norms. Technicalities in the execution of circumcision, precision in the observance of the Sabbath and the festivals,[46] matters concerning the Temple and the cult, now will achieve exceeding prominence. The opposition to *derek hattôrāh* ("the [proper] way of the Torah") will be the *derek 'aḥeret* ("another [heterodox] way").[47] The internal boundary lines between one faction and the other proved to be no less rigid than those which had separated and continued to separate all Israelites from the "other nations."

Attention should be drawn also to some, at first sight, less conspicuous but no less weighty discords that show in the Jewish-Samaritan controversy. In discussing the formative impulse that the destruction of Jerusalem and the ensuing exile gave to the emergence of the postexilic community, I singled out the transformation of the former monocentricity into a multicentricity and the unhinging of the previously balanced social structure of preexilic Judah. It is in these two spheres that the divergent developments of mainstream Judaism and the Samaritan community gradually became eminently manifest.

By claiming to be descended from the tribe of Joseph, the Samaritans also claimed a share in the history of the Northern Kingdom in which the Joseph clans predominated. They knew and told of the destruction of Samaria and of the deportation of contingents of Samarians to Mesopotamia. However, in contrast to Judah, the geographical compactness of the Ephraimites' population in the monarchical period was not transformed into a plurality of centers after the fall of their kingdom. As already stated, we have no information on any Ephraimite collectivity that was constituted outside Palestine and developed a life stance different from the one by which the Palestinian center adhered. The original monocentricity of the ten tribes, whom the Samaritans claimed to represent, became utterly fragmented. Only the population that had been allowed to remain in the territory of the former Northern Kingdom preserved vestiges of an Israelite identity. The Ephraimite Diaspora appears to have fallen prey to a process of internal dissolution, leading to its eclipse within a comparatively short time—a century or two—after the fall of Samaria. Consequently, at first the Samarians, and later the Samaritans, were never exposed to the fructifying impact of the Diaspora and restoration experience that etched the contours of the postexilic Judean community. First the Samarians and then the Samaritans persisted in their severely curtailed monocentric uniformity into Hellenistic times. Then, under the impact of various internal and external factors, dissent became rife also in the Samaritan community and generated sectarian secession in its ranks.

The nonacceptance of the prophetic and historiographical literature into the Samaritan biblical canon, and the concomitant accordance of authoritative sanctity to the Pentateuch alone, accounts for some additional conceptual divergences from Judaism. The rigorous exclusive Torah, that is to say, Pentateuch steadfastness, precipitated in Samaritanism the emergence of an utterly ritualistic religiosity lacking the inner tension that prophecy bestowed upon Judaism.[48] In the Samaritan religious stance, the exact adherence to behavioral norms takes on paramount importance. Samaritanism experienced only restricted spiritual movement, as if religious development had come to a halt already in the early stages of its genesis. Since then, Samaritan men of learning and letters have produced few new thoughts or literary innovations, certainly nothing comparable to the intellectual fecundity of Second Temple and Post–Second Temple Judaism.

It may well be that this spiritual immobility was bolstered by the nonexistence in the Samaritan world of ideas of the utopian ferment that the messianic hope imparted to mainstream Judaism, to the Qumran Community (as yet will be shown), and then to Christianity. Their opposition to the Davidic dynasty concomitant with the rejection of the biblical prophetic books and the historiographies impeded the articulation of a messianic vision in the Samaritans' conceptual universe. Although they do foresee a future time of divine mercy in which they expect to be translated from their adverse historical situation into a shining perfect eon, the depiction of that era remains rather vague, with no "royal anointed" showing on the horizon. The indistinct references to a central figure that will arise in that ideal future age seem to pertain to a New Moses (Moses redivivus) who is designated *taheb*. This latter term may be translated "restorer." The future eon is conceived as a replica of the Mosaic era in which the restorative thrust is fully dominant and which lacks altogether the utopian cosmic superstructure that prophetic inspiration had envisaged.[49]

Thus, Samaritanism emerges as an offshoot of biblical Israel that embraced only one of the two principles that became the mainstays of mainstream Judaism. Concentrating on the regulation of life in actual history by the normative Torah code, they lost the spiritual tension with which messianism and the idealistic vision of the future had imbued Judaism. While the adherence to the facticity of normative practice may well have been a major factor in the preservation of a structured Samaritan community over two millennia, it also generated a rigidity that prevented this community from creatively dealing with history by absorbing changes through an ongoing process of interpreting and, to a degree, reformulating tradition.

The above-observed "inner-group—in-group" relationship (in the framework of the proposed three-tier model), which determined the attitude of the Judean returnees toward the nonexiled Israelites, obtains also in respect to the Samaritans. Also in this case, their self-identification as *Volk und Religion*—people and confession—defined their posture vis-à-vis the contemporary Jewish nation and state. By establishing a separate central sanctuary on Mt. Gerizim as the religious pivot of their "national entity," the Samaritans in fact reactivated a political-religious pattern that arose out of the secession of the northern from the southern tribes after the death of King Solomon (ca. 900 B.C.E.)[50] and culminated in the establishment of the kingdom of Samaria and its schismatic state sanctuary, Beth-El, which was meant to serve as counterpoint to the (state) temple in Jerusalem (1 Kgs 12:25–33).

VII

Before we proceed with our investigation, it is appropriate to make reference to an aspect of the issue under consideration that Weber did not sufficiently take into account in his analysis of ancient Judaism and that is of special importance in the Second Temple period, namely, the diversity of impacts that the civilizations of successive empires which in their turn subjugated Israel had on the cultural, religious, and societal outlook of Judaism. The issue is much too multifaceted and involved to be discussed here in detail. A mere delineation of its contours and relevancy for the diversity of configurations in which Jewish schismaticism expressed itself at the time must suffice.

It cannot go unnoticed that the concept of sectarianism, as it figures in our present discussion, does not apply to cases of internal cultic-political dissent in periods in which Israel was in the sphere of the political and cultural influence of Semitic (Assyria and Babylonia) or oriental (Persia) overlords, that is, before about 300 B.C.E. After Alexander's conquest of the ancient Near East, Judaism in the land and to a large degree also in the Diaspora became incorporated in a political framework whose cultural profile was shaped by influences flowing from the Occident, from Greece-Hellas. At that juncture in history, the Samaritan schism crystallized. The situation changed radically when, in 163 B.C.E., the Hasmoneans reestablished Jewish political sovereignty for one hundred years, after which time Rome subjugated the Jewish state. It is precisely in that Hasmonean century that the commune of the Qumran Covenanters flourished. Its inception, though, may have preceded the Hasmoneans' success by a decade or two. No definite correlation between the status of political independence and the specific mode of Qumran secession can be readily established. But it must be noted that at this stage, Jewish dissent presents itself to the viewer in a makeup that differs considerably from that of the Samaritan schism, and will be reflected in the features of Jewish heterodoxies that emerged in the late Second Temple period.

VIII

We can now turn to reviewing the Qumran Covenanters' Community. The results of this case study, an exercise in microsociology, must be examined for their bearing on Weber's findings concerning Second Temple Judaism, in his macrosociological approach.

The chronological coalescence of events in the postexilic period and their recordings underscored above is even more pronounced in reference to the Commune of the Covenanters of the Judean Desert that became an object of scholarly inquiry in 1947. No other pre-Christian Jewish group or community has left for us such a rich literary legacy, authored by some and intended for all its members, which enlightens the reader on its history, societal structure, and conceptual universe. In toto, the details gleaned from these literary remains can be fitted into a mosaic that is a true-to-reality mockup of a secessionist faction in Second Temple Judaism, the life of which students of that period or, for that matter, of the entire biblical era had never encountered before. Being contemporaneous with the events described in them, the Qumran writings constitute the best conceivable basis for the study of any ancient social entity, in this instance of an early Jewish dissident movement or interlocal sect.

In addition, these materials afford the viewer a back-window view, so to speak, of the "normative"[51] Jewish society from which the Covenanters had seceded and with which they were engaged in an ideological struggle over the exclusive right to represent "true Israel" legitimately. Thus the Qumran Covenanters may be considered, in Weber's terminology, a "historical object" of interest in itself but even more so a "heuristic instrument"[52] for testing theoretical concepts appropriate to the study of Judaism in the Second Temple period, and possibly also of "sect" as a socioreligious phenomenon.

Scholars have attempted to identify the Covenanters' Commune with practically any Jewish sect or religious stream of the Second Temple period known from the ancient sources before the discovery of the new material. The most widely accepted theory identifies them with the Essenes. In comparing these two groups, one highlights affinities that by no means can be disregarded[53] but does not pay sufficient attention to telling differences.[54] For reasons of method and not only because of

605

historical considerations,[55] I prefer to view the Covenanters for the present as a phenomenon sui generis, the examination of which is bound to add a new dimension to the study of early Jewish sectarianism.

The founding members of that community can be best defined as a group of millenarian-messianic Jews who had figured out the advent of the "Kingdom to Come" by attaching a real-historical interpretation to a biblical prophecy. The utopian messianists seem to have read a message of hope into the prophet Ezekiel's symbolic act, which he performed in the face of the imminent Babylonian siege on Jerusalem and which originally was meant to announce a period of punishment that would last 390 years for Israel (Ephraim) and forty years for Judah (Ezek 4:4–6). The Qumranians interpreted this to mean that 390 years after the destruction of the First Temple in 586 B.C.E., Israel's fortunes would be restored. In anticipation of this great event, they segregated from their fellow Jews and repaired to the desert to prepare themselves there soul and body for the imminent salvation. The date at which they arrived, if one takes the prophet's visionary figures at face value, astonishingly dovetails with the dating of the emergence of the Qumran community to the beginning of the second century B.C.E., which is the common opinion among scholars. In the resulting high-tension situation the traditional forms of normal social life lost their meaning. Standing on the threshold of a new age, which they expected to be governed by an ideal code of religious, social, and political values, those millenarians saw no reason for abiding by accepted notions and maintaining established societal institutions.[56]

The millenarian spirit thus generated in the first Covenanters an anarchistic antiestablishment stance, such as can be observed also in other millenarian movements.[57] Qumran anarchism, though, was not a deep-seated principle but rather an ad hoc reaction to existing circumstances, a necessary step to be taken to pave the way leading into the messianic age. In the Qumranian's vision of the "Age to Come" the politicosocial and cultic institutions would be reinstated in accordance with their concepts, customs, and codified law. This vision was patterned upon the basically this-worldly conceptions of the Hebrew Bible, or at least of some major strata of that literature, which put a premium on a good life, on family and kinship, and on an orderly social structure.[58]

Qumran theology and the structure of the Qumran Commune, illustrate the issue of change and continuity. They oscillate between a highly idealized concept of the historical biblical Israel and a utopian vision of a future historical world conceived as a glorified restoration of the biblical past.[59] The Qumranians viewed their own community as the only legitimate remnant and representative of the biblical people of Israel. They had been chosen to experience, in an appreciably near future, a restitution of Israel's fortunes, culminating in the reestablishment of the Temple in Jerusalem.

One finds at Qumran some mystical inclinations. But these play only a minor role in that spiritual framework. The type of millennialism that flourished in that community does not dovetail with the mystical chiliasm on which Weber based his typology.[60] Qumran exhibits a quite different development: the initial temporary anarchistic posture, which never seems to have been antinomistic, will be supplanted by a hypernomistic stance, which exceeded the nomism of most if not all other religious trends in Judaism of the time, including that of Pharisaism.

The conviction that the exact details of the unfolding latter-days drama had been revealed to them appears to have induced in the Qumran membership an elite consciousness, which their Jewish contemporaries undoubtedly interpreted as a sign of unwarranted arrogance. They viewed themselves as the divinely appointed elect. They were the "Sons of Light" who had been authoritatively commanded to part company with the "Sons of Darkness," their fellow Jews, so that in their community the divine promise could be finally realized as it is spelled out in some biblical prophecies. In their communal life they perceived a revitalization[61] of biblical Israel before the conquest of Jerusalem by the Babylonians. They believed that the New Covenant which they established was the realization of the prophet Jeremiah's vision of the covenant that the God of Israel would renew with his liberated people (Jer 31:31).

The elite-consciousness, which appears to have put its stamp on the self-understanding of the Qumran Covenanters, is utterly discordant with their apparent pariah status. The Qumran Commune displays all or most of the qualities by which Weber sought to define the pariah character of the postexilic Jewish confessional community—foremost ritualistic segregation, enmity toward nonmembers and in-group morality, sectarian economic structure and lack of political autonomy.[62] The obvious contradiction between subjective self-understanding and objective classification that hits the eye in the Qumran setting altogether escaped Weber's attention and thus was not taken into account in his treatment of ancient Judaism. It would seem that the omission should be remedied and that this phenomenon should find an expression in an adjusted typology.

Like the returnees from Babylon and the Samaritans, so also the Qumranians viewed themselves as both a *nation* and a *confessional community* and thus present one more case of a mediating or mixed type that resists being subsumed under Weber's dichotomized typology. Since the antithesis nation versus religious community is founded upon and derived from the analysis of ancient Judaism, and since also later configurations of Jewry, from Pharisaism to modern times, cannot be adequately characterized by it, also in this instance, Weber's antithetical typology should come up for review.

Similarly, the Qumran Commune defies Weber's counterpositioning of "church" into which one is born and which has a "compulsory-associational" and "ascriptive" character, and "sect" which is a "voluntary association" and therefore of an "elective" nature.[63] In the New Covenant, these "polarized" principles, according to Weber, become inseparably fused: Only Israelites by "ascription" can achieve membership in this "elective" association.

The description of their life style that the Qumranians provide in their writings, and the preservation and augmentation of legislation pertaining to agriculture in Qumran law literature, prove that agricultural pursuits persisted in practically all divisions and subdivisions of Second Temple Judaism. Arguing a fortiori from the intensely nomistic Samaritans and Qumranians whom their rigid ritualistic law code did not prevent from engaging in agriculture, the—comparatively speaking—more "liberal" Pharisees certainly cannot be presented as having been estranged from such occupations. The same holds true for rabbinic Judaism: "The Mishnah knows all sorts of economic activities. But for the Mishnah the center and focus of interest lie in the village. . . . The Mishnah's class perspective described merely from its topics is that of the undercapitalized and overextended upper class farmer. . . . The Mishnah therefore is the voice of the Israelite landholding proprietary class. All Israel had was villages."[64]

According to Weber, the waning of agriculture and village orientation was contiguous with the waxing of a preponderantly urban ethic *(städtische Ethik)*. Nothing in the Qumran conceptual universe gives evidence of this transformation. Since the presumed precondition was, in fact, missing—the abandonment of agriculture—the posited development toward "urban ethics" did not materialize, neither at Qumran nor in other groupings of Second Temple Judaism. One suspects that, as already mentioned, Weber at times retrojected his own experience of denationalized and nonagrarian urbanized Jewish bourgeoisie and its ethos into earlier stages of Jewish social history.

When the foreseen date of the onset of the "Kingdom to Come" passed uneventfully, the Covenanters seemed to be losing their bearings. There and then, a Moses-like figure arose out of their midst, the Teacher of Righteousness. His origins and his biographical data are not explicated. However, he obviously was born out of the existential stress generated by the nonrealization of the Community's millenarian expectations.[65]

In Weber's conceptual framework, the Teacher would rate as a leader whose charisma resulted from societal attribution.[66] Unlike Jesus, whom

Weber considers to be representative of the religious founder type, the Teacher did not create but rather consolidated a preexisting new social community,[67] which, however, was also in conflict with family and clan. But—like the biblical prophets (see, e.g., Isaiah 3—4)—his main aim was not to undo but rather to reform the established society and its institutions, so that ultimately it would embrace and act out the traditional values that he and his followers were determined to preserve in their purity.

At the same time, in his figure are welded together characteristics that, *pace* Weber, should be ascribed separately to two different types of religious virtuosi. While the Teacher is never reported to have executed cultic functions (either as a priest or as a prophet), he is presented as a priestly preceptor invested with the spirit of prophecy. Thus, in his personality, charisma of office coalesces with personal calling. It follows that he cannot be placed securely and adequately in any one category of Weber's neat schema of four types of religious leaders: cult priest and cult prophet, teacher priest and teacher prophet.[68] While the typology in essence may be upheld in theory, more attention should be given to mixed types which in actual reality constitute the majority of cases.[69]

The Teacher seemingly did not innovate any religious concepts and maxims but rather was an inspired interpreter of the traditional lore. He was instrumental in hammering the group's anarchistic utopian messianism into the basis of a new social and religious structure. During his term of office and through him the amorphous cluster of men who had figured out the dawn of the "World to Come" by millenarian speculations developed their own religious and societal structures. The erstwhile dissenters community hardened into an institutionalized socioreligious establishment that was soon to surpass the old order from which they had seceded in social rigidity and legalistic exactitude.

The transformation sketched above generated at Qumran a gradual increase in specific Covenant precepts culminating in their codification. Before long, the particular tenets of the Covenants solidified in what may be termed a written appendix to the traditional law. Some parts of Qumran legislation are preserved in the legal portions of the Zadokite Documents, others in the *Manual of Discipline,* and still others in the Temple Scroll. With all due caution and reservations, this particular body of laws may be viewed as a sectarian parallel to the rabbinic law codified in the Mishnah. But in contrast to the Rabbinic, the Qumran Code is not formulated in the question-and-answer pattern without a specific address[70] but rather is expressly aimed at a specific audience, the "members of the Commune."

The rapid transmutation of the Qumran Covenanters, within the time span of one generation, from the status of a secessionist, anarchistic, millenarianist-inspired fellowship into a structured religious establishment again makes this phenomenon an unwilling object for inclusion in Weber's clear-cut typology of religiosocietal bodies. The dichotomy of "Cult *vs.* Word, Law *vs.* Spirit, Church *vs.* Sect"[71] simply does not apply to the Qumran Community.

The exclusive regulations at one and the same time had a centripetal and a centrifugal impact on the Covenanters. On the one hand, they effected a marked cohesion between the individual members and bestowed upon their community a distinctive uniformity; on the other hand, they clearly set it apart from the surrounding Jewish society.

In this context, the issue of "in-group—out-group morality" does not apply to the separation of Jews from non-Jews but rather pertains to the internal diversification that had manifested itself distinctly already in Judaism of the days of the return, intensified at the height of the Second Temple period, and reached its apex in the first century of the Christian era.

Thus, the nature of the Qumran ethical dualism is intrinsically different from Weber's understanding of this feature in relation to Pharisaic Judaism. The difference shows up in respect to his treatment of "inner-worldly-asceticism" which he believed to be incompatible with "in-group—out-group morality": "This all-pervasive ethical dualism meant that the specific puritan idea of 'proving' one's self religiously through 'inner-worldly-asceticism' was unavailable [for Second Temple Judaism, S.T.]."[72] This assertion has become untenable in the face of the Covenanters' theology and practice. As a matter of fact, the discoveries at Qumran have irrefutably shown that "inner-worldy-asceticism" was not first practiced by Protestantism, nor was it innovated by nascent Christianity. Rather, it is a religious stance that has its roots in a trend (or possibly some trends) that can be traced in the Judaism of the second century B.C.E. It went together with (possibly only temporary)[73] celibacy and monasticism and with "vocational" life, like that of ascetic Protestantism, which, according to Weber, "was absent [from Judaism—S.T.] from the outset."[74] While the circumstances pertaining to the genesis at Qumran of these religious facets that go counter to the family orientation predominating in the Old Testament world still escape our knowledge, the facts in themselves are indisputable.

It follows that once again, some of Weber's types are to be found in need of reinvestigation and possibly of reformulation so as to comprehend also the new phenomena he could not have taken into account.

NOTES

1. Published originally as a series of essays in *Archiv für Sozialwissenschaft und Sozialforschung* (1917–19) and republished posthumously by Marianne Weber as vol. 3 of Weber's *Gesammelte Aufsätze zur Religionssoziologie* (= *GARS*; Tübingen: J. C. B. Mohr [Paul Siebeck], 1921). The English translation *Ancient Judaism* was prepared and edited by H. H. Gerth and D. Martindale. (Glencoe, Ill.: Free Press, 1952).

2. T. Parsons, *The Structure of Social Action* (New York: McGraw-Hill, 1937) 542. Although concurring with Weber's procedure on the whole since it is based on a "well-recognized methodological principle," Parsons seems to have entertained some doubts about Weber's detailed studies. See also M. Lennert, *Die Religions-Theorie Max Webers* (Stuttgart, 1935) 3–4.

3. J. Guttmann, "Max Webers Soziologie des antiken Judentums," *Monatschrift für Geschichte und Wissenschaft des Judentums* 69 (1925) 196–97; cf. D. L. Petersen, "Max Weber and the Sociological Study of Ancient Israel," *Religious Change and Continuity* (ed. H. M. Johnson), *Sociological Inquiry* 49, 2–3 (1969) 137; F. Raphaël, "Max Weber et le judaïsme antique," *AES* 11 (1970) 334ff.; N. K. Gottwald, *The Tribes of Yahweh: A Sociology of the Religion of Liberated Israel 1250–1050 B.C.E.* (Maryknoll, N.Y.: Orbis Books, 1979) xxv.

4. Objections to Weber's "type approach" were raised already in 1924 by I. Schiper, "Max Weber on the Sociological Basis of the Jewish Religion" (trans. from the Russian by P. Glikson), *JJSoc* 1 (1959) 258ff.; see also A. Causse, *Du groupe ethnique à la communauté religieuse* (Paris, 1937) 9; W. Schluchter, "Altisraelitische Ethik und okzidentaler Rationalismus," *Max Weber's Studie über das antike Judentum. Interpretation und Kritik* = *MWSJ* (ed. W. Schluchter; Frankfurt am Main: Suhrkamp, 1978) 14; J. A. Holstein, "Max Weber and Biblical Scholarship," *HUCA* 46 (1975) 163–79; Gottwald, *Tribes of Yahweh*, 13, 627–31, offers a more balanced assessment. Some limitations of the "type approach" coupled with comparativistics were pointed out in S. Talmon, "The 'Comparative Method' in Biblical Interpretation—Principles and Problems," *Congress Volume, Göttingen 1977*, VTSup 29 (ed. J. A. Emerton; Leiden: E. J. Brill, 1978) 320–350. Weber himself was conscious of the pitfalls in his method, but this did not deter him from using it. See Weber, *GARS*, 3.13–14; idem, *Gesammelte Aufsätze zur Wissenschaftslehre* (= *GAW;* Tübingen: J. C. B. Mohr [Paul Siebeck], 1933) 213.

5. To mention only a few names and titles: W. F. Albright, *From the Stone Age to Christianity* (2d ed.; Garden City, N.Y.: Doubleday Anchor Books, 1957); M. Buber, *Königtum Gottes* (Berlin: Schocken Books, 1933); G. E. Mendenhall, *The Tenth Generation: The Origins of the Biblical Tradition* (Baltimore: Johns Hopkins University Press, 1973); Gottwald, *Tribes of Yahweh*. In this context it is noteworthy that in some "sociologically" oriented works by Old Testament scholars, Weber's *Ancient Judaism* and his other studies are referred to most sparingly, if at all. Examples are R. de Vaux, *Les institutions de l'Ancien Testament* (Paris: Editions du Cerf, 1958–60) = *Ancient Israel: Its Life and Institutions* (trans. J. McHugh; New York: McGraw Hill Book Co., 1961); Y. Kaufmann, *The Religion of Israel* (trans. from the Hebrew and abridged by M. Greenberg; Chicago:

611

University of Chicago Press, 1960); M. Smith, *Palestinian Parties and Politics That Shaped the Old Testament* (New York: Columbia University Press, 1971).

6. Weber, *GAW* 3.208.

7. H. Liebeschütz, "Max Weber's Historical Interpretation of Judaism," *Yearbook of the Leo Baeck Institute*, 9 (London, 1964) 68.

8. Research carried out since Weber's days has decisively changed scholarly appreciation of the history and sociology of Judaism in the pre-Pharisaic, Pharisaic, and rabbinic periods. In the framework of this study, even a most restricted selective listing of pertinent publications in this area of inquiry cannot be attempted. It must suffice to draw attention to only a few titles that reflect the impressive results achieved by scholars in Israel, the United States, and Europe: J. Klausner, *Jesus of Nazareth: His Life, Time and Teaching* (trans. from the Hebrew; London and New York: George Allen & Unwin, 1925); A. C. Schalit, *König Herodes. Der Mann und sein Werk* (trans. from the Hebrew and enlarged; Berlin: Walter de Gruyter, 1969); A. Ben-David, *Talmudische Ökonomie* (Hildesheim: Olms, 1974); D. Sperber, *Roman Palestine, Money and Prices* (Ramat Gan: Bar Ilan University Press, 1974); idem, *Roman Palestine 200–400, The Land* (Ramat Gan: Bar Ilan University Press, 1974); M. Stern and S. Safrai, *The Jewish People in the First Century* (Assen: Van Gorcum, 1974–76); E. E. Urbach, *The Sages, Their Concepts and Beliefs* (trans. from the Hebrew; Jerusalem: Magnes Press, 1975); G. Alon, *Jews, Judaism and the Classical World* (trans. from the Hebrew; Jerusalem: Magnes Press, 1977); idem, *The Jews in Their Land in the Talmudic Age* (70–640 C.E.) (trans. from the Hebrew; Jerusalem: Magnes Press, 1980); S. Safrai, *Das jüdische Volk im Zeitalter des Zweiten Tempels.* (trans. from the Hebrew; Neukirchen-Vluyn: Neukirchener Verlag, 1978); idem, *Die Wallfart im Zeitalter des Zweiten Tempels* (trans. from the Hebrew; Neukirchen-Vluyn: Neukirchener Verlag, 1982); S. Liebermann, *Greek in Jewish Palestine* (New York: Jewish Theological Seminary, 1942); idem, *Hellenism in Jewish Palestine* (New York: Jewish Theological Seminary, 1950); J. Neusner, *Early Rabbinic Judaism: Historical Studies in Religion, Literature and Art* (Leiden: E. J. Brill, 1975); idem, *First Century Judaism in Crisis* (Nashville: Abingdon Press, 1975); G. Stemberger, *Das klassische Judentum. Kultur und Geschichte der rabbinischen Zeit* (Munich: Verlag C. H. Beck, 1979); idem, *Das rabbinische Judentum in der Darstellung Max Webers, MWSJ*, 185–200.

9. The new insights have been fully assimilated by K. Rudolph, *Die Gnosis. Wesen und Geschichte einer spätantiken Religion* (2d ed.; Göttingen: Vandenhoeck & Ruprecht, 1980), which goes beyond the classical study of H. Jonas, *Gnosis und spätantiker Geist* (Göttingen: Vandenhoeck & Ruprecht, 1934). See further H. G. Kippenberg, "Intellektualismus und antike Gnosis," *MWSJ* 201–18. Rudolph and Kippenberg provide an up-to-date bibliography.

10. A concise description and evaluation of these discoveries may be found *inter alia* in F. M. Cross, *The Ancient Library of Qumran and Modern Biblical Studies* (rev. ed.; Garden City, N.Y.: Doubleday Anchor Books, 1961); and G. Vermes, *The Dead Sea Scrolls: Qumran in Perspective* (London: SCM Press, 1977; London: Wm. Collins Sons, 1982).

11. Weber, *Ancient Judaism*, 360ff., 415–16.

12. See S. Talmon, "Typen der Messiaserwartung um die Zeitenwende," *Prob-*

leme biblischer Theologie. Festschrift für G. von Rad (ed. H. W. Wolff; Munich: Chr. Kaiser Verlag, 1971) 571–88.

13. Weber, *Ancient Judaism*, 363–64.

14. See among others, T. F. O'Dea, "Mormonism and the Avoidance of Sectarian Stagnation: A Study of Church, Sect and Incipient Nationality," *American Journal of Sociology* 60 (1954/55) 285–93; P. L. Berger, "The Sociological Study of Sectarianism," *Social Research* 21 (1954) 467–85; B. R. Wilson, *Sects and Society* (London: Wm. Heinemann, 1961); idem, "Patterns of Sectarianism," *Comparative Studies in Society and History* III (1963); *Messianische Kirchen, Sekten und Bewegungen im heutigen Afrika* (ed. E. Benz; Leiden: E. J. Brill, 1965).

15. Weber, *Ancient Judaism*, 208; cf. 49ff., 231–32. It has been recurrently suggested that the Pentateuchal traditions about the Patriarchs, especially those concerning Abraham, are modeled in part after prototypes provided by the (Davidic) monarchy. See, e.g., B. Mazar, "The Historical Background of the Book of Genesis," *JNES* 28 (1969) 73–83, and pertinent publications cited there.

16. Such as Schiper, "Max Weber"; Holstein, "Max Weber and Biblical Scholarship"; and others.

17. Weber, *Ancient Judaism*, 61–148, 267–335.

18. See S. Talmon, "The New Covenanters of Qumran," *Scientific American* 225, 5 (Nov. 1971) 73–81.

19. Weber, *Ancient Judaism*, 267–424, 455–61.

20. See S. Talmon, "Exil und Rückkehr in der Ideenwelt des Alten Testaments," *Exil-Diaspora-Rückkehr* (ed. R. Mosis; Düsseldorf: Patmos Verlag, 1978) esp. 40–51; S. N. Eisenstadt, "Max Webers antikes Judentum und der Charakter der jüdischen Zivilisation," *MWSJ,* 162–63.

21. A more detailed discussion of this issue may be found in S. Talmon, "Kingship and the Ideology of the State (in the Biblical Period)," *World History of the Jewish People* 3/2 (ed. A. Malamat; Jerusalem: Massada, 1979) 3–26. The matter has been sometimes differently assessed in Old Testament scholarship.

22. See S. Talmon, "The Biblical Concept of Jerusalem," *JES* 8 (1971) 300–16, reprinted in *Jerusalem* (ed. J. M. Oesterreicher and A. Sinai; New York: John Day Co., 1974) 189–203.

23. The anointed King-Messiah concept has been abundantly discussed in scholarly publications too numerous to be listed here. For an overview and selected bibliography, see S. Talmon, "Kingship," 16; idem, "Typen," 578ff.; idem, "Der Gesalbte Jahwes. Biblische und früh-nachbiblische Messias und Heilserwartungen," *Jesus—Messias?* (Regensburg: Verlag Friedrich Pustet, 1982) 27–68; K. Baltzer, "Das Ende des Staates Judah und die Messias-Frage," *Studien zur Theologie der alttestamentlichen Überlieferungen* (ed. R. Rendtorff and K. Koch; Neukirchen-Vluyn: Neukirchener Verlag, 1961) 33–44.

24. See S. Talmon, "The Emergence of Institutionalized Prayer in Israel in the Light of Qumran Literature," *Qumran, sa piété, sa théologie et son milieu* (BETL 44; ed. M. Delcor; Paris: Duculot, 1978) 265.

25. See A. E. Sayce and E. A. Cowley, *Aramaic Papyri Discovered at Assuan* (London, 1906); A. E. Cowley, *Aramaic Papyri of the Fifth Century B.C.* (Oxford: Clarendon Press, 1923); E. G. Kraeling, *The Brooklyn Museum Aramaic Papyri:*

New Documents of the Fifth Century B.C. from the Jewish Colony in Elephantine (New Haven and London: Yale University Press, 1953); G. R. Driver, *Aramaic Documents of the Fifth Century B.C.* (Oxford: Clarendon Press, 1954).

26. For a comprehensive analysis of the material, see B. Porten, *Archives from Elephantine* (Berkeley and Los Angeles: University of California Press, 1968); A. Vincent, *La religion des Judéo-Aramaéens d'Elephantine* (Paris: Paul Geuthner, 1937).

27. The Book of Esther appears to reflect an "adjusted" exile community in the Persian period. It may, though, be presumed that the diaspora stance had already developed when this community was still under Babylonian rule. See S. Talmon, "Wisdom in the Book of Esther," *VT* 13 (1963) 419–45; W. L. Humphreys, "A Life-Style for Diaspora: A Study of the Tales of Esther and Daniel," *JBL* 92 (1973) 211–13; S. A. Meinhold, *Die Diasporanovelle. Eine alttestamentliche Gattung* (diss., Greifswald, 1969); idem, "Die Gattung der Josephsgeschichte und des Estherbuches. Diasporanovelle, I, II," *ZAW* 87 (1975) 306–24.

28. Some of the legal documents found at Elephantine demonstrate that also in Egypt Jews owned land and presumably engaged in agriculture.

29. This fact has been abundantly documented in post-Weberian research. See the literature cited in n. 8 above.

30. Weber's contention that "these sib registers have been fabricated" (*Ancient Judaism,* 350) and therefore can be disregarded is unwarranted.

31. As is often maintained, without any tangible evidence. See Talmon, "The Emergence of Institutionalized Prayer."

32. Weber, *Ancient Judaism,* 362–63, 417–21.

33. See J. Taubes, "Die Entstehung des jüdischen Pariavolkes," *Max Weber Gedächtnisschrift etc.* (ed. K. Engisch and others; Berlin: Duncker und Humboldt, 1966) 185–94.

34. Weber, *Ancient Judaism,* 336ff.

35. See S. Talmon, "Polemics and Apology in Biblical Historiography—2 Kings 17: 24–41," *The Creation of Sacred Literature: Composition and Redaction of the Biblical Text* (ed. R. E. Friedman; Berkeley and Los Angeles: University of California Press, 1981) 57–68, esp. 66–68.

36. For the national political nature of the returnees' socioreligious community, see S. Talmon, "Ezra and Nehemiah," *IDBSup,* 316–28; N. Avigad, *Bullae and Seals from a Post-exilic Judean Archive* (Qedem 4; Monographs of the Institute of Archaeology, Hebrew University; Jerusalem: Hebrew University, 1976).

37. Several centuries later, the Sages condemn anyone "who elicits wrong meaning or falsifies the Torah *etc.*" and deny him future salvation (*b. Sanh.* 91a; *Šeb.* 13a).

38. The "day" does not necessarily have an eschatological connotation, namely, "the end of days," but rather connotes a future-historical preordained point in time. See S. Talmon, "Eschatologie und Geschichte im biblischen Judentum," *Zukunft. Zur Eschatologie bei Juden und Christen* (ed. R. Schnackenburg; Düsseldorf: Patmos Verlag, 1980) 13–50 and bibliography adduced there.

39. Weber, *Ancient Judaism,* 382ff.

40. *Nota bene:* not "Samaritans." This latter designation applies to the

Shechemites only after their final separation from the Jews in or after Alexander's days.

41. Josephus, *Antiquities* (ed. Loeb), 11. 306–47.

42. See F. M. Cross, "The Discovery of the Samaria Papyri," *BA* 26 (1963) 110–21; idem, "Papyri of the Fourth Century B.C. from Dâliyeh: A Preliminary Report on Their Discovery and Significance," *New Directions in Biblical Archaeology* (ed. D. N. Freedman and J. C. Greenfield; Garden City, N.Y.: Doubleday & Co., 1969) 41–62; idem, "Aspects of Samaritan and Jewish History in Late Persian and Hellenistic Times," *HTR* 59 (1966) 202–11; idem, "A Reconstruction of the Judean Restoration," *JBL* 94 (1975) 4–18.

43. This was correctly pointed out by Weber, who specifies that they accepted the Torah "in the revision of the Exilic priests" (*Ancient Judaism,* 360).

44. One is inclined to find an expression of this intense Torah consciousness in Psalm 119. (See chap. 30 by Levenson in this volume.)

45. See Urbach, *The Sages,* 286–314; Safrai, *Das jüdische Volk,* 10, 39–40.

46. See *b. Sanh.* 91a; *Šeb.* 13a. Weber saw these issues entirely within the framework of the relations of Jews and foreigners, that is, in the compass of his "in-group—out-group" model (*Ancient Judaism,* 354).

47. See S. Lieberman, "Light on the Cave Scrolls from Rabbinic Sources," *PAAJR* 20 (1951) 395–404.

48. For a similar, but in details different, analysis, see F. Raphaël, *MWSJ,* 323.

49. See Talmon, "Typen."

50. See S. Talmon, "Divergences in Calendar-Reckoning in Ephraim and Judah," *VT* 8 (1958) 48–74.

51. The term "normative type of Judaism" was introduced into the discussion by G. F. Moore, who designated by it "mainstream" in contrast to "secessionist" movements at the end of the Second Temple period. See G. F. Moore, *Judaism in the First Centuries of the Christian Era, vol. 1: The Age of the Tannaim* (Cambridge: Harvard University Press, 1927) 1.3.

52. See M. Weber, *The Methodology of the Social Sciences* (trans. E. A. Shils and H. A. Finch; Glencoe, Ill.: Free Press, 1959) 156.

53. See S. Lieberman, "The Discipline in the So-called Dead Sea Manual of Discipline," *JBL* 71 (1952) 206 n. 77.

54. See S. Talmon, "The Calendar Reckoning of the Sect from the Judean Desert," *Scripta Hierosolymitana,* vol. 4 (Jerusalem: Magnes Press, 1958) 162–99.

55. As does Lieberman, "The Discipline." "Jewish Palestine of the first century [the historical horizon must be widened to include the last two centuries B.C.E.—S.T.] swarmed with different sects. Every sect probably had its divisions and subdivisions. Even the Pharisees themselves were reported to have been divided into seven (a round number of course; see *Abot R. Nat.* 37 ed. Schechter, 109 and parallels) categories. It is therefore precarious to ascribe our documents definitely to any known of the three major [I would include also "minor"—S.T.] sects."

56. A concise presentation of these aspects may be found in Talmon, "The New Covenanters."

57. See among others, N. Cohn, *The Pursuit of the Millennium* (New York:

Essential Books, 1957); P. Worsley, *The Trumpet Shall Sound* (London: MacGibbon & Kee, 1957); J. Inglis, "Cargo Cults," *Oceania* 27 (1956/57) 249–63; A. J. F. Kobben, "Prophetic Movements as an Expression of Social Protest," *International Archives of Ethnography* 49 (1960) 17–64; Y. Talmon, "Pursuits of the Millennium: The Relation Between Religions and Social Change," *AES* 3 (1962) 125–48; S. Thrupp, ed., *Millennial Dreams in Action, CSSH,* vol. 2 (The Hague, 1962; New York: Schocken Books, 1970); B. A. Wilson, "Millenialism in Comparative Perspective," *CSSH,* vol. 6 (The Hague, 1963) 93–114; Y. Talmon, "Millenarian Movements," *European Journal of Sociology* 7 (1966) 159–200.

58. See L. Dürr, *Die Wertung des Lebens im AT und im antiken Orient* (Münster: Aschendorff, 1926); S. Talmon, "Die Wertung von 'Leben' in der hebräischen Bibel" in *Der Herr des Lebens,* ed. Link (Frankfurt: Herchen, 1985).

59. See Talmon, "The New Covenanters of Qumran."

60. Weber, *GARS,* 1.553.

61. See A. F. C. Wallace, "Revitalization Movements," *American Anthropologist* 58 (1956) 264–81.

62. Weber, *Ancient Judaism,* 336.

63. See "The Protestant Sects and the Spirit of Capitalism," *Essays in Sociology* (trans. and ed. H. H. Gerth and C. W. Mills; London: Kegan Paul, 1947) 305ff.; M. Weber, *The Protestant Ethic and the Spirit of Capitalism* (trans. T. Parsons; New York: Charles Scribner's Sons, 1958) 145 and nn. 173, 152.

64. J. Neusner, *Max Weber Revisited: Religion and Society in Ancient Judaism with Special Reference to the Late First and Second Centuries* (Oxford, 1981), 19–21.

65. Since the nucleus community existed before that leader came onto the scene, he cannot be classified as an "archegetes" (Weber, *Ancient Judaism,* 331), i.e., as a "founding Prophet" (Weber *GARS,* 1.540–41), and is correctly designated Teacher in the Qumran Scrolls. See F. A. Isambert, "Fondateurs, papes et messies (XIX siècle)," *Archives de Sociologie et Religion,* 3, 5 (1958) 96–98.

66. See W. Schluchter, *MWSJ,* 65; further, T. Parsons's Introduction to M. Weber, *The Sociology of Religion* (trans. E. Fischoff; Boston: Beacon Press, 1960) XXXIIIff.

67. Weber, *GARS,* I. 542.

68. See W. Schluchter, *MWSJ* 23; D. Emmet, "Prophets and Their Societies," *JARS* 86 (1956) 18ff.

69. In other instances, as in respect to "Magic and Religion," Weber displayed interest not only in pure manifestations of the suggested types but also in mixed relationships *Mischverhältnisse.* See W. Schluchter, *MWSJ,* 23.

70. See Neusner, *Max Weber Revisited,* 3.

71. Weber, *GARS,* 3.220ff., quoted approvingly by W. Schluchter, *MWSJ,* 16; further, E. Troeltsch, *Die Soziallehren der christlichen Kirchen und Gruppen* (Tübingen: J. C. B. Mohr [Paul Siebeck], 1919; reprinted Aalen, 1977) 189.

72. Weber, *Ancient Judaism,* 343.

73. See Talmon, "The New Covenanters of Qumran."

74. Weber, *Ancient Judaism,* 343.

[Ed. note: This chapter, prepared for this volume, has appeared in a slightly different form in S. Talmon, *King, Cult, and Calendar in Ancient Israel* (Jerusalem: The Magnes Press, 1986) 165–201.]

33

Tanakh Theology: The Religion of the Old Testament and the Place of Jewish Biblical Theology

M. H. GOSHEN-GOTTSTEIN

1. This chapter[1] is a first attempt to publish in English some of my ideas on the possibility and necessity of a hitherto nonexisting area of academic study in the field of biblical religion: the theology of Tanakh.[2] Severe constraints of space limit this attempt to a few major points. These have some bearing on the issue of Bible corpus and canon in the Christian and Jewish senses, on our understanding of what the study of biblical religion is about, on the problematic use of "Jewish" and "Christian" in the context of academic study—conceived of as critical, objective, and non-denominational—and on the very use of the term "theology" in a Jewish context at a time when "biblical theology" in a Christian context has acquired both specific meanings and a problematic reputation. To put it differently: If an epithet such as "Jewish" is at all meaningful in the context of biblical studies in an academic sense and if the study of biblical religion is possibly missing a dimension, is it really "theology" that we are aiming at? Perhaps "structural phenomenology" will be enough of a contrast to comparative approaches in their evolutionary or teleological aspects.

One may suspect, from the start, that from both the Christian and the Jewish side opposition to "theology" will be considerable, since the very achievements of what constitutes much of academic Bible study as a common nondenominational enterprise may be jeopardized.[3] Moreover, the very attempt to tackle the issues that seem confined to the study of religion may spill over into various other areas of Bible studies that we like to think of as removed from any denominational bias. This may touch not only upon obvious questions, such as exegesis and history-writing, but also upon areas that seem more remote, such as canon and text.[4] Yet precisely because of the common bond that unites biblical scholars of our generation, in spite of their different backgrounds and creeds, a recon-sideration may be imperative. It would seem that while among Christian

scholars much rethinking has been going on—from W. Eichrodt, G. von
Rad, and G. E. Wright, to B. Childs and J. Barr[5]—Jewish scholars
instinctively shrink back at the very mention of "theology" in the context
of biblical studies.[6]

Our inquiry in the present outline will deal with issues in the rise of
modern biblical study, with ideologies, conceptualizations, and suggested
models rather than with fully worked out examples of what might be
achieved by a Tanakh theology. This is as yet unsatisfactory, but I hope
future detailed treatments may progressively clarify our intentions.

2. At the moment, a summary of the ups and downs of Old Testament
theology in the past must suffice as a background to our specific issues.
The critical study of the Bible and the idea of carving out a place for
"biblical" theology, as separate from dogmatic theology, rose in the
academic atmosphere as twin developments about two centuries ago. J.
Eichhorn and J. P. Gabler[7] did not work along the same lines, and Gabler
offered no more than preliminary thoughts, centering on the demand to
detelescope sayings from the two testaments and look at *legoumena* in
their own right without necessary reference to doctrine.[8] The element of
"history" introduced into theology by Gabler was almost bound to be
misunderstood in the developing historicism of the nineteenth century.[9]
On the other hand, the foundation laid by Eichhorn led ultimately to the
erection of the complex edifice of source criticism, critical history, and
critical reconstruction of the religion of ancient Israel. While "biblical"
theology was soon subdivided into its Old Testament and New Testament
components, Old Testament theology became submerged in the general
critical study. For about a century, from Vatke until Eichrodt,[10] Old
Testament theology was practically identified with a critically reconstructed inquiry into Old Testament religion.[11] True to the spirit of the
nineteenth century, this was largely along lines of the history of Old
Testament religion and, later on, comparative religion. Academic Old
Testament theology—on the Continent, and later even in Great Britain—
was de facto identified with the study of biblical religion, and it possibly
needed the aftermath of World War I in its search for meaning to bring
about a program for disengagement between the two intertwined fields of
inquiry into Old Testament religion.

In spite of the continued debate throughout the past twenty years as to
the merits or failures of Eichrodt's and von Rad's major attempts in
writing "Theologies of the Old Testament," whether they succeeded in
the task, whether "theology" has not been broken up into "theologies,"
whether "fictitious kerygmatic history" was not invalidated in its very
foundations, whether theology can be constructed around a center, and
so forth—the coexistence of two areas of legitimate inquiry into Old

Testament religion, differently aimed yet cooperating, has become a fact of the academic scene in faculties of divinity (or their equivalent). In spite of a few voices urging renewed amalgamation, it is by now a matter of individual or institutional choice whether the study of Old Testament religion is being pursued in one or both areas; the areas themselves—in spite of some overlap and argument—have been reestablished, and recent surveys of Old Testament theology, written from various points of view,[12] run into the dozens. It is only fair to emphasize—especially for the non-Christian scholar—that the position of Old Testament theology within "biblical theology," in a Christian sense, is not a settled issue and that the actual influence of "biblical theology" on systematic and dogmatic theology has hardly developed along the lines inherent in Gabler's formulations.

Allowing for considerable differences between the state of affairs in central Europe, Great Britain, and America, the rejuvenation of Reformation ideals hoped for from "biblical theology" two centuries ago has not materialized—and this may have something to do with the discussion as to whether there is a movement and whether there is a crisis in biblical theology as a whole.[13] Perhaps precisely because of the problematic interaction between biblical and dogmatic theology, it seems to the outsider that in the area of academic Old Testament studies, as it developed in most faculties of divinity, the progress of Old Testament theology not only is an irreversible fact but has become an expression of trends in Old Testament studies not to be ignored. For I would go so far as to suggest that recent trends in Old Testament studies that have gone back to stress the inquiry into the final text product instead of concentrating on pre-text forms through source analysis, redaction analysis, and the like not only are felt in approaches such as literary analysis and holistic close-reading techniques but go hand in hand with the inquiry into Old Testament theology. That is to say, the understanding of meaning and structure of the text as it stands has become at least as important as historical, pre-text analysis.[14]

To sum up: In a Christian context there exists today a field of inquiry within Old Testament studies that cannot be divorced from personal positions or even axiomatic attitudes, and I do not think I am far off the mark if I suggest that this inquiry plays a much larger role within the total academic activity than we like to admit to ourselves in our idealized picture of what modern nondenominational scholarly biblical study is about. So much, for the moment, for aspects of the study of Old Testament religion on the Christian side. It is my contention that for reasons of their own, Jewish Bible scholars have been slow to appreciate this development and have practically ignored one side of the activity of their academic confreres. I maintain, moreover, that this attitude is to the detriment of their own Tanakh study as well as to the detriment of a deeper mutual understanding.

3. Before I can proceed with my thesis, a remark on another aspect of Old Testament studies and theology is in order. Traditionally—long before Jewish scholars moved into academic Old Testament study—Christian study of the Old Testament was naturally understood as part of "theology." Perhaps it was in the very nature of Gabler's ideas of dividing the traditional field of theology that the concept of biblical theology was to undermine ultimately the previously self-evident categorization of Old Testament study as part of theology. In the twentieth century, Old Testament studies do not belong anymore to theology; rather, Old Testament theology is viewed by many as a major constituent of Old Testament studies—minor differences aside.[15] To be sure, some scholars would conceptualize Old Testament theology as an area common to both theology (as a general field) and Old Testament studies, and one could imagine that such a conceptualization could lead to interesting structures within a theory of Jewish studies, once the issue of Tanakh theology is explored in depth.[16] In any event, it is simply not feasible at this juncture to maintain that old Testament theology is outside academic Old Testament studies—a proposition that would lead to the convenient corollary that Jewish Old Testament scholars can ignore the entire field. The works of Eichrodt and von Rad, Th. C. Vriezen and Wright, E. Jacob and W. Zimmerli, and many others belong to Old Testament studies, whether written as theologies, commentaries, or monographs on Old Testament religion.

If that position is granted, no Old Testament scholar can afford to ignore the relationship existing between different parts of each scholar's work in Old Testament studies. It is my conviction that even more remote subspecializations of biblical scholarship—philology, archaeology, literary study, and others—cannot be tightly compartmentalized. In any case, areas such as literary criticism, tradition history, canonical studies, history of religion, and theology are so strongly intertwined with the paramount exegetical endeavor—the very heart of all Bible study—that it would be unacceptable for me to think of Old Testament theology as beyond the pale of academic Old Testament studies.[17] If we are forced to this conclusion in regard to non-Jewish academic study of the Old Testament—however we put the matter exactly—our analysis forces us to consider the question of Tanakh theology against the background of the development of modern Jewish Bible study.

4. It should be understood at this juncture that decades of trying to trace the rise of Bible research have convinced me that the epithets

"Christian" and "Jewish" are meaningful with regard to certain areas of today's composite field of academic biblical scholarship. When it comes to dealing with the Bible, the counterargument that there is no Christian or Jewish mathematics is simply facetious. To be sure, these epithets are not applicable to the totality of biblistics—or else international biblical scholarship could never have grown into what it is today. Moreover, scholars can carry out their entire lifework ignoring certain problematic issues, it they so wish. Yet the more we deal with aspects of meaning of the biblical text in its final form—from textual unit to canon and message—the less can we avoid our personal background and attitude. In a number of papers (see n. 1) I have dealt at some length with my view of the development of modern Bible study as undertaken by Jewish scholars. In the present context I shall simply reemphasize two points: (1) The Jewish academic professional Bible scholar is an innovation of the present century, hardly antedating the previous generation;[18] (2) no Jewish Bible scholar came to the academic scene as a trained "theologian," unlike many of his Christian confreres. Jewish scholars were by training Semitic philologists, historians, or archaeologists; they could have come from a rabbinical background—sometimes misnamed "theological"—or a national-secularistic one. The whole issue of "biblical theology" in its ups and downs was beyond their ken and interest. The study of Tanakh religion—historical, comparative, phenomenological—was an area of great importance for those scholars, continuing or correcting the work done by Christian scholars up to the very time when Old Testament theology began to reassert itself.[19] Yet the very possibility, let alone necessity, of a Tanakh theology was never as much as raised in the entire literature produced by two generations of Jewish Tanakh scholars. Judging by the material in front of us, we must conclude that Jewish biblical scholars ignored the fact that on the Christian side the study of Old Testament religion had split into twin areas. "Theology" was something that simply did not exist for Tanakh scholarship—neither the subject matter nor the term.

Perhaps the most obvious example is Y. Kaufmann, who never made a significant impact on the international scholarly scene since his work became available only belatedly and in precis form. But he was, in the opinion of many, the most original and influential Israeli Bible scholar of the past generation, thanks to his *magnum opus* "History of Belief in Israel."[20] Kaufmann had finished his own studies just before the turn of the tide in the 1920s,[21] and his work was largely a reaction to the study of Old Testament religion as shaped in the Wellhausen-Gunkel tradition. Kaufmann never found it necessary to verbalize the fact that his work was conceived as a mixture of history of Old Testament religion and monographic *Einleitungswissenschaft.* This was self-evident. But the very idea of "Tanakh theology" never occurred to him, since there simply existed only one area of inquiry. Until the first movements toward testing the idea of Tanakh theology, during the past decade or so, the bifurcation that had developed in Christian Old Testament study was never taken note of.[22] I stress the fact that there was never an issue of rejection or conscious avoidance; theology was a nonissue in an academic environment that conceived of itself as secular and objective, so that the very idea of Tanakh theology was totally unthinkable. In fact, while some of our colleagues may claim today that what they are engaged in is actually Jewish God-talk, the possibility of Tanakh theology as a conceptualized major area of biblical scholarship, both complementary and contrasting with the twin area of the study of religion, historical or otherwise, is a novelty.[23] Since the creation of such an area of inquiry would have repercussions on the entire field of Bible studies, utmost care is indicated.

5. Up to now we have tried to trace two complementary aspects of a development in the study of Old Testament religion: the rise of Old Testament theology within the Christian academic establishment as a *fait accompli,* whatever the differences and nuances, and its nonexistence on the Jewish side to the extent that Tanakh theology was a nonissue or else a freak idea. We are now ready to put two further questions: Surveying the field of Old Testament theology as it has developed over the past half century, has it contributed to the sum total of achievements of Old Testament studies in making us aware of issues that the historical-comparative study of Old Testament religion could not or did not raise?[24] Should the answer be in the affirmative, we must raise another question, probably more disturbing: If such contribution is a matter of scholarly insight—that is, a matter of academic research and not just a biblical underpinning for systematic theology—why the need for Tanakh theology? Are axiomatic positions of creed and tradition legitimate considerations in academic inquiry? Are we moving in a vicious circle when we demand standards of universal objectivity in studying the structural totality of belief? Or else, does the possibility that there coexist different truths, embedded in two millennia of history and tradition, exclude both Old Testament and Tanakh theology from the academic sanctum? If so, we would return to the pre-1930 stage, and the position would be that only the religion of ancient Israel is a legitimate subject for academic inquiry—be the method historical, sociological, or otherwise.

I submit that these are cardinal issues in our philosophical and practical approaches to Old Testament studies in general—leaving aside all considerations of the American state college and the like. There are no ready answers, only preliminary considerations, but the problem will not vanish by being ignored. For the past half century or so—roughly the period since the initial activity of Jewish professional Bible scholars—the problem of Tanakh versus Old Testament theology did not surface, and Old Testament theology could be reckoned among Old Testament studies, since no question was raised. Theoretically, it would be conceivable that as an outcome of our new awareness the internal structure of biblical studies may be in need of reexamination.

In order to answer our question we now have to stress again an additional issue that at first may sound like a terminological quibble: Why say "theology"? What is it that deserves and necessitates that name? Is it simply a terminological convention? Perhaps many obvious academic difficulties could be avoided if the field of Old Testament religion remains subdivided into two areas, but the term "theology" is sidestepped.[25] After all, both the so-called crisis of the 'Biblical Theology Movement' (if there really was such thing) and the pseudo-revisionist ideologies of nineteenth-century Jewish reformers—from A. Geiger and L. Philippson to K. Kohler[26]—make one wonder whether the aim of different types of inquiry into the religion of ancient Israel could be achieved without introducing the term "theology" into the academic study of both Tanakh and the Old Testament.

6. Since this chapter is directed to both Christian and Jewish scholars, a remark is now in order in regard to models of what has been termed "biblical theology" in its Old Testament aspects. Old Testament theology is sometimes still conceived of as little more than some kind of traditional ancilla for systematic theology—and Gablerian formulations can be construed in this way. Since the aim of putting the Bible at the center of church teaching has not been achieved—so the argument runs—it ought to be restudied, as it were, in order to correct misconceptions of systematics. This kind of concept relegates the Old Testament to a position of little consequence.[27] It follows that Old Testament theology cannot be a self-centered study, since by definition New Testament orientation is imperative if the ultimate goal is to influence systematic-dogmatic theology.[28] Not only have some Catholic Bible scholars such as P. Grelot worked at the task of Old Testament theology along these lines but also a leading conservative Old Testament specialist of Dutch Reformed background such as Vriezen is not really far from such an attitude toward Old Testament theology.[29] It goes without saying that none of these nuances of biblical theology would be of relevance for a Tanakh theology. In fact, they provide a ready argument against such an attempt. If that would be all that Old Testament theology achieves, the entire field could be left to professional Christian theologians, and Bible scholars need not bother.

Typologically different, in this rough classification, are some other volumes on Old Testament theology published over the last decades. These offer a message analysis of Old Testament sources as they stand, in their own right, yet far from a proper quantitative and qualitative evaluation of structures and of textual density of *legoumena*—a major issue to which we shall return. Moreover, most of these volumes on Old Testament theology are still organized according to the basic layout of systematic theology, even if the chapter headings do not necessarily bear titles such as God-man-salvation.[30] The arrangement in these theologies must not be overlooked; it indicates that Old Testament theology is little more than the recasting of Old Testament materials into traditional molds, in spite of assertions that it is the content of the Old Testament that is being studied. To be sure, this is a perfectly legitimate exercise for a theologian, but it has little to do with any serious attempt to understand the specific contents structure of the Old Testament in its own right. A fair number of Old Testament theologies of our generation written by leading scholars are basically executed along such lines. Most representative, perhaps, is the work of Jacob, but Zimmerli's *Outline of Old Testament Theology*[31] is also, in its essentials, a good representative. To stress our point, if this kind of treatment would be all that Old Testament theology has to offer, we could again easily ignore it in the context of academic Bible study, and Jewish scholars need not rethink their position.

This brings us to the third type—and it is here that the biblical scholar is faced with a conceptual challenge. It is not just a matter of detailed treatment or better-informed scholarship that puts the volumes of Eichrodt and von Rad in a class of their own, whatever the overwhelming conceptual differences between the two. Perhaps paradoxically—in the light of the severe criticism directed at both—it is this type of attempt at describing and conceptualizing the meaning and message of the Old Testament as a text-reading from within the community of faith, yet away from the traditional mold, that forces the issue onto the student of Tanakh as well. Both Eichrodt and von Rad have struggled—not always successfully—with three major concerns: steering, as much as possible, from the evolutionary-comparative approach and describing the Old Testament in its own terms; remaining responsible to the achievements of critical Old Testament scholarship and to write their work as part and parcel of ongoing academic discussion; and viewing the Old Testament from within a community of faith that will not accept the Old Testament without a New Testament directed meaningfulness. This last issue is ever present and cannot be simply ignored in order to make the work acceptable for non-Christian students of the Bible.[32] Nor will it do any good to pretend that Eichrodt's and von Rad's works should be left outside academic biblical scholarship. In spite of major differences, both works show that the three aspects are interwoven, and this is an integral part of their achievement. We are being offered, for the first time in the past generation, an understanding of the Old Testament analyzed from within. Christian students of the Bible may utter reservations and criticism; Jewish Bible scholarship cannot but attempt to create its alternative position. This is the development within Old Testament studies that in my submission forces us to consider Tanakh theology.

7. It would not be fair to contrast some tentative formulations and ideas with full-fledged treatments. Eichrodt and von Rad wrote *opera magna* and worked out systems. There exists still another approach that we ought to mention, but it is no more than part of a dictionary article. I refer to K. Stendahl's presentation[33] proposing the contrast that became a kind of slogan: What did/does it mean? But, then, Gabler's *Oratio* was also no more than a suggestive article. Hence Stendahl's idea is worth mentioning in the context of our inquiry concerning what Tanakh theology should be about. In contemplating Tanakh theology, can we take a step forward by considering what Stendahl may have hinted at by his contrasting formulation?[34] "What it means" represents present-directed theology. But would this imply that "what it meant" represents the totality of the theological structure of a text in the past? Does this formulation suffice to pry Old Testament theology away from both history of religion and New Testament orientation and turn it into a non-denominational theology? Could the issue be solved by shifting telic orientation, whether New Testament or rabbinic, to the pigeonhole of hermeneutics—as Stendahl seems to imply—so that "what it meant" could be inquiry into the total meaning of the text in the abstract, without denominational differences? Or would this be beyond the bounds of "theology," reduced to terminological and phenomenological inquiry, which may be precisely what is desirable?

It is extremely difficult to judge whether there is any step forward in Stendahl's formulation relevant to our problem, since no sample has been worked out.[35] But I have my doubts whether most Christian students of Old Testament religion would be willing at this point to sidestep the community of faith in favor of what seems, as described, to be a kind of "nontheology."[36] Outlines of a strictly corpus-oriented structure analysis may emerge, and "meaning" may be evaluated in terms of terminological and phenomenological quantity, subcorpus density, and inner-textual qualitative relationships (see below). Up to this point we would deal with a hitherto neglected aspect of the study of Old Testament religion. However, if relating to a community of faith is of the essence, we would have to contemplate Tanakh theology as a Jewish option—or even necessity. It would seem that, at least until now, systematic and biblical theology somehow have had in common the endeavor to give intellectual expression in some ordered way to statements about contents in the realm of faith, as understood *from inside a group.* The way of ordering may have been traditional or otherwise, but the entire enterprise grew out of the intellectual drive to conceptualize and systematize *what it is all about.* Theologizing is nothing inherently Christian,[37] but the specific way in which it has developed in the context of biblical studies is very much part of the Christian tradition of dealing with Scripture—hence the almost intuitive avoidance of the term by Jewish Bible scholars, as mentioned above. Theology seems to be what theologians have been doing and will do. Possibly this tautology is a definition. In spite of strenuous protestations, Old Testament theology has remained tied to the umbilical cord of Christian traditional theology while offering insights into the nature of Old Testament religion not offered by approaches of religious science. It is precisely this fact which makes us claim that Tanakh theology must be created as a parallel field of study. Indeed, from recent literature the astonishing fact emerges that until recently it was precisely some non-Jewish biblicists who put forward the idea, in a sentence or two, that there might be a Jewish biblical theology, because they regarded their own academic work as faith-community anchored. Little did they know what they were suggesting.[38]

8. I do not think it necessary to deal here with the kind of statement that Tanakh is not a theological system or does not intend to teach us a system. But in arguing for a field of Bible study that deals with detecting criteria for allowing the inner structure to become visible, we have to face a more serious possible source of misunderstanding. For Judaism possesses traditional "systems" that purport to be the result of authoritative interpretation of Tanakh—if not exclusively then to a large extent so. We must therefore look from a Jewish perspective at the issue of "system" understood as obligatory for behavior and observance or otherwise versus "system" to be constructed according to scholarly criteria from biblical *legoumena* as one aspect of the study of Old Testament religion, intended to be functional within a community of faith. Degrees of personal observance of *halakhah* and ideologies as to its authoritative nature, applicability or pliability aside, the traditional concept of oral law as transmitting authoritative exegesis of written law forms the historical basis of what has developed into the autonomous system of halakhic observance.[39]

On the practical level of observance, rabbinic Judaism has effectively cut itself off from further direct dependence on Scripture,[40] nor could any better modern exegetical insight into Scripture—in a Gablerian sense—make any difference to the "Scripture plus oral law" basis as filtered into the halakhic system of do's and don'ts, a very remote counter-part to practical theology. To be sure, for the past hundred and fifty years practitioners of a "liberal" ideology of pluralism of observance have chosen to proclaim the breakdown of the halakhic system in the name of historical flexibility. This remains a matter of theoretical and practical consequence for pluralism in present-day Judaism. It is not to be mixed up with the issue of "What does Tanakh mean?" The system of halakhic observance and the structure of Tanakh meaning have hardly anything in common. In any case, against the background of some fleeting flirtations of nineteenth-century Jewish Reform ideologists with Neo-Karaism, all I ought to stress at present is that in the 1980s a model of biblicistic reinterpretation of *halakhah* is the last thing we would be suggesting. Such a model of biblical theology need not be contemplated, nor would it be of any interest for Tanakh studies.

Judaism has no prior history of trying to describe the content structure of any part of Tanakh in ways other than what tradition took it to mean, and tradition was interested in the "Law" only. Contrary to popular imagination, even Karaites did not proclaim *sola scriptura*. It is correct that Judaism boasts a strong tradition of systematization, but that is a matter of law and observance and is of no relevance for us. Nevertheless, certain medieval Jewish tractates modeled on Islamic Kalam attempt to present issues of belief as a systematic description that could conceivably be termed "theological." But this amounts basically to a medieval inter-pretive selection based on selected rabbinic interpretations of biblical *legoumena* (see n. 39)—in no way near to a possible Tanakh theology. This is to say, the diachronics of Bible-based Jewish learning offer no basis for Tanakh theology, even if we may extract useful hints. "The-ology" is not essentially Christian, but in our context it must be seen as an adaptation to the non-Jewish ethos. Precisely because freely selected biblical *legoumena* provide ubiquitous underpinning of positions as *dicta probantia,* as need arises, one experiences such difficulties with the concept of a Jewish biblical theology. This concept, then, would be useful only outside the field of confrontation between Scripture and authority. This leads us back to our concept of a future Tanakh theology as a core area of the academic study of Tanakh, and it is exclusively in this area that our search will go on.

In spite of all that I have stressed up to now about the status of *halakhah,* it is Tanakh only that serves as the common practical basis for Jews; and for no one else but for Jews, Tanakh is the exclusive sacred canon. This is the precondition, justification, and prime moving force for our undertaking. If Jews are to inquire in a critical academic framework what Tanakh is all about—in what emerges as its structural totality as well as in its subcorpuses—then in spite of our hesitations Tanakh theology will have to come into being.

It would be foolhardy to announce beforehand what possible structure of contents would emerge from painstaking exegesis. The overall theme of God's ways with Israel and Israel's ways with God would possibly emerge as dominant. To be sure, covenantal aspects are part of this theme—but only part. God's self-revelation and withdrawing, creating and directing the world, instructing and reacting, demanding and retributing, succeeding and failing, compelling and allowing freedom, "running the show" and letting it run on its own, and corresponding aspects on Israel's side would probably emerge as the major themes of the totality. In this binary relationship it matters little what happens on the outside. What counts is the oneness and uniqueness of the interaction—to the exclusion of everything else. Covenant, election, and monotheism are major aspects of the one all-embracing content of "what Tanakh is all about." One God, one family, one people, one country, one way of doing things correctly—not as a static picture but in the constant dynamics of ambivalence and dilemma.

This is not a program to be carried out but a hunch, how quantity and quality of *legoumena* may guide us to recover the main structure and to subordinate side issues (see below). At present I have only a general perception of how such an approach is very different from the attempt of Eichrodt, on the one hand, and those who seek for a center of Old Testament theology, on the other.

9. It would not be too much of an exaggeration if one formulates the issue by stating that for over two thousand years, at any given time, a synchronic cut in the developing content structure of Judaism was perceived from within as being a restatement, in contemporary terms, of "what Tanakh is about." That is, for short, the central ongoing binary relationship between God and Israel. From the moment that the canon was more or less fixed—say from the period of the Qumran writings onward—sources remained Tanakh-centered, whatever their true message or reinterpretation. Tanakh is the exclusive, valid fact, and the meaning is extracted by exegesis, inspired or otherwise. If there is any validity to the model of historical layers that in their totality yield the raw material for a diachronic theology, one can hardly escape the corollary that no self-understanding of Judaism can manage without the analysis of the base corpus of biblical religion as seen from within, built on a meticulous and complete evaluation of the texts in their totality. Attempting to construe the totality of biblical *legoumena* in their interdependence and relative importance is thus as much part of biblical research as of "Jewish Theology," if we understand that term as layers of diachronic

contrasts. Thus "Jewish Biblical Theology" becomes, indeed, a necessary field of inquiry.

It is the modern scholar's prerogative to forge for himself a diachronic perspective on synchronic structures, as long as he is aware of his personal limitations, Jewish or Christian. We are concerned with one specific structure only. I emphasize again my doubt whether in the realm of the study of religion there exists "what did it mean?" in the absolute; in the realm of theology there exists the absolute in belief, not in critical inquiry. For the student of Tanakh theology, "what is meant" is ultimately as real or unreal as the attempt of the exegete to regain *ipsissima verba* or the effort of the textual critic to make his path through the maze of manuscripts to the archetype. Positivistic historicism may be utopian, and reconstructing a base line of "what it really meant" no more than a heuristic exercise. But this is precisely one of the rights and duties of modern critical scholarship: to exercise our own exegetical sovereignty[41] in order to construct our understanding of the past—if you wish, to build the best model we can for such understanding. The fact that we try to construct such a model from within our respective communities of faith makes little difference for the heuristic process as such; but it is what creates the dimension of theology.[42]

10. Tanakh theology can thus be conceptualized as an area common to biblical studies and the study of Jewish thought, possibly similar to the twin discipline, Old Testament *Religionswissenschaft*. However, our discussion cannot circumvent the delicate issue of personal commitment:[43] Are scholarly competence and a certain empathy toward the world of belief and practice sufficient for the task at hand? If Tanakh theology is to be a central area of Tanakh study, is everyone qualified to pursue it, or is a "means test" to be applied? Are the qualifications different from those expected of the student of Tanakh religion? All I am suggesting at present is that a theology developed by a member of the community of faith who totally rejects the faith would probably go astray. A field of inquiry can be central and should be understood by everyone, but it need not be everybody's business.

If the picture does not obfuscate the point I am trying to make, Tanakh theology is the business of the modern student of Tanakh religion trained in many areas of scholarship who wishes to find a place within the edifice of present-day Judaism. Yet such a student also wishes to explore for himself or herself the shape of that very edifice in its former—if you wish, original—form and to look for his or her own roots within that former edifice. As a practicing member of the community of faith—of whatever exact shade—one cannot but live in the edifice as it stands now and by the rules laid down for today's inhabitants, rightly or wrongly alleged to be based on the original "house order." But the Tanakh scholar also aims to reconstruct for himself or herself the plan and the dimensions of that very structure as it used to exist,[44] and by familiarity with the building at present may have some advantage over the stranger who dwells today in a much enlarged and changed edifice or who, in fact, dwells in a wing added later.

11. Having taken considerable trouble over suggesting what the field of Tanakh theology would be dealing with, we can now turn to some observations on method and content. Modern Bible research is based on tools developed by the humanities, philology, history, literature, and so on. In this respect there are no Christian or Jewish methods, even if there may be personal differences of attitude and application. However, as soon as we entangle ourselves in certain axiomatic presuppositions—and the very relationship between Old Testament and New Testament is a most basic one—we enter a different area of scholarship. In the light of the history of academic learning, it would be unwise to claim that theology is not part of *Wissenschaft,* just as it is senseless for natural sciences to proclaim that history or philology is not part of *Wissenschaft.*[45] Theological *Wissenschaftstheorie* functions according to its own epistemological rules, and I am not sure as yet how these would fit into the framework of Jewish Studies, heir to *Wissenschaft des Judentums,* conceived of as a branch of humanities.[46] What we are talking about, then, is a model for investigating "what Tanakh is all about" from a clear mainstream Jewish point of view—another way of saying that we shall not be satisfied with an inquiry into Tanakh religion along lines of religious studies.

I would envisage descriptivism as a necessary condition, but not a sufficient one. We must devise means to perceive the structure clearly: what is central, basic, important, what is the message repeated again and again—all over or in major parts of Tanakh—and what is mentioned rarely, incidentally, unemphasized.[47] To get away from the abstract, if the relationship of Israel and the land looms large, in most subcorpuses of Tanakh,[48] then this is for me a central issue in Tanakh theology. On the other hand, as the literature shows, this is a minor issue both in the study of religion and in Old Testament theology. A Christian Old Testament theology may play this issue down or ignore it—and it would be the task of Tanakh theology to point out that this is not just a matter of opinion, since ignoring the centrality runs counter to the facts gained by both quantitative and qualitative inquiry, that is, the number and density of occurrences as well as the issues connected with promises and threats concerning the land. "Theology of the land" is judged solely by facts gained from Tanakh, and it is a question of facts for the student of diachronics if this issue is of the same centrality in the theology gained from halakhic or aggadic sources, medieval systems (e.g., E. Halevi's *Kuzari,* Maimonides' *Guide,* etc., as contrasted with halakhic codifications), and the like.[49] An inquiry of this nature is a matter for diachronic theology—a field that can only be developed once the outlines of Tanakh theology become clearer. This example, however—and I am just hinting at the issue—should make it clear how Jewish biblical theology, once worked out, would put forth the double claim of receiving the stimulus for its way of studying facts from its own tradition and of insisting on inquiry into the meaning of Tanakh by strict procedures of quantitative and qualitative evaluation.[50]

12. Our idea of how to devise criteria for Tanakh theology[51] stands not only in contrast to the procedure of superimposing outside systems on Old Testament *legoumena*—such as the reflexes of the traditional triad, theology, anthropology, soteriology (or the same by any other name). It is equally opposed to the transfer of the idea of "Center" from New Testament theology.[52] Nor do we intend to fall into the trap of identifying critical study with any type of source criticism and introducing historicism by the back door, thus solving problems by cutting up theology into a plurality of "theologies."[53]

If I may fall back upon using my tools of trade in linguistics, the same facts may be perceived by different scholars somewhat differently, and, for example, there is no one and only correct way to decide between phonemic, subphonemic, or allophonic status. Again, there may be various legitimate alternative perceptions of morpheme structure, though not widely different, just as there are patently incorrect ones.[54] All reconstructions in Tanakh theology will be tainted by imperfections of the architect's concepts, and different architects may come up with different solutions as to how to use the main blocks in order to reconstruct the edifice. But there are blocks of majestic impressiveness that are decisive for the character of the structure, and architects should be raised to practice their art. It is precisely our constructive bias in theology that we start out with the conviction that we face not just a heap of stones but that there is an underlying plan of structure that should become visible by measurement in quantity, ubiquity, textual position, and contextual density.[55]

Again, let us make this more concrete. Any file index on Old Testament theology, however planned, will include entries that were earmarked initially "individual salvation." We all have our attitudes or beliefs concerning the subject, because of post–Old Testament systematization, both Christian and Jewish. Foreseeably, treatments of Old Testament and Tanakh theology will be different, and it is the privilege of the Tanakh theologian to maintain that the "plain sense" of the Tanakh text supports allowing little weight to this idea.[56] *Legoumena* will be evaluated as to how often they occur, in which subcorpus, in what context, in what relation and proportion, over against nonindividual (family, nation) salvation; what can be deduced from terminology, word-field density, topical constraints, and the like. I stress again, Tanakh theology as conceived here depends on the minute study of text units, aiming as much as possible for the *literal sense.*[57]

Preliminary study suggests that the position of "individual salvation" may be looming large in Old Testament theology because of its position in Christian biblical theology, not because of the facts in Tanakh, where it would probably emerge as a relatively minor issue, severely subcorpus restricted. In the totality of the structure of Tanakh theology it is of limited importance, and the quotation of, say, individual salvation in psalms with an eye toward New Testament theology is as irrelevant as Egyptian or Mesopotamian parallels of individual laments and cries for help (which, by the way, is not a matter of individual salvation). As prehistorians and comparativists we ask one set of questions; as students of the structure of Tanakh belief, thought, and teaching we ask what emphasis does Tanakh put on this or that issue, based on the evaluation of the sum total of *legoumena.* I am not suggesting that quantitative and qualitative subcorpus study is foolproof and yields definitive results, but it appears to be the best method we can follow in order to reach back into "what did Tanakh mean?"[58]

13. For the moment we can do little more than mention examples of additional themes that would emerge differently in a Jewish biblical theology. It would take a lengthy study to analyze whether what appears in the volumes of Eichrodt and von Rad is a reasonable treatment of the theme Sabbath within the context of Old Testament theology. In my submission, "explanations" based on ancient Near Eastern material are irrelevant; they belong to the comparative study of Old Testament religion. Hence, the questioning of the adequacy of an explanation such as that introduced by Eichrodt is also irrelevant.[59] On the other hand, there is an issue of Sabbath in New Testament (and dogmatic) theology, and Christian scholars cannot but be influenced by their traditions, just as Jewish scholars are. Allowing for this situation, we now ask: In which subcorpus, how, and in what context, with what reasons given, does "Sabbath" appear? How often in the Pentateuch are laws given with specific reasons appended or special rewards mentioned? How often is the similarity between divine and human introduced as a specific reason? Where and how does the text report direct divine intervention in law enforcement?[60]

What I am suggesting is this: The Tanakh theologian has to examine his texts closely in order to devise a methodology for qualification, not just quantification. It is the overall structure of primary and secondary issues that emerges when we try to take the measure of phenomena that ultimately helps us to deal with the cardinal question: What is it all about? It is my submission that Old Testament theology has not bothered hitherto to devise a method of inquiry so as to ask questions that might help us detect the structure and that the study of Old Testament religion has not progressed sufficiently because of lack of rigor in detailed work. Moreover, I claim that what I am talking about is a matter of strict scholarly methodology, which should be acceptable without denominational restriction, but I am ready to accept the judgment that I am biased by restricting myself to Tanakh in its subcorpuses, as long as we all agree to accept our respective biases as students of the Old Testament and Tanakh.

To put it differently, I would not yield on corpus-bound inquiry, and I am fully aware that what for me is the canonical totality is only a part for my non-Jewish confreres. The Tanakh theologian, like the Christian theologian, has a legitimate interest in the way a given phenomenon is mirrored, reinterpreted in a post-Tanakh structure—rabbinic, New Testament, or otherwise. The Tanakh—or Old Testament—theologian is not called upon to do the job of the student of historical layers of theology, but it is not necessary to close one's eyes to later structures even as the earlier ones are analyzed so long as one does not confuse the facts.[61]

If our programmatic examples sound challenging, I trust they are not unreasonable. Even before individual paragraphs are worked out, one should be able to visualize that the suggestions I have thrown out in regard to subjects such as land, individual salvation, and the Sabbath could be easily extended to any other central subject, for example, messianism and miracles, vengeance and prayer, sacrifice and temple,[62] life and death, and the theology of $mi\d{s}w\hat{o}t$ (commandments)[63] in general. In short, the area of inquiry we are trying to develop is Tanakh theology. In its projected difference from what has been attempted until now, it is not only possible but necessary as a new central area in biblical studies.

14. In this outline presentation I have not gone into detailed analysis of the methods used in current Old Testament theology. It is perhaps not merely the question that arises when, as a Jewish Bible scholar looking at the field of Old Testament religion, I fail to detect the kind of formulations and approaches I have hinted at. Biblical scholars who are also fellow linguists will appreciate that I am trying to reforge my linguistic tools for use in the theological workshop. If this adds some rigor to the procedure, it can be only for the good. In any event, there should be nothing specifically Jewish about this aspect. But I stress again that only a

Jewish Tanakh theology can take Tanakh in its absolute canonical finality. I cannot deal here with recent different pronouncements by scholars such as Barr, Childs, Gese, Barthélemy, or Sanders, who are struggling—each in his own way—with the issue of canon.[64] Precisely because I must respect their struggles I permit myself to define more clearly the boundary lines of mutual respect. It was probably necessary to wait for the first half-century of Jewish academic Bible study to pass until we could allow ourselves the luxury of facing the bias[65] on each side and put the question afresh: "What is Tanakh all about?" I have my ideas as to how a future Tanakh theology would be organized, based on the evaluation of *legoumena* on the relationship between God, people, and land, and how such a base line might contrast with later Jewish theologies. These and many other issues of content and method could not be raised in the first English outline which cannot be more than an attempt to direct our attention to what to me is a central and urgent issue of biblical studies. I can only hope that this essay will help to set the stage for a more realistic and deeply truthful atmosphere in the common work of Christians and Jews in the academic study of biblical religion.*

NOTES

1. The formulation offered here is a much shortened and reworked version of talks given at Harvard and other institutions in the States. Inevitably, some presentations here are similar to those made in Hebrew papers, and all are tentative formulations based on draft versions of a book on this subject. The main paper in Hebrew appeared in the Jubilee volume of *Tarbiz* 50 (1981) 37ff., and the issue of the academic study of Judaism and theology was enlarged upon in *Studies in Bible and Exegesis* (edited by myself and U. Simon) (Ramat Gan: Bar Ilan University Press, 1980). Some ideas on the rise of Jewish Bible Research were discussed in an introductory paper to a panel session on this subject at the opening session of the Eighth World Congress of Jewish Studies (Jerusalem, 1983). All of these papers as well as my "Christianity, Judaism and Modern Bible Study" (VTSup 28 [1975] 69ff.) present stages in my grappling with the subject as raised now. Certain overlaps between papers could not be avoided. For reasons of space, footnotes were kept to a minimum and standard bibliographical references were omitted.

2. I shall use "Tanakh" for what is sometimes termed Hebrew Scriptures or Jewish Bible. "Old Testament" is reserved for what is conceived of as part of the Christian Bible, without differentiation between Christian churches. In obvious contexts, "Bible" is used instead of "Jewish Bible." I am aware of ideological exercises such as indicated in the title of J. B. Payne, *Theology of the Older Testament,* but this is of no relevance for our inquiry.

3. It would lead us too far afield to explore the hang-ups of Jewish Studies in their present stage of development vis-à-vis the nineteenth-century type of schol-

arly study of Judaism that was in part connected to institutions that were Jewish "theological seminaries." Theology was sometimes used in nineteenth-century discussion as a portmanteau term for all aspects of the scholarly study of Judaism; cf. n. 27. On the other hand, the issue of "religious studies" remains perennially on the agenda of discussion concerning American institutions of higher learning.

4. While I should like to think that biblical philology, since the days of Morinus and Cappellus, has been totally removed from theological considerations, I am not convinced that our efforts have been totally successful. Out of deep respect for my colleague D. Barthélemy, I must consider seriously statements such as: "Il est évident qu'une édition de la Bible juive et une autre de l'A.T. des chrétiens présenteront des apparats critiques bien différents, puisqu'il ságira d'enregistrer les traces textuelles laissées en deux traditions religieuses distinctes." ["It is clear that an edition of the Jewish Bible and another of the Christian Old Testament will offer quite different critical apparatuses since it is necessary to record the textual traces left in two distinct religious traditions."] (*Études d'histoire du texte de l'Ancien Testament* [Freiburg: Universitätsverlag, 1978] 359). Cf. below, n. 65.

5. I mention only a few recognized scholars who are part of the mainstream of Bible studies. For our purpose it does not matter if a scholar agrees to be labeled theologian or if he feels, like J. Barr, that one should stop writing textbooks on theology. There is a fine tradition of Semitists who were biblical theologians (or the other way around), and Jewish Semitists may conceivably move in the same direction.

6. If I am not mistaken, I have been the first (and only?) teacher of Tanakh who has insisted for the past fifteen years or so labeling some of my courses at the university "Tanakh theology." I may have dared to do so because I felt securely anchored as a Semitist and biblical philologist.

7. In the same year that J. G. Eichhorn published the second edition of his *Einleitung* (1787), J. P. Gabler gave his academic talk: *Oratio de iusto discrimine theologiae biblicae et dogmaticae regundisque recte utriusque finibus* (cf. below, n. 10). Needless to say, both Eichhorn and Gabler had their predecessors, from rather different sets of attitudes. In a way, pietism and criticism had already met in the work of Semler.

8. Gabler suggested that from the text one should abstract *wahre biblische Theologie* ("true biblical theology") and by "philosophizing" on it one could distill *reine biblische Theologie* ("pure biblical theology") which in turn would clear the path for dogmatic theology. It is quite remarkable that Gabler is generally taken to be the father of biblical theology, although he never got beyond his programmatic declarations. Eichhorn, on the other hand, was conceived of as the harbinger of a new era of criticism, although his theories were challenged during this lifetime in a rapid succession of alternative critical models.

9. Gabler's demand was to describe the historical character of the ways of belief at the time of the biblical writers, and in this sense it helped to allow for the specific ways of the Old Testament. But he was not dealing as yet with Old Testament theology. As often repeated, Gabler formulated: "Est theologia bilica e genere historico, tradens quid scriptores sacri de rebus divinis senserint" (reprinted in his *Opuscula academica* II [1831] 183).

10. That is to say, roughly from the 1830s to the 1930s, or for about one

hundred years out of the two centuries separating us from Eichhorn and Gabler. To be sure, this is the period in which the academic critical study of the Old Testament became firmly established.

11. The title pages of "Theologies of the Old Testament" bear eloquent witness, mostly in subtitles, that these are critical inquiries into Old Testament religion. As in other areas, scholars on the Continent took the lead in this development.

12. This includes attempts at academic Old Testament theology that are intended for schools with a distinctly evangelical bent, such as W. C. Kaiser, *Toward an Old Testament Theology* (Grand Rapids: Wm. B. Eerdmans Publishing Co., 1978). Bible scholars belonging to the mainstream have recently felt the need to react to the phenomenon of Fundamentalism; note, e.g., J. Barr's volumes *Fundamentalism* (2d rev. ed.; London: SCM Press, 1981) and *Beyond Fundamentalism* (Philadelphia: Westminster Press, 1984).

13. The inner-Christian discussion on the nature of Old Testament theology seems to me, as an outsider, of a different character than discussion about the "crisis" slogan in biblical theology raised in the wake of B. Child's *Biblical Theology in Crisis* (Philadelphia: Westminster Press, 1970). It is possible that while Old Testament theology has developed, on the Christian side, into an area of the academic study of Old Testament religion, there is hardly any field of "Biblical religion" in a comprehensive sense (Old Testament and New Testament), so that "biblical theology" is not a sum total of Old Testament and New Testament theologies. For the student of Tanakh, none of this is of relevance.

14. I stress that I see the approaches as *complementary,* not as alternatives, just as specifically I see Old Testament theology as complementary to the historical-comparative approach to Old Testament religion. My conceptualization is thus according to the model of synchronic linguistics, complementary to diachronic. It may be that over the past decades the swing of the pendulum on the Christian side has led to a slowing down in the study of Old Testament *Religionswissenschaft;* we are very far from such a swing on the Jewish side.

15. There are specific issues on the American academic scene, due to the principle of division between religion and state. Moreover, there is no absolute line of conceptual division between schools of arts and sciences and schools of divinity, and similar formal issues can arise in other countries. To my knowledge, we have no study at our disposal that details the self-perception of Old Testament scholars in different countries and institutions.

16. In my paper on "Modern Jewish Bible Research" (§14), I have raised some issues with regard to the philosophy and structure of Jewish Studies. In that context I have considered whether Tanakh theology may be part of the branch of theology constituent of "Jewish Thought" as well as of Tanakh studies. In any event, no departmentalization should divide between the twin areas within the study of biblical religion—neither on the Christian nor on the Jewish side.

17. I am aware that a particular journal can decide that it does not publish papers on Old Testament theology. My late colleague, M. Enslin, applied this policy to the *Journal of Biblical Literature,* if my memory serves me right, and it is still followed.

18. I am speaking specifically of academic professionals, in contradistinction

to scholars who *also* dealt with some aspects of Tanakh study—such as Semitic etymology, Targum, or exegesis—as part of their duties in a seminary. For various reasons, only the growth of institutions under Jewish auspices on American soil started the trend toward opening positions for professional biblical scholars, such as M. Margolis or M. Buttenwieser. For almost a century previously, Jewish scholars who had significant contributions to Tanakh studies served as rabbis or as teachers of rabbis—from S. D. Luzzatto to Chajes and Perles. Only since the 1930s have there been chairs for Jewish Bible scholars both in the United States and in Israel. No Jewish professional was ever appointed professor of Bible on the Continent or in England. It is for this reason that those of us who started teaching around 1950 regard ourselves as the second generation. I am not sure that this position is fully appreciated, and I tend to believe that it is of importance for the subject under discussion here.

19. All this is a matter of the 1930s. I might stress that almost all Jewish Bible scholars came from European backgrounds. In a way, those who grew up in an American Jewish Reform atmosphere (like Morgenstern) were the most Germanic of all—which at that time meant true followers of Wellhausen, Duhm, and Gunkel, in the Buttenwieser tradition. For the present, I shall not raise the question whether one would find differences between Jewish and Christian scholars with regard to their approaches to Old Testament *Religionswissenschaft* in its different aspects.

20. Y. Kaufmann entered the academic scene late in life—after the retirement of M. H. Segal—at the very time when some of us second-generation biblical scholars started our careers as young lecturers.

21. Decisive papers that led to the change of direction on the Continent were published in rapid sequence by W. Staerk, *ZThK*, NF 4 (1924) 289ff.; G. Steuernagel, *BZAW* 41 (1925) 266ff.; O. Eissfeldt, *ZAW* 44 (1926) 1ff.; and W. Eichrodt, *ZAW* 47 (1929) 83ff.

22. Since I feel responsible for having raised the issue, I may add that I myself first became acutely aware of the problem when I had to teach Tanakh to the finishing class of rabbis as a visiting professor at the Jewish Theological Seminary in New York in the late 1960s. It was my own misconception of the task that forced me to study closely the books on Old Testament theology that I suggested to my students.

23. From the previous note it is clear that this statement is less correct in 1985 than it was in 1970. I venture to think that some earlier formulations of mine (in Hebrew) have left some impact and that scholars are not so frightened today. I ought to add that scholars of the past generation, such as Buber or Heschel, who worked on issues that might be said to belong to Tanakh theology, never dealt with theoretical aspects of their work, nor were they directly concerned with biblical studies as an academic field. But it is conceivable that future research will show that the sharp differences between scholars such as Kaufmann and Buber, back in the 1940s, can be understood as arguments between a historian of biblical religion and a theologian, even if no such terminology was ever employed.

24. This is not a utilitarian consideration but rather a question as to whether a certain approach is of importance to the overall scholarly effort. Of course, Old Testament theology might exist as a field of inquiry even if we deny its achieve-

ments. But in the context of this chapter in this present volume we must consider whether the inquiry into meaning and message of the text as it stands has yielded positive results, unachievable by the methods of the science of religion.

25. At least on one level any inquiry into the meaning of the text as it stands is conducted by terminological and phenomenological procedures. The price for preventing denominational division could be that we all agree to turn the clock backward in order to avoid "theology." I readily admit that while I do not think Christian scholars would give up the term, I have considered for a long time whether a terminological change would offer a solution. Cf. above, item 2.

26. The term "theology" was quite in vogue among nineteenth-century Jewish liberal thinkers. A. Geiger used the term in the title of his journal and among his *Nachgelassene Schriften* (1875) is his study "Einleitung in das Studium der Jüdischen Theologie." Other scholars used terminology of dogmatic theology such as Steinheim, *Die Glaubenslehre der Synagoge als exacte Wissenschaft* (1856). The first major theoretician of American Reform, K. Kohler, published in 1910 his *Grundriss einer systematischen Theologie des Judentums* (1910). For recent years, see titles such as E. B. Borowitz, *A New Jewish Theology in the Making* (Philadelphia: Westminster Press, 1968), or L. Jacobs, *A Jewish Theology* (London: Darton, Longman & Todd, 1973). I should stress that the only one who thought in historical terms of "layers" of theology and thus wrote of "biblical theology" was Geiger, probably the most learned among the early reformers and founding fathers of *Wissenschaft des Judentums,* in regard to biblical and Semitic studies. Nineteenth-century liberal Judaism definitely toyed with "biblistic" solutions in its quest for renewing *halakhah,* and in this context "theology" was a useful term. "Theology" is thus loaded with doubtful connotations for Jewish scholarship today, and our search for a term is not just a matter of squeamishness.

27. "Biblical theology" in the sense Gabler gave it was, at least in part, pietistically informed and was aimed at freeing exegesis from the grip of dogmatics. True biblical theology would thus revive the ideal of the Reformation that had succumbed to fossilization.

28. We cannot go into differences of dogmatic nuances between various denominations with regard to the "obscurity" of the Old Testament, to be enlightened and opened up by the key of the New Testament ("Evangelium est clavis, quae aperit Vetus Testamentum"; cf. M. Luther, *D. Martin Luthers Werke; kritische Gesamtausgabe,* 20 [Weimar: Böhlau, 1883–] 336, 24–25). All in all, Calvinistic tradition was somewhat more hesitant in this respect, partly thanks to its position on progressive revelation (note J. Calvin, *Institutes of the Christian Religion,* II. X. 2). Expositions on the superior status of the Old Testament are almost nonexistent; cf. the exceptional statement of A. A. van Ruler, *The Christian Church and the Old Testament* (Grand Rapids: Wm. B. Eerdmans Publishing Co., 1971) esp. 72. For him the Old Testament "is and remains the true Bible" and New Testament is the "explanatory gloss." But note ibid, 85.

29. Cf. P. Grelot, *Sense chrétien de l'Ancien Testament* (Paris: Desclée, 1962); T. C. Vriezen, *An Outline of Old Testament Theology* (Oxford: Basil Blackwell, 1958). While all Old Testament theologies of the past decades share in degrees of New Testament directedness, Vriezen was possibly one of the most outspoken Old Testament scholars to stress this task. On the other hand, J. L. McKenzie

tried very hard not to overstep the limits of the Old Testament (J. L. McKenzie, *A Theology of the Old Testament* [Garden City, N.Y.: Doubleday & Co., 1974]). While he formulated clearly his Christian position, his book is possibly the nearest to a nondenominational treatment. It is worth stressing that, on a practical level, scholars have not attempted in recent decades, as far as I know, to write a "Biblical Theology," composed of an Old Testament and a New Testament part. The only exception seems to be the very formal presentation in Spanish by M. Garcia Cordevo, *Teologia de la Biblia* (Madrid, 1970).

30. Some authors have managed to center their description on God-man relationships rather than on static realities (i.e., God or man). Yet *man*—taken over from traditional treatises—takes almost always the place that *people* should take, and the individual is in the center. Moreover, the third traditional component, i.e., soteriology, is usually emphasized out of all proportion.

31. E. Jacob, *Theology of the Old Testament* (New York: Harper & Brothers, 1958); W. Zimmerli, *An Outline of Old Testament Theology* (Richmond: John Knox Press, 1972), divides into: Yahweh's Gift, Command; Life before God; Crisis and Hope.

32. I entertain some doubts whether the academic study of Old Testament religion is free from bias, even though it is an accepted part of modern Old Testament research. In any event, Old Testament theology must be telic—or else it is not a statement from within the community of faith. Whatever is only part—and dogmatically mostly conceived of as the less decisive part—cannot be the same as the whole. This simple truth must be faced by Jewish Bible scholars.

33. See K. Stendahl, "Biblical Theology, Contemporary," IDB 1. 418ff.

34. *What did it mean?* stands de facto for biblical theology as a historical entity, in contrast to what the Bible means in its practical application to each generation. Of course, any "What did it mean?" contains an element of illusion. We have only our exegetical acumen to guide us, and no exegesis can fully transport us into the "then." Yet it is the business of critical historical scholarship to attempt precisely that.

35. I had the pleasure of discussing this point with Stendahl after my lectures at Harvard and I don't think his ideas would support all of these possibilities.

36. Stendahl attempted to downplay differences, but it is obvious that he did not fully consider the Jewish side. "A Christian and a Jewish Old Testament theology differ only where the question of meaning is pursued beyond the material and the period of the Old Testament texts themselves" ("Biblical Theology, Contemporary," 423).

37. Theology was part and parcel of classical pagan thought that was re-adapted, and *theologia* is not a Christian coinage but good classical Greek.

38. I stress that as far as I know such suggestions were made as *obiter dicta,* as a token of fairness toward Judaism. Obviously it was not the business of Christian students of the Old Testament to consider the problems of Tanakh scholarship.

39. This formulation sums up an inner-Jewish discussion, which cannot be gone into here. Nor shall I deal here with medieval or renaissance attempts at construing a system of teachings on the basis of rabbinic interpretations of biblical *legoumena*. The term "observance" is used deliberately in the realm of

religious practice. I need not add that the system of *halakhah* deals precisely with the "Law" that is the stepchild of Old Testament theology.

40. Tannaitic theory—though not necessarily practice—derived every detail of prescribed behavior from Scripture, as far as possible. Once the interpretation was fixed into rules of observance, however, there was no more direct appeal to Scripture. As rabbinic formulation had it, interpretation made into law is binding even if made in error, because the Torah is now in human hands—not in heaven. On principle, this is where rabbanite and karaite Judaism differed right into the Middle Ages, even if the practice was more complicated. Hence historic mainstream Judaism can have no place for "biblical theology" in the sense of an exegetical insight that would change practice. Ultimately, such ideas belong to the attempts to revive ideologies of the Reformation, and it is no coincidence that nineteenth-century Jewish Reform toyed with such ideas.

41. Exercising my exegetical sovereignty with all possible tools at my disposal constitutes for me one of the decisive differences between traditional study and modern critical research. In my submission, there can be no serious theological conceptualization without the most scrupulous detailed exegetical-textual basis—and each theologian is perforce his own exegete, guided by his own erudition and intuition. Insisting, however, on our exegetical sovereignty does not diminish our respect for the insight achieved by generations of traditional exegetes, who erected layer upon layer in their attempt at empathy into the meaning of the text.

42. In the light of what actually transpires from the vast extant literature of Old Testament *Religionswissenschaft*, the possible claim that only that branch of the study of Old Testament religion is part of critical scholarship cannot be allowed. A certain lack of "objectivity" is endemic to the entire field, as long as it is not taken over by Buddhist monks and Hindu priests.

43. I suspect that most academic students of Tanakh would be rather embarrassed by a question such as: Do you believe in the Bible? After all, religion is a private matter. Is this true as regards the Tanakh theologian? Without entangling myself in a discussion of Barthian positions on liberal theology and academic learning, I visualize something that is not just a matter of intellectual structure or Diltheyan *Geistesgeschichte*. Theology is no longer something that necessitates belief in authenticity, authority, and binding statements. From my gingerly approach it is clear that I am not sure where exactly to draw the dividing line. As is the case with so many issues, in order to create a Tanakh theology one does not have to be a believer in the divine origin of Scripture (however defined)—but it helps. At the very least, the claim that Tanakh tells us of acts of divine revelation is to be taken seriously, even though open to reformulations. In this respect I feel affinity for what I think is the approach of J. Barr. It is also conceivable that ultimately Tanakh theology can only be created by a scholar who takes canonical authority as a believed given and builds his structure within that framework. With appropriate changes, such an attitude may come near the formulation proposed for Jewish theology in general by L. Jacobs: "Jewish theology differs from other branches of Jewish learning in that its practitioners are personally committed to the truth they are seeking to explore" (*Jewish Theology* 1). At present, I would probably leave the exact character of identification to a prag-

matic self-regulation. As regards the possibility of using "phenomenology," the usage of this term in theology today rules this out; cf., e.g., the discussion of H. Kuhn in H. Vorgrimler and R. v. d. Gucht, *Bilanz der Theologie im 20. Jahrhundert* (1969) esp. 377.

44. I stress that in this specific capacity one does not inquire where the stones for the original building came from but reserves an interest as to how they were used later, because later configurations may sometimes be useful for figuring out the earlier ones. This is not to ignore the possibility that later configurations may be misleading, nor does it deny the interest in the quarry from which the blocks were hewn. But that is decidedly not the aim of the inquiry.

45. I try to avoid the terminological quibble over science, scholarship, and *Wissenschaft*. As a linguist with a developed inferiority complex about "science," I remember the feeling of relief when, in the early 1950s, I heard N. Wiener, the father of cybernetics, proclaim that physics was not an exact science.

46. Cf. my "Humanism and the Rise of Hebraic Studies: From Christian to Jewish Renaissance," *The Word of the Lord Shall Go Forth: Essays in Honor of David Noel Freedman in Celebration of His Sixtieth Birthday* (ed. C. L. Meyers and M. O'Connor; Winona Lake, Ind.: Eisenbrauns, 1983) 691ff. I am reluctant to try to express this point in Wittgensteinian formulation. Cf. also U. Koepf, *Die Anfänge der theologischen Wissenschaftstheorie im 13. Jahrhundert* (Tübingen: J. C. B. Mohr [Paul Siebeck], 1974) esp. pp. 2–3.

47. The student of Old Testament religion is often specifically interested in these latter aspects because they give information about antecedents or outside relationships.

48. Cf. W. Brueggemann, *The Land* (Philadelphia: Fortress Press, 1977), and the recent G. Strecker, ed., *Das Land Israel in biblischer Zeit. Jerusalem-Symposium 1981 der Hebräischen Universität und der Georg-August Universität* (Göttingen: Vandenhoeck & Ruprecht, 1983). Note also M. Weinfeld, *Zion* 49 (1984) 115ff. (Hebrew). Though I do not dwell on the issue of subcorpuses, I hope the point is self-explanatory (cf. nn. 50, 53, below).

49. Just as we have to allow for Christian bias playing down the issue of Israel and its land, we have to reckon with Jewish bias that might overaccentuate it. I emphasize again that it is through becoming aware of contrasting biases that combined Christian and Jewish biblical scholarship can progress. Cf. n. 56, below.

50. We do not have to carry out the full study in order to realize that the same type of subcorpuses in the *Writings* that caused problems for a unified Old Testament theology will raise problems for any attempt that does not wish to end up as "theologies." Quantity is not simply a matter of counting instances but of subcorpuses as well.

51. The only fully worked out attempt at writing a chapter along the suggested lines is the doctoral dissertation written under my direction by R. Kasher, *The Theological Conception of the Miracle in the Bible* (Ramat Gan: Bar Ilan University Press, 1981; Hebrew). His attempt naturally applies many elements of the methodological approach I had developed about ten years ago. Many problems as to how qualification is to be achieved can only be worked out in the actual writing of theologies.

52. Cf., e.g., the summary by G. F. Hasel, "The Problem of the Center in the Old Testament Theology Debate," *ZAW* 86 (1974) 65f. I have the feeling that scholars who have used this slogan did not always bear in mind its origin as vividly described by Luther *(Luthers Werke,* vol. 47, 66, 18f.): "Das Christus sej der punct im Circkel, da der gantze Circkel ausgezogen ist, undauff in sehet, und wer sich nach ime richtet, gehort auch drein. De er ist das mittel punctlein im Circkel." All in all, attempts to base Old Testament theology on an alleged center have been reduced to meaninglessness by successive suggestions. In a way, Eichrodt's initial tour de force of forcing all the facts into the mold of the covenant idea was, in retrospect, not as bad an idea as critics claimed. Also S. Terrien in *The Elusive Presence* (New York: Harper & Row, 1978) comes to grips with a basic aspect of theological structure.

53. "Historicizing" is the playground for the ingenuity of critical scholarship, apportioning data to sources (mostly assumed) that can be conceived of as following each other in time, until they were amalgamated by final editors. "Subcorpuses" are actual textual units, extant in Tanakh. Thus, e.g., Deuteronomy is a subcorpus, or even Deuteronomy 32 or 33 can be analyzed as such, because these are actual textual units. Needless to say, one of the major criticisms of von Rad has been that being convinced that we cannot detect an explicit conceptual axis in Old Testament religious thought, he ended up with a history of theologies, inspired by sources as he understood them. Perhaps I may play with the stress put on the word: Tanakh theology is not just "What is it all about?" but "What is it *all* about?"

54. Structuralists—not only in linguistics—used to speak of the relative elegance or power of a specific model, and post-Chomskyans have come to admit that all we can hope for is to improve on our models. There is not one truth waiting to be discovered. "Structure" is, in any case, something we have to discover from the text itself—and there may be legitimate competing discoveries. It is terminologically to be kept apart from "systems" that we impose from the outside.

55. I am aware that one can spend years in attempting to conceptualize an approach to opening up a new field of inquiry, only to be faced by someone coming up with a counterstatement that the Bible is not a textbook of theology. I don't think it is very useful to enter an argument at this level.

56. It is part of everyone's bias (cf. notes 49 and 64) that one is convinced that if one follows one's method correctly and does not cut corners in gathering the facts piece by piece, the final product will be a "better" piece of scholarship than the next person's. It may be this kind of creative hubris that sustains us in our work.

57. The temptation to enlarge here on *sensus literalis, grammaticus, historicus, exegesis e mente auctoris,* etc., vis-à-vis *peshat, peshatoth, peshuto shel Miqra,* etc., must be withstood. It would be of some interest to reevaluate in this context how alleged senses of words and verses would influence establishment of facts. For instance, the commentary on Psalms by the late M. Dahood would provide an excellent hunting ground for detecting a plethora of alleged *legoumena.*

58. I stress again that as Tanakh scholars we strictly follow our method. As

Jewish theologians we may or may not face a clash with results from inquiry into later historical layers, purporting to be based on Tanakh. As believers we may wish for a certain outcome of our inquiry and must beware of bending the facts of Tanakh. I shall not enter here into an argument on the issue of historical truth of constructions. It is the privilege of the historian of Tanakh religion—as of Old Testament history in general—to believe that one's model represents true facts, as they were. The Tanakh theologian builds a model to inquire into the meaning of Scripture, as it was *then*, according to *legoumena*, and must not attempt to usurp the task of the historian. But this does not mean that theology does not care for facts or that it reconstructs fiction. Considering the claims of Old Testament historians since the days of Ewald, I would even go so far as to suggest that we can be more certain about the *legoumena* than about the alleged "facts" of historians. Or, perhaps, the truth of the Tanakh theologian is not that of the historian, for the theologian looks for truths embedded in the depths of the text, not for the truth on the surface of events.

59. Since the days of Schrader and Jensen a fair number of Mesopotamian prototypes have been suggested. For a recent debunking of alleged evidence, cf. W. W. Hallo, *HUCA* 58 (1977) 17.

60. Twice in the Pentateuch, Sabbath observance is thus specifically connected. Such questions are aimed at the qualitative side of evaluation. Again, it will be a matter for subsequent comparison of layers to find out whether the position in the rabbinic (halakhic and aggadic) corpus is of equal importance.

61. Reverting to the picture of linguistics (cf. above, n. 14) I would claim that while studying the system of a synchronic cut, we must not mix in diachronic considerations. But being aware of them may help us in making better choices in formulating the synchronic description. Using diachronics intelligently for synchronic judgments has its own price, but it is worth paying. To be sure, this is why I come back again and again to the contention that what I am talking about is theology, not just structural phenomenology.

62. Again, one can understand that Eichrodt has considerable problems with the centrality of this subject. Most subcorpuses of Tanakh contain references to the subject, differing in density between legal, narrative, prophetic, and hymnic parts.

63. This would fill a volume by itself. It stands to reason that a Christian Old Testament theologian cannot ignore the Pauline pronouncements on the "Law," even if he does not share specific Lutheran accentuations. Conversely, medieval (and modern) "systems of Judaism" based on Talmudic sayings will perforce color somehow the perception of the Tanakh theologian.

64. One of the clearest formulations is that of H. Gese, *Vom Sinai zum Zion* (Munich: Chr. Kaiser Verlag, 1974) 16: "Ein christlicher Theologie darf den masoretischen Kanon niemals gut heissen, denn der Kontinuität zum Neuen Testament wird hier in bedeutendem Masse Abbruch getan" ("A Christian theology may never satisfactorily accept the Masoretic text canon to a significant degree, for the continuity with the New Testament is broken off here.") On the Catholic side, D. Barthélemy (*Études d'histoire du texte de l'Ancien Testament* [Fribourg: Universitätsverlag, 1978] esp. 15–16, 111–12) has been most outspoken in making it clear that the church should go only by the canon of the

Greek tradition of Scripture. On Childs's approach to canon as the touchstone, note the special issue of *JSOT* 16 (1980).

65. In this chapter I have used "bias" to indicate the inevitable lack of objectivity, rather than prejudice preconception, etc. G. Fohrer (*Theologische Grundstrukturen des Alten Testaments* [Berlin: Walter de Gruyter, 1972] 30) formulated a useful distinction when he wrote: "Selbst wenn man schon nicht voraussetzungslos an des AT herantritt, sollte man es wenigstens vorurteilsfrei tun" ("Even if one does not already approach the Old Testament without presuppositions, one should at least do so free of prejudgment").

*I should like to thank my assistant, Galen Marquis, M.A., for a fine job done in producing a readable manuscript for the printer and in having me reduce the number of formulations that might be too strong for some tastes.

BIBLIOGRAPHY OF
THE WORKS OF
FRANK MOORE CROSS

1947

1. "The Tabernacle: A Study from an Archaeological and Historical Approach," *BA* 10 (1947) 45–68.
2. "A Note on Deuteronomy 33:26," with D. N. Freedman, *BASOR* 108 (December 1947) 6f.

1948

3. "The Blessing of Moses," with D. N. Freedman, *JBL* 67 (1948) 191–210.
4. "Review of the *Westminster Study Edition of the Bible*," *McCormick Speaking* II:3 (December 1948) 12ff.

1949

5. "The Newly Discovered Scrolls in the Hebrew University Museum in Jerusalem," *BA* 12 (1949) 36–46.

1950

6. "Notes on a Canaanite Psalm in the Old Testament," *BASOR* 117 (February 1950) 19–21.
7. "Review of *The Bible and Modern Belief* by H. Wallis," *Religious Education* 45 (1950) 121f.

1951

8. "The Third-Person Pronominal Suffix in Phoenician," with D. N. Freedman, *JNES* 10 (1951) 228–30.
9. "Review of *Hebrew Origins* by Theophile Meek," *Journal of Bible and Religion* 19 (1951) 156.
10. "The Blessed Poor," *McCormick Speaking* V:3 (December 1951) 7–10.

1952

11. *Early Hebrew Orthography: A Study of the Epigraphic Evidence* (*American Oriental Series* 36), with D. N. Freedman (New Haven: American Oriental Society, 1952), vii + 77 pp.
12. "Ugaritic DB'AT and Hebrew Cognates," *VT* 2 (1952) 163f.

645

13. "Notes on the *Revised Standard Old Testament*," *McCormick Speaking* VI:2 (November 1952) 7–10.
14. "Review of *The Hebrew Scrolls from the Neighborhood of Jericho and the Dead Sea* by G. R. Driver," *Church History* 21 (1952) 273.

1953

15. "Josiah's Revolt Against Assyria," with D. N. Freedman, *JNES* 12 (1953) 56–58.
16. "A Royal Psalm of Thanksgiving: II Samuel 22 = Psalm 18," with D. N. Freedman, *JBL* 72 (1953) 15–34.
17. "Reviews of *Beginning in Archaeology* by Kathleen M. Kenyon and *Die Welt des Alten Testaments. Einführung in die Grenzgebiete der alttestamentlichen Wissenschaft* by Martin Noth," *BA* (1953) 43f.
18. "The Council of Yahweh in Second Isaiah," *JNES* 12 (1953) 274–77.
19. "A New Qumran Biblical Fragment Related to the Original Hebrew Underlying the Septuagint," *BASOR* 132 (December 1953) 15–26.

1954

20. "The Manuscripts of the Dead Sea Caves," *BA* 17 (1954) 2–21.
21. "Inscribed Javelin-Heads from the Period of the Judges: A Recent Discovery in Palestine," with J. T. Milik, *BASOR* 134 (April 1954) 5–15.
22. "The Evolution of the Proto-Canaanite Alphabet," *BASOR* 134 (April 1954) 15–24.
23. "Notes on Recent Research in Palestine," *McCormick Speaking* VII:8 (May 1954) 11, 14.
24. "Les rouleaux de la Mer Morte," *Evidences* VI:41 (June–July 1954) 5–12 [translation of no. 20].
25. "Review of *The Biblical Doctrine of Man in Society* by G. Ernest Wright," *McCormick Speaking* VIII:2 (November 1954) 16.
26. "The Banquet of the Kingdom," *McCormick Speaking* VIII:3 (December 1954) 7–10.

1955

27. Articles: "Inscriptions, Ancient Hebrew and Related Syro-Palestinian," "Writing, Ancient Hebrew," and "Yahweh," with D. N. Freedman, *Twentieth Century Encyclopedia of Religious Knowledge,* ed. Lefferts A. Loetscher, 2 vols. (Grand Rapids: Baker Book House, 1955).
28. "The Scrolls from the Judean Wilderness," *The Christian Century* 72:31 (August 3, 1955) 889–91.
29. "The Scrolls and the Old Testament," *The Christian Century* 72:32 (August 10, 1955) 948ff.
30. "The Essenes and Their Master," *The Christian Century* 72:33 (August 17, 1955) 954.
31. "The Scrolls and the New Testament," *The Christian Century* 72:34 (August 24, 1955) 968–71.
32. "The Oldest Manuscripts from Qumran," *JBL* 74 (1955) 147–72.
33. "Geshem the Arabian, Enemy of Nehemiah," *BA* 18 (1955) 46f.

34. "Archaeological News and Views," *BA* 18 (1955) 79f.
35. Translation (with J. S. Hazelton) of *The Nabateans: A Historical Sketch* by Jean Starcky, *BA* 18 (1955) 82–106.
36. "From Manuscripts Found in a Cave," a review article of *The Scrolls from the Dead Sea* by Edmund Wilson, *The New York Times Book Review* (October 16, 1955) 1, 31.
37. "The Song of Miriam," with D. N. Freedman, *JNES* 14 (1955) 237–50.
38. "A Footnote to Biblical History," *McCormick Speaking* IX:2 (November 1955) 7–10.

1956

39. "A Footnote to Biblical History," *BA* 19 (1956) 12–17 [reprint of no. 38].
40. "A Report on the Biblical Fragments of Cave Four in the Wâdī Qumrân," *BASOR* 141 (1956) 9–13.
41. "The Scrolls from the Judaean Desert," *Archaeology* 9:1 (Spring 1956) 41–53.
42. "La lettre de Simon ben Kosba," *RB* 63 (1956) 45–48.
43. "La travail d'édition des fragments manuscrits de Qumran," *RB* 63 (1956) 49–67, esp. 56ff. (Communications by the several members of the Jerusalem staff editing scroll fragments.)
44. "Chronique archéologique: El Bouqei'ah," with J. T. Milik, *RB* 63 (1956) 74–76.
45. "Explorations in the Judaean Buqei'ah," with J. T. Milik, *BASOR* 142 (April 1956) 5–17.
46. "The Dead Sea Scrolls, Their Significance to Religious Thought: A Symposium" with Millar Burrows, Edward P. Arbez, W. F. Albright, Amos Wilder, et al., *The New Republic* (April 9, 1956) 12–25, esp. 17ff.
47. "Qumran Cave I," *JBL* 75 (1956) 121–25.
48. "The Boundary and Province Lists of the Kingdom of Judah," with G. Ernest Wright, *JBL* (1956) 202–26.
49. "Review of the *Ancient Near East in Pictures* . . . by J. B. Pritchard," *Archaeology* 9 (Summer 1956) 150f.
50. "Lachish Letter IV," *BASOR* 144 (December 1956) 24–26.
51. "McCormick's Rehnborg Collection of Dead Sea Scrolls," *McCormick Speaking* X:4 (December 1956) 7–10.
52. "Editing the Manuscript Fragments of Qumran," with P. Benoit, et al., *BA* 19 (1956) 75–96, esp. 83–86 [translation of no. 43].

1957

53. "The Dead Sea Scrolls," *The Interpreter's Bible* (Nashville/New York: Abingdon Press, 1957) 12. 645–67.
54. "Review of *Biblical Archaeology* by G. Ernest Wright," *BA* 20 (1957) 79f.

1958

55. *The Ancient Library of Qumran and Modern Biblical Studies* (New York: Doubleday & Co./London: Gerald Duckworth & Co., 1958) xx + 196 pp.
56. "Epigraphik, semitische," *Die Religion in Geschichte und Gegenwart*[3], ed. K. Galling, vol. 2 (1958), cols. 523–26.

57. "Will You Lie for God?" Convocation Address, September 24, 1958. Occasional publication of the *Harvard Divinity School Bulletin.*

1959

58. "A Typological Study of the El Khaḍr Javelin and Arrow-heads," with J. T. Milik, *Annual of the Department of Antiquities of Jordan* III (1956) 15–23 [publication delayed].
59. "Report from the Dead Sea 'Scrollery,' " *McCormick Speaking* XIII:2 (December 1959) 20–23.

1960

60. "Will Ye Speak Falsely for God?" *Contemporary Accents in Liberal Religion* (Boston: Beacon Press, 1960) 92–105.
61. "A Ugaritic Abecedary and the Origins of the Proto-Canaanite Alphabet," with T. O. Lambdin, *BASOR* 160 (December 1960) 21–26.

1961

62. "The Priestly Tabernacle," *The Biblical Archaeologist Reader,* ed. G. Ernest Wright and D. N. Freedman (Garden City, N.Y.: Doubleday Anchor Books, 1961) [revised form of no. 1].
63. "The Development of the Jewish Scripts," *The Bible and the Ancient Near East: Essays in Honor of William Foxwell Albright,* ed. G. Ernest Wright (New York: Doubleday & Co., 1961) 133–202.
64. *The Ancient Library of Qumran and Modern Biblical Studies* (rev. ed.; Garden City, N.Y.: Doubleday Anchor Books, 1961), xxii + 260 pp. [cf. no. 55].
65. "The Study of the Old Testament at Harvard," with G. Ernest Wright, *Harvard Divinity School Bulletin,* April–July 1961, 14–20.
66. "Epigraphic Notes on Hebrew Documents of the Eighth–Sixth Centuries B.C.: 1. A New Reading of a Place Name in the Samaria Ostraca," *BASOR* 163 (October 1961) 12–14.

1962

67. "Epigraphic Notes on Hebrew Documents of the Eighth–Sixth Centuries B.C.: 2. The Murabb'ât Papyrus and the Letter Found Near Yabneh-yam," *BASOR* 165 (February 1962) 34–46.
68. "An Inscribed Seal from Balâṭah (Shechem)," *BASOR* 167 (October 1962) 14–15.
69. "Yahweh and the God of the Patriarchs," *HTR* 55/4 (1962) 225–59 [Nock Volume, ed. F. M. Cross and K. Stendahl].
70. "An Archaic Inscribed Seal from the Valley of Aijalon [Soreq]," *BASOR* 168 (December 1962) 12–18.
71. "Epigraphic Notes on Hebrew Documents of the Eighth–Sixth Centuries B.C.: 3. The Inscribed Jar Handles from Gibeon," *BASOR* 168 (December 1962) 18–23.
72. "Excursus on the Palaeographical Dating of the Copper Document," *Les 'petites grottes' de Qumran [Discoveries in the Judaean Desert* III] by

M. Baillet, J. T. Milik, et al. (Oxford: Clarendon Press, 1962) 217–21 and fig. 12.

1963
73. "The Discovery of the Samaria Papyri," *BA* 26 (1963) 110–21.
74. "The Discovery of the Samaria Papyri," *Christian News from Israel* 14 (1963) 24–35 [*manu secunda*; cf. no. 73].

1964
75. "The Name of Ashdod," with D. N. Freedman, *BASOR* 175 (October 1964) 48–50.
76. "Studies in Ancient Yahwistic Poetry," with D. N. Freedman. Johns Hopkins dissertation, 1950 (photoprint, Ann Arbor, Mich., 1964), 358 pp.
77. "The History of the Biblical Text in the Light of the Discoveries in the Judaean Desert," *HTR* 57 (1964) 281–99.
78. "The Ostracon from Nebī Yūnis," *IEJ* 14 (1964)185f. and pl. 41H.

1965
79. "The Origin and Early Evolution of the Alphabet," Hebrew Abstract in *M'rbw šl glyl wḥwp hglyl* (Jerusalem, 1965) 17–19. [Nineteenth Archaeological Convention, ed. Israel Exploration Society.]
80. *Scrolls from the Wilderness of the Dead Sea:* Catalogue of the Exhibit, The Dead Sea Scrolls of Jordan. Editor and contributor. [Published by the University of California for the American Schools of Oriental Research; Canadian edition (French and English) by the University of Toronto; British edition, by the British Museum; 1965.] 30 pp. + 19 plates.

1966
81. "The Divine Warrior in Israel's Early Cult," *Studies and Texts,* vol. 3: *Biblical Motifs,* ed. A. Altmann (Cambridge: Harvard University Press, 1966) 11–30.
82. "The Contribution of the Discoveries at Qumran to the Study of the Biblical Text," *IEJ* 16 (1966) 81–95.
83. "Aspects of Samaritan and Jewish History in Late Persian and Hellenistic Times," *HTR* 59 (1966) 201–11.
84. "An Aramaic Inscription from Daskyleion," *BASOR* 184 (December 1966) 7–10.
85. "Yahvé y el dios de los patriarcas," *Selecciones de teologia* 17 (1966) 56–60. Trans. L. Anoro [cf. no. 69].
86. "The History of the Biblical Text in the Light of Discoveries in the Judaean Desert," "The Oldest Manuscripts from Qumrân," and "A New Biblical Fragment Related to the Original Hebrew Underlying the Septuagint," *Readings on the History of the Bible Text in Recent Writing,* ed. S. Talmon (Jerusalem, 1966) 77–95, 217–54 [reprinted essays nos. 77, 32, 19].

1967

87. "The Origin and Early Evolution of the Alphabet," *EI* 8 (Jerusalem: Israel Exploration Society, 1967) 8*–24* [Sukenik Memorial Volume].
88. "Piety and Politics," *CCAR Journal* [Central Conference of American Rabbis] (June 1967) 28f.
89. *Die Antikebibliothek von Qumran und die moderne biblische Wissenschaft,* trans. Chr. Burchard (Neukirchen-Vluyn: Neukirchener Verlag, 1967), 232 pp. German edition revised from 2d English edition (+ Anhang, 219–29).
90. "The Scrolls from the Judean Desert," *Archaeological Discoveries in the Holy Land* (New York, 1967) 157–67 [republication of no. 41].

1968

91. "Mesopotamia," "Egypt," "Syria-Palestine," "Anatolia," and "The Dead Sea Scrolls," *An Encyclopedia of World History,* 4th ed., ed. W. L. Langer (Boston, 1968) 27–50, 115–17.
92. "The Structure of the Deuteronomic History," *Perspectives in Jewish Learning* III (Annual of the College of Jewish Studies, Chicago, 1968) 9–24.
93. "The Song of the Sea and Canaanite Myth," *JTC* 5 (1968) 1–25.
94. "The Canaanite Cuneiform Tablet from Taanach," *BASOR* 190 (1968) 41–46.
95. "The Early History of the Qumrân Community," *McCormick Quarterly* 21 (1968) 249–64.
96. "The Priestly Tabernacle," *Old Testament Issues,* ed. S. Sandmel (New York: Harper & Row, 1968) 39–67 [cf. no. 62].
97. "The Phoenician Inscription from Brazil: A Nineteenth Century Forgery," *Or* NS 37 (1968) 437–60.
98. "Jar Inscriptions from Shiqmona," *IEJ* 18 (1968) 226–33.

1969

99. "Judaean Stamps," *EI* 9 (1969) 20–27 and pl. 5 [W. F. Albright Volume].
100. "New Directions in the Study of Apocalyptic," *JTC* 6 (1969) 157–65.
101. "A Christian Understanding of the Election of Israel," *The End of Dialogue and Beyond,* ed. S. Seltzner and M. L. Stackhouse (New York: Friendship Press, 1969) 72–85.
102. "Papyri of the Fourth Century B.C. from Dâliyeh: A Preliminary Report on Their Discovery and Significance," *New Directions in Biblical Archaeology,* ed. D. N. Freedman and J. C. Greenfield (Garden City, N.Y.: Doubleday Anchor Books, 1969) 41–62 and figs. 34–39.
103. "The Early History of the Qumran Community," *New Directions in Biblical Archaeology,* 63–79 [see no. 102; republication of no. 95].
104. "Epigraphic Notes on the Ammân Citadel Inscription," *BASOR* 193 (1969) 13–19.
105. "Two Notes on Palestinian Inscriptions of the Persian Age," *BASOR* 193 (1969) 19–24.
106. "An Ostracon from Heshbon," *Andrews University Seminary Studies* 7 (1969) 223–29 and pl. 25.

107. Associate Editor and Translator, *The New American Bible* (Paterson, N.J.: St. Anthony Guild Press, 1969–1970) [I, II Samuel, with P. W. Skehan].

1970

108. "The Cave Inscriptions from Khirbet Beit Lei," *Near Eastern Archaeology in the Twentieth Century*, ed. J. A. Sanders (New York: Doubleday & Co., 1970) 299–306 [Glueck Volume].
109. "The Dead Sea Scrolls," *Encyclopaedia Britannica* (Chicago: Benton, 1970) 7. 117–19.
110. "Phoenician Incantations on a Plaque of the Seventh Century B.C. from Arslan Tash in Upper Syria," with R. J. Saley, *BASOR* 197 (1970) 42–49.
111. "William Foxwell Albright: Orientalist," *BASOR* 200 (1970) 7–11.

1971

112. "An Inscribed Jar Handle from Raddana," with D. N. Freedman, *BASOR* 201 (1971) 19–22.
113. "Buqei'ah" in the *Encyclopedia of Archaeological Excavations in the Holy Land* [Hebrew], ed. B. Mazar et al. (Jerusalem: Israel Exploration Society, 1971) 1. 99–100.
114. Editor with John Strugnell, *Studies in Memory of Paul Lapp* (*HTR* 64, 2–3; Cambridge: Harvard University Press, 1971).
115. "The Old Phoenician Inscription from Spain Dedicated to Hurrian Astarte," *HTR* 64, 2–3, 189–95 [Lapp Memorial Volume].
116. "ζκ['ēl]," *Theologisches Wörterbuch zum Alten Testament*, ed. G. J. Botterweck and H. Ringgren (Berlin: W. Kohlhammer, 1971) 1. 259–79.

1972

117. "The Stele Dedicated to Melcarth by Ben-Hadad of Damascus," *BASOR* 205 (1972) 36–42.
118. *Scrolls from Qumran Cave I*, ed. with J. C. Trever, D. N. Freedman, and J. A. Sanders (Jerusalem: Albright Institute of Archaeological Research and the Shrine of the Book, 1972), 163 pp.
119. "Introduction" to *Scrolls from Qumran Cave I*, 1–5 [see no. 118].
120. "Some Observations on Early Hebrew," with D. N. Freedman, *Bib.* 53 (1972) 413–20.
121. "An Interpretation of the Nora Stone," *BASOR* 208 (1972) 13–19.
122. "The Evolution of a Theory of Local Texts," *Septuagint and Cognate Studies* 2 (1972), ed. R. A. Kraft, 108–26.
123. "William Foxwell Albright," *Yearbook of the American Philosophical Society*, 110–15.

1973

124. *Canaanite Myth and Hebrew Epic: Essays in the History of the Religion of Israel* (Cambridge: Harvard University Press, 1973), xvii + 376 pp.
125. "Heshbon Ostracon II," *Andrews University Seminary Studies* 11 (1973) 126–31.

126. "Two Archaic Inscriptions on Clay Objects from Byblus," with P. K. McCarter, Jr., *Revista di Studi Fenici* I (1973) 3–8.
127. "W. F. Albright's View of Biblical Archaeology and Its Methodology," *BA* 36 (1973) 2–5.
128. "ʾēl [Dios]," *Diccionario teologico de antiquo Testamento,* ed. G. J. Botterweck and H. Ringgren (Madrid: Ediciones Cristianidad, 1973) cols. 256–75 [translation of no. 116].

1974

129. Editor of posthumous article by W. F. Albright, "The Lachish Cosmetic Burner and Esther 2:12," *A Light Unto My Path.* Old Testament Studies in Honor of Jacob M. Myers, ed. H. N. Bream, R. D. Heim, and C. A. Moore (Philadelphia: Temple University Press, 1974) 25–32.
130. "The Contribution of the Qumrân Discoveries to the Study of the Biblical Text," *The Canon and Masorah of the Hebrew Bible: An Introductory Reader,* ed. S. Z. Leiman (New York: KTAV, 1974) 334–49 [reprint of no. 82].
131. "Prose and Poetry in the Mythic and Epic Texts from Ugarit," *HTR* 67 (1974) 1–15.
132. "ζκ [ʾēl]," *TDOT,* ed. G. J. Botterweck and H. Ringgren, tr. J. T. Willis (Grand Rapids: Wm. B. Eerdmans Publishing Co., 1974), vol. 1, 242–61 [translation of no. 116].
133. "Notes on the Ammonite Inscription from Tell Sirān," *BASOR* 212 (1973) 12–15 [delayed publication].
134. "George Ernest Wright: A Tribute to Him at His Death," *Harvard Divinity School Bulletin* 5:1 (October 1974) 4, 6.
135. Editor, *Scrolls from Qumran Cave I* from photographs of J. C. Trever, with D. N. Freedman and J. A. Sanders (Jerusalem: Albright Institute of Archaeological Research and the Shrine of the Book, 1974) [Student Edition of no. 118].
136. "Inscriptions from Idalion in Greek, Cypriote Syllabic, and Phoenician Script," *American Expedition to Idalion, Cyprus. First Preliminary Report: Seasons of 1971 and 1972,* Supplement to *BASOR* 118 (Cambridge, Mass.: ASOR 1974) 77–81.
137. "Leaves from an Epigraphist's Notebook: 1. A Second Phoenician Incantation Text from Arslan Tash; 2. The Oldest Phoenician Inscription from the Western Mediterranean; and 3. A Forgotten Seal," *Patrick W. Skehan Festschrift, CBQ* 36:4 (October 1974) 486–94.

1975

138. "William Foxwell Albright, Orientalist" and "William Foxwell Albright" in *The Published Works of William Foxwell Albright: A Comprehensive Bibliography,* ed. D. N. Freedman (Cambridge: ASOR, 1975) 14–23 [republication of nos. 111 and 123].
139. "A Reconstruction of the Judean Restoration," *JBL* 94 (1975) 4–18. [The Presidential Address, delivered 25 October 1974 at the Annual Meeting of the Society of Biblical Literature held in Washington, D.C.].

140. "A Reconstruction of the Judean Restoration," *The History of Israel and Biblical Faith in Honor of John Bright, Interpretation* 29 (1975) 187–203 [republication of a corrected version of no. 139].

141. "Ammonite Ostraca from Heshbon," *Andrews University Seminary Studies* 13 (1975) 1–20, pls. 1, 2.

142. Editor with S. Talmon, *Qumran and the History of the Biblical Text* (London and Cambridge: Harvard University Press, 1975), lx + 415 pp.

143. "The Oldest Manuscripts from Qumran," *Qumran and the History of the Biblical Text,* 147–76 [see no. 142; republication of no. 32].

144. "The History of the Biblical Text in the Light of Discoveries in the Judaean Desert," *Qumran and the History of the Biblical Text,* 177–95 [see no. 142; republication of no. 77].

145. "The Contributions of the Qumran Discoveries to the Study of the Biblical Text," *Qumran and the History of the Biblical Text* 278–92 [see no. 142; republication of no. 82].

146. "The Evolution of a Theory of Local Texts," *Qumran and the History of the Biblical Text,* 306–20 [see no. 142].

147. *Studies in Ancient Yahwistic Poetry,* with D. N. Freedman (Missoula, Mont.: Scholars Press, 1975), vii + 191 pp. [publication of no. 76, with a postscriptum written in 1975].

148. "El-Buqei'a," *Encyclopedia of Archaeological Excavations in the Holy Land,* ed. M. Avi-Yonah (Jerusalem: Israel Exploration Society, 1975) 1. 267–70 [cf. no. 113].

1976

149. Contributor with Paul and Nancy Lapp et al., *Discoveries in the Wâdi ed-Dâliyeh, Annual of the American Schools of Oriental Studies* 41 (Cambridge, Mass.: ASOR, 1974) 17–29, 57–60, pls. 59–63, 80, 81 [delayed publication].

150. "Presidential Report to the American Schools of Oriental Research," *BASOR* 219 (1975) 1–3 [delayed publication].

151. "Heshbon Ostracon XI," *Andrews University Seminary Studies* 14 (1976) 145–48.

152. Editor with P. D. Miller and W. E. Lemke, *Magnalia Dei, The Mighty Acts of God: Essays on the Bible and Archaeology in Memory of G. Ernest Wright* (New York: Doubleday & Co., 1976), xii + 611 pp.

153. "The Olden Gods in Ancient Near Eastern Creation Myths," *Magnalia Dei,* 329–38 [see no. 152].

1977

154. *Scrolls from the Wilderness of the Dead Sea,* reprinted with slight revisions by the School of Theology at Claremont (Claremont, 1977), 30 pp. [see no. 80].

155. "The Dead Sea Scrolls and the People Who Wrote Them," *BAR* 3 (1977) 1, 23–32, 51 [*manu secunda*].

156. "George Ernest Wright," with P. D. Hanson, W. L. Moran, and K. Stendahl, *Harvard University Gazette* 72:27 (April 15, 1977).

1978

157. "David, Orpheus, and Psalm 151:3–4," *BASOR* 231 (1978) 69–71.
158. "The Historical Importance of the Samaria Papyri," *BAR* 4 (1978) 25–27 [*manu secunda*].
159. "The People Who Wrote the Dead Sea Scrolls," *Jewish Digest* 24:2 (October 1978) 63–70 [*manu secunda*].

1979

160. Editor, *Symposia Celebrating the Seventy-fifth Anniversary of the Founding of the American Schools of Oriental Research (1900–1975)*, vol. 1: *Archaeology and Early Israelite History;* vol. 2: *Archaeology and the Sanctuaries of Israel* (Cambridge, Mass.: ASOR, 1979), ix + 183 pp.
161. "Early Alphabetic Scripts," *Archaeology and Early Israelite History,* 95–123 [see no. 160].
162. "A Newly-Published Inscription of the Persian Age from Byblus," *IEJ* 29 (1979) 40–44.
163. "Problems of Method in the Textual Study of the Hebrew Bible," in *The Critical Study of Sacred Texts,* ed. W. D. O'Flaherty (Berkeley: Berkeley Religious Studies Series, 1979) 31–54.
164. Volume editor with K. Baltzer, *Ezekiel I* by Walther Zimmerli, trans. R. E. Clements, *Hermeneia. A Critical and Historical Commentary on the Bible* (Philadelphia: Fortress Press, 1979).
165. "Phoenicians in Brazil?" *BAR* 5 (1979) 36–43 [*manu secunda*].
166. "Two Offerings Dishes with Phoenician Inscriptions from the Sanctuary of ʿArad," *BASOR* 235 (1979) 75–78.

1980

167. *The Ancient Library of Qumran and Modern Biblical Studies,* rev. ed. (Grand Rapids: Baker Book House, 1980), xxviii + 260 pp.
168. "The Ammonite Oppression of the Tribes of Gad and Reuben: Missing Verses from I Samuel 11 Found in 4QSamᵃ," *The Hebrew and Greek Texts of Samuel,* ed. E. Tov, 105–19. 1980 Proceedings of IOSCS-Vienna (Jerusalem: Acedemon, 1980).

1981

169. "Newly Found Inscriptions in Old Canaanite and Early Phoenician Scripts," *BASOR* 238 (1980) 1–20 [delayed publication].
170. "The Priestly Tabernacle in the Light of Recent Research," *Temples and High Places in Biblical Times,* ed. A. Biran (Jerusalem: Hebrew Union College, 1981) 169–80.
171. "Foreword" in *Pottery, Poetry, and Prophecy* by D. N. Freedman (Winona Lake, Ind.: Eisenbrauns, 1981) vii–viii.
172. "Der Beitrag der Qumranfunde zur Erforschung des Bibeltextes" in *Qumran,* ed. K. E. Grözinger et al. [Wege der Forschung CDX] (Darmstadt: Wissenschaftliche Buchgesellschaft, 1981) 365–84 [translation of no. 86].

173. "An Aramaic Ostracon of the Third Century B.C.E. from Excavations in Jerusalem," *EI* 15 (1981) 67*–69* and pl. 4:2 [Y. Aharoni Volume].

1983

174. "The Samaritans [šōmerōním]," *'enṣîqlôpedyāh miqra'it* [Hebrew], ed. B. Mazar and H. Tadmor (Jerusalem: Bialik Institute, 1983) vol. 8, cols. 164–73.
175. "Alphabets and Pots: Reflections on Typological Method in the Dating of Human Artifacts," *Maarav* 3 (1982) 32–41 [delayed publication].
176. "The Epic Traditions of Early Israel: Epic Narrative and the Reconstruction of Early Israelite Institutions," in *Poet and Historian: Essays in Literary and Historical Biblical Criticism,* ed. R. Friedman, *Harvard Semitic Series* 26 (Chico, Calif.: Scholars Press, 1983) chap. 2.
177. "The Seal of Miqnêyaw, Servant of Yahweh," *Ancient Seals and the Bible,* ed. L. Gorelick and E. Williams-Forte (Northridge, Calif.: Undena Publications, 1983) 55–63 + pls. 9 and 10.
178. "The Ammonite Oppression of the Tribes of Gad and Reuben: Missing Verses from I Samuel 11 Found in 4QSamuelᵃ," *History, Historiography and Interpretation: Studies in Biblical and Cuneiform Literatures,* ed. H. Tadmor and M. Weinfeld (Jerusalem: Magnes Press, 1983) 148–58.
179. "Samaria and Jerusalem: The Early History of the Samaritans and Their Relations with the Jews" in *The History of the Jewish People: The Restoration, Days of Persian Rule* [Hebrew], ed. H. Tadmor, et al. (Jerusalem: Alexander Peli, 1983) 81–94.
180. "Phoenicians in Sardinia: The Epigraphical Evidence" in *Studies in Sardinian Archaeology,* ed. M. S. Balmuth and R. J. Rowland (Ann Arbor, Mich.: University of Michigan Press, 1983) 53–66.
181. "Studies in the Structure of Hebrew Verse: The Prosody of Lamentations 1:1–22" in *The Word of the Lord Shall Go Forth: Essays in Honor of David Noel Freedman in Celebration of His Sixtieth Birthday,* ed. C. L. Meyers and M. O'Connor (Winona Lake, Ind.: Eisenbrauns, 1983) 129–55.
182. "Studies in the Structure of Hebrew Verse: The Prosody of the Psalm of Jonah" in *The Quest for the Kingdom of God: Essays in Honor of George E. Mendenhall,* ed. H. H. Huffmon, F. A. Spina, and A. R. W. Green (Winona Lake, Ind.: Eisenbrauns, 1983) 159–67.
183. "An Inscribed Weight" in N. Lapp et al., *The Excavations at 'Arâq el-'Emîr. AASOR* 47 (1983) 27–30.

1984

184. "The Priestly Tabernacle in the Light of Recent Research" in *The Temple in Antiquity,* ed. T. G. Madsen (Provo, Utah: Religious Studies Center, Brigham Young University, 1984) 91–105 [revision of no. 170].
185. "A Note on a Burial Inscription from Mount Scopus," *IEJ* 33 (1984) 245–46 [delayed publication].
186. "Fragments of the Prayer of Nabonidus," *IEJ* 34 (1984) 260–64.
187. "Javé e os deuses dos patriarchos," *Deus no Antigo Testamento,* ed. E. S. Gerstenberger (Sâo Paulo, Brazil: Asti, 1981) 78–102 [distributed in 1984].

1985

188. "Samaria Papyrus I: A Slave Conveyance of 335 B.C.E. Found in the Wâdi ed-Dâliyeh," *EI* 18 (1985) 7*–17* and pl. 2 [Avigad Volume].
189. "New Directions in Dead Sea Scroll Research: I. The Text Behind the Text of the Hebrew Bible," *Bible Review* 1/2 (1985) 12–23.
190. "New Directions in Dead Sea Scroll Research: II," *Bible Review* 1/3 (1985) 26–35.
191. "An Old Canaanite Inscription Newly Found at Lachish," *Tel Aviv* 11 (1984) 71–76 [delayed publication].
192. "Biblical Archaeology: The Biblical Aspect" in *Biblical Archaeology Today: Proceedings of the International Congress on Biblical Archaeology,* ed. A. Biran et al. (Jerusalem: Israel Exploration Society, 1985) 9–15.
193. "A Literate Soldier: Lachish Letter III" in *Biblical and Related Studies Presented to Samuel Iwry,* ed. A. Kort and S. Morschauer (Winona Lake, Ind.: Eisenbrauns, 1985) 41–47.

IN PRESS

194. "The Origins of the Alphabet" in *Ebla to Damascus: Art and Archaeology of Ancient Syria,* ed. H. Weiss.
195. "An Unpublished Ammonite Ostracon from Heshbon" in *The Archaeology of Jordan and Other Studies,* ed. L. Geraty (Berrien Springs, Mich.: Andrews University).
196. "The Earliest Phoenician Inscription from Sardinia: The Fragmentary Stele from Nora," *The Lambdin Volume,* ed. D. M. Golomb.
197. "An Ammonite King List," *BA.*
198. "Phoenicians in the West: the Epigraphic Evidence" in *A Colloquium on Sardinian Archaeology,* ed. M. Balmuth.
199. "Inscriptions from Tel Sera‛" in *Excavations at Tel Sera‛,* ed. E. Oren.
200. "Phoenician Traders and Colonists in the Mediterranean" in E. Linder, F. Barreca, H. Edgerton, and F. M. Cross, *Mission to Phoenician Sardinia: Preliminary Report.*
201. "The Fixation of the Text and Canon of the Hebrew Bible" in *Cambridge History of Judaism.*
202. "Inscriptions from the Buqê‛ah" in L. E. Stager, *Ancient Agriculture in the Judaean Desert: A Case Study of the Buqê‛ah Valley in the Iron Age.*
203. "The Contribution of William Foxwell Albright to Semitic Epigraphy and Palaeography" in *A Symposium on the Contributions of William Foxwell Albright to Ancient Near Eastern Studies.*

INDEX

INDEX